Books by William L. Shirer

Berlin Diary (1941)
End of a Berlin Diary (1947)
The Traitor (1950)
Midcentury Journey (1952)
Stranger Come Home (1954)
The Challenge of Scandinavia (1955)
The Consul's Wife (1956)
The Rise and Fall of the Third Reich (1960)
The Rise and Fall of Adolf Hitler (1961)
The Sinking of the Bismarck (1962)
The Collapse of the Third Republic (1969)
20th Century Journey: The Start: 1904–1930 (1976)
Gandhi — A Memoir (1980)
20th Century Journey: The Nightmare Years: 1930–1940 (1984)
20th Century Journey: A Native's Return: 1945–1988 (1990)

20th CENTURY JOURNEY

A NATIVE'S RETURN

1945–1988

To Ditta —
Comme Toujours —
admiration and
love,

Bill
(author)

William L. Shirer

VOLUME III

A NATIVE'S RETURN

1945–1988

20th CENTURY JOURNEY

A Memoir of a Life
and the Times

LITTLE, BROWN AND COMPANY · BOSTON · TORONTO · LONDON

FIRST EDITION

Lines from "A Few Figs from Thistles" by Edna St. Vincent Millay, copy-
right 1922, renewed 1950 by Edna St. Vincent Millay, are reprinted by
permission of Harper & Row Publishers Inc.

Library of Congress Cataloging-in-Publication Data
(Revised for vol. 3)

Shirer, William L. (William Lawrence), 1904–
  20th century journey.

  Vol. 3: 1st ed.
  Includes indexes.
  Contents: [1] The start, 1904–1930 — v. 2. The
nightmare years, 1930–1940. — v. 3. A native's return,
1945–1988.
  1. Shirer, William L. (William Lawrence), 1904–
Biography. 2. Novelists, American — 20th century —
Biography. 3. Journalists — United States — Biography.
I. Title.   II. Title: Twentieth century journey.
PS3537.H913Z4617   1976   070'.924[B]   84-21279
ISBN 0-316-78712-4 (v. 1)

10 9 8 7 6 5 4 3 2 1

MV-PA

Published simultaneously in Canada
by Little, Brown & Company (Canada) Limited

PRINTED IN THE UNITED STATES OF AMERICA

This last volume of memoirs is for
Irina Alexandrovna Lugovskaya
who came from another world.

History, with its flickering lamp, stumbles along the trail of the past, trying to reconstruct its scenes, to revive its echoes, and kindle with pale flames the passions of former days.

— WINSTON CHURCHILL

What's important is not fame, nor glory, but the ability to endure, to be able to bear one's cross and have faith.

— ANTON CHEKHOV

The mystery and the immensity of human existence.

— RADHAKRISHNAN

Life, as it is imposed on us, is too hard; it brings us too many pains, disappointments, insoluable tasks. . . . The intention that man should be "happy" is not contained in the plan of "Creation."

— SIGMUND FREUD

No beast is more savage than man, when possessed with power answerable to his rage.

— PLUTARCH

A culture which disavowed the tragic sense of life does not find it easy to deal with life's deeper complexities without despair.

— REINHOLD NIEBUHR

Life must move forward, but it can only be understood backward.

— SÖREN KIERKEGAARD

The universe was always insecure.

— HERBERT BUTTERFIELD

Contents

Preface

This is the third and last volume recounting one man's journey through the twentieth century, a time that saw more changes on the planet than in the previous nineteen hundred years.

It saw more violence too, more bloodshed, bigger, more devastating wars.

There were, to be sure, periods of peace and growing prosperity for many, especially in the U.S.A. Science and invention exploded, utterly transforming the way we lived and altering our conception of our origins and our place in the universe. Youngsters today say they simply cannot imagine what life was like, say, back in 1904 when I was born, when people got about in horse and buggies, before the automobile, the telephone, electric lighting and power, and central heating came into general use; before there were airplanes, movies, radio and television, oil burners, electric refrigerators, air conditioners, gasoline-driven tractors, paved roads, garages, filling-stations, traffic lights, parking lots, shopping centers, airports, income taxes, social welfare, women's suffrage, computers, VCRs, jet engines, radar, moon landings, napalm bombs, nuclear bombs, space rockets, spaceships, space stations, lasers, and much else that has become commonplace today.

My father, who had a college and law-school education, and was a liberal, tolerant man — not an old fogey at all and only forty-two when he died — thought motor cars, of which there were only a few thousand in the whole land, were a menace and should be barred from the city streets and the country roads because they endangered pedestrians and frightened horses.

He also took a dim view of airplanes, of which there were only a handful — all tiny biplanes — in the whole country. The idea of travel by air, especially across continents and oceans at close to the speed of sound or beyond it, he would have dismissed as a pipe dream.

"If God had intended us to fly," he told me after we saw our first planes in a primitive demonstration of a dozen sputtering little biplanes over Grant Park in Chicago on September 27, 1910, "He would have given us wings. Let's leave flying to the birds."

Whether all these ingenious mechanical inventions and their fantastic development during the twentieth century have improved the quality of life and given it more depth and meaning, I doubt. They have certainly liberated men — and especially women — from much drudgery, opened horizons not dreamed of at the turn of the century, and speeded up living to such a frantic pace that I often want to get off the merry-go-round and catch my breath and regain my senses.

All these developments have also improved the standard of living of most people immensely, though tens of millions on earth still hunger and remain homeless, a sizable and disgraceful number in the affluent U.S.A. Most of us, at least in the West, are much better off materially than when I was born, but are we better educated, happier, wiser?

For most of the first twenty years of my adult life I worked abroad, and the previous two volumes of these memoirs have dealt largely with the world beyond our shores, principally Europe.

This book has to do with a coming home and what, after so long an absence, it was like to live and work in America during the nearly half a century since the end of the Second World War.

Luck, or fate, or God, or whatever it is that determines the extent of our lives, allowed me to live through most of this tumultuous twentieth century and through a sizable chunk of our country's existence.

In fact, as James Reston reminded me recently, our work as reporters and commentators on our times, stretching as it has over a half century or more, has covered one-fourth of the life of the Republic, in my own case sixty-four of its two hundred years.

For me it has been a long journey, full of ups and downs as with most lives, but wonderful and exciting and perplexing and troubling almost all the way.

General Introduction

The writing of memoirs, I find, is a strange and tricky business.

Can you tell the truth? Does memory, blurred and disjointed by the passage of time and fed by the imagination, lead you to recount more fiction than fact? William Allen White was afraid it did. "This Autobiography," he warned in the preface to his memoirs, "in spite of all the pains I have taken and the research I have put into it, is necessarily fiction." The reader, he said, should not "confuse this story with reality. For God only knows the truth." White was merely trying, he concluded, "to set down some facts which seem real and true to me."

That is all I have attempted to do in this memoir of a life and the times. I, too, have done years of research in a considerable pile of personal papers, though some were lost in the war and in travel, for a foreign correspondent led a nomadic life, living out of a suitcase. And I have been haunted and humbled by the warnings of poets, philosophers, and memorialists whose abilities and attainments were far above mine. Montaigne thought man was simply incapable of attaining truth because he "was the servant of customs, prejudices, self-interest and fanaticism. . . . The bane of man is the illusion that he has the certainty of his knowledge."

Isadora Duncan, who lived such a full and tragic life, used to talk to me about her memoirs while she was writing them in Paris. "How can we write the truth about ourselves?" she would ask. "Do we even know it?" Emily Dickinson thought that "truth is so rare, it's delightful to tell it." Delightful maybe, but difficult.

What is truth? To Santayana "truth is a dream unless my dream is true." And André Malraux, in writing his memoirs — or "anti-memoirs," as he called them — speculated that "the truth about a man is first of all what he hides," but he differentiated between what a man hides and what he ignores in himself. The two are not the same. Stendhal wrote one book after another about himself in an effort to understand who and what he was, but the search for the truth eluded him. "What manner of man am I?" he finally asked, and admitted: "In truth, I haven't the faintest idea."

There are other problems in writing memoirs. They have to do with the past and with time. "The past is never dead," wrote Faulkner. "It's not even past." You cannot ruminate about the past and write about it without transforming it. Immediately the imagination enters into play until it is impossible to separate memory from imagination. Or to sort out time. Einstein, for whom the conception of time was so important in his theory of relativity, and in mathematics and physics generally, thought it was impossible to sort it out. "The separation between past, present and future," he said, "has only the meaning of an illusion, albeit a tenacious one."

Rousseau, whose *Confessions* is probably the greatest and the most self-searing of all the autobiographies, thought first of writing simply a portrait of himself. He spent twelve years preparing to write it, assembling notes and mulling over notebooks, letters, and other material. In the end he rejected the idea of doing a portrait, not only because he thought it would be static but because it would present a final judgment of himself made late in life. Time would play its tricks. Instead, he decided to relate "all that has happened to me, all that I've done, all that I've thought, all that I've felt. . . . I cannot be wrong about what I've felt."

But he deceives himself. Like every other who writes of his life, he transforms it by the writing. "That is why," wrote Marcel Raymond, the editor of the Pleiade French edition of *Confessions*, "the history of his soul, which he promised us, becomes, without his knowing it, the legend or the myth of his soul."

An observation or two about my own view of life, as a background to these memoirs:

Only rarely have I paused amid the trivia of living, which makes up so much of our existence, and out of which comes the setbacks, the triumphs, the sorrows, and the rare moments of happiness, to consider how puny and unimportant we all are, how puny, in fact, is our planet. Even the solar system, of which the Earth is a negligible part, is but a dot in the infinite space of the universe. The limited space and time that we can comprehend are nothing in the incalculable extent and age of inorganic nature. Who can say, then, that the purpose of the universe, if it has a purpose, has been to create man? Who can even say that there are not billions of other planets on which there is some kind of human life, perhaps much further advanced than ours, or at least more sane, meaningful, and peaceful?

Every person's life is of importance to himself, of course; it is the only one he has and knows. But in the universe of infinite space and time, it is insignificant. *"Qu'est-ce qu'un homme dans l'infini?"* asked Pascal. Nothing. Perhaps Carl Becker, the historian, and one of the most civilized men I ever knew, grasped best our piddling place in the infinite.

> Man [he wrote] is but a foundling in the cosmos, abandoned by the forces that created him. Unparented, unassisted and undirected by omniscient or benevolent authority, he must fend for himself, and with the aid of his own limited intelligence find his way about in an indifferent universe.

And in a rather savage world! The longer I lived and the more I observed, the clearer it became to me that man had progressed very little beyond his earlier savage state. After twenty million years or so of human life on this Earth, the lot of most men and women is, as Hobbes said, "nasty, brutish, and short." Civilization is a thin veneer. It is so easily and continually eroded or cracked, leaving human beings exposed for what they are: savages.

What good three thousand years of so-called civilization, of religion, philosophy, and education, when right up to the 1980s, as this was being written, men go on torturing, killing, and repressing their fellowmen? In fact, was there not a retrogression here? In my own brief time we vastly multiplied our capacity to kill and destroy. With the advent of the bomber, we not only slaughtered soldiers but also innocent women and children far behind the lines of battle.

We could see in our own country as late as the 1960s and 1970s how good Christian and Jewish men, the pillars of our society, when they acceded to political and military power, could sit calmly and coolly in their air-conditioned offices in Washington and cold-bloodedly, without a qualm or a moral quiver, plan and order the massacre by bombing of hundreds of thousands of men, women, and children and the destruction of their homes, farms, churches, schools, and hospitals in a faraway Asian land of poor peasants who had never threatened us in the slightest, who were incapable of it. Almost as savage was the acceptance by most of us citizens of such barbarism, until, toward the end, our slumbering — or should one say, cowardly? — consciences were aroused.

Sometimes it has seemed to me that man's main accomplishment has been to tear down, rob, pollute, kill. First, his earth. Then his fellow-men. In recent years has come our final, triumphal achievement: a nuclear contraption and a guided missle to carry it, works of such incredible complexity that only our handful of geniuses could create them, works that can blow up our planet in a jiffy, snuffing out life for good. Can, and probably will, given the folly of those who rule us and who have the power to decide.

In such a world what meaning can there be in life, what purpose? All my years I have searched, like so many others, for some meaning. Seldom have I got beyond asking the questions. What is life? For what purpose? How did it originate? Where did we come from? Where are we going? Does death end it all? And what is death? The door to eternity? To nothingness? Malraux came to believe that a man "finds an image of himself in the questions he poses," that he "shows himself more truthfully by the profoundness of his questions than by his answers." As Gertrude Stein lay dying in the July heat of 1946 in Paris she mumbled to someone by her bedside: "What is the answer?" And when there was no answer she said: "Then what is the question?"

I never was able to find many answers myself. There have been some, thought up by others, though none very satisfying to me. The gloomy Schopenhauer found that life was merely the passage from being to nothingness. Sophocles, surprisingly, at the end of a long, full life in the golden age of Greece, concluded that it would have been better for man not to have been born. Sophocles had won all of life's prizes. He had captured the drama awards, been acclaimed Greece's greatest playwright and poet, was handsome, rich, and successful, and had lived in good health and vigorous mind to ninety. Yet he could write:

> Never to have lived is best, ancient writers say:
> Never to have drawn the breath of life, never to have
>   looked into the eye of day.

Solon agreed. "Call no man happy," he said, "until he is dead."

Did Solon think happiness began in the thereafter? That is a question we all have asked. The religion of the Greeks, like all other religions, answered that it did. Plato thought that heaven, the Elysian Fields, was the reward for all the injustices and unhappiness on Earth. But there were skeptics. Epicurus, for one. "There is no immortality," he was sure, "and therefore death for us is not an evil; it simply does not concern us: while we exist there is no death, and when death comes we are gone."

Without subscribing fully to his view, even after I lost my faith in the Christian certainties of the hereafter, I have always liked the way Epicurus put it.

> Faith in immortality was born of the greed of unsatisfied people who make unwise use of the time that nature has allotted us. But the wise man finds his life span sufficient to complete the full circle of attainable pleasures, and when the time of death comes, he will leave the table, satisfied, freeing a place for other guests. For the wise man one human life is sufficient, and a stupid man will not know what to do with eternity.

George Eliot was equally skeptical. For her, God was unknowable and immortality unthinkable.

Such, in part, have been the meanderings of my own thoughts as they mixed with those of others and were influenced by them. They will creep in and color, no doubt, this narrative of one life and of the times as the world moved through our momentous twentieth century. That brief whiff of time, as time goes, that has comprised my own span, encompassed more changes, I believe, than the previous thousand years. It has been an interesting experience to have been born in the horse-and-buggy age and to have survived into the nuclear era.

Luck and the nature of my job put me in certain places at certain times where some of the main currents of our century were raging. This gave me an opportunity to see at first hand, and to get the feel of, what was happening, and why. To say that "there is no substitute for experience" may be indulging in a stale cliché, but it has much truth in it. Rilke thought that to be a poet *Mann muss viele Erlebnisse ertragen"* — one has to have a lot of experience, or go through a lot. It is true for all writers and for all those who wish to have a full life.

I love books. They connect you with the past and the present, with original minds and noble spirits, with what living has been and meant to others. They instruct, inspire, shake you up, make you laugh and weep, think and dream. But while they do enhance experience, they are not a substitute for it.

I've always felt it was helpful in my understanding of our country to have been born in Chicago and to have begun to grow up there shortly after the turn of the century. Not that there were not plenty of other equally interesting and certainly more pleasant places to be born in: New York, say, or Cambridge or San Francisco. They were more civilized, probably. Still, it was in Chicago, I think, around the turn of the century, that one could grasp best what had become of America and where it was going. All the boisterousness and the raucousness, the enormous drive to build, to accumulate riches and power, all the ugliness, the meanness, the greed, the corruption of the raw, growing country was exemplified in windy Chicago. Yet some of the poetry of the land and the city were there too, in the beauty of the lake site, of slender buildings soaring to the blue sky along the water, and the quest for art and learning. You can feel it all in the poetry of Chicago's Carl Sandburg. There, and later in Iowa, I grew up with the Midwest in my blood. The Midwest, too, was not the only good place to begin life in. But it gave us something, for better or worse, that no other region had. It was the heartland. It fed the nation, mined many of its minerals, manufactured most of its goods. More than any other section, I think, it shaped the American nation and whatever civilization we have. My roots were there.

Later when I yanked them up — but not all of them, that would have been beyond me — and went abroad at twenty-one to live and work in Europe and Asia, the fortunes of my job set me down in places where some of the principal events that were shaping our world were transpiring: in India in the early thirties during the revolution for independence that Gandhi was leading; in Paris and London during the twenties and thirties when Europe's two greatest democracies were inexplicably sliding downhill; in Rome when that sawdust Caesar Benito Mussolini, after a shaky start, was fastening Fascism on a civilized people and when the Vatican was beginning to stir, to accommodate itself to the twentieth century, and the Pope was giving up the role of the "prisoner" of Rome; in Berlin during the rise and fall of Adolf Hitler and of the barbarian Third Reich; and finally in the Second World War, which Hitler inflicted on a suffering world.

Without these direct, immediate experiences I never could have gained at least some understanding of, much less have got the feel of, what happened — and perhaps why — in that troubled time. They helped later in the writing of some history.

Throughout the mature years of my life, and through the writing of these memoirs, something that Leon Trotsky wrote of our times and something else that Henry James wrote about being an American have flickered through my mind. "Anyone desiring a quiet life," Trotsky wrote shortly before he was hacked to death in Mexico by agents of Stalin, "has done badly to be born in the Twentieth Century." As for crotchety old James: "It's a complex fate," said he, "being an American." Complex or not, it was an interesting fate to be an American in the twentieth century. I am glad it was mine.

BOOK ONE

A Coming Home
1945

CHAPTER 1

Twice before, in 1940 and 1944, I had got back from the war in time for Christmas. And now, as the holiday approached in 1945, I was coming home for the third time. For good, I hoped.

The war was over. Germany, which had started it on the first day of September 1939, had surrendered unconditionally on May 7. Japan had given up on August 14.

I would never forget those first August days when the long war ended. The news was almost too tremendous to grasp. How could you be prepared for the news that burst upon us on Monday, August 6? That day we had dropped an atomic bomb on Hiroshima, a large city in Japan of which I had not previously heard, just as I had never heard before of an atom bomb. The force from which the sun draws its awesome power had for the first time, ever, been unleashed by us to slaughter human beings and wipe out their cities.

President Truman had taken to the air to tell us about it. The single bomb over Hiroshima, he said, had the explosive force of twenty thousand tons of TNT. The extent of the damage it had caused, the War Department declared, was not yet known. An impenetrable cloud of dust and smoke reaching up to the heavens had masked "the target area" from U.S. reconnaissance planes. But a bomb of such terrifying force was bound to have caused appalling loss of human life and property. The additional destructiveness of radioactive fallout was not mentioned. Only a handful of insiders, the little band of American scientific geniuses who in great secrecy had built the bomb in the sands of New Mexico, knew that radioactive fallout might in the end be the most frightful consequence of all. This would dawn on the rest of us later.

What concerned us at the time was not so much the capacity of the bomb for unbelievable destruction — no one thought of it, as we later would, as threatening to blow up the planet — but whether the bomb would terrify the Japanese into surrendering and ending the war. When that occurred after we had dropped a second bomb, this time on Nagasaki, everyone on the globe, I think, friend, enemy, or neutral, was immensely relieved that the war was over, that the mass killing and the terrible destruction would cease. We would have blessèd peace on what was left of a stricken world.

Somehow we felt, though, that the planet would never be the same again. The explosion of the two American atom bombs over Japan had ended one age for mankind. We stood suddenly, apprehensive and unprepared, at the dawn of a new one. In its editorial that morning, I noted, the *New York Times* posed *the* problem and asked *the* crucial question:

> A revolution in science and a revolution in warfare have occurred on the same day. . . . Civilization and humanity can now survive only if there is a revolution in mankind's political thinking. But can mankind grow up quickly enough to win the race between civilization and disaster?

It was a question that would hang over the rest of my life like a dark, threatening cloud, and cast its shadow over this book from the first page to the last. A half century later there is still no answer and no prospect of one. The mad race is still on and no one can yet be sure how it will end and how soon.

That spring CBS had sent me out to San Francisco to cover the founding of the United Nations. I had asked to be sent back to Europe to report on what would certainly be our final triumph over Nazi Germany. I had spent so much of my life writing and broadcasting about that country, had been in Berlin when World War II was launched six years before, and had observed at first hand Germany's amazing early triumphs in Poland and in the west, that I very much wanted to be in on its defeat, which had seemed so improbable in the first years of the war. This was not because I felt vindictive. It just seemed like poetic justice for one who had had to report for so long on the arrogance and savagery of Hitler and his thugs when they first conquered Germany and then most of Europe. But the powers-that-be at the network decided they wanted me to go to San Francisco — perhaps because I was the only one on the staff who had covered the old League of Nations in Geneva.

Now that victory over Germany in Europe and over Japan in Asia seemed certain, perhaps the most important thing to report on was no longer the war but the kind of peace the victorious Allies were going to make. Just as after World War I the victors at Versailles had set up the League of Nations, a dream of President Woodrow Wilson, to prevent further wars and maintain the peace, now they were meeting in San Francisco to establish a new world body called the United Nations, hoping it would do a better job than its predecessor. Strangely enough, I, who had seen the old League flounder in Geneva because the Big Powers were too nationalistic and too selfish to yield an inch of their sovereignty to the common good, was blandly optimistic about the chances this time for the United Nations. I was naïve enough to believe they had learned a lesson from history, especially from the suffering and sacrifice they had gone through in the Second World War. I thought their leaders, even though not very bright, knew our small planet could not survive a third world war — and this before the A-bomb was dropped and made it certain.

So from New York I set off for San Francisco on April 20, 1945, with high hopes. Not even the anticipated antagonism between the U.S.A. and the U.S.S.R., which were emerging from the war as the world's two superpowers, could dampen my enthusiasm. After all, I reflected, Americans might be hysterical about the terrible Bolsheviks, as the Russians were hysterical about the terrible capitalist, imperialist Americans, but despite the paranoia and the rhetoric, there seemed to me no fundamental conflicts of interest between the two countries. There never had been, whether Russia was Czarist or Bolshevik.

In this I would prove to be naïve, too. But, for a moment, as the statesmen from fifty nations gathered from the far corners of the earth in the beautiful city by the bay, there was an atmosphere of goodwill and a determination to succeed. Jan Christiaan Smuts, the prime minister of South Africa, summed it up. He was the sole survivor of those who had played leading parts in shaping the League of Nations at Versailles after the last war. He had seen it slowly fail. He thought the proposed United Nations was better than the old League. He also believed, he told me, that this was our last chance.

Smuts thought it would be better, for one thing, because this time the world's two greatest powers would be in it from the beginning. One of the weaknesses of the old League had been that the United States, whose president had inspired it, spurned it and stayed out, and that the Soviet Union had not been invited to join until toward the end, when it was doomed. Smuts also believed the U.N. would have more teeth to enforce the peace — even, if necessary, by the employment of armed force, which the League had never had. I could not conceive in those heady spring days that my fierce belief in the future of the United

Nations, shared by so many there, would turn out to be as illusory as that I had entertained as a youngster back in the 1920s about the League of Nations.

The conference of fifty nations opened officially on April 25, 1945, in the resplendent opera house, built as a *war* memorial. My euphoria, my high hopes, were reflected in my diary that evening.

> . . . Here were expressed today all the hopes we have of peace. In Berlin a maniac's hopes of world conquest were being buried in the debris of a once great city. [Russian troops that day were reported approaching the center of the city, where Adolf Hitler was believed holed up in the Chancellery.] Here in this beautiful community along the ocean we call Pacific, more decent hopes were being born.
>
> . . . The president of the United States [Truman had just succeeded Roosevelt thirteen days before] broadcast to the delegates: "In your hands rests our future. Make certain that another war is impossible."

Meanwhile from the war we still had, tremendous news was beginning to break. My diary tells of the climactic, blazing end.

> Sunday, April 22. The Russians are within three miles of Unter den Linden in the heart of Berlin. The city is in flames. . . . Somewhere south of Berlin a junction between the American and Russian armies is imminent. . . .

> Sunday, April 29. A weekend for you!
> American troops have entered Munich and Milan, birthplaces, respectively, of Nazism and Fascism. The British Eighth Army has liberated Venice. Nine-tenths of Berlin is now in Russian hands.
> But the greatest news of all comes from Milan.
> Benito Mussolini, the swaggering little sawdust Caesar, is dead. He was executed by Italian patriots at four twenty P.M. yesterday in a little mountain village near Como. Today his body is hanging in the Piazza Loreto in Milan. . . . According to the Milan Free Radio the Duce's mistress, Clara Petacci, was also executed, and the tyrant's body, after it was cut down, lay on hers in the Milan gutter for all to see.
> After Il Duce, Der Führer?

Indeed. Adolf Hitler's time had come too.

On Tuesday, May 1, I was lunching with some members of the American delegation at the Fairmont Hotel in San Francisco when a bellboy summoned me to the telephone. It was our local CBS office. Come quick, they said. Hitler is dead!

Though not surprised, given the latest news, I found it hard to believe. Over so many years Hitler had stridden the earth as an arrogant, ruthless conqueror, first of Germany and then of most of Europe, that I had not imagined him in my time in Berlin coming to such a sorry end, trapped at last in his lair by the despised Russians, whose country he had without provocation or warning set out to destroy four years before. Now it was his own country that was utterly destroyed, the war he had started so irresponsibly, irretrievably lost.

I hurried to the CBS studios, where they put me on the air to give some first reactions to the death of the Nazi tyrant. It was difficult to articulate them so suddenly, and I did not do very well. A golden opportunity missed! And one I had waited for so long! But it would take more than a few hours or even days to express adequately my thoughts on the impact of Adolf Hitler on his country, on me, and on the rest of the world. He had been such an evil genius.

I find a note at the end of a long diary entry for that day:

> To write some time: A summing-up of . . . Hitler. Your personal impressions . . . Remember the first time you saw him, in Nuremberg in September 1934, when he did not personally impress you so much? When was the last time you actually saw him? I think it was in the Reichstag on July 18, 1940, after he had overrun Denmark and Norway, the Lowlands and France and was making what he thought was a magnanimous peace bid to Britain.

Now the man was dead. How had he died? I wondered. And who, if anyone, had taken his place? Göring, the Number Two? Goebbels, the Number Three? Or Himmler, the chief of the Gestapo, who had been reported in recent days to be in contact with the Swedes about a surrender in the West? CBS had recorded the broadcasts from Germany telling of Hitler's end.

The news first came from the radio station in Hamburg.

> ANNOUNCER: *Achtung! Achtung!* The German Broadcasting Company has a serious, important message for the German people. It is reported from the Führer's headquarters that our Führer, Adolf Hitler, fighting to the last breath against Bolshevism, fell for Germany this afternoon in his operational headquarters in the Reich Chancellery. On April 30 the Führer appointed Grand Admiral Doenitz his successor. . . .

The admiral, a dour, thin-faced old submarine commander, came on the air. Hitler, he said, had died "a hero's death" fighting to the last "the frightful danger of Bolshevism." That struggle, he went on, would continue. Against the British and Americans only a defensive war would be fought, and if they continued to drive into Germany they would be "solely responsible for the spreading of Bolshevism in Europe."

Doenitz's broadcast, I thought, must have been written by Goebbels, the propaganda minister. Would anyone at this late date, even Russian-hating diehard Americans, fall for the old Nazi line about Hitler's fighting against Bolshevism? It was Hitler's embrace of Bolshevism in the pact with Stalin in August 1939 that had enabled the Nazi dictator to launch the war.

I doubted very much that Hitler had died "a hero's death, fighting to the last breath against Bolshevism." I was sure he had killed himself to avoid being captured by the Russians. But the lie would be necessary to perpetuate the Hitler myth, which was based on so many lies.

With Hitler gone, Germany's surrender had to be imminent. It came a week later, on May 7. The war in Europe was over — after five years, eight months, and six days of fighting that had almost destroyed the ancient continent, homeland of our Western civilization, and slaughtered millions upon millions and maimed as many more.

That summer our country did what it had failed to do after the First World War. It joined a world body that it was hoped would keep the peace. The Charter of the United Nations was signed by fifty nations at San Francisco on June 26 — "a day in history!" I noted enthusiastically in my diary. President Truman, disregarding his prepared speech to the delegates, had begun by saying: "Oh, what a great day this can be in history!" It had not been easy, as the president remarked. "That we have a Charter at all," he said, "is a great wonder!" It had come about largely because the United States and the Soviet Union, after quarreling bitterly and endlessly, had finally agreed to compose their differences.

Not a few Americans doubted that the Senate, which had refused to allow us to join the old League after the first war, would agree to our adhering to the United Nations. But the times had changed. America had matured. Franklin Roosevelt and Harry Truman, unlike Woodrow Wilson, had wisely made it a bipartisan issue by enlisting the aid of the Senate and other Republican leaders in hammering out an agreement in San Francisco. On July 28 the Senate ratified the U.N. Charter by a vote of 89 to 2.

The two nations that had not been members of the old League when it was formed after the first war, the Soviet Union because it had not been invited, the United States because it chose to stay out, were now, as the world's only two superpowers, to be the backbone of the U.N.

CHAPTER 2

At the beginning of October that year, I went back to where the war had started to see at first hand what had happened to the Master Race and its country, to get if I could the story of its last desperate hours. I wanted to find out what kind of an end Adolf Hitler really had had, and I intended to proceed finally, in late November, to Nuremberg, where the trial of the surviving Nazi war criminals was scheduled to begin. Among other things, I hoped to learn more about an unbelievable horror they had perpetrated, the news of which was beginning to surface: the destruction of the European Jews in the ovens of the Nazi extermination camps.

I have in another place described that return to Germany, which I fervently hoped would be the last before I went home for good. But perhaps a few words about it would not be out of place in this last volume of memoirs. This then can be a sort of farewell for me to the Third Reich and its barbarian leader, Adolf Hitler. There is a time to leave a place once and for all.

I got back to Berlin on Tuesday, October 30, 1945. I'll never forget that first view from the air as we circled the capital before landing. The great city was demolished almost beyond recognition. I scribbled down a few notes for my diary.

> The center of the capital around the Leipzigerstrasse and the Friedrichstrasse a vast acreage of rubble. Most of the little streets I knew, gone, erased as off a map. The railway stations — Potsdamerbahnhof, Anhalterbahnhof, Lehrterbahnhof — gaunt shells. The Imperial Palace of the Kaisers roofless, some of its wings pulverized, and here and there the outer walls battered in. The Tiergarten, like any other battlefield from the air, pockmarked with shell holes, the old spreading trees that I had known, bare stumps. And as far as you can see in all directions, a great wilderness of debris, dotted with roofless burnt-out buildings that look like mousetraps with the low autumn sun shining through the spaces where windows had been.

For days, often with my CBS colleague, Howard Smith, I prowled the ruins of the great city. My diary reminds me that the sorriest figures we saw in the streets were the demobilized German soldiers — especially the ones who had come back from POW camps in Russia and whom the Western Allied commanders were giving them their freedom, we having already more POWs than we could find accommodation for. These soldiers of Hitler had been so cocky and confident when I accompanied them through Poland in 1939 and Holland, Belgium, and France that spring of 1940. But now!

> They hobble along in their rags, footsore from walking in worn-out shoes stuffed with newspapers, their uniforms, which in my day, they kept so smart, tattered and filthy. . . . On a street in Wedding we stopped to talk to a group of them scraping along. . . . Were these the crack soldiers who goosestepped so arrogantly through Poland, France, Russia . . . ? These the *Herrenvolk?* . . . They are beat, dirty, tired, and hungry.
> "Where you come from?" I asked them.
> "From Stalingrad," they said. *"Alles kaputt."* They grinned and you could see that few of them, though they were young men, had any teeth left. They begged for cigarettes and we passed a pack around. Then they shuffled and hobbled away.

My diary for Saturday, November 3, in Berlin:

> So this is the end of Hitler's thousand-year Reich!
> The end of the awful tyranny, the bloody war, the whole long nightmare that some of us American correspondents began covering a decade ago in this once proud capital.
> It is something to see — here where it ended. And it is indescribable.
> How can you find words to convey the picture of a great capital destroyed almost beyond recognition; of a once mighty nation that has ceased to exist; of a conquering people who were so brutally arrogant and so blindly sure of their mission as the master race when I departed from here five years ago, and whom you now see poking about their ruins, broken, dazed, shivering, hungry, without will or purpose, reduced like animals to foraging for food and seeking shelter in order to cling to life for another day.

I found out something that first week in Berlin that depressed me, though it did not surprise me. The German people did not regret having started the war, only having lost it. I talked to a number of Germans about that. If only Hitler, they said, had listened to his generals during the Russian campaign; if only he hadn't declared war on the United States; if only the whole world had not ganged up on poor Germany — they would have won and been spared their present sufferings. I found no sense of guilt or remorse in Berlin. Nor any resentment against Hitler for having landed them in such a mess. As for the terrible crimes inflicted on the occupied peoples, they seemed indifferent.

On Sunday, November 4, I did my first broadcast from Berlin. It seemed a little strange to say the opening line. *"This is Berlin!"* The last time I had begun a broadcast that way had been on December 3, 1940 — almost five years before — when the Nazi German conquerors ruled over most of Europe, from the Vistula to the Atlantic, from the North Cape to Spain. Now they were too demoralized and broken to be able to rule even themselves. Germany was being run by the victorious Allies.

I spent a good deal of my time in Berlin that fall trying to find out how Hitler met his end. In San Francisco when word came in on May 1 of his death, I had been very doubtful, as I noted, of the official account. I was sure he had not died "a hero's death" at all but had killed himself to prevent being captured by the despised Bolsheviks, whose Red Army troops had surrounded his Chancellery and were about to storm it.

This turned out to be the case. The end, when it came, was bizarre enough, like so much in this strange man's life. In the golden years for Nazism, when Hitler was riding high, we correspondents in Berlin had often called him mad. But he wasn't really, at least no madder than other totalitarian dictators, Josef Stalin, for example. He had been, like the Soviet leader, a cold, calculating, brutal tyrant.

But in the last year or so, after the disasters in Russia and then in the west had doomed him and his regime, and especially in the final months, Adolf Hitler had degenerated into a wild and often insane man. The long strain of conducting the war, the shock of the defeats, the unhealthy life without fresh air or exercise in the various underground headquarters bunkers that he rarely left, his giving way to ever more frequent and violent temper tantrums, and, finally, the poisonous drugs he took daily on the advice of his quack physician, Dr. Theodor Morell, had left him a physical and mental wreck. When his headquarters in East Prussia were blown up by a bomb planted by Colonel Klaus von Stauffenberg, leader of a small group of military dissidents, he had barely escaped being killed, but he had been hurt. The explosion had not only injured one arm but had broken the tympanic membranes of both ears, which contributed to his spells of dizziness.

More and more, as the news from the eastern and western fronts grew worse, he gave way to hysterical rage. General Heinz Guderian, the next to the last of several chiefs of the General Staff, became a special victim of these tantrums. When on February 13, 1945, he insisted on trying to evacuate by sea several German divisions cut off by the Russians in the Baltic area, the Führer turned on him.

> His fists raised, his cheeks flushed with rage, his whole body trembling [the general later recounted], the man stood there in front of me, beside himself with fury and having lost all self-control. After each outburst Hitler would stride up and down the carpet edge, then suddenly stop immediately before me and hurl his next accusation in my face. He was almost screaming, his eyes seemed to pop out of his face and the veins stood out in his temples.*

On another occasion Guderian's chief of staff had had to pull him away by his uniform to escape Hitler's punching him.

It was in this state of mind and health that the Nazi dictator made one of the last momentous — and insane — decisions of his life. He issued orders on March 19 to make Germany an utter wasteland. Everything that sustained life was to be destroyed — factories, buildings, transport centers, railway rolling stock, car and truck parks, stores of food and clothing — to prevent them from falling into the hands of the enemy. It was an order condemning the surviving German people to death, for after such destruction there would be nothing left to sustain them. When Albert Speer, minister for war production, protested in a face-to-face showdown with the Führer, Hitler replied:

> "If the war is lost, the nation will also perish. This fate is inevitable. There is no necessity to take into consideration the basis which the people will need to continue a most primitive existence. On the contrary, it will be better to destroy these things ourselves because this nation will have proved to be the weaker one and the future will belong to the stronger eastern nation [Russia]. Besides, those who will remain after the battle are only the inferior ones, for the good ones have been killed."†

His own personal fate having been sealed, the crumbling dictator was not interested in the survival of the German people for whom he had always professed such boundless love and devotion.

* General Hans Guderian, *Panzer Leader*. New York, 1952, p. 343.
† *Trial of the Major War Criminals before the International Military Tribunal*. Vol. XVI, pp. 497–498.

On April 16, 1945, Zhukov's Russian armies jumped off from their bridgeheads over the Oder River and on the afternoon of April 21 they reached the outskirts of Berlin. On April 25 patrols of the U.S. 69th Infantry Division met forward elements of the Soviet 58th Guards Division at Torgau on the Elbe River, some seventy-five miles south of Berlin. North and South Germany were severed. Adolf Hitler was cut off in Berlin.

He had planned to leave the capital on April 20, his fifty-sixth birthday, for Obersalzberg and there direct the last stand of the Third Reich in the legendary vastness of Barbarossa. Most of the ministries had already moved south with their trucks full of state papers and frightened officials anxious to get out of doomed Berlin. The Führer himself had sent most of the members of his household staff to Berchtesgaden ten days before to prepare his beloved mountain villa, the Berghof, for his coming. But he kept putting off his departure.

On April 15 his mistress, Eva Braun, arrived in Berlin from Bavaria to join him. Very few in Germany knew of her existence and even fewer of her relationship to Adolf Hitler. For more than twelve years she had been his mistress. I myself that November of 1945, trying to fit together what pieces I could find to make a truthful account of the last days of Adolf Hitler and the Third Reich, was astounded to learn it. In all the years I had worked in Berlin I had never heard of this liaison. Party hacks had told me plenty of stories of Hitler's alleged involvement with other women — but never with Eva Braun. So far as I had been able to find out, Hitler's only great love had been for his youthful niece, Geli Raubal, whom he had driven to suicide in Munich two years before he became chancellor. Probably, I now learned, he never loved Eva Braun but he liked her companionship, though he kept her largely out of sight, rarely allowing her to come to Berlin.

"She was," Erich Kempka, the Führer's chauffeur, would later say, "the unhappiest woman in Germany. She spent most of her life waiting for Hitler."

Judging by photographs of her, she was not a very attractive woman. Apparently she was shallow enough, spending much of her time reading cheap novels and picture-magazines, seeing trashy films, and grooming herself. She was no Pompadour or Lola Montez. But Hitler obviously felt strongly enough about her to invite her to come to Berlin and share his end. There seems no doubt that she wanted to share it. She had no desire, she confided to an acquaintance after her arrival, to live in a Germany without Adolf Hitler. "It would not be fit to live in for a true German," she said. Dr. and Frau Goebbels agreed with her.

Hitler's birthday on April 20 passed quietly enough despite the bad news from the rapidly disintegrating fronts. All the bigwig Nazis gathered in the underground bunker to offer the Führer birthday congratulations: Göring, Goebbels, Himmler, Ribbentrop, and Bormann, as well as the military chiefs still in favor: Admiral Doenitz, Field Marshal Keitel, Generals Jodl and Krebs — the last-named the latest and final chief of the Army General Staff. (As the defeats grew, Hitler had kept sacking them.)

The Nazi dictator did not strike his guests as particularly depressed, for all the disastrous news pouring in. He was still confident, as he had told his generals three days before, "that the Russians were going to suffer their bloodiest defeat of all right here in Berlin." The generals knew better and at the regular military powwow after the birthday celebration they urged the Leader to leave Berlin for the south. In a day or two, they explained, the Russians would cut off the last escape route. Hitler hesitated. He agreed to set up two separate commands in case the Russians and Americans made their junction at the Elbe — one for the north, the other for the south.

That night of the twentieth there was a general getaway from the capital, but Hitler declined to join it. Two of the Führer's most trusted and veteran lieutenants left: Himmler and Göring. The fat, bemedaled chief of the Luftwaffe, whose failures were contributing to the German collapse, got away at the head of a long motor caravan whose trucks were filled with booty from his fabulous estate, Karinhall. Each of these old guard Nazis, it seems, departed convinced that his beloved Führer would soon be dead and that he would succeed him. They were never to see him again, they who had been at his side since the early days of the party. Nor was another notorious Nazi, the fatuous foreign minister, Ribbentrop. That night he also scurried for safer parts.

Hitler let them go. He himself had not quite given up. The day after his birthday he ordered S.S. General Felix Steiner to launch an all-out counterattack on the Russians in the southern suburbs of Berlin. Every available soldier was to be thrown into the battle, including Luftwaffe ground troops.

"Any commander who holds back his forces," Hitler shouted at General Karl Koller, the harassed air force chief of staff, who had not followed Göring to safety, "will forfeit his life in five hours. You yourself will guarantee with your head that the last man is thrown in."

All through the next couple of days the raging warlord waited impatiently for news of Steiner's counterattack. It never came. There was no Steiner attack. It had existed only in the feverish mind of the desperate dictator. When he realized it he broke down.

All day long on April 22 he had been on the telephone, as he had been the day before, trying to find out how General Steiner's attack was progressing. No one knew. General Koller sent some planes up to see, but they could not find Steiner's troops, even though they were supposed to be fighting only two or three miles from the bunker. Nor could anyone find Steiner. Not even Keitel and Jodl, the two top army chiefs. But they had further bad news for their commander in chief. The withdrawal of troops from the north of Berlin to support Steiner in the south had so weakened the defenses there that the Russians had broken through. Their tanks, Hitler was told, were now within the city limits.

Confronted with reality, the supreme commander blew up. All the surviving witnesses agree: Hitler completely lost control of himself. As one described it:

> This was the end, he shrieked. Everyone had deserted him. There was nothing but treason, lies, corruption and cowardice. All was over. Very well, he would stay on in Berlin. He would personally take over the defense of the capital. The others could leave, if they wished. In this place he would meet his end.*

The others tried to calm him down. There was still hope if the supreme commander retired to the south, where two German armies were still intact. General Jodl — and he was the only one — was brutally frank. In his view, the commander in chief was deserting the command of his troops and shirking his responsibility to them at the worst moment of the war. "You can't direct anything from here," Jodl told him to his face. "Without a staff how can you direct anything?"

But the deteriorating dictator was beyond reasoning with. He ordered Keitel and Jodl to fly south and take over command of the remaining armed forces. He would stay.

Late that night an S.S. general, Gottlob Berger, a true believer in Nazism and Hitler, arrived at the bunker. To his shock he found the Leader "a broken man — finished." Berger ventured to express his admiration to Hitler for his courage in remaining in Berlin. For a time the great man did not respond.

> Then suddenly he shrieked: "Everyone has deceived me! No one has told me the truth! The Armed Forces have lied to me!" He went on and

---

* William Shirer, *The Rise and Fall of the Third Reich.* New York, 1960, p. 1113.

on in a loud voice. Then his face went bluish purple. I thought he was
going to have a stroke. . . .*

Two days later, on April 24, Hanna Reitsch, a famed woman test
pilot, who at the risk of her life had flown in with General Ritter von
Greim of the air force, found her revered Leader in even a worse state.
She and Greim had landed their small plane on the east-west axis, the
broad avenue that ran from the Brandenburg Gate through the Tiergarten, already under Russian artillery and anti-aircraft fire. One flak
shell had hit their plane and shattered Greim's foot. Hitler came into
the clinic where a physician was dressing the general's wound.

"Do you know why I have called you?" Hitler asked Greim, who said
he did not.

"Because Hermann Göring has betrayed and deserted both me and
the Fatherland."

The news shocked the air force general and devastated Miss Reitsch,
another true believer. They noticed the Führer's face begin to twitch,
his shortened breath coming out in explosive puffs.

"Behind my back," Hitler began to shout, "Göring has established
contact with the enemy! . . . Against my orders he has gone to Berchtesgaden to save himself! From there he has sent me an ultimatum!
He . . ." Hitler stopped to gasp for breath.

This was terrible news. What had happened? After being informed
that Hitler had decided to stay on and die in Berlin, Göring had sent
the Führer a telegram from Berchtesgaden asking that, in view of his
decision, he agree that Göring take over as his deputy in accordance
with the Leader's decree of June 29, 1941, which provided for just this
contingency. If he received no reply by 10 P.M., the fat Luftwaffe chief
added, he would assume that his commander in chief had lost his
freedom of action and he, Göring, would assume the "leadership of the
Reich."

"A crass ultimatum!" Hitler yelled at Hanna Reitsch. "Now nothing
remains! Nothing is spared me! No allegiances kept, no honor lived up
to . . . no betrayals that I have not experienced! And now this, above
all else!"

He told them that he had had Göring arrested "as a traitor," had
stripped him of all his offices, and had expelled him from the party.
"That is why I have called you," he added, to Greim. Whereupon he
named the wounded general to succeed Göring as commander in chief
of the Luftwaffe.

* H. R. Trevor-Roper, *The Last Days of Hitler*. London, 1947, pp. 124–127.

On the night of April 26, Russian shells began falling on the bunker. Reitsch pleaded with Hitler to leave. "My Führer," she says she told him, "why do you stay? Why do you deprive Germany of your life? The Führer must live so that Germany can live. . . ."* He reiterated that he had decided to stay in Berlin.

"My dear girl," he said, "I did not expect it to turn out like this. I believed firmly that Berlin would be saved on the banks of the Oder." When the Russians broke out of their Oder bridgeheads he still believed, he said, that German forces, inspired by his example, would come to the rescue of Berlin. "But, my Hanna. I still have hope. The army of General Wenck is moving up from the south. He must and will drive the Russians back. . . ."

After General Steiner, General Wenck! On April 28, the Führer radioed General Keitel: "I expect the relief of Berlin. What is General Heinrici's army doing? Where is General Wenck? What is happening to the Ninth Army? When will Wenck and the Ninth Army join?"

Reitsch later described Hitler's condition that day. He strode "about the shelter, waving a road map that was fast disintegrating from the sweat of his hands, and planning Wenck's campaign with anyone who happened to be listening."

But there was no Wenck campaign. Like Steiner's "attack" of the week before, it existed only in Hitler's fervid imagination. Wenck's army already had been liquidated, as had the Ninth Army. General Heinrici's army to the north of Berlin was beating a hasty retreat westward so that it might be captured by the Western Allies instead of by the Russians.

The Führer, unnerved by the news of Göring's "treason," suspected more treachery. At 8 P.M. on the evening of April 28, when still no word of the three rescue armies had been received, he ordered Martin Bormann, his mole-like secretary, who in the last couple of years had wormed his way to considerable power, to send a radio message to Admiral Doenitz.

> Instead of urging the troops forward to our rescue, the men in authority are silent. Treachery seems to have replaced loyalty. . . . Chancellery already in ruins.

Later that night Bormann got off another message to Doenitz, this time on his own.

* All quotations from Hanna Reitsch are from her interrogation at Nuremberg, printed in *Nazi Conspiracy and Aggression*. Vol VI, Washington, 1946, pp. 551–571.

Schoener, Wenck and others must prove their loyalty by coming to the aid of the Führer as soon as possible.

And then toward midnight came another heavy blow. A radio listening post at the Propaganda Ministry across the street picked up a broadcast from the BBC in London quoting a Reuter dispatch from Stockholm that Heinrich Himmler — *der treue Heinrich* — the savage, sadistic head of the Gestapo and S.S., whom Hitler had trusted above all his henchmen, was negotiating secretly with Count Folke Bernadotte of Sweden to surrender the German armies in the west to General Eisenhower.

The news, Reitsch later said, struck "a deathblow to the entire assembly. Men and women alike screamed with rage, fear and desperation, all mixed into one emotional spasm." Hitler's spasm was the worst. "He raged," she said, "like a madman. His color rose to a heated red and his face was virtually unrecognizable." Then the Leader sank into a stupor. No one dared to speak. Finally Hitler recovered enough to curse once more his murderous secret-police chief; Himmler, he said, had committed the worst act of treachery he had ever known. He was worse even than Göring.

Himmler's liaison officer with the Führer, Hermann Fegelein, had not left the bunker on the twentieth with his chief. Like so many of his ilk, this disreputable former groom and jockey, who was quite illiterate, had risen to high position in the Nazi cuckooland; he had married the sister of Hitler's mistress and been named a general in the Waffen-S.S. Sometime on April 26 he quietly slipped out of the bunker. His disappearance was not noticed until the next afternoon when Hitler sent for Fegelein to check on what Himmler was up to. Sniffing further "treason," the Führer sent out an S.S. search party, which found the S.S. general resting in his home in the fashionable Charlottenburg quarter, apparently waiting for the Russians, who were about to overrun the area. He was brought back to the bunker, where Hitler accused him of cowardly desertion, stripped him of his S.S. rank and decorations, and put him under arrest. When the news that Himmler was secretly negotiating surrender with the Swedes broke, the raging leader, unable to get his fingers on the S.S. and Gestapo chief, ordered Fegelein court-martialed for treason. Within an hour he was found guilty, taken up to the courtyard above the bunker, and executed by a firing squad. Eva Braun declined to intervene to save the life of her sister's husband. "Poor Adolf," she whined to Hanna Reitsch, "deserted by everyone, betrayed by all."

It had not been easy to carry out the execution of Eva's brother-in-law. The ground above the bunker was now being blasted by Russian artillery. The members of the firing squad had risked their lives.

Sometime shortly after midnight Adolf Hitler was told that Soviet troops were nearing the Potsdamerplatz a block away and would probably storm the Chancellery on the morning of the thirtieth, some thirty hours hence. This seems to have at last convinced him that it was time to carry out the final decisions of his tumultuous life. He acted with dispatch.

First he dispatched Reitsch and Greim to rally the Luftwaffe for one more massive bombing of the Russians outside the Chancellery, and ordered them to arrest Himmler as a traitor. It was not easy for Reitsch and Greim to get away. Shells from Russian artillery now were landing all over the place. The two flyers were driven through the heavy fire in an armored car to the nearby Brandenburg Gate, where a small Arado 96 trainer plane had been parked behind the stout pillars. With Hanna Reitsch at the controls, the plane taxied a hundred or so yards down the east-west axis. It was night, but the broad avenue was lit up by fires from burning buildings around the Pariserplatz, behind the Gate, and just north toward the Dorotheenstrasse. The little plane had hardly climbed above treetop level before Russian searchlights picked it up and their anti-aircraft guns began to fire away. Reitsch said later the bursting flak tossed the plane about like a feather. Somehow she managed to keep it flying until it climbed into a cloud cover and the sight of the great capital burning below faded away.

Back in the bunker, Adolf Hitler, as a last award to his neglected mistress for sticking with him to the very end, married Eva Braun. It was now after 1 A.M. The shelter was shaking from the thuds of exploding Soviet shells, and there was little time to lose. Goebbels somehow had found a municipal councilor, one Wagner, who was fighting in a unit of the Volksturm nearby, to perform the wedding ceremony. The petty official was relieved to be fetched from almost certain death but surprised and awed to be called upon to perform such a task for so eminent a German.

I eventually saw a copy of the marriage document. Unusual as the circumstances were, Adolf Hitler insisted on sticking to form and observing the law as far as was possible. He did ask that "in view of developments the publication of the banns be dispensed with and all other delays avoided." The couple swore they were "of complete Aryan descent" and had "no hereditary disease to exclude their marriage." The once all-powerful dictator dutifully filled in all the forms except two: the name of his father (born Schicklgruber) and mother, and the date of their marriage. The bride, like most brides at this juncture, seems to have been nervous. She started to sign her name "Eva Braun," but stopped, crossed out the "B," and wrote "Eva Hitler, born Braun." Goebbels and Bormann signed as witnesses.

After what one of Hitler's secretaries described as a "death marriage," a macabre wedding breakfast followed in the Führer's small private apartment. Champagne was served to the guests: Hitler's two secretaries, his vegetarian cook, Fräulein Menzialy, the remaining generals, Krebs and Burgdorf, Bormann, and Dr. and Frau Goebbels. Surprisingly there was much talk, most of it about the good old times when the Nazi party was riding to power. Hitler, in an unexpectedly mellow mood, recalled fondly the wedding of the Goebbelses at which he was best man. As he had done so very often in the small morning hours of happier times, the bridegroom lapsed into a lengthy monologue, going over once more and for the last time the great moments in his fantastic life.

Now it was over, he said, as was the great movement which he had stamped on Germany, National Socialism. It would be a relief for him to die, since he had been betrayed by his oldest friends and supporters. Such talk plunged the wedding party into gloom, and some of the guests, fighting back tears, quietly left. Hitler slipped away too. In an adjoining room he began to dictate to one of his secretaries, Frau Gertrude Jung, his last will and testament.

I found copies of this document too. The testament made it very clear — to me, at least — that this man, who had ruled over Germany for more than twelve years, and over most of Europe for four, had learned nothing from his experience. Not even the shattering defeat, his disastrous final failure, had taught him anything. In the last hours of his life he slipped back in character to the primitive young man he had been in the gutter days in Vienna and the rowdy beer-hall years in Munich, cursing the Jews for all the ills of the world, spinning his half-baked theories about the universe, turning history upside-down and whining that fate once more had cheated Germany of victory and conquest. In this valedictory to the German nation and the world, which was also meant to be a final appeal to history, the doomed dictator dredged up all the empty claptrap of *Mein Kampf* and added his final falsehoods. It was a fitting epitaph of a power-drunk tyrant whom absolute power had corrupted absolutely and destroyed.

And such falsehoods!

It was not true, he said, that he wanted war in 1939. It was "provoked exclusively" by the Jews, who, he said, were thus solely responsible for not only the millions of deaths suffered on the battlefields and in the bombed cities, but for his own massacre of the Jews. He then turned to the reasons why he had decided to remain in Berlin, and to die there.

> I die with a joyful heart in my knowledge of the immeasurable deeds and achievements of our peasants and workers and of a contribution unique in history of our youth which bears my name.

He exhorted Germans not to give up the struggle. He acknowledged that Nazism was dead for the moment but "one day would have a glorious rebirth" — even in the armed forces. Finally he castigated the army, which had done most of the fighting and lost most of the men — millions of them — for having surrendered "towns and districts" in Russia, unmindful that it was his insistence that his troops never give up "a town or a district" that had contributed to the disaster in Russia, where dozens of divisions that could have retreated to fight another day were doomed because they had tried to follow the madman's suicidal orders.

With one more parting shot at the Jews, "the poisoners of all nations," Hitler finished. It was 4 A.M. He had been up all night and was exhausted. He called in Goebbels, Bormann, and Generals Krebs and Burgdorf to witness his signing of the documents and then ordered the first two to carry the testament to the new Doenitz government in the northwest. Bormann was more than willing. For all his devotion to Hitler, he did not want to share his imminent death. What he wanted was to share power, behind the scenes, with Admiral Doenitz, as he had with Hitler. But what if Göring tried to usurp the throne? Bormann got off a radio message to S.S. headquarters at Berchtesgaden, which had just arrested the Luftwaffe chief, to "exterminate" him. "Men, do your duty!" he exhorted. As soon as his Leader had carried out the last act of his life, Bormann would leave for safer parts.

Dr. Goebbels had no such intention. He did not want to live in a Germany from which his revered Führer had departed. For the first time in his life, he said, he would disobey his Master. He sat down and scribbled out his own valedictory to present to future generations. In it he announced that he, with his wife and six young children, would die by the side of their beloved Führer.

During the afternoon of April 29, one last piece of news came in over a makeshift radio from the outside world, and it must have unnerved the stricken dictator further. Benito Mussolini, his fellow Fascist dictator and ally, had met his end in Italy. I never found out how many of the details of the Duce's shabby end were given to Hitler. But one can surmise that whatever he learned only strengthened his resolve not to be made "a spectacle" of, as he had written in his last testament.

He now hastened to make his final preparations. He had his favorite Alsatian dog, Blondi, poisoned and two other dogs shot. He distributed capsules of poison to those of his staff who might want to use them rather than fall into the hands of the Russians. To each he expressed his appreciation for long and faithful service.

Evening now approached, the last of Adolf Hitler's life. He ordered the destruction of his remaining papers and sent out word from his apartment that no one was to go to bed until further orders. This indicated to the others that this was the end. So they waited, not knowing what to do. It was not until around 2:30 A.M. of April 30 that Hitler emerged and appeared in the dining passage. Some twenty persons, mostly women members of his staff, had assembled there. He shook hands with each, mumbling a few words that were inaudible. His moist eyes, Frau Jung remembered, "seemed to be looking far away, beyond the walls of the bunker."

After Hitler retired, there was a bizarre scene in the bunker. The tension, which had become almost unbearable, broke, and several couples started to dance! And to drink! And to talk wildly! The weird party became so noisy that word came from the Führer's quarters requesting quiet. But the dancing went on — through the rest of the night.

Next day at noon, the last daily military "situation" conference of the war was held as usual. Hitler came in to hear the bad news, for the very last time. The Russians had now reached the eastern end of the Tiergarten and broken into Potsdamerplatz. They had surrounded the Chancellery. Hitler realized he had to act — quickly. Still, he insisted on lunch first. Apparently his bride had no appetite, and Hitler ate his last meal with his two women secretaries and his cook.

While they were finishing lunch, Erich Kempka, Hitler's chauffeur, who was in charge of the Chancellery garage, was busy trying to round up gasoline for the funeral pyre. He himself did not yet know its purpose; he had simply received orders to find two hundred liters — no easy task in the besieged bunker — and deliver it in jerricans to the doorway leading out on the garden above. After some difficulty, Kempka managed to scrape up one hundred eighty liters, and with the help of three aides, carry it to the emergency exit.

Meanwhile Hitler had fetched his bride for a final farewell with those who had long been in his inner circle: Dr. Goebbels, Generals Kreb and Burgdorf, the secretaries, and Fräulein Menzialy, the cook. Frau Goebbels did not appear. Like Eva Braun, this much more formidable and attractive woman had found it easy enough to make the decision to die with her husband. But unlike the Hitlers, the Goebbelses had six young children.

"My dear Hanna," Magda Goebbels had said to Hanna Reitsch two or three evenings before, "when the end comes you must help me if I become weak about the children. . . . They belong to the Third Reich and to the Führer, and if these two cease to exist there can be no further place for them. My greatest fear is that at the last moment I will be too weak."

Alone in her little room at this last moment she was striving to overcome her greatest fear.

Eva Braun and Adolf Hitler had no such problem. They had only their own lives to take. They said their last farewells and retired to their quarters. Outside in the passageway Goebbels, Bormann, and the others waited. A revolver shot was heard. They waited for a second shot, but it did not come. They opened the door. The body of Adolf Hitler was sprawled on the sofa dripping blood. He had shot himself in the right temple. At his side lay Eva Braun. A second revolver lay on the floor but it had not been used. The bride had swallowed poison.

The men checked their watches. It was 3:30 P.M. on Monday, April 30, 1945, ten days after Adolf Hitler's fifty-sixth birthday, and twelve years and three months to a day since he had become chancellor and had begun to make a shaky Germany into the conquering Third Reich. It would survive him by just one week.

The Viking burial and cremation took place to the accompaniment of exploding Russian shells in the garden above the bunker. During a lull in the bombardment the two bodies were placed in a shallow shell hole and ignited with gasoline, as the mourners, led by Goebbels and Bormann, stood at attention and raised their right arms in the Nazi salute. But not for long. Red Army shells again began falling and as the flames commenced to consume the bodies of the great dictator and his bride, the little band of henchmen withdrew down the steps to the safety of the bunker.

It was now time for Goebbels to follow suit. He waited until the next day, May 1, when it became evident that the Russians were about to burst into the last stronghold of the Third Reich. Toward evening he called in a physician to give his six children lethal injections. To the last moment they had been romping about the complex of underground corridors and rooms, playing hide and seek, oblivious to this final act of history being played out by their parents and the man they knew only, and affectionately, as "Uncle Adolf." I found no eyewitnesses to their end. Helga, the oldest, was twelve; Hilda, eleven; Helmut, nine; Holde, seven; Hedda, five; Heide, three.

Then Goebbels summoned his adjutant and instructed him to fetch some gasoline. "This is the worst treachery of all," he told him. "The generals have betrayed the Führer. Everything is lost! I shall die with my wife and family." He did not mention that he had just had his children dispatched. At about 9:30 P.M. on May Day, just as it was getting dark outside, Joseph and Magda Goebbels, arm in arm, mounted the steps leading to the emergency exit, ducked out to the gardens amid exploding shells and, standing side by side, braced themselves for the adjutant — S.S. Hauptsturm Führer Günther Schwaegermann — to carry out their orders: a shot each in the back of the head.

Such was the sorry end of Hitler and Goebbels, victims of their lust for power and conquest and of their reversion to barbarism. The other two Nazi bigwigs who had been accomplices in their crimes, Göring and Himmler, did not survive them very long. Both were captured by the Allies. Both cheated justice by swallowing poison.

Himmler first. Dismissed on May 6 by Admiral Doenitz from his rump government, which had been set up at Flensburg on the Danish border, the S.S. and Gestapo chief, who had sent so many millions to their deaths, wandered about the frontier for days seeking some way out that would allow him to live. On May 21, having shaved off his mustache, tied a black patch over his left eye, and donned an army private's uniform, Himmler set off with eleven S.S. officers to try to pass through the British and American lines to his native Bavaria. The party was stopped the first day at a British control point between Hamburg and Bremerhaven. After a brief interrogation, Himmler admitted his identity and was taken away to Second Army headquarters at Lüneburg. There he was stripped and searched and made to change into a British army uniform to avert any possibility that he might be concealing poison in his clothes. But this was not precaution enough. Himmler kept a vial of potassium cyanide concealed in a cavity in his gums. When on May 23 a British army doctor started to examine the prisoner's mouth, Himmler bit on his vial and was dead in twelve minutes.

This cold-blooded killer had never looked his part. I saw him from time to time and he first struck me, with his pince-nez spectacles, as looking like a harmless schoolmaster. But behind the façade was a ruthless man, the most evil of all the Nazi thugs, responsible more than any other German for the massacre of millions of Jews in the ovens of the extermination camps, and also for the deaths of two million Russian prisoners of war.

Göring, perhaps a little more human but scarcely less ruthless, shared responsibility for letting Russian POWs die of exposure and starvation in their shelterless camps; he met his end somewhat later, on October 15, 1946, around midnight. Two hours before his turn would have come to be hanged at the Nuremberg jail along with ten other Nazi leaders found guilty by the four-power Allied tribunal of various crimes against humanity, Hermann Göring, once so fat and bemedaled and all-powerful, swallowed a vial of poison that had been smuggled into his cell.

For weeks I had sat in the courtroom in Nuremberg, covering the trial. For me it was the last chapter of a story that had begun eleven years before in this very city when as my first assignment in Hitler's Germany I had been sent there at the beginning of September 1934, to cover the annual Nazi party rally. It was in this old medieval town of narrow winding streets that once saw Hans Sachs and the *Meistersinger* that I had got my first glimpse of Adolf Hitler and his henchmen (Göring, Goebbels, Himmler, and Hess, principally) and launched myself into covering the rise of the Third Reich for the next six years. The men had been so arrogant then and they had become even more so in the ensuing years of triumph — what a contrast to the way they looked in the Nuremberg dock, shabby and down at heel, and beaten.

It was here in Nuremberg, I remembered now as the trial ground on, that at the end of the frenetic party rally in early September 1934, I had suddenly begun to realize that Adolf Hitler, loathsome as he was, had a hold on the German people that no other German had ever had, and that they were prepared — no, willing and happy — to follow him loyally and obediently like sheep but also with all their power and ability on a great adventure that bade no good for the civilized world nor even, in the long run, for themselves or for Germany.

CHAPTER 3

It was at the Nuremberg trial that I at last learned for sure about the "Final Solution," the diabolical plan of Hitler, carried out so ruthlessly by Heydrich and Himmler, to get rid of all the Jews of Europe by massacring them. Our own State Department and the British Foreign Office had done their best to keep the news of the Nazi slaughter of the Jews secret until the Allies had won the war, but a good deal of the truth had gradually filtered out to the West. Only, it had not been believed. It had been too horrendous for ordinary mortals to grasp. I myself at first had been skeptical, despite all my years in Nazi Germany. The extermination camps in Poland, where the Jews were gassed, had not yet been set up when I left Berlin in December 1940. Construction of them had begun only the following year.

But looking back, I have to admit a terrible failure on my part. I should have remembered what Hitler said in his speech to the Reichstag on January 30, 1939, the sixth anniversary of his taking over the German government, and the beginning of the year in which he would launch the Second World War: "If the international Jewish financiers . . . should again succeed in plunging the nations into a world war the result will be . . . the annihilation of the Jewish race throughout Europe."

By that time, after five years in Nazi Germany, I knew well enough that there was little hope for the Jews. But for some reason this publicly expressed threat by the dictator did not register very strongly with me, perhaps because he had again pulled the old poppycock about the "international Jewish financiers" starting a world war, when everyone knew that if war came it would be Hitler who started it. For all the persecution of the German Jews up to 1939, at least there had not yet been any mass killings. Probably even then I could not quite grasp that such a thing could occur in this nation, ruled though it was by ruthless, fanatical anti-Semites. After all, Germany was a Christian country with a very deep and rich European culture. Hitler repeated the threat five times in subsequent public utterances that year, and there is no excuse for my not having taken notice.

Back home after I left Berlin at the end of 1940, I should have done much more than I did to get the facts of this terrible genocide and then report it. I should not have been so easily put off by the State Department and the Foreign Office. I should have pressed the White House, where I had good contacts in Harry Hopkins and Bob Sherwood, and in Felix Frankfurter at the Supreme Court, who was close to the president. But even Justice Frankfurter, himself a Jew who as a youth had emigrated from Austria and who was very much concerned with the fate of Jews in Nazi-occupied Europe, was put off by President Roosevelt, who kept telling him that according to his information the Jews were being transported "to the East" to provide cheap labor for the Nazis and not to be destroyed.

So the revelations at Nuremberg of the "Final Solution" burst upon me like a thunderbolt and left me numb for several days — my mind, my imagination, unable to cope with their enormity.

There was that almost incredible confession of a Nazi thug by the name of Rudolf Hoess, commander of the Nazi extermination camp at Auschwitz. Hoess, a convicted murderer at twenty-three who had served five years of a life sentence before being amnestied in 1928 by the easygoing Weimar Republic, had joined the S.S. two years later, and after the Nazis came to power in 1933 had served as a guard and later as an official in the concentration camps. Thus he spent almost his entire adult life first as a prisoner and then as a jailer. At Nuremberg he seemed most anxious to tell his story, both in affidavits for the prosecution and then on the stand. He seemed proud of his achievements as one of the greatest killers of all time.

For one thing, he boasted, it was he who had introduced a much better means of mass extermination at Auschwitz than was offered at other Nazi death camps in Poland: Belzec, Treblinka, and Wolzek.

> I visited Treblinka to find out how they carried out their exterminations. The camp commandant there told me he had liquidated 80,000 in the course of half a year. . . .
> He used monoxide gas and I did not think that his methods were very efficient. So when I set up the extermination building at Auschwitz I used Zyklon B, which was a crystallized prussic acid, which we dropped into the death chamber from a small opening. It took from three to fifteen minutes to kill the people in the death chamber, depending upon climatic conditions.

Herr Hoess said he knew when the people were dead "because their screaming stopped." After the bodies were removed, he said, his "special commandos took off the rings and extracted the gold from the teeth of the corpses." Always Herr Hoess kept making "improvements" in the art of mass killing.

> Another improvement we made over Treblinka was that we built our gas chambers to accommodate 2,000 people at one time, whereas at Treblinka their ten gas chambers only accommodated 200 persons each. . . .
>
> Still another improvement we made over Treblinka was that at Treblinka the victims almost always knew that they were to be exterminated, while at Auschwitz we endeavored to fool the victims into thinking that they were to go through a delousing process. Of course, frequently they realized our true intentions and we sometimes had riots and difficulties. Very frequently women would hide their children under their clothes but of course when we found them we would send the children to be exterminated.*

Two of Germany's greatest industrial firms, Krupp and I. G. Farben, had set up plants at Auschwitz to take advantage of cheap Jewish labor. How were the selections made, Hoess was asked, of those picked to work and those to die?

> We had two doctors at Auschwitz to examine the incoming transports of prisoners. They would be marched past one of the doctors, who would make spot decisions as they walked by. Those who looked fit to work were sent into the camp. The others were sent immediately to the extermination plants. Children of tender years were invariably exterminated since by reason of their youth they were unable to work.

But even those "fit" Jews who were sent to work as slaves in the very profitable enterprises of Krupp and I. G. Farben did not live very long. After they had been worked to exhaustion, they were returned to Herr Hoess and his colleagues for the "Final Solution."

---

* Before they were herded into the gas chambers, over whose entrances were signs "BATHS," the victims were told they would simply go through a "delousing." But Hoess cooked up even more macabre deceptions. For example, hardly had the captives left the freight trains in which some of them had been transported a thousand miles or more without food or water, than they were given pretty picture postcards marked "Waldsee," a typical name for a vacation spot in Germany, to be signed and sent back home to their relatives. The printed inscription on the card read: "We are doing very well here. We have work and we are well treated. We await your arrival."

Finally, while the selection was being made for the gas chambers, light music was rendered by an orchestra of "young and pretty girls all dressed in white blouses and navy-blue skirts," as one survivor remembered. The musicians were chosen from young Jewish women inmates, whose lives, for the moment anyway, were spared. Thus the death marches at Auschwitz and at other Nazi extermination camps were carried out to the merry tunes from Viennese and Parisian operettas.

Not all the Jews were killed in the gas chambers. In the beginning the Nazi Germans used another method of extermination. It came to light in Nuremberg.

One day, some weeks before the trial began, American prosecutors were questioning a German named Otto Ohlendorf on his wartime activities. The prisoner was typical of many who had risen to eminence in Himmler's S.S. A university graduate, with a doctorate in jurisprudence, an intellectual, a brilliant economist, he had served most of the war as a foreign trade expert in the Ministry of Economics in Berlin. But for one year he had taken on an assignment away from the capital.

What kind of an assignment? he was asked.

"I was chief of Einsatzgruppe D," he said.

By this time the lawyers on the U.S. prosecution staff had become somewhat expert on the subject.

"During the year that you were chief of Einsatzgruppe D," Lieutenant-Commander Whitney R. Harris, a young lawyer on the American staff, asked, "how many men, women, and children did your group kill?"

Ohlendorf, Harris later reported, shrugged his shoulders and with only the slightest hesitation answered:

"Ninety thousand."

The Einsatz groups had first been organized by Himmler and Heydrich to follow the German armies into Poland at the outset of the war in the fall of 1939 and there round up the Jews and place them in ghettos. But with the beginning of the Russian campaign nearly two years later, their function was changed. They were ordered to follow the combat troops and carry out the final solution.

There were four such Einsatzgruppen, A through D. The last one, which Ohlendorf commanded between June 1941 and June 1942, was assigned to the southern sector in the Ukraine and attached to the Eleventh Army. Thus the German army knew what these Einsatz thugs were up to. On the stand at Nuremberg Ohlendorf explained, adding that among the Jews, women and children were not to be spared.

"For what reason were the children massacred?" the Russian judge, General I. T. Nikitchenko, interrupted to ask.

OHLENDORF: The order was that the Jewish population should be totally exterminated.

THE JUDGE: Including the children?

OHLENDORF: Yes.

THE JUDGE: Were all the Jewish children murdered?
OHLENDORF: Yes.

In an affidavit and on the stand, Ohlendorf described how the Einsatzgruppen killed. They would round up the Jews in a town, seize their valuables even to their "outer clothing," and then transport them in army trucks to the place of execution, usually an antitank ditch, which often the victims were made to dig themselves. The German guards would then push them into the ditch. Then, said Ohlendorf, "they were shot, kneeling, or standing, by firing squads in a military manner."

And the ditch was bulldozed over the corpses.

In the spring of 1942, Ohlendorf revealed, the method of execution for women and children was changed, on the orders of Himmler. Instead of shooting them, the Nazi exterminators dispatched them in gas vans especially constructed for the purpose by two Berlin firms. When the motor was started, the fumes from the gas exhaust were piped into the hermetically sealed van. Death came after "ten to fifteen minutes," Ohlendorf said.

But this method was entirely too slow for the massacres the Nazis now planned — quite inadequate, for example, for the slaughter at Kiev, the capital of the Ukraine, shortly after its capture by the German army. There, according to an official Einsatz report, 33,771 persons, mostly Jews, were executed by shooting in just two days, September 29 and 30, 1941.

The total number of Jews and Soviet commissars done away with by the Einsatzgruppen could not be completely computed at Nuremberg. Ohlendorf's Group D did not do as well as some other groups. Group A in the north reported on January 1, 1942, that it had executed 229,052 Jews in the Baltic area and in White Russia. By November, Himmler reported to Hitler that 363,211 Jews had been killed in Russia from August through October, 1942.

Adolf Eichmann, by that time the leading S.S. manager of the Holocaust, later testified that two million persons, almost all Jews, were liquidated by the Einsatzgruppen in the East. But this probably was an exaggeration — the Nazi killers often gave swollen figures to impress the bloodthirsty Hitler and Himmler. According to Himmler's own statistician, a Dr. Richard Korherr, a total of 633,300 Jews in Russia were "resettled" — that is, executed — up to March 23, 1943. Probably by mid-1943, when the murderous duties of the Einsatzgruppen were taken over by the extermination camps, which could carry them out more efficiently on a larger scale, the number of their victims had passed one million. One million innocent, defenseless human beings shot to death in cold blood by the Germans! Five million more Jews would be slaughtered in the gas chambers of the death camps.

Hoess and Ohlendorf did not escape justice. The latter was found guilty by a U.S. military tribunal at Nuremberg along with twenty-one other Einsatz group leaders, fourteen of whom were sentenced to death. Only four, Ohlendorf and three other group commanders, were hanged — at Landsberg prison on June 8, 1951. (This was the prison where Adolf Hitler had served two years for having led the Munich Beer Hall Putsch in 1923.) Hoess, the terror of Auschwitz, was turned over to the Poles, who tried him and sentenced him to death. In the spring of 1947 he was hanged at Auschwitz, the scene of his crimes.

While I was in Nuremberg covering the trial, my mother died in Cedar Rapids, Iowa. I was down with the flu, the worst case I had ever had. Early on the morning of Tuesday, November 27, in one of the crowded bedrooms of an old palace where the correspondents were put up by the army, Howard Smith leaned over from his cot to wake me up. "I'm sorry," he said, "but I have some bad news for you. Your mother died yesterday. New York told me over the feedback last night." He had done the midnight broadcast to New York from the courthouse downtown. I wondered how the end had come. Quickly and without pain, I hoped. She had not been recently ill, so far as I knew. My worries had been about my wife, Tess, in New York, who had pneumonia.

If Mother had died on the Monday, funeral services would be on Wednesday or Thursday. With luck, if I could wrangle transportation and the doctor's okay, I might make it back to Iowa in time for them. I dragged myself out of bed and dressed and went down to see the army physician.

"You're in no shape to make the long flight home," he said, "even if you can get transportation, which I hope you can't. I know how you feel, and I'm sorry. But I urge you not to go." He took my temperature. It was still 102°. "Go back to bed," he said.

I hooked a ride to town to the army transport bureau. A young lieutenant said he would do what he could, but there was little chance. He might get me on a plane to London or Paris the next day or the day after. But he could not guarantee a connecting flight to New York before the weekend, at the earliest. Beaten, I returned to the press

camp and went back to bed. A cable from Tess had come in. Mother's
end was swift and painless, she said.

> MOTHER FELT WELL UNTIL LAST MINUTE, FAINTED SUDDENLY IN
> THE MIDDLE OF A CHAT WITH A NEIGHBOUR, NO PAIN, DID NOT WAKEN
> AGAIN, DIED TWENTY MINUTES LATER.

I kept after the transport office the next two days but there were no
planes. On Thursday I had a cable from Tess dispatched the evening
before — the time difference between Nuremberg and New York was
six hours — saying the funeral had been set for Friday in Cedar Rapids.
She was too ill to go. My brother and sister had left by train from the
east to help arrange it.

I wondered if I had been able to make it whether I would have been
able to express what I felt very strongly about my mother at the funeral
service, which would be attended by her friends, a number of whom
I had known while growing up in Cedar Rapids, though of course I had
not seen them for twenty years — I had been twenty-one when I left
the place. Probably not. It was not customary, even at a Presbyterian
service in those days, for a relative, even a son, to deliver a eulogy. But
perhaps I could get in a word by long-distance cable. I scrawled a few
lines and got them off to my brother in Cedar Rapids.

> PLEASE CONVEY TO MY FRIENDS THERE ALSO THE PASTOR MY DE-
> SPAIR AT NOT BEING ABLE TO BE PRESENT LAST RITES FOR MOTHER
> TOMORROW. I WOULD HAVE LIKED TO SAY A FEW WORDS RECALLING
> HER INTEGRITY HER COURAGE HER WISDOM HER SELF-SACRIFICE HER
> TOO GREAT MODESTY AND WONDERFUL INSPIRATION SHE WAS TO US.

Later, I was told that the pastor of the First Presbyterian Church
opened the service by reading my cable. It was little enough tribute to
a wonderful woman, who had struggled through a difficult life bravely
and with great fortitude. She had lost her husband in Chicago in 1913,
when both were forty-two, and he already launched on a brilliant career
at the bar. She had raised three children alone on the most slender of
means and seen them through college. She had endured the loneliness
of widowhood for thirty-two years after a marriage of less than half that
length, never complaining of her fate. She accepted it with grace and
wisdom.

On Sunday, December 9, I did my last broadcast from Nuremberg.
A couple of days before, it had turned bitter cold, and the medieval city,
or what was left of it, was blanketed in snow. Paul White, the CBS news

director, had ordered me home. I felt a little guilty. Probably I could make it home for Christmas. Most of my colleagues and hundreds of Americans on Justice Jackson's prosecution staff would have to spend the holiday in the frigid, bleak ruins of this old town. Still, none of them had been in this country anywhere near as long as I had. Fascinating as the trial was, I was glad to get out. My diary:

> Nuremberg, Sunday, December 9 (after midnight). Exhausted from writing the broadcast, giving it twice (recording and "live") and then finishing the last take of the long cable to the *Digest*, which went off at midnight. Must pack now and be up at six to catch the courier plane to Paris. . . .
>
> A strange feeling of relief to be leaving this tortuous, tragic land again — perhaps for the last time. Its fate, its spirit, its character, its culture, its people and their barbarian excesses (and now their excessive self-pity) and finally their ghastly war have absorbed my own little life for nearly fifteen years. I seek a release. . . .
>
> It is almost five years to a day since my last going away from Germany. It seemed then that the evil in the German had not only triumphed over himself but was about to triumph over the world. . . .
>
> What seemed like certain doom when last I left did not come off. Those who sought to destroy the rest of the world are themselves destroyed. . . .

They would eventually recover and rebuild, of course. Had they learned anything from the thirteen years of the Third Reich, which most of them had enthusiastically supported? I found little evidence of it. They had never really minded the barbarism of the Nazi regime. They seemed uninterested in the horrors Hitler had perpetrated in the occupied lands and in slaughtering five or six million Jews in the gas chambers. Or they didn't believe such things had happened: it was all enemy propaganda. The Allies had hoped the revelations of the Nuremberg trial would arouse the Germans to a realization of what had happened. But so far as I could see, it had not. More than once I had gone out into the streets and asked ordinary Germans what they thought of the trial.

"Propaganda!" they said. "You'll hang our leaders. So why go on with this farce of a so-called trial? It's propaganda!"

The Germans were not the only ones who had learned little from the war and the Nazi crimes against humanity. There were some Americans, especially in the army. For instance: at Dachau, the notorious concentration camp near Munich, an American military court was trying a certain Dr. Schilling, actually well known to Germans as a scientist, who was accused of having murdered three hundred prisoners at Dachau by using them as guinea pigs for experiments in the study of malaria. The good doctor freely admitted what he had done but justified it on the grounds it had advanced the study of the disease. Unbelievably, he was backed by an American army officer, who was quoted as saying that the U.S. surgeon general's office had found the results of the Dachau "research" worthwhile because they had contributed to the cure for malaria. I doubted that the surgeon general had made any such finding. Another U.S. Army officer, I noted, was going around Munich saying he didn't believe the atrocity stories about Dachau anyway.

CHAPTER 4

London, where I was to pick up an army plane for home as soon as space was available, was damp and chilly and gray as usual at this time of year. But the English were looking ahead to their first peacetime Christmas in six years and the miserable weather, which they were used to anyway, did not bother them. Nor did much else, though they knew that after all the sacrifices of the long war, grim years lay ahead in which they would have to rebuild the bombed-out cities and somehow put together a new economy, the old one now in shambles because of the cost of war and the loss of most of the Empire, which formerly had been so profitable.

It would be their first Christmas, I reflected, since 1938 that the lights would be on in the city streets and merrymakers could go caroling as they had before and one could look through the windows, so heavily curtained during the wartime blackout, and see the lights of Christmas trees. I began to think that I would be spending this Christmas in London, but the U.S. Army finally came through with a place on a plane that would get me home in time.

On the way to the airport, a headline in the *Daily Telegraph* caught my eye. John Amery, son of an eminent Tory politician and former cabinet member, had been hanged the day before for treason. He had broadcast for Hitler. The British were certainly being tough on their radio traitors. William Joyce, whom the English had dubbed Lord Haw-Haw and listened to in great numbers during the Phony War, had just been condemned to death for his broadcasts from Berlin against his own people. I wondered if the United States would be as strict with its radio traitors when they came to trial. Eight of them had been indicted for treason two years before, but none had yet been tried. I had known a number of these miserable men and women, American and English, in Berlin.

John Amery, whose father had been home minister during much of the time I had worked in London, had arrived in Berlin after I left, but I had learned about him later. He seems to have been somewhat of a spoiled child. Declaring himself bankrupt at twenty-four, he had left

England, worked for Franco in the Spanish Civil War, frequented French Fascist circles during the first two years of the world war, and gone on from France to Berlin in 1942 to broadcast for the Germans. He also became involved in trying to recruit British POWs for an anti-Bolshevik Free Corps to fight with the Germans in Russia. At his trial, to the surprise of the court and his own defense lawyers, he pleaded guilty to all counts. This was committing suicide, for under English law a plea of guilty in a treason case brought a death sentence automatically. A judge could not substitute a sentence of imprisonment, and there was no appeal from the sentence. So John Amery, at thirty-three, had gone to the gallows that chilly, gray December day.

William Joyce would quickly follow him. He had been tried for treason at Old Bailey in September, found guilty, and sentenced to death. He had appealed and his case was reviewed in November by the Court of Appeal, which confirmed the verdict and the sentence. In a desperate move to cheat the gallows, Joyce appealed to the House of Lords, where five judges heard his case for a week in December. His main defense was that he was an American citizen, having been born in Brooklyn in 1906 of Irish parents, and therefore could not be tried for treason against the British king. But the prosecution showed that he had always traveled with a British passport, had proclaimed that he was British, and once, in order to run as a candidate in municipal elections, had sworn that he was a British citizen. Apparently, according to friends who had covered the trials, Joyce believed to the last that his plea of American citizenship would enable him to escape the gallows. But in all three hearings the courts held that Joyce, while admittedly "an American subject, by reason of his birth in the United States, had put himself under the protection of the Crown by obtaining and using a British passport, and therefore owed allegiance to the Crown at the time he was broadcasting from Germany."

I got to know him in Berlin at what must have been the high point of his strange life. This was during the "Phony War," that strange interlude between September 3, 1939, when World War II broke out upon Hitler's attacking Poland, and the summer of 1940, when the Germans overran the West. Scarcely a shot was fired on the western front between the belligerents. Not a bomb was dropped. Only leaflets. The British were bored. William Joyce's broadcasts to them from Berlin helped fill the void. On the air he affected the voice, mannerisms, and accent of a rather decadent English lord. The caricature amused the British listeners. According to Ed Murrow, about half of those who turned their radios on during the evening switched to Haw-Haw. This represented an immense following. But he did not hold it very long. When the war became serious and the real fighting began, first in Norway and then in Holland, Belgium, and France in the spring and summer of 1940, and London and much of Britain began to be heavily bombed, Joyce lost his audience. His quips no longer amused a people suddenly concerned with fighting for their survival.

I used to see Haw-Haw at the shortwave center of the German Broadcasting House, where he went by the name of "Froelich," the equivalent in German of his English name, for it means "joyful." Later, when the British began to bomb Berlin, we found that we shared a distaste at being herded by bullying S.S. guards into the air-raid shelter when the alert sounded. We would sneak out of the cellar and usually end up in his office, where we would douse the lights, pull aside the heavy curtains on the windows, and watch the fireworks. When they were over and while we were waiting to go on the air, we had much good talk. I had a sneaking liking for the man; he was amusing and not unintelligent. But he was the victim of a twisted mind, which instilled in him a violent hatred of the Jews and the British upper classes and a childish adulation of Adolf Hitler and National Socialism.

He had not turned traitor for money — or for love.* He received, I

---

* His compatriot, Norman Baillie-Stewart, whom I also saw on occasion around Broadcasting House, where for a short time he wrote broadcasts for the English-language section, sometimes under the direction of Joyce, whom he detested, had done it for love. And twice! A 1927 graduate of Sandhurst and soon a captain in the Seaforth Highlanders, he had been found guilty in 1932 of betraying military secrets to Germany (Weimar Germany then) and sentenced to five years' imprisonment in the Tower of London. The girl who had led him to this was German, and on his release from prison he set out to find her or another like her, for apparently he had a fixation on German women, which also caused him to have the same feelings for Germany — any Germany, Weimar or Nazi. In Berlin I got the impression that the Germans found Baillie-Stewart difficult to deal with — his Scottish nature, they said, was unbending — and he was transferred from the broadcasting service to the Foreign Office, where he was employed as a translator.

In the end, due to the strange vagaries of British justice, Baillie-Stewart escaped the fate of Amery and Joyce. The original charge of high treason against him was reduced to an offense against the Defense Regulations, for which he was found guilty and sentenced to five years in prison.

There was a third British radio traitor I used to see at Broadcasting House, Jack Trevor, an English actor. I wondered what had happened to him. I never heard he even had been arrested. Perhaps he died in Berlin after I left, and the war became more grim, even in Germany. He popped up a couple of times in my diary of those days. On Christmas Eve, 1940, in the midst of the *Sitzkrieg*, as the Germans called the Phony War, I had dropped in on a party at the Rundfunk. Joyce and his wife had come in to drink champagne and dance. Jack Trevor soon joined them, "much in his cups," I noted. Later, when I was commenting on the British radio traitors, I jotted down this note about Trevor in my diary:

His one burning passion is hatred of Jews. Last winter it used to be a common sight to see him stand in the snow, with a mighty blizzard blowing, and rave to an S.S. guard outside the studio door about the urgent necessity of liquidating all Jews everywhere. The believe, the customary thousand marks a month (roughly four hundred dollars) and his Nazi employers threw in a free apartment. As for love, he had brought with him from England his wife, with whom he seemed very much in love.

Why then was he committing treason? He denied that he was, saying that he had renounced his British citizenship and become a German citizen. But still — why, I would ask him, was he spouting Nazi propaganda to his own people?

"I believe I'm broadcasting the truth," he would say. Probably he actually thought so. He had become a fanatical true-believer. He felt that Hitler, he said, was trying to save the world from "the forces of darkness." He seemed hurt when I said I couldn't understand how a man of his intelligence could believe in such nonsense.

The main reason he was broadcasting to England for Hitler, besides ideology, I concluded, was that it offered him for the first time in his life recognition as someone of some importance. He was listened to by a large number of his fellow countrymen. This had never happened to him at home.

In Britain he had never made it, try as he had. After grade and high school in Ireland, he had studied at the University of London and in 1923, at the age of seventeen, he joined the British Fascists and got his first taste of street brawling, scars of which were still visible on his face when I saw him years later in Berlin. This first British Fascist organization did not thrive, and ten years later, in 1933, the year Hitler took power in Germany, Joyce joined Sir Oswald Mosley's British Union of Fascists and soon became its director of propaganda and one of its leading speakers, pamphleteers, and street fighters. He broke with Mosley four years later and, with John Beckett, a former Labour M.P. (Mosley had also been a Labour M.P.), formed a Nazi party of his own, the National Socialist League. But it did not thrive, nor did he.

"To me it was clear on the morning of August 25, 1939," he once said to me, quoting, as I later saw, from his book *Twilight Over England*, published in Berlin in 1940, "that the greatest struggle in history was now doomed to take place. England was going to war. I felt that if, for perfect reasons of conscience, I could not fight for her, I must give her up forever."

He fled, crossing over the Channel and heading for Berlin to take

---

guard, who undoubtedly had no special love for the Jews, but whose only thought was how much longer he must stand guard on an unholy wintry night, would stamp his freezing feet in the snow, turn his head from the biting wind, and mutter: "Ja. Ja. Ja. Ja," probably wondering what freaks Englishmen were.

part in what he called the "sacred struggle to free the world." He was already blinded by his adulation of Adolf Hitler. I found him tiresome on the subject. The Führer, he held, was the greatest leader the century had produced. His "heroism" was "superhuman." I remember him pointing out, when he gave me a copy of his book, the last sentence, which constituted, he said, his supreme belief: that there were two guarantees of the future of mankind, "the greatness of Adolf Hitler and the Greater Glory of Almighty God."

Through his trial and the appeals Joyce behaved, English reporters who covered the case told me, with courage and even humor. He would go with the same courage, I was told later, to the gallows at grimy Wandsworth Prison on the bitter cold morning of January 3, 1946. He made no apologies for what he had done.*

Until Germany declared war on the United States on December 10, 1941, and brought us into the conflict, there was nothing treasonous about Americans broadcasting for Hitler on shortwave to the United States from Berlin. One could question their taste, but not their loyalty to their native land. There were three of them who began broadcasting Nazi propaganda early in the war, and I occasionally ran into them and learned a little of why they were doing it.

The most effective of the three, at least on the air, was Fred Kaltenbach, of Dubuque, Iowa. He was a fanatical convert to Nazism. He really believed in it. Born of German immigrant parents, he remained very German in outlook and, like so many Germans in the Fatherland, he was early attracted to Hitler's movement. He had a good education in America, studying first at Grinnell, one of the best of the small liberal arts colleges in the Midwest, and then at Iowa State Teachers College in Waterloo, where he earned a B.A. in 1920 (after serving a short time as a second lieutenant in the Coast Artillery during the First World War). After receiving an M.A. in history at the University of Chicago, he returned to Dubuque to teach in the high school. He followed avidly Hitler's rise to power in Germany. In 1933, the year his idol became

---

* On the contrary! He was defiant to the last. "In death as in this life," he said in a last statement issued by his brother Quentin immediately after the hanging, "I defy the Jews, who caused this last war, and I defy the power of darkness which they represent. . . . May Britain be great once again and in the hour of the greatest danger to the West may the standard of the Hakenkreuz (swastika) be raised from the dust crowned with the historic words: '*Ihr habt doch gesiegt!* (You have conquered nevertheless!)' "

Like the maniac he worshipped, Adolf Hitler, William Joyce, intelligent though he was, had learned nothing from recent history, from the recent war which Hitler had started and now lost, from the exposure of Nazism as a fraud and a barbarism. He was the victim, as so many are up to this very moment, of a mindless devotion to an outlandish ideology.

the German chancellor, Kaltenbach organized a group of high-school boys into a hiking club that he called the "Militant Order of the Spartan Knights." He modeled it after the Hitler Youth, even to brown shirt uniforms. The school authorities in Dubuque showed better sense than their counterparts in Germany. They ordered Kaltenbach to disband his "knights." Rebuffed if not disheartened, he departed Dubuque and indeed his country, and set out for his beloved Nazi Germany. There he enrolled at the University of Berlin and eventually earned a Ph.D. When the war started he offered his services to Dr. Goebbels and began to broadcast on the German shortwave radio service to America.

It was not at first easy for him or for his new masters. It sounds almost unbelievable, but Nazi officials in the Propaganda Ministry and at the Broadcasting House found the American "too Nazi." He quarreled with them over the purity of their National Socialism.

That quarrel was still going on when Kaltenbach showed up at Compiègne, where on June 21 and 22, 1940, Hitler dictated his armistice terms to the French after their terrible defeat. The German radio people had barred him from covering the event and refused him transportation from Paris. But he hooked a ride with some army officers and sneaked into the little clearing in the woods at Rethondes outside of Compiègne. All during those two days he was continually being ejected from the grounds by M.P.s and continually slipping back. I remember Kaltenbach standing by my side that first day when Hitler arrived. The Führer was surrounded by his military officers; opposite him sat the dejected members of the French delegation. Kaltenbach, as if in a trance, gazed longingly at his Führer. He would have died for Adolf Hitler.

And actually he did. He elected to stay on in Germany after Hitler declared war on America. His broadcasts to America now became virulent. He spouted out his glorification of Hitler and Nazism and his hatred of the American democracy. He urged Americans to turn against President Roosevelt and to desist from the war effort.

At the war's end, Kaltenbach, who had remained in Berlin, was captured by the Russians, who refused to turn him over to the Americans. Perhaps they thought his fellow countrymen would not be as tough on him as he deserved. On this last assignment to Berlin I made inquiries as to what had happened to him. The Americans didn't know. The Russians wouldn't say. I presumed he was dead.*

---

* This was finally confirmed by the Russians in July of the following year. The Soviet Army Command in Berlin informed the American authorities that Kaltenbach had died in a Russian detention camp "of natural causes."

Edward Leopold Delaney, who was known at the Propaganda Ministry in Berlin as E. D. Ward, broadcast under the latter name for Goebbels. At home he had been a struggling actor, touring the country in such plays as *Get-Rich-Quick Wallingford*. He was also an author of two books, *The Lady by Degrees* and *The Charm Girl*, the latter advertised as the "scream-line correspondence of a radio charmer and her girl friend." According to a note I made of him in my Berlin diary in 1940, "he has a diseased hatred for the Jews, but otherwise is a mild fellow and broadcasts the cruder type of Nazi propaganda. . . ." Like Kaltenbach, he chose to remain in Berlin after the United States entered the war, and in 1943 he was indicted for treason along with seven other Americans who had broadcast to the United States.*

The third American broadcaster indicted for broadcasting to the United States from Berlin after 1941 was a woman, a Miss Constance Drexel of Philadelphia, where Drexel is a famous name. She had once written, she told me, for the *Public Ledger* there. The Nazis hired her, I think, because she was the only woman in town who would sell her American accent to them. I suspected she did it, in part, because she needed the money. At least, in pestering me for a job on CBS, she said she needed some. The Nazi Germans at the Broadcasting House complained that she was a lousy broadcaster, with no style or personality to project. But she stayed on after America got into the war. In time, the Justice Department would drop its indictment of her and she would return, so the department later informed me, to the United States.

There was a fourth American broadcasting for the Nazis when I was still in Berlin before we got into the war, but unlike the others he was a combat radio correspondent with the German army whose front-line battle recordings were played to America on the shortwave. This was Charles Flicksteger, who wrote and broadcast under a shortening of his name to "Flick." I knew him rather well. In fact, I replaced him when I went to Berlin in 1934 for the Universal News Service.

Flick's chief interest was music. Married to a retired Munich opera singer, he composed operas, one or two of which, I believe, were produced in provincial German opera houses. He used to tell me that Germany was the only country in the world where a struggling com-

---

* In 1945 the Justice Department dropped the indictment against him and in 1951 he surfaced as a broadcaster for a Tucson, Arizona, radio station. He admitted he had broadcast for the Nazis, but denied that he was anti-Semitic. In fact, he posted a thousand-dollar bond for anyone who could "prove" he was anti-Semitic. Queried by the *Arizona Daily Star* about that, I replied I stood by what I had written about Delaney in *Berlin Diary*.

poser had a chance to have his opera performed — the country had more than a dozen good opera companies, subsidized by the government. Flick would contrast this with America, which, outside of New York and Chicago, he said, had no opera companies, and even those rarely played a new work by an American composer.

Flick, who had many friends in the Nazi party, including Göring, got into some kind of trouble with them during the June 1934 blood purge of the S.A. leaders and found it necessary to get himself transferred from Berlin to Vienna. There the Austrians promptly arrested him as a Nazi agent and expelled him. He returned to America to see if he could make a go of it at home as a journalist and a composer. Apparently he couldn't, and sometime before the war he returned to Berlin, soured on his native land. "I just couldn't make it over there," he complained to me.

When I saw Flick next — and for the last time — he had made his decision. It was a curious meeting. It was June 1940, and the German army, which I had followed across Holland, Belgium, and France as an American correspondent, had just marched into Paris. I came back to the hotel one evening and slipped into a seat at a large table in the dining room of the Hotel Scribe. The table was full of happy German army officers, most of them in their cups. One of them with the insignia of a first lieutenant looked familiar. He was grinning at me.

"Guess you didn't expect to see me, Bill, in this," he said, pointing to his gray German army uniform. He had given up his American citizenship, he added, and become a German. He seemed pleased with himself. After all, the German army had just conquered France in six weeks. And he was now a part of it.

Toward the end of the war, I heard, Flick had somehow got out to China, where he was manager of a German-owned radio station, XGRS, which poured out anti-American propaganda from Japanese-occupied Shanghai. He was arrested by the Americans in Shanghai at the war's end, I believe, but later released.

None of these Americans, as I have said, who were broadcasting to America in the service of Nazi propaganda were involved in treason during the time I knew them. America was not yet in the war. Flick apparently escaped indictment later, when we did get into the war, because he had become a German citizen — a defense similar to the one that did not save Joyce's life. But Kaltenbach, Delaney, and Miss Drexel apparently took no such step before Germany and the United States became formally at war, and they were indicted in 1943 for

treason. In the meantime, other Americans, on the whole more effective, had joined them in Berlin.

I knew two of them rather well. One was Robert Best, who had been
the United Press correspondent in Vienna during the years I had the
Chicago Tribune and CBS bureaus there. The other was Donald Day,
for twenty years the *Chicago Tribune*'s correspondent in Riga, from
which he poured out richly imaginative stories about the troubles of the
nearby Soviet Union, including lurid tales of uprisings that were about,
he reported, to overthrow the godless Bolshevik regime. These tales
made him a great favorite of our boss, the imperious, anti-Red Colonel
McCormick, proprietor, editor, and publisher of what he insisted was
"The World's Greatest Newspaper." Day was a big, boisterous, boyish
fellow, rather liked by most of his American colleagues despite his
deplorable reporting and his making his hatred of the Bolsheviks in
Moscow into a sacred crusade. It was this fierce zeal that propelled him
late in the war into the service of Hitler against his native land.

The end that Bob Best chose surprised me and, I believe, the rest
of his American colleagues who knew him and liked him in Vienna.
Born in Sumter, South Carolina, in 1896, he had graduated from
Wofford College in Spartanburg in 1916, served as a lieutenant in the
Coast Artillery during the First World War, and had then enrolled in
the Columbia University Graduate School of Journalism. He was a
promising student and in 1922 he set off for Europe on a year's Pulitzer
traveling scholarship. He soon landed in Vienna, got a job as a United
Press stringer, holed up in the Café Louvre, where the foreign correspondents hung out and where he wrote his dispatches and held forth
at his *Stammtisch* in one corner. He rarely left it except late in the night
when he went home to his apartment, which he shared with an aging
woman of mysterious but probably Levantine origin, whom we called
"The Countess" but whom none of us correspondents ever saw.

In those days Bob Best was the most genial and generous of fellows.
He would not only share his news stories with you, but file for you when
you were ill or out of town. Though not a good writer or a very good
reporter — he was too lazy to check up carefully on a story or to go out
and dig for information — he was a mine of information and misinfor-
mation about Vienna, Austria, Central Europe, and the Balkans. He
seemed to know everyone in town, including the most murky agents
of the Comitadji and other Balkan conspiratorial groups. American
visitors invariably looked him up at the Louvre, especially the well-

known foreign correspondents who came and went — Dorothy Thompson, H. R. Knickerbocker, John Gunther, and others — and noted writers such as Sinclair Lewis (married to Dorothy) and H. L. Mencken, who showed up fairly regularly in Vienna to sample the beer, brush up his German, and chew the fat with the American newspapermen.

Bob Best's closest friend in Vienna was a Jew, a learned Hungarian who became a correspondent for British and American newspapers, and not only helped Bob in his job, but lent him money and regularly invited him for drinks and meals. In fact, many of Bob's friends among the journalists in Vienna were Jews. I mention this because ultimately he was to become the most virulent anti-Semite of all the anti-Semitic Americans broadcasting for Hitler.

How he got that way in the end I never could completely figure out. In my various tours of duty in Vienna from 1929 to 1938 I never would have suspected that Bob Best could become a vicious Nazi. I saw him for the last time on the evening of March 11–12, 1938, when Hitler took over Austria. He kept hoping against hope that the Nazis would fail. Once during the hectic evening, he came back from a telephone booth in the café and announced that the Austrian chancellor, Kurt von Schuschnigg, had regained power. Once before Schuschnigg had put down a Nazi coup. The news was false, as Bob's news often was. But it expressed his hope. Later that evening, his friend Major Goldschmidt, Catholic but half Jewish and the leader of the Austrian legitimists who wanted to bring back a Hapsburg monarchy, came in and sat down next to Bob to check on the news. By this time Best, like the rest of us, knew that it was all over for Austria. The Nazis had taken over the capital and the country. Major Goldschmidt rose from Bob's table and said quietly: "Most of you have not agreed with me, but we've been friends. I say goodbye to you. This is the end for the monarchy and for the Jews. I will go home and get my revolver."

Best took the lead in trying to dissuade him. I remember that shortly afterward on that nightmarish evening, the wife of Best's closest friend, a beautiful Slovak, came into the Louvre. She was worried that her husband would be arrested as a Jew. Nazi thugs were reported to be already rounding up the Jews. Bob Best comforted her. Secret arrangements were being made, he assured her, for the American minister himself to take her husband out to Bratislava on the nearby Czech frontier.

After the Austrian Anschluss I moved my CBS headquarters to neutral Geneva and did not see Best again. But I kept in touch with him by letter and telephone, especially after the war started and I had to spend most of my time in Berlin. Three or four times I phoned him to ask him to broadcast for us on stories breaking in Central Europe that I could not get down to cover. On the phone he seemed his old self, and there was no trace of Nazi bias in his broadcasts for us.

Shortly before I left Berlin at the end of 1940, I had a letter from Best. He was in Vienna, and he wrote that he would stay on there "even if we get into the war." That was the first inkling I had that something might be happening to him. For if America "got into the war," it could only be against Germany, and that would make Bob an enemy alien unless . . . The thought bothered me. I had heard he had a new girlfriend, Austrian or German, who was an ardent Nazi.

When we did get into the war at the end of 1941, Best, like other Americans, was interned at Bad Nauheim until such time as Germans caught in the United States could be repatriated. Most of the internees were American diplomats and journalists, and I heard that Best soon began distancing himself from them. When in the spring of 1942 the Americans were finally allowed to leave Germany, Best chose to remain, "in the interest of history," he said, in an open letter to the American chargé d'affaires. By this time, the Nazi poison had taken effect. Best peppered his letter with anti-Semitic outbursts against his native land, which he said was being destroyed by "the Rascal-Roosevelt's Jewed-up Administration." Best lit out for Berlin and got a job as an American commentator on the Nazi propaganda broadcasts beamed on shortwave to America. Dr. Goebbels apparently liked Best's violent anti-Semitic vocabulary in denouncing the "Jew-nited States." The American turncoat soon became Berlin's star Jew-baiter.

At first he did not identify himself. He was introduced from Berlin as "Mr. Guess-Who." One spring evening in 1942 we identified him at the CBS Shortwave Listening Post in New York. The man on duty that evening happened to be an Austrian friend of mine who had been a newspaper editor in Vienna. He was a Jew and Best had befriended him. In fact, he told me later, the night the Nazis took over in Austria, Best had lent him a month's salary and helped him escape across the frontier to Czechoslovakia. He felt he owed his life to Best. Suddenly on this evening my Austrian friend burst into my office. He was excited and disturbed.

"There is someone talking from Berlin," he said, "who calls himself 'Mr. Guess-Who.' He sounds to me like Bob Best. But I can't believe it. Please come and listen."

I hurried to the booth, put on earphones, and listened. There was no doubt. It was Bob Best. He was thundering away at the Jews in America. My Austrian Jewish friend was in tears.

Once a week, on Sunday, I had a column in the *New York Herald-Tribune*, which also syndicated it around the country. It dealt largely with enemy propaganda. On Sunday, May 31, 1942, it began:

> So Bob Best has turned traitor and decided to join Haw-Haw, Kaltenbach, Ward, Chandler and a few other English and Americans who have sold their native accents and their souls to Dr. Goebbels's short-wave propaganda station in Berlin. . . .
> Why did he do it?

Ever since that spring evening of 1942 I had mulled over that question. Why did Bob Best — why did Donald Day and the other Americans — do it? Most men turn traitors for money. Best never had much, but he didn't seem to mind. Nazi money couldn't have tempted him. I believe he got no more than the others, a thousand marks a month and perhaps a free apartment. In the end, I think, he did it out of ideology. He had finally been bitten by the Nazi bug, and it destroyed him.

One trouble with Best was that he stayed in Central Europe too long. He never went home to renew his roots, and gradually he put down new ones in the worst weedy patches of Mitteleuropa. He became alienated from his native land and its values, which he had absorbed in the small towns of the Carolinas in his youth. He became more and more Austrian at a time when the Austrians, like the Germans before them, began to see Adolf Hitler as a savior. There had always been a good deal of anti-Semitism in Vienna — that was where Hitler had first absorbed it as a youth — and apparently after the Anschluss in 1938, when Best's Jewish friends fled to escape what they knew would happen under Hitler, the American, now pretty much alone,* drifted more and more into Nazi circles, accompanied by his fiancée or perhaps led by her. At the same time, judging by his later broadcasts from Berlin, he reverted to the fundamentalist Christianity of his youth in the American South, where his father had moved from one small town to another as a Methodist preacher. But in his sick, Nazified mind

---

* After the Anschluss in the spring of 1938, the American newspapers closed down their offices in Vienna and assigned their correspondents to other capitals. I myself, with most of the European continent to cover, moved my CBS headquarters from Vienna to Geneva, where communication facilities were free of Nazi control. The news agencies, with the exception of the United Press, hired local nationals to provide them with the news. Best, reduced now to being a "stringer" for the United Press since there was little news from the former capital, which had now become just another provincial German city, became, I believe, the only American journalist there.

fundamentalist Christianity, like America, like Western civilization, became threatened by sinister, Christian-hating Jews.

I wondered as my plane took off from London for home whether Bob Best and the others would be brought back home for trial. The British radio traitors had been swiftly tried, sentenced, and executed. Best and his American colleagues were still incarcerated in an American military prison in Germany. Why the delay? I wondered. I thought of something else. If Best were tried for treason in America, as the indictment called for, would I, as one who had known him, who had first identified him for the press and the U.S. government as the one who was broadcasting for Hitler, be called to testify against him? I could not excuse what I believed was his treason. Nevertheless, the prospect bothered me. He had been a friend and colleague.

The trip home in an army transport C-54 was uneventful. A group of Irish-American merrymakers from Boston, led by Mayor James M. Curley, came aboard. They had been in London to try to get the Preparatory Commission of the United Nations to locate the organization's world headquarters in their fair city. In London a week before, the commission had voted to make the permanent seat of the U.N. in the United States.

In Shannon, Ireland, where we stopped to refuel, the Boston delegates tanked up at an airport bar for the long hop across the ocean. They were in a festive mood and already filled the plane with the spirit of Christmas, which with luck and good weather we would get home just in time to celebrate.

I was excited at the prospect. I was going home this time for good. In fact, this was for me a farewell to Europe, to being a foreign correspondent. It had taken me a long time to come to a decision, but I had made it in the last months of the war. The twenty years abroad — my entire adult life — had been wonderfully full. A reporter's life had been interesting and sometimes exciting. I had come to feel at home in Europe, in London, Paris, Rome, Vienna, Berlin, Madrid, had picked up four languages in order to do my job and to get to know and enjoy different cultures, especially their rich literature. I had liked the work and the life. In Vienna I had married a Viennese and we had our first child there. It would have been easy and even pleasant to drift into staying on in Europe forever. CBS had offered me just that prospect: to succeed Ed Murrow, who was going home, as chief correspondent in Europe. It was tempting, but I had turned it down.

Instinctively, toward the end of the war I came to the realization that when it was over I must go home for good. Fascinating and fulfilling as my years in Europe had been, I would always be a stranger there, an eternal observer, unable to participate really in the life of any nation or people. It was difficult at first to admit this. But I had to face the truth that actually I had not put down any deep roots in Europe, not even in Paris and Vienna, which I loved and loved to live in, and where I felt more at home than in any American city.

After so long a time abroad I scarcely knew my native land. But that was where my roots were, that was where in the end I belonged, that was where I wanted to make my way for the rest of my life. I was forty-one. There was still time to start out afresh at home.

I was not alone in these feelings. Two of my closest friends and colleagues, John Gunther and Jimmy Sheean, had already made that decision, John before the war, and Jimmy, like me, before the war was over. Edgar Snow, another old friend, had felt similarly, I would find out later. He had spent most of his journalistic life in China, which he loved passionately and understood deeply, and which in turn had left an indelible impression on him. Later he would put it eloquently in his memoirs:

> China had claimed a part of me even if I could make no claim on her. Part of me would always remain with China's tawny hills. . . . Yes, I was proud to have known [the Chinese], to have struggled across a continent with them in defeat, to have wept with them and still to share a faith with them.
>
> But I was not and could never be one of them. A man who gives himself to the possession of an alien land . . . lives a Yahoo life. . . . I was an American.*

So I had turned down the chance to stay on in Europe. In London Ed Murrow and I had had a long talk about it. He himself — mistakenly, I thought — was going home to become CBS vice-president in charge of news and public affairs. I told him I thought it was foolish to give up what he had done better than any of us on the air to become a network executive.

"Stay on the air!" I had urged him. "You're the best there is. Besides, you're a lousy executive."

But Ed had made up his mind. He was confident he could shape the future of radio as a medium of the news better as an executive than if he remained on the air as a commentator. Even more important, he

* Quoted from Edgar Snow's memoirs by his widow, Lois Snow, in an article in the *New Republic*, January 26, 1974, entitled "The Burial of Edgar Snow."

said, television was looming in the near future and in his new job he felt he could help develop it into a tremendous force in purveying, as no other medium could, the news. Why not join him, he said, as his assistant? We could do great things together.

But I was an even worse executive, I told him, than he was. I had no competence whatsoever. I would like to stay on the air as a reporter and a commentator, continue my Sunday column for the *New York Herald-Tribune* and its syndicate, write an occasional piece for the magazines, and, if I could find time, do another book. My first book, *Berlin Diary*, published in 1941, had done quite well. I did not tell Ed that my secret passion was to write books and that ultimately I hoped to end up doing just that. I didn't quite trust myself. Like most other journalists I would probably put off writing books simply because a steady job gave one some kind of security. I doubted that I had the guts to give up a regular salary check and strike out into the uncertain world of writing full-time.

Ed did not like my reply, and asked me to think it over. But I, too, had made up my mind.

Some of the members of the Boston party became so ill and unruly in the plane during the night that the pilot decided to make an unscheduled landing in Boston and get rid of them. One had suffered a heart attack and looked as if he might give up the ghost any moment.

My wife Tess, Eileen Inga, who was seven, and Linda, who was four, were at the airport in New York when we landed. Tess had found a beautiful apartment in an old house facing the East River at 50th Street and had just moved the family from Bronxville. She and the children had already decorated a large tree in one corner of the living room that faced on the river. Eileen and Linda scarcely recognized me.

"You going to stay home now?" they asked.

"Absolutely," I said. "No more wars. No more going away."

They dragged me to a Christmas service at Dalton, where they had recently enrolled, insisting that I keep my uniform on. They wanted to show me off, I guess. Then over to Fifth Avenue to see the brightly decorated shop windows. We mingled with the throngs of merry shoppers along the street and then we walked over to Park Avenue in the bracing December air just as the Christmas lights went on. Christmas Eve we sat around the fire and Tess and I read to the children from Dickens's *Christmas Carol*.

This was heaven. This was the good life. And it was easier than I thought at this Christmas reunion to erase, at least for this happy moment, the memory of the nightmare years in Europe that had led up to the war and into the war and that had robbed us, as it had millions of others, of this kind of a decent life together.

But from now on, I swore to Tess and Eileen and Linda, we would have it. There would be peace and some decency in the world and we would have it.

BOOK TWO

The First Two Years
1945–1947

CHAPTER 1

It felt good, though a little strange, to be home for good and working, and no job or war in Europe to go back to.

The adjustment, so difficult for some of my returning colleagues and impossible for a few who drifted back to Europe and uncertain existence, was easier than I expected. True, I missed the life we had led before the war in Paris, London, Vienna, Rome — even in Berlin. But not as much as I feared. New York, I found, had practically all the things I liked in the Old World capitals: good libraries, art museums, theaters, symphony orchestras, chamber music ensembles, ballet, and opera.

And there was in the air of New York City an electricity, a surging vitality, that the cities of Europe lacked and that made living vibrant and stirred you up and made the blood tingle. It made you feel as if there was nothing impossible under the sun if you wanted it badly enough in your work and in your life.

While I was overseas Tess had found an ideal place to live in Manhattan — a part of an old house in Beekman Place that overlooked the East River. It gave us the sort of home that ordinarily we could not have afforded even in those days, long before rents in Manhattan soared far beyond the means of those with modest incomes. Antoine de Saint-Exupéry, the French writer and aviator and the previous tenant before he returned to the war and death in 1944, had paid a thousand dollars a month rent for it. The gracious owner, whose husband and sons were also overseas in the war, had given it to Tess for three hundred dollars. She was one of those rare persons of wealth who was completely unostentatious about it. Nothing that we could afford to pay meant the slightest thing to her. She wanted someone compatible to live in the large house while her husband and sons were away in the war, and she found in Tess just what she wanted. She tossed aside as irrelevant, I learned later, her attorney's protest that she was *giving* our quarters to us. Her husband did not survive the war and her two sons preferred to live elsewhere when they returned. So we stayed on there, practically rent free, for our payment was soon reduced to two hundred fifty dollars a month when we relinquished two small rooms on the fourth floor, which we had not used anyway.

It was a lucky break, and one we much appreciated, especially in the ensuing years when rents began to soar and the going got rough for us in other matters. But I had always believed in luck, that there was bound to be in anyone's life the good and the bad. At the moment, as we settled down to life at home, we were on the upswing. Good fortune was favoring us.

I loved the work and the life. At CBS I had a fifteen-minute sponsored Sunday broadcast of news and news analysis, so called, that alone paid me all the money I needed or wanted — much more than I had ever made before. It relieved us of any money worries. For the first time in our life, almost, it gave us a certain feeling of security. I had gradually built up the audience to a point where the broadcast enjoyed the highest rating of any daytime network show on Sunday. Two or three sponsors were waiting in the wings to back the program in case the present one faltered. With the country going over to peacetime production for a people starved of civilian goods for four years, there were more applicants for sponsorship of radio programs than there was time on the air. Everyone wanted to advertise his wares. Aside from the Sunday show I also did brief, unsponsored commentaries three times a week on the 11 P.M. news.

The work in radio kept me busy enough, but I had added other jobs to it. In 1942 the *New York Herald-Tribune* had asked me to do a weekly syndicated column on propaganda, which the belligerents, especially Nazi Germany, were using widely as an important weapon of war. The paper called it "The Propaganda Front," which I did not like, but in time I strayed widely from the subject, writing what I pleased about the war and the eventual peace and other aspects of foreign affairs, which in a sense had become, after twenty years abroad as a foreign correspondent, my principal lifework. This column enabled me to keep my finger in print journalism, my first love, where I had got my start. It kept sharpened my facility to write.

Broadcasting regularly, I found, gave one a peculiar notoriety. Invitations to speak, to lecture, to debate, poured in. And just to keep my finger in that world, too, I accepted a few. For me it offered a chance to do what, among other things, I had come home to do: participate, however modestly, in the affairs of my country. On the platform, especially in rough-and-tumble debates, you could express your opinions more thoroughly than on radio. CBS was still, quite unsuccessfully, trying to prevent us from expressing opinions on the air. I did not particularly like to lecture or to deliver a long set speech. For one thing, it took me weeks to prepare. Unlike some of my colleagues on the lecture circuit, such as Eleanor Roosevelt, I could not talk at length ad lib. But I found I could do it when I got caught up in debate. The debates were also humbling. Sometimes I got clobbered. There is an entry in my diary for Thursday, April 11, 1946. "Got quite a drubbing at Town Hall [New York] tonight." It was a debate over a popular radio program, "America's Town Meeting of the Air," on the Russian-Iranian dispute, with Max Lerner and me pitted against two old friends, Louis Fischer and Edgar Mowrer, both veteran European foreign correspondents. "I was booed by the audience," I noted. It was easy, with the notoriety and the constant publicity that radio brought, to get puffed up about yourself. The public debates brought me down a notch or two.

So the work — the broadcasts, the talks, the lectures, the debates, the weekly newspaper column — brought a good life and kept me busy.

To my joy, I found that many of my friends from the years in Europe were now also back home, most of them settling in the New York area. John Gunther and Vincent Sheean, two of my oldest friends — all three of us had come originally from Chicago and worked abroad for Chicago newspapers — had returned before the war, though both had gone back to it frequently to do newspaper and magazine articles, and Jimmy Sheean had ended up, of all things, as a lieutenant colonel in the Army Air Corps. Both already had written and published brilliant books that had attracted a wide audience at home and in England, John with his "Inside" volumes of which *Inside Europe* was the pioneer in a new kind of book journalism; Jimmy with his autobiographical *Personal History*, which had been a huge success. Dorothy Thompson, who had reported so brilliantly from Berlin, from which Hitler expelled her, already had a widely syndicated column and was becoming a new star of radio. Her Sunday broadcasts attracted a vast audience. She also lectured and made speeches. Dorothy was a very close friend of Gunther and Sheean. I did not know her nearly so well, but we were good friends — I admired her greatly.

Only, Dorothy and I had a problem. Though we were both violently anti-Nazi, we disagreed about the Germans, with whom Dorothy, it always seemed to me, had a passionate love-hate relationship, as indeed she acknowledged. We had violent disputes about the Germans and about what to do with them. Sometimes we got into shouting matches that we soon regretted, for we were fond of each other. Finally, in a moment of wisdom, we agreed to forgo discussing the

Germans. The subject was verboten. And we continued to see each other to the end.

Joseph Barnes, a former Moscow and later Berlin correspondent of the *New York Herald-Tribune*, was now back home as foreign editor of that civilized liberal journal. We had become close friends in Berlin, and would remain so. Though Joe used to pride himself on being "just a good reporter," he was in fact the most scholarly of us foreign correspondents, with an original and brilliant mind.

Jim Thurber was my oldest friend. It was he who had been sitting around the copy desk of the Paris *Chicago Tribune* one sweltering August evening in 1925 when I, age twenty-one and just out of a small Iowa college, having wangled a job at the last moment before a scheduled departure for home,* had slipped into the slot next to him. We had become good friends in Paris and kept in touch after he went home toward the end of the 1920s and eventually, after the usual struggle, became a well-known writer and cartoonist, perhaps the best humorist in the country and a bright light at *The New Yorker*. Now we renewed our friendship. His eyesight was failing him; he had lost one eye in a freak accident in his youth. And though this was a blow to him as a creator of wonderfully humorous cartoons for the *New Yorker*, he did not complain. He and his wife, Helen, spoke of leaving New York soon and settling in West Cornwall, Connecticut.

I already had acquired new friends in that beautiful countryside in the northwest corner of the state. The first was Lewis Gannett, the genial, erudite daily book reviewer of the *Herald-Tribune*, who had bought a farm that once had belonged, I believe, to one of his ancestors, a president of Yale. (Lewis himself had graduated from Harvard in a class that included John Reed and Walter Lippmann and that had been lucky in having a whole bag of great teachers, among them Copeland in English and Santayana and Royce in philosophy.) Lewis and his wife, Ruth, a talented illustrator, were by now veteran gardeners and historians of this particular Yankee area.

Down the road from them lived Irita Van Doren, the beautiful and gracious editor of the *Herald-Tribune Sunday Book Review*. Through Irita, I met her former husband, Carl Van Doren, the biographer, and Carl's younger brother, Mark Van Doren, the poet and one of the most lovable human beings I have ever known. For these friends their rocky, hilly farms were weekend and summer havens. The Van Dorens and the Gannetts lived in the city, where they worked five days a week.

* See Volume I of these memoirs.

Tess and I began to look for a place in the neighborhood. New York would be all the better if one could escape it occasionally. It would be a relief to get away briefly from the enormous pressures and drive of the big city and the heat of July and August.

At the *Herald-Tribune* we also made other lasting friends. Besides Irita Van Doren and Joe Barnes there was the couple who owned and ran the newspaper, Ogden and Helen Reid. Ogden was not the most brilliant publisher in the business, but he had an instinctive wisdom that led him to hire some of the best reporters and editors in the field. Though he and the paper were Republican, albeit of the liberal branch that then dominated the party, Ogden didn't much care what a person's politics were. He was more interested in good writing. Helen, his dynamic wife, a small handsome woman no more than five feet tall, really ran the newspaper. She was its chief strength, and in my time there and thereafter we became warm friends. Even more than Ogden, Helen was eager to listen to opinions other than her own and to discuss problems with a frankness I never experienced with the proprietors of other big enterprises. Bill Paley at CBS had been this way in the beginning, at least with Ed Murrow and me, particularly so with Ed, but he changed as the network grew in size and wealth.

Also at the *Tribune* was Geoffrey Parsons, the learned, tolerant editor of the editorial page. He was one of the wisest men I ever knew. I first met Geoffrey when he came to Berlin in August 1939, on the eve of the war. He struck me then as a man of great good sense in the midst of phonies and hysterics. He befriended me when I returned first at the end of 1940, and it was largely he who persuaded me to contribute a Sunday column to the newspaper and its syndicate. Often I went to him for counsel.

Kay Boyle was one of the oldest of the friends I met again. We had met in Paris during the late 1920s. She was a well-known, flamboyant figure among the Left Bank Americans then, but more serious than most, fiercely devoted to her writing and to the new currents that were stirring in Paris in those days from James Joyce, Gertrude Stein, *transition*, Hemingway, and others. She was a close and devoted friend of Joyce (but not of Stein) and worked with Jolas and his collaborators at *transition* to shake up our language — *transition* was fiercely devoted to what it called "the revolution of the word." It seemed to me in those heady days on the Left Bank that Kay Boyle was the most talented of the American women writers in Paris. Fifty years later, I would say that there can be no doubt of it. She has continued over half a century to turn out notable fiction, nonfiction, and poetry. At eighty-four, as this is written, she is still going strong, writing and teaching.

During the war Kay had married Joseph von Franckenstein, who came from an old Austrian family in the Tyrol. His cousin had been the Austrian ambassador in London at the time of the Anschluss in 1938 when Hitler grabbed Austria, and he had immediately resigned his post rather than serve the Nazis. The British paid him an unusual honor. They gave him British citizenship and a knighthood to boot. Kay brought Joseph to America early in the war. Soon he helped organize a unit of ski troops for the U.S. Army that trained in the Colorado Rockies. He went to Italy with them, fought against the Germans there, and as the war moved toward its climax volunteered to parachute behind German lines in his native Tyrol to organize the Resistance forces there, sabotage the retreating Germans, and furnish intelligence by radio for the advancing American troops. He was captured, however, by the Waffen-S.S., court-martialed as a spy, and sentenced to death. Miraculously, he was rescued by an American patrol just as he was about to be shot. How the United States government rewarded this hero who had risked his life for his adopted country will be duly recounted. It is a shameful and shabby story.

It is not the only one of its kind I shall have to tell in these pages. Equally shameful and shabby treatment would be inflicted by our government on another old friend from Europe, John Carter Vincent, whom I had met while he was U.S. consul in Geneva, but who had spent most of his diplomatic career in China, one of a small group of American diplomats who really knew the country, spoke its language, and dared to predict at the end of the war that unless Nationalist China, under Chiang Kai-shek, the darling of President Roosevelt and of most Americans, especially on the right, cleaned out the vast corruption and did something for the war-torn people, it might fall to the Communists.

Ed Snow, the best journalist we had on China and a friend of the unfortunate "China hands" in the diplomatic service, would suffer too for telling the truth, not from the government but from the tycoons who ran so much of our press. He had been the author of that great pioneering book, *Red Star Over China*, the first account the outside world had of the historic trek across the vast hinterland of Mao Tse-tung's Communist forces and of the founding by Mao of a fledgling Marxist regime in Yenan, which eventually would take over all of China. No other American correspondent seemed to have such a grasp of the country, its politics and its splendid civilization, and none other wrote so well and so authoritatively about it.

I had first met Ed in Simla, the summer capital of India, in the days of the British Raj. It was in 1931, and I had helped arrange for him an interview with Gandhi. To my surprise, they did not get along very well. Ed was not as impressed by him as I was. Perhaps it was partly because Ed's great love was China, to which he shortly returned. He went back to India after the war, by which time he was a roving correspondent for the *Saturday Evening Post*. In fact he was standing a few feet away from Gandhi when the great Hindu leader was assassinated in Delhi on January 30, 1948. (Jimmy Sheean was also standing nearby.) By that time, after a number of talks with Gandhi, Ed, as he later told me, had recognized at last the man's true greatness.

During the war he had taken a house near Nyack and attempted to settle down there, though he was often off to Europe and Asia to do special stories for the *Post*. I gathered from my occasional talks with him that he was having difficulties with his editors. Ed did not seem to be the ideal correspondent for a magazine like the *Post*. He was not conservative enough; he delved too deeply in his reports for readers more attuned to the shallow and the superficial. He was too liberal, too easy on the Reds, who had taken over China. At any rate, he eventually found himself unemployable not only on the *Post* but on any other American publication. He went into exile in Switzerland, scratched out a living writing for European publications, and died on the shore of Lake Geneva of cancer, his last days eased by the presence of Chinese doctors flown out from Peking by Mao and Chou En-lai. Irony of ironies, Ed Snow, one of the greatest American journalists of our time, forced into exile essentially for being too liberal and, as the idiotic witch-hunters said, "too easy on the Communists," was hailed just before his death and just after by an archconservative and anti-Communist, Richard Nixon, who said he had not only learned a great deal about China from Snow but gave him credit, through his contacts with Chou and Mao in Peking, for helping him open the door to Communist China. To think that Edgar Snow, in the end, had to be rehabilitated by Richard Nixon!

A year or so after I returned for good, there was a meeting with one of the most remarkable women of our time. Van Wyck Brooks, at that time a neighbor in New York, invited me to have dinner with Helen Keller. Never had I looked forward so much to meeting someone, with the exception of Gandhi, when I went out to India. Like everyone else, I knew her story, but I never could quite believe it. I simply could not comprehend how a child, deprived when she was nineteen months old, through a severe illness, of sight and hearing, which soon made her also mute, could then be taught to read and write and talk. But more than that! To become well educated, a *cum laude* graduate of Radcliffe College, well versed in literature and history, a master of several foreign languages. It was an almost unimaginable achievement. And it was due not only to Helen Keller's genius but to the genius of her teacher and companion, Anne Sullivan, later Mrs. John Macy, who took over her pupil at the age of seven and remained with her until her own death in 1936 when Miss Keller was fifty-six. She was replaced by another remarkable woman, Miss Polly Thomson.

Miss Thomson was at Miss Keller's side the evening early in 1947 when we all met at an East Side restaurant in New York for dinner. Instantly I found Helen Keller beautiful and gracious, and before I realized it we were deep and passionately in a conversation. Unfortunately my diary account of the evening has been lost. I recall it, in part, from memory and from a beautiful letter Miss Keller sent me afterward.

I was so carried away by her personality and wonderfully quick mind that I did not recall until later just how it was we conversed. As I remember it, I could not understand very well Miss Keller's words. They were spoken in a well-modulated voice (which of course she could not hear), but the words were blurred. So Miss Thomson repeated them. Sometimes when I spoke, Miss Thomson tapped out my words on the hand of Miss Keller. At other times, when our talk became animated, as it often did with such an eager and passionate woman, Miss Keller would put her fingers to my lips and lip-read.

To my surprise, she said she had been an "avid listener" to my broadcasts from Berlin (and to those of Ed Murrow from London), and she wanted to know, she said, how I had managed to survive the long years in Nazi Germany. She of course had not actually heard our broadcasts, but Polly Thomson had communicated them to her by what they called the "manual alphabet" — the tapping out of the words on her hand.

I began to realize that her hands, with the long, sensitive fingers, were the key to her communication with the outside world. She used them not only to receive and to give information through the manual code but to lip-read. "My hands," she once said, "have never been still, except in sleep, since I was two years old. They mean the world I live in — they are the eyes, ears, channels of thought and good will."

I was amazed how rapidly she absorbed what was being said at the table and how quickly she came back with her thoughts. The conversation went back and forth so naturally that most of the time I was unaware that Miss Keller and Miss Thomson were tapping each other's hands with lightning speed. Miss Thomson would keep relaying her friend's comments not only from the words she got from the tapping but from Miss Keller's oral comments, which she could understand.

There were also vibrations. Her handicaps had made Miss Keller supersensitive to vibrations, and I began to feel that these played an important part in her communication with others. She seemed to be getting a feeling of me as much through vibrations as from what I was saying.

In her letter about our meeting, dated February 8, 1947, and mailed from her home in Connecticut, she mentioned this phenomenon. "Memory has preserved for me vibrations from your brave search for truth amid falsehood." Apparently she had felt these from my broadcasts from Germany.

I had mailed her after our dinner meeting an inscribed copy of my book, *Berlin Diary*, and also a copy to Polly Thomson. She thanked me warmly: "It is not easy to thank you for a gift so eloquent of your warm-heartedness. . . . When I feel the pages of your diary again under my fingertips, I shall be able to gain fresh instruction from the facts you recorded, though caught in an iron ring of surveillance and reviving barbarism. What a rare urge to opportunity and adventure it must have taken to stay as long as you did in that hell on earth."

At one juncture in our talk, Miss Keller had expressed a passionate desire to visit Russia. She thought the Russian people had shown extraordinary bravery during the war and she was anxious to talk to some of them and to see what they were doing for their blind. She feared the war had probably left thousands of soldiers without eyesight. I suggested that perhaps Joe Barnes, a former Moscow correspondent of the *Herald-Tribune* and fluent in Russian, might be of help to her and might even go along with her as interpreter and guide. He had served Wendell Willkie in this capacity there early in the war.

"I am most grateful to you," Miss Keller wrote, "for approaching Mr. Barnes on the subject of Miss Thomson's and my going to Russia. I have long had a deep affection for the Russian people . . . and if we may have the privilege of visiting their blind and understanding their needs, that will be among the dearest gratifications of my already full life."

I was unable to facilitate the visit to Russia, though Joe Barnes and I worked on it for several months. I told Miss Keller that evening that it was a pity she had never been able to visit Russia years before in time to meet Tolstoy. The great Russian author had lived on, vibrant to the last, to 1910. Perhaps in 1904, the year Miss Keller had graduated *cum laude* from Radcliffe, would have been a good time. It would have been, I ventured to say, a famous meeting. They would have got along. They would have set sparks a-flying in each other.

CHAPTER 2

B*erlin Diary*, which Helen Keller overpraised so much that evening and in her letter, was my first book to get published. Our talk propelled my memory back to my struggles with it and how it saw the light.

Ever since my high-school days and my childish attempts at soldiering at Camp Funston, Kansas, at the end of the First World War when I was fifteen, I had kept, on and off, a diary. Later, as my job as a roving foreign correspondent swept me through Europe and parts of Asia at times of great upheaval and change in the late 1920s and through the entire decade of the 1930s, it occurred to me that these journals, recording events on the spot, might not be of use to only me as the raw material of contemporary history for writing books, but might themselves eventually be made into a book.

I was particularly conscious of this when I arrived in Berlin at the end of the summer of 1934 and began to report on the rise of Adolf Hitler's paranoiac Third Reich. It was an interesting and sometimes an exciting but also depressing story to cover, first for American newspapers and then, in the fall of 1937, for CBS, when I switched over from print journalism to radio, then in its infancy as a medium of reporting the news. And it became obvious to me that this mad and violent Nazi dictator, who had bamboozled the German people into giving him their fanatical support and into following him blindly and obediently no matter where, was going to decide before long the fate of Europe and perhaps the world. He was lurching down the road to conquest and war. He was threatening to exterminate all those who stood in his way, at home and abroad, and even those too unempowered to stand in his way, the Jews. However unpleasant, however much it sickened, this was becoming the most important story an American reporter could cover.

Jotting down in my journal the day's happenings after I was dead tired from digging for news in a hostile environment and from batting out dispatches and broadcast scripts was not easy. But I was young, apparently possessed of a great deal of drive and energy, and usually

I was able to do it late at night after the day's work was over, or early the next morning before it had begun. In a diary I could get in so much that I had to keep out of my dispatches and broadcasts. There was no prior censorship in peacetime Nazi Germany of my cables, and, later, of my broadcasts. But I knew — every American correspondent who worked in a totalitarian country, Fascist or Communist, knew — that there was a fine line beyond which one did not go — if one wished to remain and work in the country for any time at all. If one stepped over the line, one was expelled. It happened all the time in Nazi Berlin. I was warned and threatened, and once the hysterical Nazi press called for my expulsion, but I managed to stay on. Probably, I figured, Dr. Joseph Goebbels, the head of the Propaganda Ministry, who with Hitler decided who among the foreign correspondents would stay and who from time to time would get booted out, concluded that the advantages of allowing a correspondent who obviously detested the regime to remain (it showed that Hitler could take criticism, at least from a foreigner, and that he had nothing to hide) outweighed the disadvantages of having unpleasant happenings reported abroad.

In July 1940, I had returned from Paris to Berlin after the fall of France, despondent at the turn the war had taken. The supposedly strong French army had been easily routed in six weeks. Actually, as I had seen while racing through France as an American correspondent with the great German Sixth Army (great until it was destroyed at Stalingrad some three years later), the French had really not fought, as they had so valiantly against the Germans in the First World War. The month before, Hitler had conquered and occupied Denmark and Norway. He now stood astride most of Europe, from the Vistula in Poland to the Atlantic, from the Norwegian North Cape to the Pyrenees along the French-Spanish frontier. Only England stood in his way of total conquest of Europe. And the British, having lost most of their arms in the miraculous but costly evacuation of Dunkirk, seemed hardly able to repel the invasion of what now we had to accept as the most formidable army of all time. Faint hearts were predicting that the British would have to capitulate too, as the French had.

It was warm and muggy in Berlin in July and the beginning of August and there was not much news except the increasing bombing of England by the Luftwaffe and the preparations the Germans claimed to be making for the invasion of the British Isles. Until I took off to cover that story, there was little to do in Berlin. So I brooded about the predicament of what was left of the Western World. And to seek relief from my depression I wrote up my diary notes, scribbled into little pocket notebooks during the Battle of France. The Germans, after all, had invented and carried out a new and revolutionary kind of warfare — the *Blitzkrieg*. Determined not to get bogged down by the trench war of 1914–1918, they had raced down the roads of Holland, Belgium, and France, softening up the resistance by saturation bombing and then hitting what was left with swarms of tanks. It had been almost a parade. The Netherlands had been overrun in less than a week, Belgium in two, and France in six. I was one of the few neutral observers who had followed at first hand this formidable army and observed its completely new tactics of attack. I thought my diaries of the campaign in the west would make a good story for American magazines and incidentally interest our military people.

I sent the diaries off to my agent in New York and urged him to try to sell them to one of the "slick" magazines. I needed some money to finance the trip home for Tess and our two-year-old child, Eileen Inga. Tess had kept open our CBS bureau in Geneva while I was away in Germany, but she had received no compensation. We decided, in view of events, that it would be better to close the bureau and give up our house, and for Tess and our child to get off to America until we could see what the situation would be in Europe. The prospect of Tess and Eileen leaving relieved me, but it also depressed me. I would no longer be able to get out periodically from Nazi Germany to Geneva to see them and restore my frayed nerves. There would be an end to even the little family life we had been able to preserve since our marriage nine years before.

Late in August, the Germans flew us correspondents up to the Channel to watch the Luftwaffe begin its all-out onslaught on Britain and to prepare to cover the invasion. A couple of weeks there convinced me that the Germans were not going to invade, though they urged us correspondents to say so, to scare and pressure the British. The Germans simply did not have the shipping to move a large army across the choppy Channel. That was the first good news for me since the war began. While in northern France, I also learned that the army was beginning to send a number of divisions from the west to the "eastern front." Since there was no eastern front, this could only mean the Germans were beginning to mass troops against Russia, then a virtual Nazi ally. To me, this was also good news. It meant the unholy alliance of Stalin and Hitler was breaking up. If Hitler took on the Soviet Union before Britain was conquered in the west, he would, I thought, be biting off more than he could chew.

Back in Berlin there was word from my agent in New York, Carl

Brandt. The "slicks" had all turned down my diary of the Battle of France. "No longer timely," their editors said. The battle, after all, was over. Brandt cabled he was offering the diaries to the *Atlantic Monthly*. It wouldn't pay much, but at least it would assure us publication.

Tess and Eileen Inga left Geneva for home that fall. It was a sad parting. I had no idea if their bus would get through to Barcelona as it struggled through German-occupied France. It was a two-day trip. The bus took along its own gas, and food and water for the passengers. There had been a mournful scene at the bus station in Geneva. Scores of Jews, desperate to get away, had tried to climb on the bus, and because it was full had been turned away.

Back in Berlin I had increasing battles with the Nazi censors. The Germans were resentful that I had not fallen for the propaganda all autumn that they were on the point of invading Britain. They began to cut more and more meat out of my broadcasts. Some evenings, when they hacked out most of my text, I refused to go on the air. Once, when this happened, the German Broadcasting Company cabled CBS in New York their "regret" that I had "arrived too late to do the broadcast." By October I knew my usefulness as an American reporter in Berlin was over. A German friend in a position to know tipped me that the government was cooking up an espionage case against me. I was to be accused of being a spy, of using my broadcasts to CBS to get out coded messages to enemy intelligence. I decided to go home.

The good ship *Excambion*, a small American freight and passenger vessel out of Lisbon, pitched and rolled slowly toward New York and we finally made it by Christmas Eve. I was arriving in Washington for a happy holiday reunion with my family: Tess and Eileen, my mother, who had journeyed out from Iowa — I had not seen her for five years — my sister and my brother, John, his German wife, and their daughter, who was the same age as Eileen. We had a great time, prolonging our get-together until the day after New Year's.

Back in New York, I had a hard time convincing CBS that I was not going back to Berlin — that I had used up my chances there both of surviving and of being able to report enough of the truth to make it worthwhile. The Nazis were on to me. I no longer could get anything past the censors. Goebbels would cut me off the air completely with his espionage frameup. Even if that failed — and it was a risk that I was not prepared to take in that cuckooland — the Nazis would not let me say anything that mattered or that contradicted their brazen propaganda.

I would not broadcast their garbage. All this I told Paul White. Paul was a genial guy and a good editor of domestic news. But Hitler and Nazi Germany were something beyond his comprehension. It had been one of my problems with him. It was White who, during the previous fall, when the Nazi censors started to stifle me, had cabled that he wanted me to stay on in Berlin even if I was restricted to merely broadcasting the official Nazi communiqués. I had told him then that I would not do it and I told him again now.

Anyway, I wanted a rest. Six years in Berlin had worn me down — how much, I was just beginning to realize. Passing over Paul White, I applied to Bill Paley, who owned and managed the network, for a three-month leave of absence. Reluctantly, he granted it, but pointed out it would have to be a leave without pay, without, that is, the $154.23 a week I was earning. He was not a man, I could see, who was careless about CBS money. Neither he nor White made any mention of reemploying me at the end of my leave in June if I did not return to Berlin.

But I did not care. It appeared that nearly every publisher in New York wanted to publish my Berlin diaries as a book. They wired, telephoned, and wrote me. Even the magazine tycoons were interested. Henry Luce, over at *Time* and *Life*, sent two of his top editors to my hotel to persuade me to do an article. DeWitt Wallace, editor and owner of *Reader's Digest*, came over himself to my cubbyhole of a temporary office at CBS and demanded I do a piece for him. William Shawn, managing editor of *The New Yorker*, wrote, "Please keep us in mind."

This was quite a contrast to my experience of some years before during the year off in Spain, when we were broke and couldn't interest a single American editor or publisher in anything I was writing. It was different too from a few months before when all the big magazines, including *Time, Life,* and the *Digest,* had turned down my diaries of the German triumph in the west. I can't say I didn't enjoy this sudden and unexpected attention. I even got a kick out of a weekend out at Oyster Bay as the guest of Kermit Roosevelt, then a power in a large New York publishing house, who was also pressuring me to give him the book. I shall never forget one elderly, white-haired, strong-faced woman of the T. R. Roosevelt clan sitting for hours embroidering a pillow on which was stenciled the face of Franklin Roosevelt. She kept jabbing the handsome likeness of the president of the United States with her needles, exclaiming with each strike: "That's for you, my dear Franklin! That's for you!" Having been away from the country since the days of Calvin Coolidge, long before FDR appeared on the scene, I did not know of the feelings of the Oyster Bay Roosevelts for their kin at Hyde Park.

From the beginning I had pretty much made up my mind to give the book to Knopf. This was not because of Alfred Knopf, whom I did not know but whom I admired for the kind of books he published — especially those of some of the great writers abroad such as Thomas Mann. It was because of Blanche Knopf, his wife, who used to call on me in Europe, as she did on many other American correspondents, and encourage me to write books. During our year off in Spain in 1933, after I got fired by the *Chicago Tribune,* I had churned out my first book, a very autobiographical account of my assignments in India and Afghanistan, disguised as a novel and written in the taut, spare style most of us were copying from Hemingway in those days. It was terrible, though I did not realize it for a long time. Blanche read it once on a visit to Berlin and urged me to rewrite it. She kept in touch thereafter and we occasionally met not only in Berlin but in Paris and London, to which, from time to time, I escaped from the lunacies of the Nazi capital. Just before Christmas she began to pester me about "the diary book."

I was not aware until later that Blanche and Alfred Knopf were not on speaking terms once they left the office. I did become aware — and quickly — that Alfred, once Blanche had offered me an advance of ten thousand dollars for the diaries (a large amount in 1941), did not like it one bit. Only H. G. Wells, he said, had ever received such an advance. And I was only a journalist, not a writer. But Blanche prevailed and I signed a contract, taking the first payment of twenty-five hundred dollars to pay the rent and living expenses at a house in Chappaqua I rented from a friend, Ferdinand Kuhn, of the *New York Times.* There I settled down with paste and scissors to try to make a book out of the diaries.

At the end of a couple of months I sent off to the Knopfs half of the manuscript. Blanche liked it. Alfred was silent. Early in April, with my leave running out, I took the rest of the manuscript to New York. I was to depart the same day on a two-week speaking tour that CBS had organized to promote its local stations. I did not look forward to it. And I was depressed about my book. The diaries had not turned out to be very gripping. Two or three books about the war had recently appeared, including one called *Out of the Night* by a refugee German writing under an assumed name. Most reviewers had found it sensational. It was jammed with adventure and violence and suspense, and made an exciting story, though I had some doubts about its authenticity. In contrast, my volume seemed tame, lame, not even very interesting.

In a black mood I lugged the manuscript up to the Knopf office on Madison Avenue, just across the street from CBS. Alfred Knopf would have to fork over twenty-five hundred dollars, which was due on submission of the completed manuscript. He would probably be in a worse mood even than I was.

This turned out to be an underestimation. He was sitting at the head of a large table, surrounded by three or four editors and promotion people and Blanche. As I took my place opposite him, I shoved the box of manuscript toward him. He did not even deign to glance at it. He just pushed it over to the edge of the table, as rudely as he could. I thought for a second it was going to fall to the floor, the yellow sheets scattering about the room.

"Bill," said Alfred, "it won't do. I've been thinking about it —"

"Have you been reading it?" I interrupted.

"I've been thinking about it," he resumed. "And I tell you, Bill, you can't get a book out of a diary —"

"What about Samuel Pepys," I again interrupted, "or the journals of André Gide? I believe you published the latter."

"Well, that's another story," said Alfred, obviously affronted that I should dare to consider myself, even by implication, in the company of such greats. "Almost invariably a diary doesn't make a good book."

"Why?" I put in. I resented that he was making a judgment before reading the script. I doubted that he had even glanced at the first half, which I had sent him several weeks before.

"I'll tell you why! A diary doesn't have a beginning, a middle, and an end. A good book, Bill, has to have a beginning, a middle, and an end."

He grabbed the box that had almost fallen to the floor and shoved it back across the table at me.

"Take this. Scrap it and write me a straight book — with a beginning, a middle, and an end."

"Straight books, Alfred," I said, "about Germany or Britain or Russia or the war are a dime a dozen these days. Every returning correspondent is rushing out with one." I was really aroused. "What I've given you here in my diaries," I said, "is something original, Alfred. Something you won't find in other books."

Alfred obviously was not impressed. I knew I had him, in one way. Before I walked out of this boardroom he had to hand me a check for twenty-five hundred dollars. On the other hand, I hated to have such poisonous relations with a publisher, especially for a first book. So I tried to smile.

"Besides, Alfred," I said, "my three months' leave with CBS is practically over. It would take me another six months, probably a year, to write you a straight book. I don't have that time. I've got to get back to CBS and broadcasting. There's a war on, you know."

Alfred was not impressed with this response either. As if he hadn't heard me, he said: "Tell you what I'm going to do." He looked out the window to the CBS building across Fifty-second Street. "I'm going to call up my old friend, Bill Paley, over there, and get you a further leave. I know you've got a good book in you, Bill. You just have to take out time to write it."

"Sorry," I said, shoving the typescript back across the table in his direction. "I contracted to give you my diaries. I've kept my part of our agreement. I know you're going to keep yours."

I was sure he had the check in his coat pocket all the time.

"Very well," Alfred said. He walked over to me and handed me the check. "You'll regret it," he announced, and stalked out of the room.

I felt terribly down. All my hopes for my first published book were dashed. And by my publisher, of all persons. He hadn't even read the damned manuscript. I walked across Fifty-second Street to CBS and went up to my cubbyhole on the seventeenth floor. I had lugged a big suitcase in from Chappaqua and left it at the office. I was due to open my lecture tour that night in one of those New Jersey towns across the Hudson. In those days a dinner jacket was obligatory for a lecturer. I shut the door, opened the suitcase, pulled out my tux, a dress shirt, and a black tie, and changed. Colleagues from the newsroom came by to chat (I had been away for three months and they were welcoming me back), but I cut them short. I couldn't remember ever having been in such a foul mood. Down on Madison Avenue with my big bag, I hailed a taxi, drove to the ferry, crossed the river, and took another taxi to the lecture hall. It was early. Down a rather dilapidated street I spotted a rundown bar. I left my bag at the hall and strolled to the pub. I had an Irish whiskey, then two, then three. I began to feel better. I snatched a sandwich. Finally it was 8 P.M. and I walked back to the hall. It was tough going getting through the talk. Good thing I had made copious notes. I practically read the speech, though the lecture contract forbade it. Somehow I got away, after the usual question period, to the railroad station in Newark, where I was to catch a train for Chicago. At the station I had time to have a Scotch.

I no longer recall much of that lecture tour or even many of the towns. It was a nightmare. I couldn't shake my depression. Two or three times I was on the point of wiring Alfred to forget the diary book. I'd take it back and shop elsewhere. But there never seemed time — even for that. Lecturing was more strenuous than I had expected. After a week of it I was dead tired. Occasionally I did get a lift. At Kansas City, the local CBS station had put on a furious publicity campaign, rented the largest auditorium in the city, and filled it with sixty-five hundred people. I remember walking out on the platform and facing that huge audience and freezing with fright. But thanks to an excellent loudspeaker and a desperate effort, I was able to come to, and wobble through the talk.

My last lecture was in Memphis on April 25. While in the bar of the Pearson Hotel gobbling down a sandwich and a Scotch before my sponsors arrived to drive me out to the lecture — and I thanked God it was the last — a bellboy brought me a telegram. I started to open it and then desisted. Since bad luck often comes all at once, I was sure it was a wire from Tess saying that Eileen Inga had been run over by a bus or that she, Tess, had. I would postpone the bad news until I had finished the cursed lecture and come back to this bar and fortified myself. On the way to the lecture hall we were halted by a hose that firemen had laid across the street. One of my hosts got out of the car to phone the hall that we had been held up. Sitting there in the car waiting, I became uneasy about the telegram. I took it out of my pocket. I might as well face the bad news now rather than later. If it was shattering, I could simply cancel the talk. I tore open the telegram. We had been stopped underneath a streetlight, so there was enough light to make out the words.

It was from Alfred Knopf and there were two pages of it. Just as he had expected, he said, the Book-of-the-Month Club had taken my book for its July selection. It had happened very fast. Three days after he himself had received the manuscript, the club had made its decision. This was most extraordinary because the book club always demanded to have a book in proofs before it would consider it. But this time the Book-of-the-Month Club had acted after seeing only the typescript. And for the very first time. Alfred sent me his heartfelt congratulations. It was a grand book, etc.

I sailed through the final lecture, returned to the bar, shed my hosts, called Tess, and that night for the first time during the trip had a sound, pleasant sleep. Next morning, refreshed and happy, I caught the first train to New York. My first book, even though it was a paste-and-scissors job, was not going to be a disaster after all. Alfred had said selection by the Book-of-the-Month Club, besides paying well, guaranteed a good sale. That was fine. I needed the money. We were almost broke. There had been no salary from CBS and I had not heard whether they had a place for me. But what of the reviews? I wondered. Would I get clobbered? Would the reviewers maybe agree with what Alfred had thought in the first place? That the book had no beginning, middle, and end? Many writers, I knew, claimed they never read the reviews of their books and couldn't care less what the reviewers wrote; for the most part reviewers were miserable little worms, ignorant, illiterate, and envious. But this first time I had to admit I cared. I had heard that lousy reviews in the *New York Times* and *Herald-Tribune* Sunday book sections could destroy a book — and its author.

The reviewers were kind, and their editors were generous in the space they gave. Both the Sunday *New York Herald-Tribune Books* and the *New York Times Book Review*, the two most influential literary publications in the nation, devoted their front pages to the book. I had not expected much from George M. Shuster, president of Hunter College and an authority on Germany, who I heard would write the piece for the *Times Book Review*. I knew he had been deeply sympathetic with the old Germany and with the Germans and I had heard in Berlin that he had been a little late in facing the facts about Hitler and the Third Reich. In the beginning, it was said, he had pleaded for a "better understanding" of them. Besides, American academic historians tended to look down on American journalists who tried to write history. But Dr. Shuster turned out to be surprisingly enthusiastic about the book and its author — even about journalists.

"Shirer and his [journalistic] friends saw through the Nazi hocus-pocus; the trained diplomats frequently did not," he wrote, and went on: "There is nothing stranger in all history than the ability of relatively untrained newspapermen to diagnose Hitler correctly, while the statesmen and the editorial writers were led around by the nose."

The piece in the *Herald-Tribune*, written by Joe Barnes, was full of understanding, because Joe had been there. And full of praise. But despite our friendship Joe could be quite objective, and he was.

PM, the maverick New York daily that Ralph Ingersoll had recently started with the financial help of Marshall Field (for one thing, it took no advertising), gave me most of the front page of the paper itself, as if the publication of the book that day, June 20, 1941, was big news. *Time*, which had been rather critical of me as a broadcaster in the past, was surprisingly sympathetic. Its review began: "This diary is the most complete news report yet to come out of wartime Germany."

And so the reviews and the comments went. Not all, I hasten to add. In my very own home state of Iowa the esteemed *Herald* of Bellevue lashed out in an editorial entitled "Shirer Is out of Place over Here."

> When William Shirer gave his short wave radio reports directly from Berlin earlier in the year, people excused his pro-Hitler reports on the grounds that he was in the midst of the Hitler nest and had to say what the Nazi propaganda machine ordered. But Mr. Shirer, the alleged ace reporter, is in the United States now and his isolationist propaganda continues over the radio and his book, "Berlin Diary," with its Nazi poison is for sale on all book stands. Unfortunately Shirer has become widely known and thousands of people listen to him. It's too bad that he returned to the United States: a pro-Nazi sympathizer like him should remain in Berlin.

I cannot remember anything about me, before or since, in any language in any country, that was so absurdly wrong on every point. It was something of a small-town masterpiece.

There was a spate of anti-Semitic letters and so many telephone calls in the dead of night from rabid anti-Semites that I had to have our telephone number changed and made unlisted. Most of these notes and calls came from New Jersey, where the pro-Nazi Bund, I believe, was at its strongest.

One of the more moderate anti-Semitic attacks against this Presbyterian-born correspondent was printed in pencil on an advertisement of *Berlin Diary* that appeared in the July 20, 1941, issue of the *Herald-Tribune Books* and mailed to me by an anonymous correspondent.

> The poor Germans! How they put up with a little kike like you for two years, I don't see. I wouldn't call them intolerant after that if I were you. They were too patient, harboring a spy like you all that time, and your return for their hospitality is just what one might expect.

A strange thing to me: because I expressed my outrage at the Nazi Germans and at Hitler in this and two subsequent books, including *The Rise and Fall of the Third Reich*, many Americans, including some Jews, assumed that I was Jewish. What puzzled me, and still does, is that so many concluded that you had to be a Jew if you wrote like that about the Third Reich and its gangster leaders. It was rather disturbing.

Everyone, incidentally, thought I had picked a wonderful title for the book, *Berlin Diary*. Actually it had been plucked out of the air at the last moment. Until the last minute we were going to call the book

This Is Berlin, the words with which I opened my broadcasts from the German capital. Then we discovered Ed Murrow was about to publish a book titled *This Is London*, an expression he had made famous by the way he started his broadcasts, with a crisp emphasis on the word "This." (He had made it so unique that in Berlin I changed to stressing the last word: "This is — *Berlin.*" But it didn't work for me as it had for Ed. I lacked his great histrionic talents on the air.) The Knopfs had summoned me to the office for a conference on what to do. We agreed we had to change our title. The printer was about to begin setting the type. Alfred, Blanche, and I racked our brains. I finally proposed "Berlin Diary." It did not enthuse me, nor did it the Knopfs. But we were desperate. And because Alfred didn't like the book anyway, I thought, What difference does it make? I put the question to an old friend, Paul Gallico, a Knopf author.

"It doesn't make any difference at all," Paul said. "If the book sells, people will think the title is a natural. If not, they'll quickly forget it."

The reviews in London that fall were equally flattering. This was also a pleasant surprise — I was having a string of surprises. In the summers I had worked in London during the late 1920s, British book reviewers, I thought, were unnecessarily condescending to American authors. Perhaps the terrible bombing that the British were taking so coura- geously had knocked out some of their temptation to patronize us. At any rate, the reviews of *Berlin Diary* were kind and understanding. One, in the much esteemed and sober *Times Literary Supplement* (in those days its reviews were never signed) began:

> Mr. Shirer's "Berlin Diary" stands out from all the books about the war. . . . For one thing few chroniclers have had the same experience of the European scene for so long a space as he has. For another, he had exceptional opportunities for inquiry, first as a foreign correspondent and later as Berlin reporter for the Columbia Broadcasting System. For a third, there is the rare quality of a man who, though he may not have always known his own mind (a hopeless affair in the censor-ridden and Gestapo ruled Reich), certainly always knew his own feelings and con- victions and in his day-to-day record of epochal events ("the deeper story of this great land in ferment") expresses them fearlessly and memorably. It is a human as well as an historical document. . . . Every entry in the diary grips, both for the matter recorded and for the manner of record- ing.

This was heady stuff for an author to read about his first book, and I tried not to take it too seriously. The reviewers were seeing a lot of things in the diaries that I had not been conscious of.

At least two reviews, one in the *New Statesman*, a second in the *Observer*, mentioned something that kindled my pride in my profession. They pointed out that America had produced between the wars a unique group of foreign correspondents to whom not only the Americans but the British owed a debt of gratitude. Said the piece in the *Statesman*:

> Shirer is typical of a group to whom we owe a great deal. They are the professional American correspondents in Europe, very objective in their reporting, highly competent on the technical side, fearless and immensely industrious.

F. A. Voight, himself once a British foreign correspondent, wrote similarly in the *Observer*. "England," he said, "owes much to these men and women." I took it as a British tribute to so many of us: John Gunther, Vincent Sheean, Dorothy Thompson, Sigrid Schulz, Walter Duranty, H. R. Knickerbocker, Ed Murrow, the Mowrer brothers, and others.

When you had worked, largely unknown, in the wilderness so long, perhaps you could be excused for enjoying this fleeting limelight. I thought what I liked most was the reaction of certain individuals to the book. Some items in my old folders remind me of them.

There is a copy of a letter to Alfred Knopf from Carl Becker, the historian from Cornell, who writes that he is reviewing *Berlin Diary* for the *Yale Review*.

> It must be a great satisfaction to publish a book that is not only a great book but a best seller as well.* In the review I've tried to explain why the book is a good one, and to convey something of the fine intelligence and character of the author. I don't know when I've come to admire an author so much from simply reading his book.

There was a curious experience with President Roosevelt. Knopf had sent him one of the first copies of *Berlin Diary* off the press. One day a few weeks later I received it back. It had been signed by the president. I was puzzled. Was this some kind of rebuke? A letter from Stephen Early, FDR's press secretary, tried to clear the matter up. Perhaps I was naïve. He said the president had "requested" him to send it back to me.

> Of the hundreds of books the President has received in the more than eight years he has been in the White House, this one is the first, to the

---

* By August 7, 1941, when the letter was written, *Berlin Diary*, I believe, had climbed to the top of the best-seller lists in the *Times* and *Herald-Tribune*.

best of my knowledge, that he has ever asked to have returned to its author.

This still left me wondering. Then Steve explained.

It is returned to you for your signature, at least, and if the signature includes an inscription, I think the object of sending this book to you will have been happily achieved.

I did not return the book. It had been slightly damaged in the mail. I sent another copy, inscribed to the president, which Alfred Knopf lugged down to Washington and personally delivered to the White House. By now Alfred was very happy about *Berlin Diary*.

In a second letter to me, Early described Alfred's arrival.

Alfred Knopf came in yesterday and brought a first edition of your *Berlin Diary*, inscribed by you. The President was delighted — perfectly satisfied with the exchange but a bit sorry that the copy I had sent you had arrived in a slightly damaged condition.

Knopf gave me a very enthusiastic report on the sales of *Berlin Diary*.

I hope you make a million!

So I kept the copy signed by Franklin Roosevelt. It was the only copy of a book of mine ever autographed for me by a president.

One of the most eloquent tributes to the book came from Ed Murrow. One late afternoon in July up on Cape Cod, Tess and I were driving to the summer playhouse in Dennis to see Moss Hart in *The Man Who Came to Dinner*. He was making his debut as an actor, I believe. On the way we turned on the car radio to catch the CBS evening news. Ed came on from London. There was no bombing to report that evening. He was going to devote his part of the broadcast, he said, to talking about *Berlin Diary*. Ed was very moving: about the book, about me, about our friendship, about the way we had worked together in Europe.

Tess and I had pulled off to the side of the road and shut off the car's motor so we could hear the broadcast more clearly. There was almost always some static in these transatlantic transmissions. We were so emotionally drained, each of us, by what Ed said that after he had finished speaking we sat there on the side of the road a long time, unable to move or to speak. We could not find words for what we felt.

My euphoria over the apparent success of my first book was balanced by disappointment that CBS had not yet given any indication that I still had a job. I had made it plain I could not return to Berlin. Neither

White nor Paley nor the array of vice-presidents that a network carried had accepted my word as final, nor offered me any alternative. I had to start thinking about trying to find a job elsewhere.

One day before Tess and I left for the Cape, I talked it over with Raymond Gram Swing, an old friend from Europe, a former foreign correspondent from World War I days, and now the most popular radio commentator in America. The country practically came to a standstill every night at ten when he began his broadcast. Raymond advised me to try to get a job on some small-town radio station "in order to gain experience." This was surprising — and discouraging. I thought I had had a good deal of experience in big-time broadcasting. I was not as eminent as Raymond. But I had earned a modest reputation, I thought, from three years of broadcasting from Europe, especially during the first year and a half of the war. I suppose I could have turned to NBC. I knew Abe Schechter, Paul White's opposite number as news editor. But I thought it might be disloyal to CBS. (I was still naïve about such things as company loyalty.)

I quickly forgot about the problem once we reached the Cape. The reviews of the book started pouring in, and cheered us up. And I was having a glorious vacation at Chatham with Tess and Eileen, the first one we had taken together in three years. We lolled on the beach, swam, sailed, hiked, motored around the Cape, picnicked all over the place, savored Provincetown. In a rash moment, I even played a round of golf. Occasionally a reporter or book reviewer came down from one of the Boston papers or radio stations to talk and take a few photographs of our happy family life. Sometimes Tess and I stole away to see a play at one of the summer playhouses. I was hungry to see American plays. I had seen a lot of theater in London, Paris, Vienna, and Berlin. But except for a very few in London, I had seen no American plays since *What Price Glory*, in the summer of 1925 when I stayed briefly in New York on the way to catch my cattleboat for Europe at Montreal.

As the month's vacation on the Cape neared its end, I began to wonder what I was going to do about a job. Tess thought that perhaps the reception *Berlin Diary* was getting might interest CBS in considering further employment for me — and if not, then NBC. But I heard nothing from either. Perhaps the people who ran radio did not read books.

Then one morning at the beginning of our last week, Paul White dropped in at our bungalow. He was carting several copies of *Berlin Diary* that he said he wanted me to autograph for CBS "clients." We gave him some breakfast, chewed the fat a little, and at Paul's suggestion he and I adjourned to a nearby golf course for a round. It was on the eighth hole, as I remember, after we had putted the green, that Paul suggested we take a break. There was a bench near the next tee and we sat down. Paul started to talk about the book.

"All of us at 485* have been damned happy, Bill, at the success of *Berlin Diary*," Paul said. "Everyone at the office is talking about it. It has not only given you a lot of prestige, but us, too. We would have got in touch with you earlier, but we wanted you to enjoy your vacation and have a good rest. But don't think we haven't been thinking of you. We have. And we want you back at CBS. In fact," and he picked an envelope out of his inside pocket, "I've brought you a contract to sign."

That evening at dinner we talked it over. There was a small raise and a promise of a Sunday show of my own, originating in New York, that Paul said eventually they would find a sponsor for.

"That means perhaps a thousand a week extra," Paul said, beaming. He did not mention going back to Berlin.

I felt relieved. I liked broadcasting. I wanted to get back to it. Maybe someday I would turn to writing books, though I still did not know yet, even at thirty-seven, whether I had it in me to really write well. *Berlin Diary* had been mostly a job of assembling and cutting my journals. Still, the book consisted of my writings. Apparently these had some appeal. In my first years in Paris, sixteen years before, I had aspired to be a writer. It was in the Paris air then. Scott Fitzgerald had already made it and Hemingway soon followed with *The Sun Also Rises*. And Kay Boyle and Djuna Barnes and Archy MacLeish and Elliot Paul and others were attracting attention. I had tried to write some poetry and fiction, but it was no good, and I had made up my mind by 1927, when I graduated from the Paris *Trib* and became a foreign correspondent for the *Chicago Tribune*, that journalism, the recording of history as it happened, was the field for me. I still thought so.

Though radio broadcasting had come to fascinate me and though it seemed to have much more of an impact on the public than newspapers, I nevertheless missed writing for the printed press. The weekly column for the *New York Herald-Tribune* had given me a chance to get back to it in 1942. The column, syndicated to some fifty major newspapers, had also augmented my income. In fact with that, the book sales, and the new sponsored Sunday broadcasts, I would soon find myself making more money than I had ever imagined. In the fifteen

* 485 Madison Avenue, New York, was the CBS office.

years I had worked abroad up to this time, I had never been paid more than a hundred and fifty dollars or so a week. I had started on the Paris edition of the *Chicago Tribune* in 1925 on a salary of fifteen dollars a week. When I graduated to the foreign service and began roaming the world for the *Trib*, my salary was increased to fifty dollars a week. CBS in 1937 started me at a hundred and fifty dollars a week and raised it by $4.25 by the time I came home from Berlin three years later. Perhaps the $4.25 was a weekly bonus for covering the war.

Obviously a reporter did not become wealthy laboring for an American newspaper or broadcasting network. I guess most of us didn't much care. Perhaps we never had time to. Maybe we were a little gullible.

After a year, Knopf got out a press release on how *Berlin Diary* had done over the first twelve months. Not badly. The publisher said it had sold 298,490 copies. It did not know how many the Book-of-the-Month Club had sold but noted that the club had printed 296,490 copies. It was "safe to assume," Knopf added, that the club had sold most of those copies. Knopf itself had printed 308,185 copies in nineteen printings. So between them they had printed 604,615 copies of which 595,000 had been sold.*

Eventually I made, if not a million, at least a sum that seemed astronomical to me — more than I could grasp. But the government didn't let me keep very much of it. The tax collector brought me down to earth and quickly demolished the dream that the good luck I had had with this first book would make me financially independent. My federal and state income taxes on the first year's sales came to 82 percent. The literary agent took another 10 percent. That left me in the end with 8 percent.

I suppose the dream of writers and of reporters who became writers of achieving financial independence if they had a best-seller was universal among us. And perhaps for reasons somewhat different from other people's. If lightning struck, it meant that you could henceforth devote all your time and energy to writing. You would no longer have to depend for a living on a regular job in journalism, advertising, teaching, or whatever, which took most of your time and almost all of your energy. And you would no longer risk getting fired or laid off.

* The book sold at $3.00 in the bookstores, of which the author received a royalty starting at 10 percent, rising to 12½ percent after the first 5,000 and 15 percent after the first 10,000 copies. The Book-of-the-Month Club paid, so far as I recall, a straight 25 cents per copy, divided equally between publisher and author.

The experience with *Berlin Diary* taught me that this was no longer possible in America, no matter how well a book did. Income taxes took the bulk of your royalties. There were no "tax havens" for writers. These were reserved for wealthy investors, bankers, businessmen.

Hemingway wrote me from Havana urging me to take the matter to court, to become a test case in the fight of authors to get a fair shake with taxes. What the IRS refused to recognize was that an author, after a long dry spell, might make a pile in one year — and make nothing for years thereafter. The bad years should be balanced with the good. This seemed only just, but it was not apparent to the IRS, the Congress, the Treasury, or the White House.*

I would have liked to become financially independent of the owners of newspapers and networks. I had already learned with the *Chicago Tribune* how frivolously they could throw you out. And until recently, apparently, one best-seller would have guaranteed setting you free. Sinclair Lewis had told me once that he himself had become financially independent with his first big success, *Main Street*, on which he paid, he said, if I remember rightly, 6 percent income tax.

I told Hemingway and the Authors Guild, which I had just become eligible to join and which had also urged me to be a guinea pig, that I would not go to court, or even publicly protest what I thought privately was an outrageous treatment of an author by our federal and state governments. It would be unseemly with a war on. Our country had already been drawn into it in December 1941, six months after the diary was published, by Pearl Harbor and Hitler's declaration of war on us. Millions of Americans were going to be drafted to fight and risk their lives — practically without pay. It was not the time to squabble with the government over taxes.

---

* Later, to some extent, it would be. Authors were allowed to balance income, for tax purposes, over five years, though this was eventually reduced to three years. And the 50 percent lid on income taxes helped in a big year. But the big years were few and far between. Very few authors in America could live on their royalties and thus devote full time to writing. They had to make their living elsewhere.

CHAPTER 3

By the end of 1946, I had settled down in New York as a network radio commentator and, for one day a week, a syndicated newspaper columnist. I was also doing an occasional article for the magazines and some lectures and speeches.

The work kept me busy. There was little time to bask in the notoriety and publicity I found, to my surprise, one soon got in America from such public activities. This helped me to avoid getting unduly puffed up and taking myself too seriously, though looking back I can see that there were times when I became rather pleased with myself and enjoyed the limelight, unmindful that in America, especially in the world of broadcasting and newspapers, fame and notoriety are fleeting. The flattery heaped on me was embarrassing. I had to keep knocking it into my head that it was superficial, shallow, and meaningless and could be poisonous if you believed in any of it for one second. This was a time when the newspaper gossip columnists were at the height of their popularity. Amazingly, a vast public eagerly devoured their tidbits about the rich and famous, who in turn, for the most part, relished the spotlight the gossip-writers gave them. Ever since some of my broadcasts from Nazi Germany and from the war in Europe had attracted some attention, as had my first book, my name kept creeping into the nationally syndicated columns, not only of those of the gossipmongers such as Walter Winchell and Leonard Lyons, each of whom had millions of readers from coast to coast (Winchell also had a Sunday evening broadcast that for years ranked among the ten top-rated shows on the air), but into the columns of the book critics, the radio critics, the entertainment editors.

This was heady stuff for one who had lived in obscurity throughout his career. I suppose the truth was, however much I denied it to myself, that I rather liked emerging for the first time into the public glare with the broadcasts, the book, the newspaper column, and the public speeches. I noted the mention I got in the columns and rather warmed to seeing my broadcasts, writings, and speeches quoted in the daily press. I admit — at least now, forty years later — that I got a kick out of speaking at a huge rally at Madison Square Garden in New York on behalf of Republican Spain on January 2, 1945, and earlier from filling the large convention hall in Kansas City and the spacious Shrine Auditorium in Des Moines, Iowa, by appearing for talks on the war promoted by local CBS stations. Though the first sight of such vast audiences when I stepped up on the platform petrified me and for a few seconds left me speechless, it also gave me a thrill I had never felt before. To go on and move so many thousands of people by your mere words and your mood and by the mystery of communication was a new experience for me. For twenty years all over the world I had reported others doing it. Now it was happening to me.

I was also pleased, I have to concede, to be invited to address a dinner at the Waldorf honoring the great German writer Thomas Mann on his seventieth birthday. (He had befriended me and more than any other author had kept encouraging me to write.) And I was flattered to be asked to speak at various banquets to honor General de Gaulle, Mahatma Gandhi, and others, or to say a few words on behalf of some cause or institution.

Looking back on my schedules of those years, I wonder how I got the time and energy to do all these things. I was still young, only forty-two, I probably told myself as I fell into the American habit of driving myself to the limit. It gave me a varied, full life.

I did not go in for another American habit, a passion really, to join a lot of clubs and organizations. I had never been a joiner. But I did become a member of the Century Association and the Council on Foreign Relations, not at all suspecting that they were, or would shortly become, or so it was said, two of the most "establishment" groups in the country. The Century seemed full of men who shared a good many of my tastes — many were writers and artists. This, plus the good and inexpensive food and the excellent wines, made it a pleasant place to drop in for lunch.

Hamilton Fish Armstrong, the editor of *Foreign Affairs*, recruited me into the Council on Foreign Relations. It was a much smaller organization than it is now, and only gradually did I become aware that it was a growing force in shaping American foreign policy and influencing the men who made policy — indeed in picking some of these men. To me the council offered a number of opportunities, above all the chance to dine and talk off the record with visiting foreign statesmen — they became more numerous after the establishment in New York of the U.N. Once or twice a week there was a meeting with a visiting prime minister or foreign minister or other such dignitary. To have sought them out in their native lands would have taken much time and trouble.

The council also gave one an inside view of what was going on in Washington. Secretaries of state and their assistants and ambassadors came to speak to us.

Radio broadcasting, which had come of age during the war, was at the height of its popularity in those first postwar years. Considering that it was pure pioneering, radio had done a pretty good job in reporting from Europe the road to war from the time of the Anschluss in Austria in the spring of 1938, to the fatal day of September 1, 1939, when Hitler sent his troops into Poland and launched the Second World War. Radio had brought the war into the living rooms of America, along with the voices of the statesmen pleading their causes: Roosevelt, Hitler, Churchill, Mussolini, Stalin, and lesser fry. There was an immediacy in radio that the printed newspaper could not provide. The morning newspaper could give you an account of a Hitler speech, and even the text, announcing his latest act of aggression. But with radio we could bring the speech into twenty million American homes, just as he was pronouncing it, with all his shouting and venom, along with the frenzied reaction of his immediate German audience. A listener in faraway America could thus participate in the scene, as if he were there.

But radio, despite a myth to the contrary, had not covered the war very well. This was mainly because of a ridiculous, self-imposed rule by the networks that forbade the use of recordings. Every report we made of a bombing or a battle had to be transmitted *live*. To use a recording for background to show you the true sound and fury of modern *Blitzkrieg* was verboten. This idiotic rule tied our hands. We could not, we quickly learned, report a modern war, *live*. You could not take one end of a telephone line to the front and broadcast from there, as you might have done from the trenches in the First World War, had there then been commercial broadcasting. In the Second World War, for the most part, there was no "front." Armies advanced and retreated on wheels at great speed down the main roads. The only way you could cover them was with a portable recorder. You could take a telephone wire up to the roof of a building to catch the sound of a bombing. But all too often when your time came to broadcast there would be a brief lull. No bombs. No sound. Just a rare silence.

Ed Murrow experienced this in London. He was a genius in describing the terrible bombing of London in 1940. Few who heard these broadcasts will ever forget them. But Ed felt terribly frustrated because he could not use a recorder. Night after night during the worst bombing any city had ever taken there would be a lull just as he went on the air. If he had been allowed to record, he could have caught the awesome sounds immediately before: of exploding bombs, of the intense fire of the anti-aircraft batteries, of fire engines and ambulances shrieking up and down the blacked-out streets, and then he could have blended them into his report.

I did not have this particular problem in Berlin since the Nazi authorities forbade me to even mention that an air attack was in progress, as it sometimes was during my late night broadcasts. Once when the sound of exploding British bombs and the response of the flak guns nearby penetrated through to my mike in the studio and emerged loud and clear in New York, causing the anchorman there, Elmer Davis, to remark that by the sound of it Berlin was being heavily bombed as I spoke, German engineers on orders from the Propaganda Ministry installed a lip microphone that picked up no sounds at all beyond a foot from your mouth.

But I had plenty of opportunity to broadcast the sound and fury of modern combat at the front, in Poland, in September 1939, after the Germans attacked, and in the west when spring came the following year. Early in the German drive through Belgium and France in May there was a great tank battle just west of Dinant as German armor broke over the Meuse River, a major Allied defense line. Some two thousand German and French tanks were locked in what was the greatest tank battle ever fought up to that time. The sound, the fury, was indescribable in words, but a recording would give you some idea of it. Foreign correspondents were not allowed to get near the place. At any rate it would have been impossible to get a telephone line up to the blazing scene, which moved back and forth in the dust and smoke. German army combat correspondents made recordings of the battle. The German army offered them to me. I urged CBS in New York to make an exception of their idiotic rule in this case. It was refused.

Indeed, a good many months later, after France had been conquered and there was a lull in the war except for the Battle of Britain in the skies, I received in Berlin a cable from Paul White: "It is against the rules to use recordings on network. . . ." As if I had forgotten. At the end of the Battle of France I had scored a notable scoop in broadcasting the signing of the Franco-German armistice at Compiègne. How much more impressive that broadcast would have been had I been able to use the recordings secretly made by the Germans of what went on in the famous railroad car during the armistice negotiations. Hitler's remarks, the arrogant talk of the Germans, the weeping of the French. I had heard it all outside a German army van that was recording the historic scene.

As soon as the war was over — after all the lost opportunities! — the American networks junked the rule against using recordings. Too late! I did note the decision. I find a diary entry, from London, on Sunday, October 13, 1945:

> For the first time since I've been broadcasting, CBS allowed me to do
> an early recording in case my live broadcast later broke down.

That had been another disastrous consequence of the ban on using recordings. Because of atmospheric changes and differentials of light, shortwave broadcasts from Europe to America got through better at some times than at others. (Medium-wave transmitters cannot cover the distance across the Atlantic.) For example, transmission often was surer if we broadcast from Europe in daylight when it was also daylight at home rather than when it was night in Europe and day in America, as it was during most of our regular live broadcasts. Murrow and I had begged CBS in New York to allow us to record earlier to take advantage of this situation. Then if our live broadcasts didn't get through they could use the earlier recording. It seemed so reasonable. But not to the CBS brass at Madison Avenue.

The first year back home after the war I spent a lot of time covering the rather uncertain beginnings of the United Nations, which finally, for better or worse, had settled in New York. It was the hope of the world in those early days. Most people, including myself, believed that, unlike the old League of Nations, the U.N. would succeed in keeping the peace.

At the founding of the U.N. in San Francisco the year before, I had been impressed by Field Marshal Smuts of South Africa, the only statesman there who had played a major role at Versailles in shaping the League of Nations at the end of the First World War. This time, he insisted, we must not fail. He had tried to put more teeth in the new world body. And he never lost sight of what had to be its goal: "to save succeeding generations from the scourge of war which twice in our lifetime has brought untold sorrow to mankind." He had succeeded in getting those words into the preamble of the U.N. charter.

The League of Nations had officially expired as the clocks of Geneva struck midnight on April 18, 1946. But it had long been dead. I, who had often covered it between the wars and for a time had lived in the old Swiss Calvinist city, had witnessed its last sad days and demise. Its death did not, as Woodrow Wilson, its founder, predicted, break the heart of the world. But it saddened many of us, I think, who had watched at first hand its early efforts to live up to our hopes and then witnessed the failure of the Big Powers, who dominated it, to live up to their noble commitments. I noted the League's imminent passing at the end of my Sunday broadcast on April 7. And I quoted from an entry I had made in my diary in Geneva six years before, on July 5, 1940. I had returned there from Berlin, after covering the Battle of France, to see my family and get a little rest. Late that afternoon Tess, Eileen, and I had gone for a walk down by the lake.

> In the sunset the great white marble of the League building showed through the trees. It had a noble look, and the League had stood in the minds of many as a noble hope. But it had not tried to fulfill it. Tonight it was a shell, the building, the institution, the hope — dead.

Despite that terrible disillusionment with the old League, I remained hopeful about the new U.N. On December 15, 1946, for example, I began my Sunday broadcast with this rosy picture:

> The U.N. Assembly is nearing the end of its first historic session on our shores. . . . This has been a momentous session, if only because it set the world on the road toward general disarmament, including the outlawing of the atomic bomb.

If only it had! I was unduly impressed by the unanimous vote — 54 to 0 — in the U.N. Assembly the day before to press forward for general disarmament, including the abolition of the atom bomb and the establishment of an on-the-scene inspection to see that no one cheated. At that time, of course, only the U.S.A. had the bomb and it was willing to give up its monopoly and put the bomb under the control of the U.N. If that had happened, we might not face such a grim nuclear future as we do today.

The atom bomb provoked in our land much silly — and dangerous — talk about war with Russia. This came not only from ordinary people, who probably did not have the facts, but from top people in government, including a former president, who presumably had them. The latter, especially, were becoming gung-ho on going to war with Russia, though the sounds of battle and bombing from the war with Germany and Japan had scarcely died down. Indeed, former President Herbert

Hoover would return from a quick visit to Germany and propose to President Truman that the Allied agreement at Potsdam for the treatment of defeated Germany be scrapped and that German heavy industry, which had helped Adolf Hitler come within an ace of winning the war, be revived. We would need a restored Germany, I heard him say in private, to help us cope with the Russians. Others wanted to give more help to revive prostrate Japan, for the same reason.

Talk of going to war with Russia, especially in Washington where our brass should have known better, was utterly irresponsible. I remember a dinner given by Hamilton Fish Armstrong to honor two Supreme Court justices, Robert H. Jackson and Felix Frankfurter. A number of prominent men were there, including Henry L. Stimson, Roosevelt's secretary of war, Lord Inverchapel (Clark-Kerr), the new British ambassador in Washington, who had just arrived from serving in Moscow, Henry Luce, the *Time-Life-Fortune* tycoon, and Myron Taylor, former head of U.S. Steel and until recently U.S. observer at the Vatican. Justice Jackson, just back from heading the U.S. prosecution at the Nuremberg trials, tried to explain what he had done in handling Nazi war criminals. Taylor said he himself opposed the whole idea of prosecuting the Nazi leaders. What we ought to be concentrating on, he said, was war with Russia. He became so rabid on the subject that John Gunther shouted across the table at him that his talk was "shocking."

So, I thought, was a piece by a Cold War columnist for the *New York Daily News*, which had the largest circulation in America. I called attention to it in a broadcast I made on March 17, 1946.

> World War III due to be touched off in April or May when Russia moves into Turkey and the British come to Turkey's defense, according to Washington's hottest rumor.

From the capital the Alsop brothers reported in their widely syndicated column that there was "only one reason why war was not expected": because to stop the Bolsheviks would bring "the most violent kind of crisis."

Even the *New York Times* lost its bearings. On page one it ran this banner headline:

HEAVY RUSSIAN COLUMNS MOVE WEST IN IRAN:
TURKEY OR IRAQ MAY BE GOAL: U.S. SENDS NOTE

At 8 P.M. on March 12, an unusually late hour for such things, the State Department had called in the reporters and told them that "Soviet troops in Iran were moving westward toward Turkey and Iraq."

Then the State Department lost track of them. I kept phoning in vain for further news of this ominous military threat. Where were the Bolshevik troops? Had they reached Iraq? Had they pushed on to Turkey? No one at the department or anywhere else in Washington would say. Military experts in London, less hysterical about the Bolsheviks than their opposite numbers in Washington, finally reported that the roads westward from Tabriz toward Iraq and Turkey were snowbound and had been for days. Perhaps the Russian troops had been caught in the snows. Or had they ever started? There was never any further word from the State Department. It left those Russian armies in thin air, whence it had launched them.

One veteran Associated Press reporter in Moscow, who had no illusions about the Bolsheviks, was depressed at all the talk of war with Russia. Eddy Gilmore, returning to his post after several months' leave at home, reacted with a dispatch that expressed his bewilderment and concern — and Gilmore was one of the least emotional and most matter-of-fact of all the American correspondents in Europe.

> In Russia there is little or no talk of war. On the contrary, there is much talk of peace. There is no anti-American feeling as such in Moscow. There are articles of criticism of the United States . . . but I would be a very untruthful reporter if I did not say there is three to five times as much anti-Russian sentiment in the American press and on radio as there is here against our country. I've heard no one in Moscow express a desire for war with the U.S. . . . , which is more than I can say of what I heard in Washington.

The American people apparently were not falling for the war propaganda in Washington. According to a University of Denver poll in the fall of 1946, some 73 percent of Americans did not think the present difficulties with Russia were worth going to war over. The Federal Council of Churches, which spoke for the majority of the Protestant churches in America, made public a plan for peace with the Soviet Union. "War with Russia," it said, "can be avoided, and must be avoided, without compromise of our basic conditions."

Still, the talk went on, especially in the nation's capital, though by the end of 1946, I noted, it was beginning to shift toward fear of Russian spies. Wild charges were beginning to be made that some of our most eminent statesmen were agents of Moscow and participants in a Communist conspiracy. Certain politicians were drumming up fear that our Communists, who couldn't elect a dogcatcher in any state of the Union, were about to take over the Republic.

I had not heard such idiotic talk since my early days in Nazi Germany.

Toward the end of the war the House Un-American Activities Committee, which had become almost extinct, was rescued from oblivion largely by John E. Rankin (D–Miss.). As the hysteria about Communism and Russia increased, the committee, which by its very nature had been something of a joke (who is to decide who and what is un-American and on what basis?), took on a new life and gathered so much power that few congressmen dared to oppose it or even criticize it. The press was equally craven.

Though a man of almost unbelievable narrow-mindedness, Rankin provided me with many good quotes for my Sunday broadcasts and newspaper column. He had a marked talent for the utterly ridiculous. He described the Fair Employment Practices Commission as "the beginning of a Communistic dictatorship the like of which America never dreamed!" Communism, he said, "had hounded and persecuted the Saviour during his earthly ministry, inspired his crucifixion, derided him in his dying agony, then gambled for his garments at the foot of the cross." Rankin once proposed a bill that would make schoolteachers liable for ten years' imprisonment if they "convey the impression of sympathy with . . . Communist ideology."

It was Rankin who once asked the House Un-American Activities Committee's chief counsel, one Ernie Adamson, about the chairman of the British Labour party, Harold Laski. Labour had been voted into power in England at the end of the war. Though Laski was a distinguished economist and academician from the University of London, the author of many books, a friend of two U.S. Supreme Court justices (Holmes and Frankfurter) and of many other prominent Americans, Rankin spoke as if he had never heard of him.

"Who is Mr. Laski?" the congressman asked his counsel.

Adamson: "Mr. Laski is, I believe, one of the leaders in England of the Communist movement."

Rankin: "Is he an American?"

It was Mr. Adamson who wrote a strange letter to an American veterans' group.

> I note that you refer to democracy several times. I wonder if you are sufficiently familiar with the history of the United States to be aware that this country was not organized as a democracy?

This must have confused our war veterans, who apparently believed that democracy was one of the things they had fought for.

By this time I was becoming confused myself. For the nonsense went on, taken seriously by grown-up men and women, many in positions, private and public, of great importance. There was Representative Harold Velde (R–Ill.) claiming that "Soviet spies were infesting the entire country, like gypsy moths." There was Congressman Robert Rich (R–Pa.) charging that Dean Acheson, undersecretary of state, was on Stalin's payroll. There was the inimitable Senator Jenner (R–Ind.) calling General George C. Marshall, whom I regarded as one of the greatest Americans of my time, a "front man for traitors, a living lie who had joined hands with this criminal crowd of traitors and Communist appeasers who, under the continuing influence of Truman and Acheson, are still selling America down the river."

In the U.S. Senate, President Truman was denounced as one of the "egg-sucking phony liberals" whose pitiful squealing would "hold sacrosanct those Communists and queers" who had "sold China into atheistic slavery." The choicest phrases were reserved for those "prancing mimics of the Moscow party line in the State Department" who were "spewing the Kremlin's malignant smear" while "the Red Dean [Acheson] whined and whimpered and cringed" as he "slobbered over the shoes of his Muscovite masters."

As I struggled through my first years back home, trying in my broadcasts and newspaper columns to make some kind of sense of what was going on, I began to wonder if my beloved country was turning into a lunatic bin. I had lived through the nightmare years in Nazi Germany. Were there to be nightmare years at home?

BOOK THREE

Ousted by CBS

The End of a Career in Broadcasting

1947

CHAPTER 1

O_n Monday, March 10, 1947, a vice-president of the advertising agency that handled the sponsor of my 5:45 P.M. Sunday broadcast over CBS telephoned me that I was being dropped from the program. He explained that the sponsor, a manufacturer of shaving cream and other shaving products, was pleased with the commercial rating but wanted now to appeal to a younger audience — perhaps with an entirely different kind of a show that would feature a jazz orchestra in place of my weekly analysis of the news.

I was skeptical of such an explanation. I also was taken aback and depressed at being thrown off the air suddenly and without warning. And I was surprised that there was no word from CBS about this. I knew enough about the broadcasting business by now to realize that, despite all the brave words by the networks, especially by CBS, claiming that they and not the commercial sponsors determined who and what were heard on the air, it was in fact the advertiser who almost always called the tune and made that decision.

Still, I thought, CBS might make an exception in my case. Over the past six years, I had built up the 5:45 P.M. spot on Sundays to have the highest Hooper rating of the day. The present sponsor had had nothing to do with this, though he had benefited. And, as my agent, MCA, recently had reminded the network, I was something of a bargain. My broadcast cost less than any other commercial program on CBS Sunday afternoons and yet had the highest rating. In fact, said MCA, it had several companies waiting in the wings to sponsor my broadcast. There was no danger that CBS would lose any money on me.

I was puzzled that the shaving-cream company would suddenly drop a show with high ratings. Ordinarily a sponsor abandoned a program only because it felt the ratings were too low to justify the expense. Could it be, I began to wonder, that the sponsor, though pleased with the ratings, didn't like my supposedly liberal view of the news?

The tensions of the Cold War already had made themselves felt in our country. There was a growing intolerance. There was increasing pressure, especially on independent and liberal journalists, to conform to the conservative views of Big Business and Big Government.

NBC had cleaned out its last two liberal commentators, John Vandercook and Bob St. John, the year before. CBS recently had edged Quincy Howe out of his 6 P.M. daily spot as soon as a sponsor had bought it and had given it to Eric Sevareid, the new head of the Washington bureau. The era of McCarthy lay just ahead, but already there were signs foreshadowing it. I had not taken the change of climate as seriously perhaps as I should. I had been through it all before — in my years in Nazi Germany.

Recently, I had begun to notice a growing criticism of my broadcasts from the right. The archbishop of New York, Cardinal Spellman, did not like some of the things I was saying on the air. His criticism was shared by other conservatives. Even the vice-president of the ad agency that handled the shaving-cream company account began to hint that I was "too liberal." He himself was rising in Connecticut Republican party circles.

It occurred to me then, as I reflected on the matter, that since the sponsor was not dropping me because of low ratings, he could be taking such action only for some other reason: to silence me.

If this were the case, I doubted that the powers-that-be at CBS would stand for a sponsor's doing that. I was, I thought, on extremely good terms with the two most important of them: William S. Paley, principal owner of CBS and chairman of the board, and Edward R. Murrow, vice-president and director of news and public affairs.

For ten years, ever since I had joined the network, I had had easy access to Bill Paley whenever anything was on my mind. He seemed like a good friend, in the counsel he gave and in the back talk he accepted from me when we disagreed. He had invited me socially, as he had Murrow, to his town house and to his home in the country, an invitation he extended to few other CBS employees, even the top brass.

Ed Murrow, my immediate boss in New York as he had been in London in our days in Europe together, was, as readers of earlier volumes of this memoir know, one of my closest friends. We had been through a lot together in the years we were building up from scratch CBS News from abroad. We had forged a bond that to me, at least, was very rare between two friends and colleagues. I had an enormous admiration for his work — he was the best by far of all the American broadcasters — and I had great respect and liking for him as a human being. Like all friends and co-workers, we had had our differences. But this had never shaken my feelings for him, nor, I had gathered, his for me.

It was, therefore, with considerable confidence that I phoned him, told him my sponsor was dropping me despite good ratings, that there were other advertisers waiting to buy my Sunday spot, and would he advise me whether the program belonged to me or to the sponsor? To put it bluntly — as he and I had always put such matters between us in the past — would he and Paley allow an advertiser to throw me off the air?

To my surprise, Ed, who began to sound somewhat officious as our conversation proceeded, said he would get back to me — in a day or two.

I next called Paley. He was brisk and businesslike. He said the decision about my Sunday broadcast was up to Murrow. Ed was in charge of CBS News.

For a week there was no word from Ed. His silence puzzled me. So, on March 19 I wrote to him and asked if he had come to any decision. The shaving-cream company had informed me in writing that I was through after the broadcast of Sunday, March 30. I would appreciate his informing me, as he had promised to do, whether this was Columbia's decision, too, since, I added, "Mr. Paley informs me that the final decision is yours and not, as I had first believed, the soap company's."

A day or two later Ed finally phoned. He was crisp and cool — most unlike the Ed I had known for ten years. He had made his decision, he said. I would be replaced on the Sunday afternoon program by another commentator. He offered no explanation.

On the following Sunday, March 23, I said at the end of my talk: "Next Sunday I will make my last broadcast on this program. I have been informed by the sponsor and by the Columbia Broadcasting System of that decision." After much wrangling over the phone, Ed had finally approved that statement. At first he had tried to make me agree not to say a word about disappearing from CBS on Sunday afternoons. I had insisted on at least mentioning it.

I had scarcely signed off with those words at 6 P.M. that Sunday afternoon when the storm broke.

So much that was false, misleading, and one-sided was subsequently written in newspapers, magazines, and later in books about the break with Murrow and my ouster from CBS, which destroyed my career in broadcasting and almost destroyed me, that I shall set down here for publication for the first time my side of the story: the facts as I saw and understood them. I've waited a long time to do this.

It is not because I consider what happened to me personally very important to the public, though the destruction of a man's career is important to him, but because the issues involved were of considerable importance to broadcasting in this country, then as now. Murrow, toward the end of his own career at CBS, would raise them himself in numerous speeches and interviews. Those issues concern the question of who decides whom and what you hear on the air, whose wavelengths belong to the people and not to the network, station, or advertiser, though all three of them make billions in profits from their use.

Involved above all is news and comment. Should a shaving-cream company, or any other company that advertises on a network, determine whom the public should hear broadcasting news and comment, and by its selection make certain that the public will hear what the company wishes it to hear — most likely a narrow and conservative view of events? Or does the responsibility belong to the network? And should it stand up to the advertisers' pressure and to the pressures from government, business, labor, churches, veterans' organizations, and other institutions — especially during a period of national uncertainty, witch-hunting, and hysteria such as we were approaching in 1947?

In January of that year, three months before my fall, the *New York Times* had raised the question in an editorial headed "Sponsored News." Writing of the "relationship between a news or comment program and its sponsor," the *Times* declared: "Advertisers are being permitted to say what news is to be put on the air and who is to put it on the air. No newspaper would tolerate for a moment such control of its news and opinions."

Ed Murrow, prompted, I believe, by Paley, promptly got off a letter to the *Times* on behalf of CBS, criticizing the editorial's views. In the opinion of most of us on the news staff, it was hardly the kind of forthright letter we would expect from Ed. A little pompous and self-righteous in tone, the letter, we thought, skirted around the truths that Murrow knew as well as any of us. What had happened to him, we wondered, since (foolishly, I thought) he had chosen to go off the air and become our news director?

"Under no circumstances," Ed wrote, "will we sell time for news and permit the sponsors to select a broadcaster who is not wholly acceptable to us or to influence the content of the broadcast."

This was stretching the truth a little, we thought. Money talked, and a big advertiser could and did pick whom it wanted to be its newscaster and commentator from Columbia's large staff. This was a fact of life on network broadcasting, and none knew it better than Murrow. It was almost the same, Jack Gould, the *Times* radio critic, observed in answering Murrow's letter, "as if an advertiser were permitted to say which member of a newspaper staff should or should not be responsible for an editorial assignment." And he reminded Murrow of the case of Quincy Howe. If CBS had regarded Howe as eminently qualified for the news spot when it was unsponsored, Gould asked, "why should he not be retained in that period whether or not a prospective advertiser happened to concur in the network's decision?" The answer was that if the sponsor preferred another commentator, it got him. Ed Murrow knew all about that. As news director he had been directly involved in the Howe decision.

Ed certainly knew, too, of a recent instance of Phil Wrigley, the chewing-gum king and, I believe, the largest single advertiser on CBS, insisting that I come out to Chicago to do a news and comment program that he would sponsor. Paley had practically ordered me to comply — he could not afford to "cross" Wrigley, he said — but I had refused. I did not want to live in Chicago, and I did not want to become identified as working for Phil Wrigley and his chewing gum. Much later David Halberstam, in recounting my downfall at CBS in *The Powers That Be*, concluded that my defiance of Paley in this instance paved the way for my ultimate dismissal — one did not "cross" the chairman either.

The controversy stirred up by the *Times* and Murrow's response did not, I admit, cause me any concern. Perhaps it should have, but in those days, if not arrogant, I was rather self-confident. Perhaps I was guilty of a little of what the ancient Greeks called hubris. That may explain why the blow, when it came, seemed harsh, unfair, unreasonable.

Beyond the issues involved in my case there was a very personal matter: the destruction of a great friendship. Ed Murrow had hired me in Berlin in 1937 when I was out of a job, and for that I was grateful. For ten years we had worked closely together in pioneering broadcast journalism. It had been a fascinating and exciting experience. Murrow had been an interesting, inspiring, and forthright man to work with.

And he had proved to be, I thought, a close and loyal friend. Reticent though I was about such things, I had more than once in my diary reflected on our friendship. One such reflection had formed part of the last entry I published in *Berlin Diary* in 1941.

We had spent four days together in Lisbon early in December 1940, when we had flown down from London and I had flown out from Berlin on my way home, if I could make it, for Christmas. It had been another fine reunion and we had sat up each night till dawn talking — talking a year of the war out of our systems, comparing our work and our lives in the two wartime capitals. We had said good-bye at the dock in Lisbon as I took ship for New York.

> Aboard the *Excambion*, December 13 [1940] (midnight).
> All day both of us depressed at leaving, for we have worked together very closely, Ed and I, during the last three turbulent years over here, and a bond grew that was very real, a kind you make only a few times in your life, and somehow, absurdly no doubt, sentimentally perhaps, we had a presentiment that the fortunes of war, maybe just a little bomb, would make this reunion the last. . . .*
> We paced up and down the dock in the darkening light of dusk, waiting for the ship to go. . . . Soon it was dark and they began pulling the gangway in. I climbed aboard and Ed disappeared into the night.

In his letters to me Ed often reciprocated my feelings. I remember a letter he wrote from London on July 27, 1941. The worst of the Luftwaffe blitz on England was over. The Germans were deeply involved in Russia, which they had attacked five weeks before, and they had few bombers to spare for London. Ed was coming home for a long leave. In the meantime he had just received a copy I had sent him of *Berlin Diary*, which had come out at the end of June.

> July Twenty-seven . . .
> Dear Bill: . . . Want to tell you how much I liked your book . . . not easy to write about such things, but it reveals in print the honesty, charity, tolerance and humor that is you. . . . Of the things you said about me I am very proud. . . . In fact the job we did together gives me more pride than you can know. Since you left much has gone out of this job for me. . . .

He was lending his copy of my book, he continued, to Harold Laski and others, who "are enthusiastic . . . and want to review it when it's published over here. . . . Shall probably bankrupt myself presenting copies to friends of mine saying . . . look, this is what my colleague and

---

* Two days before he had received a wire from London telling him that his new office had been bombed and demolished by the Germans. His old office had been destroyed only a couple of months previously.

friend wrote." He hoped I would join him in London after his return from leave.

> Maybe we could come back and do this job together starting about first of March. . . . Why not sit down and write me a letter . . . don't forget how lonesome and isolated one feels over here. . . .

From the very first I had noted a dark side to Ed that only those very close to him were aware of. He could be morose, depressed, despairing, sad. He did not find life a picnic. He had few illusions about the human race. Some of this lugubrious side of Murrow, which I liked and respected because I shared his dim view of life, came out in this letter, as it did in nearly all his letters and in our talks.

> I am very discouraged . . . the old let down has come back to England since the Russians started fighting. . . . Me, I feel pretty low right now. . . . When the pressure is on there isn't much time to think but now one is too much inclined to try to look into the future and dear God what a future it's going to be. . . . Famine, plague, down into the mud . . . whole economy being so geared that the powers that be will fear peace more than a continuation of the war. Most people here talk of peace as though it would be something like the last peace. . . . Some of the stuff that's going on in these shadow governments here would make you laugh . . . or cry. . . .

After the war Ed had abandoned broadcasting, at which he was so good, and returned to New York from London, where he had won such fame as was accorded to no other American journalist in England, ever, to become the CBS vice-president in charge of news and public affairs, a post in which I thought he would be wasting his talents.

I gathered Paley had pressured him to take the job — against his better judgment — telling him he was absolutely indispensable in it if CBS were to maintain the lead in radio news that it had gained during the war, largely because of Murrow, and if it were to keep that lead when broadcasting moved into television. It was the challenge to his imagination, I think, that appealed to Ed. Besides, at that time he had such an admiration for, such a feeling of loyalty to, Paley — it was mutual — that he simply could not turn him down.

TV lay not far ahead. Paley had often talked with Ed and me about the prospects of television in the many bull sessions we three had in Europe during the war. He had urged us to start thinking of how news would be presented on the tube. It would be a new challenge — much greater and more exciting than radio had flung at us.

Ed was not so sure. He was skeptical that television would have much place for news, any more than the movies did. But he was giving it considerable thought. We occasionally discussed it during that first year at home.

I saw less of Ed now than I would have liked. But I realized he was busy and absorbed in his new job. And not too happy in it, perhaps. There was some office gossip that Ed might be resentful of my making more money as a sponsored newscaster than he did as a vice-president. But I did not believe this for an instant. It would have been most unlike Ed. He had never seemed to me to care any more about money than I did. I recalled a letter he had written me from London on September 4, 1941.

"I am frankly not very much interested in making a lot of money," he had written, "although I would like to have a small nest egg so I won't be forced to look for a tin cup when I decide to come home for good."

Seconds after I finished my broadcast that Sunday afternoon of March 23 with the simple statement that CBS and my sponsor had decided that the following Sunday would be my last, the telephone switchboard at CBS began to light up. Five minutes later the calls were swamping the network's lines. Thousands of listeners were phoning in, or attempting to, to ask why I was being taken off the air or merely to squawk and protest. Thousands of angry letters began to pour in at CBS and the offices of the sponsor.

By Tuesday after the broadcast, picketers were marching back and forth before the entrance to CBS, flaunting their signs of protest. A committee, mostly clergymen, was formed to take up my case with the chairman of the board himself. The director of the CIO Political Action Committee issued a statement condemning CBS for ousting me and demanding an investigation by the Federal Communications Commission.

"The action of CBS," said the statement, "appears to be part of a plan to rid the airwaves of all commentators who share progressive views or whose opinions are not those of their sponsors."

Several well-known writers agreed. As one New York newspaper (*P.M.*) put it: "Prominent figures in the fields of politics, literature and the stage and screen were rallying behind William L. Shirer, CBS commentator, in an effort to prevent his going off the air. . . ."

Dorothy Parker, chairman of the Voice of Freedom Committee, a sort of watchdog of the airwaves, got off a telegram to Paley.

THE DROPPING OF WILLIAM L. SHIRER FROM HIS SUNDAY AFTER-
NOON CBS PROGRAM OF COMMENTARY COMES AS A SHOCKING BLOW TO
THOSE WHO HAVE FAITH IN THE FREEDOM OF THE AIRWAVES.

SHIRER'S HONESTY AND STEADFAST SEARCHING FOR THE TRUTH IN
ALL MATTERS HAVE WON HIM ONE OF THE WIDEST AUDIENCES ANY
COMMENTATOR HAS EVER HAD. *TIME* MAGAZINE ONCE DESCRIBED HIM
AS "AN AMERICAN EVERY AMERICAN CAN BE PROUD OF."

WHAT IS THE REASON THEN FOR HIS GOING OFF A PROGRAM ON
WHICH HE HAS MADE A HOOPER RATING OF 6.9, ONE OF THE HIGHEST
AMONG CBS'S SUNDAY AFTERNOON SHOWS?

IF THE ADVERTISER IS DISPLEASED WITH SHIRER'S VIEWS, THEN WE
APPEAL TO YOU TO DISREGARD THE ADVERTISER, LEST IT BE SAID THAT
HE CAN DETERMINE WHOM THE AMERICAN PEOPLE SHALL HEAR — OR
SHALL NOT HEAR — ON THE AIR.

CBS HAS LONG TAKEN PRIDE — AND PROPERLY SO — IN ITS PRO-
GRESSIVE OUTLOOK. DON'T LET THE SHIRER EPISODE BE THE FIRST
BLACK MARK ON THIS RECORD.

Dorothy Parker, whom I did not at that time know personally, but whose caustic wit in her short stories and reviews I had long admired, certainly outdid herself. Her telegram of protest was signed by several dozen well-known writers and actors, including Gregory Peck, John Gunther, Vincent Sheean, Lewis Gannett, Ring Lardner, Arthur Miller, Edward G. Robinson, Judy Holliday, José Ferrer, and Margaret Webster.

They were joined in separate protests by a number of others. Robert E. Sherwood, playwright and confidant of President Roosevelt, wired Paley that it would be "a tragedy if CBS lost the broadcasts of William L. Shirer." Archibald MacLeish, the poet, also a confidant of Roosevelt and a personal friend of Murrow, wired Ed that the action of CBS "will be interpreted . . . everywhere as another retreat by the networks before the pressure of advertisers." He was sure, he told Murrow, "that you have done everything possible to prevent [such] an action." He couldn't have been more wrong.

Ralph Ingersoll, former editor of *P.M.* and of some of the Luce magazines, and also a friend of Ed, was more skeptical with his old friend. He wrote him:

Dear Ed:
I've just read the shocking news of Bill Shirer's being dropped by Columbia and I want to tell you how appalled I am. What have they done to you since you came back from England, that you aren't out in front fighting for him?

It was a question I kept asking myself — what had they done to Ed Murrow up on the nineteenth floor amid the nineteen vice-presidents? — as he began to issue statements not only justifying my ouster from the Sunday broadcast but trying to destroy me as a broadcaster, dressing up his assertions in the most amazing half-truths, evasions, and downright lies. He turned out to be uncharacteristically slick in trying to confuse the public, diffuse the protests, and finish me off at CBS. I was appalled by his disregard for the truth. It was a side of Ed that I didn't suspect existed. Was it worth it to him, I kept thinking — was it necessary — to lie for the corporation? Did he owe this to Paley?

Fortunately for me, his pronunciamentos were so devious and so contradictory that in the end, I think, judging by the comments in the newspapers and magazines, they indicted him. The utterances did not fool the press or the public, whose condemnation of CBS, Murrow, and Paley, was practically unanimous. But they did confuse some writers who later wrote of these events in magazine articles and books and who simply took Ed's company line.

In the midst of the hullabaloo about the shaving-cream company and CBS dropping me, the president of the esteemed concern, laden down with thousands of angry letters and telegrams protesting its action, called on me at my apartment in New York and offered to rehire me. He seemed desperate. He would do anything, he said, to stop the avalanche. The company could not afford, he added, such adverse publicity. The resentment expressed in the letters and telegrams by thousands of listeners was bound to hurt business. The company wished at all costs to avoid public controversy.

I confess the president's call and his eagerness to reinstate me cheered me up. It looked as though I would have my job back after all.

I told the president I would convey the good news to Chairman Paley and call him back at the end of the day. Unfortunately, I had to rush out to lunch with Elmo Roper, the pollster who was also a consultant to CBS, a friend of Paley and of me. He had invited me to lunch at the Rainbow Room atop Rockefeller Center to see if there was anything he could do to help solve my problem with Columbia. When I told him of the visit of my sponsor's president, he agreed with me that this probably would settle the whole matter. Elmo seemed relieved and happy about this unexpected turn. Though our food had not yet arrived, he urged me to go to a nearby pay phone and tell Paley the good news. He was sure Bill would be highly pleased.

But Bill Paley was not. His voice and manner were ice-cold. The sponsor could not reinstate me in the Sunday afternoon period, he said. CBS had decided otherwise. I was definitely out, so far as that spot was concerned.

"Thank you for calling," he said, and hung up. Elmo Roper could not believe it. But I was beginning to. I was beginning to see that Paley could not forgive me for having crossed him. You did not do that to the chairman of the board of a big corporation. For a day or two perhaps he had hesitated until he saw whether Murrow would be loyal to him and the company or to an old friend. Now that Ed had made it clear where he stood, Paley did not hesitate. He would show me the cost of insubordination.

And he would put out of his mind, as the imperious Colonel Mc-Cormick of the *Chicago Tribune* had done fifteen years before, as all the great American tycoons did, any thought of the services one had rendered the company over the years, the risks a foreign correspondent had taken to get the news, to cover the war, the lack of normal personal and family life, the long hours of toil seven days a week, week after week, month after month, the prestige one had brought the organization by one's work, the loyalty and devotion one had showed it. I shouldn't have been surprised. I'd been through it all before with Colonel McCormick, as had so many of my colleagues with their respective press lords. Bill Paley was just another one of the breed. With Ed Murrow, of course, it was different. I was still baffled by his behavior.

Paley and Murrow blamed me for stirring up all the rumpus and were furious with me, though they knew that I had had nothing to do with the reaction to my ouster from the Sunday afternoon spot. I never asked one person or organization to do anything at all. What took place was spontaneous and surprised me as much as it surprised and displeased the chairman and his news director.

Their displeasure, which quickly turned to resentment, was soon manifested. Apparently what irked Paley the most was the picketing before the CBS premises. That had never happened before. It was giving Columbia a bad name, and I was responsible for it. Paley also, I was told, bitterly resented having to receive a committee of distinguished citizens who called on him to protest my ouster and to urge him to reconsider it. That, too, had never happened to CBS before, and he was sure that I was behind this embarrassment to the chairman of the board.

Paley's feelings came blurting out at a meeting in his office with Murrow and me. He angrily informed me that my "usefulness to CBS" was over. Ed said nothing. His silence, I thought, was revealing. In fact, both men later denied that the boss had said any such thing to me. This was when they adopted a new company line: that I had not been "fired" and that the both of them had sincerely desired me to stay on at CBS — albeit not in the Sunday spot where I had an audience of five million listeners. They said this — my boss and my close friend — at the same time that they were telling the public that I had been replaced on Sunday in order to "improve Columbia's service of news and news analysis," in effect saying that I had become incompetent and, therefore, had to be replaced. And yet they expected the public to swallow the yarn that they were most anxious for me to remain at CBS and to continue to broadcast "in a different time period," as Ed put it in one of his public statements.

> It would be foolish indeed [Murrow argued] for CBS to ask Mr. Shirer to continue as its news analyst, as we did from the outset, if we intended to gag or censor him. . . . We had hoped that Mr. Shirer would continue to broadcast over CBS in a different time period.

Both Murrow and Paley kept stressing that they had offered me "a different time period." But this was as false as were many of their other statements. Ed had at one stage said CBS would create a period for me on Saturday afternoon (when listeners wanted sports news, not analysis of world news), but Paley had overruled him on that. He had then spoken vaguely of my broadcasting on part of the period between 11 and 11:30 P.M. (after most listeners had gone to bed), but even this was not a firm offer. No assignment of a definite time period was ever made by CBS after the sponsor decided to take me off the Sunday spot. Yet Ed, in his statements to the press, continued to contend that in my case CBS had simply made a "change in assignment," the kind of expert judgment a newspaper might make in transferring a columnist's space to another page. "In fact," he added, "CBS changed the time period of Mr. Shirer's broadcasts several times in years gone by."

This was untrue. The time of my Sunday broadcast had never been changed since its inception six years before. And there was a difference, Ed well knew, between taking a commentator off a sponsored broadcast for which he had over the years built up a mass audience and simply moving him around in the unsponsored news periods at hours when there were few listeners.

Of all Ed's various statements to the press on behalf of CBS, I think I resented most the following one:

> In shifting Mr. Shirer's assignment, CBS exercised its informed editorial and managerial judgment, with a view to improving its news analysis service in the Sunday afternoon spot. This was not a sudden decision but was based on careful, expert study of this program over a long period of time.

The first sentence put me down and, as Ed realized, made my working for CBS any longer impossible. It was as if the *New York Times* had yanked Scotty Reston off the op-ed page and told its readers such a move was done to "improve" the page.

The second sentence was a pure lie. The truth was that it *was* a sudden decision, set off, as Paley admitted in a moment of candor when he received the committee of protesters, by the sponsor's decision to drop me. No "study" of the program — careful, expert, or otherwise — was ever made, over a long period or a short period of time. Ed invented this one out of whole cloth. I checked this fully after my ouster. No one at CBS had ever heard of this alleged "study." Neither Murrow nor Paley, with whom I'd been very close, had ever even mentioned any dissatisfaction with my broadcasts on Sunday after- noon, though God knows they were far from perfect. Indeed, both men, right up to the last (before the sponsor acted), had constantly praised the Sunday show. It added, they said, to the prestige of CBS in the field of news, which was considerably higher than NBC's, and they especially had liked its high ratings. Not many radio news shows brought in more dough than they cost.

On March 25, five days before the broadcast the sponsor (not CBS) had designated as my last on Sunday afternoon, Murrow announced my replacement to the press. He was Joseph C. Harsch, a veteran *Christian Science Monitor* correspondent in Washington who also broadcast part-time for CBS. Joe was an old friend. He had arrived in Berlin for the *Monitor* at the beginning of the war and I had hired him there as a part-time broadcaster for CBS. He was a good journalist, not brilliant or flamboyant, but sound. Joe was also a decent and honorable man. He phoned me immediately from Washington and said he would not accept replacing me unless I consented, which I did.

Ed Murrow used the announcement of my replacement to rub it in again. "We believe," he said, "that Mr. Harsch, with his long expe- rience in Washington and abroad and his access to news sources in

Washington, will improve Columbia's news analysis in this period."

Joe Harsch, as a broadcaster on my old spot on Sunday afternoons, quickly faded out. He soon was dropped.* The period, reserved for me for news and comment so many years, soon gave way to a program of pure entertainment. It did not take Murrow and Paley long to lose their zeal to "improve Columbia's news analysis in this period."

In my case it had been a red herring and a lie, but I could not say so publicly. I had to leave that to others. Several radio editors and columnists on the metropolitan newspapers quickly exposed the Paley-Murrow hypocrisy. But support from another and unexpected source soon made the network look ridiculous — to the embarrassment of both executives.

The bizarre scene in the CBS studio and control room in New York at my final broadcast that Palm Sunday of March 30, 1947, was unbelievable. It brought back memories of broadcasting for CBS from Berlin in the Nazi time.

Ed Murrow had been at his worst when I phoned him on Saturday morning about what I would say at the end of this farewell broadcast. Ed at first had insisted I say nothing, as he had about the broadcast the week before, but I had balked at that. I thought I owed it to an audience of five million listeners to say a word about my departure. To have said nothing would have been too cowardly. Ed and I had finally worked out a statement. And though I did not like it — I had made most of the concessions — I had in the end accepted it as the best I could get from the CBS management in the present circumstances.

And then, Saturday evening, friends in the news department had phoned me to say the place was full of rumors I was going to depart from my script and blast CBS before I finished my last broadcast. I phoned Murrow Sunday morning to reassure him.

"You son-of-a-bitch! You better not try anything funny today," Ed had responded. "You better stick to the script — or else!" he warned.

"No problem, Ed," I said. "Look at all the experience I've had in sticking to scripts. In Berlin. Remember?"

I had often told him of how some little Nazi always sat opposite me in the studio in Berlin, following a copy of my script word for word, and

---

* In a letter to me Harsch wrote that, "anticipating events," he asked out. "CBS would have booted me out had I not got in the first blow. It seems that they considered me an expensive luxury. The one thing I resent above all is that they took the Sunday show away from me on the ground that I had not been able to attract a sponsor when they themselves had deliberately withheld the time from sale. . . . Then they announce that I am unsalable. . . . It's kind of good to be an honest reporter again."

ready to cut me off with a little switch at his hands if I deviated from it by a single word. I had had to use various inflections of the voice to get through what I wanted to say.

Ed ignored the allusion to the capital of the Third Reich.

"For your information," he said sternly, "I've got things fixed so we can shut you out in a split second."

"Just like in Berlin," I could not keep from saying.

The resemblance held to the very end. In my tiny office fifty feet from the news studio, I sweated out the writing of the last broadcast, as I had all the others, incorporating late news from the wire services into the text of a few things I wanted to say that last time. I finished writing earlier than usual — generally I was still at work on the broadcast up to a few seconds before airtime at 5:45 P.M. Ted Church, our chief editor, and Dallas Townsend, the editor of the day, both good friends, both appalled at the turn of events, had told me they were under pressure from Murrow to read carefully every word of my script. So for the last ten minutes before airtime, they sat in the news studio, one on each side of me, and combed through the script — as if they were looking for time-bombs.

I was getting very close to a state of nervous exhaustion, after battling the corporation, Paley, and Murrow. John Gunther, one of my oldest friends from our days together in Europe as foreign correspondents for Chicago newspapers, had volunteered to come in and help me through that last time, though I realized he also was a friend of Ed, who had often given him opportunities to broadcast and keep his name before the public.

My editors finally finished going over my script. I glanced at the clock. We had about ten seconds to go. I looked into the control room where my old colleague, Henry, the engineer who threw the switches and gave us our cues, and who had been doing this broadcast for years, greeted me with the wave of a hand and a smile. Two or three unfamiliar men stood behind him. Ed's henchmen, apparently, who were there to see that Henry, out of a warm feeling for me, did not hesitate if they told him to throw the switch that would instantly silence me. Ed, I heard, was directing operations from his office on the nineteenth floor. I had hoped he would come down and face me personally that last time. Church and Townsend joined the others in the control room. By now they formed a squad. This was a much larger force than had ever been summoned to keep check on me in Berlin. It was all very familiar. But I had not quite expected it here. I felt slightly repelled but also slightly amused by the way these figures — they looked like sleuths in a bad film — began to crouch over the one carbon I had made of my script.

I got through the thirteen and a half minutes of reading it about as well as I expected, considering my feelings, which I was determined must not show. I came to the last page, paused, and then read the lines as unemotionally as I could.

> This is my last broadcast on this program.
>
> The issues involved, which make it my last broadcast, are — so far as I'm concerned — important, but I believe this is not the place nor the time to discuss them. I realize you listen in on this program to hear the news.
>
> In conclusion, I would like only to say this: To you who have followed these Sunday afternoon broadcasts since 1941 — through the years of the war and the beginning of the peace — I thank you for having listened.

Immediately after the broadcast I ran into a group of reporters waiting for me outside the studio. To them I read a brief statement I had knocked out the day before saying that because CBS had made it plain by the public statements of Paley and Murrow that my usefulness at CBS was over, I was resigning.

Perhaps this was a tactical mistake. Murrow and Paley quickly seized on it to "prove" that I was not fired. Hadn't I resigned? Even Eric Sevareid, thirty years later, would publish an article in the *New Republic*, adopted from remarks he delivered before the Washington Journalism Center, in which he declared it to be a "*myth* that William L. Shirer was fired by Ed Murrow and fired because he was politically too liberal. He wasn't fired at all. . . ."*

Sevareid's loyalty to CBS to the very end apparently blinded him to the way corporations, especially among the media, got rid of employ-

---

* Sevareid, too, had been an old friend. I had known him just before the war when he was working on the Paris *Herald* and at the U.P. bureau in Paris, and had urged Ed to hire him as our correspondent in France, which Ed had done. Eric wrote me a day after my last broadcast reiterating his "loyal" friendship, wishing me well but sticking up for CBS. He accused me of wronging the corporation. He did not feel that I had been "done an injustice" nor could he "go along," he said, with my "accusations against CBS." Three months later he again wrote: "I still think you were a crazy bastard to do what you did and say what you said; I still think you were wrong. . . ."

Alexander Kendrick, an old colleague on the foreign staff, in his biography *Prime Time — The Life of Edward R. Murrow*, written and published while Kendrick was still an employee of CBS, was as misleading as Sevareid. He had Murrow declaring that my sponsor "had clearly expressed their displeasure at not selling more shaving cream." The charge was not true, and could not be true, given the high Hooper rating of the program. Neither the sponsor nor Murrow had ever complained about the ratings. As far as my departure from CBS was concerned, Kendrick wrote: "Murrow tried to persuade him [Shirer] to stay. . . . Murrow was sure moreover that Shirer would soon find another sponsor and wanted him to remain on the air." Nothing could be farther from the truth.

ees. Technically they seldom "fired" one. What they did was to make his staying on untenable and thus force him to resign. It was an old trick. I had no intention of staying on with CBS so that Paley and Murrow could humiliate me further.

A few days after I was replaced, the press announced that I would be the recipient of what was then radio's highest honor, the George Foster Peabody Award for "outstanding reporting and interpretation of the news," at the seventh annual presentation of the awards on April 17 at the Hotel Roosevelt in New York.

I went to the luncheon determined not to gloat over the award, though I appreciated receiving it, especially at this particular moment. In the audience below the speaker's platform I noticed Ed Murrow and a group of his men from CBS occupying one of the large round tables. Ed seemed very nervous. He glowered at me as though he was expecting me to get up and, pointing at him, rub it in about my award. He need not have worried.

Edward Weeks, editor of the *Atlantic Monthly* and chairman of the Peabody Advisory Board, got up to read the citation.

> One of the great team of news gatherers . . . for CBS . . . William L. Shirer won the gratitude of American listeners for the truth he told us about Hitler and Germany despite the opposition of censors during those crucial years, 1938–1941. We are equally grateful to him as a commentator for his recent warning of the trouble arising in Central Europe.

Ted Weeks paused, a smile breaking over his face, which he directed first at Murrow just below him and then turning his head at me at his side at the speaker's table.

"To Mr. Shirer," he said, ". . . and may his voice be heard again! . . . the Peabody Award for the outstanding interpretation of the news in 1946."

I must confess that this was a sweet moment for me. What the audience of men and women from the world of broadcasting seemed to like about Weeks's remarks was not so much that I had received the award but Ted's felicitous note that my voice might be heard on the air again. The audience had broken into a loud and prolonged applause at the words, so that Weeks had had to pause and wait until it subsided to complete his sentence.

The account of the incident in the *New York Herald-Tribune* the next day noted the burst of clapping at this juncture and continued:

Mr. Shirer rose, accepted the bronze medal and said: "I want to thank this committee for this honor and for their good wishes." Without further comment he sat down.

Out of the corner of my eye I could see Murrow breathing a sigh of relief. A couple of days before, in a speech to the Overseas Press Club, he had made a snide remark about the Peabody Award being given to me. He had received it three years before, in 1944, he said, "at a time when I was no longer doing my best broadcasts." The implication was clear. But making it in public was most unlike the Ed Murrow we all had known up to this point.

But by now he was spewing forth in public almost daily his and the corporation's poor opinion of me. It was as if the sponsor's dropping me had aroused some old and fierce animosity in Ed that none knew had existed. As a parting shot, the day he and Paley forced me to resign after my last broadcast on March 30, 1947, he had issued another public statement that concluded:

> The Columbia Broadcasting System and no one else decided to place another news analyst in the period that has been occupied by Mr. Shirer, and Mr. Shirer doesn't like it, and that's all there is to it.

The words were so bland, so smug, so deliberately misleading that even on this last day, after all that had happened, I found it difficult to believe that they could come from Edward R. Murrow. Sad . . . that they had.

The Peabody Award was not the only timely recognition I got about my work as a radio journalist during those tense days when Paley and Murrow were doing all they could to denigrate it and publicly humiliate me. In June that year *Billboard's* sixteenth annual poll of some one hundred newspaper radio editors selected me "as the most interesting news commentator on the air," and this was duly reported in the daily press. And on March 10, the day the sponsor notified me I was through, the secretary of the Alfred I. duPont Radio Awards Foundation wrote to tell me that the Committee of Awards included my name "prominently among those considered for the 1946 Award." Although it went to Elmer Davis, "the Committee has requested me to advise you," the secretary wrote, "of their appreciation of the excellent work you have done in line with the objectives of this Foundation. With our best wishes for your continued success. . . ."

CHAPTER 2

N̲o doubt in the next few weeks and months and even for a
year or two I felt sorry for °myself, suddenly deprived of a career after
having practiced it, not without some modest success, for twenty-two
years — ever since I had turned twenty-one and finished college and
set out for Europe.

My ouster, I believe, marked the beginning of a new CBS policy of
knuckling under to what it thought was the temper of the times. That
Murrow would go along with it saddened me. Soon, with the arrival of
Senator McCarthy on the scene as the great exposer of Communism
and Communists in America, CBS would actually stoop to investigate
the loyalty of CBS employees, especially those in the news department. After that, CBS compelled its employees to sign a loyalty oath,
the only network that did. Whatever Murrow's private feeling, he went
along with the corporation. There is no record of his publicly protesting
this shabby investigation. He himself signed the humiliating loyalty
oath and advised his colleagues to do likewise. By this time he had given
up his executive job as head of news and, happily, returned to the air.
He also became a director of the corporation. As even Kendrick, the
most sympathetic of biographers, wrote: "In becoming a member of
the CBS Board of Directors, Murrow placed himself within the CBS
decision-making apparatus that instituted the loyalty oath, engaged in
blacklisting. . . ."

By this time I had given up trying to understand what had happened
to my old friend. I was out of CBS, out of broadcasting, and I no longer
saw the man who had hired and fired me. But for some time after my
departure I did try to fathom why Ed Murrow turned on me so savagely
that spring of 1947. Others tried too, but with no more success than
I had.

David Halberstam in *The Powers That Be*, published thirty-two
years later, suggested that though Ed and I were good friends, we had
been, "in a subtle way, rivals as well."

Murrow, deft, civilized, the ultimate gifted broadcaster in projecting mood and feeling; Shirer, a far better writer, more cerebral, a more penetrating journalist in dissecting ideas and issues. It had been a friendship not without its edge, but they were men bound to each other by a transcending common experience which had evoked the best of each of them. More, they were identified with each other completely in the public mind, for in those dark days at the start of World War II it had been their two voices, Murrow and Shirer, that the nation had listened to: listeners could not think of one without thinking of the other.*

Be that as it may, I had never felt myself to be a rival of Ed. Our talents, I thought, were complementary. Ed was incomparable on the air. He had a feeling for communication by radio that amounted to genius. He had the manner, the voice. I did not. What I brought to fledgling radio journalism was a broad experience as a foreign correspondent. Murrow had had no journalistic training, either at home or abroad. He had joined CBS as an educator. I had spent twelve years before coming to CBS as a newspaper correspondent in all the important European capitals and, more briefly, in large parts of Asia. I knew Europe: its languages, its culture, its history, its national rivalries. That was why, I believe, Ed had taken me on in the first place.

As Halberstam indicated, our friendship had not been without its edge. We had had our disagreements. Once, before the war came, Ed had complained bitterly that I seemed to be more loyal to Paul White, director of news in New York, under whom I supposed we both worked, though I realized Ed loathed him, than to him, as European director of a staff that consisted only of him and me. Ed had a slight jealous streak.

Some at CBS thought Ed had been jealous of the success of my first book, *Berlin Diary*, which came out shortly after his own first book, *This Is London*, in 1941 and quickly outsold it, climbing to the top of the best-seller list. But I did not believe it. No one could have written of that book and its author as movingly and as generously as Ed had to me.† He was just as generous, as we have seen, about the book in public.

Murrow, I was told, had resented my not joining him in London after I left Berlin at the end of 1940. I had explained to him that I had been away from the United States for too long — some fifteen years, compared to his three — and that I needed to live and work at home for at least a short while. With a lull in the war, after the fall of France and

* David Halberstam, *The Powers That Be*. New York, 1979, p. 132.
† See p. 98.

Hitler's abandoning any attempt to invade Britain, it was a good chance for me to get acquainted with my native land and to see a bit of my family for the first time. When the lull was over, especially if America got into the war, I would return. He himself, now that the news in London had become somewhat routine for the moment, was coming home on extensive leave. I doubted if I could make much of a contribution in London, where he had become a legend. For the time being, I thought I could contribute more in New York. One had to know and understand the militarist, aggressive dictatorship, which now had conquered most of Europe and posed a threat not only to Britain and Russia, but to America, though our good people were blind to it. None of the men broadcasting for CBS from New York had my experience and background. None of them knew Nazi Germany, or the rest of Europe, at first hand. Paley and Paul White, our news director, agreed that the best place for me at the moment was New York. I had explained all this to Murrow in London.

He had replied that while he regretted my decision he respected and understood it. Later, even when the war was over, after I'd returned to Europe twice, in 1943 and 1944 to help cover, first, the Eighth Air Force, which had begun its big bombing of Germany in 1943 from its bases in England, and then the American army, in 1944, after it landed on the Continent and drove toward Germany, my failure to join Ed in London earlier still seemed to rankle him.

One night shortly after the end of the war, when we had journeyed back together to Europe from New York on the old *Queen Mary*, still converted to a troop ship, Ed had suddenly turned against me with an astonishing fury. Driving up to London from Southampton, where we had disembarked, Ed had suddenly lurched at me and tried to pummel me, cursing me. He had been drinking heavily that evening — we both had — but nevertheless his strange behavior surprised me. He was rather incoherent and I was not sure what was upsetting him, though later it dawned on me that it had to do with what he called my letting him down after I left Berlin and decided to stay at home for a while. Next day he called at the flat where he had put me up in London and apologized, and I put the incident out of mind. Like some of my other good friends, such as Jimmy Sheean, one of my closest and oldest, Ed sometimes got a bit belligerent when he had downed too many.

So, as I tried to sort out what had affected Murrow that spring of our break, I put down that first resentment at my not going over to work with him in London after my Berlin assignment was over. There had been a similar experience, after the war, when I declined to join Ed as his assistant when he abandoned broadcasting to become director of news and public events. I did think he understood when I told him then that I was an even worse executive than he was.

There was one other incident I recalled that took place after Ed had settled down on the nineteenth floor at CBS headquarters. AFRA had threatened to strike the networks on behalf of its members, actors and other performers on the air. Murrow had called us news commentators in and told us that in case of a strike we would have to fill in the time — if necessary around the clock — reading news and commenting on it. I told Ed flatly I would not strike-break against AFRA. I would respect its picket lines. Ed had not liked that.

So, though I was not conscious of it, there had been perhaps an accumulation of grievances against me in Ed's mind that had long simmered and that happened to boil over at the moment the sponsor decided to drop me. I was taken aback, I must admit, at the lengths they drove him to. I was surprised that his loyalty to the corporation and to its chief was so total. It was not necessary. His place with the company and with Paley was secure.

At least for a long time to come. I don't think Ed looked beyond that. Who would? In the next few years in New York Ed would enjoy a new and even dizzier success in broadcasting than he had had in London during the war. But his turn would come, as mine had. I mentioned this to him in one of the last talks we had, a day or two before my exit, and he would remember it, years later.

"I've been through this before," I said, "with the *Chicago Tribune.* Every newspaperman has, if he has been around long enough. You can't possibly imagine it now, Ed, but your turn will come. Someday you'll get just what I'm getting."

One thing puzzled me about Murrow's zeal in dumping me. Sensitive and intelligent as he was, Ed knew what was in the wind, knew that we were entering a period of growing intolerance and hysteria, of witch-hunting and Red-baiting — some of the very things he had been passionately against all his adult life. For all his wild and misleading statements about me, he knew in his heart that, our friendship aside, this was no time for him or CBS to knuckle under to the hysterical forces of reaction that were beginning to take over the country by ousting me because a shaving-cream company and its Madison Avenue advertising agency thought my views a bit too liberal. I would be among the first victims, but he must have known that others would follow, though I do not believe he had the faintest inkling, as I did, that he himself eventually might meet a similar fate.

Still, the signs were there.

The previous fall, the November 1946 congressional elections had been a disaster for the Democrats. For the first time in eighteen years the Republicans had captured both houses of Congress, much of its majority the result of its candidates winning on a platform of clearing the Communists out of the government in Washington, its "communistic" targets including such staunch patriots as General G. C. Marshall, Undersecretary of State Dean Acheson, and President Truman himself. This Congress was bitterly reactionary. Its Republican majority proclaimed that it was not only going to clean the Communists out of Washington but also repeal all social and welfare legislation passed since the beginning of the New Deal. The clock was going to be set back with a vengeance, if not back to McKinley, at least to President Calvin Coolidge.

Among those elected that fall of 1946 was a little-known local judge, Joseph R. McCarthy of Wisconsin, to the Senate, and an even lesser known local politician in California, Richard M. Nixon, to the House. Both had accused their opponents of sympathy with Communism and of having "Communist" support. The voters had fallen for it, as they usually do in this country.

To take the steam out of Republican charges of being soft on Communists, President Truman had himself ordered all federal employees to take a loyalty oath. Those suspected of disloyalty were fired. Their hearings, when granted, were a farce. To add fuel to the fire, the attorney general, Tom C. Clark, had issued a list of ninety organizations which in the opinion of the Justice Department were subversive — mostly because they were allegedly "Communist Fronts." Every month or so, Clark would expand his list, until it included dozens of innocent groups. No matter. Any government employee who had belonged to one of them, or contributed funds to it, or been sympathetic, might be held to be disloyal and discharged. The witch-hunt had begun. Distinguished careers were beginning to be destroyed. The House Un-American Activities Committee leaped in. The FBI, often in cahoots with Senator McCarthy and the committee, lent its aid, and took the lead in checking up on hundreds of thousands of suspected subversives. Soon McCarthy would push his way to the front of the pack, exposing alleged "Communists" in government.

Eventually Murrow realized where such hysteria was taking the country. And in the end he would turn on the shabby senator from Wisconsin in a memorable broadcast that exposed McCarthy for the mountebank he was and indeed hastened his end. But to some, Ed's move came late. David Halberstam, researching his book *The Powers That Be,* noticed it. It was "significant," he thought, "that Murrow's broadcast attacking McCarthy took so long in coming."

McCarthy was getting away with murder, "yet he [Murrow] did not act. McCarthy had given his first speech in March 1950, and that year had passed, and then 1951, and then 1952, and then 1953. Starting in 1952 friends began to ask Murrow and Friendly when they were going to take McCarthy on."

Halberstam thought Murrow became "seriously disturbed by the company's and his own failure to move earlier on McCarthy. . . . Murrow's own failure to act had become an issue among journalistic colleagues. Afterward [he] was haunted by the fact that the program was so late."

But better late than never. No other network then, or later, allowed one of its commentators to take on McCarthy. The broadcast of Murrow on his *See It Now* program devastated the Red-baiting senator from Wisconsin, and he never recovered from it.

But it turned out also to be the first step in Ed Murrow's fall from grace at CBS. Several members of management and the board of directors were far from pleased. Frank Stanton, president and the righthand man of Paley, returning from a business trip to the Midwest, called in Fred Friendly, Murrow's collaborator on *See It Now*, and told him that several affiliates there thought the broadcast had been bad for business. Some went further. They thought Murrow's attack on McCarthy "might cost the company the network."

Indeed, Ed soon confronted the same sponsor problems that had helped terminate my career at CBS. Alcoa, which had stuck by Ed through many a public controversy, decided the next year not to renew *See It Now*. Then, in a series of moves that resembled those he and Ed had taken against me, Paley decided to phase out *See It Now*, despite its enormous prestige as by far the best public affairs program on TV. Soon it was gone, and a poor substitute show was given to another (Friendly) to produce, and Ed found himself on the way out.

A few months after ridding CBS of me, Murrow returned to broadcasting. First on radio, and then on television, he was again a glittering success. He was the best there was. He pioneered boldly in TV news as he had in radio news. Much more than any other he shaped the nature of the presentation of news and the covering of public events, including wars, on television, to which, the surveys tell us, most Americans now go to ascertain the happenings of the day. His failure to achieve more in the face of the stupidity and greed of the networks, especially his own, broke his heart and broke him in the end.

In those first exciting years of television, which brought into the home not only the voice but also the face, not only the sound of a city or a battlefield or whatever but also the sight, Ed Murrow became more famous than ever, his finely chiseled, brooding countenance familiar in every household in the land.* He was said to be making millions. But the commercial corruption and cheapening of the medium that had brought him such overflowing awards finally sickened him, gnawing away at his insides. However belatedly, after how many millions, he turned on the huckstering broadcasters in a speech to them at Chicago on October 15, 1958, and publicly condemned them and their broadcasting stations and networks for their inanity, timidity, avarice, and irresponsibility.

Paley never forgave Murrow for the Chicago speech. From that moment on their unique relationship started to cool and dissolve. Or, perhaps it had begun to go a few months before when Paley had thrown Murrow's trail-blazing program *See It Now* off the air after seven lively years of life as the best public affairs program on TV.

Ed, I heard, felt this was "the end" for him. He was bitter. To Charles Collingwood, his protégé whom he had hired in London during the war, he confided: "You're only important around here as long as you're useful to them. . . . When they're finished with you they'll throw you out without a further thought."[†]

He took a year off, a sabbatical, to think things over. He traveled leisurely around the world. When he returned, he found himself virtually through at CBS. His last program had been taken off the air. A new program, *CBS Reports*, which he had thought he would head, was given instead to another, his old collaborator on *See It Now*, Fred Friendly. The year off, the trip around the world with his wife and son, had not helped him, physically or mentally. Friends at CBS said he was exhausted and depressed and looking for a graceful way out.

I ran into Ed one day on Madison Avenue. It was a cold, dark day in December 1960, shortly after the publication of my *Rise and Fall of the Third Reich*, on which I worked night and day for ten years. I had not seen Ed during that time. We had never become reconciled. I had not sought or wanted reconciliation, though I heard from mutual

---

* In January 1952 the number of TV sets in use during the evening hours surpassed for the first time the number of radio sets, though radio was still ahead of TV in advertising revenue.
† Halberstam, op. cit., p. 150.

friends that he did. What had happened thirteen years before had receded in my memory but it could never be undone.

Ed was in a somber but relaxed mood, reminding me of how he had been in the old days when we were eager young colleagues. But his looks shocked me. His deeply lined face was emaciated; his trim body seemed shrunken. A cigarette dangled from his lips. He coughed.

He congratulated me on the reception of my book on the Third Reich, which had just crept to the top of the best-seller list and which had been accorded some esteem by various reviewers and which promised for the first time since my end at CBS to give me an assured income for a few years.

"It's a tremendous achievement," Ed said. "Far greater than anything we've done on the air. You ought to be proud of yourself."

I mentioned that I had followed his dazzling career on TV. He thanked me and then his face darkened.

"I'm through at CBS," he said. "Washed out."

I told him it was hard to believe. He had given almost his whole adult life to Paley and the network.

"In the end, I got what you got," he said. "I remember you told me I would. I should have known it."

He seemed uncharacteristically bitter at CBS. And he told me briefly how he had been squeezed out. Luckily President-elect Kennedy had offered him the directorship of the U.S. Information Agency and he was accepting. He was going to resign from CBS, after twenty-seven years with the network. He was fifty-three and in poor health — mainly, his associates thought, from years of overwork and too many cigarettes.

One warm day in August 1964, nearly four years later, Janet Murrow, Ed's wife, with whom we had also been very close — she was the godmother of our second daughter, Linda — phoned from their country place near Pawling, New York, and spoke to my wife. She said Ed very much wanted to see me and asked if we could drive over the next day from our farm, which was an hour away in Connecticut, and have lunch.

I had heard he was dying of cancer. He had given up his job at USIA, despite President Johnson's urging that he remain, after the assassination of President Kennedy. He had gone to a hospital and had one lung removed. We accepted Janet's invitation immediately.

As we drove over to Pawling the next day — it was one of the loveliest days of the summer, pleasantly warm, dry, and sunny — I told Tess that I would not discuss, nor let Ed discuss, our break. I had heard again recently that he wanted a reconciliation.

Tess and I were taken aback by Ed's appearance. He was a mere shell of the man we had known in our youthful, golden years in Europe together. His body had shrunk and seemed even thinner. His face, pale and bloodless, was also much thinner, the cheeks hollow, the furrows deeper in his forehead and around his eyes, which were still bright. Though he had given up smoking, he coughed a great deal and seemed to have trouble breathing. That probably was due, I thought, to his having only one lung. Perhaps also the cancer was spreading.

We had much good talk at lunch in the old but elegant farmhouse, though Ed seemed a bit on edge. Still, he talked warmly of those first years in Europe when all four of us were young and excited about life. We laughed nostalgically as we recalled some of the good and crazy times together in Berlin, Geneva, Vienna, London, and the first year in New York after we came back from the war.

After lunch Ed said he would like to take me around in his jeep and show me his farm. We had compared notes about the joys and sorrows of two city slickers trying to farm, though on my one hundred acres in Connecticut, I did little more than garden and cut firewood, while Ed had a going farm twice as big with a couple of hundred head of pure-bred cattle and good haying fields.

I suggested that the jeep ride over the rough terrain might be too tiring for him. He seemed so frail and spent. Also I was uneasy that he wanted to get away from Janet and Tess so that he could have a heart-to-heart talk with me about the past. But he insisted on our going and we drove off over the fields, Ed at the wheel. It was a rather rough ride and soon Ed was perspiring profusely. But he kept bravely on. Twice as we mounted a ridge where you could look over the surrounding country, Ed stopped the jeep, sat back, caught his breath, pointed out the view, and started to say something about the old days together. I changed the subject as quickly and gracefully as I could.

We fell silent and Ed drove back to the house. There we joined our wives for tea. Later Ed and Janet came out to the driveway to see us off. We all agreed it had been a good reunion.

"After much too long a time," Ed put in, his face lighting up for an instant. He was breathing hard and looked terribly tired.

He had not mentioned his health except to joke about giving up cigarettes after chain-smoking through his adult life. He was facing dying with the same courage he had faced life, with the same simple courage he had shown during the war when he had roamed the streets of London with the bombs falling all about him or when he went off, once, on an RAF bomber on a mission over Berlin, from which only half the planes returned.

It was the last time I saw Ed Murrow. The next spring, on April 27, 1965, he died of a brain tumor.

BOOK FOUR

Down and Out:

The McCarthy Years

The Struggle to Survive

and to Write and to Publish

1948–1959

CHAPTER 1

Perhaps it was a bit of bravado. The first thing we did after I got kicked out of CBS was to buy a farm in the hills of northwestern Connecticut near some of our closest friends: the Thurbers, the Gannetts, the Van Dorens, the Barneses.

It did not cost very much — $9,500 for one hundred acres, a beautiful old eighteenth-century saltbox house, and a big red barn. We paid in cash. And though I had been somewhat surprised at not being immediately offered a job at NBC or ABC, I was assured by my agent there was nothing to worry about. I'd soon be back in broadcasting.

"Go and take a long vacation," he urged. "You've earned it."

So, after working out plans for doing over the farmhouse, we went up to Lake Placid for the summer, where I finished putting together a second book of diaries that would be published as *End of a Berlin Diary*. In the meantime a local contractor was renovating the farmhouse. We were quite innocent about that, despite a good deal of advice from our friends, who said they spoke out of bitter experience. Though the old farmhouse was in fairly good shape, it lacked plumbing, electrical wiring, and central heating. Also, we soon learned that the chimney, which helped to support saltbox houses, was a fire hazard and had to be torn down to the cellar and rebuilt and that the roof leaked and had to be completely reshingled. We tore out one wall to enlarge the living room and — against the raging of Ruth Gannett, a purist in regard to eighteenth-century houses — put in two large picture windows to give a better view over the Litchfield hills. By the time the contractor was finished, we owed him four times the cost of the house and the one hundred acres.

But it was worth it. In the years to come, when the going got rough, it was a haven. Here, at least, no matter what happened, we had a roof over us and enough land to grow a lot of the food we needed.

The farm gave us an idyllic place in which to live and work and rest, to get back in touch with nature, to get the feel and smell of the woods and fields, to see the seasons change and unfold, to know what it was like to plant and to harvest, if only, as in our case, a large vegetable garden, a small orchard, a modest berry patch, a haying field or two.

My diaries over the next twenty years would be full of ecstatic jottings about the sheer beauty of what one saw and felt in this rural place: a field deep in snow sparkling under a near-full moon on a cold, clear January night; the smell of the fresh air and the land in the spring as the barren ground came to life and the soil was plowed and harrowed, and the trees budded and burst into bloom and then their leaves into bright green, and the birds sang and in the pond below at night the frogs croaked shrilly.

Summer had its delights, too, as we mowed the fields and breathed in the sweet, unforgettable odor of freshly cut grass drying, picked the fruit and berries and vegetables, carted them into the house, and froze what we could not immediately eat. And then before the late September frost, there were grapes to be harvested and flowering plants to be brought in.

October was the most colorful month of the year, with the maples turning into bright reds and scarlets and the aspen, poplars, and other trees into yellow. There is nothing more magnificent than a New England autumn. In November nature began to quiet down, and by Thanksgiving the trees were bereft of their plumage except for the pines and the hemlocks in the woods that began beyond the pastures.

Soon the snows would come and we would say that despite the sometimes bitter cold and fierce winds we liked winter on the farm best of all. Perhaps this was partly because we could be there only weekends and during the Christmas vacation and were spared the ordeal of surviving seven days a week the long, hard, blustery, frigid winters in the hills of northwest Connecticut.

As it was, we loved cutting down our own trees and cutting up our own firewood for the two large fireplaces in the living room and the kitchen. The one in the kitchen was immense as high as my head — and had an old Dutch oven at one end, so that together they formed the entire wall on the interior side. In former, simpler times the good people had done their baking and cooking in this fireplace.

In the winter, when the snows piled up sometimes from Thanksgiving to Easter, we did a lot of skiing about the place, which was dotted with hills — the children learned their skiing here. And on the driveway that led down to the country road we tobogganed until our faces were blue from the cold. It was wide enough for two sleds to race — down a hundred yards to the road and then for another two hundred yards to the pond below. Sometimes we would skate on the pond. Finally, in March, as the snows began to melt, there was maplesugaring for the children to do. The place had been primarily a maple-sugar farm — there were dozens of maple trees near the house. The children loved tapping the trees and boiling the sap, but I groaned at lugging mountains of firewood to their kettles. It seemed to me they burned a cord of wood to get a quart of maple syrup.

For the two girls the farm turned out to be a wonderland. They loved it. No matter how inclement the weather, no matter how hard it was snowing, they would insist on our setting out from New York in the car every Friday afternoon as soon as school was out. And we could hardly pull them away from the farm on Sunday afternoons for the three-and-a-half-hour trek back to the city. They demanded that we spend not only the long summer vacations there but also all the briefer holidays, especially Christmas and Easter.

Christmas in the country would be the high point in their young lives. They loved playing in the snow, skiing, and tobagganing; and when these did not tire them out, they would build snowmen and snow forts. Just as in the summer they did not seem to mind weeding the garden (the bane of most children and, indeed, of most grownups) and picking the vegetables and berries and helping to freeze them, so in the winter they did not grumble — after they had frolicked in the snow — at having to carry in firewood and helping with the other chores. They would never forget, they later said, the rituals of the day before Christmas, which began in the morning when we went out into the woods to find and cut down a pine or a spruce tree, lugging it on a sled over the snow to the house, setting it up in the living room, and decorating it while a fire roared in the fireplace.

It began to grow dark shortly after four o'clock on Christmas Eve, and we would set off with presents for the farm families nearby. After dinner we gathered around the fire, exchanged presents, sang carols, and took turns reading the Dickens classic and from a fabulous collection of Christmas stories we had picked up. Outside, the winter wind would be howling and the snowflakes blowing against the window-panes.

Christmas Eve in the snowy Connecticut hills! It brought us much happiness. It brought us very close to each other.

From the years on the farm — and they only left it to go off to college and then to get married — Inga and Linda would say they got a number of things: good health, a feeling of family, a love of nature and of the land, a passion for growing things, especially flowers, all of which, they thought, helped to deepen and enrich their lives.

Their parents got the same thing and more. The farm became not only our haven, but a place to live and work. Soon, in a study I fixed up in the barn for the summer and in a bedroom-study in the winter, I would be doing much of my writing, and Tess would be painting summers in a studio we built for her up in the woods. To have a pleasant place in the country to work and to get the peace and tranquillity we needed to offset the tensions of the city became more and more important as the years slipped by and our fortunes fell.

I returned to New York in the fall of 1947 to find that the NBC and ABC radio networks were not so keen about taking me on as my agent had thought. In fact, we never heard from them. My agent said he had kept after them. They never responded.

I did get an offer, not to join ABC but to do a Sunday broadcast on that network that would be sponsored by the United Electrical, Radio and Machine Workers of America. With a half-million members, the UE had by that time become the only important Communist-led union in the country. For me, that was the problem. Part of the reason for my forced departure from CBS, I was sure, was that I had been not only labeled a "liberal," which I was proud to be called (though I made no claims myself to be anything), but also accused in some reactionary quarters of being a "Communist sympathizer" and perhaps (horrors!) even a secret "Commie." It occurred to me that if I were sponsored on the air by this union, the lunatic forces of reaction would proclaim gleefully that their accusations were confirmed: I was a radio commentator broadcasting for the "Commies."

I talked it over with Albert Fitzgerald, president of the union, and Julius Emspak, the secretary-treasurer, who, I gathered, was the real spark plug of the organization. Fitzgerald, I believe, was not a Communist; but Emspak made no secret of his beliefs, which were shared, I was told, by another dynamic figure in the union, James B. Matles, director of organization. I told Fitzgerald and Emspak that I appreciated their offer to put me back on the air but that, because of the issues raised in my ouster from CBS, I could not accept it. I recommended Leland Stowe, an old friend from our days as correspondents in Europe, for the job; and, being unemployed at the moment, he took it. Lee was a staunch liberal, and he was very good on the air during the year or two that the union sponsored him. Unlike many commercial sponsors, the UE gave him complete freedom of expression. Certainly his opinions must have rankled the dominant Communist wing of the union.

Eventually Stowe became disillusioned with where his liberalism had landed him — or failed to land him. While at the University of Michigan, teaching journalism, at which he was very successful, he became a roving correspondent for the *Reader's Digest* and gradually, judging by what he wrote, adapted to its conservative views.

I returned to the air on November 30, exactly seven months after my exit from CBS. The president of a medium-sized company that manufactured shirts offered to sponsor me on a fifteen-minute program of news and comment over the Mutual Broadcasting System. The executive was an old-fashioned liberal who wanted me back on the air. He also wanted to expand his business and develop, I believe, a nationwide market for his shirts.

Though MBS had a large number of radio stations, it lacked the prestige and the following of the other three networks. It made no pretense of having a news-gathering organization that could compete with them. It was a cooperative enterprise, not a corporation as were the others; and its management was pretty much dominated by the largest station members, for instance, WOR in New York and WGN, the organ of the *Chicago Tribune*, in Chicago. It had a good many commentators but a very small news staff. For direct broadcast reports from abroad it depended mostly on stringers. I never became a staff member as I had at CBS. I was not entitled to use the MBS news staff, however inadequate, or its wire services. I subscribed to the United Press for news and paid for it out of my own pocket.

The program was finally set for 1:00 P.M. on Sunday — not the best time to build up a sizable audience. Not many Americans seemed to be in the mood at that Sunday hour to listen to news and comment. People were more interested — and I didn't blame them — in the sporting events of the day or in getting out to the park or the country for some fresh air and exercise. Or maybe they were lingering over their ample Sunday dinner . . . or recovering from one. In contrast, my broadcasts on CBS Sundays at 5:45 P.M. had come at the end of the afternoon when many were wondering what the news might be — there were practically no news broadcasts during the day on Sundays.

I had no illusions that I could swiftly build up the ratings I had had. But I wanted very much to give the job a try. Perhaps it would ultimately lead me back to a job on NBC or ABC.

One thing I liked about MBS was that, unlike CBS, it gave me complete freedom, including freedom to express my opinions. CBS had forbidden us to air an opinion; and though Murrow and I had often broken the rule, we had been under increasing pressure to knuckle under.

Indeed, Ed, who had finally given up his job as vice-president in charge of news at CBS and returned to the air in September, had gone out of his way, I thought, to assure his listeners in his first broadcast that he would not be expressing any personal opinions. His contract, portions of which he read, forbade it.

> It says that news programs are broadcast "solely for the purpose of enabling listeners to know the facts — so far as they are obtainable — and so to elucidate, illuminate and explain facts and situations as fairly to enable the listener to weigh and judge for himself."
>
> Now that's pretty complicated language — the kind that lawyers like to write. My own interpretation of it is that this program is not a place where personal opinion should be mixed up with ascertainable facts. We shall do our best to identify sources and to resist the temptation to use this microphone as a privileged platform from which to advocate action.

Listening to his initial broadcast, I was surprised that Murrow had gone along formally with this limitation by CBS on his freedom of expression. His equating the expression of personal opinion with "advocating action" seemed misleading. Since when was airing a personal opinion equivalent to asking for action? Ed's great wartime broadcasts from London had been full of his opinions. He had been far from "objective," as indeed had I, broadcasting from Berlin.*

Harriet Van Horn, radio critic of the *World-Telegram*, noted this in a piece about Ed's return to the air. She wondered why he had stressed that his contract forbade him to express his opinions.

> If you recall Mr. Murrow's magnificent broadcasts from London during the blitz, they were impassioned in their nonobjectivity. Mr. Shirer's Berlin broadcasts made no secret of his personal sympathies either.

At any rate, I had no restrictions on my freedom to express opinions at MBS and I said so in my first broadcast on November 30, 1947:

> . . . There has been a good deal of controversy and misunderstanding about a commentator's right to express his honest opinions on the air.

---

* "I remember you once wanted me to be a preacher, but I had no faith, except in myself," Ed wrote his parents from London during the war. "But now I am preaching from a powerful pulpit. . . . I am trying to talk as I would have talked were I a preacher." — William Manchester, *The Glory and the Dream*, p. 514.

It has been argued that a commentator should not be allowed to express any opinions — that he should leave the listener to form his own.

But there's a fallacy in that argument, it seems to me.

Surely the American public makes up its own mind on issues after it has listened to the opinions of a good many persons — very conflicting opinions, as befits a democracy — but opinions nevertheless. I doubt if the American people ever got much help in trying to make up their minds by listening to speakers who have no opinion, or are afraid to express it, or are not allowed to.

I said I recognized, of course, the tremendous responsibility of one who, through his broadcasts, had access to the ears of millions of listeners and that I would do my best not to abuse that privilege and that responsibility.

> I shall not try to make up your minds for you. But I shall not be dishonest with you by hiding my own opinions, which, I recognize, are, like everybody's, only human and, therefore, often wrong.
>
> In these Sunday broadcasts, therefore, I shall try to present all sides and all the facts, so far as I can ascertain them. The opinions I arrive at will not necessarily be yours. A democracy has gone pretty stale when everyone agrees.
>
> But you have a right to know that such opinions as are expressed in these broadcasts are my own, and not anyone else's — not those of the network, or the station, or any sponsor, or any political party, or any pressure group, or of the government.

A year later, in a broadcast on Sunday, January 2, 1949, I found it necessary to reiterate the freedoms I had at Mutual. During the fall elections I had had a number of letters saying in effect: "Of course you can't give us the whole truth. The network or the sponsor won't let you."

> New Year's may be a good time to get this straight. Neither the Mutual network nor the sponsor . . . has ever censored me or faintly hinted or suggested that any change whatsoever be made in the text of these Sunday broadcasts. I've been absolutely free to give the facts as I found them — all of them. And utterly free on this network to utter my honest opinions, including the unpopular ones and what turned out to be some wrong ones.

I continued my Sunday broadcast over MBS for a year and a half, until mid-April 1949, when the shirt manufacturer ceased sponsoring it. A once-a-week broadcast at a not very good time was hardly enough to boost his business across the nation. A biographer of Murrow has insinuated that the sponsor dropped me because my "ratings continued to drop," the same explanation offered by some for another sponsor dropping me from my CBS Sunday show. Again this was scarcely the truth. According to my agent, MCA, the Hooper ratings for Mutual were "terrific," starting at 3.9 and jumping early to 4.8. Considering the time spot, they were not bad.

Raymond Gram Swing, the veteran journalist who had had enormous ratings for his evening commentaries over MBS during the war, now could not even find a sponsor for his Sunday broadcast over ABC at 1:15 P.M., immediately after mine. He had ruminated about this in his farewell appearance on January 25, 1948. I had caught his last broadcast that afternoon; and his departure and his words saddened me, for we had been friends for fifteen years and I had greatly admired him, first as a foreign correspondent, then as an editor of *The Nation*, and finally as a broadcaster. He was completing forty-one years in American journalism. And, as he said, with this broadcast his "regular contribution to American radio comes to an end after more than twelve years."

> My Sunday broadcasts did not find a sponsor. . . . I am not at all sure that I would have continued for another year. . . . But I wasn't asked. . . .

Strange — or was it not so strange? — how fickle, how forgetful the American public could be. That afternoon I kept remembering that Raymond's evening broadcast during the war had had a very special place in the lives of millions of Americans, who broke off from whatever they were doing at 10:00 P.M. to listen to him.*

Raymond went on to broadcast for the Voice of America but soon ran afoul of right-wing bigots, who frothed at the mouth at his rather old-fashioned, middle-of-the-road liberalism. In 1953, I heard, Swing was being considered for a news spot on CBS but was held to "be unacceptable to the network," an industry code word for "blacklisted."

Murrow generously came to his rescue and offered him a job on the staff that prepared Ed's evening broadcasts. Soon Swing would be writing many of the "think pieces," the commentary Ed did after recounting the hard news. Swing got no credit on the air for these

---

* He had a special place in the lives of Britons, too. According to a poll taken by the BBC in 1940, some 30 percent of the adult population, or about nine million persons, listened to Swing's once-a-week broadcast to Britain. A lengthy portrait of Swing in the *Saturday Evening Post*, December 14, 1940, observed that "today Swing reaches more listeners than any other person in the world who speaks over radio." And eight years later in America he couldn't find a sponsor and was dropped!

contributions, so listeners got the impression they were written by Murrow himself. With one exception, I believe, the great veteran broadcaster never spoke on Ed's program. Nor did he ever complain.

By the time I was through at MBS, I had already lost my Sunday column on the *New York Herald-Tribune*, which that newspaper had syndicated in other papers from coast to coast. The country was going more and more conservative — or at least the powers that controlled the newspapers and radio networks were. This was true of the *Herald-Tribune*, which under the long administration of Ogden and Helen Reid had carried the banner of a liberal Republican party. (It had almost single-handedly put across the nomination of Wendell Willkie in 1940.) Now the running of the paper had passed to their elder son, Whitelaw Reid; and it was moving toward the right. My kind of commentary was not in tune with what it wanted. I had sensed that for some time.

I was now out of journalism completely, and apparently I was unemployable in either broadcasting or the newspapers. American journalism had given me a good and interesting life over a span of twenty-four years. And I thought I had made at least a modest mark in it. But the newspaper editors and the broadcasting executives obviously did not agree. Through the grapevine I learned that they thought I was finished, washed up, a has-been — though I was only forty-four. Or if none of those, perhaps something worse: a "pink" or perhaps even a "Red." Out of step with good old patriotic Americanism.

The Cold War was already upon us. There were astonishing cries in Washington — and not only there — for war with Russia to finish off the Bolsheviks once and for all.* *Life* magazine, with its enormous readership and influence, would soon come out in a full-page editorial demanding the destruction of "the Soviet Union and Soviet Communism." Even so knowledgeable a man on Russia as George Kennan had in 1947 published an article in *Foreign Affairs* (identifying himself only as "X") calling for American containment of the Soviet Union and Soviet Communism within Russia's borders "at every point where they show signs of encroaching" — a policy warmly embraced by the Truman administration, most of the press, and the public but deplored by Walter Lippmann as "a strategic monstrosity."

* The yelping in Washington for war with the Soviet Union had plunged Albert Einstein into gloom. Harlow Shapley, the Harvard astronomer, who was also deeply concerned at the war cries, had sent me the contents of a letter he had received from Einstein: "I now feel sure that the people in power in Washington are pushing systematically toward preventive war."

I think Kennan had been provoked, at least in part, by a hard-line speech by Stalin to his party officials in 1946, in which the Soviet dictator denounced the idea of coexistence with the West and renewed his determination to further world revolution.

Then Stalin, following his seizure of Czechoslovakia in February 1948, had in June begun the blockade of Berlin in the false belief that he could drive the Americans out of the Allied-occupied city. We had replied with the Airlift and had flown into Berlin from Western Germany enough food, clothing, and coal to sustain the city's population of two and a half million.

But for several months it looked as if the two superpowers would be drawn into war. I flew into Berlin that fall of the blockade, and though Allied planes, chiefly American C-54s, were bringing in enough supplies to keep the Berliners from freezing or starving, the great fear in American circles was that some mad Russian would shoot down an American plane and war would follow. I spent a tense evening in Berlin with a grim General Lucius Clay, the American high commissioner for Germany. He feared the Russians might provoke an incident any moment that would lead to war. In the end the Russians gave up after eleven months — probably because if it had come to armed conflict, they realized the consequences of our having the atom bomb and their not having it, not for a year or two more. But it was a close call in Berlin.

The Cold War continued. And if, among other things, it brought terrible repression in Russia by a paranoiac dictator, it also began to spread intolerance at home. Loyalty tests, first instituted by President Truman for federal employees in 1946, were increasingly demanded of employees of private companies.* Arch-conservatives were calling President Truman, Secretary of State Acheson, and even General Marshall traitors and agents of the Moscow Bolsheviks. A move was begun in the U.S. Senate to "drive the Communists out of the State Department." Pearl Buck, a Nobel Prize laureate, in literature, was barred from addressing a Washington, D.C., high-school commencement — she was not anti-Communist enough, especially on China, where she had spent most of her life and which she knew very well and which was now, in 1949, about to be taken over by the Communists, whom she didn't like.

McCarthyism and its un-American reign of terror in our country lay just ahead.

---

* Few seemed to realize that loyalty tests would never uncover Communists or hamper them in the slightest way, since they would have no qualms about swearing that they were not now and never had been party members.

CHAPTER 2

U nable to find a job on a newspaper or radio network, I turned of necessity to what deep down for a long time I had wanted to do most: writing books. Perhaps — probably, even — I did not have the talent for it; though my first two books, *Berlin Diary* in 1941 and *End of a Berlin Diary* in 1947, had been well received and had reached a large audience — especially the first, which by now had had sales in the Knopf and Book-of-the-Month Club editions of nearly a million copies. Still, as I have noted, they were scissors-and-paste jobs. I still had to write a "real" book, as Alfred Knopf had reminded me: one with a beginning, middle, and end.

I turned first to fiction.

The idea of trying a new field had been sprouting slowly in my mind for a long time. Somehow it began to dawn on me that you could get closer to the truth about life in our time in a novel than in a work of nonfiction. My feeling for nineteenth-century Russia, France, and England, I noted, had come largely not from books of history and biography — though I had read a number of them — but from the novels: in Russia from those of Tolstoy, Dostoyevski, Turgenev, Chekhov (his short stories and plays), and Gorky; in France from those of Balzac, Stendhal, and Zola (and for the turn of the century, Proust); in England from the works of Dickens, George Eliot, Jane Austen, the Brontë sisters, Thackeray, and Hardy. They were the ones who illuminated the century for me, leaving indelible impressions of what life was like in that time and what the human experience, with its comedies and tragedies, its ups and downs and uncertainties, and its baffling mysteries, was. And to boot, the novelists usually told a good story.

I, of course, did not pretend for one minute that I could come within miles of reaching the level of these giants of literature. I lacked their talents, let alone their capacity for greatness. Still, within my limitations I thought that one day if I had the chance, I might try to set down in a series of novels whatever experience had taught me about life in the turbulent, strife-torn years I had lived through in the twentieth century.

Another correspondent, I eventually learned, had returned from the war with the same idea. One evening I had run into John Hersey. We were speaking at a meeting for some good cause at Carnegie Hall in New York. Afterward we adjourned to a nearby bar. And in answer to each other's questions as to what we wanted to do now that the war was over, it quickly developed that our answers were surprisingly similar. Hersey said with great determination that he was not going to write any more nonfiction. He was going to write novels. This somewhat surprised me. For he had just come out in *The New Yorker* with his memorable account of what had happened at Hiroshima after our first atom bomb dropped on that city. It was a brilliant piece of journalism.

"You mean after *Hiroshima* you're going to write fiction?" I asked.

"Exclusively, I hope," he said.

Hersey had more grounds for his decision than I had. He had already written and published during the war a very good novel, *A Bell for Adano*, based on his experiences as a war correspondent in Sicily. I had written a novel back in 1933 during our year off in Spain, drawing on my two years in India and my friendship with Gandhi; but it had turned out badly, and I had not tried to publish it. John and I parted, wishing each other luck. And he went to work at once to fulfill his ambition. I waited, as most journalists do in such circumstances, because I was still broadcasting and writing a column, earning a good living for the first time in my life. Now, as the summer of 1949 began, loss of both jobs had forced me to begin writing a book.

Actually I had been at work on a novel in my spare time since leaving CBS. At first it took the form of a play. I thought that this was a good way to develop my characters and the plot for eventual use in a novel. Beyond that, in whatever form, I wanted to fathom the motives of the chief figures in the story for behaving as they did.

It was to be a fictionalized account of the American and, to a lesser extent, the British radio traitors in Berlin, the small group of men and women who turned against their countries and broadcast during the war for Adolf Hitler. (I have written about them previously in these memoirs.) In the play and novel, especially the latter if I could get to it, I wanted to penetrate, if possible, into a phenomenon that is as old as mankind: treason. Why do men and women commit it? For money? For love? Out of hatred, for some reason, of their native land? Or because they become obsessed with some new ideology — in this case Nazism and racism? Treason, like prostitution, is one of the oldest human practices. Why is this?

Since you can only write well about what you know, I based the work on my acquaintance with the radio traitors in Berlin; most of whom I knew to some extent and two of whom, William Joyce ("Lord Haw-Haw"), the Englishman, and Robert Best, the American, I knew very well, especially the latter.

In March 1948, I had been subpoenaed to testify in Boston at the treason trial of Bob Best.*

At the trial in Boston not much light was shed by Bob or by anyone else on why he had committed treason. He himself defended himself with the old argument that he must have felt an American jury would fall for, as the American public often had, that in his broadcasts from Berlin he was only fighting "godless Communism," which he said had become a "holy cause" for him. The jury was not taken in by this old Nazi line, and on April 16 it found him guilty of all twelve counts of treason in the indictment. It was his fifty-second birthday.

Best was sentenced to life imprisonment and began to serve his time at the federal prison at Fort Leavenworth. Later, after a series of cerebral hemorrhages, he was transferred to the U.S. Medical Center for Federal Prisoners at Springfield, Missouri, where he died from another attack on December 15, 1952.

Five days later, on December 20, the *New York Times* published a report of his death under the following headline:

R. H. BEST, TRAITOR
DIES IN FELON WARD
JOURNALIST WAS SERVING LIFE
TERM FOR NAZI BROADCASTS
FROM GERMANY IN WAR

I was up on the farm with my wife and children preparing to celebrate Christmas. That evening I wrote in my diary:

> . . . Thus, sadly, ends the life of a man I knew. . . . I was subpoenaed to testify against him during his trial, which I did, though my testimony was minor. He avoided looking at me while I was on the stand, but I looked at him a long while, scarcely recognizing the very decent chap we all had known in Vienna. He had — or assumed — the fanatic's eyes, but otherwise his face had wasted away, mirroring what had happened to him as a person. It did not give you any pleasure . . . to see an old friend in the dock, his life at stake in a trial for treason (one of the few treason trials in American history), despite what he had done.

Ten months before, a former Baltimore newspaperman, Douglas Chandler, who broadcast from Berlin for Hitler under the pseudonym

* The story of his wartime activities is on pp. 43–47.

"Paul Revere," had been tried in the same federal court in Boston, found guilty of treason, and sentenced to life imprisonment. He was the first person ever convicted of treason in Massachusetts and the first American ever to have been found guilty of treason for having broadcast over the radio against his own country. Best was the second.*

Other Americans who were indicted for the same offense got off more easily. Ezra Pound, the distinguished poet who broadcast for Mussolini from Italy during the war, was adjudged insane and mentally unfit for trial in 1945 and committed to St. Elizabeths Federal Hospital in Washington. He was released in 1958 and returned to Italy.

For reasons never officially or otherwise explained, Donald Day, who always began his broadcasts from Berlin by identifying himself as "Donald Day, correspondent for the *Chicago Tribune* for twenty years in northern Europe," was never prosecuted. After being held in custody in Berlin for nine months by the U.S. Army, he was released on Christmas Eve, 1946, on instructions from the U.S. Department of Justice.

There were reports in the press that the imperious Colonel Robert M. McCormick, who owned and ran the *Tribune*, had brought pressure on the Truman administration to get Day off the hook, though this seemed unlikely in view of the colonel's jaundiced view of President Truman and, especially, of his predecessor. Day never returned to his native land. He lived in Bad Tolz, West Germany, until 1962 when he moved to Helsinki, where he died four years later. Sometime after Colonel McCormick's death, around 1962, the *Tribune* put Day on its payroll as a stringer in Helsinki, at first at twenty-five dollars and then fifty dollars a month.

Why there were different forms of justice for the Americans who broadcast for Hitler during the war — some considered traitors, others not — has always been a mystery to me. Down through history, I guess, justice has always been that way. Erratic. Uneven.

In England, remember, William Joyce and John Amery were hanged for broadcasting for Hitler.

How my first novel, *The Traitor*, took shape is briefly noted in my diary.

* They had been tried in Boston because their plane from Germany had been forced by bad weather to land there. Its destination had been Washington, where both men had been indicted and where the government had intended to try them. The defendants, as I recall, dug up some ancient law that said that in a case of treason an accused person brought back from a foreign land must be tried in the place where he lands.

Farm, August 6, 1948. First draft of the Traitor play finished. God knows if there is any worth in it. I feel it is not as good as had hoped. . . . Some things did not come off.

The work was still in the form of a play, but I was thinking more and more of novels. ". . . Projecting a series of novels, the whole to be subtitled 'Glimpses of the Times of the World Wars.' "

I seemed to be burning with wild ambition during the summer of 1948, the first we had had on the farm, the first time since our year off in Spain fifteen years before that I had been able to write continuously, day after day.

Farm, September 1, 1949 . . . A good summer. 100,000 words on the novel, and still three weeks to go before we return to N.Y. The first time I can remember when I had nearly three months which I could devote to writing without the distractions of earning a living: broadcasts, columns, articles, etc. THIS is what I would like to do for the rest of my life. But how to live? To feed the hungry mouths? And, of course, the fact that I have written 100,000 words does not prove that they are any good.

I plugged on and on.

New York, February 23, 1950. Birthday. 46 . . . Finished the last chapter of the "Traitor" novel at noon. Much revision of the book needs to be done and I would like to rewrite the first 100 pages, if I knew how. . . . When I think I have devoted the better part of two years to this book. And yet it is not as good as I had hoped. . . . Raced through the last pages this morning. The ending had finally got into my head and I wanted to get it down on paper before I lost it. . . .

Finally:

New York, April 4, 1950. Signed a contract for the novel today with Farrar & Straus. While this does not mean that it will amount to anything, it does help to bring me out of the depths of depression I have felt these past weeks. When Cass Canfield [head of Harper's], to whom I had sent it as a friend — he had badgered me to write it and to show it to him when it was finished — sent it back saying it was "not saleable," . . . and then when my own publishers (Knopf) turned it down with a curt note (from Blanche Knopf) saying it hadn't "come off" and "was not even a novel," I felt somewhat down.

I guess what irked me was that neither Canfield, who was a friend, nor the Knopfs, who had done so well with the diary books, offered even to discuss the book. Canfield's brief note had been formal and cold, as if I had submitted it formally to Harper's. Blanche's letter had been exactly like it. Not a word from Alfred Knopf. He had not liked *Berlin Diary* either, but it had helped carry him nicely over a rough financial period. I wondered if his silence had anything to do with his feelings about the novel and me, which he aired to Irita Van Doren, editor of the Sunday *Herald-Tribune Books*. He had bitterly protested her giving me John Hersey's novel *The Wall* to review. He had told Irita I did not read novels, was wholly uninterested in them, and, therefore, incompetent to review them — especially one so important as Hersey's book. This had surprised me, since he knew that I was passionately interested in fiction and had read a great deal of it. On more than one occasion on weekends at his country house in Purchase, New York, I had sat up half the night with him and other writers talking of novels: on one occasion with Sigrid Unset, the Nobel Prize–winning Norwegian novelist; on another occasion with Willa Cather, whom I much admired. Knopf had published both.

I ruminated in my diary

> that I had pretty well wasted two years of work . . . and that my whole project to turn to novels . . . had begun to be a dismal failure. If I could not write even a *publishable* novel at 46, I had indeed failed miserably — failed in knowing, in judging myself and my work.

Then my agent, Paul Reynolds, sent the manuscript to a new publisher, Farrar & Straus. John Farrar and especially Stanley Young, who had just joined the firm, read it, liked it, and offered to publish it.

It came out in November 1950; and though the reviews on the whole were quite good, it did not at all stir the country. It hit the best-seller list; but the sales were modest, nothing like those for the diary books. No magazine was interested in serializing it. A typical comment came from an editor of the *Saturday Evening Post*. The "consensus" at the *Post*, she wrote, "was that the theme, as a whole, is dated and old hat." The age-old theme of treason and why men commit it "dated and old hat"? And in its latest form, when for the first time in history men were convicted of treason for having broadcast for the enemy in wartime and hanged or given life imprisonment?

I was intrigued by the reviews. What I had not quite realized was how differently reviewers could see a book. Some thought *The Traitor* had not come off as a novel, that the characters were cardboard, and that I should stick to nonfiction. Others reacted quite differently. Joseph Henry Jackson, whom I much admired as a literary critic (he was one of the few we had in our country), wrote in the *San Francisco*

Chronicle that I had written "a rapid, full-packed, thoroughly readable novel" that had "meaning as well as being a lively tale." Lloyd Morris, also a critic I admired, wrote in the *New York Herald-Tribune* "Books" that my "first venture in fiction is a powerful, absorbing, extremely provocative novel . . . that keeps the reader under constantly increasing tension until the final page."

The comment that meant most to me came from the great German novelist Thomas Mann. In the midst of a lecture tour that brought me out to the Pacific Coast, I was invited to lunch with him and his family at their home in Pacific Palisades. I noted it in my diary:

> Hollywood, November 28, 1950 . . . I was overwhelmed by the way Mann spoke of my first novel, *The Traitor*. While one must make allowances for the politeness of one's host, what pleased me above all else was that the whole Mann family had evidently read the book, or a great deal of it, and discussed it, its characters and story, at some length. [His wife, Kattya, and daughter, Erika, were present.]
>
> The old man said he could not believe it was a first novel. He said he thought I had succeeded in creating some good characters and that he was surprised that I could write of Germany and the Germans so well.
>
> He wanted to know how long I had worked on the book. And when I said I had worked at the actual writing for two years and had thought a lot about it and had made countless notes for it for another two years previous to sitting down to it, he gave a great affirmative grunt.
>
> "Ja," he said. "Two years. It takes that to write a novel. But there are many who try to do it in less time."
>
> . . . He told me about his new novel, just finished, and how it was based on a medieval poem in which some character marries his mother and there is a murder in the family. . . .
>
> We talked about the fact that Hollywood had never tried to do a film based on a novel or a short story of his.*
>
> He laughed and shrugged his shoulders and said: "I guess everything I've written is unsuitable for the films. In fact, I can't think of any story of mine that would make a motion picture. But I like the films," he added quickly as if he feared I might misunderstand him. "They've had a great influence on the modern novel. The flashback technique, which you use so effectively in *The Traitor*, stems from the movies, for instance."
>
> That led him to talk about my picture of America in my novel, which he said he had found particularly interesting. At first, he said, he thought I was going to create a too idyllic picture of it out of a sort of nostalgia of one who has lived mostly away from it. But then the picture had taken on depth and truth — "very good," he said.

---

* Later I saw a beautiful film based on his novella *Death in Venice*. I believe it was done in Europe.

So despite its turn-down by my own publisher and by Harper's and notwithstanding its modest sales, I felt good about the reception of my first published novel. Most of the reviewers had a good word for it, albeit with reservations. It might not be any great shakes — it certainly was not so good as I had hoped. But it was a start. It helped to make that year of 1950 memorable for me. In fact, the year turned out to be one of the more memorable of my life, and in one instance brought on a personal crisis that I would have to struggle with over the next ten years, at times in lonely desperation.

On New Year's Day, 1950, up on the farm, I had noted in my diary (perhaps a year too early) the passing of the first half of the twentieth century. What enormous changes it had brought in human life! When it started we were still in a horse-and-buggy age. And now we had leaped into the atomic age and learned how to wipe out human life on the planet in a mere hour or two. That was progress?

The Farm, New Year's Day, 1950. The first half of this century gone. What will the last half be like? I will die in it. That is the only thing I know for certain. . . .

We saw the first half of this epic century out last night quietly. A nearly full moon in a heaven ablaze with the winter stars was out, lighting up the green hills, which we had hoped might be white with snow, but weren't. At 11:10 P.M., in the very last hour of the century's first half, we (Tess, Eileen and I, and the dog) walked down the road to the pond. The ice glistened in the cold moonlight. We slid on it. The dog barked. Eileen called out. The great hemlocks cast their shadow. And then we walked back to the house to see the New Year and the last half of the century in. I went upstairs and waked Linda, as we had promised, and carried her downstairs. Finally the stroke of twelve and we toasted the future with champagne. . . .

I was thinking of nearly half a century of my own life almost gone (46 years) and of my present eclipse in radio and journalism (after a certain notoriety!) and whether my present writing (the novel and those I still hunger to write) would turn out to be any good. . . .

But after nearly half a century of existence have you come any closer to [solving] the riddle of life? Its meaning? Purpose?

I doubted it.

I have learned only that one's personal happiness, which is such a relative, nebulous thing, must come from within — from contemplation, from love, from honesty with oneself, from renunciation of worldly success, from acceptance of fate and the senseless, cruel disorder of life.

New York, February 23, 1950. Birthday. 46. And did not feel much like celebrating . . . I did not want to think of it. Why? Are you afraid of the race of time past you? Not afraid, exactly. But certainly conscious of [it] in relation of what one wants to accomplish. So little time, and so much you want to do. So much time passed already, and so little done.

Not that I was bothered, I went on, by lack of "success."

What is called "success" is really little better than notoriety. I had a little . . . with the first book . . . with the radio. . . . But I did not deliberately seek it. Nor do I now. What do I want? A means of earning a reasonable living that will still give me time to continue writing. I do not want to write in a vacuum, as I seem to have been doing the last three years. Anyone who writes wants some sort of recognition.

Often in my diary that year I kept coming back to the problem of beginning to live in the atomic era.

Perhaps the last half of the century will be dominated by it [I had written at New Year's]. It is conceivable that this brief span of time, a mere pinpoint, will see our world destroyed (by the bomb). An atomic war would do it. . . .

The year before, in 1949, the Russians had themselves got the atomic bomb.

New York, September 24, 1949. . . . A historic day yesterday! President Truman announced that "we have evidence that within recent weeks an atomic explosion occurred in the USSR."

Abruptly the balance of power in the world was upset. Since Hiroshima in 1945 we alone had possessed the bomb. During all the time since — five years — we could have annihilated the Soviet Union with it. That was the chief reason, I was sure, why Stalin abandoned his foolish blockade of Berlin. But now we had lost — or would shortly lose — that staggering advantage. Either the two rival superpowers would now have to work out some agreement to coexist in the atomic age. Or they would collide and blow up the planet.

I think Truman understood that at once. It seemed surprising that he was still president. On the eve of the 1948 elections he had not been given even an outside chance by anyone. I had helped cover that strange campaign for MBS. My diary recalls its climax:

New York, Tuesday, November 2, 1948. . . . A presidential election today. Dewey and Truman. No one gives Truman a chance. All the pollsters and newspapers say it's a walkaway for Dewey. . . .

I can't even vote, and this is the first time I've been home during a presidential election since I was old enough to vote. Four years ago on the Western front. Eight years ago in Berlin. And this time I was away in Europe on a brief assignment when registering took place. Hence I lose my vote.*

I resented it. I had been deprived of the vote once before, in the midterm elections of 1942. I was back home from the early part of the war then; and when I went to register in Tuckahoe, New York, I was challenged by a Democratic watcher on the grounds of illiteracy. From the looks of me he must have thought I was a Republican, though I intended to vote Democratic. I must admit the challenge on such grounds took me by surprise — I had published my second book recently, *End of a Berlin Diary,* and I also thought my broadcasts would indicate I could at least read and write. But the Board of Registration insisted that I must pass a literacy test — its members had never heard of my book; they did not read books. I was told that this was the last day for such a test, that it was given only at an address miles away; and that since I could not reach it in time, I would not be permitted to register. I protested long and bitterly. At forty-four I thought it was time I be given the ballot in my native land.

But at least I could report on the election.

Probably be up most of the night broadcasting the results [I noted at the end of the entry on November 2], though most think it will all be over, the results known (i.e., Dewey's victory) before midnight.

All during the campaign I had accepted, as had all other reporters, editors, commentators, and columnists, the conventional wisdom that Dewey would win, probably by a landslide. We were all taken in by the polls. As early as September 9, nearly two months before the election, Elmo Roper, one of the most highly regarded pollsters, had declared that Dewey had an unbeatable lead over Truman of 44 percent to 31 percent. Roper said he would, therefore, issue no more polls. Despite reports as the campaign progressed through the fall that Truman was attracting large and enthusiastic crowds, the polls continued to show Dewey as a shoe-in. On the eve of the voting, they issued their final predictions. The Gallup Poll gave Dewey 49.5 percent of the vote, Truman 44.5 percent, with the rest going to Wallace, the Progressive party candidate, and J. Strom Thurmond, the Dixiecrat. Roper, who

* Permanent registration, at least in the states in which I voted — first New York and then Connecticut — was then unknown. You had to register for each new election. Also during the years I worked in Europe, from 1925 on, there was no absentee ballot.

had continued in business after all, gave Dewey a clear majority, 52.2 percent, and Truman 37.1 percent. "I stand by my prediction," Roper said. "Dewey is in."

I was struck during the last days of the campaign how the pundits of our press, undoubtedly swayed by the polls, took Dewey's victory for granted. I admit I did not question their wisdom. Indeed, I quoted them in my Sunday broadcast. I had not bothered as I should have to go out into the country to try to see for myself. Thus on October 26, a week before the polling, I noted a column by Walter Lippmann, the doyen of the columnists, saying that the "whole relationship between East and West will be greatly affected by the decisions [of] the Dewey Administration. . . ." Like everyone else, he assumed without question that Dewey would soon be in the White House. Like the brothers Alsop, who in an article in the *Saturday Evening Post* of October 16, written probably four weeks before, entitled "What Kind of a President Will Dewey Make?" wrote: "Dewey will be ready to seize the Washington hydra by its thousand throats." In their nationally syndicated column of October 27, they began: "In the sea of troubles into which Thomas E. Dewey will soon be placed as President of the United States. . . ." Even the liberal Max Lerner in the *New York Post* wrote a column entitled "Dewey and the Interregnum." He was apprehensive about the seventy-eight days between Dewey's election and his taking office. "Thomas E. Dewey's election as President is a foregone conclusion," Leo Egan wrote in the *New York Times*. *Life* magazine captioned a photograph of Dewey: "The Next President of the United States." On the eve of the election, the *Times* predicted that Dewey would win 345 electoral votes from twenty states, while Truman would receive only 105 electoral votes from eleven states. "The Democratic Party," wrote Ernest K. Lindley in *Newsweek*, "is shattered." And finally, just before the polling, Lippmann chipped in with a warning that "the course of events cannot be halted for three months until Mr. Dewey has been inaugurated. . . ."

The columnists were so confident that in the pieces they had to write the day of the voting, for publication in the newspapers that would appear the next day with the actual results, they did not hesitate to mention Dewey as president-elect. Thus the Alsop brothers, whose column appeared in many newspapers the morning of November 3: "The first post-election question," they wrote, "is how the government can get through the next ten weeks. . . . Events will not wait patiently until Thomas E. Dewey officially replaces Harry S. Truman." Drew Pearson's column also appeared in newspapers announcing the election result on November 3. He wrote of "Tom Dewey, who will take over the White House 86 days from now."

But Tom Dewey did not take over the White House. It remained the residence of scrappy Harry S. Truman.

My diary for Wednesday, November 3:

> The incredible has happened! Truman has won! Dewey finally conceded shortly before noon today. . . . The pollsters, the newspapers, the radio commentators, including myself, were utterly wrong.
>
> We broadcast at MBS until six this morning from the ballroom of the Ritz-Carlton. . . . At first none took seriously Truman jumping into an early lead. As soon as the first scattered returns came in, Brownell, Dewey's campaign manager, appeared before the press at the Hotel Roosevelt headquarters and pompously announced that the expected Republican sweep was coming off and that Dewey was taking two-thirds of the states.
>
> But about 10:00 P.M. I went out on a limb and said that though the returns were still fragmentary, they already were a surprise and that, contrary to all predictions, it was a close race. Some [of the brass at MBS] did not like what I said; put it down to my naïveté in domestic affairs. For the next hour I was not asked to take my regular turn at commenting on the election trends.

Because I spoke German and French, I was shunted off to do interviews with correspondents of the German and French broadcasting companies on how the polling was going. My bosses at Mutual apparently did not mind my misleading the Germans and French as long as I didn't mislead our American public. But by midnight

> it was evident to all that the voting was not going Republican, as predicted. Even Brownell, a smooth Wall Street lawyer, stopped coming out and making silly predictions. Word did come that the *Chicago Tribune* was on the streets with a first edition whose front page headline read: "Dewey Defeats Truman."
>
> But almost at the same moment our station in Chicago, WGN [for "The World's Greatest Newspaper" and owned by the *Tribune*, which pretended to such stature], came through with the news that Truman was running well ahead of Dewey in Illinois.

This was a key state, which like the others in the farm-belt Midwest Dewey had been confident of carrying. But many commentators, especially Fulton Lewis, Jr., the right-wing Mutual broadcaster, and Hans Kaltenborn over at NBC, kept saying that we must wait for the down-state vote in Illinois and the rural vote elsewhere. This would melt Truman's lead and put Dewey way ahead.

But soon after midnight it was evident that the rural areas were not clinging to Dewey. Just the opposite. In rock-ribbed Republican Iowa, my old home state, Truman was also leading.

Still, no one, myself included, could quite believe the figures now racing in over the teletypes. For me personally they were too good to be true. In the end, as everyone at Mutual still was sure, Dewey would squeak through.

Dog-tired, we finally stopped broadcasting at 6:00 A.M. and MBS went off the air. I came home and went to sleep. All now depended on the final count in Illinois, Ohio and California. Probably [I thought as I dozed off] Dewey would squeeze in.

I awoke about 11:00 A.M., turned on the radio and learned to my joy that it was all over. A few minutes later — at 11:10 A.M. — came word that Dewey had conceded.

And so the little man that everyone said couldn't make it did make it because he had guts and confidence and fought on the issues while Dewey, depending on the polls' certainty that he would win easily, went about mouthing pious platitudes and refusing even to discuss the issues. He has only himself to blame, though his mistake was human. It must be a bitter pill for him, for he had taken it for granted from the moment he was nominated that he would be in the White House on January 20. . . .

The people have confounded the wiseacres, the smoothies. Perhaps they have shown that the day is past in America when the wealthy, through control of the media of information — press, magazines, radio — can bamboozle the citizenry into voting for reaction and greed.

In this, looking back from the Reagan years of the 1980s, I was, I can see, indeed naïve.

CHAPTER 3

With the loss of my syndicated *Herald-Tribune* column and soon afterward of my Sunday broadcast over Mutual, I could no longer avoid facing the problem of earning a living — enough to support a family of four. Nearly every month as the year 1950 raced by we had to sell some of the few stocks we owned to pay our bills. We realized our modest life savings would not last long at that rate. Unless *The Traitor* went better than my agent and publisher estimated, I would have to try to scratch elsewhere to make ends meet. Perhaps I could get more lectures, but that would mean a lot less time for writing.

In the meantime that summer came an offer from a pair of movie producers in Hollywood to consult on a film about Adolf Hitler, which they were going to shoot in Vienna, and to act in it in a minor role — that of myself as a foreign correspondent in Nazi Germany. My agent had some doubts about the producers, but he finally secured an agreement for round-trip tickets to Vienna for Tess and me, expenses in Vienna, a payment to be made in Paris, and a small percentage of the film's profits. If the film was a success, we stood to make a considerable sum. For the time being the job would enable Tess to return to her native city and visit with her parents — her younger brother, drafted into the German army, had been badly wounded on the very last day of the war and died two years later — and it would allow me, after the filming was over, to work in Paris, Bonn, and London on the book that had been turning over in my mind: *Midcentury Journey*. (I had no illusion that my acting debut in an American movie would lead anywhere at all.) The project would tide us over until late fall; my sister would look after the children on the farm while we were gone.

There was another purpose in making the trip: to see if, as many feared, the Russians would take advantage of our having just become tied down in Korea and move westward into the heart of Europe. That would certainly bring on war in Europe between the United States, with its Western Allies, and the Soviet Union. The Russians, with their satellites, certainly had land forces enough to advance swiftly westward, but we had the atom bomb with which to retaliate. (Moscow had not had time enough — in a year — to match our stockpiles or our means of delivering the bomb.) New York and Washington had been rather panicky about the possibility of the Red Army's moving in Europe. My plane from New York to London had only a dozen passengers; most had canceled their passage. Americans did not want to fly into the teeth of the Bolshevik advance. My own hunch was that out of fear of the A-bomb, Stalin would not move. But with him and the Russians you never knew. I myself recalled that memorable night in Berlin in August 1939, when we got the unbelievable news that the Soviet dictator, the great anti-Fascist champion, had signed a pact with Hitler that made the latter's launching of World War II a few days later inevitable.

A couple of weeks in Vienna, waiting for the work on the film to start, convinced me that the Russians were not going to move. Allied Intelligence Services, which were on the front line — so to speak — with Soviet troops but a few miles to the east of Vienna, were unanimous about that. They had detected no signs that the Red Army was preparing to strike.

I had arrived in Vienna just a bit too late to convince our film director of that. The day before my arrival he had fled in the greatest secrecy to Paris, from which he wired us that he (and his wife, who was in Hollywood) were sure the Russians were going to march, that they would quickly overrun Vienna first, and that he was lighting out for home on the first available plane. This held up shooting on the film while our producer tried frantically to find another director. But it gave Tess and me time to revisit some of our old haunts in Vienna.

The city was still nursing wounds from the war, but it was recovering and frantically rebuilding. Much of the baroque charm was still there. Baroque had always been the key to the character and the life of the Viennese.

> In Vienna, at least, [I had once written] it made for a special and peculiar vision of life, at once spiritual and material. It managed through the harmony and fantasy of form to bring heaven and earth together, to abolish the boundary between life and the dream, between the real and the unreal, and to reconcile for man the antagonisms of pain and joy, death and life, nature and man, faith and knowledge; Baroque was a dynamic thing, full of passion and sensualism, for it recognized the human longings and the deep creative urges as well as the frailties. Above all, it was a call to dream.

For centuries they had dreamed on in Vienna, the imperial center of the sprawling Hapsburg Empire, passing the pleasant days and nights waltzing and wining, in light talk in the congenial coffeehouses, in viewing the make-believe of the theater and opera and operetta, in flirting and making love. To be sure an empire had to be governed, an army and navy manned, business transacted, and labor done. But as little as possible of the mind and energies was devoted to such prosaic things. The real life of the Viennese in the old days began with the fun and the pleasures and the dreams.

Suddenly the first of many rude awakenings came. In November 1918, with the war lost after four years of bitter fighting, the ancient House of Hapsburg came tumbling down, ending a golden epoch and a way of life that this city — like the imperial capitals of Berlin and St. Petersburg — would never see again. Over the next three decades these lighthearted and attractive people would, in fact, go through a damnation unequaled in the West in our time: revolution; blockade; hunger; cold; the bloody shooting down of workers, women, and children; Fascist oppression and Nazi savagery; bombing and bombardment and finally Russian occupation. And yet in 1950, as we roamed the streets, we could see how splendidly these people had survived; their buoyant spirits restored their lust for life after such hardship and sorrow still wonderfully strong. It was an experience, I remembered, that we in America had never had to go through. I wondered how we would have taken it had it happened to us; since character is mostly formed in adversity, and we had had so little of it, never having been conquered nor — since the British burned Washington in 1812 — occupied.

For the first time since the war, life had returned to something like normal in Vienna. There was plenty to eat, and work was well along on rebuilding the city from the ruins left by bombing and bombardment.

Once Tess and I stopped at the corner of the Kaertnerstrasse and the Ring to watch the workers restoring the bombed-out State Opera House, the pride of the Viennese. Austrian friends had told us of what had happened there on the night of March 12, 1945, the seventh anniversary of Hitler's taking Austria. Swarms of American heavy bombers, flying up from Italy, had turned the city into a fiery inferno. Hundreds of flaming buildings toppled over into the streets. Buses and streetcars and all other traffic came to a halt. The people huddled in their air-raid shelters. Then a rumor began to spread. To the Viennese it was too horrible to believe.

"The opera has been hit!"

From all corners of the burning city the citizens converged on the

Ring, unmindful that their own homes might be going up in flames or that they might get killed in the street from the falling bombs, spent anti-aircraft shells, and collapsing walls. All through the night and the next morning they tried to save the stately musical shrine that meant so much to them, forming bucket brigades to help the firemen, doing whatever else they could. But it was hopeless. The State Opera House had been shattered by four direct hits of high-explosive American bombs. Slowly, reluctantly, thousands of Viennese abandoned the scene, their smoke-blackened faces, we were told, still full of anger and resentment but even more of sorrow. You could pulverize their homes and offices and all the old imperial state palaces, but to destroy this temple of music — this was barbarous.

Tess and I stood for a few minutes watching the men and women working behind the immense scaffolding that surrounded most of the Opera House. They were toiling like beavers. Already they were taking down the scaffolding in front of the façade facing the Ring, so that we could see the new brightly colored pillars and colonnades. A crowd applauded them as they worked. These good Viennese would have to live awhile longer in their patched-up dwellings, but the beloved Statsoper must be made whole again as soon as possible.

While our film producers were still searching for a new director, Tess and I stole off to Salzburg for a weekend. It seemed as we looked back that we had always been stealing off to Salzburg at this time of year to take in the music festival, which now had just been revived after having been shut down since the beginning of the war.

Salzburg, in the western section of Austria, was still under American military occupation. Indeed, Tess and I had been put up at a palace outside town taken over by the American military commander, one of whose aides had procured us tickets to the opera. We were driven to the theater by an obnoxious young American lieutenant, who was resentful at having to miss a Saturday evening's officers' dance at the palace. As we made our way with him to the box of the American military commander, once reserved for the Hapsburgs, an attendant whispered to us in German that the Austrian minister of economics and his wife were sitting in the American general's box. For some reason this infuriated our lieutenant when we told him, though there was plenty of room in the box for all of us.

"Throw them out!" he shouted.

Apparently the attendant understood very little English, and it was obvious that the lieutenant spoke no German — or almost none.

"*Aus! Aus!*" he yelled. He knew that German word, at least.

"But the governor of Salzburg Province put them in there, sir," the attendant replied in German.

"What did he say?" the lieutenant, now red-faced, his eyes almost popping out, said, turning to us. Tess, highly embarrassed, translated the words.

"Tell him I don't care who put them in there. Tell him they have no right to be in the general's box. Out with them!"

Tess and I tried to duck away.

"Just a moment," cried the lieutenant. "You've got to help me. I don't speak the damned language. Tell that guy, whoever he is, to get the hell out of the general's box."

"You'll have to tell him yourself, Lieutenant, though I think you are being extremely foolish," I said. "There is plenty of room in that box for all of us. Why don't you just calm down?"

For a moment the lieutenant was so taken aback he became speechless. In the meantime Tess told the attendant in German what the young American officer had said. By this time we had advanced to the back of the box, in full view and within easy earshot of fifteen hundred people in the auditorium below, who had turned to take in the scene. The attendant went down to the cabinet minister and his wife and whispered in their ears. They had heard the fuss but apparently had not understood what it was all about. Now, obviously highly embarrassed but determined to show as much dignity as they could muster, they got up slowly and left their places.

"I am terribly sorry," Tess whispered to them in German as they passed us.

"We understand," the wife whispered back. After all, I thought, the Americans have been here for five years. The Austrians are used to us.

The lights in the house started to dim, and we slunk into our seats. I guess only Beethoven (or Mozart, a native of Salzburg and around whose music the festival is built) and this great opera, the only one, I believe, he ever completed, could have restored us that evening.

Returning to the palace after the opera, we had a drink with some of the American officers. The regular Saturday-night dance was in full swing. I mentioned to a colonel what had happened at the opera. Before I could add how ashamed I was, he replied, "Good for him! That's the way to treat these people!"

I was ashamed all over again.

*   *   *

Back in Vienna, we finally started shooting the film. Luther Adler, a fine actor, played Hitler. Why an American Jew would want to play the mad, sadistic, barbarian, anti-Semitic Nazi dictator, who had almost wiped out the Jews of Europe in his extermination camps, puzzled me. Perhaps Adler was interested in the irony of it. But he confessed to me that he had long had a burning desire to play the part. He threw himself into it with great zeal and soon was looking and talking like the psychopathic Führer I had known in my Berlin days.

Vienna, August 8. Have made my film debut! From 7:00 to 10:00 P.M. last night we shot the scenes in a Vienna hotel room (erected in the studio) with Patricia Knight, a blonde beauty, who has the leading female role in the film. It was all new to me — and fun — the scenes being worked out on the spot by the director and ourselves, which gives little time for the subtleties one can achieve in the theater. I was less nervous and self-conscious than I had feared; and though it gets on one's nerves to do the same scene over a dozen times first in rehearsal and then in shooting, we got through in fairly good time.

This morning I did the opening scene in the ruins of a building that is supposed to be the entrance to Hitler's bunker in Berlin. Actually it was a battered building on the Jacquingasse, on which we used to live at the time I had my ski accident. While the camera people were setting up their lights and gadgets, I strolled up the street to find our apartment house. It was still standing but completely gutted, the windows bricked up.

The film, called *The Magic Face,* was certainly no masterpiece, even by Hollywood standards; but it did well at the box office and even better later when it was shown repeatedly on television. Somehow the producers never got around to divvying up the agreed modest percentage of the profits owed to me; and I heard that Luther Adler and Patricia Knight, who had a much larger share, fared similarly. My first inkling of the hesitation of the producers to part with their cash came toward the end of August when we arrived in Paris and found the one thousand dollars in francs, due us on arrival under our contract, failed to materialize, as did a few weeks later a thousand dollars payable in pounds sterling in London. We got stranded in both capitals until my New York agent came through with hasty advances.

Aside from making the film in Vienna and seeing whether the Russians would march through Western Europe that summer while the United States was tied up in the war in Korea, I had a further reason for making this journey. I wanted to find out, if I could, where Western Europe stood at the midcentury mark. More precisely I wanted to probe into the state of France, West Germany, and Britain. Could they (with Italy, which was also trying to rise from the ruins of the war) revive the former power and perhaps even glory of Western Europe, which had been the center of Western civilization so long? If I was lucky, if the material I could dig up proved good enough, I might get a book out of this midcentury journey. If so, that would be the title: *Midcentury Journey.*

It began to grow in my mind. After recounting the day's doings and thoughts in my diary, I found myself adding "Ideas for Book."

Paris, August, 1950 — Book. To make it in diary form? "Journey Back Through the Years." The outer frame being diary of this trip to Europe. (You could even use from diary "Thoughts in Plane Coming Over" . . . then digress into story of what happened to Europe last 25 years — Br., Fr., G., Austria . . . two clips — possibly for book. [They were about General de Gaulle saying he was "available" and an editorial from *Le Monde* asking why the U.S.A. never sent its intelligentsia — writers, artists, intellectuals — abroad to represent it, as European countries do and as America once did] . . . the incredible lies of the Communists Press in Europe. . . .

Frankfurt, West Germany, Sept. 10. Book. Get in: When you first came over in 1925 the position of U.S. was that of an isolated land whose leaders had scant understanding of the world. . . . In London and Paris there was resentment of war debt settlements. (In Paris in '27 buses of American tourists stoned.) In Germany, U.S. regarded as something of a wealthy sucker whose investments would (and did) retool and modernize German industry and would, probably, never have to be repaid, which they weren't.

An American traveler in Europe in 1950 was struck by how all this had changed, how every country in Europe, incl. Germany, esp. Germany, looked daily to the U.S. for help & advice, recognizing its undisputed leadership of the Western World, apprehensive of its gropings and mistakes, but realizing that its future depended largely on U.S.

London, Sept. 20. Diary and Book. Article: "A Visit to the House of Commons."

My visit to the Commons the previous day was one of the most interesting I had ever experienced. For nearly eight hours the august chamber debated whether to overthrow the Labour government for its decision to go ahead with the nationalization of the iron and steel industry. It was a particularly interesting session for me, because not only was Winston Churchill leading the debate for the opposition Tories but also one of my closest friends in England, Russell Strauss, the labor minister in charge of taking over the nationalized industry, was making the principal speech for the government. It turned out to be one of the bitterest debates I had ever heard in the Commons. Most political pundits thought it well might end in the defeat of the Labour government, the dissolution of the House, and the calling of new elections. But Labour squeaked through by a vote of 306 to 300. Churchill, whom I had not seen speak in the Commons since the war when he was prime minister, was in good form though not in his best form. Russell Strauss, no rival in oratory (as was another old Labour friend from my young days in London, Nye Bevan, Churchill's great tormentor), did very well in defending Labour's nationalization program. Though on the extreme left of the party at that time along with Bevan, Jennie Lee (Bevan's wife), and a few others, Strauss, who had inherited a family fortune and metals business, knew the capitalist business world as few other Labour M.P.s did.*

On one subject that summer I turned out to be wrong and on another perhaps a not very good prophet. The first concerned General de Gaulle.

My diary, Paris, August 18:

> De Gaulle came out with a long bombastic statement warning of the danger of the hour and — typically — offering to take over power again. He talks a queer kind of pseudo-authoritarian jargon and I doubt if many Frenchmen will take his declaration seriously.

Ever since the war I had been an admirer of the strange general, applauding his brave feat in striking out alone against Marshal Pétain and General Weygand, the two most prestigious military figures in France, for signing the armistice with Germany. From London and later from Algeria when that African province was liberated by the British and American armies, he had presided over the "Free French"

---

* Some years later, when Labour was out of power and Strauss had more time to devote to his business, he made a trip to Pittsburgh to confer with a group of American steel magnates there, who wanted to increase their orders from his firm. They did not connect him with the left-wing labor minister who took over and managed the nationalized iron and steel industry in Britain. All through his talks with them he listened to them cursing that minister and his Socialist party and urging him to help the Tories (at the moment in power) get the industry back into private hands. Strauss never divulged his identity to them. He had never, he told us later, enjoyed so much an attack on him. He was tempted, he said, in the end to tell the American tycoons who he really was but desisted out of fear of provoking a series of apoplectic strokes, if not worse.

movement, often at odds with Churchill, his chief backer among the Allies, and harshly opposed by President Roosevelt, who did not believe he had any right to speak for the occupied French. During the war I had written, broadcast, and spoken on behalf of his movement. But I had always had misgivings about his imperiousness, his appetite for political power, and his somewhat authoritarian program. I didn't like his obsession with the leadership principle — on this he was almost as bad as Hitler. Some of his writings on the subject reminded me of *Mein Kampf.* "Men need leaders," he had written. "The leader is distant, for authority cannot be without prestige, nor prestige without distance. . . . Confident in his own judgment and conscious of his strength, the leader makes no attempt to please. . . . All that he asks is granted. . . ."

"Unless things turn very much for the worse," I concluded in my diary August 24 in Paris, "I do not think de Gaulle can come back. If conditions become desperate, he well may."

The latter would happen. In 1958 the fledgling Fourth Republic would falter over trying to hold on to Algeria and Indochina and over its inability to assure some kind of peace and order among the warring classes at home; and General de Gaulle, who had stepped down as provisional president in 1946, would come back as president of the Fifth Republic and restore domestic tranquillity, and some of France's former prestige, if not grandeur. My opinion of him changed again into skeptical admiration for the vision he had and for the restraint he showed. He did not abolish the political parties, as many had feared. He was authoritarian, a man of the right, to be sure, but acted always within the framework of a new constitution that guaranteed to the French their cherished freedoms.

Despite the illusions of grandeur of de Gaulle, who labored mightily to restore France to her former power and greatness, it was plain to me that he would never entirely succeed. Like Britain, France had been drained almost to death by two world wars and in her case by four years of German occupation, during which much of her wealth was siphoned off or stolen by the occupiers. Also like Britain, France was losing her vast overseas empire; in her case: Morocco, Algeria, and Tunisia in North Africa and Indochina in the Far East.

As the result of the war, leadership in the world had passed from Western Europe to two non-European giants, the U.S.S.R. and the U.S.A. De Gaulle, with his keen intelligence and grasp of history, recognized it. He did not like it, but he adapted to the inevitable. The British, too, though a little more slowly. In Paris and London at midcentury you could feel how difficult it was when your country had ridden so high for so long to admit that the golden days were over and could never return.

As for Germany you could see now that she, too, was finished as one of the world's great powers. This was caused not only by another lost war. She had lost the First World War in 1918 and come back under Hitler only two decades later to make another attempt to dominate the continent.

What gave the rest of the continent some assurance that it would not happen again was that Germany was now divided and that as long as she remained cut up into two Germanies neither one would ever be strong enough to reach out again to try to subdue Europe and Russia. Being split into two nations was obviously painful to many Germans, but I found the rest of Europe breathed easier because of it and wanted it to continue indefinitely.

This was also because Europeans felt that the Germans had really not changed very much. Polls taken in Germany disclosed that most Germans still believed that Nazism had been a good idea, though badly carried out. One poll taken not long before my return that year asked the Germans: "Do you believe that the Germans can govern themselves democratically?" Less than one-half answered in the affirmative. Already, I noted in my diary during a stay in Frankfurt, Bonn, and Berlin, the old gang was back in control of the German economy. These, for the most part, were the industrial magnates who had made Hitler's rule possible. Now they had become the darlings of the Americans and British, who had helped them regain their old holdings.

Once before, following 1918, the victorious Allies, especially the Americans, had rebuilt Germany after they had conquered it in war. They had hoped the country would keep the peace, but it had not. Now we were again rebuilding Germany in the same hope. As I left West Germany in 1950, I was skeptical of our success. It was difficult for one who had covered Weimar and then Hitler's Germany to have much confidence in the future of this talented but unstable people.

Once again I was wrong. Thanks to some unusual leaders, Konrad Adenauer, Willy Brandt, Helmut Schmidt, and a few others, the Germans for the first time in their history began to make democracy work. (It had not worked well the first time in the Weimar Republic, and Hitler had destroyed it.) The Federal Republic (West Germany) turned out to be a success. It soon became the most prosperous and economically powerful country on the continent.

*   *   *

Britain turned out to be the most interesting country of all for me this time. The changes were much more profound than in the other lands. Somehow I liked London much better now. In three of the years between the wars I had been yanked from Paris or from Vienna, both of which I loved, to the drab British capital to work for two or three months relieving the *Chicago Tribune* correspondents stationed there while they were on vacation. Instantly I took a dislike to the city, the country, the people, and life in the British Isles. The English, I thought, were unnecessarily condescending to Americans. The snob-bishness of the upper classes, their atrocious manners, astounded me. The food was bad; and the blue laws, passed during the First World War, when perhaps they made sense, but were never repealed, made life miserable, especially Sundays when I was forced to remain in London because of my work. The city closed down on the Sabbath: transportation, restaurants, theaters, bars, and almost everything else you could think of except, of course, churches. My only consolations in those days — besides Zora, my Hungarian friend who came out one year from Vienna to share the miseries of London — were the inex-pensive French restaurants in Soho. God knows they were not exactly gourmet; but they were better than almost any English restaurant dispensing its cold mutton, boiled-to-death brussels sprouts, and taste-less, starchy desserts. It was at modest little French restaurants in Soho that I first met some of the British trade union leaders, young Labour M.P.s (class of 1929) like Nye Bevan and Jennie Lee, and visiting American artists such as Paul Robeson, who was under suspicion at home of being a "Red" but who had taken London by storm with his singing in *Showboat.*

During the war the English changed. The terrible pounding they took from the German bombing seemed to have knocked some of the stuffiness and the snobbishness out of them. Suddenly they were friendly to Americans and even hospitable. American correspon-dents who had never previously been invited socially to anything suddenly found themselves deluged with invitations to dinner or weekends in the country. I remembered my astonishment at finding, a week or so after my arrival in London in 1944, that I had met at lunch or tea or dinner nearly every cabinet minister, politician, writer, playwright, actor, and actress in the country. It was all very helpful and pleasant.

By 1950 there had been a considerable social revolution in Britain. It had not demolished the class structure but it had shaken it. And it had transformed the economy and the social contract. In five years the

Labour government had nationalized the Bank of England, coal mining, transportation, civil aviation, international communications, electricity, gas, and just now the iron and steel industry. And it had given the United Kingdom the most comprehensive health insurance system in the world.

At home, American critics of that system, especially in the American Medical Association, had derided British "socialized medicine" as impossible and unwanted. But this was not true. It was extremely popular among all classes, all parties. While I was in England, even the Conservative party, girding up for the next year's elections, had adopted a platform that said: "The Conservative Party is wholeheartedly in favor of a National Health Service available to all."

Could England ever recover her former greatness? I discussed it through many a night with my friends and acquaintances, Tory, Liberal, Labour. By 1950, five years after the end of another devastating war which again had bled the country grievously, most Britons were becoming reconciled to a more modest role for the nation. It did not seem likely to them that England could ever again be what she had been, say, up to the beginning of the First World War in 1914 or even up to the beginning of the second one in 1939. The sources of power and wealth which had made her supreme were no longer there. They had been destroyed in two world wars and their aftermaths. Already India, the jewel of the empire, had broken away two years before.

The fate of England had been suffered, of course, by other empires. What stirred this traveler was that with Britain it had happened so quickly, within one's own lifetime, so that one could say, however sadly, what none could have said about the Romans or the Greeks: that he had seen with his own eyes the dissolution of a fabulous empire and the descent from the heights of a great nation.

As everyone said, there would always be an England. The indomitable spirit of this unique island race would long endure. But I could not help thinking as I departed its shores that I would never see England as it had been, even in 1925, when my own little journey through the second quarter of our century had first taken me there; nor would I see the splendor — and exploitation — of empire as I had seen it five years later in India, where the British raj still reigned supreme. The majesty of empire, the splendor, the power, the wealth, were lost forever.

CHAPTER 4

Sorting out my impressions of two months in Europe at the midcentury as my plane headed home over the North Atlantic, I remembered a small item of news that I had not had time to jot down in my diary. While in Frankfurt, I had noticed in the European edition of the *New York Times* a letter from Howard Lindsay, the playwright and actor, protesting the inclusion of my name and the names of some other writers in an obscure publication I had never heard of called *Red Channels*. Apparently we were accused of having some connection with Communists or with Communism or both. Well, almost everyone in America was being accused of being a "Red" by some crackpot. A hitherto unnoticed junior Republican senator from Wisconsin by the name of Joseph R. McCarthy, I remembered, had in February accused the State Department of harboring two hundred and five "card-carrying" Communists. He had the names in his pocket, he claimed. And while a few reactionary know-nothings had raised a hue and cry in support of the senator, I thought he had been pretty well disposed of just before I left by the Senate Tydings Committee, which after due investigation had held that McCarthy's allegations "constituted the most nefarious campaign of half-truths and untruths in the history of the Republic."

In the plane as we approached our shores I dozed off and the *Red Channels* connection faded from my memory.

But not for long.

"One's feeling about this country after a short absence," I wrote in my diary a few days after my return, "are mixed."

We had behaved admirably in Korea, I thought, in stopping Communist aggression there. If we had intervened so decisively and promptly against Hitler's aggression, I noted, there might not have been a Second World War.

On the other hand, I found the country

in a state of the worst intolerance I have ever known. The false and phony "super-patriots" are attempting under the fake guise of anticommunism to set up a thought-control in this country which sickens the heart of one like myself who lived through it in Nazi Germany. And the craven men who control American business, the advertisers who dominate our means of communication, newspapers, magazines, and especially radio, are surrendering to these bigots so completely, so abjectly, that if we are not careful we shall soon be committing most of the worst faults of the totalitarians whose way of life we claim to oppose.

I came home last week to find myself a personal victim of this situation.

I recounted being listed in *Red Channels*. For the first two or three days I did not, I could not, take it seriously. Then I began to circulate about New York, especially around Madison Avenue where the ad agencies and CBS were. And I learned to my utter astonishment that to be listed with one hundred and fifty others in this obscure publication as being involved with Communism or Communists was to be blacklisted from employment in broadcasting, the entertainment world, and journalism in general. Unbelievable! This two-bit publication had become the bible of Madison Avenue and the networks. If your name was in it, no advertising agency — and in those days they produced many of the leading shows on radio and TV — and no network executive would hire you. You were condemned to unemployment in your field — with no chance of explaining or defending yourself.

I must have enlightened myself very quickly that first week at home as a glance at my diary shows. The phoniness of *Red Channels'* charges

has not prevented the radio industry — i.e., the networks, the advertising agencies, the companies that advertise on the air — from accepting *Red Channels* as a blacklist so authoritative that a top official at CBS tells me no man on the list has a chance of being employed henceforth on radio.

In fact, the blacklisting was already operating.

General Foods, a billion dollar corporation, and NBC, one of the giants of the radio industry, I learn, dropped a lady actress from a show, in fact, postponed the opening of the show, because twenty — twenty! — telephone calls came in protesting the presence of the lady in the cast because her name was listed in *Red Channels*.*

* I believe I was referring to the case of Jean Muir. Listed in *Red Channels*, she was dropped from the popular daytime serial *The Aldrich Family*, sponsored by General Foods.

I myself found in opening my mail last week a cancellation of the one radio show I was scheduled to appear in: an interview with Martha Deane apropos of my first novel coming out November 3. Of course, she did not say it was because my name was on the blacklist. That might have made her liable to a lawsuit. She merely made up some excuse.

It became obvious that CBS was the main target of the publishers of *Red Channels* and of their weekly sheet, *Counterattack*. The latter had charged that "all networks let some Communists and Communist fronters get on their programs, but CBS is worst of all." The response of CBS to this shocked many. It hired the publishers of the scurilous sheet that had attacked it to investigate the loyalty of its employees! CBS had capitulated to the hysterical vigilantes.

What was this *Red Channels*, which dictated to the mighty moguls of the advertising agencies, the networks and even the movies whom they might employ?

It was the work of three former FBI men, Theodore C. Kirkpatrick, John G. Keenan, and Kenneth M. Bierly, who had resigned from the agency shortly after the end of the war. Early in 1947 they had set up a firm called American Business Consultants with a capitalization of $15,000, most of it provided by a wealthy importer, Alfred Kohlberg, the head of the China Lobby, which accused the State Department of "losing" China to the "Reds." A staunch backer of Chiang Kai-shek, he was also a supporter of Senator McCarthy.

The purpose of the new enterprise was to attack Communism in America; and with this in mind it brought out a weekly newsletter called *Counterattack*, which it said contained "Facts to Combat Communism." Targets of the newsletter included Trygve Lie, secretary general of the United Nations, whom it dubbed "Stalin's choice," the U.N. itself, William L. Green and Philip Murray, heads of the AFL and the CIO, the Blatz Beer Company for sponsoring a "fellow traveling" actress in one of its shows, the book review sections of the *New York Times* and *New York Herald-Tribune*, the Yale Law School for harboring "Reds" on its faculty, the Associated Press — the list was endless, including also *The New Yorker*, *Time*, *Life*, *Look*, and the *Atlantic*, and even U.S. Steel.

Counterattack was an immediate success. It brought the three ex-FBI men a good living and increasing power as the advertising agencies, sponsors of programs on the air, and the networks began to heed its warnings of "Reds" fouling up the entertainment industry, especially broadcasting.

To increase its profits and its prestige, in June 1950 American Business Consultants brought out *Red Channels* in magazine form, under the subtitle "The Report of Communist Influence in Radio and Television" and with an illustration on the cover showing a large red-stained hand clutching a microphone. There were one hundred and fifty-one names listed, and after each name was noted the organization the person was "reported as" having once belonged to or supported. Declarations that the suspects were "reported" as subscribing to were also listed. The publishers obviously got their list from the House Un-American Activities Committee (which had been aided by the FBI), the Tenney Committee in California, and the *Daily Worker* — the last, the organ of the Communist party in America.*

To avoid libel suits, the publishers printed a disclaimer to the effect that they were not accusing any of the listees of being a Communist or even a Communist sympathizer.† They also stated their belief that in screening personnel, every safeguard must be used to protect the innocent. They did not say they had followed this practice. Obviously they hadn't, for none of those listed — I later found — had even been questioned by them. Amazingly, some courts of law would, in the Red-baiting hysteria of the early 1950s, accept as sincere these phony disclaimers.

Red Channels made three "charges" against me:

1. that I had been chairman of "The Friends of the Spanish Republic";
2. that I had attended a dinner of, and had been supported by, "The Voice of Freedom Committee"; and
3. that I had signed an amicus curiae brief to the Supreme Court on behalf of the Hollywood Ten.

The first and third "charges" were true; the second partly true. But wait a minute!

I was proud to have headed up "The Friends of the Spanish Republic," a not very effective organization that tried in vain to help save the Spanish Republic and prevent the rebel general Franco from turning Republican democratic Spain into another Fascist country on the model of Italy and Germany. I had lived in Spain for a year just prior

---

* Among others listed in *Red Channels* were: Howard K. Smith, my former colleague at CBS, who had succeeded Ed Murrow as chief of the London CBS bureau; the writers and playwrights Arthur Miller, Lillian Hellman, Abe Burrows, and Irwin Shaw; Olin Downs, music critic of the *New York Times;* the musicians Leonard Bernstein and Aaron Copland; and the actors Edward G. Robinson, Orson Welles, Gypsy Rose Lee, Hazel Scott, Judy Holliday, Burl Ives, and Lee J. Cobb.
† The distinguished actors Frederic and Florence March had sued *Counterattack* for having labeled them as Communists, and the publishers had settled out of court.

to Franco's rebellion, and I had admired the stumbling efforts of the Spanish Republic to establish a democracy after King Alfonso had abdicated and fled. There was nothing Communist about our little organization. It was not listed among the alleged "front" groups in the back of *Red Channels*. It was not mentioned on the attorney general's list of "subversive" organizations.

Neither was the second group, "The Voice of Freedom Committee." It was true I did attend one of its meetings. In May 1947, shortly after my ouster from CBS, this committee announced that it was holding a public meeting to discuss my controversy with the networks. It said that Ed Murrow, representing CBS, and a commissioner from the Federal Communications Commission (FCC), which had jurisdiction over the networks and radio stations, would appear. It invited me to come to speak for myself.

I went. Commissioner Clifford J. Durr turned up for the FCC. Ed Murrow did not show. Durr and I spoke our pieces. During the session I got the impression that the committee was chiefly interested in exploiting me. And I began to suspect it might be a front organization. That was the end of my connection with it.

The third "charge" against me turned out to be the most effective: that I had signed an amicus curiae brief to the Supreme Court on behalf of the Hollywood Ten. I had.

One morning, a year or so before, I had received a call from Professor Zachariah Chafee of the Harvard Law School. I knew him by reputation but not personally. He told me that he and some of his colleagues had drawn up an amicus curiae brief to the Supreme Court urging a fair hearing on certain constitutional points for the Hollywood Ten on their appeal of a conviction for contempt for having refused to answer questions about their Communist affiliations before the House Un-American Activities Committee. He said he had lined up a dozen impeccably non-Communist notables to sign it but had discovered that they were all Republicans. He wanted some Democrats to round out the list. Two publishers in New York, he added, had agreed to sign: Cass Canfield, the head of Harper's, and Bennett Cerf, who ran Random House. Would I join them in signing?

I told him that I had not followed the trials of the Hollywood Ten and knew very little about them, but that if he read me the brief, I would consider signing it — after I had talked to Cass Canfield, an old friend. The text of the brief seemed innocuous enough, in essence asking for a fair hearing. I got Cass on the phone and he urged me to join him and sign it. I did. Cass, who got around more than I did, said that most, if not all, of the Hollywood Ten probably were, or had been, members of the Communist party. But he thought that in the present atmosphere of anti-Red hysteria it was important for non-Communists to stand up and remind the wavering courts that Communists were citizens too and had a constitutional right to fair trial. I agreed.

Though I had not followed the proceedings closely, I doubted if the accused screenwriters had received a fair hearing before the House Un-American Activities Committee. Back in December 1947, the Authors League, of which I was a member, had protested the action of the House committee in citing the ten for contempt. The league stressed that the House inquisitors had denied the Hollywood writers the right to call witnesses in their own defense and to cross-examine hostile witnesses. Most of them had not even been allowed to read statements prior to testifying.

I knew none of the Hollywood Ten writers personally. I seldom went to the movies and had been working as a correspondent in Nazi Germany during most of the thirties. In Berlin, American films were *verboten*. I had no idea who was writing them. The only names in the ten I recognized were Ring Lardner, Jr., because I had been an avid reader of his father, and John Howard Lawson, whose book on play-writing I had once read and who, I believe, never made any bones of not being a Communist. The other eight, I was told when I finally asked, were well-known Hollywood screenwriters: Albert Maltz, Al-vah Bessie, Adrienne Scott, Edward Dmytryk, Dalton Trumbo, Samuel Ornitz, Lester Cole, and Herbert Biberman. In my ignorance of the movies and of Hollywood, they were just names to me. I knew nothing of what they had written.

So much for my signing an amicus curiae brief to the Supreme Court for the Hollywood Ten. I learned later there were many similar briefs submitted by others in the country. But my signature on one of those briefs, along with fourteen or fifteen other people, mostly conservative Republicans, was to cost me for the next ten years' employment in American journalism: both broadcast and print. No executive from the networks, ad agencies or sponsors, no editor of a magazine — with one or two exceptions — to whom I submitted manuscripts would touch me with a ten-foot pole.

It was as if I had committed some heinous crime against my country and had been convicted without trial. This puzzled me. I was not and never had been a Communist, nor had I ever been accused, even by the most hysterical witch-hunters, of being one. My political views had been expressed in hundreds of dispatches, broadcasts, articles, and diaries. A liberal sampling of the last in a book, *Berlin Diary*, had been read by millions. I had never hidden what I thought. No congressional committee, not even the notorious House Committee on Un-American Activities nor its rival, the Senate Internal Security Subcommittee, nor any other government group obsessed with Communists and Communism ever expressed the slightest interest in calling me before them.

How then could one defend himself? I decided to ask my lawyer to sue *Red Channels*. I was not interested in damages, though it looked as though I would certainly be damaged unless I could force *Red Channels* to issue a public retraction and erase my name from its blacklist.

Morris Ernst, my lawyer and a friend, was one of the foremost champions of civil liberties in the country. As counsel to the American Civil Liberties Union, he had long played an important and well-publicized part in that worthy organization's fight for civil rights. He was a friend of President Roosevelt, of Justice Felix Frankfurter of the Supreme Court, and of many other notables in Washington. He had backed Roosevelt's New Deal. He had espoused many liberal causes* but above all the civil rights of all Americans. I had not a doubt in the world that he would push my suit against *Red Channels* with his accustomed zeal and skill.

To my astonishment Morris Ernst refused to sue *Red Channels* on my account.

"I won't take your money," he said, explaining that in his opinion it was almost impossible to win a libel suit against the blacklisters.

I said I would still like to take the chance. I asked him to think it over. He said he would write me more fully.[†]

"Dear Bill," he wrote me on May 16, 1951:

> As I told you . . . I see no valid basis for letting you spend your money on a libel suit. . . . Above all, it would be long drawn out and expensive. . . . Incidentally, no one that I have heard of has developed a bit of social engineering to cope with movements such as *Counterattack*. . . .

---

* And he had waged mighty battles against censorship. In one of them he won the reversal of the ban on bringing James Joyce's *Ulysses* into the United States, a landmark case that began the loosening of book censorship in our country. In another case he fought successfully against the suppression of Marie Stopes's *Married Love*. As counsel for the Authors League, Dramatists Guild, and the Newspaper Guild, he triumphed in many a court battle for the rights of authors and dramatists, and for the right of newspaper people among other things, to organize.
† "Morris does not seem to realize," I noted in my diary, "the enormity of the crime involved or the real danger to American liberties of such bigots and the facility with which they can stampede the bizmen who today run America."

I didn't see that "social engineering" had much, if anything, to do with it. It was a matter of the law. I tried to needle some of Ernst's law partners to put a firecracker under him on my behalf. But he came back with the same stock answer:

> October 30, 1951
>
> Dear Bill: In regard to your footnote to your letter to Harriet [Pilpel, a partner], may I say I also have regrets that neither I, nor you, nor anybody else has developed any satisfactory technique for coming to grips with *Red Channels*. As I told you before, I am loath to advise a libel suit not only because of the burden of time and money, but primarily because the courts are no good for handling libel matters. . . .

Still, I thought, the courts were all we had "for handling libel." I knew they were currently in the grip of the anti-Red hysteria, like most other institutions. But I myself was willing to have a try with them. Ernst wouldn't listen.

> Don't be sore at me [he went on] because I won't take your money by advising you to start a libel suit. On the other hand I would not relish, even if you so desire, trying to work out a deal with *Red Channels*. I would not relish it because I know that those who have tried are not only not better off but are worse off. . . .

Strangely, in view of those last two sentences, Ernst called me up a few weeks later and proposed that I meet with him and the publishers of *Red Channels* for lunch at "21" to discuss my problem. He seemed surprised when I indignantly refused.

I never underestimated the difficulties of suing *Red Channels*. The judiciary was showing no more courage than any other group in these McCarthy days. I would soon be following with increasing incredulousness the Julian case, in which a judge of the New York State Supreme Court dismissed a libel suit against *Red Channels* without even calling on its publishers to enter a defense.* The judge, who before being elevated to the bench had been a successful and much-publicized prosecutor in the trials of some accused Communists, argued — to the surprise of many in the bar — that the publishers of

---

* This was Justice Irving Saypool in the suit of a CBS actor, Joseph Julian, against the publishers of *Red Channels*. To A. M. Sperber, biographer of Murrow, who testified for Julian and was constantly harassed by the judge, "the trial was a disaster, the presiding judge Irving Saypool . . . making no pretense to impartiality . . . narrowing admissability to zero levels, sustaining objections so as virtually to gag testimony on the blacklist, taking over cross-examination, like a prosecutor, from the bench, in tandem, at times, with the defense." A. M. Sperber: *Murrow: His Life and Times.*

Red Channels, before listing names, specifically disclaimed any intent to specify that those mentioned were Communists or even sympathizers with Communism. The judge accepted this at its face value. He went further. He cited in defense of the blacklisters their statement that in screening personnel, every safeguard must be used to protect the innocent. That a judge could take that statement seriously shocked me.

The Julian case seemed to prove that Morris Ernst, in refusing to take my money to sue *Red Channels*, was right. Later, as John Henry Faulk's 1962 libel suit against *Aware*, a blacklisting outfit similar to *Red Channels*, would show, you could win a case against them. Faulk, host of a talk show on CBS, was awarded over two million dollars in damages — a figure later cut down by the New York Court of Appeals to half a million, but a notable victory nevertheless because it appeared to help to end the era of blacklisting and its acceptance by the powers-that-be in broadcasting, films, and certain areas of journalism. A brilliant, flamboyant New York lawyer, Louis Nizer, had represented Faulk and, against all the odds, won.

I kept after Morris Ernst for years and finally gave up toward the end of the 1950s. But I remained puzzled at his reluctance to go forward.

Thirty years later I wondered if some revelations about Ernst's close relations at the time with the FBI and its director, J. Edgar Hoover, which were too shocking for me at first to believe but which turned out to be fully documented, explained in part his refusal to take on *Red Channels* for me.

Morris Ernst, the scrappy champion of civil rights, a power for decades in the American Civil Liberties Union, of which he was also counsel, the lawyer who fought notable battles in the courts against censorship of books and for the freedom of expression for writers, who had represented many a liberal target of the hysterical right, men like Heywood Broun, the wonderful columnist of the old *New York World* and founder of American Newspaper Guild, Edward R. Murrow, and Raymond Gram Swing — this sterling defender of the Bill of Rights *in cahoots* with J. Edgar Hoover, who opposed almost all that Ernst supposedly held dear* and who for years secretly aided the witch-hunters, Senator McCarthy, the House Un-American Activities Committee, the McCarran Senate Subcommittee, and others, including probably *Red Channels*, founded by three of his former FBI operatives, to smear and ruin many of the very men Ernst befriended and repre-

---

* They did share a hatred of Communism.

sented or publicly supported?! Morris Ernst *in cahoots* with a cop like that?!

That was what came out of the revelations, thanks to FBI papers obtained through the Freedom of Information Act by Professor Alan Theonaris of Marquette University, Harrison E. Salisbury, the former *New York Times* correspondent and editor who relied heavily on Theonaris, and others.

At first I could not believe it.

Even when Salisbury came out in *The Nation* on December 1, 1984, with his devastating report on "The Strange Correspondence of Morris Ernst and John Edgar Hoover — 1930–1964," I did no more than make a note to read *The Nation* piece sometime (I had noticed a story in the *Times* about it) and check with Salisbury, a friend, who lives not far from me in the Berkshires of Western Massachusetts and Connecticut. I had known Salisbury since World War II days overseas, admired him, respected his integrity, and liked his liberal outlook. But I thought maybe he had gone overboard this time, as all of us journalists did occasionally. I did not catch up with him and his article until the fall of 1986. Reading it and talking with him at length about it one evening left no doubt in my mind that he was revealing some truths about Ernst that none of his friends and clients like me had ever faintly suspected.

Salisbury's sad tale is based largely on the correspondence between these two quite different men. Of the many telephone calls and personal visits they had, there is less documentation. But the odd exchange of letters between the two men over twenty-five years offers enough to make us see Ernst in a somewhat new light; and it set me to wondering why, in my own case, he gave me a runaround in a matter that he knew almost destroyed me over a desperate decade.

The first thing that bothered me about the correspondence was Ernst's unbelievable fawning before the FBI director and his flattery of him. "Of course a lot of people think I am just a stooge for you, which I take as a high compliment. There are few people I'd rather support," Ernst wrote Hoover in January 1948. Between that date and 1952, Ernst would write — though I must admit I did not take notice — a number of articles, speeches, and books in which he lauded the FBI. Where his writings dealt with Communism, Ernst received a good deal of help, we now know, from the FBI and its files. He was duly grateful.

"You are a grand guy and I am in your army," he wrote Hoover on November 29, 1948. A year later he mused to the director that "I am fast becoming known as the person to pick a fight with in relation to the FBI."

All through the correspondence "What can I do for you? Can I help?" was a constant refrain in Ernst's letters. When Ernst went to Europe in December 1949, he wrote the director to ask if there was anything he could do "for you or your boys." He referred constantly to "your boys." In 1950, after Hoover had received a decoration from the king of England, Ernst wired him: "Congratulations, dear Knight. I will be in Washington tomorrow, Thursday. If you or any of your boys want to see a lowly layman, let me know."

Perhaps all this fawning and flattery before a very nasty cop was harmless. But it does not ring well in the ears of one who had admired and respected Ernst, as I had.

What *was* reprehensible in his relationship to Hoover, in my opinion, was that he sent the FBI director copies or originals of many confidential letters addressed to him (Ernst) without the knowledge, much less the consent, of those who wrote them. And in doing so, and on other occasions, he became what can only be termed an informer to the FBI.

There is, as Salisbury writes, "something unnerving about the spectacle of Ernst — Mr. Civil Liberties — sharing with Hoover this stream of intimate material" — for the lawyer turned over to the FBI on his own and without the knowledge of his colleagues a great deal of confidential material about what went on in the ACLU: memoirs, reports, minutes of meetings, copies of the correspondence of its various executives, including those of the grand old man of the organization, Roger Baldwin, its long-time secretary. What would those men and women, including many outside the ACLU, have thought — as Salisbury asks — if they (Arthur Garfield Hays, co-counsel of the ACLU; Roger Baldwin; Senator Wayne Morse; the editors of *The Nation* and *The New Republic,* and many others) had known that Ernst was secretly bringing their letters to the attention of the head of the FBI?

Even worse, to me, was the outright informing. Several examples of it come to light in the Ernst–Hoover correspondence. Once he gave Hoover the names of four associates of William Remington, a career government official convicted of perjury for having denied he turned over confidential documents to the Communists. Remington was sentenced to three years in the penitentiary at Lewisburg, Pennsylvania, where Alger Hiss was also confined and where Remington was murdered by an inmate.

On September 7, 1948, Ernst wrote the FBI director that he wanted to talk to him "in regard to a dame." Ernst said her brother was an important Communist party official. "I would like to talk to you," he added, "about this lady if you are in a position to let me give you some information." In 1953 he also wanted to give some information to the FBI about a man whom President Truman was considering as secretary of labor. The man's wife, Ernst reported, had been a Communist twenty years before. (Guilt by marriage?)

Sometimes Ernst was confronted with a conflict-of-interest problem, but he managed to handle it in his own way. When Hoover complained to Ernst that Murrow in his broadcasts was becoming critical of the FBI, the lawyer, who represented the broadcaster, replied that he would ask him to halt the criticism. Murrow's biographer reports that in 1951 Ernst "sold" Murrow the idea of doing a *See It Now* show about the FBI. Later he tipped Murrow off that CBS was hiring a former FBI man to screen its files.*

I did not care much either for another revelation in the Ernst–Hoover papers: that the lawyer on several occasions asked the FBI for advice as to whether he should take on a client. On May 17, 1944, he wrote Hoover for his opinion in regard to his accepting a prospective client, a German who had visa problems. An FBI memorandum of November 12, 1953, tells of Ernst's firm being asked to represent a man involved in the Alger Hiss case. "Morris may want to call us later about this when they get further details." The implication is that Ernst wanted FBI approval before taking on the client. Another FBI memorandum of June 1, 1950, indicates Ernst sought the Bureau's guidance about possibly representing Harry Gold, a confessed spy for the Soviet Union, who was implicated in the famous cases of Klaus Fuchs and the Rosenbergs. Fuchs would confess to delivering atomic secrets to the Russians; the Rosenbergs did not confess, and after being convicted had been sentenced to death. For a time Ernst was drawn even further into the Rosenberg case and was in touch with the FBI about it, informing Hoover's office that Julius Rosenberg's sister had asked him to do what he could to save her brother's life.

Ernst told the FBI that he indeed had an idea that might save Rosenberg's life: to obtain a confession that would reveal the Soviet atomic espionage ring in the United States in return for which Rosenberg would be spared being sent to the electric chair. If Julius Rosenberg "breaks and tells all he knows, this would be a terrific story

* Sperber, op. cit., pp. 371, 364.

and probably would be most helpful to the Bureau," he told Louis B. Nichols, a close aide to the FBI director. But he would not enter the case, Ernst added, unless "it was agreeable" to the FBI. In the meantime, could it send him as much information as possible on the Rosenbergs before going further?

Most people would agree — I certainly did — with something that Morris Ernst had repeated in private and public a thousand times: every accused person, no matter what he has done or who he is or what his beliefs are, has the right to the best possible legal defense. It was the credo, I believe, of the American bar. But as Salisbury asks: Is it usual for lawyers to consult the police before deciding whether or not to represent a client? Is it — I would add — ethical?

There is nothing in the FBI records so far revealed that Morris Ernst ever consulted Hoover about suing *Red Channels* on my behalf. Perhaps my case was regarded by both as not important enough to take up their time, though the files contain a good many requests for FBI advice about Ernst's representing clients on much smaller issues, such as visas. All I can say is that had I known of Ernst's cozy relationship with Hoover and the FBI, I would have given up on him and asked another lawyer — perhaps Louis Nizer, who was an acquaintance — to take my case. But to me, Morris Ernst was more than a lawyer. He was my friend. I believed in him as a great fighter for civil liberties. Including my own.

What baffled and saddened me about Harrison Salisbury's revelations was that Ernst, in view of his formidable battles for our constitutional freedoms, which I'm sure he regarded as the greatest achievement of his life, did not recognize what kind of a person he was dealing with in J. Edgar Hoover — a man who, as Salisbury reminds us, would eventually be "exposed as a primitive racist, a wiretapper of presidents, a blackmailer of politicians and a sympathizer of McCarthy." Morris must have known — every reporter and congressman knew — that Hoover was secretly assisting, with all the resources of the FBI, the various witch-hunters, especially Senator McCarthy, Senator McCarran, and the House Un-American Activities Committee. Ernst knew that the publishers of *Red Channels* were three former FBI employees of Hoover and that the FBI reportedly had helped them compile their list.

He repeatedly told me that despite all his efforts he could simply not come up with any idea to "cope" with *Red Channels*. Did he ever consult his friend Hoover? I now wonder.

*　　*　　*

Eventually, over the years, I recognized that though Ernst's refusal to take legal action against *Red Channels* was a setback in a situation that cost me dearly, the main guilt in the whole matter had to be assigned not so much to a hesitant lawyer or even to the publishers of the scurrilous blacklist, trying to make a buck from the anti-Communist hysteria, but much more to those powerful men who enforced the blacklisting: the executives of the radio and television networks, of the advertising agencies, of the corporations who sponsored programs on the air, the moguls of Hollywood, and the editors of some of our magazines.

They were the shabby cowards. If just one of them had shown a little courage and decency and said he was going to hire people on their merits and not on whether they were in *Red Channels*, the blacklists would have faded away. But none dared. Not one.

There were a few with guts in those dismal days. One was Jack Gould, the radio-television critic of the *New York Times*. He never ceased attacking *Red Channels* and exposing the hollowness and cowardice of those who caved in to it. And the *greed!* They did not do it, he said, out of any zealous patriotism in the face of what they perceived to be a Communist threat.

> . . . The governing motive was commercial expediency in desiring to avoid any controversy lest customers for a sponsor's product be offended.
>
> There was no real concern whether a person in *Red Channels* was guilty or innocent; either way he was "controversial" because he was in the book. . . .*
>
> With *Red Channels* the business community in broadcasting simply abdicated its citizenship in as dismal an hour as radio and TV ever had.†

A few others spoke up against the McCarthy delirium of the times. Foremost for me was a man I much admired and whom I knew slightly, federal judge Learned Hand, one of the most distinguished members of the bench in America — many lawyers rated him above any current

---

* Some of the perpetrators of *Red Channels* eventually broke away and went into the business of clearing (for a fee) some of those they had implicated in its pages. One of Kenneth M. Bierly's first paid jobs was clearing names for Columbia Pictures. He did this notably for the film actress Judy Holliday. "You can say," he told the press, "that Miss Holliday is not a Communist and neither are a lot of other people in it [*Red Channels*]."

"It was immaterial," he once explained, "whether they [the 151 listed in *Red Channels*] were Communists. . . . In the first place we don't know who's a Communist. In the second place, we couldn't find out if we had asked them. . . ."

† *New York Times*, June 6, 1954.

member of the Supreme Court. Learned Hand thought the American community was "in peril."

> I believe that a community is already in a process of dissolution where each man begins to eye his neighbor as a possible enemy, where nonconformity with the accepted creed, political as well as religious, is a mark of disaffection; where denunciation, without specification or backing, takes the place of evidence; where orthodoxy chokes freedom of dissent; where faith in the eventual supremacy of reason has become so timid that we dare not enter our convictions in the open lists to win or lose. Such fears . . . may in the end subject us to a despotism as evil as any that we dread. . . .
>
> Risk for risk, for myself I had rather take my chance that some traitors will escape detection than spread abroad a spirit of general suspicion and distrust, which accepts rumor and gossip in place of undismayed and unintimidated inquiry.

Henry Steele Commager, the great historian and an authority on the Constitution, also took a dim view of the predicament. "We are now embarked," he said, "upon a campaign of suppression and oppression more violent, more reckless, more pervasive and ultimately more dangerous than any in our history." He called on Americans caught up in the anti-Red convulsion to come to their senses.

Even President Harry Truman, who felt he had been obliged to institute loyalty oaths for federal civil servants in order to counter the rightist charges that he was "soft on Communism," spoke out. We were defending ourselves against Communism, he said. But we were also under another kind of attack: from those who were

> trying to create fear and suspicion among us by the use of slander, unproved accusations and just plain lies. . . . These slander-mongers are trying to get us so hysterical that no one will stand up to them for fear of being called a Communist.

He inveighed against "character assassination and guilt by association," against "slander and lies. These things are a threat to every single citizen. . . . When even one American, who has done nothing wrong, is forced by fear to shut his mind and close his mouth, then all Americans are in peril." He did not flinch from saying this to the American Legion.

I kept making notes of such statements. They gave me a little hope that the unholy spectacle would pass.

There was Robert M. Hutchins, chancellor of the University of Chicago, saying at its 237th convocation:

> Every day in this country, men and women are being deprived of their livelihood, or at least their reputation, by unsubstantiated charges. . . . We do not throw people into jail. . . . We throw them out of work.

And there was that old curmudgeon, Bernard de Voto, a kind of dyspeptic man I often disagreed with, writing in *Harper's* magazine words that warmed my heart. Announcing that he would no longer talk to the FBI or other official investigating bodies "about anyone whomsoever," he added:

> I like a country where it's nobody's damned business what magazines anyone reads, what he thinks. . . . I like a country where . . . what we say does not go into FBI files along with a note from S-17 that I may have another wife in California. I like a country where no college-trained flatfeet collect memoranda about us and ask judicial protection for them, a country where when someone makes statements about us to officials he can be held to account. We had that country only a little while ago and I'm for getting it back. It was a lot less scared than the one we've got now.

I noted in my diary at the farm on May 21, 1950, the eloquent words of Gerald W. Johnson, one of the grand old men of the *Baltimore Sun*, reviewing in the *New York Herald-Tribune Sunday Book Review* the first volume of the papers of Thomas Jefferson. He cited the famous letter Jefferson wrote to Dr. Benjamin Rush on September 23, 1780: "I have sworn on the altar of God eternal hostility against every form of tyranny over the minds of men."

To Johnson, this was

> the greatest thing that Jefferson ever wrote. Consider the impact of that assertion upon Americans of 1950. When in our country . . . have so many people so arrogantly assumed the right to tyrannize over the minds of men, dictating what they shall think, what they shall speak, how they shall vote, with whom they shall associate, and imposing moral obloquy, if not the pains of law, upon any who dares to question the dictum that all is for the best in the best of all possible worlds?

Appended to that diary entry is a clipping of an editorial in the *Washington Post*. It began:

> For weeks the Capitol has been seized and convulsed by terror. . . . What has permitted this thing to come to pass?
> The rising distrust, the roaring bitterness, the raging of Americans against Americans, the assault on the freedom of inquiry, the intolerance

of opposition — all this malaise, it seems to this newspaper, has its roots in a deep and troubled state of the Nation's mind.

So there *were* Americans — even newspapers — who still had guts, who still cared about our freedoms and realized how gravely they were threatened in this intolerant time. Amid the discouragements of those days I needed to be reminded of it. I needed to remind myself, too, that there were other Americans — including two friends of mine — who were faring much worse. I was being deprived of employment. They were, too. But they were also being publicly disgraced and destroyed.

The two friends were John Carter Vincent and Joseph Francken- stein. Both were distinguished members of the foreign diplomatic service — John Carter, a veteran of twenty-nine years, most of them spent in China; Joseph, a relative newcomer, who had arrived in America from his native Austria early in the war.

How our nation repaid these two men for their loyal service to their country still rankles in my blood. It was shabby, disgraceful, and unforgivable.

On April 27, 1954, Kay Boyle, Joseph's wife and an old friend since our Paris days in the late 1920s, wrote to me about her husband.

> Dear Bill:
> I shouldn't write you when I'm in a depressed state, as I am today, but I'm doing so anyway. On Saturday, Joseph was advised by the State Department that he has been suspended from the Foreign Service as a security risk, that new charges will be brought against him within thirty days, and that a hearing will be held in Washington. When will this madness end?

At the moment Joseph was teaching at a private school in Rowayton, Connecticut, being "on leave" from the Foreign Service pending further review of charges that had risen first in 1952 in Germany where he was head of Amerika Dienst, which supervised and aided American- sponsored newspapers and periodicals in our occupation zone. The charges were vague, to say the least. Apparently the chief accusation was that Franckenstein's loyalty to his country was subverted by his loyalty to his wife, who was targeted as being a Communist or Com- munist sympathizer. Guilt by marriage! The U.S. Consular Board, which conducted hearings, unanimously cleared Franckenstein of all charges. But in those days Senator McCarthy was the real power in America. Two of his minions, Roy Cohn, the McCarthy committee's consul, and his young friend G. David Schine, whose combined ignorance of foreign affairs was second to none, intervened during a junket to Europe to ferret out Communists from the ranks of American officials abroad — the "junketeering gumshoes," the reporters called them — and Joseph was suspended pending further inquiries in Washington as to his loyalty.

I remember my boiling resentment when Kay wrote me of what happened. How many Americans, I thought, would have had the guts to volunteer, as Joseph had, to be parachuted behind the enemy lines during the war and risk being captured, tried as a spy, and executed? Not I, certainly. And surely not his hysterical accusers. In fact, McCarthy and Cohn were protesting loudly at Schine's being drafted, charging that it must be due to some Communists in the U.S. Army, which they were about to take on as their next victim.

So Joseph Franckenstein was out of a job and so was his wife. For *The New Yorker,* which had accredited Kay Boyle as its correspondent in Germany, withdrew her accreditation as soon as her husband was in trouble — an act for which Kay never forgave the magazine and its editor, William Shawn.

Over the next years Kay and Joseph spent all their spare time and all their money collecting papers and documents to prove Franckenstein's loyalty to his adopted country. And that he was not a Communist! The charge seemed so senseless to those who had known him. For Joseph came from an old and conservative Catholic family in the Austrian Tyrol. His cousin, George Franckenstein, had been the Austrian ambassador in London, and when the Nazis took over in Vienna in 1938, he had promptly resigned. In recognition of his integrity the British government had knighted him — a rare honor.

I marveled at the zeal and persistence of Kay and Joseph, year after year assembling an immense dossier to support his defense. They were fiercely determined to prove one thing at least: that Joseph had always been a loyal citizen and official. It was a question of personal honor. In my impatience with the cowardly officials in Washington who lived in unholy fear of McCarthy (even President Eisenhower for too long was intimidated), I thought it would be enough for their lawyer to get up at a public hearing and simply ask — as I had asked myself — who could be more loyal to his country than a man who had risked his life for it, as Joseph had done, and had come so close to losing it?

Kay and her husband toiled away for nine years to clear his name. Their lawyers, Edward Greenbaum in America and Benjamin Ferencz in Germany, aided them immensely — and without pay. Finally, in 1962, Joseph Franckenstein was cleared of all charges. The State

Department apologized for the long ordeal it had put him through and reinstated him . . . but in what at that time was certainly not one of its most attractive posts: he was sent to Teheran as cultural attaché. He might be exonerated, but he was not exactly welcomed back by the State Department. Teheran was considered a faraway, primitive post. Few of the embassy personnel brought along their families. And for a man who had ruined his health in his fight for honorable survival it was a cruel exile. Six months after he went to Teheran, Kay and their son, Ian, joined him. But they found a dying man. He was flown to an American military hospital in Germany and operated on for a malignant brain tumor. When he was brought back to Walter Reed Hospital in Washington, it was discovered that he also had lung cancer.

It was obvious that he would not recover. Kay searched around for a job to support them and found one as a professor of English (though she had no academic degrees) at San Francisco State College. They flew out to the West Coast together in September 1963 — she to her new place of work, he to the army hospital in the Presidio in San Francisco. There he died a few weeks later at the age of fifty-three.

Though John Carter Vincent had spent most of his career abroad in China, Tess and I met him in Geneva in 1939 when he arrived to serve on the American delegation to the International Labor Organization, of which John C. Winant, a former governor of New Hampshire and a wonderfully Lincolnian sort of a man, was president. John Carter seemed to me more Jeffersonian in his views and his nature, reflecting the soft accents of the South and an old-fashioned American liberalism. His wife, Betty, was a vivacious, dynamic, attractive woman. We all quickly became fond friends.

Shortly after I returned home from Germany at the end of 1940, I found that John Carter was off again to China. During most of the remaining war years he was counselor of the American embassy in Chungking and became influential in working out what American policy there was toward Nationalist China. (Under Roosevelt and Hull it was confused.) Returning home, he became chief of the Office of Far Eastern Affairs in the State Department, then minister to Switzerland and finally minister to Tangier.

He was in Tangier on the night of December 15, 1952, when he received a telegram from the secretary of state informing him that the Civil Service Commission's Loyalty Review Board had found that there was "reasonable doubt" of his loyalty to the United States. The board recommended that his services be terminated. The department was suspending him immediately.

This was not the first time Vincent had been in trouble. Ever since the end of the war he had been attacked by right-wing Republicans, by their supporters in the press, and by the China Lobby as having helped to "lose" China to the Communists. Silly as this charge was — since "winning" or "losing" China was beyond American power — it had been taken up by a surprisingly large number of influential Americans. In 1947, Republicans in the Senate had held up for six months John Carter's appointment as minister to Switzerland. In 1950, McCarthy had publicly branded Vincent as a "Communist spy" and sent an emissary secretly to Europe to get the goods on him.

In those years after the war John Carter and I were drawn closer together by this shared fate: we were both victims of McCarthyism and of the anti-Communist hysteria that swept across the nation. But I soon began to realize that my friend was in a much worse predicament than I. The witch-hunters were out to ruin his career, drive him from office, disgrace him by questioning his loyalty to the country he had served so well for so long, and destroy him.

What happened to this gallant, decent, patriot I summed up with sadness in a letter I wrote to the *New York Times* on December 6, 1972, and which was published on December 14.

> To the Editor:
> The death this week in Cambridge of John Carter Vincent marks the passing of one of the last of that small group of brilliant Foreign Service officers who spent most of their professional lives representing their country in China and who, because they tried to tell their Government the truth about that complex country, were shabbily dismissed as disloyal and probably Communist, their careers ruined in the Joe McCarthy–John Foster Dulles time. . . .
> Vincent, in fact, was a rather old-fashioned Southern Jeffersonian Democrat of the Woodrow Wilson stripe and to accuse him of being a Communist and "disloyal to the United States," as Senators McCarthy and McCarran did, seemed ludicrous to those of us who had known him for a long time.
> What hurt him most was the charge of disloyalty, sustained by a 3-to-2 vote of the Civil Service Loyalty Review Board, for he was passionately devoted to this country and had spent the best years of his life trying to serve it in a dozen posts abroad and at home.
> What hurt him too — and outraged me — was Dulles' asinine charge in dismissing him that Vincent had "failed to meet the standard demanded of a Foreign Service officer." Everyone knew he was one of the very best in the service.
> Dulles knew it too. Not long after he fired Vincent "for incompetence"

in 1953, he pleaded with him . . . to meet him secretly in the privacy of his home to help him find a way out of what he called the "China mess."

Though his friends, I among them, advised him against it, Vincent, out of stubborn loyalty to the country and perhaps because he believed he had been right about China all along (he had predicted Chiang's quick collapse after the war), swallowed his pride and accepted the secretary's call for help.

An ungrateful nation retired Vincent, after 28 years in the Foreign Service, on a pension of $6,200 a year. This, it seemed to me, was the final insult. (Dismissed generals would get a great deal more, and tax free.)

John Carter was puzzled by all that had happened to him, but he was not bitter, though his career had been ruined and his reputation as a decent citizen smeared. For the last nineteen years he cultivated his garden in Garden Street in Cambridge, played with his grandchildren, continued his Chinese studies, did a little work at Harvard and Radcliffe, tried to learn more about his own country whose Government had cast him out — an intelligent, scholarly, tolerant, courtly gentleman with a slight Georgia drawl and an integrity that could not be shaken to the last.

William L. Shirer
Lenox, Mass., Dec. 6, 1972

CHAPTER 5

All through the 1950s I found myself struggling to earn a living, finally forcing myself to realize that further regular employment in the profession to which I had given my life for a quarter of a century was now pretty much out of the question. I had not waited around for something to turn up. I had spent ten hours a day writing away at books. They were being published. But they were not bringing me a living. I did not need much. We lived, as we always had, a modest life. We did not have to have much to pay the nominal rent in New York, the taxes on the farm, part-tuition for the girls' school, and the bills for clothing, food, and drink.

On New Year's Day, 1951, at the farm I reviewed, as usual, the year just gone by. Outwardly it was dominated by the Korean war, which I supported. In my own life it was noteworthy for the publication on November 3 of my first novel, *The Traitor*.

It has sold fairly well but . . . obviously I cannot live from novels. . . . And I have to confess that at 47 (which I'll be next month) I have not yet solved the problem of making a living. . . . Radio would help . . . but I seem to be blacklisted from that. It is puzzling how journalism, in which I made a certain mark, I think, has so little use for those who not so long ago were hailed as being near the top. (I think of Sheean, who complains of being broke, and of Dosch-Fleurot, a great correspondent of the old *World*, starving away in Madrid. . . .*

My only course, as I see it this New Year's Day, is to struggle along making what I can from lectures and mag. articles, keep my eye out for radio or TV, and ABOVE ALL ELSE, continue to *write, write, write*. . . .

On February 23, my birthday, I went up to Cambridge to speak to a Harvard Law School Forum.

* Vincent Sheean, a *Chicago Tribune* colleague of mine and a lifelong friend, was one of the most distinguished journalists of our time, the author of a number of fine books, including his autobiography *Personal History*. I have written of him in the first volume of these memoirs. Of Dosch-Fleurot, too, who gave me the chance to return to Berlin in 1934 and begin a new reporter's career in the Third Reich.

47 today! . . . Nearly 50, nearly an old man; and nothing substantial accomplished yet. A slow starter, perhaps?!

At the end of the summer of 1951 at the farm I summed up the year thus far:

Farm, August 31. The summer over, the first maple leaves starting to turn, . . . and I have let the summer flit by without accomplishing much. Wrote about half the "Journey" book, and broadcast three times a week for a sheer cash income for a living.

The broadcasts were for Gordon McClendon's short-lived "Liberty" Radio Network, for which such liberals as Raymond Swing and John Vandercook also broadcast that summer. I guess this was too big a dose of "liberalism." I forget how soon Raymond and John faded out, but I was replaced at summer's end by John Flynn, whom I described in my diary as "a pseudo-Fascist, . . . pro-Jap and pro-Nazi." So once again, after a summer's reprieve, I faced a "cash-flow" problem as autumn came.

It was cold and rainy today, and dark, and I gave some thought to how I should earn a living this year, and I was depressed. Then I read from Joseph Conrad. He cheered me. . . . For Conrad in his novels was concerned primarily with how man meets adversity. It is only at the moments of crisis that he proves himself as a person of character, even of worth. "We begin to live," he says, "when we have conceived life as a tragedy. . . ."

Often I wrote rough memos to myself on "projects" that might bring in some money.

August 27, 1951:
Money . . . with radio over, must find means.

1. TV bites, but nothing to count on.
2. Radio. Not much prospect . . . *Red Channels.*
3. Book. Will finish "Midcentury Journey." But you can't live off books.
4. Mag. articles. But I dislike doing them, and have no entry to the mags. that pay.
5. Play. Finish the "diplo" one. But it's a long chance.
6. Better. The Hitler Play.
7. Play on native's return. See notes.
   "A Coming Home"
   "Return of the Native"
   "A Native's Return."

8. Movies . . . Again have no entry there.
9. Lectures. Good. But not enough to live on.
10. A "column." I'd like this, next to writing books. But small chance. Field already is overcrowded.

I peppered my literary agent, Paul R. Reynolds, with memos full of ideas for magazine articles, stories for the films and TV, and formats for an evening TV news roundup. I kept after him about selling my books abroad, to paperbacks here, and to the movies. I had a thousand ideas.

I even turned to writing plays — an old weakness of mine. I had found three years earlier, while working on *The Traitor,* that I could best develop my characters and the plot by doing it first roughly as a play. This had been mentioned in the press, with the result that one evening at dinner Armina Marshall, associate director of the Theatre Guild, had brought it up and followed with a letter that greatly cheered me.

> The Theatre Guild, Inc.
> July 31, 1948
>
> Dear Mr. Shirer:
> Remember our conversation over dinner not so many months ago . . . when you told me you were going to do a play, and promised that we might have a look at it? How is it coming along, and what about letting us see it?
>
> Warm personal regards,
> Armina Marshall

This was encouraging. Armina Marshall was the wife of Lawrence Langner, co-director with Theresa Helburn of the Theatre Guild, which had brought good theater back to this country, beginning with the plays of Eugene O'Neill, our greatest playwright.

I got the first draft of the play, rough as it was, typed and at the end of August sent it off to Armina Marshall. On September 22, 1948, she wrote back at considerable length.

> Mr. Langner and I both enjoyed reading THE TRAITOR and think you have done an extraordinarily good job. From a standpoint of structure and suspense interest and technique, it is quite professional and definitely shows you know your way about the stage.

They had plenty of specific criticism, chiefly that the main character was not sufficiently developed.

The incidents in the play are strong. Whether they register as melo-dramatic or dramatic depends on the depth of characterization, and here is where we think the work should be done.

We also think that the play might be marketable in its present form for it certainly is a stirring and an exciting picture. If, however, you should feel that some rewriting is necessary, we hope you will give us an opportunity of reading the play again.

Making allowances for the Langners' obvious gentleness and tact toward an aspiring playwright, their response had been one of the few bright spots in my life at that time. I no longer remember why I did not take up their challenge to work on the play. It certainly needed it. Perhaps there was at the moment no time, what with deadlines to meet on the novel and the necessity of working at other things to bring in some cash. It was probably too early for me to recognize that my talents did not lie in writing fiction. I went ahead doing play versions of the other novels I wrote and published in the 1950s, one of which actually received a semiprofessional production at a small theater in a provincial American town.

In my determination to exist, I also turned again to the radio-TV agents. Television had not yet been developed far enough to have regular news shows. I spent months working out plans for first a Sunday TV thirty-minute review of the week and then, when that had been established, for a regular thirty-minute news roundup each evening. Nothing ever came of it. One of my former agents, at least, did not give me the runaround. Herb Rosenthal at MCA had represented me in the big-money days. When I asked him whether he would like to take me on again, he replied frankly that "MCA would not find it to their advantage to represent you today."

But usually it was the runaround. For two or three years, as tele-vision was coming in, I took my ideas to an old friend of mine, a former vice-president of CBS who had moved over with the same title to NBC. He was always most cordial and interested. He said he liked my ideas. He hoped he could bring me into NBC soon to develop them further. TV would be the future medium for news, he agreed with me. But I should be patient. The networks were still groping with the problem. I fed the man my ideas for a couple of years before another friend at NBC, more honest, took me aside one day and said I was wasting my time. My vice-president friend would never do anything for me at NBC. On account of *Red Channels*. Of course, he would never say so. Afraid.

By 1952 I was beginning to try to face reality. An entry in my diary recalls it. One week that spring I had lunched with a well-known radio-TV agent. He had been decent enough to suggest I concentrate on some other activity — "writing, for example," he said — for a living. I had also lunched with my literary agent to discuss my dreary prospects as a writer.

New York, April 10, 1951. . . . Somehow these two luncheons this week helped me to bring on another spell of depression. . . .

I know what I want to do. Continue writing. But I have a . . . family to support. . . . When I try to think merely of how I am going to earn a living during the next six months — until the fall lecture season begins — I am completely baffled — for the first time in my adult life, I think.

When you are considered down, if not out — and I suspect most people who know me, or of me, have written me off * — one's friends drop away. . . . It has happened now. Not only with our general friends; but with the three or four closest friends. Even the Gunthers have become chilly and avoid us. I have seen them once, I think, in six months.

Tess says: wait until you have a book that goes. They'll all come tripping back then.

I found a way out, sort of, in lecturing. The Red-baiters had invaded this field, too, and were trying to hound anyone left of McCarthy out of business. A handful of lecture dinner clubs and similar groups did cancel when the vigilantes brought pressure on them. But thanks to the colleges and universities, which sponsored most of the lectures those days and which had more guts than the advertising agencies, sponsors, networks, and filmmakers, they were thwarted. In the McCarthy time they were a bastion of free speech and the only one we had.

* In those days *Newsweek* ran a column entitled "Where Are They Now?" Each week it named a couple of persons it pointed out were once prominent in their fields but who had not been heard of in some time. It was not malicious in tone or content but, as the title indicated, insinuated that its subjects had hit the end of the trail and were has-beens if not failures. No one heard of them anymore. What had happened to them? Where were they now? In *Newsweek*, November 25, 1957, the column featured two persons under the rubric "Where Are They Now?" Elmer Davis, my former colleague at CBS, director of the Office of War Information, a distinguished writer and caustic wit and a wonderful man; and me. Davis had retired from radio because of ill health and was living in Washington with his wife.

About me: "William L. Shirer, made famous by his nightly radio reports from Berlin during the early days of World War II and by his book 'Berlin Diary,' has been off the air nearly ten years and is now a writer and part-time lecturer." It said I was "presently working on a book," and gave its title.

Wasn't that what the press usually said about someone consigned to oblivion? That he "was working on a book"? A sort of face-saving expression for those considered "finished"?

One thing consoled me about "making" that column. I was proud to be coupled with Elmer Davis.

Some of my correspondence about the lecture cancellations makes amusing reading today. A Marshall I. Hewitt, M.D., chairman of the program committee of the Knife and Fork Club of South Bend, Indiana, which had booked me for a talk on October 16, 1951, hastened to write in May calling attention to an attack on me in *Counterattack*. Among other things, I was accused of speaking at a dinner given "by the pro-Communist 'Churchman' "in 1948. I had, indeed. It happened to be a dinner the *Churchman* gave to honor General Eisenhower, who was present.

"We have been very cautious," Dr. Hewitt wrote, "in screening the prospective speakers for the South Bend Knife and Fork Club in our attempt to weed out those who were pink or even faintly pink-tinged. Obviously, we do not desire to have speakers of a questionable background."

I replied to the good doctor that my background was well known, having been built up in countless newspaper dispatches, radio broadcasts, speeches, lectures, and books. I could not hide it if I wished. In view of his doubts, however, I canceled the talk. When I challenged the doctor to release the exchange of letters to the press, he replied that he "had no right to."

A couple of years later the Dallas Council on World Affairs lost its nerve when some vigilantes threatened to picket an address it had booked me to make. The frightened executive director had first written imploring me not to mention "World Government" in my talk. He did not want to censor me, he said, but explained that the council was "facing a very peculiar situation . . . in which a small but vociferous group of fanatics are creating a great uproar about 'world government.' " A week before my scheduled performance the poor director became frantic. He called my lecture agent and asked to cancel. It would be "disastrous" for me to appear in Dallas, he said. The council's office had been picketed and he feared the worst — apparently a bloody riot. By this time I had already canceled the engagement, along with some others, having come down with the flu.

The esteemed Dallas Council on World Affairs need not have been so fainthearted. I usually had problems when I spoke in Dallas, but they were easily handled. Once at a lecture at Southern Methodist University a white-haired, rambunctious aged lady of the Dallas right had sat in the front row and heckled me throughout my talk. I had simply turned up the microphone and gone on speaking. Few people in the hall could hear the good lady's ravings. At the end, though, she provided a hilarious scene. Despite her age, she leaped to the platform as I finished speaking, grabbing the microphone with one hand and the lapel of my dinner jacket with the other. (Before leaving on the tour, my wife had affixed on the lapel, as she usually did, the red ribbon of the Legion of Honor, which the French government had given me at the end of the war.)

"What is that red ribbon?!" my charming heckler asked, yelling into the microphone and tugging at my coat lapel so firmly she was almost choking me. I was surprised at the strength of a woman so old.

"Why, madam," I said. "That is the *Order of Lenin!*"

"Did you hear that?" she cried to the audience. "I tried to tell you he was a punk Communist. Now he admits it. He confesses that that red ribbon, which I hold in my grasp" — at which point she tried to rip it off — "is the Order of Lenin."

She stepped proudly aside to await the applause of all true patriots. Instead, the audience roared with laughter.

Dallas in the 1950s was full of rather fanatical conservatives, it is true; and many of them were mindless or loony and very rich. The main currents of American thought, in all their diversity, had not reached them. They did not have much sense of history. It did not surprise me that one of Dallas's sterling citizens — a woman at that, as I recall — spat upon Adlai Stevenson when he was running for president. But I always liked the rough and tumble of speaking there. Maybe I was lucky: no one ever spat on me. And I was never run out of town on a rail.

Except that it took a great deal of time from writing, I rather liked the first couple of years of lecturing. For one who had been away so long, it provided the opportunity of seeing large parts of the country for the first time. There were very few colleges, universities, cities, and towns I did not visit over the lecture years. I got acquainted with the South, which was almost like a foreign land, and with the West, which I loved; and I got renewed contact with my native Middle West. There were not many spots in New England, my postwar home, that I missed. I summed up my first impressions of my new calling in a letter of December 27, 1949, to Howard Smith, who had replaced Ed Murrow for CBS in London.

I have just returned from a long lecture trip of one-night stands through your own deep South. And while it is very interesting to get reacquainted with your native land after a long absence, lecturing is no leisurely way of life. One comes back exhausted. It does have its point though. . . . For one thing you can say pretty much what you damn please. And that's becoming a luxury in this country.

A year later I was writing in my diary:

Farm, Sun., Dec. 10, 1950. Finally finished six weeks of lecturing in the West and Southwest, a little tired. . . . It's a rugged way to earn a living . . . Hope to skip it next year, if I can earn more of my living writing — or perhaps go back to broadcasting, part-time — for I will NOT give up writing. . . .

Sometimes I noted how it was, rushing up and down the land. Nostalgia crept in when I came across familiar places.

Sunday, October 29, 1950. On the Union Pacific between Chicago and Portland.

So many spots along the way bring back memories. Now at 3 P.M. coming into Sidney, Nebraska, where one summer during college I worked in the harvest fields. Yesterday evening coming into Chicago on the N.Y. Central and the train stopping at 63rd Street and Woodlawn. I sat there for a moment trying to grasp that it was here, on this spot, that I was born and grew up until I was 9. Last night it looked utterly strange. There seemed no connection between this place and me. And I thought of how much change and wandering there is in life, for at 8, say, when my father was still alive and young and progressing in his profession [law] and very much rooted to this city, it would not have occurred to me or to him that one could wander so far from this neighborhood that in time it became completely lost, so that when you passed by many years later there was nothing to identify you with your birthplace except a cold calculation in your memory.

Last night sometime after midnight the train passed through Cedar Rapids, Iowa, where I grew up, but I was asleep. . . . My mother lies buried there — and my father — and it was my home from 9 years of age to 21, when I left and struck out for Paris.

Reading Mark Twain on the train brought my thoughts back to Cedar Rapids:

In a letter to William Dean Howells he gives a clue to something that has always puzzled me: why when I go back to C.R. everything there — the two homes we lived in, the parks, the business district, the leading hotel, the college campus, the town itself, all seem so SMALL . . . much smaller than when I knew them as a youngster. Says M.T.: "When a man goes back to look at the house of his childhood, it has always *shrunk:*

there is no instance of such a house being as big as the picture in memory and imagination calls for."*

And always impressions of the people and the wonderful land.

Farm, Sun., Dec. 10, 1950. . . . To remember from the last week of the lecture tour: the sun in Tucson . . . and Frances O'Brien painting my portrait and making me look like Yeats, which I don't, and the talk with her coming back from Mexico about Freud and Jung and Catholicism (she wanted to convert me). . . . And the madonna-like faces of the Mexican women in the streets of Nogales . . . and the faces of the greedy, selfish little men gathering around the new governor-elect of Arizona (Howard Pyle) in the hotel lobby in Phoenix. . . . And a Mrs. Parsons, who had driven me in from the airport, remarking on the necessity of impeaching "that Jew Frankfurt on the Supreme Court" . . . and Pyle, a radio commentator, who seemed like a nice, sensitive fellow tho not very strong, confessing to me that the grab for spoils was getting him down, and he looked down. . . .

The winds of Amarillo blowing steady in gale force the whole time, unlike any other I have ever felt anywhere in the whole world. . . . Talullah Bankhead making her debut in Dallas as a lecturer, chain-smoking the entire time. . . . The five-hour bus ride from Odessa, Texas, to Alpine across the arid land . . . the dazzling sun and the fatigue and yet the beauty of it, esp. when the mountains, which I had not expected, appeared on the horizon and we started to climb. . . .

"We have such a wonderful country to live in," I wrote in my diary in Los Angeles, Sunday, November 12, 1950, "as one who has just crossed it from coast to coast can see."

And we have a fine people, sober, well-meaning, generous, full of good humor. And we are ruining ourselves by our outrageous hysteria and suspicion. And by our attempts at thought control.

I had got the results of the midterm national elections the Tuesday before when I arrived in Oakland, California. In this state Congressman Richard Nixon had beaten Congresswoman Helen Gahagan Douglas in what local newspapermen told me was one of the nastiest campaigns the great state had ever seen. Nixon, already making his

---

* As I noted in the first volume of these memoirs, André Maurois made a similar observation, inspired by Marcel Proust's attempt to recapture the past in À la recherche du temps perdu (Remembrance of Things Past):

It is vain [he wrote] that we return to places we have loved: we will never see them again because they were situated not in space but in time, and the man who looks for them will be no more a child or an adolescent who embellished them with his imagination.

name in the House of Representatives as a Red-baiter, had smeared Mrs. Douglas with the Communist label; and in the present hysteria, it had worked. But not only in California. Republicans had clobbered the Democrats, especially in the Senate races, on the "Communist" issue: Taft in Ohio, Dirksen in Illinois, for example. They, with Nixon, Capehart and Jenner of Indiana, McCarthy and others like them were going to take over the Senate and then, they hoped, the country. Did they really believe what they bellowed: that the Communists were about to take over the country? What Communists? There weren't enough in the United States to elect a dogcatcher, much less a congressman.

In Los Angeles, I stayed with Bob Ardrey, the playwright and film writer, and his wife.

> The Ardreys gave me an almost unbelievable picture of the pressure here on everyone to conform, and of the wild and reckless branding of liberals as Communists. Famous actors, they say, who used to support liberal causes are frightened to death. . . . Movie producers and directors . . . are likewise gripped with fear that they may be tabbed as "Commies.". . .

It was no better in Hollywood four years later, judging by a little experience of my own. A Hollywood film producer had gone overboard, I thought, about doing a picture based on my novel *Stranger Come Home*. Then he had had second thoughts. Perhaps there was something subversive in it after all that had escaped the first reading. But it wasn't that. My Hollywood agent explained to my New York agent.

> Wray Davis and Tom Gries were in this afternoon. Davis now feels he was a little impetuous about Shirer's *Stranger Come Home*. He would like to test a few organizations, such as the American Legion, to find out if they would actively demonstrate against such a film.

Lecturing never gave me quite a living, but it provided most of it through the hysterical 1950s. Lecture agents were a particularly greedy breed. They took fifty percent of your fee for booking you and for paying your transportation. You yourself paid the biggest part of the expenses, food and lodging. A fifty percent fee hurt. But it provoked in me a strange illusion. My agent would book me, say, for five lectures a week (in five different towns) for five hundred dollars a lecture. This meant twenty-five hundred dollars a week, which seemed a lot of money for me; and if you multiplied it by the six weeks you were out in a season, it came to fifteen thousand dollars — almost all I needed for the year. I kept forgetting that I would receive only half of that, or seventy-five hundred dollars; and that the bill for hotels and food would knock off another two thousand dollars, so the net was not so big. I also kept forgetting the bite of federal and state income taxes. Even for two seasons, the spring and autumn tours, the net — after taxes — was hardly enough to keep us above the official poverty level.

Once in a great while I got what for me was a whopper of a fee.

This happened, for instance, the time I became a last-minute substitute speaker for Mrs. Eleanor Roosevelt. One early winter evening in New York she telephoned me. She had a bad case of laryngitis and put her secretary on the phone to explain that she was due to address a Hadassah group at luncheon the next day in Buffalo. Could I replace her? There were no night planes to the city. It was snowing and it was doubtful if there would be any flights the next morning in time to get me into Buffalo by noon. The last night train left in an hour. I hurriedly packed, had trouble finding a taxi, but finally caught the train as it was pulling out of Grand Central Station.

I'll never forget the faces of the fifteen hundred good women of Hadassah in the ballroom of the hotel in Buffalo when they saw me, instead of Mrs. Roosevelt, emerge from a side room and take my place with the officers of the organization at the speaker's table. There had been no time to inform the membership of the last-minute change. I glanced across the room at the sea of faces. In all my life I have never seen such expressions of surprise, letdown, disappointment, even pain. But the good ladies were game. They heard me out. They applauded warmly, even if it was hard to do. I made it a little easier for the organization by offering to take just half of Mrs. Roosevelt's fee of twenty-five hundred dollars. At that, it was more than twice what I usually got. It became less, of course, as you forked over fifty percent to the lecture agent.

Once in a while a quite unexpected person would show up in the audience at one of my lectures. And this would help compensate for the dreariness and frustrations of the one-night stands. I have a note saying that

former President and Mrs. Truman came out to hear my address to a district conference of Rotary at Independence, Mo., April 26, 1957. Following the speech we had a good talk [over drinks at their home, as

I remember] about foreign affairs, the subject of my talk, and about the
Truman Library . . . which will be formally opened in July.

Next morning Mr. Truman personally guided me through the library. He was terribly proud of it. The former president could be much
too generous in his comments about me as a journalist on whom, he
would say, he had often depended in the past for information on what
was going on in the world. Seeing my present eclipse and indeed
expulsion from my old profession, this was bound to buck me up. On
one occasion Mr. Truman went a little far. This was at Chicago, where
he told the annual convention of the Booksellers Association that in the
years that led up to the war — and especially in the war years — he
had regularly read copies of my dispatches and broadcasts and often
found them of much more worth than the dispatches reaching him from
the State Department. It was a whopping exaggeration and embarrassing for me to hear.

Also friendly to me was General George C. Marshall, whom I did not
know personally until he turned up at a lecture of mine to some group
at Pinehurst, North Carolina, composed almost entirely of retired army
officers, who naturally were rather conservative and rigid in their
views. Most of them disagreed strongly with some of my views on
foreign affairs, and there was a lively question-and-answer period at the
end of the talk. At one point, General Marshall, who had been sitting
in the front row, jumped up to defend me. After the meeting we
adjourned for a drink and some private talk. He complimented me for
speaking out. He seemed depressed about the state of the country,
which McCarthy and his supporters were terrorizing. The witch-
hunting senator from Wisconsin had accused Marshall of "treason" and
proclaimed that he had made common cause with Stalin. Even President Eisenhower, in fear of McCarthy, had once dropped from a
speech a defense of the general who had been his boss and benefactor
during the war as chief of the Army General Staff. For my money,
General Marshall, who also had served as secretary of state and secretary of defense and who received the Nobel Peace Prize in 1953, was
one of the great Americans of our time, not only a patriot but a man of
integrity and decency at a lamentable time in our history when those
qualities were in short supply among the men who were running our
country.

Often when I got weary of the lecturing and frustrated, I would tell
myself that more important writers than I would ever be had had to

lecture for a part of their living. The list was long but it included Emerson, Mark Twain, and, in my own time, the wonderful lyric poet Edna St. Vincent Millay.

Still, I kept chafing at the burden. Up at the farm on New Year's Day, 1953, while doing my annual review of the previous year, I tried to face up to the problem. I had written sixty thousand words up to Labor Day on a new novel, but lecturing from early October until mid-December had drastically reduced any further writing.

> The catch is the damned lectures, which break up the continuity and the rhythm and the discipline of writing. . . . An occasional tour would still be beneficial to any writer or journalist who lives in N.Y. But I have seen every section of the country now and talked to tens of thousands of people, and the lectures largely bore me and they fill me with a terrible frustration because they make continued writing impossible.

I also began to realize that there was something insidious and terribly harmful in lecturing. Morris Ernst had warned me of it years before. With all the adulation you got, you risked taking yourself seriously. There was no real debate to keep your wits sharpened, your ego dampened, and your mind clear of cobwebs. And practically repeating the same lecture night after night, week after week, was stultifying.

Vernon Louis Parrington, the great but largely unrecognized historian of American thought, had pointed out the consequences of lecturing to John Fiske, a philosopher and historian who in the beginning had possessed one of the finest American minds of the nineteenth century and who as a young man had proved too radical and daring and modern to be accepted at first on the faculty at Harvard, as he had hoped.

> Driven to other means of support he turned to lecturing . . . and thereafter to the end of his life suffered much of his vast energy to drain off into that most fruitless of jobs for a creative mind. A certain genial egoism was to blame for his playing willingly the role of lackey to women's clubs. He liked to talk to sympathetic audiences, and he was greatly effective on the platform. The inevitable result was that he fell short in accomplishment of the fine promise of his early years. His style became diffuse, his materials picturesque rather than solid, his thinking flabby. Pretty much all his significant work was done before he was forty.

Lecturing had had a similar effect on William Jennings Bryan. I had seen it myself as a high-school youth working Chautauqua, where Bryan for years lectured daily to throngs of delirious listeners, for he was a dazzling spellbinder. He had been, after all, as I mentioned in the first volume of these memoirs,

> one of America's foremost political figures — three times the Democratic candidate for President, and Secretary of State, for a time, under President Wilson. . . . He had been the idol of millions, including me.

But after a quarter of a century of lecturing he had become, it seemed to me, "an empty shell, a vain and foolish old man, blabbering banalities." Lecturing had destroyed him.

> It had stultified his mind, deadening it against the reception of new ideas as the world continued to change. He repeated the same speech, day after day, year after year, to the same roaring applause, which fed his vanity but left his mind emptied and dry. There was no one against whom he could sharpen it. His eloquence remained unimpaired, as did his magnetism at the tribune. But even as he continued to sway the masses with his repetitious oratory, he retreated more and more from reality, perhaps unaware of the banality, the triviality, of the haven he had found under the Chautauqua tents.*

"Still, few writers . . . can live exclusively from writing," I noted again in my diary of January 1, 1953, at the farm as I tried once more to figure out what to do.

> . . . I had no employment in radio or TV during the past year, except for a few guest appearances mostly in connection with the publication of *Midcentury Journey.* CBS canceled the two or three I had been scheduled for on its network.
>
> Quite obviously I am (still) banned . . . because of *Red Channels.* It has been as effective in "free" America as an official list in Germany or Russia under Hitler or Stalin. No executive in radio or advertising DARES hire anyone thus blacklisted. . . . It is the law of the U.S. radio and TV . . . and it has deprived me of the living I formerly made in the medium. I think it has also made it next to impossible for me to sell anything to the big magazines, and it must have something to do with the iciness of the *Herald-Tribune* proprietors, who formerly, when I wrote regularly for the paper, were so warm and friendly. . . .
>
> This being driven out of my profession by . . . the hysteria of the times has puzzled and troubled me. . . . And I have had to fight hard — inside — to make sure it did not DEFEAT me.
>
> I do not think it has.
>
> What is important . . . is not to give in, not to surrender, not even to withdraw from the fight, as one is tempted to do. . . .

* William L. Shirer, *20th Century Journey, The Start.* New York, 1976, pp. 162–163.

In the meantime one can achieve some sort of happiness in one's personal life. You can keep on building an inner life. I still get much out of books. . . . And there is music. And the land here: nature, the soil, the woods, the flowers, the plants, the trees, the changing seasons. They have been very important the last few years.

And the family of course, the center of my personal life.

And a few friends remain true; not many but a few. And as one grows older so many tragedies befall those you have known that at times you think that you yourself have been lucky.

We saw the old year out at the Thurbers' last night. The first snow of the season began to fall as we drove over. But coming home the snow had stopped, the sky had cleared and a nearly full moon had come out, lighting up the snow-mantled countryside. It was quite beautiful.

Thurber, blind, is rather petulant, but I try to take it good naturedly, being full of admiration for the pluck he shows in continuing to work at his writing despite his handicap — the great, awful, continuous darkness in which he must always live. Humorist that he is — perhaps the greatest in the country — he feels fiercely that the world has gone to hell, that there is very little hope for this country, now seized by unbelievable intolerance. We talked in the New Year rather lugubriously, but I had the feeling that neither he nor I felt as bad about it as we *said* we did. Have not all great humorists been incurable pessimists at heart? Mark Twain? Was Rabelais?

Not all my diary entries in those days were given over to somber reflection on trying to survive. I noted parties, holidays, meeting new people, seeing old friends, the triumphs and setbacks of writers I had known or admired or both, and their deaths, the foibles and follies of the mighty, domestic and world events, the joys and sorrows of raising a family, the hectic life in New York and the more tranquil one on the farm, and much else. Once in a while my luck took a good turn. And there was never in our lives a dull moment. I knew worry but never boredom.

There was the night I first met Greta Garbo. Like millions of other men I had worshipped her on the screen as the most beautiful and fascinating, if enigmatic and elusive, woman in the world. "New York, April 15, 1950. To the Gunthers last night . . . Greta Garbo was there. . . ." She was as beautiful face-to-face as on the screen. But I reported I was "crushed" by my "disillusionment." She was not exciting to talk to, and the way she laughed somehow grated on me.

I had a better time earlier that day, my diary says, at the circus at Madison Square Garden, to which I repaired with Eileen (Inga) and four of her young friends from school.

It was more fun than I expected. I even got a kick out of the man who stood on one finger (balanced on a crystal ball), and the Spanish lass who performed on an ordinary swing just under the roof, swaying back and forth, her feet clinging to the board of the swing, her hands free in the air. Probably, tho, the biggest kick was just watching the youngsters.

The wonderment of the five twelve-year-olds, their excitement — I still remember it when I go to the circus.

Though I had soured on broadcasting and broadcasting had soured on me, I noted some of the humorous and bizarre — even hilarious — aspects of it. There was a fine scene, my diary reminds me, on the evening of September 11, 1952, when a popular TV program called *Author Meets the Critic* did a show on *Midcentury Journey*, published that very day. The format called for one defender and one prosecutor of the book. The former was the lovely Doris Fleeson, one of the first women correspondents and columnists in Washington; the latter was — or was supposed to be — Henry J. Taylor, an arch-conservative who had often attacked my views. There was no love lost between us. Taylor breezed in fifteen minutes before air time and, to the consternation of the show's producer and director, announced that he would not attack the book, that he liked it very much, agreed with most of it, and would say so. The producer and director appealed to him in vain to change his mind. They had hired him, they said, to criticize the book; Miss Fleeson would do the defending. Without an argument, without debate, the show would be a flop. But Taylor, to everyone's surprise, was adamant. So he joined Miss Fleeson in praising the book. The director and producer wrung their hands. One of them was so wrought up I feared he might have a stroke.

My diary ends with another kind of comment on the show:

Typical of TV and radio. Neither of the two producers of this book program had bothered to read the book.

Actually it was a work of philosophical reflections on what had happened since the war to the countries I had just visited: Austria, Germany, France, and Britain, with an additional chapter about America in the first grip of the McCarthy hysteria. But the program's producers had written Doris Fleeson in Washington that the book was about the "Marshall Plan." And since they had neglected to send her the book and she could not find a copy at the Washington bookstores she had boned up on the plan, discovering only on the train coming up to New York, after she had finally procured a copy of the book, that it was about something entirely different.

A few days later I added a note in my diary.

New York, Sept. 18, 1952. Not only do radio and TV people who interview you about the book almost never read it. They can't even give the title correctly. Nancy Craig on TV Thursday called it "Mid-Journey." Last night George Combs over at ABC began by talking about "Mid-century Journal." Not important, of course, but typical of how slipshod radio and TV have become.

Two days before:

An amusing and typical incident at NBC today. I sat around with the producer of a book program, a director of the Talks Department, and one or two other NBC moguls waiting for the man who was supposed to interview me for a recording to be broadcast Saturday. After half an hour, they started telephoning for the man; finally reached him at his home. He had, he said, not come to the broadcast for the simple reason that NBC had fired him the week before!

My diary changed subjects quickly.

Friday, May 5, 1950. We measured Eileen (Inga) today and found she is taller than her mother!

There was also occasionally good news, even from the tough world outside that had thrown me, for the moment, for a loop.

New York, Sunday, January 13, 1952. *Midcentury Journey* finally finished, and a load is off my mind, tho I feel depressed as I always do at the end of doing a book. Depressed, I suppose, because I keep wondering whether it was worth the effort, the time, the suffering — and what it took out of me and my life. Wondering whether it is even publishable; worth reading. It may be the best book I've done; the most thoughtful, the best written. Yet I feel it is not up to what I had hoped.

I worked feverishly to finish it all through the holidays up on the farm . . . from early morning through the whole day and then . . . in the kitchen where I could make a log fire in the Dutch-oven fireplace to 3 or 4 A.M.

We'll see now what the publisher says. I've already spent the advance. . . .

New York, April 14. Roger Straus phones this morning. "I don't see why you shouldn't sweat this out too."

"Sweat what out?"

So he explodes his little bomb. . . . The Literary Guild, says he, has suddenly decided . . . to consider *Journey* for its main selection.

"I don't believe it," I say. "And please don't do this to me."

"It's God's truth," says Roger.

New York, April 17. A letter from Roger asking me to keep my fingers crossed. He has had to hold up binding the book until the Guild makes up its mind. He will press for a decision by Monday, the 21st. . . . I wish to hell he had never told me about it. So hard not to count on. It would solve so many of our problems. Of course, it really is quite out of the question. . . . Must put it out of my thoughts; forget it completely. . . .

New York, April 22. Roger phoned early from Augusta, his voice full of gloom.

The Literary Guild has decided NOT to take the book. . . .

This evening to the Council for a dinner for Chester Wilmot, who has just published here a remarkable book on the war, *The Struggle for Europe*. . . . Afterward with Cass Canfield, head of Harper's, Prof. Commager and Wilmot to the Plaza for some beers and more debate on Wilmot's book. This took my mind off my own and the disappointment.

New York, April 23. I must really get down to figuring out a living through the next six months. I had hoped to spend the summer on the farm writing on the novel. . . . All day I kept whistling to keep my courage up. . . . Day after tomorrow I must go up to Cambridge to talk at Harvard. Scarcely feel in the mood.

New York, April 24. About 4:30 P.M. I walked home from the Waldorf, where I had gone to have a haircut. . . . When I opened the front door, Linda, who had just come back from school, was jumping up and down excitedly and murmuring something about wasn't it fine news about the book. Actually I didn't pay much attention to her, as she is full of youthful enthusiasms these days. She is 10½. . . .

Upstairs Tess rushed to greet me. She was practically incoherent. But this much soon came out: Straus & Reynolds both had been phoning for the last hour . . . madly. The Guild, they said, had changed its mind. It was taking *Journey* after all.

Occasionally in my diary I reflected on a writer I had known.

New York, Thurs., Jan. 11, 1951. The papers tell of the death of Sinclair Lewis in Rome yesterday. He would have been 66 on Feb. 7. The dispatches say he died alone. No friends or relatives were there; only the doctors and nurses. I guess he had been a very lonely man for a long time . . . a curious irony for one who fundamentally was so gregarious. . . . Perhaps Marcella departing from him to marry a younger man brought on the final loneliness. It was also ironic that Red, who was so thoroughly American, lived more and more in Europe after the last war. Even there, I gather, despite his enormous world reputation (Nobel Prize and all) he was a lonely figure, for he does not seem to have established many friendships with writers in Europe.

I remember him the year he spent with Dorothy [Thompson] in Vienna . . . 1932 it must have been. Already one felt his loneliness. For months at a time, as I recall, he holed up in a villa on the Semmering. It was winter, the snow deep, and he rarely went out.

I remember spending a day with him there. He was drinking heavily . . . (from depression over the imminent breakup of his marriage to Dorothy, who was away most of the time in their apartment in Vienna) and he seemed at loose ends. To pass away his time, he said, he had bought the entire set of English novels published by Tauchnitch [which printed paperback English-language books sold on the Continent] and was already well through them.

He talked too that day of his great ambition, which unhappily never came to fruition: to write a novel which would be a sort of history of the U.S.A. and of the American people from the first days. . . . He was the one writer who could have done a masterpiece on this subject — even if his style, his photographic approach, was temporarily outdated in Amer. writing.

I pondered why he had never been able to write the book.

Excessive drinking, for one thing, prevented it, though later on, when I saw him in America during (and after) the war, he was usually on the wagon. He looked very emaciated then, his gaunt face pockmarked. But of course it must have been more than drinking. Other things threw him off: his infatuation for Marcella, his writing plays for her and acting in them with her.

The day on the Semmering we also had a long talk about one of my pet themes: Why American writers stop writing (or stop writing anything good or important) at middle-age, in contrast to Europeans, who usually just get into their stride at 45 or 50. He had some theories but the answer escaped him, as it did me. In his own case he kept on writing with prodigious energy, even if in the last 15 years his talent seemed to have dried up.

If he enjoyed (or however he felt about it) world fame he also experienced being in the troughs when the public seemed to have forgotten him and the critics, reviewers, dismissed him with condescension. . . .

A great loss, his death, though I believe he had said about all he had to say. I wonder how much happiness he had.

Most of my diary for 1957 is missing, so I have no record of my reaction to the dispatches for May 3 that year that told of the death the day before of Senator Joseph McCarthy. His eclipse had already begun in 1954 when he took on the U.S. Army and during the hearings of a Select Senate Committee exposed himself in the glare of the TV lights for the fraud he was. A few months later the Senate voted to censure him. Thereafter he faded rapidly and his already heavy drinking increased. But the hate and the fear and the intolerance he ignited and fostered lingered on in the country until the end of the decade when finally Americans, even the frightened rabbits in radio and TV and the films, not to mention those in the press and in the Congress, began to come to their senses again.

Into my diary crept notice of the death of a terrible tyrant who played a major role in our times and an evil one.

> Farm, New Year's Day, 1954 . . . One great event of 1953: Stalin finally died. But the jungle world he built up in Russia goes on unchanged. His body was hardly cold before Malenkov, apparently the top man in the succession, framed his chief rival and had him shot on Christmas Eve.* What will Stalin's place in history be? Distasteful as the tyrant was to us, it will probably be big. He built up the Soviet Union into one of the world's two great powers.

True. But over the bodies of millions of Russians. I did not realize then the extent to which Stalin, in his paranoia, went in literally wiping out millions of his fellow countrymen until I read Khrushchev's account at the Twentieth Party Congress and George Kennan's devastating revelations in one of his books. Stalin's tyranny was as brutal as Ivan the Terrible's and more massive; and its cost to Russia physically, morally, spiritually, and culturally was incalculable. I was wrong about Stalin's place in Russian history. In the Soviet Union he was finally exposed for what he was under the Gorbachev regime.

Ironically his death kept me from entering Russia. Stalin died on March 6, 1953. I happened to be in Finland where I had been told in Washington by the Russian embassy I could pick up a visa for my first visit to the Soviet Union. (For years my application had been rejected.) But the nearby Soviet frontier was closed for several days after Stalin's death. I had to wait until the 1980s to get in to the U.S.S.R.

I think life would have been unbearable in those days without the return from the long fall lecture tours in time for the Christmas and New Year holidays with the family on the farm. I continued to jot down

---

* This was Beria, the sinister chief of the Secret Police. Malenkov himself soon disappeared from office. But he was not shot, ushering in a new era in Moscow in that regard.

in my diary on New Year's Day how we had seen the old year out and what had happened during the previous year.

Farm, January 1, 1954. To Rose Algrant's last night to see 1953 out, and there were there: Jim & Helen Thurber, the Lewis Gannetts, Mark Van Doren and Dorothy & others who usually forgather together on this occasion, including the younger generation. Stella Adamic came with the Gannetts. I had never met her before, though I felt I knew her through his (Louis Adamic's) books. He killed himself a couple of years ago, apparently unable to bear existence any longer. He had been very popular with his books about the emigrant American (himself) from about the beginning of the Depression in 1933, but after the war he felt himself, I think, becoming isolated because of his strong liberalism which the witch-hunters equated with Communism. She seems a lovely girl: dark, sensitive, simple, intelligent.

Jim Thurber more mellow than on previous New Years. Up to a year or so ago he was very combative and evenings often ended up (after an argument) with him stalking out. (I never blamed him, feeling it was a release of his pent-up resentment and frustration at his blindness, tho God knows he has kept up with his writing despite it.) Jim talked well of writing and writers, esp. humorists, and of the position of humor in literature. "Humor is a mystery, beyond analysis. It aims at truth, and sometimes comes near." etc. He spoke at length of writers fearing death. (I noted how I pay much more attention to the *NYT* obituary columns than formerly.)

Mark Van Doren, who has been taking his sabbatical year up at his farm here, looked young and almost dapper. . . . He told me of the publisher's letter he resented most. He had sent a novel to Thayer Hobson some years ago and got the manuscript back quickly with a curt note saying: "I am not going to publish this and I hope for your own good you will not show it to any other publisher." . . .

This year I shall be 50!

A good deal of the past year, that inexorable FACT stared me in the face. . . . It is said that a writer's creativity starts to taper off after 50. Am I naïve in thinking that because I developed (matured) slowly and got down to book writing late (*Berlin Diary* was published in 1941, when I was 37 — my first book) that I may have my ten best years between 50 and 60?

I certainly was not having my ten best years at earning a living. As the decade of the 1950s slipped past the halfway mark our financial situation continued to deteriorate. My diary kept track.

New York, June 1, 1955 — My book on Scandinavia out May 23, and so far the *NYT* . . . has completely boycotted mention of it. . . . I must reluctantly face the fact that there is no living — even a modest one — for me in books. . . . We exist mostly from my lectures, but that also is a diminishing return, and I must turn to some other field of writing. Few writers in America now earn their living from books. Almost all have to do something else: journalism, teaching, advertising, lecturing. Problem is to find something else that will still leave time and energy for writing.

Still to try: a play.

And to look into writing plays for TV.

I am still blacklisted from performing on radio-TV and, I reluctantly conclude, from most of the popular magazines.

But I must strive to take the present defeats decently. How many other writers have gone through this! I recall Henry James' sense of frustration when he seemed to have lost contact with his public. And only last week I was reading Stefan Zweig's account of the bitter despair of Kleist and Nietzsche when neither could even get their masterpieces . . . published or produced.

It was a good summer on the farm that year. I labored on a new novel, the first one I had ever attempted which was not autobiographical; and I began to have high hopes for it. Working the fields and the big garden, sawing and getting in the wood for the winter, and swimming with the girls kept me in good shape. I also continued jotting down ideas for making some money and got them off to my agent or directly sometimes to editors and publishers of my acquaintance. Nothing came of it. No money came in. It continued going out. We had to live, though by mid-June we were eating mostly from the vegetable garden.

Farm, September 18, 1955. Another summer's end. Back to New York tomorrow. . . .

I have written the bulk of five books here (and in 1950 and 1953 I spent most of summer in Europe, and in 1951 I was broadcasting for "Liberty" and stayed in New York.)

1. *The Traitor* (novel)
2. *Midcentury Journey*
3. *Stranger Come Home* (novel)
4. *The Challenge of Scandinavia*
5. *Pawancore* (working title of novel just finished).*

Writing is what I wanted most to do — and I've done it. But two questions!

1. Were books any good?
2. Am I not going broke writing?

* Published as *The Consul's Wife*.

Only the lectures have saved me financially — but each year we bite into our capital — and this cannot go on much longer.

Try and lick that problem this year.

But I couldn't. In fact, each successive year the latter half of the decade things got worse.

New York, February 16, 1957. 53 next Saturday (Feb. 23) and beset by financial difficulties such as I've never seen before. . . . T. has panicked, can't sleep, is down in bed ill since a week. . . .

'Tis just 10 years since I was thrown out of CBS and my fortunes faded. I'd hoped to live from writing, with the help of lecturing. But it has been a losing race — we've spent some $45,000 of our modest capital, which is almost gone. Present crisis came when the lectures, which had grossed some $20,000 a year (about $10,000 after agent's commissions) suddenly this year, without warning, dropped off to nothing. . . .

'Tis obvious we cannot go on this way. Obvious too from the experience of writing over the last ten years that the kind I have done will not give the living we've tried to keep up. Either I have to change the type of writing into some kind that pays a decent living. . . . OR get some kind of work — besides lecturing — that would permit me to continue writing honestly, OR get work that demands full time and abandon, at least for the present, any writing at all. . . .

What to do? And what not to do? Don't panic! . . .

Appended to the diary of that bleak February day are three pages of notes, partly handwritten, partly typed.

wls. Feb. 16, 1957.
A Way Out.
General.
    1. To tide us over from May to Dec., when should finish book.
        1. Foundation help. Need $8,000 for the 8 months
        2. If that impossible, will have to abandon book temporarily and find a job.
            1. Jobs? Radio-TV. NBC? ABC? Dumont? Luce? Dewitt Wallace? Mike Cowles?*
        3. 1957–58 lecture season. $7,000. Estimated.

Expected Income, without a job immediately.

March 1.	$ 720.00	(S&S)
	472.00	(England)
March 25.	525.00	(local lectures)
April 10.	236.00	(England)

* Owner-publishers of *Time-Life*, *Reader's Digest*, and *Look*, respectively.

	1,200.00	(lectures: net, after commission & expenses)
April 26.	250.00	(lecture)
	280.00	(lecture)
May 10.	236.00	(England)
	200.00	(lecture)
	500.00	(Hillman Jury)
	$4,539.00	

On another sheet I toted up estimated expenses for 1957. Rent, college and high-school tuition for the girls, insurance, taxes, and food came to $11,750. One item was $1,080 for a part-time maid. We had quarreled over that, but Tess insisted she could not do without. Over most of the ten years we were going broke she had insisted on a full-time maid. And on a full-time Swiss governess for the children, long after they had outgrown her.

We had begun to clash over other aspects of our deteriorating financial situation. As our affairs grew steadily worse, Tess seemed to resent my inability to earn enough to keep us in a comfortable state, free of worry. It was a husband's duty, she kept saying, to support his family. Recently she had bridled when I suggested that she take a temporary job to help tide us over until a new book, in which I had high hopes, was finished. She had so many talents, artistic and linguistic; she knew several foreign languages — it would be easy, I said, to find something. She had never worked for pay since we were married twenty years ago. But now, I pointed out, our situation was desperate.

As with so many other spouses everywhere, our squabbles over money, or rather the lack of it, began to erode a long and pretty solid marriage.

The next year, 1958, I had hoped would be better. Perhaps the novel just out, *The Consul's Wife*, would sell — it was by far the best fiction I had yet written, I thought. Perhaps we could sell it to Hollywood. I urged my agent to redouble his efforts. Maybe the magazines would buy some pieces from the new book I was feverishly working on.

No luck.

New York, January 2, 1958. Another year gone by . . . I continue to lose ground. . . . My capital is almost exhausted. . . . For the last ten years . . . I have simply not earned enough to meet our modest expenses.

Our furnace at the farmhouse had blown out and we did not have the money to buy a new one. Nevertheless, Tess and I had gone up to the farm for New Year's Eve with the Thurbers and other friends in

Cornwall. A fire in our living room fireplace and another in the stove in the kitchen reduced the cold somewhat.

We found Jim Thurber in good spirits.

> Jim completely blind now. . . . He told me he had now published more books since he went blind than when he could see. A tribute to his guts.

> New York, January 10. Paul Reynolds [literary agent] sends in the record (for income taxes) of what my writing (books and mags) earned this past year. $6,640.79. . . . But two-thirds was in advances. . . . Received but really not yet earned.

> Fifteen years ago when I was making too much money from my writing (journalism, the book *Berlin Diary*, & broadcasting) I remember thinking: Well, whatever problems lie ahead, in one's life, in one's work (& there would be plenty, I imagined), at least I had solved the problem of earning a living. . . .

> Now earning enough to hold on . . . has become a major problem and the cause of much worry in this house. . . .

> Tuesday, February 15. Curious how these notes seem given so much to money problems. I had so long been without them. Last week I closed out my account with the broker. . . . My last liquid capital (gone). Once, eleven years ago, that capital came to 40 or 50 thousand. . . . From now on I must make both ends meet. . . .

> Have now done 235,000 words on the book. . . .

For some time I had been working, on and off — and for the last year and a half, full time, fourteen hours a day — on a long and difficult book that almost everyone told me was well worth doing but would not sell. They would look at me and shake their heads, as if to say: When will he come down to earth and try to write something that will give him a living? Doing this long book is only putting him further in debt.

I knew what they were thinking. But I persisted.

I was sure I had found a subject for a book that might be very important as contemporary history and that, through the circumstances of my work in the last years leading up to World War II and because of an unprecedented break that never before had come to historians, I was in a rather unique position to write.

I was not a "professional historian," as the academics would say. For them, for some reason, you had to *teach* history to be a "pro." I knew better. Some of the greatest historians had never been in academe — Herodotus, Thucydides, Gibbon, to name the first three that come to mind.

I cared not a whit about a classification. What was important was not whether you were called a "historian" but that you wrote good history. And the field was open to all, especially, I thought, to former journalists. As a reporter I had watched history being made in India when Gandhi began his revolt against the British; in Germany when Hitler took over; and in Great Britain and France when the Western democracies began to slide downhill; and in Italy when Mussolini strutted about.

At Nuremberg at the end of the war, covering the trial of the Nazi war criminals, I had learned that almost all the confidential records of the German government during the Nazi time, including those of the Foreign Office, the army and navy and of the Nazi party, had fallen into the hands of the Allies. Such a treasure had never before become to writers of history available in their lifetime. And in my case I had the advantage of having lived through at first hand the nightmare of the Third Reich. Memories of it were still fresh in my mind, my blood, and my bones. Academicians might scoff at the value of such an experience. But I remembered that Thucydides, one of the first and probably the greatest of historians in the Western World, had justified his writing the history of the Peloponnesian War by reminding his readers that he had lived through it, "being of an age," he had added, "to comprehend events and giving my attention to them in order to know the exact truth."

All through the 1950s, I had labored at sifting through the mountains of German documents, classifying them, translating them and making notes. Some time in 1955, I had started to write — at first in time snatched away from other work, later full-time, which came to mean night and day. Friends later said I seemed to be living and working those years in a daze, as if I were in a trance, no longer in touch with the real world.

I was not aware of it. But I realized I was consumed by a burning desire to master the vast material (millions of words of documents), organize it, write the book, and survive until I had finished it. Most of my friends and acquaintances, and my agent, thought I had gone a little crazy.

And my publisher refused even to consider bringing out the book!

When the Scandinavian book was ready for the press, I had met Stanley Salmon, chief editor and executive vice-president of Little, Brown, at Sturbridge, midway between the farm and Boston, for a weekend to go over the proofs and various editorial problems and, above all, to discuss what I would do next. Salmon knew I was well into a novel and hoped to finish it soon.

"What I'm most interested in," he said, "is after that. What are you going to do? You mentioned recently you had a big book in mind."

"Stanley," I said, "for once in my life I know exactly what I'm going to do. I've been working on and off on it for years. I even know the title of the book, and this time you're not going to talk me out of it."

He had just done that with the Scandinavian book, getting me to substitute a terribly pedestrian title for a rather poetic one I had wanted.

"Stanley," I started to go on. "It's going to be the biggest, the most important book I've ever —"

"What's it about? What are you going to call it?" he broke in.

"*The Rise and Fall of the Third Reich.* It's going to be a history of Nazi Germany based on the captured secret documents and on my own personal experience in Berlin in the Hitler time. It's an opportunity, Stanley, that comes once in a lifetime, if that. With any luck, it's bound to be a pretty important book."

Stanley listened patiently, but to my surprise his face grew cold. I had thought at first he would leap up from the table in great excitement at the news I had just given him. But instead he was frowning.

"Dear Bill," he finally said. "Please don't ask Little, Brown to publish a book to be called *The Rise and Fall of the Third Reich.* Really! We're not interested!"

I was stunned. I couldn't believe his words.

"You're not serious," I said.

"I'm deadly serious," he said.

"Will you put it in writing?" I asked.

"You'll have a letter first thing next week."

BOOK FIVE

"The Rise and Fall of the Third Reich"

A Turning Point

1954–1960

CHAPTER 1

Toward the end of January 1954, I tossed into my diary folder a note scrawled on the back of a sheet torn out of my desk calendar:

January 24, '54.
To Do
    A book to be called "The Rise and Fall of the Third Reich."

In the midst of trying to scratch out a living lecturing and of getting on with writing books apparently I forgot the item. For up on the farm six months later, on a piece of yellow copypaper, I scribbled out again the identical words.

Farm. June, '54.
To Do
A Book. The Rise and Fall of the Third Reich

At least I had a title.

Actually, I had been tossing around in my mind the idea of doing such a book ever since covering the Nuremberg trial of the chief Nazi war criminals nearly nine years before, in the late fall of 1945. *Berlin Diary,* published in 1941, had been a sort of a day-to-day eyewitness account of the Nazi conquest of Germany and then of most of Western Europe from 1934 to 1940. It was what I personally had seen and experienced as an American correspondent in Berlin. But it had been impossible in a totalitarian dictatorship to penetrate very deeply under the surface. We journalists watched and recounted events: Hitler's tearing up the Versailles Treaty in 1935 and proclaiming, in violation of it, a large new conscript army; his occupation of the Rhineland the next year, 1936, in violation of another treaty; the Nazi invasion and occupation of Austria in 1938 and of Czechoslovakia the spring of the next year — a prelude to Hitler's invasion of Poland on September 1, 1939, and his launching of World War II.

I covered these events as a correspondent. But I did not know — none of us, journalists and diplomats, knew — what went on in the secret meetings and conferences of Hitler with his generals and Nazi cronies where the Nazi aggressions were plotted nor the secret diplomatic exchanges between Hitler and Mussolini, Chamberlain, Daladier, and Stalin, which largely determined what took place in that time of upheaval and deceit. We saw the Jews being hounded and persecuted, their property and savings stolen by the state; and we saw them being carted off to concentration camps. But we could not follow them to see how barbarously they were being treated, nor did we know of the decision on high, about the time I left Berlin at the end of 1940, for the "Final Solution" that would consign them to extermination camps nor, until it was much too late, did we learn that they were there massacred on the order of the popular government of this ancient Christian nation.

There was so much we didn't know, and we knew it.

Then at the war's end in May of 1945 the whole vast secret record of what we had not known, set down in millions of confidential records of the Nazi German government, party, military establishment, ministries and the leaders, fell into the hands of the victorious Allies.

Before I left Nuremberg at the end of 1945, my duffel bag stuffed with the first few hundred thousand words of secret Nazi papers already released, I knew that with such material at hand someone would soon be able to write a fully documented history of Nazi Germany packed with revelations so shocking that the world would scarcely believe. One of the documents had indicated the kind of material a historian would be dealing with. It was the deposition of a Nazi party hack I had never heard of named Rudolf Hoess telling proudly of how at Auschwitz he personally had supervised the extermination in the ovens there of more than two million Jews. Other initial documents included the minutes of the most secret meetings which led up to Hitler's making his fateful decision to go to war.

For the first time — ever — historians immediately after the event could now write the definitive history of the rise and fall of a great nation.

Was it something I should tackle? I had seen a good many of the events unfold. That would give me an advantage over those who had not been there. But questions immediately popped up.

Upon my return home I had jobs that took all the time I had: broadcasting for CBS and writing a column for the Herald-Tribune. What time could I possibly snatch to write books? Maybe, I thought, when I've saved up enough money I would take a year or two off and do the book on Germany.

With the loss of my broadcasts and columns, that possibility went out the window. Due to that and the blacklisting, I had to scratch harder each year to eke out a living. There was nothing left to save. I could try to do the shorter books and hope that one of them would sell. But how could I find the time to sift through the immense piles of confidential Nazi papers and then get on to writing the big book? That would take years. Did I have it in me; did I have the discipline and the know-how to write a historical work whose subject and the materials to support it were so vast?

As late as the spring of 1956, after I had already waded into the Nazi documents, I had my doubts.

> New York, Tuesday, April 25, 1956. . . . Book is overwhelming. Can I master it? Can I take advantage of this unprecedented, rich store and of my own experience of working and living in the Third Reich and do the book? . . . We shall see. I have many misgivings as to my own shortcomings; but also a certain confidence. . . .

Many professor-historians could easily get the time off for such a project. They had their sabbaticals and other subsidized leaves from the classroom in which to write their books. And they seemed to have little trouble in getting foundation grants and various fellowships to finance their time off. Moreover, many of them had already published works of history. They knew how to write them.

Given all that and the precariousness of my own situation I decided to wait to see if the academic historians would take on the job of doing a serious history of Nazi Germany based on the avalanche of new material. I had little doubt they would come forth. Their opportunity was unique. No other generation of historians — ever — had had such a find. I was quite content to leave it to them.

I waited. And waited. No one stepped forth. A few American academic historians dabbled around the periphery. One, whom I got to know and admire, turned out some excellent articles and an interesting monograph on the Eher Verlag, Hitler's publishing empire, which had made him a millionaire. An English historian turned out an excellent little book — so far as it went — on the rise and fall of Nazi Germany. But at three hundred pages it was too short to go very far or to encompass the vast subject and the immense documentation available to sustain it.

In England, Alan Bullock's biography of Hitler, published in 1952, was excellent; but it did not purport to be a history of the Third Reich nor did John W. Wheeler-Bennett's brilliant *The Nemesis of Power*, which concentrated on Hitler's successful quest for absolute power and came out in 1953.

You might have expected the Germans to take the lead in writing the great, documented history of their country under Adolf Hitler. But they were avoiding the subject like the plague. Perhaps it was too soon for a German. Perhaps German historians first would have to come to grips with the enormity of the barbarism their nation had plunged itself into and their own responsibility for it.

Nine years after the end of the war and the fall of Hitler, I decided to take the plunge — since no one else would. I would not write around the subject. I would tackle it head-on. I would try to write for the first time a fully documented and complete history of the rise and fall of the Third Reich. Somehow I would find the time to do it and still support my family. *

The first thing to do was to find a new publisher, my old publisher having turned down flat the very idea of such a book.† I would have to ask for a sizable advance to help tide me over the next couple of years. To find a new publisher that would be excited enough about the book to pay such an advance turned out to be more difficult than I had expected.

Cass Canfield at Harper's, an old friend, was not interested. I decided next to try a small publisher, in the belief that such a one might be more tempted to take a chance on me. I invited to lunch an old friend, Harold Guinzburg, the founding head of Viking. We had seen a bit of each other during the war in England where he was an overseas director of the Office of War Information. On one occasion he had called me in to help him out with a difficult problem. Harold was responsive enough during the lunch. The food was good and we washed it down with a smooth dry Burgundy white wine. He thought the idea for the book was pretty exciting. But when I began to talk about the necessity of a relatively large advance — at least $10,000, I said — Harold's face paled and then, it seemed to me, began to turn a rather sickly green. Plainly I was making him uncomfortable.

"Bill," he said, "I like the idea of your book. Very much. And I'm definitely interested. But I can't give you a large advance nor, in fact, any advance at all on so risky a venture. But I hope you'll let me have first crack at the manuscript when you've finished."

---

* I was further emboldened by the plaint of E. H. Carr, the British historian, in his fine book on German-Soviet relations between the two world wars published in 1951. "No serious attempt has yet been made," he wrote, "to write a history of Germany under Hitler."
† Stanley Salmon suddenly resigned as editor-in-chief at Little, Brown early in 1955. But neither his successor nor anyone else at the firm showed any more interest in publishing the book.

This struck me as a wholly unreasonable request. I tried to smile. There was no use saying anything more.

Convinced by that experience that I could only get a decent advance from a large house, I turned to another friend I admired, Ken Mc-Cormick, editor-in-chief of Doubleday, the biggest trade publisher in the country. Ken was a likable, civilized, warmhearted man and an editor whom every writer who dealt with him respected. He liked the idea of the book, said he would try to get a $10,000 advance, but warned that book publishing was in the doldrums for the moment and that he might have difficulties. Rather apologetically he called me a few days later and said that the most Doubleday could offer was $7,500.

I was a little surprised that a publisher as large and as well-off as Doubleday would turn me down on a matter of only $2,500 — especially since their chief editor was so enthusiastic about the book.

"I'm tremendously enthusiastic about *The Rise and Fall of the Third Reich,*" McCormick wrote me a few days later,

> but since I couldn't get the kind of money you needed to write it, I can certainly understand your looking elsewhere to find it. I think it's a terrific idea, and you're the one to do it.

I had turned finally to one of my closest friends, with whom, as a friend, I had already talked about the book. This was Joe Barnes, who had left the *New York Herald-Tribune,* to become editor of the ill-fated *New York Star,* and when that folded, had moved over to book pub-lishing and become an editor at Simon and Schuster. At some point in our informal talks he called in Jack Goodman, the dynamo of S&S; and one evening at my home over drinks the three of us came to an agreement. Simon and Schuster would advance me $10,000 ($9,000 after the agent had taken his commission). Since such books never sold, they said, they asked me to make a couple of concessions that I had never previously made: give them ten percent of foreign and movie rights. For a book they were sure they could never sell, it seemed odd to me they would ask for this, since nonfiction works were almost never bought by Hollywood; and there seemed little prospect of making anything out of foreign publication. But I would not be losing much, if anything; so I agreed.

I called in my agent, Paul R. Reynolds, to work out the rest of the details. He had stuck with me through the last five books, the com-missions on the sales of which probably had not even equaled the expenses he incurred. This was the first sizable advance he had seen for me and it meant a thousand dollars for him. But I got the impression he figured that it was the last compensation he would get from such a book. Like everyone else who knew me, he seemed to be wondering, I felt, when I would snap out of it and settle down and write a book he could sell and that would relieve me of the constant strain of trying to earn a decent living. He had no idea, nor did I, nor anyone else, how long I would become buried in churning out this new book. I myself assured him and S&S I would do it in two years. The contract so stipulated. Little could we foresee!

My diary:

> New York, Tuesday, April 24, 1956. . . . I have now signed up with S&S to do a book, "The Rise and Fall of the Third Reich," which . . . — the thought sobers me — will take the next one and a half to two years out of my life. At my age — 52 — that is something to contemplate. It isn't that there is anything else I would rather do; there isn't. But there is the problem of supporting the family during that time; and I have not come near to solving it.
>
> Because of the hundreds of tons (millions of words) of captured German documents, the material for the book is overwhelming. Can I master it? . . . We shall see. . . .
>
> S&S will pay me $900 a month (after the agent's 10 percent commission). For the next eleven months that should give me a basic living. . . .

For a year at least. Who dared look further than that?

> New York, October 1, 1956. Began actual writing of book — 3 R. . . .

All that summer I had slaved away at the documents. During a trip to Washington in August, I made a very helpful contact. I found a scholar at the Library of Congress who could lead me to the documents I wanted. Since there was no index to them, this was invaluable. Of even more worth, he had a scholarly background in the culture and politics of Central Europe.

This was Dr. Fritz T. Epstein of the Slavic and Central European Division of the Library of Congress in Washington. Of Czech-German descent, Dr. Epstein was a distinguished linguist, a man of deep learning in history; and he had made himself an authority on the captured German papers. Though I must have seemed to him a rather unlikely person to be attempting to master the massive documentation of the Third Reich and then to write its history, he befriended me from the first and far beyond the call of duty he spent a great deal of his time and energy over the next three years guiding me through the forest of documents and retrieving those which were of primary importance to me. Epstein himself, under the auspices of the Human Resources Research Institute of the Air University, had compiled the only guide there was to the captured German documents. This was far from being the index really needed, but it proved to be of immense help.

Soon after the Nuremberg trials two separate series of volumes stemming from them had been published by the Allies. The first was the forty-two-volume *Trial of the Major War Criminals*, of which the first twenty-three volumes contained the text of the testimony at the trial and the remainder the text of the documents accepted in evidence, which were published in their original language, mostly German. Additional documents, interrogations, and affidavits collected for the trial and translated rather hurriedly (and often badly) into English were published in the ten-volume series *Nazi Conspiracy and Aggression*. There was no index to either of these series. It took some wading through to find what you wanted.

After the major Nazis had been tried, there were twelve subsequent trials at Nuremberg conducted by United States Military Tribunals, from which duly emerged fifteen bulky volumes called *Trials of War Criminals before the Nuremberg Military Tribunals*. Bulky as they were, they contained only one-tenth of the material used in the trials. This series, too, had no index.

By the time I first started plowing into the documentation for my book, all these volumes had become available and you could assemble them at home and work on them. But they covered only the material released at Nuremberg. Vast quantities of Nazi documents did not figure in the trials. One gigantic collection of them had been stored for years in a large U.S. Army warehouse in Alexandria, Virginia. No one in our great government had shown the slightest interest in opening the hundreds of packing cases to see what of historical interest might lie within them. It was only in 1955, ten years after their capture and the year before I contracted to write my book, that the American Historical Association took the initiative to look into the Alexandria papers. Its members got little help from the government. But a handful of its scholars, giving freely of their time and helped by a few modest grants from foundations, finally got access to the documents and began to sift through them. For a time the air force loaned them a couple of photographers to microfilm the papers. It was slow going; but these valiant researchers, under the leadership of Dr. Gerhard Weinberg, were spurred on by the threat of their own government to return the Alexandria documents to Germany before they could be duplicated. Secretary of State John Foster Dulles seemed completely insensitive to their task. He was constantly and publicly assuring the German chancellor, Konrad Adenauer, that he intended to give the Alexandria papers back to Germany without further delay. There was no reason to hurry and good reason not to. American scholars feared that once the captured documents were returned to Germany they might not find access to them all for some time — or ever. After the First World War, the government of the liberal Weimar Republic, which had succeeded the Hohenzollern monarchy, had released only a few confidential papers, thus stifling the work of scholars, German and otherwise, trying to write the history of the last years of Kaiser Wilhelm II's regime and of the First World War.

Though I had begun the actual writing of my book in the fall of 1956, I spent a great deal of my time henceforth, long hours day after day, in research. In Washington I worked in the Library of Congress, in the Archives, in the Historical Division of the State Department, and in the office of the Chief of Military History at the Department of the Army, making myself a pest at each of these learned places but obtaining a vast amount of material.* I flew twice out to Palo Alto to labor in the Hoover Library at Stanford, which had, among other treasures, the files of Heinrich Himmler, the dreaded chief of the Nazi Gestapo and one of the great German killers of the Jews.

I worked long hours in the library of the Council of Foreign Relations and in the New York Public Library. Luckily I was able to do a great deal of research at home, poring through the sixty-seven unindexed volumes of the Nuremberg trials, the ten volumes of secret papers of the German Foreign Office (published jointly by the British and American governments) — the latter a great treasure for one who, as a correspondent in Berlin, had spent endless hours covering that shrine in the Wilhelmstrasse — and finally the papers collected for me from a myriad of sources by Dr. Epstein and others, including Telford Taylor, chief prosecutor at the twelve subsequent trials at Nuremberg.

Historians here and abroad generously and patiently answered my ceaseless queries, but I groaned at the time I had to take off from research and writing to handle this correspondence. A secretary for such things would have been of immense help, but I could not afford

* I was surprised — and I admit somewhat relieved — to find how little American historians had poked into the vast historical treasure of the captured Nazi documents. One day a group of the ranking librarians at the Library of Congress, obviously pleased that someone was interested in their unique holdings, trundled out a whole hand-truck full of Hitler's personal papers. I was astonished that they had not been opened since being catalogued. We took to untying the ribbons that bound them. Out fell what to me were priceless objects: among others, scores of drawings and paintings that Hitler had done in his vagabond youth in Vienna.

one. At one juncture I had to appeal for aid to the former chief of the German Army General Staff. The very title had been rather awesome in German history; one thought of the great German chiefs of staff: Field Marshal Count von Moltke, who had received the surrender of Napoleon III at Sedan in 1870; of his nephew, Helmuth von Moltke, who had commanded the German armies that swept almost to Paris only to be turned back at the Marne at the beginning of the First World War in 1914; and of Field Marshal Paul von Hindenburg, who had taken the post in 1916. The one whom I now asked for help was General Franz Halder, chief of the German Army General Staff from August 14, 1939, a fortnight before Hitler plunged the world into its second world war, to September 24, 1942, when the Russians had begun to seal the fate of the hitherto invincible German Army. He had never been promoted to field marshal, as were so many German generals in the Nazi time. Hitler never liked nor fully trusted him. And he felt the same way toward his leader.* He struck me, in my years in Berlin, as a very unusual type of military man, reflective and intellectual. His appointment as General Staff chief had been unusual. He was the first Bavarian and the first Roman Catholic ever to be named to that key post. It had been a severe break with Prussian-Protestant tradition of the officer corps.

I wrote to General Halder because I had not understood why Hitler, on May 24, 1940, just as his armored forces were closing in on the surrounded British and French armies on the Channel coast at Dunkirk at the climax of the Battle of France, had ordered them to stop in their tracks. The delay allowed the British to evacuate the bulk of their expeditionary force that had been fighting in northern France and Belgium and also enabled several thousand French troops to get away. I knew from Halder's diary that he had been flabbergasted by the decision. But I wanted more light on why Hitler had issued the crucial order, which Field Marshal von Rundstedt later called "one of the great turning points in the war."

Halder replied almost immediately and in detail.

His diary, jotted down in old-fashioned Gabelsberger shorthand not only from day to day but also at crucial moments from hour to hour, was a unique source of information for me, for he was in constant touch with

---

* In 1938, when Hitler almost pushed Germany into war over Czechoslovakia, a war the German generals knew the country was not prepared for and which they feared might lead to a European war and another defeat for the Reich, General Halder, according to his own account, led a conspiracy to overthrow Hitler. Plans to arrest the dictator were abandoned, Halder said, when Prime Minister Chamberlain agreed to go to Munich to appease the mad Führer. This meant that there would be no war — for the moment.

Hitler and the other generals and top officials at the great occasions when fatal decisions were made.

Another primary source was Hitler's daily calendar book, snatched from the ruins of the Chancellery bunker in Berlin where the vanquished dictator had killed himself, by an American soldier, though the Russians had been in possession of the bombed-out building for weeks before the Americans arrived. This book enabled me to keep track of Hitler's whereabouts and settle controversies over where he was on such-and-such occasion and whom he saw and what he was up to.

There were other informative diaries available besides those of General Halder. I was surprised at how many Nazi bigwigs kept them. Halder was not the only general to indulge in the practice. General Alfred Jodl, chief of operations of the High Command of the Armed Forces (OKW), wrote almost daily in his diary at moments of crisis. OKW itself kept an official diary of events, as did the Naval High Command. Indeed, I found that the Allies had captured at Schloss Tambach near Coburg some sixty thousand files of the German Naval Archives. This was a lucrative find. The files contained practically all the signals, ships' logs, diaries, and memoranda of the German Navy from April 1945, when they were found, back to 1868, when the modern German Navy was founded.

The diaries of Dr. Joseph Goebbels, the minister of propaganda, survived. So did those of Count Schwerin von Krosigk, the minister of finance throughout the Hitler reign. Despite having been a Rhodes scholar, he was one of the most muddled aristocrats who faithfully served the Führer; but his diary, reflecting his weakness, still provided a good deal of evidence of Nazi skulduggery, especially in the last desperate months of the crumbling regime.

Throughout the years of research I continually stumbled onto papers that threw a bit more light on the bizarre goings-on in the Third Reich. A typical example was the unearthing of transcripts of telephone conversations of the Nazi leaders taped by a special office secretly set up by Hermann Göring at the Air Ministry. Once, the special office blundered into taping not only the telephone talks of officials Göring wanted to get the goods on but also of the field marshal himself. This was on the afternoon and evening of the Anschluss, March 11, 1938, when Hitler forced the Austrian chancellor to resign and sent in Nazi troops to take over his native country. Twenty-seven telephone conversations between Göring in Berlin and his Nazi agents in Vienna on the fateful day were taped and transcribed by his own Air Ministry. They tell a graphic story of how Austria's fate was settled by telephone from Berlin. If the results had not been so tragic, some of Göring's conversation would have sounded comical.

Once, for instance, when the Austrian Judas, Arthur Seyss-Inquart, reported from Vienna that he could not get the stubborn Austrian president, Wilhelm Miklas, to appoint him the new chancellor, Göring got on the phone.

> GÖRING: Well, that won't do. . . . The president has to turn the powers of the chancellor over to you. . . . Tell him this is no time for joking.

If Miklas did not give in, Göring added, the German troops would march in. But still the stubborn president held out, even after his chancellor had resigned. He refused to appoint a Nazi to succeed him, and he declined to resign himself. This was reported to Göring by the German military attaché in Vienna, General Wolfgang Muff.

"He will not give in to force?" Göring could not believe it.

"He will not yield to force," the general repeated.

"So he just wants to be kicked out?"

"Yes," said Muff. "He is staying put."

"Well, with fourteen children," Göring laughed, "a man has to stay put. Anyway, tell Seyss to take over."

Hitler intended to justify his invasion of Austria by having the new Nazi cabinet in Vienna send him a telegram asking him to send in German troops to quell disorder and "prevent bloodshed." But since there was no disorder, no bloodshed, as I myself could testify (the local Austrian Nazis had captured the streets of Vienna quite peacefully), Seyss-Inquart stalled in sending the telegram. Hitler was enraged and ordered Göring to do something. So the fat field marshal phoned Vienna and dictated the text of the telegram the new Nazi regime was to send Berlin. The German agent taking the call promised he would show Seyss-Inquart the text of the "telegram" immediately.

"Well," Göring said, "he does not have to send the telegram. All he needs to say is 'Agreed.' "

Thus it was that when I passed through Berlin the next day on my way to London to do an uncensored report on Hitler's takeover of Austria, I found the German morning papers screaming their headlines: GERMAN AUSTRIA SAVED FROM CHAOS! There were incredible stories hatched up by Goebbels describing "Red Disorders," fighting, shooting, pillage in the main streets of Vienna. And sure enough on each front page in bold type was the text of the "telegram" sent to Hitler from Vienna calling on the Führer to send in troops to save Austria from bloodshed. The text was identical to the one dictated that night by Göring in Berlin. This false telegram was subsequently cited by the German Foreign Office to foreign governments to justify Hitler's invasion.

Göring's telephone conversations that night would be used as evidence against him in the Nuremberg trial seven years later.

That his secret office for taping telephones dared even to record Hitler's most confidential telephone conversations surprised me. I found, for example, a lengthy transcript of a call from Hitler to Prince Philip of Hesse, whom he had dispatched by plane to Rome on March 10 with a personal letter to Mussolini, full of the most outrageous lies and telling him that he would invade Austria and hoped for the Duce's understanding. Four years before, at the time of the Nazi murder of Chancellor Dollfuss in Vienna and the threat of German takeover, Mussolini had mobilized four divisions on the Brenner Pass to discourage Hitler from invading. Now on the night of March 11, four years later, as his troops stood poised to cross over the Austrian border, Hitler waited with increasing uneasiness for a response from the Italian dictator. At 10:25 P.M., according to the transcript, Prince Philip called the Chancellery in Berlin from Rome. Hitler himself grabbed the phone. The Duce, the prince reported, "had accepted the whole thing in a friendly manner."

> HITLER: Then please tell Mussolini I will never forget him for this!
> PRINCE: Yes, sir.
> HITLER: Never, never, never, no matter what happens! . . .
> PRINCE: Yes, sir. I told him that, too.
> HITLER: As soon as the Austrian affair has been settled, I shall be ready to go with him through thick and thin — through anything!
> PRINCE: Yes, my Führer.
> HITLER: Listen! . . . You may tell him that I do thank him from the bottom of my heart. Never, never shall I forget it. . . .

This was the sort of material which understandably we newspapermen on the spot at the time could never get. Only the captured documents could reveal what went on inside the cuckooland of the Third Reich. Every week, even after I had started writing, I made new discoveries as I continued to wade through the documentation. My excitement grew. I was, I hoped, transmitting it to the pages I was writing. And I was glad I had attempted this formidable task. If I could hold out and somehow keep my family from starving, I would have, I began to think, a good book and perhaps the first to reveal the inside story of the Third Reich, which had so disgraced the German people, their history and culture, and had caused so much suffering in this world.

We could pinpoint at last, for example, the exact moment and occasion when Adolf Hitler made his fateful decision to go to war and, as it happened, eventually plunge most of the world and all the major powers into the deadliest armed conflict the planet had ever seen. Early in his political career as a Nazi rabble-rouser, Hitler had talked about the necessity of Germany's waging war, once it became strong again. War would be necessary in order to reoccupy the Rhineland, take over his native Austria and eliminate Czechoslovakia, fall upon France to revenge the defeat of 1918, and then attack and destroy Poland and Russia, which had the *Lebensraum* he said Germany needed.

But these were his general ideas formulated when he was writing *Mein Kampf* after the fiasco of his Beer Hall Putsch in Munich in 1923. Not even many Germans had taken him seriously. But now he was Master of Germany and on assuming power he had begun at once to rebuild the armed forces in defiance of Versailles. What, we wondered, had happened to his military ambitions? Had they become more precise? Or had they mellowed?

It was not possible for us correspondents in Berlin to find out. We knew he had bluffed his way into reoccupying the Rhineland in 1936. The French easily could have repelled him had they had the will. It was not difficult to know where the Nazi dictator would strike next: at his native Austria, where he was already stirring up trouble. Then at Czechoslovakia. With Austria in his hands, the Czechs would be surrounded on three sides and doomed.

But each such move would risk war. Was Hitler prepared to take the risk? Most of us thought not, not for the time being, simply because Germany, despite its feverish rearmament, was not yet strong enough to take on the major powers — Britain, France, and Russia — should the war spread, as it seemed likely to. This was in 1937. That year there was no further Nazi aggression, and we felt somewhat confirmed.

The captured Nazi documents revealed that we were wrong. They showed that it was indeed in 1937 that Hitler made his fateful decision to go to war. We have the date: November 5, 1937.

On the afternoon of that autumn day Adolf Hitler called in to the Reich Chancellery in Berlin six individuals: Field Marshal Werner von Blomberg, minister of war and commander in chief of the armed forces;

Colonel General Baron Werner von Fritsch, commander in chief of the army; Admiral Dr. Erich Raeder, commander in chief of the navy; Colonel General Hermann Göring, commander in chief of the air force; Baron Konstantin von Neurrath, foreign minister; and Colonel Friedrich Hossbach, military adjutant to the Führer. Colonel Hossbach was not a name I recognized, but he had played an important role that day. He took notes of what Hitler said and five days later wrote them up in a highly secret memorandum, thus recording for history one of the decisive turning points in the life of the Third Reich. The Führer himself regarded his remarks as so important — they were the fruit, he said, of "thorough deliberation and the experience of four and a half years of power" — that, in the event of his death, he explained, they should be regarded as his last will and testament. The colonel's minutes showed up at Nuremberg. As I sat writing in my barn at the farm some twenty years later, I had on my desk a copy of the minutes and also of another captured document which told of what led up to the day of Hitler's decision.

Some six months earlier, on June 24, Field Marshal Werner von Blomberg on the orders of Hitler had given the commanders of the three armed services a directive marked "Top Secret" preparing them for what the Führer would now, in November, lay down as his irrevocable goal. Strangely enough, the directive began by assuring the generals that the general political situation was such that Germany "need not consider an attack from any side." Neither the Western powers nor Russia, it explained, had any desire for war nor were they prepared for it. Nevertheless, the German armed forces must be ready to exploit "politically favorable opportunities should they occur. Preparations . . . for a possible war in the mobilization period 1937–1938 must be made with this in mind." For war right away, that is.

What possible war, since Germany need not fear an attack "from any side"? Well, Blomberg laid it down, several wars. A war on two fronts, with the French fighting in the west and Czechoslovakia in the east, with perhaps Poland and England drawn in. There could be a surprise German attack on Czechoslovakia, which, said the directive, "must be eliminated from the very beginning." Then the generals must get ready for "armed intervention" in Austria and Spain.

So the top German generals had had advance warning of the Führer's thoughts as they assembled at the Chancellery in Berlin on the afternoon of November 5, 1937, to hear him expound them. It was 4:15 P.M., and they listened to their Master for four hours, the meeting, according to the minutes, breaking up at 8:30. They heard a mouthful.

Germany had to have more space, Hitler said, and not in some faraway African colonies but in Europe. "Germany's problem could be solved only by force," he explained, and the only "question was when and where." Germany's vast armaments would begin to become obsolete by 1943. And in the meantime, Germany's enemies, France, Britain, and Russia, were beginning to rearm. So he was resolved, he said, to wait no longer than 1943–1945 to "solve Germany's problem of space." If favorable circumstances arrived, such as the French being paralyzed by internal strife or tied down by war with Italy, he would strike sooner against Austria and Czechoslovakia — "as early as 1938," he said, which was only two months away. The conquest of "the Czechs would have to be carried out with lightning speed." He assured his generals that Britain, France, and Russia would not move against him.

So as evening fell over Berlin that autumn day of 1937, it was clear to the German generals and the German foreign minister that Adolf Hitler had crossed his Rubicon. Germany would go to war, if necessary the very next year, at the latest in 1943.

To judge by the Hossbach minutes of the meeting, the raw decision stunned them. Not, it is clear, because of any doubts about the morality of German aggression against its neighbors. But because they knew Germany, for all its frantic rearmament, was not yet ready for war. On that ground Blomberg, Fritsch, and Neurath dared to object to Hitler's decision. They represented what they must have thought was a powerful opposition: the army and the Foreign Office. It was the last time they or anyone else in Germany talked back to the Nazi dictator. Within three months all three were gone from office.

We knew of their departure when it happened: it was publicly announced. What the correspondents — and I think that was also true for the diplomats — did not know were the weird events that led to the fall of the two ranking generals. Nor, of course, did we know that Hitler had made his irrevocable decision to go to war. How different history might have turned out had it become known!

The stories eventually revealed by the Reich's secret archives of how Field Marshal von Blomberg and General von Fritsch — the latter the epitome of the Prussian army officer — were disposed of were almost unbelievable, even to us old hands in the Third Reich. I inserted them in the history I was writing to show how Hitler and his psychopathic Nazi party cronies operated by 1938, just five years after grabbing power in this great nation.

What drove the two highest-ranking officers out of the German army had to do with, of all things, matters of sex — true and untrue. I don't believe this had ever happened before in Germany. The army, still dominated by the rigid Prussians, was proud of its old traditions of strict personal morality. An officer had to be and behave like a gentleman. For one thing, he should not marry beneath him.

Field Marshal von Blomberg was well aware of that when six years after the death of his wife of twenty-four years in 1932, he married his secretary, a woman named Erna Gruhn. The very prospect raised more than eyebrows among the old officer corps. A Prussian officer, and certainly a field marshal, did not marry his secretary, a mere commoner. But Hitler, an Austrian, distrusted the stiff officer corps. Its aristocrats, he felt, had never fully accepted him, a plebian from the ranks, a mere corporal in the Great War. He heartily approved of the marriage; and to show it, joined by Göring, he attended the wedding on January 12, 1938, as the chief witness, wishing the couple well as they departed on their honeymoon in Italy. Göring himself had been especially accommodating to the field marshal. When it was discovered that the army chief had a rival for the affections of Fräulein Gruhn who might cause trouble and even attempt to block the marriage, Göring had the man shipped off to South America with a warning not to return.

All seemed well for the field marshal and his commoner bride. But not for long. Soon rumors spread through Berlin that Fräulein Gruhn had an unusual past — hardly one that would fit her to be wife of the commander in chief of the German army. At police headquarters a brief investigation turned up a file marked "Erna Gruhn" that revealed her as a former prostitute. She had grown up in a massage salon run by her mother, which, in Berlin as elsewhere, was merely a camouflage for a brothel.

The police chief gave the file to Göring, who hurried to show it to Hitler, who, after perusing it, blew up. What enraged him particularly was that he had been the chief witness at the wedding. If the news became known, he would be almost as much a laughingstock as the field marshal. He summoned Blomberg, who could not believe the charges against his wife, but who offered nevertheless to divorce her forthwith. But this, Hitler now told him, was not enough. The officer corps itself, he said, was demanding the field marshal's removal. The chief of the General Staff, General Ludwig Beck, had laid it down that "one cannot tolerate the highest-ranking soldier in the army marrying a whore." So Hitler dismissed his field marshal — and however shocked Blomberg may have been about what he had learned of his bride's past, he was still sufficiently enamored to join her in Capri and resume their honeymoon.

The obvious candidate to succeed Blomberg was the commander in chief of the army, General von Fritsch, a gifted but unbending officer of the old school — "a typical Army General Staff character," Admiral Raeder had called him. But Hitler had not forgiven him for opposing his decision of November 5 to go to war. Nor was the dictator unaware, I am sure, of Fritsch's contempt for Nazism and the Nazi cronies who surrounded the Leader. In fact, the general made no bones of his feelings toward the Nazis. Once, at Saarbrücken — it was the day Germany took over the Saar — I had stood next to Fritsch in the reviewing stand as we waited for Hitler to appear. Although he scarcely knew me except as one of the American correspondents in Berlin, he poured out a flood of sarcastic remarks about the Nazi bigwigs, from Hitler on down. He was especially contemptuous of Heinrich Himmler, the chief of the S.S. and the Gestapo. It was the latter who now framed him and brought him down in ruin.

On January 27, 1938, the very day Göring was showing Hitler the police record of Field Marshal von Blomberg's bride, he also produced a still more damaging document against General von Fritsch. It had been provided by Himmler, and it alleged that the army chief had been guilty of homosexual offenses under Section 175 of the criminal code and that for the last two years he had been paying blackmail to an ex-convict to hush the matter up. When the word got out, Fritsch's brother officers demanded that Hitler receive him and give him a chance to answer the charges.

This Hitler agreed to do and summoned the accused general to the Chancellery. A scene took place there that an officer of Fritsch's background was hardly prepared for but which by this time, I believe, had become common among the gangsters who ran the Third Reich. The meeting began reasonably enough. Fritsch gave the Führer his word of honor as an officer that the charges were completely untrue. But Hitler was skeptical. Himmler now produced from a side door in the Chancellery a strange, shuffling, degenerate-looking fellow — Fritsch must have wondered how such a disreputable-looking character ever was let in the Chancellery of the German Reich. He gave his name as Hans Schmidt and admitted to a long prison record dating back to a boys reformatory. His chief interest for years, it developed, had been spying on homosexuals and then blackmailing them. He glanced at General Fritsch and said he recognized him as the army officer whom he had caught in a homosexual offense in a dark alley near the Potsdam railway station in Berlin with an underworld character named "Bavarian Joe." For years, Schmidt said, turning to the three most powerful men in Nazi Germany, Hitler, Göring, and Himmler, this officer had been paying him blackmail to keep quiet.

General von Fritsch was outraged. The spectacle of the head of the German nation bringing in such a shady criminal to such a place on such an occasion for such a purpose rendered him speechless, which Hitler took as a sign of guilt. He thereupon asked for his resignation. Fritsch indignantly refused and asked for a trial before a military court of honor. But Hitler had no intention of giving in. He ordered Fritsch to go on indefinite leave, which meant that the general was suspended as army chief.

There was talk among the senior generals of staging a military revolt and removing Hitler — but it was only talk. For a moment the officer corps thought it had gained a victory and that Fritsch would be restored to his post and Himmler destroyed. A preliminary joint investigation by the army and Ministry of Justice quickly established that General von Fritsch was the victim of a Gestapo frame-up conceived by Himmler. It found that the ex-convict Schmidt had indeed caught an army officer in a homosexual act in a dark alley near the Potsdam station and had successfully blackmailed him for years. But his name was not Fritsch but Frisch, and he was now a bedridden retired cavalry officer listed in the army rolls as Rittmeister von Frisch. The Gestapo had known this, but it had arrested Schmidt and threatened him with death unless he pointed the finger at the army chief. The ailing Rittmeister had also been taken into custody to prevent him from talking, but the army eventually had seized both men from the Gestapo and hidden them until they could testify at the general's hearing before a court of honor, which the Führer had finally promised.

Like so many other promises of his, this was not kept. The court of honor was never allowed to proceed; and the whole matter of military leadership was solved on February 4, 1938, when Hitler announced that he personally was taking over command of the armed services. He relieved sixteen senior generals of their commands and transferred forty-four others. As for Blomberg and Fritsch, he announced that they had resigned "for reasons of health."

Not a word of the real reason for their fall ever reached the public. It remained a top secret until revealed by the captured German documents.

CHAPTER 2

I now had at hand such vast material that the problem was to work one's way through it without getting lost in the forest. It was a constant temptation, to remain lost; for to one who had lived and worked in Nazi Germany, it was utterly fascinating to keep turning up documents that shed a blazing light on events that had long perplexed us or about which we had not known at all. It soon occurred to me that we journalists had really known very little of what was going on behind the scenes in Hitler's Germany.

I began to write — and more rapidly than I had ever been able to do before.

By the fall of 1957, after one year, I had written 500 pages, or about 150,000 words. This was a record for me; I had always written slowly, painfully. But now — and it astounded me — the words came pouring out. Some days I could scarcely come to a stop. By the spring of 1958, I had turned over 805 pages to my editor at Simon and Schuster, Joe Barnes.

Was it any good? I was fairly sure it was. But a writer is rarely a good judge of his handiwork. Joe was an old friend; but, as I have mentioned, he had always been a sharp critic of my work. I sounded him out. And one day he sent over from his farm, which was not far from mine in northwest Connecticut, two memos he had written to Max Schuster, the Simon and Schuster chief. They surprised me. And they gave me the encouragement I needed to plunge on.

The first one, dated September 26, 1957, began:

Dear Max:
    As you know, I don't often do this, but I feel I should let you know, even at this early date, that I have revised sharply my estimate of Shirer's *The Rise and Fall of the Third Reich*. I was always certain that it would be a good and useful book, but after having read 500 pages of the first draft — approximately half the book — I now think of it in terms which I haven't felt like using about any book I've read in a long time.
    It seems to me now that Bill has here the making of a really great book, in many ways but chiefly in two — its true scholarship and its readabil-

ity. . . . He has written it with a good deal of gusto and passion. . . . As you can see, I'm more enthusiastic about this book than anything I've read for a long time.

My editor's enthusiasm did not wane as I fed him more pages. Seven months later, on April 11, 1958, Joe again got off a memo to Max Schuster. He had now read, he said, 805 pages.

> My enthusiasm for the content grows. It seems to me an extraordinary and unorthodox combination of personal reporting and scholarship. . . . The readability, interestingly, seems to me to come from the research even more than from the personal reporting. I am more than ever struck by the fact that this will be the first book on Germany to be based on *all* the records. Whatever else the unconditional surrender did to the world, it gave historians the most detailed record of an entire regime, and Shirer has quarried material from it all. . . .

In his first memorandum the previous fall noting that half the book still remained to be written, Joe had suggested that Simon and Schuster might think of ways of helping me get through it.

> If we could get an advance on serial rights for him, it would speed up the book by releasing him from the need of lecturing and writing magazine articles, but so far I've had no luck. . . . I think he agrees that he oughtn't to take from us any bigger advance than we've already given.

This last was news to me. I would have agreed readily to a further advance! I think Joe, a very subtle guy, was trying to hint to Schuster that if he shared Barnes's enthusiasm, Simon and Schuster might fork over another $10,000 to enable me to work full-time on the rest of the book. The publisher must have been skeptical. At any rate he was not moved by Joe's encomiums to risk any more of his money on the book. In some circles publishers were said to be gamblers, but I did not believe it. They rarely took a chance and backed it with a bit of their capital. Like everyone else, they wanted a sure thing.

By 1957, as I have mentioned, my finances were again becoming disastrous. The $10,000 advance had been spent. I did manage to break through one *Red Channels* barrier and sell two magazine articles: one to *Good Housekeeping* for $2,000 and a second to the *American Weekly* for $1,000.

This saved my life because the lectures were beginning to peter off. My agent warned that he simply could not continue to book me talking on Adolf Hitler and the Third Reich. There was no longer any interest in America in either, he said.

Then why was I taking four or five years out of my life and going broke to write a history of the Third Reich, which would contain necessarily a biography of Hitler? It was a question that kept popping up more and more in my mind. As I approached my fifty-third birthday in February that year I could see no way out of my financial situation. My diary entries became more and more depressed.

In my desperation I turned to the foundations for help. First to the Guggenheim Memorial Foundation. A good many of my friends and acquaintances had received Guggenheim grants and I thought I would have little difficulty. The main objective of the foundation, printed in its brochures, was to give "Fellowships to Assist Research and Artistic Creation." In its application forms it said:

> The Fellowships are awarded to men and women . . . who have already demonstrated unusual capacity for productive scholarship. . . . The Committee of Selection seeks evidence that the candidates are persons of unusual capacity for research, demonstrated ordinarily by the previous publication of contributions to knowledge. . . .

I thought my published works and my research and writing of the Third Reich book qualified me for a grant. Also, I knew the director — or thought I did. This was Henry Allen Moe, with whom I had had on occasion a drink and a little talk at a club we belonged to. I wrote to him and got several of my friends who had already received Guggenheims to write to him about a fellowship for me. He kept putting me off. A letter of June 27, 1957, was typical:

> Dear Mr. Shirer:
> I had expected to be able to see you long before this, but there has been no chance. And now tomorrow I must go off to South America for five weeks. . . .

An earlier letter from the gentleman should have warned me.

> February 20, 1957
> Dear Mr. Shirer:
> I have been up to my ears with things that had to be done. . . . Tonight I have to go away on a trip for the Foundation, but I shall give you a ring when I get back. Please accept my apologies for the delay in replying to your letter.

I never got the ring. And I never got a Guggenheim Fellowship.

Someone suggested that I might fare better with the Ford Foundation. As it happened, I knew one of the directors there also — Shepard Stone, whom I had known when he was an editor on the *New York Times*. I had also seen a lot of him in Germany a few years previously when he was serving as an assistant for press affairs to John J. McCloy, the U.S. high commissioner for Germany. Stone had been very helpful there.

I got in touch with Shep, explained what I was working on, and told him I needed some ten thousand dollars to finish the book. As early as April of 1957 he wrote me he had discussed my case with his colleagues and "found at least some interest." Soon there was at least enough new interest to bring Shep over to my house two or three times to look at what I had so far written on the book and to acquaint himself with the vast documentation with which I was working.

Shep was a somewhat emotional man, and his enthusiasm for my project mounted. Finally one day he dropped by our apartment in New York.

"Hell, Bill," he said. "I can't get you a measly ten thousand dollars. The Ford Foundation doesn't deal in such trifles. But I think I can get you a million bucks."

A million bucks! I was stunned.

"Shep," I said, when I had recovered, "I don't need, or want, a million bucks."

"You don't understand," he said. "What I want to see you develop is a big project. Get a dozen good academic historians from the universities to take over the research under your direction. They can comb through all those hundreds of packing cases of German documents you say are in an old army warehouse in Alexandria, Virginia. If you'll head such a team, I think I can get you a million dollars. But ten thousand? That's out of the question."

I could not envisage myself riding herd on a dozen university professors, who would certainly not like working under a nonacademic writer, a "journalist" at that. I knew what documents I needed and where they were. I could best do my own research. I simply wanted relief from lecturing and writing magazine articles long enough to complete it and finish the book. Ten thousand dollars this year and perhaps another ten thousand the next year would really see me through.

But apparently for the people at the Ford Foundation this was too small an amount to warrant their attention. In the end I never got a cent.

I went back to the magazines. By the summer of 1958, I had advanced far enough to be able to offer them pieces from the book based on material from the secret papers never published before. The skulduggery — the lies and deceit — in which Hitler engaged to take Austria and Czechoslovakia and Poland; the revelations of the secret Hitler-Stalin pact in which the great ideological adversaries agreed to divide up Poland between them; why Hitler decided not to try to invade England; why he went to war against Russia and took on the United States. One section of the book, I thought, "The Road to War," would make a good magazine serial. At last, after years of work, I had produced an account of how the mad Führer had secretly and deliberately taken that road. It was a story not yet known.

For several months it looked as if *Life* would take the last piece. At one point its editors spoke of paying ten thousand dollars for the section. But in the end they turned it down.

The *Saturday Evening Post* was especially frosty — and, I thought, high hat. One of its editors, Robert Murphy, wrote my agent on April 9, 1958.

> I am returning William Shirer's book chapters which you sent over the other day. I am afraid that we can't excerpt anything from it, because that would rob the material of the only thing that really sets it apart from earlier recaps and that is the documentation.

So except for documentation, my opus, which I thought was so new and original and revealing, was to the *Post* merely another "recap"!

A little earlier, in January, another *Post* editor, Richard Thruelsen, had rejected the manuscript on different grounds.

> We all agree that you have a very good book in this Shirer material (if you can judge by a chapter), but it doesn't appeal to us as *Post* material. It's a little too journalistic for our editorial project and overly historical for our regular article list.

Roger Straus, who had remained a friend despite my departing his publishing house, suggested to me that I get the *Reader's Digest* to advance me a sizable sum in return for the exclusive rights to magazine material from the book. Paul Reynolds, my agent, was on particularly good terms with the *Digest* editors; and I had seen something of its owners and publishers, DeWitt Wallace and his wife, Lela Acheson, at the time of *Berlin Diary*. But the best we could get out of the *Digest* was their agreement to take one short piece for from fifteen hundred dollars to two thousand dollars, "if the writing is satisfactory."

With the foundations and the magazines out, my prospects of being able to finish the book became more and more dim. At some point soon, it seemed fairly certain, I would have to lay it aside and get a job of some sort to keep my family afloat. My diary in 1958 is full of accounts of wild attempts to come up with something that would enable me to go on writing — now that I was so near the end of the book. I had invested so many years in this work it seemed outrageous not to be able to finish it. I simply couldn't afford not to.

All that year, while researching and writing twelve to fourteen hours a day, I thrashed around for some solution. There had to be a way out! I suggested to the people at *The Nation* — old friends — that they make me foreign editor. The magazine had been without one for years, and showed it. A diary note recalls a grandiose project I began cooking up in which I hoped to draw Joe Barnes as a partner.

March 3, 1958.
To discuss with Barnes.
PROJECT for a Publishing Venture.

IDEA: To set up a small company here to follow new books, new writers, in Europe thru literary and book-publishing periodicals there, through our contacts abroad, and to have read HERE by our own staff the foreign books that look promising.

I went on to note that American publishers were not "equipped" to comb foreign countries for new writers, new books. For one thing, they didn't know the languages. Foreign agents sent them some suggestions but were not very enterprising. So we published a few well-known European authors but were ignorant of the young, unknown ones who were beginning to be published in their native lands. Our company would sell these last to American publishers.

Joe and I could follow books and writers in England, France and Germany — and Joe in addition, in Russia.

And I mentioned friends who could cover the various countries and languages in the rest of Europe, including the Scandinavias.

Joe thought it a good idea but one that would take years really to launch. In the meantime, he said, I had to finish the book. He was wracking his brains to find some magazine that would give me the advance I needed to pull me through. He had not given up entirely, he said, on *Look*.

The author with elder daughter, Eileen Inga, Cape Cod, Massachusetts, 1941

The author with his family, Bronxville, New York, 1941 (l–r) Inga, Shirer, Tess, Linda

Proud father with Inga
and Linda

Tess Shirer at the time of her
marriage, 1931

John Gunther

Edward R. Murrow
and the author aboard
the *Queen Mary*, 1945

The author and Murrow at work after the war

The author with Elmer Davis and Rex Stout at
a Yankee baseball game

With Kay Boyle in
Stamford, Connecticut,
1978

Clipping the newswire
at CBS

Radio years at MBS

The author working in his study, Bronxville,
New York

On a visit home with the author's mother

The farmhouse in
Torrington, Connecticut

Shirer and his granddaughter, Deirdre, in
Torrington, 1966

The author's home in Lenox, Massachusetts

Christmas dinner with Inga (l),and Linda (r), 1975

With grandchildren
Christina and
Alexander

The author in the
country with Linda
and her children

The author with Marge Champion at the Winter
Palace, Leningrad 1982

At Saint Isaac's
Cathedral, Leningrad,
1982

On the bank of the
Neva, Leningrad 1982

The author on his sailboat, Stockbridge Bowe, 1980

Hamilton Fish Armstrong, editor of *Foreign Affairs* and an old friend, also began to be concerned about my not finishing the book. He had been helpful in dozens of ways and had got the Council on Foreign Relations, which published *Foreign Affairs,* to cooperate with me in the research through its excellent library. When I told him at the end of the summer in 1958 that I did not see how I could support my family over the winter without getting a job and abandoning the book for the time being, he suggested that if I asked the council to appoint me a "Historical Research Fellow," they might do it. I applied formally for the place; but apparently it did not yet exist, and I heard no further about it.

I began to look around for a job. A friend at the Mutual Broadcasting Company tipped me off that the network was looking for a full-time commentator and that perhaps the *Red Channels* ban could be breached. I did a couple of trial broadcasts, but some vice-president did not much like my voice and even less my delivery. It was too slow, too reflective, he said. Still, the job hung in the air for several weeks, and it looked as if I might possibly get it.

I called up Ham Armstrong. I was flat broke, I said. I might possibly get a job, which I hated, at Mutual. But that would mean abandoning the book — at least for now.

"You can't do that!" Ham said sternly. "You've got to finish the book."

"I've also got to eat," I said. "And my wife and the kids have to eat."

"How near are you to finishing the book?"

"I need one more year," I said.

"How much do you need to tide you over for the year?"

"Ten thousand dollars would do it," I said.

"Well, that's not a fortune. There must be some way of raising ten thousand." He hesitated. "Have you tried the small foundations?"

"No. Not after the big ones, Guggenheim and Ford, turned me down."

"Do you know Frank Altschul?" he asked.

"Yes. But not well."

"He has some small family foundation, I believe. I'll get to him and then back to you."

Altschul had made, I believe, a fortune in business. He was now retired and spent a good deal of time at the council of which he was currently president. I had met him there. Armstrong quickly ascertained that Altschul maintained a modest family project called the Overbrook Foundation. At Ham's urging, he agreed to have the foundation advance me five thousand dollars immediately and a further five thousand six months later if I could show that I had made progress on the book and was within a half a year or so of finishing it.

This saved my life and my book. We quickly paid what we owed on our grocery bills, assured the girls they could remain in school — Inga was a junior at Radcliffe and Linda a senior at the Dalton School in New York — and I settled back to fourteen hours a day of writing. I had reached a point in the book where the tide of war had changed; the once invincible German army was now in retreat in Russia and in North Africa; and I was about to halt the narrative to write a long and terrible chapter about Hitler's barbarous so-called New Order in Europe, including the "Final Solution" for the Jews. The revelations of a vast array of secret Nazi documents not only about what Hitler had done in the conquered lands but, worse, what he intended to do, were so shocking that I could scarcely believe them. He planned to make Europe, including Russia, a gigantic land of slaves to serve their German masters. The Jews were to be completely exterminated. The Slavs were to be starved down to a manageable level of lowly toilers for the Third Reich. Russia as a nation would, in the Nazi phrase, cease to exist.

For years the prospect of such a hell, worse than anything our poor planet had ever suffered before, had kept me in a state of depression. Then in 1942, with Hitler's first military reverses, one could begin to hope that that world might be saved from this calamity after all. With 1943 bringing Germany's fateful defeat at Stalingrad, the worst disaster to the German army in its history, the clearing of the Germans out of North Africa by the Anglo-American armies, and the Allied landings in Italy, it became certain that the New Order was doomed. But it was a fearful chapter in history nevertheless, and it had to be set down. Then in 1944 came the Anglo-American landings in France, the sweep across that country past Paris to the German frontier. The Russians, for their part, neared the old German border in the east. The end could not be far off; and it came at 2:41 on the morning of May 7, 1945, when in a little red schoolhouse at Reims, Germany surrendered unconditionally to the Allies and repeated the act in Berlin a couple of days later.

The war against Germany, the most destructive, the most savage warring that Europe had ever seen, was over. And as I got to that point, my book was finished too. I had watched the rise and some of the fall of the Third Reich over the years. Hitler had boasted it would last a thousand years. It had expired after exactly twelve years, four months, and eight days. Still, it had seemed an age to those who suffered its outrages, an Age of Darkness. Now a bleak night was descending on the Master Race, which had perpetrated so much evil.

All that autumn of 1958, I wrote and wrote, and all that winter of 1958–1959 and the spring that followed and the summer. My family and friends said later I batted away at my typewriter as if I were possessed. For the first time, I did not jot down a line in my diary. When I first started checking over my journal for this book, I noted that since I could find nothing for 1959, that year's entries "were missing." And then I realized that most likely there had never been any. An entry on April 12, 1960, explained: "Very few entries in recent years. Most of my time and energy for more than five years has gone into research-ing and writing the Third Reich book. . . ."

There is not even a diary entry for the day I finished the book. But two letters, one to Kay Boyle and the other to Ham Armstrong, tell a little of how it was and identify the date. The letters were written on Monday, August 31, 1959, from the farm and reveal that I came to the last page of the book just a week before, on Monday, August 24.

Dear Kay:
    . . . Last Monday evening, a little after seven, after a last twelve-hour stretch, I came to the last line on the last page! The youngsters . . . raced down to a drugstore and produced a bottle of champagne. That last page was Number 1795, so you can see what I've been through. There still remains some revisions and cutting to do, but the load is off my back and mind. At that, it is a jolt to part with something you've been living with daily for five years. . . .

I wrote Armstrong similarly, adding:

Since you have sustained me over the years with your encourage-ment, wondering perhaps whether I would ever finish the damn thing, I hasten to give you this news, and I would appreciate it if you passed it along to Frank Altschul, whose aid helped me through the last and most difficult year.

I felt exhausted but exhilarated at finally coming to the end. And I felt good about the book. I was sure it was the best I had ever written. It was certainly the most ambitious in its sweep of history. It was by far the longest. I thought it might interest a lot of people not only because of its revelations based on the secret documents but also because of the way I tried to write it: history as literature, not cut-and-dried history as so many academics wrote.

But I had no illusions that it would sell. Everyone connected with it — my publisher, my editor, my agent, and my close friends over in West Cornwall, Jim Thurber, Mark Van Doren, Lewis Gannett, who had read part of it — had assured me that it would not. And I had no reason to doubt them.

Indeed in my letter to Kay Boyle on finishing the book I had, after remarking on what a jolt it was to part with something you had been living with so closely for years, added:

> But I must get back to making a little money, if that is possible, what with two girls in Radcliffe this year [Linda had joined Inga there the previous fall].

For not only the book was finished that summer's end but also the ten thousand dollars from the Overbrook Foundation that had enabled me to wind up the five years' toil on the work. An advance of five thousand dollars had in the meantime come in from Secker and Warburg in London for the British rights to the book. So we could get by until the end of the year. But after that?

Publication by Simon and Schuster would come in the spring of 1960. But the book would have to pay back in royalties the ten thousand dollars originally advanced by the publisher before it would begin paying me anything. And everyone concerned said it would be lucky if it managed to pay back the advance. I began to see that soon I would be back to where I had been for the last dozen years: struggling to make ends meet and not quite making it. The wonderful feeling I had had at finishing the book began to turn to ashes.

Then luck again turned my way.

Back in 1957, Joe Barnes, in his memo to Max Schuster about his reassessment of the book after reading the first 500 pages of manuscript, had mentioned his "hope of getting Bill Attwood, Leo Rosten and Mike Cowles excited about it." Joe apparently had kept after them gently but firmly through the years. I had mentioned what I was working on two or three times to Mike Cowles, the owner and publisher of Look, when I ran into him. I did not know him well; but out in Iowa when I was young, I had met the Cowles family, who were building up the Des Moines Register to be the best daily newspaper in the state. From this connection I had written a few pieces for the Cowles magazine when it was in its infancy and not doing very well.

Early that summer of 1959, we sent Look a chunk of it entitled "The Road to War" (the part that Life had turned down). I was so buried in my writing as I was coming down the home stretch of the book that I remember only vaguely that the people at *Look* bought one piece from it and rushed it to press in time for the twentieth anniversary of Hitler's launching of World War II. It was published in the September 1, 1959, issue — exactly twenty years after the Führer marched into Poland and plunged the world into war. It appeared as the first in a series called "Untold Stories of World War II" and was subtitled "How Hitler Launched World War II." A picture of Hitler adorned the cover.

This angered and frustrated the circulation manager of the magazine. I was having a drink one day in the first floor café in the *Look* building with Mike Cowles and two or three of his editors who had worked on the script when the circulation chief burst upon us. He was waving an advance copy of *Life* and one of *Look*.

"Hey, boss," he said to Cowles, "how in hell do you expect me to sell our mag against *Life* when we come out with a cover like this?" He flaunted it before us. It showed a stern-looking Hitler. Next to him was a German general with thin lips and a grim expression, whom I took to be Field Marshal Walther von Brauchitsch.

"Now take a look, for Christ's sake, at what the opposition is giving us." He held up the cover of *Life* depicting a beautiful young woman clad in one of the most fetching bathing suits I had ever seen. The bathing suit was a wonderful marine blue.

"Tell me, boss," he practically yelled at Cowles, "how I'm going to sell that bastard Hitler against that lovely bathing beauty. Just tell me, please!"

"Let's wait and see." Cowles smiled. He gave the impression of knowing something the rest of us did not know.

I do not recall my agent's telling me of how much he had got out of *Look*. Perhaps he didn't want to distract me from finishing the book. It was certainly not the ten thousand dollars *Life* had at first talked to us about. It probably was twenty-five hundred dollars — a tidy, timely sum to us at any rate.

More good fortune — and from *Look* — was to follow. There had been some opposition among the editors at *Look* to taking a piece from the book on the grounds that, as my lecture agent had found, there was no American interest in Hitler or Nazi Germany. But Mike Cowles, a keen journalist, had not agreed. He had had some testing done, he told me later, the results of which gave him a contrary view. The reception of that September 1, 1959, issue of *Look* convinced him. Apparently it outsold *Life*. This was good news to me. Maybe that five years out of my life given to writing the history of Nazi Germany had not been spent in vain. There was some interest in the subject after all.

A few days after the typescript of the book was finished, Mike Cowles took the copy I had promised him, split it up into five sections, and asked his five top editors to each take one section home for the weekend, read it, and report back Monday morning to him whether any more of the book was suitable for further pieces in *Look*. I regretted that the gentlemen had to spoil their weekend, but I was also hopeful that some good might come of it. Hopeful but not very confident. My editor and publisher at Simon and Schuster and my agent shared my feelings.

On September 24, exactly one month after finishing the book, I went up to the *Look* offices on Madison Avenue, opposite the CBS building where I had worked for so long, and signed a contract to write a piece of some 25,000 words by the end of December on the life of Adolf Hitler, based on the book. The magazine would extract three articles from the manuscript at five thousand dollars apiece. It also had the right to publish a fourth piece at the same price. We had not seen such sums since the golden days of radio and of *Berlin Diary* ages before. We were once again, after such a long drought, in clover! The feeling of relief was indescribable. I went around the streets of New York in a great white, shining cloud for days thereafter.

There remained, of course, concern over the publication and reception of the book in the following spring. I thought the interest of *Look* was a promising sign that perhaps the book would go well after all. But I soon found that this was not the view of some at Simon and Schuster.

For one thing, the book was awfully long. With notes and index, it would come to over 1,200 printed pages. Joe Barnes sent me a copy of a sarcastic letter from A. J. P. Taylor, the British historian at Oxford, sneering at the length of a book by Max Lerner, which Simon and Schuster had sent him. Taylor, never very friendly to his rivals in America, wrote:

> . . . The industry, grasp and range of the author stagger me. The mere physical effort is more than I could undertake in a lifetime. But all the same: the book is too long and too large at any rate for feeble members of an old continent. I cannot even hold it with comfort. How then can I read it?
>
> With great respect, American writers and publishers who produce books of this size earn from me condemnation, not praise. You are killing literature. But, of course, you are an outsized nation; and maybe it is all right for you. We have abandoned projects of this size. We jog along from

day to day, enjoying what comes — including books of reasonable compass — until you or the Russians press the button.*

Some American reviewers were declaring that they would no longer read books with an array of footnotes. My God, I thought, my book must have at least a thousand. I had tried to document each fact and had noted it in a footnote.

And then the only quarrel Joe Barnes and I, close friends since our days in Berlin together on the eve of the war, had ever had broke out. One day in the country Joe and his wife Betty dropped over for a drink. Joe and I had a few editing chores to chew over and we went upstairs to my small study. Suddenly Joe lit into me for signing the contract to give *Look* three more pieces from the book.

"I know you've been broke for a long time and need the money. But dammit, you've ruined the sale of the book for us. After *Look* has published three or four more pieces, who is going to buy the book?"

Joe was angry. And he soon reduced me to the same state. He accused me of short-sighted greed, of not remembering how much I owed to Simon and Schuster.

I suddenly realized why Joe was so furious with me. The bigwigs at Simon and Schuster had failed to tell him that they themselves had encouraged our negotiations with *Look* and approved them. They thought publication in a mass-circulation magazine of a few pieces from the book would immensely help it by bringing it to the attention of millions of readers. Joe found it hard to believe; he simply could not imagine that his bosses would deliberately, as he said, ruin the sales of the book. He became even more angry, and I resented it. We almost came to blows. We were saved by our spouses. Betty and Tess had heard our shouting and rushed upstairs to separate us. We all four took a walk in the woods so that Joe and I could cool off, returned to the house for a drink, and before the evening was out we were old friends again.

As encouraged as Simon and Schuster was by *Look*'s interest in the book and the resulting massive, free publicity it would bring, it none-theless decided to launch the book with a printing of only 20,000 copies. It was not a bad beginning; but it showed, I thought, the publisher's lack of confidence in the book.

My English publisher was even more cautious. One day Fred War-burg, head of Secker and Warburg in London, came to lunch at our place in New York to discuss his publishing the book in England. It was

* The Oxford don's loathing of long books did not prevent him from writing a book, *English History, 1914–1945*, published in 1965, that was 708 pages in length.

a great book, he said; he was proud to publish it but . . . he hesitated.

"But what?" I asked.

"Like many wonderful books," he replied, "I'm afraid it won't sell. It's awfully long, you know. And studded with footnotes." Once more he paused. "I'll tell you, Bill, what we're going to do. We're not going to print it ourselves in England. We're buying sheets from Simon and Schuster."

"But printing costs in England are less than half what they are here," I protested. "Besides," I said foolishly, "Simon and Schuster are only printing twenty thousand copies to begin with. They won't have any to spare for you."

"Well, they've just sold me seventy-five hundred copies," Warburg said, rather smugly, I thought.

"But that leaves Simon and Schuster with only twelve and a half thousand copies." I was naïve, I can see now.

"That's right," Warburg said.

I felt like ushering him out of the house before Tess could serve the dessert. Especially after he added insult to injury by saying that because of the high price of the Simon and Schuster sheets he would have to charge the British equivalent of ten dollars for the book, the same as Simon and Schuster. That, I argued, was pricing it beyond the means of most book buyers in England. Even here in America the ten dollars Simon and Schuster was going to ask for the book practically guaranteed a small sale. No book at that price, I was told, had ever done well. Warburg, if he printed in England, I pointed out, could bring the book out at half that price. But he was adamant, and I got rid of him as soon as I could. After he left, I took a long walk up First Avenue to cool off. The roar and fumes from the trucks, bumper to bumper, did not improve my spirits. When the money from *Look* is gone, I thought to myself, I'll really have to look for a permanent job. I had been trying to write for twelve years; in fact, I had been trying to write all my adult life. It had given me a living in journalism but not in books. I would never give it up, but I had to abandon the idea that I could live by it. Well, how many writers could? Damn few. Maybe a couple of hundred, according to the studies we had made at the Authors Guild. A couple of hundred out of maybe ten thousand.

Simon and Schuster now set publication for June 1960. Friday, April 1, was April Fool's Day, though I had forgotten it. I was alone at the farm preparing to return to New York for a few days. I had spent the week plowing and harrowing the vegetable garden, planting some early lettuce, peas, and onions, and trimming the berry bushes. It was outdoor work I loved, and it had given me time to contemplate. I would spend the summer trying to get a regular job. Perhaps I could get back into broadcasting. Television was starting to break through, and I had some ideas about it as a news medium. Maybe teaching was the answer. I could never get a job as a history professor at the college level because I lacked a graduate degree. But the journalism schools in our universities were at last reaching out for veteran journalists as teachers. Perhaps I could get a job at the Columbia University journalism school, one of the best in the country. That way I could remain in New York and keep the Connecticut farm.

With these thoughts in mind, I started putting a few things in my suitcase for the sojourn in New York. The telephone rang. It was Joe Barnes, and he was excited.

"Bill, I've got some news for you. The Book-of-the-Month Club has just taken *The Rise and Fall*. Congratulations!"

I was speechless.

"Well . . . uh . . . that . . . uh is good news," I stammered finally. I could not believe it.

Then I thought of the date.

"Come on, Joe," I said. "This is no time for an April Fool's joke. I'm not in the mood."

"It's God's truth," Joe insisted.

"Well, thanks for telling me," I said and hung up.

I called my agent. It was news to him, and he very much doubted it.

"I sure hope it's true," he said. "But I think if it were, Book-of-the-Month Club or Simon and Schuster would have called me."

I got back to Joe at Simon and Schuster. He was a little annoyed at my disbelief. "Why don't you call Irita?" he said. "Maybe you'll take her word for it." Irita Van Doren, editor of the Sunday *Herald-Tribune* book section, was an old friend.

"It's true," Irita said when I reached her by phone. "I was about to call you. I'm organizing a little party for you this very afternoon — at my house. Can you make it to New York by six or so?"

"I'll try," I said.

My agent called back. He at last had the news too. He rattled off a few details.

"To start with," he said, "there's a guarantee of twenty thousand dollars for you. But the big thing is that a Book-of-the-Month Club selection means Simon and Schuster will sell a lot more copies than they ever expected. It will give a tremendous sendoff to the book. But publication date will have to be postponed. Simon and Schuster has just called that they're putting it off from June to October or November."

So we would have for the first time in ages — thanks to *Look* and the Book-of-the-Month Club — a good summer. No more money worries, at least for a couple of years. I was back in the clouds again, and I had to be careful driving the three hours back to New York not to veer off the road. At Irita's, I drank too much.

CHAPTER 3

Despite the Book-of-the-Month Club's taking the book and all the publicity from the *Look* piece, Simon and Schuster stuck with its print order of 12,500 copies (after selling 7,500 to Warburg) when the book finally came out on October 17, 1960. I wondered about it but I concluded that the publisher knew what he was doing. My chief concern now was how the book would be received. A good many writers claim they never read their reviews. I do read them. And in this instance I felt some trepidation. I remember hearing from the grapevine that the Sunday *New York Times Book Review* had given the book for review to a prestigious Oxford historian, H. R. Trevor-Roper, whom I much admired. I had freely quoted from his brilliant book *The Last Days of Hitler*. But I had misgivings about what kind of a piece he would write. British book reviewers had been very tough recently on American writers. Trevor-Roper's colleague and rival at Oxford, A. J. P. Taylor, was a good example. In deploring American books and authors, especially those concerned with history, they seemed to me to be taking out their resentment at the way America, not Britain, was now the world power of the West. Also I was aware of the disdain of academic historians for former journalists like myself who tried to write history. This was particularly virulent in America. In England it was not so bad but still . . . was an eminent Oxford historian, himself an authority on Nazi Germany, likely to look kindly and with understanding on an American journalist daring to write the first fully documented history of the Third Reich?

I remember thinking that, well, the *Times* never did like me. It never forgave me writing for its rival, the *Herald-Tribune*. I had once exchanged some harsh words in correspondence with Arthur Hays Sulzburger, the *Times* publisher, whose family owned the newspaper. The *Times* had not even reviewed two or three of my last books. So now it had gone to an Englishman and a university professor to write about this one. That probably meant two strikes against me. And in the one publication that counted most.

H. R. Trevor-Roper's review of *The Rise and Fall of the Third Reich* was spread all over page one of the Sunday *New York Times Book Review* of October 16, 1960. It flabbergasted me. I could scarcely believe it. The editor's caption gave the first hint.

LIGHT ON OUR CENTURY'S DARKEST NIGHT
The Awful Story of Hitler's Germany
Is Movingly Told in a Masterly Study

How can we look objectively on the Third Reich? the Oxford historian asked.

> It was the greatest, most horrible phenomenon of the twentieth century. . . . In ordinary circumstances it would be impossible, only half a generation after its end, in the twilight period between the passion and documentation, to write its history. But with the Third Reich nothing was ordinary, not even its end. . . . In that total annihilation all the secrets of [Hitler's] rule were broken open, all the archives captured, their truth tested in court, their contents made public.
>
> Now, as never before, the living witnesses can converge with the historical truth. All they need is a historian. In William L. Shirer they have found him.

I had to stop there. It was almost too much for me.

> He was himself in Germany from 1934 to 1941 — need we refer to his "Berlin Diary"? Since the war he has studied the massive documents made available by Hitler's total defeat. And now he has brought together his experience and his study in a monumental work, a documented 1,200-page history of the whole episode of Hitler's Third Reich.

"Of course, he will have his critics; every author has," Trevor-Roper went on and proceeded to note some criticisms of his own.

"But these are trivial criticisms in view of the greatness of his achievement," he said. "This is a splendid work of scholarship, objective in method, sound in judgment, inescapable in its conclusions."

A little dizzy from reading the *Times* and immensely grateful to Trevor-Roper, I turned to the Sunday *New York Herald-Tribune Book Review*. I was not personally acquainted with the editor of the Sunday *Times Book Review*, but the editor of the *Herald-Tribune*'s rival review, Irita Van Doren, was one of my dearest friends. She, too, had given my book the entire front page with a review by Gordon A. Craig, a professor of history at Princeton and a well-known author of books and articles on Germany.

It was quickly apparent that Professor Craig did not agree with

Professor Trevor-Roper that the Third Reich had found its historian in me. By no means! He conceded that I had written "an immensely readable book." But he did not think it was much good as history. For one thing, it was too long. Professor Craig thought I should have shortened it by cutting and paraphrasing "in most cases" the voluminous documents such as secret speeches, diplomatic notes, military directives, and even the unique personal correspondence between Mussolini and Hitler.

The book also, he thought, "was out of balance." The reviewer would have organized the material differently, putting more emphasis on Nazi activity during the Weimar Republic and the first years of power.

Despite the mountains of documents on which I had drawn, Craig thought I had missed some important material; and he regretted that I had not read the book of a German historian on the Weimar period. (I had read him though I had failed to note it in my bibliography.) Craig thought it "a pity" that I had not used more material recently published in Germany, especially by the *Vierteljahrheft für Zeitgeschichte*, which I did not consider very objective. (It would later devote an entire issue to attacking the book, something it admitted it had never done before.)

Irita wrote me immediately that Craig's review was "a matter of great distress" to her. But, of course, she respected his right to set down his own views of the book, as I did. Irita's headline scarcely reflected the contents of the review. It read:

SHIRER'S VIVID, MONUMENTAL CHRONICLE OF NAZI GERMANY.

It was fine for me but not very accurate in view of what Craig actually wrote.*

To my surprise I fared well in the *Chicago Tribune*, whose lordly owner, Robert Rutherford McCormick, had fired me in Vienna back in 1932 when I was the paper's correspondent there. Perhaps in the long

---

* In a letter to the *Herald-Tribune*, Kay Boyle, the novelist and a friend of Mrs. Van Doren, protested Craig's review. (She had reviewed the book in the *New York Post*.)

> Gordon A. Craig's review of William L. Shirer's "The Rise and Fall of the Third Reich" is indeed a poor tribute to Mr. Shirer's monumental accomplishment.
> The patronizing attitude of the review and Mr. Craig's listing of the journals, documents and books which Mr. Shirer *should* have read might be seen to have a humorous side if it were not for the fact that the book is, just as Mr. Shirer wrote it, a vitally important contribution to the history of our time. . . .

Miss Boyle also objected to Craig's "dismissing" the book as "a commendable job of research." She thought it was considerably more than that.

interim he had forgotten. (He had forgotten once before, a few days after giving me the gate, when he had written me asking why he never saw my byline in the *Trib* anymore.)

Like the two leading New York Sunday newspapers the *Tribune* devoted all of page one of its Sunday "Magazine of Books" to my opus. The headline read: "Shirer Crowns His Career with Superb History." The reviewer was another academic historian, S. William Halperin, editor of the *Journal of Modern History*. Though the professor contended that the book contained "little that was new or original" (and I had thought that it was bursting with new revelations and insights due to its use of massive documentation never published before in one book!), he was generous enough. He thought that I had "put together a comprehensive, perceptive and highly readable history. . . ."

> The author's erudition is impressive without being obtrusive. The psychological insights are superb. The descriptions of situations and events are among the finest in contemporary reportorial writing. For these reasons "The Rise and Fall of the Third Reich" may be regarded as the crowning achievement of Shirer's distinguished career.

By this time such comments were beginning to endanger my balance. They were puffing me up. A little more and I might begin to take myself much too seriously. The review in *Time* brought me back to earth. The news weekly, with its usual pompousness, thought that "what was needed" to write the history of the Nazi time was not me, but "another Dante or a new Wagner"; and, of course, that left me out — I was far from being any kind of a Dante or Wagner. So . . .

> To his task Shirer brings only modest writing gifts, but he has an advantage that swamps all shortcomings: his material is horribly fascinating. The book may lack literary stature and new insights, but it seizes the reader's interest and holds it to the end.

Time concluded: "Rise and Fall acts as a breezy, journalistic surrogate for better books on specified aspects of Nazism." I would have very much liked to know — and perhaps many readers would have, too — the titles of some of the "better books." But the *Time* reviewer named not a single one.

Time's rival *Newsweek* was somewhat kinder. Its anonymous reviewer thought I had "produced an impressive historical thriller" and that I had "transformed enormous research into orderly drama."

Some months later, in its issue of January 23, 1961, in a piece about such a long and expensive book as mine becoming a best-seller, *Newsweek* recalled the day it had counted me out.*

> Three years ago Shirer was so far out of the limelight that *Newsweek* listed him among famous missing persons in its weekly feature, THE PERISCOPE, "Where Are They Now?" As it turned out, Shirer was . . . toiling away at a book of no very sensational promise.

The reviews in the daily press, on the whole, were more favorable than I had expected. Orville Prescott, who did the daily book column in the *New York Times* and who was no great lover of my previous work, showed a surprising enthusiasm for *The Rise and Fall.* He did note that my opus was almost as long as Gibbon's *Decline and Fall of the Roman Empire* and that it was not written with the formal elegance of that eighteenth-century classic.

"But it is written well, smoothly and lucidly, with a steady narrative drive."

As he proceeded, Prescott became more enthusiastic until he concluded his piece: *"The Rise and Fall of the Third Reich* is one of the most important works of history of our time."

Prescott's opposite number on the *New York Herald-Tribune*, John K. Hutchens, called the book "a masterly performance."

There were brickbats, too, in the daily press, especially if the reviewers were academic historians. Some were closing ranks to rake it over the coals and dismiss it.

Thus Walter Helbronner in the *Richmond News-Leader:* "There is nothing new revealed in this book," he wrote. He did not like my "occasional sweeping statements" and as an example he cited my eyewitness description of some of the English soldiers captured while the German armies were romping through Belgium and France. I had been struck by their poor physical state and had speculated that it was one consequence of England's shameful neglect of its youth between the wars. The professor thought this was typical of "my sweeping statements."

This seemed to me to be characteristic of much of the academic criticism. The professors nitpicked on one small point or another often with reason and just as often, I thought, to show off their learning; but invariably they refrained from giving the reader any perception what-

* See page 183.

soever of the nature and scope of the book or what it tried to cover. They skipped mention of the great historical events that shook Germany, Europe, and the world through the Nazi nightmare and that constituted the heart and core of the book.

George L. Mosse, whom I admired and from whose works I had benefited, was typical, I thought, in his review in *The Progressive*, a periodical I had always liked. He thought my attributing to the Germans "a slavish obedience to the state and a clumsiness in diplomacy" was "distorted" and "not very helpful" in explaining Nazism. He said I seemed "to forget that, as one eminent professor had put it, 'National Socialism gave meaning once more to life for the Germans.'"

I had, in fact, written at length on that subject. But I was still too naïve to realize that many reviewers saw what they wanted in a book and were often blind to what they did not want to see.

Professor Mosse's criticism fascinated me the further I read.

"It is incorrect to say," he went on, "that Germany stressed the state and not the individual. Nazi ideology saw itself as the ultimate fulfillment of the individual."

This was astonishing to one who had lived through the years of frightening regimentation in National Socialist Germany — and from an academic whose writing on the Germans had been much respected. But Mosse grew more astonishing with each paragraph.

> Many an American like Shirer finds it difficult to grasp that the horror that swept over Europe was not madness at all. . . . Few between the wars defended representative and parliamentary government anywhere in Europe.

Few? I don't know where Professor Mosse was, but I was working in Europe in those days and — outside of Germany, Italy, the small countries of the Baltic and the Balkans, and, at the very end, France — I found that the vast majority defended parliamentary democracy: in Great Britain certainly and the Scandinavian countries and in Czechoslovakia, Belgium, Holland, Switzerland, and in Spain during the Republic until Franco, with German and Italian help, overthrew it, and in France until the war came and defeat and parliamentary democracy was destroyed by the German conquerors and their French stooges. The professor's assertion, I thought, was not only highly inaccurate but also a poor explanation for the horrors of Hitler. And I was sure that the horror that swept over Europe *was* a madness and that it came primarily from Berlin where a madman ruled.

The hostility of the American academic historians puzzled me. I had not and would not experience such prejudice from their brethren in Europe. In England, academic historians such as John Wheeler-Bennett, the great authority on the Weimar Republic and the coming of National Socialism as well as on the German military and on the Treaty of Brest-Litovsk, treated me with a great deal of understanding in their criticism.

It was the same in France, where not only the university historians but also some of the principal political figures in my history, former premiers Paul Reynaud and Edouard Daladier, for instance, welcomed my contribution to the history of the times. Daladier, who was premier in the last years leading up to the war, wrote in the Paris *Candide* that he would have acted differently had he known of certain things disclosed in my book:

> We did not know then (1938) [Daladier wrote] the documents published by William Shirer in his . . . history of the Third Reich: the resignation of the Chief of General Staff, General Ludwig Beck on August 18, which was kept strictly secret on the menacing order of Hitler; the declarations to Hitler of General von Weitersheim on August 10 and of those of General Adam, Commander in Chief in the West that the fortification [of the Siegfried Line*] would not be completed by the end of August and that he had not been given enough troops to hold them.
>
> We remained ignorant also of what Shirer has written in his book on the birth of a conspiracy [the military plot to oust Hitler if he ordered an attack on the Czechs — a conspiracy led by General Beck's successor, General Halder].

Daladier was particularly resentful, he told me later in a conversation, that the British government, to whom the German conspirators had confided, had not tipped him off.

In Britain and in France, then, the statesmen involved and the academic historians took my book seriously; though, naturally, they found parts to criticize. They were not suspicious of a work of history simply because it was a "best-seller." One of my American academic friends reminded me that this was not so among many of his colleagues here at home. One evening he telephoned me from the annual meeting of the American Historical Association, then holding its Christmas-week convention in Washington.

---

* The Siegfried Line was supposed to be the German equivalent of France's famed Maginot Line. Begun on the western German border after the Nazi reoccupation of the Rhineland in 1936, it was never completed. But Hitler bluffed France and Britain into believing that it was a formidable barrier.

"Good thing you're not here!" he exclaimed. "The professors are clobbering the hell out of you!"

"Still?" I asked. "What's bothering them now?"

"They can't forgive you for making the best-seller list." He paused. "There's another reason why they can't forgive you."

"And what is that?"

"Because, dammit, you wrote the whole damn history of the Third Reich before any of them had even started to think of doing it. They say you should have left it to them."

"I tried," I said. "I waited and waited for them."

"I know. That bugs them, too. During all that time, they realize, they were sitting on their behinds. Too lazy or too timid to attack those mountains of Nazi documents and organize and write the book."

The childish prejudices of the professors aside, I began to marvel at the wonderful variety of reactions to the book. Lively, individual, differing opinions were, after all, the yeast of our American democratic life.

I had wanted, within my limitations, to write narrative history as literature; and I hoped I had succeeded to some extent. (*Time*, among others, did not think so. But some did. Alden S. Wood in the *Boston Herald*, for one, concluded that I had made "a major contribution to history and literature." Ernst S. Pisko in the *Christian Science Monitor* thought the book secured the author "a front place among contemporary historians.") One thing that bothered me about a good many of our academic historians was they did not seem to connect history with literature. This was painfully evident from the books many of them wrote, in which there was no respect for the beauty and the subtleties and the rhythms of our language nor any feeling for them. Almost all good narrative history, it seemed to me — especially that written for the general public, from Herodotus and Thucydides on — had been good literature as well.

Fellow writers were much kinder than my critics from academe. One of the nicest letters of all came from a novelist I had long admired but did not know personally.

> You have just given me eight days of steady reading, during which I did not want to do anything else but read, and I must thank you most sincerely for this rare pleasure. I was conscious all the time that I was reading of the enormous amount of work you had done, as well as of your unremitting care, and that impression is still with me today, after a night spent away from the Third Reich.

It was acutely (almost painfully) interesting to read the conclusion you drew from your data, and if I felt like disagreeing with you occasionally (we are all of us human when we are not sub-human) the occasions were very few indeed; nearly every time I was converted to a fresh point of view. May I thank you for the great pleasure I personally have experienced from your very remarkable achievement.

Yours sincerely,
C. S. Forester

Terrence Prittie, the *Manchester Guardian* correspondent in Germany after the war, had concluded in his review in the December 1960 issue of the *Atlantic Monthly,* that in my book "there is history which might do the most good after all in Germany. For nothing comparable has been written there; and if anyone ought to read *The Rise and Fall of the Third Reich,* it is the Germans themselves."

But it did not do much good in Germany. As I expected, *The Rise and Fall* had rough sledding when it was published there in translation a year later.* Sixteen years after the Allies had destroyed the Nazis (the Allies, *not* the Germans), the Germans were still not able to face up to the ghastly truth of the barbarian rule of Hitler, which most of them — so far as I, who had lived and worked among them, could see — had supported, often with surprising zeal. By this time the bombed and bombarded land had been largely rebuilt from the ashes and the debris with much Allied help; and the Germans, or at least the West Germans, were regaining their self-confidence and forgetting their past. They were becoming prosperous again in their newly built homes; and they resented being reminded of that terrible past, which was just what they said *The Rise and Fall* did. The newspapers and magazines, and even the chancellor and his government, fell on it with a vengeance. Their anger and hysteria was something to behold, though it did not much surprise me.

The pack was led by a mass-circulation weekly illustrated magazine of supposedly liberal tendencies called *Stern,* which honored me with a long review and an even longer cover story filled with wonderful vituperation and the most amusing personal attacks. A second weekly of conservative bent, *Aktuell,* devoted parts of two issues to clobbering me and suggesting that for such an anti-Nazi book I deserved to be awarded the Order of Lenin. *Der Spiegel,* a weekly whose format had been borrowed from *Time,* joined in assailing me as an "amateur

* *Berlin Diary* was never published in Germany. No German publisher would touch it.

historian" surrounded by "critics and amateur historians who have joined his bandwagon." The first of these it cited it called "the Jewish critic Eliahu Ben Horin," followed by the *New York Times*. The review in the *Stern* was almost a masterpiece in misrepresentation and in what I could only believe, in some instances, was pure invention. "For the American, William L. Shirer," it began, "the war against Germany goes on." (The book actually concluded with the end of World War II and the fall of the Nazi Third Reich.) "He has at his disposal a dangerous weapon: a book in which he tells a million times stories as history. Too many have already taken it as the classic history of the Nazi time."

This was a theme, among others, that ran through most of the diatribes against me in the German press — the resentment that the book had sold a million copies in America and thereby misled so many Americans about the Germans and their history. A second theme followed, apparently even more important for the Germans; for it was belabored not only in the German press but also by the German chancellor and the German government. This was — and *Stern* said it was embittered by it — that publication of my book once again raised anti-German feelings in America and in England.

Distortions in the *Stern* review abounded.

> The book declares that the Germans since Luther were criminals, that under Hitler they could be nothing else and that they always would be. The author in his introduction admits that he hated the Germans. He is silent about whether he still does.

Noting that I had cited Goethe as saying: "I have often felt a bitter sorrow at the thought of the German people, which is so estimable in the individual and so wretched in the generality," *Stern* quipped: "Now, we have seldom read a work of history so full of faults in its details and so wretched as a whole."

Stern next turned to my background as an American correspondent in Berlin and said my own American colleagues there had deplored my untruthfulness in reporting from Nazi Germany.

> Quite independently of the other, two of his correspondent colleagues in Berlin declared: "Shirer is a German-hater.". . . Shirer's book shows his hatred of all Germans. When one asks him about this, he replies that some of his best friends are German. His work is really an invented piece of Nazism.

It went on to question my veracity in reporting the Franco-German Armistice at Compiègne in June 1940. Why, it asked, had I claimed I was able to follow what went on in the famous Armistice car of Marshal Foch when the Germans laid down their terms to the French? "All the other American correspondents swore that a thick cordon of German troops had been drawn around the railroad coach to prevent the foreign press correspondents from getting too close and overhearing what went on inside. Yet Shirer claimed he was the only reporter who found out what was going on." *Stern* doubted the explanation I gave in *Berlin Diary* since, it said, I cited no witnesses.

There had been no mystery about what had happened. A German army communications truck near where I was preparing to broadcast was recording the proceedings from hidden microphones inside the coach. I merely stood by the truck, listened, and took notes. But *Stern* found it an unlikely story.

"A lucky guy, this Shirer," it said, "a real daredevil." Incidentally, *Stern* either invented or misunderstood what the American correspondents allegedly "swore" to. None of them were present that day in Compiègne. They had all been flown back to Berlin by Hitler. I had intentionally escaped his net.

Stern's blasts against me in its lengthy review were preceded by an onslaught on me in an earlier issue in which it gave over its cover to me and my nefarious anti-German works. I felt honored. No other magazine, anywhere, had ever before put me on its cover, nor has one since. Here I was, on one side of the cover, shown broadcasting from Berlin during the war. On the other half was a headline, part in white, part in yellow against a black background:

SWASTIKA OVER NEW YORK
SHAMEFUL STORIES FOR AMERICANS
INVENTED BY WILLIAM L. SHIRER

Below the headline was shown a cover of *Look* with the headline:

IF HITLER HAD WON WORLD WAR II
BY WILLIAM L. SHIRER

This was a piece in a series on the "Ifs" of history which *Look* had asked me to do. MacKinlay Kantor, for instance, had written one called "If the South Had Won the Civil War." But the point of such pieces escaped the German mentality of the editors and reporters of *Stern*, who belabored me in column after column of its pages for raising hatred anew of the Germans and the Fatherland.

I had based this imaginary happening on the brutal way Hitler had actually treated the countries of Europe he had conquered and on his secret plans, which were among the captured Nazi documents, for what he would do when he occupied Britain, which at one juncture he thought imminent. It was just a piece of fancy, which many history buffs were interested in; but in this case — perhaps more than in other articles in the "If" series — it was supported by the hard facts of what we knew had already happened to other countries unlucky enough to be taken by the Nazi Germans and which surely would have happened to us had we been conquered too. I had documented the facts in the book and taken a few of them for examples for the article.

At the very start of the Second World War after Germany attacked Poland, Admiral Wilhelm Canaris, chief of German Military Intelligence and secretly an anti-Nazi, had noted in his diary, on September 12, 1939, that "extensive executions are planned for Poland and that particularly the nobility and clergy are to be exterminated." When he protested to Hitler, the dictator answered with a secret directive:

> . . . The Polish gentry must cease to exist. [Also] all representatives of the Polish Intelligentsia are to be exterminated. This sounds cruel, but such is the law of life.

That "law of life" was next applied to the Soviet Union. In 1942, after Hitler had occupied a large part of western Russia, he gave a general outline of his ideas:

> The Slavs are to work for us. Insofar as we don't need them, they may die. . . . Education is dangerous. It is enough if they can count up to 100. . . . Every educated person is a future enemy. . . . As for food they won't get any more than is absolutely necessary. We are the masters.

Actually, as Hitler's Master Plan for Russia evolved, millions of Russians were not even to get enough food to keep alive. Hermann Göring was quite frank about it. One month after the invasion, he forbade any attempt to "mitigate" the famine in Russia, which he predicted would undoubtedly take place as a result of the military campaign. "There is no doubt," one of his secret memoranda stated, "that, as a result, many millions of persons will be starved to death if we take out of the country the things necessary for us." That the Germans would take them out, said Göring, "must be clearly and absolutely understood."

In the autumn of 1941, as the armored German columns rolled on toward Leningrad, Moscow, and the fertile Ukraine, Göring told Count Galeazzo Ciano, the Italian foreign minister: "This year between 20 and 30 million persons will die of hunger in Russia. Perhaps it is well that it should be so, for certain nations must be decimated."

On September 18, 1941, as Hitler's armies approached the two cities after only three months of campaigning, the Führer issued strict orders: "A capitulation of Leningrad or Moscow is not to be accepted, even if offered." What he had in mind for them he made clear in a directive to his commanders on September 29. It looked on that day that Leningrad would be the first to fall.

> The Führer has decided to have Leningrad wiped off the face of the earth. The further existence of this large city is of no interest once Soviet Russia is overthrown. . . .
>
> The intention is to close in on the city and raze it to the ground by artillery and continuous air attack. . . .
>
> Requests that the city be taken over will be turned down, for the problem of the survival of the population and of supplying it with food is one which cannot and should not be solved by us. In the war for existence, we have no interest in keeping even part of this great city's population.

Was there any reason to believe, I asked, that Hitler would have treated the United States more tenderly than Russia? Hitler had a certain respect for the Soviet Union and especially its dictator, Stalin. But he had nothing but contempt for America and the Americans. He thought better of Britain, but that would not have spared the British, as we know from the Nazi secret plan for the occupation of that country, which to Hitler, at least, seemed imminent after the fall of France in June 1940. Some twenty-three hundred persons led by Prime Minister Winston Churchill, his cabinet, Parliament, the clergy, and others including writers prominent in British life were to be arrested immediately. As in Poland and Russia the terror in Britain was to be carried out by the S.S. Six S.S. *Einsatzgruppen* were to do the main job. Their labors in Russia had pleased the Führer. There, *Einsatzgruppen* had killed, by their own account, three-quarters of a million people. (Eichmann put the figure at two million, but he was given to boasting about such things.)

The German Army, which in Poland and Russia had appeared anxious to leave the dirty work to the S.S., was not above sharing it in Britain. Among the captured Nazi documents is an army order signed by Field Marshal Walther von Brauchitsch, commander in chief of the German Army, on September 9, 1940, when his troops were poised for the Channel crossing to conquer Britain. It directed that every able-bodied man in Britain between the ages of seventeen and forty-five be rounded up and shipped out of the country to the German-occupied Continent. That meant they were destined for slave labor. The field marshal also stipulated that hostages would be taken, and he proclaimed the death penalty for any Briton caught posting an anti-German placard or who failed to turn in firearms and radios within twenty-four hours.

Such was the way the Germans had behaved in the occupied land; such were their plans for Britain. I cited them as examples of what certainly would have happened to America had Hitler won the war and occupied our land. As was the case with my book on the Third Reich, there was not a word in the article about postwar Germany or the Germans. Yet just as with the book, *Stern* fumed and fretted in column after column that the dreadful piece showed not only my undying hatred of Germany and the Germans but also showed my unfitness for writing their history during the Nazi time.

Though *Stern* did not find anything funny in my article, it recommended that "this and other stories of William L. Shirer be banished to where they belong: among the comic books" — if I translate *Groschenschmoker* correctly.

In the daily press in Germany the attack was led by Paul Sethe, a German historian and an editor of the independent Hamburg daily *Die Welt*. His lengthy review, however, appeared in a weekly newspaper *Die Zeit*. Since Dr. Sethe wrote well and had a reputation as a historian, his piece entitled "Shirer's Half-Truths" created a deep impression in Germany. Unlike the tone of the criticism in the weekly press and in most of the dailies, it was not hysterical. In fact, the historian seemed to come to his conclusion rather reluctantly. For he started out by saying that I had "written one of the most important books in years . . . a work of industry and patience, overwhelming in its wealth of detail, overwhelming also in the impression it gives of intensive research and contact with innumerable first-hand sources." But then, almost as if he felt in his duty as a patriot of Germany, he drew his dagger and assailed me for my "half-truths" and distortions and mean spirit in writing what I did. I thought his diatribe was, as an American historian protested to *Die Zeit*, itself full of distortions.

Walter Goerlitz, another well-known historian who specialized in military history and who was an editor of *Die Welt*, wrote an attack on the book in that journal which was headlined: "How One Should Not Write History." Sethe had said my book was full of errors. Goerlitz thought they were so numerous that merely to enumerate them would take a whole book. "Shirer," he wrote, "is not a good scholar of German history. What he brings forth about it springs from the clichés of Allied propaganda in two world wars."

Others, as if in chorus, after declaring the book was full of "mistakes," added too that it was made up of clichés. Hermann Eich in the *Dusseldorfer Nachrichten* assured his readers that "no cliché about the supposed or real inferiority of the German character was left unsaid by the American author."

Some reviews advised the readers not to take the book seriously; because the author was a mere journalist, not a historian. "He writes journalism, not history," they said.

A few reviews were favorable, especially in the Social Democratic press. They pointed out that the massive negative criticism in Germany had failed to give any idea whatsoever of the scope of the book and its range of contents. An editor of *Die Zeit*, in presenting a few excerpts from the German reviews, pro and con, called attention to this. He differed with Dr. Sethe's criticism in the same publication.

> Shirer's book has been greeted by "bravos" and "boos"; outside of Germany by "bravos," in Germany by "boos" (with only a few exceptions). We learn little more about the content of the book than what stands in the title. And we learn practically nothing of how it actually came to be. The number of reviewers who do not hide the occupation of the author is great — as if it matters here, or in any literary work, who or what the author is. Truly this is always easier to confront than the question of the quality of a book.

A handful of German reviewers dared to buck the tide. Michael Freund in *Die Politische Meinung* of Bonn felt that "the book remains an account of German history from 1933 to 1945 that no German should be allowed not to read."

Some reviewers asked why no German historians had written a history of the Third Reich. After all, it was their country. "We are forced to answer sadly," Bernd Nelessen (who did not like my book) wrote in *Die Welt*, "that this theme has not yet engaged any German author who deserves to be taken more seriously than Shirer."

> While it is true that the lack of competition from a great German historian does not make Shirer's book any better, it would be easier to dismiss it in good conscience as a bad piece of work if we could cite another book on the same subject that had the authority and renown of a German scholar behind it.
>   . . . The fame that Shirer's book has enjoyed forces German historians to face up to this situation. For Shirer's book on Germany is not the scandal. The scandal is the lack of German historians willing to accept a great challenge. . . .

A critic who was more favorable to my work, "CH" in the *Sud-deutschen Zeitung*, brought up the same subject.

> It's a shame. We allow the great subject of our current history . . . to be taken away from us by foreigners. And when the "foreign perspective" is put forward, we turn around and complain righteously that the author lacks the necessary insight. . . . Understandably [Shirer's book] is aggravating. The aggravation is primarily because we did not produce an attempt of equal merit. No total picture from a German pen exists for comparison. . . .
>
> The journalist Shirer understands his work, and he has diligently rummaged through mountains of documents. He quotes in abundance from these documents, against which there is no appeal. . . .

But such comments in Germany were few and far between. Most of the reviewers fumed that I was a German-hating monster and my book on the twelve-year nightmare of Nazism a monstrosity and an insult to the German nation and people. The fact that the book concerned itself with the behavior of the German people and their nation only under Hitler was evaded. The reviewers made it look as if I were attacking the nation and the people as they now were, struggling in the Western part to make democracy work for the first time in German history.

I was struck by the fact that the outbursts against the book and me seemed to be of one piece, as if orchestrated and directed from some center. All the criticisms resembled each other. The book was full of errors. The author did not understand the Germans or their history. He was mean in spirit, full of hatred for the German people and their behavior down the ages.

An American historian at Ann Arbor, Dr. Ernest G. Fontheim, also noticed the unanimity of the German reviews. In a letter to the Sunday *New York Times Book Review* published on April 8, 1962, apropos of an article from the *Times* Bonn correspondent about the reception of my book in Germany,* he observed:

---

* "Sixteen months after its publication here . . . ," Sidney Gruson cabled the *Times* from Bonn, "William L. Shirer's 'The Rise and Fall of the Third Reich' continues to roil West Germany."

> Although the argument concerns the historical and literary value of the work, it is centered on why Shirer wrote the book and why it was such a success in America.
>
> In effect, the book is taken in Germany as a current political document. . . . Germans took the book as both a cause and symptom of what they consider to be a new anti-German campaign in America . . . stimulated by what are always tartly called "certain circles.". . .
>
> There has probably been no other book published here since the war which had so great an impact with so relatively small a sale. Only about 14,000 copies have been sold in the German edition, but the reviews, criticisms, articles, letters to the editor and letters answering the letters to the editor continue without let-up.

The article "Germans Don't Always Like What They Read" by Sidney Gruson comes as no surprise to those who follow the German newspapers. . . . For example, the usually very sedate *Die Zeit* of Hamburg published a review [of Shirer's book] by the German historian Paul Sethe. A letter to the editor of *Die Zeit* pointing out, and refuting, only the most-important distortions of Shirer's work contained in the review, was refused publication with the excuse that it had been submitted over two months after publication of Sethe's review.

The German illustrated weekly *Die Stern* was even less restrained than *Die Zeit*. It published a vicious personal attack against Shirer . . . by accusing him of lies (without proof, of course) in his earlier work "Berlin Diary."

There should definitely be no objection to balanced and sober reviews of Shirer's book pointing out both its positive and negative aspects. But when practically the entire press of a nation in rare unanimity tears a book to pieces by resorting to distortion and unfair personal attacks on the author, then one starts to wonder. . . .

I had begun to wonder myself, but soon the mystery began to evaporate. In fact, as early as December 3, 1961, shortly after publication in Germany, Gaston Coblenz, the Bonn correspondent of the *New York Herald-Tribune*, cabled his newspaper that

The West German government has adopted the unusual expedient of attacking William L. Shirer's best-selling "Rise and Fall of the Third Reich" in an official Bonn publication.

The occasion for the action has been the appearance of Mr. Shirer's account of Nazism in a German language edition. . . .

The German government has been dismayed at the success which the book has enjoyed in the United States. They regard it as having played an important role in keeping unpleasant memories of the past alive among the American public.

The government publication lodged a charge of anti-German bias against Mr. Shirer by printing an array of quotations by German and other critics who have reviewed the book.

Actually, in the copy I have, which Chancellor Konrad Adenauer later had printed in Switzerland in March 1962 and issued by the German embassy in Bern, the publication did not itself directly attack the book. It printed without comment a number of German reviews and in addition the foreword to the German edition by Golo Mann, son

There is a single theme to all this comment — that Shirer equates Nazis and Germans in such a way as to imply that the German character made Hitler's rise and rule inevitable. The current complaint further is that the logic of such a view must create a view that Germans can never be trusted, nor eventually reform.

of Thomas Mann, and a respected historian. It also published excerpts from my introduction to the book. But it carried in full the most prestigious attack on the book, the review of Paul Sethe entitled "William Shirer's Half-Truths" and the piece that also dismissed the book by Nelessen, balancing it with two other reviews, one of which was quite favorable. An English translation of the twenty-four-page pamphlet, my publishers believe, was mailed to thousands of American newspaper editors and book reviewers by the Bonn government.

Chancellor Adenauer made no bones about his position. He attacked me on television. He raved to anyone who would listen, I was told, especially on his visits to America, against the book and against me. And once when he was in New York, he called Mike Cowles to his suite at the Waldorf, angrily denounced him for publishing pieces from the book, and demanded that *Look* cease publishing further extracts. Cowles, who could be hard as nails, was not intimidated by the angry German chancellor. He told me afterward that he said to the German:

"Sir, are you telling me that the Shirer book is not truthful? If so, *Look* will print a retraction."

"Mr. Cowles," Mike swore the chancellor answered, "you do not get the point. The point is not whether it's truthful or not. The point is that it is turning out to be extremely harmful to German-American relations. It is stirring up in America hatred of the Germans. Mr. Shirer is a German-hater, a *Deutschhasser!* You must not publish any more of his trash."

"That is something for us to decide, Herr Chancellor," Mike said he replied. "As I said, show me proof of lies or distortions and I'll correct them. But we shall go on publishing the rest of the pieces from the book as scheduled. We believe they are based on the documented facts. Incidentally, Herr Chancellor, did you note that the book is about Germans under Hitler, not about the Germans today?"

In Washington, Konrad Adenauer was always treated with kid gloves. He was the darling of the State Department. And the Washington establishment. Mike Cowles turned out to be different. Adenauer's anger and bluster had not intimidated him.

Listening to Mike's account and ruminating over the reception of the book in Germany, I recalled some words I had recently read in *Encounter* from Karl Jaspers, the German philosopher. I had been maligned by the German chancellor and the German press for what I had written of the Germans during the savage Nazi time. But here was a German philosopher writing about them today as the 1960s began.

We Germans have still to achieve our own integrity as a prerequisite of our new liberty. . . . Both truth and political education are the victims of our German amnesia.

. . . Our political freedom is not of our own doing. . . . We received freedom as a gift from the conqueror. . . . By the will of the victors we have been given the opportunity of democracy, a democracy which did not emerge from some struggle for liberation but was decreed for us at a time when we were simply a huddled mass of German survivors.

Does Germany yet know what freedom is? Political liberty was created by Europeans in struggle. [And in] America. . . . Today we Germans are only enjoying the political fruits of these events. But can we become true democrats? Up to now ours is only a superficial relation to democracy.

At home I began to learn a little more about "success." The editors of *Reader's Digest*, it will be remembered, had not been impressed by the early samples I had shown them from my book. They had turned down my proposal, when I was desperate, that they give me an advance to enable me to finish the work in return for exclusive magazine rights. The most they did, as I have mentioned, was to offer to buy one short piece "if the writing is satisfactory."

Whether they took it I no longer remember.* What I do remember is that as the book began to mount the best-seller lists toward the end of 1960 and soon reached the top, the editors of the magazine changed their minds. They bought the rights to reprint a condensation that was spread over three successive issues of March, April, and May of 1962, a year and a half after book publication. Never before, I believe, had the *Digest* condensed a book over so many issues. A special sheet pasted on the cover called attention to the pieces. And now the *Digest*, once so cool about the book before it was published, grew exceedingly warm. Its introduction to the first condensation went a bit overboard, I thought. But after the clobbering I was taking in Germany that spring of 1962, I did not complain.

"For the past year," said the *Digest* in introducing the first install-ment,

"The Rise and Fall of the Third Reich" has been the best-selling non-fiction book in print. Its prominence is no accident, for it is a masterful telling of one of the most gripping dramas of all time . . . the story of a man, a nation and a world gone mad. . . .

* Sometime after writing the above I came across a diary entry for January 1, 1961, saying that the *Digest* bought it but never published it.

[Shirer's] book will long stand as the definite record of this incredible era. . . . Here for the first time are revealed the secret decisions, the intrigues, the behind-the-scenes machinations of the Nazi movement. The result is a work of profound scholarship enlivened with the journalist's eye for striking anecdote and incisive detail.

My agent extracted from the *Digest* what seemed to me an astronomical sum of money; and coupled with the revenue from *Look* and the sales of the book this meant that at last, for the first time in my life, despite having to pay well over half of what came in to the tax collector and the usual ten percent to my agent, I had achieved financial independence, at least for a while. I could continue to write and not have to spend half my time scratching for a living by doing other things. I gave up lecturing and writing magazine articles. I abandoned any idea of returning to broadcasting. It had been a long haul. But finally I seemed to have made it as far as supporting my family by writing was concerned. I felt a load off my back. I looked forward to whatever life still might bring, not even minding that old age lay just around the next turn of the road. I thought maybe the next years, even in the twilight, might turn out to be the best years of my life.

"We've had one of the most beautiful Christmas holidays on the farm in memory," I wrote in my diary of January 1, 1961, a couple of months after the book first came out in America. We had not been able to spend Christmas on the farm for two or three years, because the furnace had blown out and we could not afford a new one.

Wonderful snow, clear cold weather, a full moon, and much skiing and sledding with the children, who came back from Cambridge.

And heat in the house! New furnace!

BOOK SIX

The Running Out of Time

1960–1975

CHAPTER 1

I was fifty-six when the Third Reich book was first published in 1960, and fifty-eight when the to-do over its appearance here and abroad subsided and I could turn to other things: principally to the next book and to figuring out my working and personal life now that fortune, after so long a drought, had smiled on us.

Writers do not retire at sixty-five — though some think they should — but that age nevertheless is a milestone, and for me it loomed not so far ahead. With some money in the bank, we need no longer worry about having enough to pay the rent, the groceries, and the tuition of two girls in college.

I could scarcely realize our good fortune. It had come so suddenly and unexpectedly — against all the odds and the predictions of everyone. It took time to adjust to it, though the adjusting was pleasant. It also took time to wind down from the grinding pace I had set year after year. To help me slow down, Bennett Cerf had phoned one day and suggested I do a couple of juvenile books for Random House's Landmark Series for youngsters between ten and fourteen. A child's biography of Adolf Hitler to start with.

It was not so easy as he assured me it would be. I suffered the first writer's block of my life, sitting for days with a blank piece of paper in my typewriter, unable to create a line. How did you write for young people? You couldn't be condescending. You had to respect them. But you had to keep it simple enough for them to understand. I read and reread other Landmark books by my friends to try to find out how it was done. John Gunther had written one about Alexander, another about Caesar. Pearl Buck had done one about Martin Luther. But these were authentic heroes, figures in history youngsters looked up to. I didn't want them looking up to Hitler or seeing in him a hero. He was a genius, but an evil one. Finally I got the knack and did the book. And for good measure, to completely unwind, I wrote a second book — about the sinking of the *Bismarck,* on which I had accumulated some documentary material for the Third Reich book and then not found the space to use.

And then I succumbed, briefly, to the temptations of Hollywood.

In my diary of January 1, 1961, reviewing the past year's turn of good fortune, I had noted: "It even looks as though we might get a movie sale."

Up until then my agent had advised me that this was not likely. "They almost never buy a work of nonfiction," he said, "and I do not expect them to take this."

But "they" had.

"Unfortunately, for peanuts," my agent later lamented. He had been so surprised when an offer came from MGM, of all studios, that he had taken what they first offered, which was "a disgrace," he said. But at that time, after so many lean years, the offer — and I have forgotten exactly what it was — seemed big enough to me. And it would be interesting, I thought, to see if Hollywood could do a film about so vast and terrifying a subject.

"They'll do plenty," my friends said. "You won't recognize your book when they get through with it, especially at MGM."

But I felt I had some protection. Two friends, who were quite serious about such matters, were to produce and direct. Both had made a mark in the theater, and one had also done well in the films. The producer was John Houseman, a veteran of the stage and lately head of the American Shakespeare Theater at Stratford, Connecticut. He had also directed a number of films. The director was George Roy Hill, who recently had done two plays by Tennessee Williams on Broadway and was regarded as "a comer" in the theater world. He had not, I believe, had any experience in films but he was anxious to try his hand at them.

I was pretty sure that with Houseman and Hill running things, we would get at least a serious film out of the book. MGM had never made a documentary. This came out at our first meeting with the head of the studio, a man who was trying to fill the shoes of the famous Louis B. Mayer. It was my first encounter with a Hollywood movie mogul. His office, big as a barn, was painted a garish pink. He kept us waiting just long enough, I suppose he thought, to impress us. He was more than cordial as we shook hands. He was effusive.

"My dear Mr. Shirer, you've ruined my sleep for the last three nights. You can ask my wife. I tell you, I've sat up through three nights reading *The Rise and Fall*. I couldn't put it down. But it's long. It left me no time to sleep. It's . . ."

He turned to pick up the phone, which had just buzzed.

Jack Houseman, sitting at my side, whispered in my ear: "Don't believe a word of it. The son-of-a-bitch can't read!"

Turning again to us after a few crisp words on the phone, the great man resumed. "Yes, sir, it's a great book. If I may say so, I think it's a masterpiece. And MGM is proud to have bought it . . ."

"For a song, my agent says," I wanted to break in to say, but I resisted.

"Now, Mr. Shirer," he went on, "you're in good hands here. Jack Houseman has made some wonderful films for MGM. And we welcome you, Mr. Hill," he added, turning to my director, "to Hollywood. We've already heard of the great things you've done in the theater."

He paused to screw up his face.

"As a matter of fact, Mr. Shirer, I have to tell you that MGM has never made a documentary. We've made great films, but they were not documentaries. Your masterpiece cries out for a great documentary. That's why I'm happy to see you in such good hands. If anyone can do it, Jack Houseman and George Roy Hill can do it.

"Thank you very much for coming in." He rose and dismissed us. Already, Houseman informed me, he had approved an initial appropriation of one million dollars. I was to write the script. A little later we would scour the archives in Washington and in Europe for new film. I was sure there were masses of it that had never been shown.

The next few days I was initiated into a familiar Hollywood scene. The three of us would sit around a swimming pool, usually at the swank hotel where I was staying, and discuss the picture we would do and the script I would write. Often toward the end of the afternoon we would adjourn to John's place on Malibu Beach for further talks and further drinks. It was fun, but so far as developing a script, a pleasant waste of time. Finally I moved out to a motel at Palm Springs to really get into the script, and John and George flew off to Washington to see what kind of film was available there.

Later when I returned to Hollywood I met some of the celebrities at various parties and occasionally on location. Since in twenty years in Europe there had been very few American films to see and since I had been too busy, or too uninterested, after my return to see many more, I was woefully ignorant of the "stars" and what they had played in. This could prove mildly embarrassing. I would be introduced to some obviously important actor or actress. I might recognize the names but I had never seen them on film. Through some lapse, for instance, I had never seen Judy Garland on the screen and had scarcely heard of her.

But one day when I went out to Universal Studios to watch Stanley Kramer shooting *Judgment at Nuremberg*, she was sitting in the witness box playing the part of a Berlin prostitute and being questioned by an actor I did know, Dick Widmark, who was playing the prosecuting attorney at Nuremberg. After the scene Dick introduced us. She said she wanted to talk. I wondered what I could say. I couldn't say the usual thing in Hollywood: "You were perfectly wonderful in such-and-such picture." So I waited for her to begin. She did not hesitate. I found her most natural and pleasant. She wanted to know what Berlin prostitutes were like. How did they dress? How did they walk? Talk? And so forth. Actually, I couldn't remember.

The film had an all-star cast, so on that one day I got in a word with several persons who were obviously notable film personalities. Spencer Tracy, playing the part of a judge at Nuremberg, wanted to know how the actual judges there had looked and spoken and gestured. I liked him at once. Burt Lancaster, at one point a bit miffed at the slow pace of the shooting, wanted to know if the actual proceedings at Nuremberg could possibly have gone so slowly. "I'm getting bored!" he shouted at Kramer.

After dispensing a million dollars, MGM gave up on the film of the Third Reich book. John Houseman and George Roy Hill took off to greener pastures. In the end MGM sold the rights to David Wolper, who made of it a very good documentary film. It was an impossible task, really, to compress the history of Nazi Germany into a two-hour film. But Wolper did wonders. It is still shown in colleges and universities and occasionally on television.

I never tried to write for the films again. Hollywood was not my dish. It was unreal. I could not connect with it.

I returned from the make-believe land, anxious to get started on a new book. But what book? Doubleday had been after me to do one on my time with Gandhi in India. After having been immersed so long in writing about Europe, it seemed a welcome change. The idea for it had long been buzzing in the back of my mind. In fact, there had been a sort of draft in the autobiographical Indian novel I had written the year we took off in Spain. But that book — my first — had not come off. It was really terrible, and I had put it aside when I returned to newspaper reporting in 1934. Now in 1961, after the long years on the Third Reich book, I felt receptive to Doubleday's prodding, and I signed a contract to write the book. But after looking through my papers, I realized I was not yet ready to recount the experience with Gandhi and with the revolution he led that had brought India independence. It needed more reflection. The Mahatma had made such a tremendous impact on me. I could not yet get it down in words. I must find another subject.

I must also, I knew, face up to the state of my personal life, which seemed almost to have been held in abeyance during the long years of toil on the German book. There had been tensions between Tess and me, largely, I thought, over finances, or rather the lack of them. Now there was no longer any excuse for that. We need no longer worry or quarrel about where the next meal would come from. We could relax and be happy.

Linda had gone up to Radcliffe in September 1959, to join her sister there, just as I had finished the German book. For the first time in the last twenty-one years of our married life there were no children around the house. Tess and I were again alone, and this presented problems that neither of us had given much thought to.

The next June, Inga graduated from college and married.

> Wed., Aug. 3, 1960. Farm. Eileen Inga was graduated from Radcliffe College on June 15 and married three days later, . . . at the Church of St. Mark's in the Bourie in New York. . . .
>
> The rector, Episcopal, was Michael Allen, son of Jay and Ruth, whom Tess and I had known since he was a tot (in Europe) and who gave up journalism to go into the ministry. . . .
>
> St. Mark's is an old run-down church, the second oldest in New York. Inga had liked the look of it when she was doing social work there some years ago. . . .

It had been founded by Peter Stuyvesant, and the old one-legged Dutchman, who had ruled New Amsterdam so sternly, was, I believe, buried there.

The ceremony, I noted, went off nicely, though our little bridal procession could not get into the church until Michael, I, and a few brawny friends of the bride and groom from Harvard cleared out a half-dozen Bowery bums who were sleeping under the roof that covered the entrance. We did it gently and I gave each of them a couple of dollars to buy a beer and a sandwich around the corner.

> And so a rather closely-knit family of four is now only three. . . . It seems only yesterday that Inga was a tot, fooling about the place with her younger sister, even more a tot. And soon — in three years — Lin will graduate from college and probably marry. And a cycle will have been completed, one that absorbs most of your adult life. And we will be left to ourselves again, as we were in the beginning. Then we will be

grandparents — a second but outer cycle — and shortly thereafter pass along. It seems so short, this life-span upon the earth. To me at 56, despite all the well-filled years, life seems scarcely to have begun. There is so much I would like to do. But not much time remains and most of the doings, I begin to realize, will never get done.

Learning Russian, for example. Now, I realized, I probably would never learn that subtle and beautiful language. I had wanted to, ever since I had first read in English translation the great nineteenth-century Russian novelists, Gogol, Dostoyevski, Tolstoy, and Turgenev (and the poetry of Pushkin, the short stories and plays of Chekhov) in the high-school days in Iowa. George Kennan, when he was in the U.S. embassy in Berlin at the beginning of the war, had told me I would never really understand the great Russian writers unless I read them in the original. I had begun in Paris in the mid-twenties, exchanging English for Russian lessons with an attractive young Russian woman then studying at the Sorbonne. But I had had to spend most of my spare time first learning French. My job as a correspondent had taken me away from Paris and from this teacher, and there was no time or opportunity in the next hectic years as a roving reporter to find another.

More important than learning Russian were the books I still wanted to write: about the experience in India with Gandhi, about the fall of France in 1940, about World War II, about the future of Europe, still recovering from the devastations of the war, and finally about my own country, now that I had been back long enough to get the feel of it. And I wanted to return to doing novels, despite my lack of success in this field, and I wanted to write some plays, though the three or four I had done had been worse than I expected. Perhaps if there were time, I could write some poetry, having got some very bad verse out of my system in the Paris days.

And I wanted to make my marriage survive, overcoming the difficulties of recent years that had been caused by a number of unfortunate things besides our poverty, including the frequent separations that stemmed from work and the war, and my own occasional wanderings.*

Tilly Losch had come into my life at the end of the first part of the war after I came home from Berlin. It was the late summer of 1941; my family was still on the Cape and I had returned to New York to resume

---

* There were other causes and their consequences too intimate to expose, ever, to the outside world. I am attempting to keep in mind the words of Shaw that "no man is bad enough to tell the truth about himself during his lifetime, involving, as it must, the truth about his family and his friends and his colleagues. This is especially true about a spouse."

broadcasting. One warm August evening just before my 11 P.M. broadcast at CBS, John Gunther, Tola Litvak, and Frank Capra, the latter two noted film directors, had dropped by my cubbyhole of an office and asked if they could sit in the studio to hear the news show and then take me out for a drink. In their tow was an extremely attractive-looking woman of about forty whose soft, slight Viennese accent I detected at the very instant she was being introduced. It was Tilly Losch.

She had already become a legend in Vienna when I began working there in 1929. She had been, people said, the most dazzling prima ballerina the venerable State Opera had seen in ages. A dynamic dancer and a great beauty. She had "retired" early, shortly before I arrived in Vienna, and gone on to London where she married a rich Anglo-American there and resumed dancing. But this time it was in popular musicals. It was a new and second career for her and she was again a great success.

That summer of 1929, I had had to leave Vienna for a long assignment in London. Zora, a Hungarian friend I had met in the Austrian capital, joined me in Britain and shortly after her arrival we went to see Miss Losch in a Noel Coward musical, *This Year of Grace*. Zora had seen her dance in Vienna shortly after the end of the war and raved about her.

"You must see her!" she said, but it took no urging. I had heard so much about her that first winter in Vienna.

Tilly Losch turned out to be the star of the Coward show. In fact, later in his autobiography, Coward wrote that she had saved it. She was the most dynamic dancer I had seen since Isadora Duncan. And much more beautiful. At the end of the show, Zora, noting my enthusiasm, suggested I go backstage and meet Miss Losch.

"She will appreciate your telling her how bowled over you were by her," Zora teased me. But I was much too timid to go backstage. A few days later there was a lengthy piece in one of the weeklies, handsomely illustrated with photographs, about Miss Losch and her career. I clipped it out, wondering at my hero-worship of this fascinating woman. I was twenty-five and in love with Zora, I thought, and here I was falling madly for someone I had not even met, and probably never would. I never quite recovered from that first fever.

And now suddenly and unexpectedly, out of the blue, on this hot August night of 1941 in New York, we were introduced for the first time. In an instant I felt myself falling in love with her.

They listened to my news broadcast and then we went off to "21" for a drink and a bite to eat. I was enthralled. Tilly and I sat at one end of the table engrossed in talk, oblivious of the others. I became aware of my state when John Gunther, rather annoyed, suddenly yelled at us and asked if it wasn't time that we joined them — he had a story he said that he thought we wouldn't want to miss.

It was an exciting nightcap for me. In the week that followed Tilly and I exchanged rather formal notes, and she invited my wife and me to tea when Tess returned from the Cape. I thought the two women, being Viennese, would get along well, but they did not. I was being naïve, of course. Tess, who was much shrewder in such things than I, apparently detected instantly the electricity sparkling between Tilly and me. She did not like it. And she began to object to the three of us continuing to meet.

So the two of us began to meet, and rather quickly Tilly Losch and I became close to one another. Two years later when I went off to England for a time to cover the U.S. Eighth Air Force, then beginning its daylight bombing of Germany, we started to talk of marriage. She was divorcing her second husband, an English lord, she said. She asked me when I got to London to urge her lawyers to speed it up. But love her as I did, I would not break up my family for her. Linda was not quite two and Inga was only five. Whatever our mounting differences, Tess had stood by me over a long and difficult time. I remembered the dedication only two years before I had made in *Berlin Diary*.

To Tess, Who Shared So Much.

Tilly did not like my stand. She said she wanted all or nothing. We began to have our problems. I preferred to drift along, as before. This was unsatisfactory to the two women closest to me. In my foolishness I thought them both unreasonable. I was stubbornly determined though to keep my family together, but I would not give up seeing Miss Losch. Sometimes she seemed to solve my problem by breaking off. But there was always a making-up. And so it continued for the next few years, with much hurt to each of us three and with Tess so resentful as time went on that life at home became more and more difficult. As we have seen, that life was not improved by our bickering over my difficulties in making a living while I was at work on the Third Reich book. Or by the strain of trying to write that opus.

Not long after I finished that writing I finally broke for good with Tilly. It was a terrible wrench for me. But I decided that it was the only way I could save my marriage. By this time I was sure it would not be much of a blow to Tilly. Though she was always very mysterious about her life, she was becoming more and more involved, I felt, with other men, for which, given my own indecisiveness, I did not blame her. I still loved her, but it had become obvious to us both that we would never make it together. She was tired of waiting for me.

For years there was no further contact between us. We dropped out of each other's lives. Then one day early in 1975 I received a telegram from Tilly. "PLEASE CALL ME," it said. "SITUATION SERIOUS."

I was then living in the Berkshires in western Massachusetts and I took the first plane I could get for New York. Tilly seemed desperate. A doctor had diagnosed cancer but she said she did not have much confidence in him. She wanted me to find her another doctor. I phoned around to friends and found her one.

Tilly had changed a great deal. Much of the fire had gone out. Her face looked waxen but she was still beautiful, I thought. And whatever men had come into her life, she seemed terribly lonely. There was no attempt to bridge the gulf between us since I had last seen her. But there were no recriminations either. We spoke lovingly but not sentimentally of the past, remembering some of the good times.

"It seems so long ago," she said, sadly.

"It was," I said.

"We were rather silly sometimes," she said, a wan smile gently breaking out on her face.

"Maybe it was because we were in love."

"Yes." She whispered the word.

There was a silence. She seemed lost in her thoughts.

"I've often wondered," she said, "why we didn't make it."

"We almost did," I said. I thought it better to leave it at that. She knew. But perhaps she did not remember. Or want to.

Tilly Losch died on Christmas Eve, 1975, in New York. Next morning as our family gathered at the home of one of my daughters in a nearby suburb to celebrate the holiday, Tess broke the news to me. She handed me a copy of the *New York Times* folded over to the obit page. The report of Tilly's death — and life — ran nearly three columns under the headline

Tilly Losch, Exotic Dancer, Is Dead

One forgot how varied, as well as distinguished a career she had had — not only as a dancer but as an actress, a choreographer and a painter. The *Times* obit recalled it. After her years in Vienna as a prima ballerina she had played at Salzburg in Max Reinhardt's production of *Everyman*, had choreographed and danced in his production of *A*

Midsummer Night's Dream, and danced in *The Seven Deadly Sins* by Kurt Weill and Bertolt Brecht, which George Balanchine choreographed in Paris in 1934.

In her post-Vienna days she had also danced with Harold Kreuzberg at the Berlin State Opera and, in a lighter vein, on Broadway, with Fred and Adele Astaire in *The Band Wagon,* a performance that moved Brooks Atkinson, the *Times* drama critic, to write that "Tilly Losch raised musical show dancing to the level of a fine art."

In a state of some shock I stumbled through the *Times* obit. Though we had been separated for years and had only this year resumed seeing each other — and then very occasionally — I felt a tremendous loss. And I felt remorse. I had gone off to Europe with a friend and spent most of the summer of 1975 there. I had not called Tilly on returning to see how she was. This was all the worse, since I knew she was stricken with cancer. The doctor I had recommended had confirmed it. That fall I did not call either. My personal life at that moment was in a mess. I didn't want to see anyone. A fortnight before Christmas I sent Tilly a Christmas card with a letter suggesting that we get together soon. A few days before Christmas I phoned her at her apartment in New York. There was no answer. I telephoned a New York florist and ordered a Christmas bouquet sent to her. I had no idea that she was in the hospital, dying.

Tilly Losch was buried in a public park in her beloved Salzburg in Austria. On the fireplace mantel in my living room I keep a photograph a friend took of her tombstone. Beside the engraved figure of a dancer, taken from a drawing Tilly once did, are the words:

TILLY LOSCH

NOV. 15, 1903–DECEMBER 24, 1975

DANCER ACTRESS ARTIST

The wording is in English rather than in her native German, the language of Salzburg. I'm sure she wrote it herself.

The final break with Tilly, fifteen years before her death, did not bring the expected relief at home. Perhaps it was too late.

CHAPTER 2

Through it all one had to work. I finally hit upon the book I wanted to write and got down to work on it.

The idea for it had come to me first twenty-one years before, in that sad June of 1940 when as an American correspondent with the German army I came into conquered Paris and witnessed the fall of France. It was an awesome spectacle.

In the space of six weeks during that spring and early summer of weather more lovely than anyone in France could remember since the end of the previous war, this great democracy, the world's second largest empire, one of Europe's Great Powers and perhaps its most civilized and possessing what was supposed to be one of the finest armies in the world, went down to utter military defeat, leaving its proud citizens dazed and then completely demoralized.

"It was the most terrible collapse," a French historian concluded, "in all the long story of our national life." In the fallen capital on June 17, I noted in my diary:

> I have a feeling that what we're seeing here is the complete break-down of French society — a collapse of the army, of government, of the morale of the people. It is almost too tremendous to believe.

On the roads south of Paris, between the Seine and the Loire rivers, and beyond, there were now some eight million panic-stricken refugees, fleeing for their lives to keep out of the hands of the Germans. Those who were old enough, remembered the brutal treatment at the hands of their old enemy in the last war, when thousands of French hostages had been shot.* Of Paris's five million inhabitants, only 700,000 had remained by the time I arrived. The rest, the police said, had fled.

No provision, the correspondents reported, had been made for food, drink, or lodging for so vast a throng. Those who had no cars slept at night in the fields next to roads. By day they scrounged for food, and

---

* In all, 29,660 French hostages would be executed by the Germans during World War II.

in their desperation some of them pillaged, and many fought for water. Along the roadside a few peasants sold food and even water — at highly inflated prices. But this took care of only a few.

By this time there was little left of the vaunted French army. A million men had been taken prisoner after the Germans had broken through and encircled them with their swarms of tanks. The rest were retreating southward, mostly in disorganized ranks. Along the congested highways the demoralized soldiers blended into the streams of refugees. Many of them threw away their arms and uniforms, hoping to avoid being made prisoners of war and shipped to Germany. Some of the top generals were already pressing the government to give up and sue for peace. General headquarters, moving south nearly every night and reduced to chaos, had little contact with the crumbling remains of the retreating army.

The government itself, like the Army High Command, was in disarray. Since fleeing Paris it could hardly function at all. Its members had arrived at the Loire on June 11 and scattered to various châteaux in the region of Tours, apparently to safeguard against the whole government being wiped out by one little bombing. But there was little communication between cabinet members, between them and the army, between the government and the outside world. How could there be?

Most of the châteaux had only one antiquated telephone on the premises, usually located in the downstairs toilet and not in good working order and connected only with the nearest village, where the operator insisted on shutting down for two hours at lunch and for good at 6 P.M.

The only source of outside news for the traveling French Foreign Office was a portable radio which the British ambassador had thought to bring along. Apparently no one in the Foreign Office had thought of such a thing. When its undersecretary called on the president of the Republic at the Château de Cangé, he found the nation's chief magistrate, as he reported later, "entirely isolated, without news from the premier, without news from Supreme Headquarters, depressed, overwhelmed. He knew nothing."

Parliament, which might have helped to sustain the wavering government and encouraged it to fight on, even if it had to be from the colonies in North Africa, could not be assembled in the midst of the headlong flight. Many of its members had lit out for Bordeaux, which the government and High Command reached on June 14, the day the German army entered Paris.

Two days later Premier Paul Reynaud, who wanted to move the government to North Africa to continue the war from there, resigned. General Maxime Weygand, commander in chief, and Marshal Henri Pétain, the hero of Verdun in the First World War, had gained control of the cabinet. They were demanding the government ask for an armistice. This it did early the next morning, June 17. By that time Pétain was in as premier and General Weygand as his minister of defense.

I got the news the next day. German army engineers had set up loudspeakers in the vast place de la Concorde:

Paris, June 18 — Marshal Pétain has asked for an armistice! [I noted in my diary.] The Parisians, already dazed by all that has happened, can scarcely believe it. . . . I stood in a throng of French men and women . . . when the news first came. They were almost struck dead . . . Pétain surrendering! *Pourquoi?* No one appeared to have the heart for an answer.

The end for France now came swiftly. I kept noting it down in my diary.

Paris, June 19. The Armistice is to be signed at Compiègne! In the *wagon-lit* coach of Marshal Foch that witnessed the signing of another armistice on November 11, 1918 in Compiègne Forest.

I went out to Compiègne that afternoon and watched German Army engineers work merrily at demolishing one wall of the museum where the Armistice car had been preserved. Before I left they had finished their job and were inching the car out to the old siding outside.

Paris, June 22 (midnight) The Armistice has been signed!

France had taken itself out of the war. Only Great Britain now stood out against Hitler.

Less than three weeks later, on July 10, 1940, the French National Assembly, frightened by the Germans and by their own new leaders, Pétain, Weygand, and Pierre Laval, voted to abolish itself and the Third Republic and replace it with a dictatorship that shabbily tried, with the backing of a surprisingly large number of Frenchmen, to ape that of the conquering Germans.

By that time, July 19, I had returned with heavy heart to my post in Berlin. With France out of the war, there was no military action for the moment. I had time to ponder the fall of France. How, I wondered, had it happened, and so swiftly? How was it possible? What were the flaws in this great nation and in these gifted people that had brought them to such a low and pitiful state? What had really happened to the French army, which had held off the Germans for four years the last time and finally, with the help of the British and, at the end, the Americans, triumphed over them? Had the French truly fought, as they had between 1914 and 1918? I myself had seen little sign of it. The German armored columns, which had simply driven *through* the French, had moved too fast to catch up with.

Who was responsible for the quick collapse of the army and the government? In the first instance, was it the generals, who had prepared and led the troops so badly? Or the politicians, as the Fascists at Vichy were beginning to charge, who had failed to provide the army with the necessary arms — the planes and tanks which for the Germans had spelled the victory? Or could a good deal of the blame be put on the French people themselves, who, as the defeatists on the right were beginning to say, had gone soft under the "godless" Republican regime? What about the right, with its antipathy to the Republic and its democracy, its sympathy with the totalitarian dictatorships? Or the Communist left, which had shamefully followed the directions of the Kremlin, even when, as with the Nazi-Soviet Pact of August 1939, they opposed France's vital interests? Did the fall of France prove, as Laval and his henchmen were now saying, that the democracies were doomed and that they could not match the dictatorships? Was Western democracy lost? Was Nazism, as Anne Lindbergh would come to believe, judging by her book of that name, "the wave of the future"?

Maybe, I thought, France's fall was inevitable. The price it paid for victory in 1918 was too high — nearly a million and a half Frenchmen killed in battle — to enable it to recover sufficiently to oppose the more numerous and more highly industrialized Germans so soon on anything like equal terms. Perhaps if the British had contributed as much as they had in the first war, the result would have been different. And if the Americans had come in time, as they had in 1917.

Sitting in Berlin that dismal late summer of 1940, a time of heartbreak for me, I pondered these questions. I had lived and worked in France for many years. I had come to love it. It was my second home.* I had learned its language, absorbed some of its culture, studied its history, and as an American correspondent reported daily on what it was up to. When I arrived in 1925, France was the greatest power on the Continent. Its army, which had borne the brunt of the fighting

---

* "France is every man's second home," Thomas Jefferson once wrote.

against Germany between 1914 and 1918, had no equal in Europe — or in the world. It stood watch on the Rhine. It guaranteed France's hegemony in Europe. The devastated towns and cities, roads and railways had been rebuilt. The economy was recovering. Germany, the old enemy, which twice, in 1871 and in 1914, had attacked France, was on its knees. For Frenchmen the future seemed bright.

That had been the way it was when I first left the country for other assignments in 1929. But I returned often to Paris in the following years, and in 1934 spent most of the year there. By then France had drastically changed — for the worse. It had become a house divided. Frenchmen were lambasting each other, in the streets, in the press, in Parliament. Rancor and intolerance poisoned the air.

I came back to Paris too after France and Britain had sold out the Czechs at Munich in 1938. To my horror, most French welcomed the sorry deed, arguing that it had saved them from another terrible war. They were now hopelessly ready, it seemed to me, for peace at any price. Still, when the war came in September 1940, I was sure that the French, as they always had, would fight to the last to defend their country. They would be outraged by this third German attack in little more than half a century. But this had not happened.

This pondering about the French was cut short for the moment in August that year when the Germans took us up to the Channel to cover what they thought would be the invasion of Britain. Waiting for the invasion that never took place, I began to think of what I would do if this war ever came to an end. Maybe, I thought, if I could dig up the material and achieve some understanding, I would do a book on the fall of France. It was one of the great dramas and, to me, one of the great tragedies of the twentieth century. There would be a second book to write. On the rise and fall of the Third Reich. Perhaps, though, you could write only the first half of that story. Nazi Germany had not fallen. In fact, there seemed no prospect at all of that. It was now the master of most of the old Continent — from the North Cape of Norway to the Pyrenees on the Franco-Spanish border, from the French Atlantic coast to the Vistula in Poland. The French were finished, for the time being anyway. But the Germans were at the height of their power.

Absorbed though I had been in writing books about the recent past and scrounging for a living, I had tried to keep up with what was going on in the world, noting developments usually in my diary, filing away newspaper clips about them, listening to the evening news on radio, and then TV, and cursing or rejoicing or wondering as the case might be. After a quarter of a century of reporting events firsthand, I was now a more distant observer. But my passion for following the news remained. Sometimes it involved a personal friend.

Martha Dodd was a good friend of mine from our days in Berlin where her father, Professor William E. Dodd, a noted historian at the University of Chicago, was American ambassador. I got to know the family well and liked it very much. It was solid as a rock and closely knit. Dodd was a southerner, with the courtly manners of the South, a fine historian's mind, and a liberal outlook on life that had made him a friend and a mentor of Franklin Roosevelt, who had named him to the Berlin post. I admired him for the way he stood up to Adolf Hitler. I appreciated the support he gave me. Bill Dodd, his son, was struggling to get his Ph.D. at the University of Berlin. Martha, not long out of college and a brief stint on the *Chicago Tribune*, my old paper, was the joy of the family. Attractive and vivacious, well read and an aspiring writer, she was a popular figure in Berlin and made many friends and contacts that were helpful to her father in his mission.

Two of her closest friends turned out to be prominent Nazis, Putzi Hanfstaengl, Hitler's party foreign press secretary, and Rolf Diels, the sinister head of the Prussian Secret Police. A third friend was Colonel Ernst Udet, a much decorated flyer from the First World War and after 1933 a brilliant achiever in building up the Luftwaffe under Göring. Of Prince Louis Ferdinand, eldest son of the crown prince, Martha would write: "He was one of the most interesting men I was to know in Germany and one of my dearest friends. . . ."*

She saw, of course, a good many Germans who did not like Hitler — the ambassador was often host to them and it was at his home that I met a number of them. And though, as she admitted, she had been a little naïve politically when she arrived raw and inexperienced out of Chicago and thought she had an open mind about Nazism, she soon matured. On the whole she shared her father's liberalism and his growing hatred and fear of Fascism during her four years in Germany. I do not recall her ever expressing much enthusiasm for Communism, even after she visited the Soviet Union, even after her friendship with a Russian diplomat at the Soviet embassy, who was much liked by most of the American correspondents in Berlin, who resisted his charming way of trying to convert them. Years later, after the war, when Martha

* Martha Dodd, *Through Embassy Eyes*, p. 69. The book is an account of her four years in Germany.

and I ran into each other occasionally in New York or Connecticut, I do not remember her even mentioning the subject of Communism. Nor did her husband, Alfred Stern, a former Chicago businessman, whom she had married on her return. They would talk of liberal causes they were interested in. Alfred seemed almost apolitical, interested more in the market and economics than in politics. Part of his career had been in public housing.

In the light of all that, I was all the more flabbergasted by what now happened.

One crisp evening in 1953, Tess and I ran into Martha and her husband during the intermission of a Broadway play. We had not seen them in some time. So we agreed to meet after the theater for a snack and a drink at a nearby restaurant and catch up on each other's news. Actually, during the repast, they said little of what they were up to. We talked mostly of old times in Berlin. Since Alfred had not been there, he was rather silent. He seemed a little preoccupied. Martha was her usual self, I thought, vivacious, warm, and charming. And relaxed. We parted at midnight, promising, as we always did, to get together again in the not-too-distant future.

A couple of mornings later, while I was having an early breakfast with the children before they caught their school bus and glancing as we talked at the front page of the *New York Times*, my eyes caught a headline that struck me dumb. Martha Dodd and Alfred Stern, it said, had been charged with spying for the Soviet Union and had fled the country — presumably for Mexico.

I had hardly bundled the children off to the school bus and returned to reread the amazing story about my old friend, which I could not believe, when the doorbell rang. Two young men flashed their FBI badges, showed their identification cards when I asked for them, and said they had to talk to me. I took them up to the second-floor living room, which overlooked the East River.

"Did you know Martha Dodd?" one of them immediately asked.

"Very well."

"*How* well, would you say?"

"Very well, as I said. Her parents, especially her father, the eminent historian and our ambassador in Berlin when I was there, were close friends of mine. Martha, too. I was very fond of Martha Dodd."

"You were fond of Martha Dodd?"

"Very."

"Do you know that she stands accused, along with her husband, of espionage for the Soviet Union?"

"I was just reading about it in the *Times* when you gentlemen rang my doorbell. It astounded me. I cannot believe it."

"You can't believe it?" My interrogator looked shocked. "Why?" he asked.

"Because it's the last thing in the world I would expect her to do."

"She was a Communist, wasn't she?"

"Not to my knowledge."

"You didn't know she was a Communist?"

"No. Never."

One of the agents took out of his pocket a small looseleaf notebook and started to flip the pages over rapidly. On each page there seemed to be a woman's photograph.

"I would like you, sir," he said, "to identify Martha Dodd, if you can. Just stop me when you think you see her photograph." He began to turn the pages rapidly, the photos flying by.

"Gentlemen," I said. "Can't we cut the comedy? I told you I knew Martha Dodd rather well." I grabbed their portfolio, or whatever it was, flipped through the pages of photographs, found Martha's, and identified it.

"You say that's her?"

"I say that's she, yes."

There was a moment's silence. Then one of the men turned quickly to me, eyed me closely for a moment, his eyes squinting.

"Have you seen the Sterns recently?"

"As a matter of fact, I have."

"When? Where?"

By this time I realized that the FBI must have been tailing Martha and Alfred. After all, this could be a capital case. Congress had passed a law providing the death penalty for espionage. The Rosenbergs had gone to the electric chair at Sing Sing on just such a charge — spying for the Soviet Union. My two questioners knew perfectly well when and where I had very recently seen my friends.

"Can't we really cut the comedy?" I said again. "I'm sure you know the answer to that question. But I'll give it anyway. My wife and I ran into Martha and her husband at the theater here in New York two or three evenings ago. We talked with them in the lobby during the intermission and, since we hadn't seen each other in some time, agreed to have a snack and a drink at a nearby restaurant after the theater."

"What restaurant?"

Though Tess and I had often gone there after the theater, I couldn't recall the name.

"Was it the Blue Ribbon?"

"I think that was the name of it. It's on Forty-fourth Street, I think, just east of Broadway."

"So the four of you went to this restaurant. What did you do there?"

The questions were getting more and more idiotic.

"We ate."

"What else?"

"We drank . . . beer."

"Yes?"

"And we talked."

"What did you talk about?"

"Of old coins . . . and the weather . . . ," I started to say.

"Tell us frankly what you talked about," one of the agents asked.

"I really can't recall exactly," I said. "I think we talked mostly of old times in Berlin."

"In Berlin? What were you doing in Berlin?"

"It's really no secret, gentlemen. I mean, I was not there as a spy or anything like that."

The ignoramuses obviously had not read my books. The illiterates!

"I was an American foreign correspondent in Berlin," I said.

"And you knew Martha Dodd and her husband in Berlin?"

"I knew Martha and her parents and brother. Her father, as I told you, was our American ambassador in Berlin."

The louts! Couldn't they even get that straight?

"I did not know Alfred Stern there."

"You did not know her husband?"

"No. He was not in Berlin. I believe they married after she returned to America. But surely the FBI knows all that — and a lot more that I don't know."

"We're asking you!" one of the louts said, trying to be sharp, I suppose.

"You knew that Alfred Stern was a Communist, didn't you?"

"No. I knew he had been a businessman and probably still was. I didn't know him well. But I'm sure he was not a Communist."

"And you claim you didn't know Martha Dodd was a Communist?"

"I'm making no claims, gentlemen. I've told you what I know and what I don't know. And I think this has gone on long enough. If you have any more serious questions, shoot. Otherwise I shall bid you goodday. I would like to get to work."

Finally they left, leaving me to wonder — and not for the first time — why J. Edgar Hoover didn't recruit more knowledgeable men. Was it perhaps because he didn't want to?

Tess, when I told her of what had happened, could not believe it either. She, too, had known the Dodds very well and with her Viennese charm and beauty she had been a great favorite of theirs.

"Is there anything you know about Martha from our Berlin days, or from the few times we've seen them here since we returned, that would make you even faintly suspect that she could be what she is accused of being?" I put it to Tess.

"Absolutely not," she said.

Martha and her husband moved on quickly from Mexico, where they may have feared extradition, to Cuba and from there to Prague. Next, I heard, they went to the Soviet Union but, apparently not liking it there, returned to Prague where they settled down. It was from there, some years after her flight and our after-theater repast, that Martha began writing me. The correspondence broke off when they returned to Cuba for seven years — from 1963 to 1970 — and resumed desultorily when they went back to Prague and settled there for good. For years her letters — judging by the envelopes — were opened by both the Czech and American censors. I assumed my letters to her got the same treatment. I suppose the FBI took a dim view of my corresponding with one indicted on so serious a charge (formal indictments had been handed down in 1957). But I considered Martha innocent until proven guilty — that was the law in our country.

From what I knew of her I could not conceive of her spying for the Soviet Union. What possibly could she, or Alfred Stern, know that would interest the Russians? The couple seemed to live a quiet life. Later I would learn a little more about the accusations. The Sterns were charged mainly with being couriers for Soviet espionage in this country, using their home in Ridgefield, Connecticut, as a meeting place for Soviet agents.

In her letters to me Martha never discussed the charges, in fact, never even mentioned them. Nor did she complain about their lives as exiles behind the Iron Curtain. As the years went by, I gathered, their lives became increasingly lonely. Martha, I also gathered, yearned to visit the West — West Berlin, which she knew so well, Vienna, Rome, Paris, London. But for fear of extradition they had to confine their travels to Hungary, Yugoslavia, and the rest of the Balkans, or to Poland — rather drab lands except for Hungary. And they wanted, I judged, to do something more with their lives than just exist as lonely exiles. Martha was a gifted writer, as her book on her years in Germany showed. But in Prague and Havana her talent apparently was not put to use. For years after their return to Czechoslovakia from Cuba, she wrote, she was quite content to be a hausfrau. Most unlike her!

And so the Sterns lived on, an American woman and man without a country.

Then in the spring of 1979, a quarter of a century after their hasty departure from our shores, Martha and Alfred were once again on the front page of the *New York Times*. The U.S. government announced it was dropping the espionage charges against the Sterns and quashing the indictment because the most important witnesses in the case were no longer alive.

Martha wrote from Prague jubilantly, asking whether I thought they could safely return home and inquiring what life was like now in the U.S.A. and especially in New York, from which they had been separated so long. They took off at once for visits to Paris and London. But they did not return to their native land. "We are really too old," she wrote, "to pull up roots."

Alfred Stern died of cancer in Prague on July 24, 1986. He was eighty-eight and had lived in exile for thirty-three years. He left no public word about his plight. Martha wrote that she would never fully recover from this loss. They had been married for nearly half a century and she was now paying a penalty, she said, "for too long and too devoted a marriage and living in a foreign country whose language neither of us was able to learn."

Once, in 1985, Martha wrote me a long letter, which perhaps shed a little light on her story. She had recently been working, she said, "on that big romantic-tragic thing in my life in the thirties." She made it plain it had to do with her experience with the first secretary of the Soviet embassy in Berlin, which I have already mentioned. He was a brilliant, attractive Russian named Boris Vinogradov, whom even the most conservative American correspondents in Berlin hailed as a friend, although knowing that he was a dedicated Communist who believed in the greatness of the Soviet Union. He had gone on from Berlin to Warsaw as chargé d'affaires of the Russian embassy there. I remember he was warned by one of his American correspondent friends, who, on his way back from Moscow, stopped over in Warsaw to see him, against returning to the Soviet Union. Stalin was beginning his reign of terror, dispatching by firing squads hundreds, then thousands, of the party faithful. But the young diplomat was too devoted a

Bolshevik to be frightened by such a threat. Continuing the Revolution, he said, was more important than any man's life, including his own. He went back. After the war we learned that he had been liquidated by Stalin.

Martha now added that "despite rumors to the contrary," her affair with the young Soviet diplomat in Berlin "had nothing to do with later developments and faiths. These came from hatred of the Nazis, the [civil] war in Spain and deep respect for the Soviet Union as the biggest opponent of Hitler. *You* understand, I'm sure."

I shared her hatred of the Nazis and her sympathies with Republican Spain, betrayed by Franco and destroyed by the armed intervention of Fascist Italy and Nazi Germany. But respect for the Soviet Union as the biggest opponent of Hitler?

For the Soviet Union that in August 1939 had signed the infamous pact with Nazi Germany, which enabled Hitler to launch World War II a fortnight later? Was the Soviet Union at that moment of shame "the biggest opponent of Hitler"? On the contrary. The U.S.S.R. became the biggest ally and collaborator of the Nazi tyrant. It became his "biggest opponent" only after Nazi Germany turned and attacked it on June 22, 1941, when it had no other recourse but to defend itself. Only then, with its very survival at stake, did it become "the biggest opponent" of Hitler.

So how could I understand — in the light of the facts of history? Furthermore, there could be no understanding when one did not know what had led Martha and her husband to flee the country and to spend the rest of their lives in lonely exile in the Communist lands. Did they believe they could not get a fair trial amidst the hysteria of the McCarthy time? Did they want to escape the fate of Alger Hiss, or even more, of the Rosenbergs? So far as I know, they never publicly denied, as Hiss had done, the charges of espionage for the Soviet Union. Once in Prague, Alfred was quoted in the press as saying the charges were "fantastic" and "extraordinary." Fantastic and extraordinary they certainly were. But were they false? Or true? The government never took its case to court. And Alfred Stern, dying at eighty-eight, carried his secret to the grave. Now only Martha could reveal it.

CHAPTER 3

The 1960s raced by. My days were full of work and of wonder at what was going on — in our country and abroad — and how swiftly and dramatically life was changing. A new generation was taking over our country, as the election in 1960 of John F. Kennedy, forty-three, as president showed. Its men and women were born well into the century. A still younger generation, the one that had reached the colleges and universities, was in revolt. It was stirring up the campuses and provoking fear and resentment among the old fuddyduds of the Establishment. Changes that would deeply affect the lives of Americans were sweeping the old away.

The 1950s, for instance, had seen television replace radio as the chief purveyor not only of entertainment but also of news and sports over the air. At the beginning of the 1950s, there had been only three million television sets in America. In the very first year of the decade another seven million sets were added. By the beginning of the 1960s there were forty million sets. Nearly every American family had one. Whether you liked it or not, television had come to occupy and dominate the lives of most Americans. They spent five or six hours a day gazing at the tube. They got most of their entertainment from it. By the 1970s it was the chief source of news for our citizens, and for many the only source — an appalling development, it seemed to me, and not the only one. Members of families, their eyes glued on the TV set, lost the art of conversing with each other. They sat in silence for hours before the horrible shrine. Not only families but friends. A social evening for many now consisted of gathering to listen to two or three favorite programs. In the course of an evening hosts and guests would exchange scarcely a word.

Most programs on commercial television, it seemed to me, were trash. They appealed to a lot of people, to be sure, and there was nothing wrong with that. What was wrong was that the three big commercial networks, enjoying a monopoly of the air and interested only in making money, would present little or nothing that appealed to a large minority that wanted some substance in their programs. I could not believe that their day-time soap operas and evening "sit-coms" contributed much to civilization and enlightenment in the U.S.A. Or even to adult entertainment. Later, cable TV offered the prospect of a change for the better, but in practice it turned out to be disappointing, at least to me.

Public television, too. Except for news and sports, I listened to it most. Its broadcasts from the New York Metropolitan Opera and the New York Philharmonic Orchestra were fine but infrequent. One remembered that radio offers these programs every weekend. Public television also offered interesting programs of animal life and others on the origin and development of life on the planet, but who wanted to watch animal life night after night? There was no balance in the programs. If the commercial networks avoided controversy so as not to frighten advertising sponsors, the Public Network also avoided it because, I suppose, it did not want to offend Congress, which supplied some of its funds, or the corporate "supporters," whose contributions grew substantially.

I watch weekend sports and the daily evening news on network TV and a play, an opera, a symphony concert occasionally on public television. There is not much real news on the evening shows — there is not time to treat it more than superficially — but from them I get a certain feel for people and places. For news I have to turn to my local paper, and since I live in the northeast, to the *New York Times*. That still leaves me a good deal of time for reading. I gather there is not much general reading, at least of books, in our country anymore. Gazing at the tube has replaced it as it has replaced social conversation. Are the consequences not predictable: a country of illiterate boobs sitting dumbly around the TV set, like ancient cavemen around a fire, unable to communicate or articulate, stupefied by inanities?

In the fall of 1962 an event occurred that sobered up the country and forced it to face a grim reality: our very extinction no less. A nuclear war between Russia and the United States was narrowly averted. This time Americans suddenly woke to the threat of a nuclear exchange and its consequences.

I was up on the farm doing some fall chores. But when the crisis broke, I abandoned them to stay glued to a TV set. On Tuesday, October 23, 1962, I began my diary:

A possibility of nuclear war and the end of the world. Pres. Kennedy last night broadcast the information that Russia was building missile bases in Cuba capable of delivering nuclear warheads on the nearby U.S.A. and Latin Amer. countries. He demanded Russia dismantle U.S.A. bases, and he clapped on what he called a "quarantine" — actually a naval and air blockade — of Cuba, shutting off all offensive weapons. If and when American naval vessels stop Russian ships, what happens?

It seems obvious to me that no American president could sit idly by while the Russians set up nuclear missile bases which might destroy us in a few minutes. Not to defend against that would be criminal negligence. . . .

On the other hand, one thing can lead to another in this situation, with each side refusing to back down, until you get the nuclear war that will blow up the planet, though neither Russia or the U.S.A. wanted to go that far. That is the chief danger. . . .

Friday, October 26. New York. Back from lectures Wednesday and Thursday evenings at universities in Pennsylvania. For first time the possibility of utter destruction weighs on our people. At Susquehanna U. last night the president and one of the deans approached me before the lecture to say their students were in a state of shock, could not study all week and deeply feared that nuclear war was about to come and that it would wipe us out. . . . The president and dean asked me to reassure the students in my talk, but this was impossible. I had been deeply depressed myself all week. But I tried to point out (in my talk) . . . that Russia's head, Khrushchev, had miscalculated in regard to us, that miscalculation has always been the greatest danger. The only comfort I could offer was a guess that Mr. K. might realize his miscalculation and draw back — since he didn't want to see Russia destroyed.

Farm, Sunday, Oct. 28. — About noon, while I was out in the front yard raking leaves, Tess called out from the living-room window that there had been a break and that it looked like peace. I rushed in. She had just picked up a broadcast that Mr. K. had backed down, that he had agreed to dismantle the Russian missile bases in Cuba. . . . Apparently at the brink of nuclear war the Russians drew back. . . .

Two days later the Defense Department announced that air photographs disclosed that Russians were swiftly dismantling the bases. The world's first threat of nuclear extinction had been averted. But it was a close thing. Would we be so lucky the next time?

The following year, 1963, the country was again thrown into shock. And this time there was sorrow too and despair. The young president was assassinated at Dallas.

It was a Friday in late November, and I had gone up to the country the day before for the weekend. There was some wood to saw up and split, so that we would have enough to last over Christmas. About 1 P.M. I knocked off and went into the house for a bite of lunch. I was just finishing when the wife of a farmer down the road phoned to say she had just heard the last part of a bulletin on TV. Apparently the president had been shot. I turned on my set. Walter Cronkite, so stunned he could hardly speak, was saying on CBS that the president was being rushed to the hospital in Dallas but that it was not known whether his wounds were serious. So there was hope, and I grasped it desperately and clung to it. I remained sitting immobile, stricken, before the tube the rest of the afternoon and all through the evening, refusing at first to accept the truth of what happened and then trying to cope with it. Only the next day could I collect myself enough to put something in my diary.

Farm. Saturday, November 23, 1963. Pres. Kennedy was shot and killed by an assassin at Dallas, Texas, yesterday.

I have never before felt such a personal loss in the death of a president or public figure — not even the time in April, 1945, when F. D. Roosevelt, a beloved figure to my generation, suddenly died when I was on leave in Cedar Rapids. . . .

Personally I had never even met Kennedy, except for a brief hand-shake some years ago in New York when as senator and author of a best-selling book called *Profiles in Courage,* he made the major address at the Annual Book Award ceremony. I believe he received the award that year . . . for nonfiction. . . .

And though I had some reservations about him as president these past three years (I had voted for him), he was the first occupant of the White House since FDR who inspired me with much confidence and hope, and even affection. . . . He had a spontaneous sense of humor that added to his attractiveness. It bubbled over in his last public appearance at a [breakfast] speech at Fort Worth an hour or so before he was murdered. Thanks to TV we saw that appearance — after the sudden death was reported, and this juxtaposition, this seeing him in such a radiant mood just before death, made the tragedy almost beyond bearing.

As I sat watching the little screen, I kept thinking that this was the clinching proof that not only is there no sense in human life but that all the talk of the religious men about there being a righteous God that rules the universe is humbug. If there is a God and he can permit such an insane, inane ordering of human existence, then God is not what the Christians or the Jews or the Moslems or the Buddhists teach and think he is. Still the Masses and the memorial services went on last evening and today — there were several on TV — as if somehow this murder of this decent young man in such a position was part of a divine justice which we on earth do not understand. I cannot follow that.

By nightfall the scene had shifted to Washington.

Lyndon Johnson, the V.P., who took the oath of office in the president's plane at the Dallas airfield — apparently the authorities were afraid he might be shot if he appeared in a public building — spoke a few words at the Washington airport as he alighted after Mrs. Kennedy had departed with her husband's body. The din of the motors was so great that you could scarcely hear him. . . . He said simply: "I will do my best. That is all I can do. I ask for your help — and God's."

Scotty Reston had a very good piece that morning on the front page of the *New York Times*.

America wept tonight, not only for its dead young president, but for itself. The grief was general for somehow the worst in the nation had prevailed over the best. . . . For something in the nation itself, some stain of madness and violence, had destroyed the highest symbol of law and order.

Television that dark November weekend showed us the actual killing of the man who killed the president.

Farm, Sunday, November 24 . . . Shortly after noon in full view of the TV screen, which I was watching, a man stepped forward in the basement corridor of the Dallas city jail and shot the man accused of assassinating Kennedy. He fired one shot into the man's stomach from about one foot away. This assassin too seems to have been a shady character, one Ruby, alias Rubinstein, owner of a strip-tease night-joint in Dallas, and a holder of a police record.

Later — an hour or so later — in the same hospital — and about ten feet away from — where Kennedy had died Friday, he too died. His name was Lee Harvey Oswald. He was 24.

Oswald had been picked up by the Dallas police a couple of hours after the president was shot, at first accused of slaying a policeman. He was formally charged with killing President Kennedy shortly before midnight. On this Sunday just before noon he was being moved from the city to the county jail.

A loner and a drifter, Oswald had served in the Marine Corps and then taken off for the Soviet Union, where he worked in a factory for nearly three years, married a Russian woman, and applied for Soviet citizenship. This was refused. Oswald soon tired of living in the Soviet

Union, applied to regain his American passport and returned to the United States. He was obviously a very confused young man. His motives for shooting the president were not known, or at least never made public, and with his murder it was unlikely that they ever would be. Thus suspicions were aroused that never quite died down. I noted them in my diary that very day I saw him on TV being murdered. There were some seventy Dallas police guarding him in the jail's basement corridor through which he was being whisked. Not one of them lifted a finger, much less a gun, to stop the assassin. And what was Ruby doing there in the first place? The public had been excluded. Only reporters were allowed entrance. And the Dallas police knew the man.

Was it a cover-up? I wondered in my diary, noting the suspicious behavior of the Dallas police. For years some Americans wondered, even after a Presidential Commission headed by Chief Justice Earl Warren had, after long hearings, confirmed that in its opinion Oswald was the lone assassin, firing the fatal shots from the sixth floor of the Texas School Book Depository, where he was employed. My diary for that day, Sunday, November 24, ended:

> We seem to have shown the world and ourselves these past two days what savage, unlawful, unrestrained people we are.

The assassination of the young president, the slaying of his assassin, was too much to comprehend at once. As David Brinkley put it on NBC:

> The events of those days don't fit, you can't place them anywhere, they don't go in the intellectual luggage of our time. It was too big, too sudden, too overwhelming and it meant too much. It has to be separate and apart.

So many who had meant much to me, either as friends or notables, or both, were passing away. The last of the giants who had shaped the world in the years that led up to and through the Second World War died at the beginning of 1965. After Hitler and Mussolini and Roosevelt, whose lives came to an end in 1945, the last year of the war, and Stalin, who died in 1953, Winston Churchill, whose courage, eloquence, and fierce determination, had kept Britain in the war against the conquering Nazi Germans until the final Allied triumph, died in London at ninety on January 24.

He had survived the end of an era after the First World War and the end of another after the second war. In some ways, though, he was a character out of the eighteenth century, especially in his vision of the world and in his use of the English language in his speeches and writing. Perhaps it was this which caused him to have one shocking blind spot in his view of world affairs. This was his implacable opposition to Britain's giving India its independence. He had a romantic eighteenth-century idea — perhaps partly from his military service in India as a young man — that most Indians loved to be ruled by the British and that if they were set free, the various peoples and religious sects would fly at each other's throats and destroy the country. He talked a lot of nonsense about the "warrior races" of India wanting to serve under the British raj. A great politician himself, he had nothing but contempt for the Indian politicians who were pressing for self-government for their country. Contempt for Gandhi above all, whom he never understood or tried to understand.

I remember in 1931, while I was covering the Indian revolution, Churchill's complaining bitterly to the House of Commons that Gandhi was being allowed to negotiate on equal terms with the viceroy of India — at that time Lord Irwin, later Lord Halifax. The spectacle, Churchill claimed, nauseated him.

Gandhi took Churchill's attacks on him with typical good humor. I remember his chuckling when an aide read to him the outburst of Churchill against him in 1931 in the Commons. Gandhi had been meeting with the viceroy in Delhi in an attempt to reach a peace settlement. Day after day the frail little Hindu leader trudged up the marble steps of the Viceroy's Palace.

Churchill couldn't stand it. Rising in the House of Commons, he expressed his revulsion at "the nauseating and humiliating spectacle of this one-time Inner Temple lawyer [Gandhi], now a seditious fakir, striding half-naked up the steps of the Viceroy's Palace, there to negotiate and parley on equal terms with the representative of the King-Emperor."

In great contrast to his primitive views on India, Churchill saw very clearly and very early the threat of Nazi Germany. And because of this he became a pariah in his own Tory party, a lone voice in the wilderness as the party under Neville Chamberlain blindly opted for disarmament at home and appeasement of Hitler abroad.

It was during this period, in 1938, that I had a rather droll experience with Churchill. I thought of it as I read through the obituary and an account of all the worldwide tributes on this great man's death. It happened a day or two after I had flown from Vienna to London to give an uncensored report on the Anschluss. CBS, for which I was a correspondent in Europe, asked me to get Churchill to broadcast on the crisis, but it would pay him only fifty dollars. When I phoned

Churchill at the House of Commons, he agreed to do a broadcast; but he wanted more than fifty dollars, which was a ridiculous sum. From the way he talked I concluded he would accept five hundred dollars. But William Paley, the head of CBS, was adamant. He would not pay more than fifty, and we lost the broadcast.

When the Germans attacked in the west on May 10, 1940, the hapless Chamberlain was thrust aside and Churchill finally attained his lifelong ambition. He became prime minister. And just in time! For it was he in those dark months that saw the fall of France, the mass bombing of Britain, and the threat of a Nazi invasion who held the country together and galvanized it into defiance of Hitler. Without his indomitable spirit all might have been lost before Russia and the United States were drawn into the war the following year. And along with Franklin Roosevelt he was the architect of the Anglo-American triumph over Hitler in the west.

Churchill, in my observation, was the greatest orator of our era. In my time in Nazi Germany, I heard almost all of Hitler's principal speeches between 1934 and the end of 1940. They were tremendously effective, at least with the Germans. I heard Mussolini orate in Italy and once in Berlin. I listened a good deal to the golden voices of Aristilde Briand and Paul Boncour in France, and, of course, to many broadcast talks of President Roosevelt. But of all these Churchill, I thought, was the greatest public speaker. His mastery was due not only to his voice but also to other factors. He had a wonderful sense of timing. His eloquence lay not only in the way he expressed himself but also in his words — words that would live in one's memory.

Few who heard them at the time or read them will ever forget the words he spoke to the Commons when he took over the government as the Germans began to sweep westward through Holland, Belgium, and France those May days.

> We have before us an ordeal of the most grievous kind. We have before us many long months of strife and of suffering. . . . I would say to the House: I have nothing to offer but blood, toil, tears and sweat.

Even more eloquent were his words to the Commons on an even darker day a few weeks later, after the Germans had conquered France and the Low Countries and driven the remnants of the British expeditionary force off the continent. Britain stood alone against the triumphant Hitler, who was poised to launch his Luftwaffe bombers against Britain and then invade it. It was one of Britain's darkest hours in all her long history. Churchill stood up in the Commons and said:

> We shall not flag or fail. We shall go on to the end; we shall fight in
> France; we shall fight on the sea and the oceans; we shall fight with
> growing confidence and with growing strength in the air; we shall defend
> our island, whatever the cost may be; we shall fight in the fields and in
> the streets; we shall fight in the hills; we shall never surrender; and even
> if, which I do not for a moment believe, this island or a large part of it
> were subjugated and starving, then our Empire beyond the seas . . .
> would carry on the struggle, until in God's good time, the new world
> with all its power and might, steps forth to the rescue and the liberation
> of the old.

And there was his tribute to the fighter pilots of the RAF who turned
back the Luftwaffe in the greatest air battle ever fought: "Never in
history have so many owed so much to so few." And his much-quoted
crack that Russia was "a riddle, wrapped in a mystery inside an
enigma."

Public speaking came naturally to him, but he also worked hard at
it. Though he rarely, if ever, read a speech verbatim, as most American
politicians do (it was forbidden in the House of Commons, I believe),
he made copious notes and had them well in mind before he got up to
speak.

"Never rise to speak," he once admonished a group of us correspondents, "unless you know precisely what you want to say — and have the
notes to remind you of it."

Some of his colleagues thought he overdid it. Once in London in
1943, halfway through the war, I recall Anthony Eden, the foreign
secretary and eventually successor to Churchill as prime minister,
complaining that the P.M. had secluded himself for three days in order
to draft a crucial speech to the Commons.

"He has disappeared from sight!" Eden said. "None of us can get to
see him. A lot of important matters have to wait."

Churchill was stunned that at the very moment of triumph over
Hitler in 1945, for which he had labored so hard and long, the voters
in Britain turned him out in a national election and elected a Labour
government instead.

I watched him in the Commons a few months later speaking for the
Tory opposition against a Labour bill to nationalize the steel industry.
(An old friend, G. R. Strauss, a wealthy but left-wing Labourite, was
the minister in charge of the nationalization.) Churchill seemed much
older — perhaps the burden of the war years, of seeing his country

through one crisis after another, was largely responsible. He was stooped and the fire seemed to have died down and words came with surprising difficulty. Perhaps the subject bored him.

The last time I saw him was in New York in 1946 when he invited a few of us former correspondents in for a late breakfast in his suite at the Waldorf. He was attired in the coveralls he had worn so often during the war and he was sipping from a wineglass full of brandy. Apparently he noticed surprise on the faces of some of his guests that he would be imbibing such strong drink at such an early hour. At any rate, with a twinkle in his eye he quipped that, as he once said, he neither wanted nor needed brandy but that it was pretty hazardous to interfere with the ineradicable habit of a lifetime.

Churchill seemed full of life again, content with the role of opposition leader in the Commons, which he said gave him time to finish his war memoirs, do a little painting, and spend much of his time in his beloved country home, Chartwell, which he had helped to build with his own hands. But I suspected that his exuberant spirits were due largely to his zest for the controversy that a speech he had made a few days before had aroused not only in the United States but also throughout the world. He had spoken at Westminster College, a small institution at Fulton, Missouri, with a beaming President Truman looking on.

Stalin, his armies having installed puppet Communist regimes in Eastern Europe, was becoming more and more belligerent toward the West in his speeches and actions. In Fulton, Churchill rose to take issue with him.

"From Stettin in the Baltic to Trieste in the Adriatic," he said in a peroration that reverberated around the world and gave it a new term for the line separating the East and West in Europe, "an iron curtain has descended across the continent." The Soviet Union constituted "a growing challenge and peril to Christian civilization." He thought that the Russians could be halted only if the English-speaking nations stood together against them.

Though this was pretty much the line of the Truman administration and the Congress, the speech caused an immediate furor in our country. The wartime hero was accused of wanting to foment another world war — this time against Russia. Even true-blood anti-Communists criticized Churchill for wanting to shore up Britain's waning power by provoking America into joining her in an anti-Soviet campaign. The speech, said Walter Lippmann, our dean of columnists, was an "almost catastrophic blunder," and he reminded his readers that British imperial interests and American vital interests were far from identical.

I have mislaid my diary notes on this last meeting with Churchill. But, as I recall, he feigned surprise at American reaction to his speech. It was not "anti-Russian" at all. Had Americans read the headlines but not what he actually had said? He had specifically declared that he did not believe the Soviet Union wanted war — only the fruits of war, that is, the expansion of its power.

If my memory is at all correct, Churchill grew more somber before our talk was over. Obviously he had been bitterly disappointed that the Allies, who together had brought down Hitler and the Third Reich, had fallen out as soon as the peace came. I think that despite all his long experience with the cussedness of mankind and the deceits of many, he believed that the Allies could have made a peace that would be lasting and offer security to all nations, large and small. But this had not happened — just the opposite. This had depressed him. Two years later, as he finished the sixth and last volume of his memoirs, he could not help stating its theme as follows:

HOW THE GREAT DEMOCRACIES
TRIUMPHED,
AND SO
WERE ABLE TO RESUME
THE POLICIES
WHICH HAD SO NEARLY
COST THEM THEIR
LIFE.

I found a certain inconsistency in this. It was he himself who was now stressing that it was not because the triumphant democracies had fallen out — they really hadn't — but because Stalin had opted for hostility to the Allies, which had helped save his country, that we owed the mess we had made of the peace. I did not believe that our side was blameless. Many a powerful figure in the West was already pushing for what soon would be called a Cold War. Some were even calling for a preventive war against the Soviet colossus while the U.S.A. still was the only power to have an atomic bomb. The distrust was mutual. For as long as Stalin lived, better relations with the Soviet Union were impossible.

Churchill's great wartime antagonist, Aneurin Bevan, the fiery-tongued old warrior of the Labour party, had died five years before, in 1960, at the age of sixty-two. I had first met him in 1929 when he was elected to the House of Commons for the first time, and we remained in touch as long as he lived. I paid a brief tribute to him in the first volume of these memoirs, but I would like to add this.

He had come out of the Welsh coal mines to become a dominant figure in British politics. He had been elected from the Welsh constituency of Ebbw Vale, which continued to send him to Parliament to the end of his life. Nye, as he was known to almost everyone, was a ball of fire in those days, determined to right the wrongs of society and especially to alleviate the plight of the poor. Though the fire died down somewhat — though not by much — as he grew older and matured and mellowed, he never abandoned for a moment his fierce concern for the underdogs of our world.

I had a feeling in 1929 that though he would stumble he would go far. Stumble he did, finding himself often at odds with his own Labour party, whose left wing he led. Once, in 1929, he was kicked out of the party and in 1951 he resigned from a key post in the Labour government. But he always came back. At his death he was deputy leader of the party, and its most prominent figure. Yet the goal he sought most eluded him. He wanted eventually to become the leader of the Labour party and prime minister. Perhaps he would have, had his life not been cut short by a fatal illness.

Nye Bevan's feuds with Churchill added much spice to the debates in the House of Commons, where his oratory rivaled that of the great wartime prime minister. He could be as sharp and as witty as the old Tory antagonist. "You are the chief architect of our misery!" Bevan would shout at Churchill, who once called *him* "a squalid nuisance" and at another time assailed him as "this evil counsellor . . . this gamin from some Welsh gutter." Actually, I believe, the two warriors had a great admiration and respect for each other.

For a man who went to work in the coal mines when he was thirteen and had only two years of higher education at a labor college in London, Nye was an astonishingly well-read man. He devoured books, especially on history, politics, economics. And he had an immense intellectual curiosity, constantly widening his horizons not only from books but also from meeting new people of all sorts. Once in London, in 1943, he phoned to say he heard John Steinbeck was in town and he would like to meet him. The three of us sat up all one night in my room at the Savoy discussing everything under the sun and sometimes arguing issues with such passion and heat that tempers flared.

Bevan turned out to be my most provocative friend. Some of our arguments went on for years, and at times we fell into shouting matches. One of our differences was over military conscription. With the growing menace of Hitler's Germany, I thought Britain should introduce the draft in order to build up an army. I would fly over from Berlin to London to try to persuade Nye to get the Labour party to back it. But he was violently opposed. We fought over it until the war came.

In 1955, when Bevan visited America for the second time, he seemed slated to become the next British foreign minister if Labour were returned to office soon, as seemed likely. With that in mind, John Gunther and I set up a meeting at John's house for him to meet Adlai Stevenson, whom we thought might become secretary of state if the Democrats won the White House after Eisenhower's second term. Curiously, the two did not seem to hit it off. As it turned out neither ever got the job to preside over foreign affairs.

Nye Bevan's greatest accomplishment was in fighting for, and largely setting up, Britain's National Health Service. Often berated for being too negative because he was always on the attack, Bevan now showed great creative powers. As minister of health from 1945 to 1951 and then as minister of labor and national health services, he was in charge of instituting this most drastic social change in British society. Criticized though it has been for its many flaws, Britain's National Health Service, which gives every citizen free medical, dental, and hospital service from the cradle to the grave, has become an unshakeable part of British life, supported and maintained even by the Tories in their long spells of power. In America, the most affluent nation on earth, we offer a watered-down version of this service only to our elderly.

In 1929 in London, I also met Jennie Lee, the daughter of a Scottish coal miner, who too was elected by Labour to Parliament that year for the first time and so at twenty-four became the youngest member of the Commons, one of its few women and certainly the most beautiful. It had to be that she and Nye would marry, and they did in 1934. They made an attractive pair. Jennie too rose in the Labour party and finally became a minister in a Labour government.

Tess and I had a deep affection and admiration for her, too, and in the foreword she asked me to write for her second book, *This Great Journey*, I could not help remarking that she was "one of the remarkable young women of our time — our own country has had no one quite like her" — and alluding to her "dark, laughing, Scottish beauty and great charm."

*　　*　　*

On the afternoon of July 14, 1965, Adlai Stevenson collapsed on a London street and died. He was sixty-five — "only four years older than me," I noted in my diary.

> I kept thinking last night of what strange and ironic tricks fate plays on men. Stevenson, who wanted to be president, and was nominated twice for the office by the Democratic party, never made it because he had the bad luck to run each time against a war hero, Eisenhower. Against any other Republican candidate . . . he would have made it. Eisenhower, who probably never thought of becoming president and probably wasn't much interested, became president twice. Johnson got to the White House two years ago by accident, the death of Kennedy.

I often thought from talking with him that Stevenson wanted even more to be secretary of state than president. But in this quest too he lost out. President Kennedy, out of pique at Stevenson's defying him at the 1960 Democratic convention, and President Johnson, out of ignorance probably, named another, genial but mediocre Dean Rusk, to the office. This was to cost them dearly and was a disaster for Johnson. They did appoint Stevenson U.S. representative at the United Nations and then, at least in Kennedy's case, double-crossed him, especially in the Bay of Pigs crisis when the president deliberately misled him.

Scotty Reston, in an appraisal on page one of the *New York Times*, made a good observation. Stevenson, he wrote, "was the man of thought in an age of action. He was in tune with the worldwide spirit of the age, but not with the spirit of his own country." To the *Times* of London, Adlai Stevenson was a "tragic figure" in American history, "a prophet before his time, who received honor but not power" and who died "full of disappointments."

In the last year or two he scarcely hid these disappointments. A few weeks before, after attending the funeral of Ed Murrow in New York, we had walked down the street together. He seemed strangely tired — strangely because he usually was so bouncy — and very subdued. I was aware from random remarks he had made and from what friends said that he felt frustrated with his work as U.S. representative at the United Nations. Both the White House and the State Department often either misled him or kept him in the dark as to U.S. policy. He did not like that or having to defend policies he personally opposed. His views were more and more dismissed or ignored in Washington. But on that stroll after Ed's funeral he obviously did not feel like talking of his problems. He seemed too depressed.

To Eric Sevareid, who had a long talk with him in London three days before his death, he confided that he was tired and expected to resign his post at the U.N. within a few days. He would retire from public life, he said, practice a little law in Chicago and New York, visit with his grandchildren, "his greatest delight," and "sit in the shade with a glass of wine in his hand and watch people dancing."

Some things puzzled me about Adlai Stevenson and I noted one or two of them in my diary that day after his sudden death.

> A strange and contradictory man. . . . He had great wit — a rarity in the U.S.A. today, a sparkling sense of humor that was always erupting in his public speeches and private conversation. He was an intellectual, an egg-head — a type considered suspicious in America. . . . But he was indecisive. He found it hard to come to a final decision. And while this often shows one's intelligence — since things are rarely black and white — it is a handicap to a man in high public office. . . .

Though he fell short of attaining the great prizes he sought, he was a good loser. Few who heard and saw him on TV will forget his graceful words the night he first lost to Eisenhower. After congratulating the general he added:

> Someone asked me as I came in, down on the street, how I felt, and I was reminded of a story that a fellow-townsman of ours used to tell, Abraham Lincoln. They asked him how he felt after an unsuccessful election. He said he felt like a little boy who had stubbed his toe in the dark. He said that he was too old to cry but it hurt him too much to laugh.

CHAPTER 4

So many writers — poets and novelists mostly — who had helped enrich my life were dying in those postwar years.

H. G. Wells, who had seemed such a towering literary figure at one time to my generation, died in London in the summer of 1946. I had run into him in London during the war and this once-idol of mine had been bitter and somewhat lost, I felt. The world had not turned out as he had hoped.

Rebecca West, in the years that she befriended me, talked often of Wells. They had been lovers before the First World War when she was young and beautiful, and I gathered she had very much wanted to marry him. But, married at the time, he had held off. Later, after his wife died, he had wanted to marry Moura Budberg, complaining to George Bernard Shaw that "she will stay with me, eat with me, sleep with me. But she will not marry me," which pleased the great playwright. Wells had brought Baroness Budberg, a charming Russian, who was also the lover of Maxim Gorky, to Vienna when I was stationed there; and John Gunther and I saw a bit of them during that visit. Wells was still hopeful that a world government would bring peace and happiness to the world, though Moura, who had lived through the Russian Revolution, was skeptical.

I was fascinated by a woman who could be at the same time mistress to two of the leading writers in the world. We kept up an acquaintanceship to near the end of her life. One of the most interesting evenings I ever had occurred in New York after the war when I had dinner with Moura Budberg and Rebecca West, each a little wary of the other, and they reminisced about Wells. But even more fascinating, after Rebecca had left, was sitting up all night with Moura to hear her recount the night in 1936 that Maxim Gorky died in his dacha outside of Moscow. She was with him. And she believed that he was poisoned by Stalin, who could no longer stomach Gorky's refusal to support fully his bloody dictatorship. Again, as after the Bolshevik Revolution in 1917, which had caught her in Petrograd, she was forced to flee in the dead of the night. Stalin would surely kill her, to silence her, if he could find her. She somehow made her way safely out of Russia.

H. G. Wells died bravely and with his sense of humor intact. When an old friend, toward the end, kept breaking in on a monologue he was delivering, Wells retorted: "Don't interrupt me. Can't you see I'm busy dying?"

Ernest Hemingway passed on in July 1961, just short of reaching sixty-two. Reading the obits and the tributes from all over the world, I wondered what time would do to his reputation. I myself believe that he must be considered our greatest contemporary writer, who created a new style, a new language, with his lean, fast-moving, hard-bitten prose. His fame, I believe, did him in in the end. He began to believe in his own myth, and this was fatal. But he had known greatness. And he had given us some of the finest writing of our time.

Thomas Mann used to say that our country seemed hardly aware that it had produced between the two world wars four of the greatest novelists in the West: Hemingway, Fitzgerald, Dos Passos, and Faulkner.

William Faulkner, who like Hemingway won a Nobel Prize, died the next year on July 6. "Probably our greatest writer," I noted in my diary the next day, "one of the last of the American giants who came up after the First World War."

John Dos Passos died on September 28, 1970, at the age of seventy-four. Over half a century he had drifted from the far left to the far right. It was not so important that the man who in early life had contributed to the Communist *New Masses* ended up writing for the reactionary *National Review* or that he who had once supported William Z. Foster, the Communist candidate for the presidency, became an ardent supporter of the presidential candidacy of Barry Goldwater. Most important and depressing to me, at least, was that the author of the *U.S.A.* trilogy of novels, completed in 1936, could later write such a different trilogy, *District of Columbia*, finished in 1949. The first had been a brilliantly written and passionate account of the injustices of life in industrial America in the first third of the twentieth century. The second had been, at least to me and even to most of the sympathetic critics, a rather bloodless but acerbic assault on President Roosevelt and the New Deal. Twelve years later came the long novel *Midcentury*, a one-sided attack on the trade unions, for which Dos had been so zealous in his earlier years. Never had a great writer, so far as I remembered, spent the last half of his life assailing what he had thought and written during the first half. And in the process Dos had lost the magic that had made him such a fine writer in the 1920s and 1930s. As a writer he had faded away, the sap gone out of him.

Scott Fitzgerald had died in 1940 at forty-four, burnt out at middle age by drink, early success, and the burden of later failure. Thomas Mann once told me he thought Fitzgerald was the most graceful writer of the great quartet. Perhaps he was, but he had abused his talents and wasted them. Still, his *The Great Gatsby*, published in 1925, seemed to me as good as anything Hemingway or Faulkner ever wrote.

John Steinbeck, also a Nobel laureate, died in 1968 at sixty-six. I noted it in my diary on Christmas Eve, John having died on December 20.

> I . . . saw something of him when he lived around the corner [in New York] during part of the war when I was home, and in London in 1943.

We had gone over there that year as war correspondents to cover the U.S. 8th Air Force, which was just beginning its massive bombing of Germany. I had introduced him to some of my friends, chiefly among the Labour party but he was not very much interested in politics. He was almost apolitical. What concerned him chiefly was the sociology of our society, the plight of the poor and forsaken, as he showed in his great novel *The Grapes of Wrath*.

For years I was puzzled that Steinbeck, like Fitzgerald and Hemingway, had slid downhill after writing his great work early in his career. It had happened to Fitzgerald after *The Great Gatsby* in 1925; to Hemingway after *For Whom the Bell Tolls* in 1940; and to Steinbeck after *The Grapes of Wrath* in 1939.

Was that the inevitable fate of American novelists in our time? It seemed to be becoming a pattern. Steinbeck tried valiantly to go on: *Cannery Row, The Wayward Bus, East of Eden, Sweet Thursday*, and *The Winter of Our Discontent*. One gathered he was bitter and frustrated that they were not very well received by the reviewers and the public.

In 1962, John won the Nobel Prize for Literature, the sixth American author to receive it. Paradoxically this highest of honors for a writer, the most coveted prize of all, though it brought him much acclaim and the satisfaction of literary achievement recognized worldwide, also brought a further slacking in his creativity.

"The prize did terrible things to John's ability to create fiction," said Harold Guinzburg, the head of Viking, Steinbeck's publisher. "He felt very frustrated and he would fool around with an entertainment, or something light, to break the tension."

Poets I liked were making the front pages with notices of their deaths. Edna St. Vincent Millay had gone in 1950 at fifty-eight. Some of her peers, though praising her, did not think she was the greatest of our contemporary poets. But I thought she was one of the best. It was she who, more than any other, had awakened my interest in modern poetry during my college days. She had come once to my campus in Iowa to read her poetry and later at a reception spoke with some of us students. It was not only that she led me to poetry but also that she helped liberate me by her poetic voice and the example of her life, from the Midwest puritanism and stodginess in which I had grown up. I and a few kindred spirits at the college never tired of reciting her verse, beginning with the lines

> *My candle burns at both ends,*
> *It will not last the night;*
> *But, ah, my foes, and oh, my friends —*
> *It gives a lovely light!*

Her lyric love poems, I think, touched the whole country and her sonnets were to me as moving as those of Keats. I worshipped her and her genius from afar. The three or four times I met her in New York were fleeting.

Steepletop, where Edna Millay lived her later life and died, lies only a few miles over the mountain from where I have resided the last twenty-one years. Each spring I make a pilgrimage across the mountain to visit her grave, listen to poetry readings by some of her surviving friends and, until her death recently, chat with Edna's sister Norma, who lived on and on in the beautiful hills at Steepletop.

I liked Carl Sandburg and his poems too, though at this writing (the latter 1980s) he seems not to be held in such esteem as he was when I was growing up in the Midwest and he was a sort of poet laureate of Chicago, whose clatter, rawness, dynamism, violence, corruption, and poverty, but also whose beauty, promise, and excitement he expressed so movingly.

His great six-volume biography of Lincoln, in which there was so much poetic prose, made it biography as literature. Some academics came to scoff at it, complaining of its flawed scholarship and showing no appreciation of its greatness as literature and apparently not knowing that Sandburg spent two decades of his life in research. I believe it will live.

I remembered Sandburg from my youth as a great bard. He too came to our campus, strumming his guitar and singing his folksongs and declaiming his verse. Later he gave me much moral support in the blacklisting days when I was down. He feared no one, certainly not Senator McCarthy and the witch-hunters of the intolerant years. Sadly I began my diary:

> Farm. July 23, 1967 (Sunday). — Carl Sandburg dead at his goat farm in North Carolina.
> 89. A long life. And full.

T. S. Eliot, the American expatriate who became a British subject in 1927 and was one of the greatest poets in the English language of our time and certainly one with tremendous influence on poetry and poets in the twentieth century, died in London at the beginning of 1965 at seventy-six. His impact on my whole generation was enormous. We read and pondered especially *The Waste Land*, which came out in 1922, with its air of despair and disillusionment at the way our world had turned out: the horrible blood-letting of the First World War — for what? — and the botch the so-called statesmen had made of the post-war peace. One remembered the famous lines, the opening of *The Waste Land:*

> *April is the cruellest month*

and from *The Hollow Men:*

> *This is the way the world ends . . .*
> *Not with a bang but a whimper.*

It was long whispered and eventually confirmed that Eliot's American friend, Ezra Pound, had saved *The Waste Land* from disaster by urging extensive revisions. Pound died in Venice in 1972 at eighty-seven after an extraordinary life. I never cared much for his poetry but I admired his devotion to it and his generosity in encouraging and helping other poets and writers. In Paris in the 1920s, when one could not help bumping into Pound here or there, I knew of his generosity to James Joyce — somehow he wangled for him a government grant — his encouragement of Hemingway. And one heard of his bullying Harriet Monroe into publishing Eliot's first big poem, "Love Song of J. Alfred Prufrock," in her *Poetry* magazine, of his getting Frost first published by sending off some of his poems to a magazine without consulting the poet, of his early recognition of William Carlos Williams and many others.

That was the good side. He had another. Even in the Paris days, before he settled in Italy, I noted his megalomania, his craving for self-advertisement, his hunger for the grandiose. Worse was to come. Years later, after World War II had started, when I had a small office near the CBS shortwave radio listening post in New York whenever I was home, I listened to Pound's outrageous broadcasts from Italy for Mussolini against his native land. He had become a crackpot, and a nasty one, fuming at the Jews on whom he blamed most of the world's ills, especially the war, which Hitler had started and Mussolini, like a jackal, had joined. He cursed Roosevelt and those around him and praised Mussolini, blind to the phoniness of this sawdust Caesar.

In wartime, this was treason — working for the enemy against your own country — and after the war, when Pound was picked up by American troops in Italy, he was duly indicted in Washington. At least two Americans, Best and Chandler, who had broadcast for Hitler from Berlin, got life sentences, but Pound was declared insane and incarcerated in St. Elizabeths Hospital for the Insane in Washington. For years there was much controversy among American writers over whether they should help get Pound pardoned and released from the asylum. It was a difficult problem for me. I had loathed Pound's broadcasts at a time when this nation was fighting for its life against the two Fascist dictatorships, which Pound was defending. But he had long been a bit of a crackpot. Probably few Americans heard his shortwave broadcasts from Rome, so the damage was slight, though I did not forgive him for it. But I felt sad that we were keeping an influential poet and a generous man locked up in a lunatic bin for the rest of his life, crazy as he might have been. The government had dropped indictments against several of the American radio traitors, just as much to blame as Pound. So in the end I joined with other writers trying to obtain Pound's release. After long delays it proved successful. The indictment was dropped in the spring of 1958. Pound was freed, and he returned to his beloved Italy and died there.*

*   *   *

* Two days after his eighty-seventh birthday which, according to his biographer, "was full of joy, cake, champagne, neighboring children, friends." On his return to Italy twelve years before, after being released from St. Elizabeths, he had greeted the press on disembarking at Naples with a Fascist salute and told the reporters: "All America is an insane asylum."

Inanimate things die too, and sometimes I noted them in my diary. The death of a famous train, of a famous magazine, for instance. Both reminders of an ever-changing world.

On May 29, 1961, I pasted in my diary a clip of a Reuter dispatch from Paris to the *New York Times.* It began:

> "The Orient Express is no more.
> After a service that has lasted 78 years, the train was on its last journey today [the 28th].

It had left the Gare de l'Est in Paris the night before for Bucharest by way of Basel, Zürich, Innsbruck, Salzburg, Vienna, and Budapest, a journey of sixty hours.

Reading this brought back memories.

> How often I have taken that train . . . from Paris to Istanbul down through Switzerland and Austria to Vienna and then down the Danube to Budapest and then southeast to Bucharest and Istanbul — a journey of 67 hours and usually a pleasant one. Some of the cars branched off to Italy and Yugoslavia (and even to Greece). In my Vienna days I traveled on it frequently to and from Paris.

But there were times when assignments took me on it to Milan and Venice and Rome, to Belgrade, to Athens.

The Orient Express was a comfortable all-Pullman train with good food and wine served in the dining car. It took you through picturesque landscapes, especially the mountains of the Alps from Basel to Salzburg, then the hilly valley of the Danube down through Vienna to Budapest and thereafter the mountains, hills, and valleys of the Balkans, with their quaint villages and colorfully dressed villagers.

What killed the Orient Express? The airplane, no doubt, and to some extent the Iron Curtain. It became much quicker and a bit cheaper to travel by air. After the war it proved exhausting and frustrating to cross the frontier of a Balkan Communist country. You were hauled off the train, even in the dead of the night, to open your baggage to inspection — it too had been removed — even if you were only passing through the country.

Agatha Christie wrote a fine murder thriller set on the Orient Express. I often found the train full of mysterious-looking characters, I noted in my diary, "but I never myself saw a crime perpetrated." Shenanigans, yes, and sudden romance or at least sex, for somehow on that wonderful train the customary restraints, all the taboos, which still existed in that old-fashioned golden time of one's youth, did not stop you.

> Lenox, Saturday, December 9, 1972.
> *Life* magazine folded yesterday after 36 years.
> Though it was terribly flawed . . . it made a mark in American journalism as a great picture magazine. Thus goes the last of the great weekly or biweekly national magazines, a victim mainly of TV, with its greater advertising potential. *Life's still* pictures could not compete with the *moving* pictures on TV. And the magazine in the last years could not compete with TV for advertising. *Look*, which published a good deal of my stuff . . . folded a year ago. And before that the *Saturday Evening Post* and *Colliers*.
> Probably the mass of Americans has ceased to read even the magazines. It does not read books. It prefers to gawk at the idiot-box — for free.
> Sad, though, the passing of another great magazine.

Years later *Life* reappeared in the form of a monthly, but it was not the same.

There were two Germans whose deaths I noted in my diary. Neither of them was very well known in America, but I had followed them at close hand when I lived and worked in Germany.

One was Dr. Hjalmar Horace Greeley Schacht, a gangling banker with a long neck he covered with a high collar and who I thought had one of the most nimble minds of the century. He knew how to land on his feet, no matter what the setback. In fact, he prospered under every regime Germany knew from Kaiser Wilhelm II through the postwar Weimar Republic and Hitler's Third Reich to the time of Chancellor Adenauer in the 1950s. Like a cat, he had nine lives. Or more.

He was credited with restoring the German currency after it slid to a trillion marks to a dollar in the 1920s. Under Weimar he was for years president of the Reichsbank. He became in my time in Germany the architect of Hitler's war economy in the 1930s. He served the Nazis well. Found not guilty of being a war criminal at the Nuremberg trials at the end of the Second World War, he went back to banking; and after most of his Nazi colleagues had either been hanged, jailed, or forgotten he again prospered.

I saw him occasionally in Germany before the war, sometimes at official ceremonies but mostly at lunches or dinners at the American embassy in Berlin when William E. Dodd was the ambassador. There he liked to pose as really anti-Nazi despite his posts as Hitler's president of the Reichsbank and Nazi minister of economics. He would crack jokes at his Nazi party bosses and occasionally give me a clue to a good story. He was finally fired and arrested by Hitler during the latter part of the war and was confined to a concentration camp from which he was liberated by American troops. I saw him last at Nuremberg, where he sat in the dock with Göring, Hess, Ribbentrop, and other Nazi criminals, fuming that the Americans and British would try *him* along with such Nazi riffraff. We correspondents were not permitted to talk with the defendants; but through his lawyer Schacht sent word to us of the terrible injustice he felt had been done him by the Allied conquerors. We knew how anti-Nazi he had been. It was hard for me to sympathize; I had always thought that without him and his financial wizardry Hitler's Third Reich would have gone bankrupt by 1939 and been unable to plunge us into another world war.

I saw him in Vienna right after the Anschluss in March 1938, and concluded he had arrived from Berlin to seize Austria's gold. But he would not speak to the foreign press, not even to those of us who had known him in Berlin. I knew what he was up to, but I did not know how low he could stoop to kowtow to Hitler when he thought it necessary. Years later, while researching the Third Reich book, I came upon an account of Schacht's speech at that time to the employees of the Austrian National Bank, which he was incorporating into his German Reichsbank, along with its gold and other assets.

After attacking the foreign press for the way it reported Hitler's military takeover of Austria, Schacht defended it as the "consequence of countless perfidies and brutal acts of violence which foreign countries have practiced against us." This was pure nonsense, but the inimitable Dr. Schacht went on to worse.

> Thank God! . . . Adolf Hitler has created a union of German will and German thought. . . . And he finally gave the external form to the inner union of Germany and Austria. . . .
>
> Not a single person will find a future with us who is not wholeheartedly for Adolf Hitler. . . . The Reichsbank will always be nothing but National Socialist or I shall cease to be its manager.

Dr. Schacht then forced the Austrian staff to take an oath to be "faithful and obedient to the Führer."

"A scoundrel he who breaks it!" he yelled and then led his captive audience into shouting a triple "Sieg Heil!"

This great survivor finally died in Munich on June 4, 1970. He was ninety-three.

General Franz Halder, chief of the once-vaunted German Army General Staff at the beginning of World War II, did not live quite so long as Schacht. But he was eighty-seven when he died in Bavaria on August 2, 1972. He was generally considered the brains behind Hitler's early military victories: the three weeks' conquest of Poland in September 1939, the six weeks' overwhelming of France in the spring and early summer of 1940, and the rapid German advance in the summer and fall of 1941 to the gates of Moscow. I followed his career rather closely in my years in Germany. He was most generous in helping me solve some military puzzles of the French campaign while I was writing my history of the Third Reich. And when all around him in Germany, especially some of his former fellow generals, were fuming at that book, he publicly defended it.

Hitler sacked him in the spring of 1942 for protesting too much against the warlord's strategy to "finish off" the Russians that summer. The General Staff chief tried to tell the Führer that the German Army simply didn't have the strength. The dictator probably had taken more criticism from General Halder than from any other officer or official. But by this critical time he could no longer stand it, and Halder was relieved of his post. This turned out to be a loss not only to the German Army, which soon would suffer at Stalingrad the worst defeat in its history, but also to historians. For Halder's diary is a unique source of concise information for the period between August 14, 1939, when he began the diary, and September 24, 1942, when he was sacked as chief of the General Staff. All that crucial time he was in daily contact with Hitler and the top men around him, military and civilian. I found its three volumes invaluable in writing the history of Nazi Germany; and I have been amazed that no American publisher had it translated and published over here, for it would have given American readers a unique insight into a very important chapter of history.

General Halder was arrested in 1944 at the time of the attempt of a few army officers to assassinate Hitler. Placed in solitary confinement in a pitch-dark cell for several months and then confined to the Dachau concentration camp, he, like Schacht, was liberated by American troops advancing through the Tyrol on May 4, 1945. Himmler is believed to have ordered the execution of the whole lot, which included Schuschnigg, the former Austrian chancellor who had at first defied Hitler.

At Nuremberg, General Halder stunned the court by submitting a report telling of how, shortly after he became chief of staff in 1938, he had conspired with a group of fellow officers to arrest Hitler and depose him if he attacked Czechoslovakia and got Germany involved in a war the generals felt could not be won. Halder insisted that they were on the verge of carrying out their plan when word reached them in Berlin on September 28, 1938, that Chamberlain, the British prime minister, and Daladier, the French premier, had agreed to go to Munich to meet Hitler and Mussolini in what could only be a sell-out of Czechoslovakia. Since Hitler, thanks to Chamberlain, was going to get what he wanted in Czechoslovakia *without war,* the conspirators, Halder said, called off their plans to arrest Hitler. This was later confirmed by several of the other conspirators. It was interesting, at least to me, that they had planned to get rid of the Nazi dictator only because he threatened to launch a war the army was doubtful it could win. I would have thought there were even better reasons.

CHAPTER 5

On Monday, December 11, 1972, I ended my diary for that day: "Four of my oldest, closest friends . . . All dead."

One of them, Mark Van Doren, the poet, had died the day before in West Cornwall, Connecticut, at seventy-eight. Just a week before, on December 3, John Carter Vincent, whose career as an American diplomat Senators McCarthy and McCarran and their fellow witch-hunters had ruthlessly destroyed, had gone.

It had been a bad year for losing friends. Ed Snow, the great foreign correspondent and China hand, died of cancer in February in Switzerland at sixty-six; and Miriam Hopkins, the fiery actress, in October, just short of her seventieth birthday. And now in December, besides Van Doren and Vincent, Jay Allen, an old colleague and friend since our Paris days, and close also to John Gunther and Jimmy Sheean, had died.

And what was going to be a sad Christmas for me because of these losses was turned into a terrible Christmas that year when President Nixon and his scheming secretary of state, Kissinger, began their devastating Christmas bombing of Hanoi, hitting among other things the city's main hospital and massacring many of its patients and staff. They tried to deny it at first, but Telford Taylor, our chief American prosecutor at Nuremberg, happened to be in Hanoi, witnessed the carnage, and reported it to the *New York Times*, though he was not a correspondent.

Such a Christmas message!

Such American barbarism!

I wrote in my diary that ensuing New Year's Eve: "It makes one feel terribly guilty to be an American." One could not help but feel ashamed. In my German years I had cursed Hitler for his savagery; now I was cursing Nixon and Kissinger (himself a Jewish refugee from Hitler) for theirs. And I mourned for the days when I could go over from my Torrington, Connecticut, farm to West Cornwall to commiserate over such outrageous deeds with three of my oldest friends (three of the four mentioned in the diary): Jim Thurber, Lewis Gannett, and Mark

Van Doren. Jim had died sometime back, in 1961; Lewis in 1966; and now Mark in this Christmas season of 1972.

For years, until Jim went, we four, with our wives, would meet Saturday evenings to dine and drink, chew the fat, reminisce about the good old days, curse the phonies who had now made the present so bad, and settle the world's more pressing problems.

Thurber was my oldest friend. We had met, as I have recounted,* one August evening in 1925 nearly half a century before when I, a raw youngster just out of college in Iowa, had reported for work on the night copydesk of the Paris edition of the *Chicago Tribune* and a lanky, owl-eyed man with thick glasses in the slot next to me had introduced himself. "I'm Jim Thurber," he said. The name did not ring a bell. He was, in 1925, not yet known. But he was doing, he soon confided, a lot of writing on the side. What he showed me of it that fall was very good and very funny — obviously he was a born humorist. But he was not getting anywhere, he felt, and he was in despair.

He did an amusing stint on the Riviera that winter editing an absolutely zany edition of the *Tribune* there — he wrote most of the copy himself out of his impish fantasies — but when he returned to Paris in the spring, he was again despondent. We had some long talks.

"Goddammit, Bill," he would say, "I'll be thirty-two this year. And what have I accomplished?"

He would answer himself. "Nothing.

"A guy has to face it," he would go on. "I'm nearly thirty-two and I ain't going to be no novelist. It's certain I ain't going to be no Fitzgerald or Hemingway. Look what they've done, and they're not even thirty."

Fitzgerald, we figured, would turn thirty that year, but already at twenty-four, Jim reminded me, he had published his first novel, *This Side of Paradise*, and his really great novel *Gatsby* when he was only twenty-nine. Hemingway was even younger. And though he had only published up to now three slim books brought out by small American presses in Paris, everyone knew that he had just finished his first novel, *The Sun Also Rises*, which those who had seen it — writers like Gertrude Stein, Fitzgerald, Dos Passos, and MacLeish — said contained the best writing of any of the younger generation.

"He's only twenty-six, and he writes, apparently, a great novel!" Jim exclaimed. He was not jealous, I could see, just full of admiration.

One evening, in exasperation, I turned on Thurber. "So what the hell! You're nearly thirty-two and you haven't yet written the great

---

* Volume I of these memoirs.

American novel. Most of the great writers were late starters. Hemingway and Fitzgerald are the exceptions. They've had early success but maybe they'll peter out. At least you're on your way. And you're going to stay the course."

He would not agree. I had never seen him in such a dark mood. He announced he was through with Paris. It might be good for Fitzgerald and Hemingway and the others. It was not getting him anywhere. He was going home. To New York. Broke and despondent, he took ship home at the end of June 1926, leaving his wife in Paris until he could earn enough in New York to pay her passage back. He told me later he landed in New York with just ten dollars in his pocket and, of course, without a job, without prospects. But in a cheap, furnished room in the Village he settled down and wrote and wrote, and received rejection after rejection, twenty of them from a new magazine, *The New Yorker*, which had been started the year before.

Eventually, as everyone knows, he finally got a job with that surprising magazine and began a wonderful career that soon would make him our country's greatest humorist, not only in his writing but also in his deftly drawn, strange, outrageous cartoons. Soon he would become the creator of the unforgettable Walter Mitty, of seals in the bedroom and unicorns everywhere, and of hilarious battles between the sexes in which the woman usually got the upper hand. No one, not even Chekhov, could write of dogs and draw them as Thurber did. They were very strange beasts, more human than not.

We kept in touch, though the Atlantic lay between us and we were both very busy in those years that led up to the war. I followed with growing wonder and admiration his work: the pieces and cartoons in *The New Yorker* and the books, with wonderful titles, that began coming out every year or two — *Is Sex Necessary?* (with E. B. White), *The Owl in the Attic and Other Perplexities*, *The Seal in the Bedroom and Other Predicaments*, *My Life and Hard Times*, *My World and Welcome to It!*, and others.

During the war, whenever I was back in New York, we renewed our old ties and after the war we both settled in the hills of northwestern Connecticut — he, full time; I, like Gannett and the Van Dorens, with our jobs in the city, weekends and vacations. By this time Jim was going blind. Like me, he had lost one eye and, in his case, the other was deteriorating. Finally the light went out altogether.

I remember one evening at his house in West Cornwall a few years before his death. We had gathered at his place for our customary Saturday get-together. Threatened with blindness myself and wondering how I would take it if it came, I had marveled that while Jim had chafed at it — it had slowed up his writing and ended his drawing completely — he had never become bitter about it or uttered one word of self-pity.

On this evening he seemed in unusually good spirits.

"I feel pretty good tonight," he said, taking me aside. He had just finished another book, he said.

"With this one, Bill," he said, "I have now written more books since I couldn't see than before."

It was a great triumph.

Two other old friends in West Cornwall died in 1966, Lewis Gannett and Irita Van Doren. They were both veterans of the same newspaper.

Lewis had retired ten years before at sixty-four after twenty-seven years as the daily book reviewer for the *New York Herald-Tribune*. During that time, he estimated, he had written six thousand columns reviewing eight thousand books. And books of every conceivable kind! For despite his insistence that he was only a "newspaperman," he was very erudite. Erudite but not pedantic — ever. And always informal, interesting and full of a wonderful curiosity about men, life, literature, history, nature, the world.

One wondered how he could do it. For the first eighteen years he wrote a book column five days a week, which meant he had to read a book, no matter how long or weighty, and write about it in one day, with two days off on weekends, in his case, for gardening on his beloved farm in Connecticut. To read a book a day and review it was an impossible task. I learned this myself in 1947, just after I got fired from CBS, and the *Herald-Tribune* asked me to substitute for Gannett for a month. (He had suffered some kind of a breakdown from overwork and had to take a three-month sick leave. John Hersey and Malcolm Cowley also did a month's stint each for him.) I am a slow reader and a slow writer, and after a month of trying to make the daily deadline I had a mild breakdown myself. When we had finished, Hersey, who was also exhausted, and I called on Helen Reid, who by that time was pretty much running the newspaper, told her that what they were asking of Gannett was too much, and persuaded her to hire an assistant reviewer, which she did. Thereafter Lewis had to do only three reviews a week and the letup proved wonderful for his health and his peace of mind.

I have never known a man as generous, gentle (and yet tough-minded), warm, genial, broadminded, and unstuffed as was Lewis Gannett. He loved discovering new writers and encouraging them. In

1932, when he was relatively new at reviewing books daily, he wrote a column about a novel whose author, he said, he had never heard of, *Pastures of Heaven.*

"I would recommend to editors," Gannett wrote, "a name I have never met before, that of John Steinbeck."

Lewis helped launch the unknown Steinbeck on a career that brought the novelist the Nobel Prize. By that heady time Steinbeck had ceased seeing Gannett. Early on Gannett championed Faulkner and Dos Passos. When Dos moved from the far left to the far right in his politics, Gannett was saddened but kept in touch with him. Toward the end of their careers, Gannett invited Dos, whose latest books were being ignored by reviewers and critics, to write a volume for the *Mainstream of America* series, which he was editing; and he worked with him very closely to help make it, a work on Jefferson, one of the best books Dos Passos wrote in his declining years.

Gannett loved his farm on Cream Hill in West Cornwall and wrote lovingly of it, especially in his last book, *Cream Hill: Discoveries of a Weekend Countryman,* in which he told of the unfolding of the seasons — May and October were his favorite months, as they were mine — of his puttering in his gardens. He and his wife, Ruth, had the most spectacular wildflower borders in the county; but Lewis also was proud of his vegetable garden in which, among many other things, he grew the best Golden Bantam sweet corn of us all.

Retiring in 1956, he was able to spend the last ten years of his life on his farm — full time. It is not always that the last years of a man or woman are very happy or fulfilling — life becomes so full of sorrows, aches and pains and other physical ailments, and shortcomings, disappointments, the sense of failure, of goals never attained. But Gannett seemed very happy, finding time not only for growing crops and flowers but also for contemplating the other wonders of nature. Time too for leisured reading, for seeing old friends. I find in my folders of those days a letter he wrote to Tess on November 3, 1965, exactly three months before he died, that reminds me of his warmth and friendship.

> It is a month since you and Bill were here. . . . A few days ago a postcard arrived indicating that Bill was in Paris, and whether you are in Greece, Paris, New York, or where, we do not know.

I had given him a copy of the Persian edition of *The Rise and Fall of the Third Reich* for his birthday in October.

> . . . The Persian edition of Bill's book has been one of the most effective conversation pieces we have ever had in this house. I won't say

that I have been reading it; but I have been looking at it, and so has everyone else who comes to the house.

. . . I don't suppose you will be coming up (soon), but if you do, please drop by. No visitors would be more welcome.

And then two Van Dorens, who summered and weekended on their farms in West Cornwall, went.

Farm, Sunday, December 18, 1966. — Mark Van Doren phoned from his place over by Falls Village this morning to say that Irita had just died in New York.

Irita Van Doren, a beautiful, witty, warm, gracious, intelligent southerner and the divorced wife of Carl Van Doren, was editor of the Sunday *Herald-Tribune*'s weekly book review for thirty-seven years — from 1926 to 1963, when she retired at the age of seventy-two. Thus she served the paper even longer than Lewis Gannett, who indeed she selected as the *Tribune*'s first daily book reviewer.

I owed her much. She became not only a good friend but also one of my mentors, sometimes a stern one because underneath her softness and charm was a vein of iron, but always most devoted and helpful. Like scores of others of her friends — she was close to many in our circle, Gunther, Sheean, Dorothy Thompson, Hamilton Fish Armstrong — I adored her. No matter how busy I might be, I could never bear to turn her down when she asked me, as she frequently did, to do a review for *Books*. She was the one who insisted I take over Gannett's book column for a month.

"The discipline will do you good," she said with a smile. And it did.

I saw a good deal of Irita in New York and even more at her farm in West Cornwall. Often Wendell Willkie would be with her. For years until he died they were inseparable and Willkie owed much to her. She introduced him to the world of books and writers and eventually, I think, became his best political adviser. She also helped him with his speeches and, I think, was largely responsible (with Joe Barnes) for the quality of his book *One World*, which he wrote after a round-the-world trip early in the war and which was very good and became a best-seller.

The obituaries of Irita spoke of their close "friendship" but in truth they were not only "friends" but lovers. And it was one of the remarkable things about the times that even when Willkie ran for president in 1940, none of his political opponents, including Franklin Roosevelt, whom he was challenging, though they knew the secret, mentioned it publicly. And it never became public. I occasionally saw Mrs. Willkie in those days, and she seemed to accept the situation bravely, though she did not like it. I remember one sad moment at the end of an evening in New York in which at some meeting Willkie had been honored and had made a speech. Both Mrs. Willkie and Irita were there, but Willkie had gone off with Irita at the end. I took Mrs. Willkie home in a taxi. "How I love that man!" she kept saying, fighting back the tears.

Lenox, December 14, 1972. We went over to Cornwall yesterday for the memorial service for Mark Van Doren. A gray wintry day . . . but it gradually cleared. . . .

Mark was the third member of our Cornwall quartet to go, after Thurber and Gannett.

"My turn soon?" I asked in my diary that night. That was sixteen years ago, as this is written.

Mark Van Doren had died on December 12 at seventy-eight. He was a gentle, sensitive, beloved man, a great teacher and a fine poet. I loved and admired him. And he befriended me and kept after me to go on writing, especially during the years of discouragement. Mark also wrote novels, short stories, and literary criticism; and he would complain that teaching, though he loved it, kept him from his writing. And each summer that I knew him from the early 1940s on he would swear that he was going to give up teaching and spend all his time writing. But he kept putting it off. And this was a boon to Columbia, where he taught for thirty-nine years, and to its students. Indeed, several of his students, who later became writers, would acknowledge their debt to him: John Berryman, Thomas Merton, Lionel Trilling, Allen Ginsberg, Louis Simpson, and Jack Kerouac. Whitaker Chambers, the nemesis of Alger Hiss, called on his former teacher years after he left Columbia and asked him for help in returning to the world of letters after years in the underground of the Communist party as a spy for the Soviet Union. Van Doren gave him letters to literary editors saying that Chambers wrote well. It was the beginning of Chambers's new life.

After the memorial service we went for a wake at the Van Doren house, a lovely eighteenth-century colonial structure in the midst of a hundred acres. The farm was mostly woods but Mark and his two sons, Charles and John, kept the fields around the house mowed. A good many of our Saturday evening powwows had been held here. And now with the passing of this good man, they would become only a memory.

There was one other in Cornwall. On a page of my diary is pasted a clip from the *New York Times* for February 15, 1961, telling of the death there at fifty-one of Stella Adamic, widow of Louis Adamic, the wonderful immigrant writer from Yugoslavia who burst upon the literary scene at the beginning of the 1930s with his book *The Native's Return*. She was an attractive character in that book which told of Adamic's return with his young American wife to spend a year with his relatives in the old country. After his death — Stella thought he killed himself out of despair at becoming a victim of the postwar witch-hunt — she settled in Cornwall where she was a close friend of the Gannetts and the Van Dorens. Like others of my friends, Stella had been a dancer; later she became a teacher and then a librarian, having returned to college at fifty to earn a master's degree at Columbia in Library Science.

More than eight years later I typed on that old 1961 diary page with the *Times* clipping an addenda:

> Lenox, August 22, 1969. I remember the shock and then the hurt of reading that, as I browsed through the *New York Times* on a plane headed west out of Chicago. I loved her. I don't think that anyone but us ever knew.

I was now the last of our old Cornwall group, and I would soon become the last survivor in my immediate family. My younger brother, John, had died suddenly of a heart attack at sixty-two in March of 1969; and my older sister, Josephine, went at seventy-three in October of 1973, as the result of the same thing.

I loved them both and often ruminated on their lives. My brother had a fine mind and a sterling character, and though he had a more distinguished career than he realized — he rose to the top of the U.S. Civil Service as an economist in various federal agencies and for some years was a much respected professor of economics at the University of Arizona — I think he felt frustrated at the life he had lived. Actually, he wanted to be a writer. He took early retirement at fifty-nine and settled down to write a novel and a play, some short stories and essays. But it was too late. You had to start earlier.

My sister taught school all of her life after graduating from college, the last quarter of a century at a high school across the Hudson from New York, and she was very good at it and quite content to remain at that level. I suspect it was a lonely life though — no husband, no family, but love perhaps twice, with long years between. She had been engaged in college and found love, I think, in middle age that continued to her death.

My brother had died in California and I was too ill at the time to fly out for the funeral, but for my sister I arranged the things you have to attend to when a member of the family passes away and you are the only one left. I think she would have liked the informal little memorial service at the graveside in Westwood, New Jersey. A fellow teacher and a former student spoke briefly but eloquently on what my sister had meant to the school, its teachers and students. My two daughters each read a poem that I knew my sister had liked, one from John Donne, the other from Dostoevsky. I read one from Euripides: "Not To Live in Darkness."

My diary for Thursday, November 1, 1973, after describing the little ceremony:

> . . . There had been a storm blowing all day Monday and Monday night, with torrential rains and driving winds. But for a few hours on Tuesday morning the storm subsided, the winds died down, the sun came out, the autumn was crisp and clear, as if Providence had smiled on this fond farewell.

And finally I parted with my three closest surviving friends, two of whom I had met in the mid-twenties in Paris, when we were struggling young newspapermen, the third toward the end of my years in Berlin.

The first to go was Joe Barnes. He had been transferred by the *New York Herald-Tribune* in 1939 from Moscow to Berlin, where he replaced another Barnes and another old friend from the Paris days, Ralph Barnes, who had gone on to London and who would shortly, when the war came, be killed in an RAF bomber shot down returning from a bombing mission against the Italians in the Balkans.

In coming to Berlin from Moscow, Joe Barnes had exchanged one totalitarian dictatorship for another. From the brutalities of Stalin to those of Hitler. He knew the Soviet Union well, spoke fluent Russian, and loved the people and the culture. Germany was new to him, the people as well as the language. And it puzzled him. Yet such was his intelligence and burning curiosity that soon he was writing some of the most perceptive dispatches from Berlin as Hitler pushed Germany ever closer toward war. We soon became fast friends, sharing the same hostility and also, I think, the same fascination, in regard to a regime that in so short a time and with so many ruffians as its leaders had turned the Germans into sheep who would do the bidding of Adolf Hitler, no matter how criminal and barbarian.

In the last summer weeks, full of tension, before the Nazi dictator plunged the world into war on September 1, 1939, Joe and I met nightly after I had done my broadcast and he had finished his dispatch. Often we would walk through the Tiergarten where we could talk without fear of hidden microphones and end up after midnight at the Taverne, a café where the American and British correspondents met after work and where we could chew the fat with our colleagues, exchange ideas and information and escape for a moment the tensions of living and working amid the paranoiac Nazis.

Joe left Berlin that first fall of the war, returning to New York to become foreign editor of the *Tribune* and then taking leave of that job to become head of the New York branch of the Office of War Information when we got into the war. We saw each other in New York whenever we could and then at the first U.S. Army front in western Germany in 1944 when Joe returned briefly as a *Tribune* war correspondent. After the war he was again foreign editor of the newspaper, but left it in 1948 to become editor of the *New York Star*, the successor of *P.M.*, which Marshall Field had bankrolled. The odds against its survival were too great and it folded the next year. Joe then went over to book publishing, joining Simon and Schuster as one of its key editors. It was Joe, as I have mentioned, who interested S&S in publishing *The Rise and Fall of the Third Reich* and for years he worked closely with me on that book as an editor and friend.

In the years after the war we were neighbors in the country; and it was on his farm or mine in the hills of northwest Connecticut that we often got together to talk about our garden crops, solve the world's problems, commiserate about the intolerance of the McCarthy time — Joe too became a victim — work on the book of mine he was editing, drink a little and laugh a lot, despite, or perhaps because of, the wretched state of the world.

Joe Barnes lay dying from cancer when we finished work on getting to press the next book. He died on February 28, 1970, at his home in New York. He was only sixty-two.

I spoke at the memorial service for Joe Barnes in New York on the afternoon of May 6 that year. The hall was crowded, for he had many friends and many more admirers. Rarely what you say on such occasions is adequate but I did my best to recall an old friend who had touched me profoundly and many others.

And I brought up something I had often ruminated about: the fate of men like Joe Barnes who never quite, I thought, got their due in life. Here was one who had had four distinguished careers, as a foreign correspondent, a newspaper editor, a book editor, and a gifted translator, especially from the Russian. And yet . . .

The ups and downs of fortune often play havoc with the use and the impact of the talents of a man. And there were some among Joe's friends and admirers who thought his brilliant gifts had sometimes gone wasted. If so, I would say it is our country's, our society's, loss.

Joe lived in a time when this country squandered — or ignored — the contributions of many a gifted citizen, when what a man like Joe had to offer: a keen intelligence, a lucid mind, an incorruptible character, vast experience of the world, a capacity for penetrating the cant — when these qualities were not often appreciated.

But if Joe had any feelings of this — and I never heard him express them — he would have said, I think, that THAT was the luck of life. He did not complain. He worked; he thought; he taught; he reasoned. He did what he could to shed a little light in the darkness. . . .

After the memorial service John Gunther and I walked over to a pub on Lexington Avenue for a drink and a chance to catch up on each other's news. We had not seen much of each other recently for certain personal reasons and because I was now living permanently in the country and he had stayed in New York. John was just back from Australia and to my surprise I saw that he was a sick man. It wasn't only that he was exhausted from the strenuous labors in Australia and the long trip back. His face had no color and he was breathing heavily as he talked, and coughing. He said he had given up smoking but it was obvious he was not cured of an old emphysema. We had a few drinks, discussed the going of Joe Barnes and of so many other old friends and colleagues. We updated each other on our personal lives — mine had changed the most. He congratulated me on the France book, which had just come out.

"Don't pay any attention to the brickbats," he added. There had been plenty of these this time. "Remember, we all get them."

Then he talked of what it had been like in Australia. I had nagged him for years to do one final book in his famous "Inside" series. That would be *Inside Australia*, the last continent to be covered, the last of the "Insiders." He had run out of continents. Though not in the best of health — he had been in the hospital to try to find out what was ailing him and he was still having problems with his eyesight after cataract operations in both eyes — he had plunged with his usual energy and high spirits into research for the Australian book and then spent several exhausting months roaming the continent from one end to another, moved on to New Zealand and finally to New Guinea. A postcard dated February 2 from Kuala Lumpur in Malaysia alerted me that he was on his way home. Now this spring he had started writing. He was tired but, as always when he began to write an "Inside" book, full of enthusiasm for it.

"And when THAT'S finished," he said, half exploding, "I'm going to take a hell of a long rest. No more continents to conquer. No more 'Inside' books to do." They had brought him fame and fortune.

We finished our drinks and our talk and departed. I was glad I had seen him again. In Vienna, where we'd both been stationed in the 1930s, he for the *Chicago Daily News*, I for the *Chicago Tribune*, we and our wives had seen a great deal of each other. And it had been the same when we came back to live in New York. Our tastes were hardly the same. John loved to give big parties to which he invited celebrities. (It was at his house that I had met Greta Garbo.) I preferred a quieter, simpler life. John liked to go with friends to plush restaurants. With that boyishness which he never entirely lost he would confess that he got a kick out of being made something of by a head-waiter. I rather disliked plush restaurants and their kowtowing headwaiters.

I loved the country, the more so as I grew older. John preferred the city. After he married Jane, they used to spend part of the summer at her parents' retreat in northern New Hampshire. But I gathered John was never very enthusiastic about spending too much of the summer there, or in any other rural place. He would grow restless to get back to the Big Apple. For years we tried — in vain — to interest him in buying a place in Cornwall — he was also a good friend of Gannett and Irita Van Doren there.

Still, we had a lot in common: our long experience together in Europe, a hunger for history and literature, pride in our journalism and in our books, a burning curiosity about people and life and the world. And we had had a lasting friendship over nearly half a century.

I thought of these things as I walked back in the failing light of a lovely spring afternoon in New York to where I was staying. Twenty-two days later John Gunther was dead. Cancer had struck him. It was May 29. He was sixty-eight.

It was cancer too that killed the last of my old friends and colleagues, Vincent Sheean. Jimmy died at Arolo on the shores of Lago Maggiore on March 15, 1975. He was seventy-five. Unlike John, he saw it coming. He had come back to New York the previous fall for treatment and stayed until the first of the year, when he gave it up as hopeless and returned to Italy. We had talked frequently on the phone and despite his ailment and the debilitation of the treatments (cobalt, for one) he was in high spirits. I planned several times to go into New York to spend a few days with him but something at the last minute always prevented it. Later I would bitterly regret it. When I flew over to Europe that spring for what I had first hoped would be a reunion it was too late.

In Europe some used to call us the "Chicago Kids." John Gunther and I had been born in the city and Jimmy, who grew up in a nearby town in Illinois, had come to Chicago to attend the university, where he met John. All three of us worked abroad for Chicago newspapers.

Four years older than I, Sheean had gone to Paris in 1922, got a job working part-time for the Paris edition and part-time as assistant to the *Chicago Tribune*'s Paris correspondent, Henry Wales, and by the time I arrived in 1925 he was already a legendary foreign correspondent, more famous than his boss. That year he had penetrated the French and Spanish lines in Morocco to interview Abd-el-Krim, the rebel leader who had driven the Spanish army out of the Riff Mountains and was holding his own against the French, commanded by no less a figure than the great war hero of Verdun, Marshal Henri Pétain. Several times Sheean had narrowly escaped death as he came under fire from Spanish and French artillery and bombs, and twice he had almost been executed as a spy by the Arabs. His talk with the rebel leader, then very much in the news, and his reporting in depth about the revolt in the Riff was a world scoop and made Sheean famous overnight.

Shortly after his return to Paris from the Riff, he was fired by Wales for taking too much time off for dinner one evening — or so Jimmy always claimed.

"I was never again employed in a newspaper office," he wrote later in *Personal History*, "and never wanted to be."

But that did not end his journalistic career. Though from that time on he would devote most of his time and energy to writing books, he took on important reporting assignments from such agencies as the North American Newspaper Alliance and contributed dozens of articles to the magazines.

In *Personal History*, Jimmy did not mention that he did indeed return to employment in "a newspaper office." This was on the *Paris Times*, a fantastic sort of non-newspaper that Jimmy, with a number of other writers, worked on in 1926. Most of the copy came out of their heads since the newspaper had no news sources. It was a place Sheean and others went back to, they said, when they were broke and wanted to spend a few months in Paris between books or assignments. It was, in fact, in 1926 in Paris that Jimmy and I first became good friends; and though there were years when we were operating on opposite sides of the globe, we remained in touch. Then there would be times, after the Second World War, when we lived in the same city, New York, and saw more of one another.

I always thought Sheean was the best writer of us three "Chicago Kids," certainly the most graceful; and though a few regarded him as something of a hard-drinking playboy, he was strangely enough the most learned of us three. He was a much better linguist and he knew better his history and philosophy. But there was never any conscious feeling of rivalry or even of competitiveness among us. Our books certainly did not compete. And even when Gunther and I were stationed in Vienna for rival Chicago newspapers, neither of us felt any personal rivalry or competitiveness, a situation that would have displeased our editors, had they known of it. I think we all felt that luck had smiled on us when our early books, Jimmy's *Personal History* in 1935, John's *Inside Europe* in 1936, and my *Berlin Diary* in 1941 made the best-seller lists and gave us financial independence at least for a while.

Vincent Sheean, to use the name he wrote under (it was his middle name; his first name was James, hence "Jimmy" to his friends), had an uncanny sense of when certain world figures were about to die. The most notable example of this involved me. One morning in November 1947, in New York, Jimmy phoned and insisted I come over for lunch.

"I'm trying to finish a book," I said. "Like you, I never break for lunch."

"It's terribly urgent," Jimmy said. "You must come. I have to see you. Today! For lunch!"

So I went over to his apartment, cursing him as I came in.

"I'm sorry," he said. "But I had to see you. I want to talk to you about Gandhi, with whom you spent those two wonderful years. He is going to die! Soon!"

"How do you know?" I asked. India that late fall was in upheaval. It had gained its independence from Britain on August 15, 1947. Gandhi had won his revolution but he was heartbroken that the Moslems had broken away to form the Islamic nation of Pakistan. Deeply religious though he was, he had fought for a united, secular, independent India. Worse to him, Hindus and Moslems were now butchering each other, especially in the Punjab and Bengal. There was chaos and wholesale murder. Gandhi was fasting "unto death" to try to stop the carnage. It was a weapon he had often used to obtain his goals. He had always recovered from his fasts. He always looked frail, but he was made of iron.

Jimmy ignored my question.

"I have to see Gandhi before he dies. There is something that he can teach me about the meaning, purpose and significance of life."

He asked me to give him a letter of introduction to Gandhi and another to Jawahrlal Nehru, who was now India's first prime minister. Jimmy left a few days later for India. But he dawdled in Europe, as he often had, and in Egypt, and lingered on in Pakistan. The Moslems had always fascinated him. He later said he needed time to prepare himself for Gandhi. Though he still had a premonition of Gandhi's imminent death, he thought he had a little time.

Not much, as it turned out. Not as much as he had hoped.

Gandhi had returned from Calcutta to Delhi in the fall of 1947. Unable to stop the Hindu-Moslem slaughter in the new nation's capital, he had once more begun a fast on January 13, 1948, in order to bring the two peoples together. Jimmy arrived in Delhi from Pakistan the next day, but Gandhi was already too weak to see him. On January 17, Gandhi's doctors issued a bulletin saying the Mahatma would not survive more than two or three days longer unless he gave up his fast. He was seventy-eight and already exhausted by his struggles to halt the killing. Next day the Hindu and Moslem leaders signed an agreement for peace and Gandhi gave up his fasting. But he was not strong enough to see Sheean until January 27, when they had their first talk. There was another the next day and they arranged to meet again on Friday, the thirtieth, immediately after Gandhi's evening prayer meeting.

Sheean and another old colleague, Edgar Snow, waited in the crowd of some five hundred worshippers who assembled for the prayer meeting on the lawn of Birla House for Gandhi to appear. They stood by the small platform from which Gandhi conducted the prayers and the singing of hymns. Gandhi, still very frail from his fasting, arrived, leaning heavily on the arms of two young women aides. He greeted Sheean and Snow and others clustered by the platform. Suddenly three shots rang out. Crying "He Ram!" ("O God!") Gandhi fell to the ground, dead. (The assassin, a crackpot Hindu, was caught, tried, found guilty of murder, and executed.)

For two days Sheean, in shock, wandered about Delhi in a daze, unable to speak. He said later he had no memory of those forty-eight hours. But later he had a wonderful memory of what Gandhi had meant

to him finally, especially after those two meetings in Delhi just before
the great man died, and he wrote beautifully of it in a book that came
out the next year, *Lead Kindly Light*. It had been Gandhi's favorite
Christian hymn. The Mahatma had often joined heartily in singing it
at prayer meetings I had attended in Delhi in an earlier time.

"Depressed at thinking of Jimmy gone," I wrote in my diary. "He
filled so many bright spots in my life — often in his letters, though our
correspondence was desultory over nearly fifty years." Leafing through
a file, I came across a letter from Jimmy from Rome in November 1963
that I thought was typical and that tells something of the man. I copied
it down in my diary. It came in response to a review I had written of
Jimmy's book *Dorothy and Red*, a wonderful tale of the stormy and
disastrous marriage of Dorothy Thompson and Sinclair Lewis. Jimmy
had been one of Dorothy's closest friends and he and Lewis were
friends also.

Dear Bill:

. . . I wanted to thank you for the *kindness* of your review of my book,
D&R. . . . I don't mean that it was a favorable review (although it was
that also) but just that it was *kind*. . . .

But you've always been like that. I have never forgotten when you first
came to us in Paris with your eagerness and aspiration, cheeks like
famine and eyes like the far-off stars. . . .

Do you know the difference between life and time? I've only just
found it in Seneca, in pursuit of my present endeavors. Life is the
moment of *knowing* (it is, however briefly, wisdom) and all the rest of
the mortal existence is simply time, a notation. Seneca quotes a Greek
poet (now lost) who is thought by some to be Menander, by others to be
Euripides, who says in one line, *We live the smallest part of our lives,
the rest is only time*. . . .

Thanks for the lurid postcard from Paris last year when you said This
is a nice city, Remember? I do remember.

My diary that day ended:

I am the last of the three of us (Gunther, Sheean and I) who came to
Europe in the early or mid-twenties out of raw, wild Chicago (in my case,
also from Iowa — in any case, out of the Midwest) and made a certain
mark first as correspondents and later with our books. John and Jimmy
were a little older, by four or five years.

It leaves me lonely.

Dinah, Jimmy's widow, felt it.

Arolo, 16th April, 1975.
Darling Bill,

Thank you for your lovely cable. Now you are the only one of the great ones left. Hold on, my friend, and don't you dare quit.

Love,
Dinah

Hold on with what? With whom? I have now to go back six years to my diary.

Lenox, Feb. 3, 1969 — At 1:15 P.M. today I finished the France book, writing "The End" on page 1618. . . .

By that time my personal life was in shambles, and I had moved to a new place. Tess and I had broken up after a marriage of thirty-six years.

BOOK SEVEN

Past Hope or Fear

Twilight and the Gathering Night

1975–1988

CHAPTER 1

There be many shapes of mystery;
 And many things God brings to bear,
  Past Hope or Fear.
And the end man looketh for cometh not,
 And a path is there where no man thought.
          — Euripides

Tess and I began to reach the end that blizzardy Christmas Eve in the country in 1966, the night it all ended for Gilly.

My first meeting with Gilly in Vienna went back thirty-four years. We had not become friends until fifteen years later, after the war, when we were both back from our long time in Europe. But only friends. Not more. Then suddenly, to our complete surprise, only a year or so before this fateful Christmas Eve, we had fallen in love. We had resisted it. I did not want to break up my marriage, and she did not want to play any part in it. But our resistance crumbled.

There had been no hint in the beginning that we would end up this way. She had come to Vienna in the fall of 1932 to write a novel; I had been stationed there since 1929 as a correspondent for the *Chicago Tribune*. I did not meet her until the Christmas holidays that year when John and Frances Gunther gave a small party for her. She was certainly a very attractive American woman — tall, statuesque, with bright hazel eyes and brown hair and a radiant personality. She spoke well and was full of life. Frances had told me that Gilly had come to Vienna not only to write but also to ponder marrying a Polish prince whom she had met and become engaged to nine years before when they were students at the University of Grenoble. The parents of both of them had opposed their marrying; and Gilly, in despair and defiance, had married a young American writer with whom she soon broke up. She and her Polish prince had kept in touch, and now in Vienna she was trying to decide whether she wanted to marry him if he again proposed, as he seemed on the point of doing. I do not remember having much talk with her that evening at the Gunthers'. During the Christmas holidays that year I was preoccupied by my own situation. I had just been fired by the *Chicago Tribune;* and Tess, my Viennese wife of less than a year, and I were trying to decide how to survive in a world already wracked by the Great Depression. I do remember that Gilly struck me as much too sophisticated and too much the polished New Yorker to spend the rest of her life in the stagnant, primitive, backward world of rural Poland — even in a castle with a charming prince.

The prince had telephoned her a few days later, on New Year's Eve, and again proposed and again she had accepted. They were married in London the following summer, after which she set off with her bride-groom to begin life in Poland as a princess. She later wrote of that experience in a book, *Polish Profile*, published in 1940 and in a second, franker book, *A Matter of Life and Death*.

As with many marriages there was early disappointment and disil-lusionment. Gilly would write in the second book that "precisely when and precisely why the light went out and the house, once warm, now grew cold" no one could say. But she came to believe herself that the "loss of my husband's love [came] after our first child was born." Loss of love does not necessarily end a marriage, especially in the old, rigid, very Catholic aristocracy in Poland; and the American princess and her Polish prince lived on together in Poland. She had another child and gradually accustomed herself, as far as a young American woman could, to the isolated, narrow, routine life of the country's nobility.

The people the couple associated with were so isolated, she later said, that they did not see the war coming or realize that Poland would be its first casualty, though that was plain to everyone but an idiot after Hitler consolidated his hold on Germany and turned abroad for new conquests. It also was obvious that Poland could not afford the luxury of being at odds with both of its giant neighbors, Germany and the Soviet Union. Obvious, that is, to all but the privileged class.

Gilly herself, she later wrote, was blissfully apolitical and, like the Poles, did not at first see the threatening clouds gather over central Europe. She was rudely awakened one day in March 1938, while on a visit to Vienna to consult a doctor. It happened to be the day Hitler marched in and took over Austria. She suddenly became aware that the Nazi dictator wanted much more than Austria. Czechoslovakia, now surrounded by Germans on three sides, would be next and then Poland, when she too became outflanked. But Gilly was not listened to when she returned. The Poles would continue to blind themselves to the very end.

That end came for Gilly and her Polish family in the humid, warm days of September 1939, when Hitler's armies smashed through Poland in three weeks. She and her two children escaped from their castle in Silesia to Rumania and eventually to Paris, where her husband, after Poland had been gobbled up by Germany and the Soviet Union, joined her.

I had not been in touch with Gilly after she left Vienna to get married. We had met, after all, casually; and it was no wonder that she forgot me, though the remembrance of her beauty, her charm, her bright, original mind, lingered with me. I too had been in Vienna the night of the Anschluss when the Nazis took over; but I did not know until years later, when she told me, that she too had been there that hectic night.

One day in 1947 in New York, I received a business letter from her in which she addressed me as "Mr. Shirer," a total stranger. She was then publicity director of a New York publishing firm, and she was asking me for a blurb for a book by a friend of mine which they were publishing. With the blurb I sent a note to which I attached a postscript:

> Are you not the same Virgilia Peterson whom I met at the Gunthers' in Vienna in 1932, who was on her way to Warsaw?

"Yes," she answered, "I am the female on her way to Poland whom you saw at the Gunthers'." She added that she had also seen me recently at a party "at the Plaza."

With that breaking of the ice we finally met again in New York and once more became casual acquaintances, meeting occasionally at parties and literary gatherings and exchanging the time of day. We got better acquainted after she invited me to participate in a popular TV program, *The Author Meets the Critic*, which she began moderating in 1952 and at which she was very good. This was a time when the McCarthy hysteria had put me down if not out, and I found that Gilly was very sympathetic to those of us caught in that bind. Against great opposition from her sponsors she had insisted on devoting one program to a book of mine. Later I learned that Gilly was largely responsible for my getting the National Book Award in 1960 for *The Rise and Fall of the Third Reich*. She had badgered her colleagues on the judges panel into voting for the book.

By that time Gilly had divorced her Polish prince and married Governeur Paulding, a magazine editor and writer and one of the most civilized men I ever knew. Tess and I began to see something of them.

We four became good friends. I remember once, when "Govey" lay dying of cancer and Gilly was spending all her time, night and day, in caring for him and easing his slow, painful exit from life and working herself into exhaustion and a near breakdown, that Tess insisted I take Gilly out to a lively little French restaurant we knew to help relieve her of her tension.

"Govey" died a few weeks after, in August of 1965. Though she could not know it, nor could I nor anyone else, Gilly herself had but sixteen months to live. In response to a note of condolence she answered that when she had cleared up Govey's affairs, she was going away for a couple of weeks and then would return to New York to "take up whatever life I can lay my hands on."

I no longer remember, if I ever knew, just when or how Gilly and I, after so long and beautiful a platonic friendship, fell in love. All I know is that it happened suddenly, sometime in the early part of 1966. All at once we saw in each other something we had not seen for thirty-four years and felt some powerful chemistry that had not existed before, transforming us from old friends to lovers. It seemed absurd, unreal. We could not understand it. And we fought to repress it. We would swear not to see any more of each other until our passions had cooled and reason had restored us to sanity. But it was no use. We began to contrive to see each other more and more frequently. Any excuse. Any lie. Mutual friends in New York put their country home in Connecticut, which they rarely used, at our disposal. It was not far from my farm. We snatched as many days and nights there as we could.

But in the midst of the explosion of a great love, we were sorely troubled. Difficult as life for me was at home, and increasingly so, I still felt a loyalty to my wife. I did not want to abandon her after so long a marriage — some thirty-five years by now. True, we no longer had to stay together for the sake of the children. Both Inga and Linda had graduated from college, married, and were living their own lives. Inga's first child had come in August that year, making us for the first time grandparents.

On the other hand, I was deeply in love with Gilly and wanted to share the rest of my life with her. She herself felt miserable about my breaking up a marriage for her. But as the year progressed she apparently decided she wanted all of me, whatever the consequences. I failed to notice this, though probably she told me. Finally that fall I told her that I did not yet want to break up my marriage but that I would try to see as much of her as possible.

"But why," she would ask, "do you want to continue a marriage when love has gone out of it?" And I would remember what she had written in *A Matter of Life and Death* when the love went out of her marriage to her Prince Charming. "There is only one certainty: No marriage, when dead to either participant, can be raised again." And on love: "Love comes and goes willy-nilly as the wind. . . . And when it is gone it is gone for good."

I realize now I was insensitive to her feelings that fall. We saw more of each other those autumn weeks than ever before, usually at our friends' farmhouse. It obviously was not enough for either of us, but especially for her. But Gilly had a Spartan quality about her and she did not complain. And I, in my ignorance and complacency, was not fully aware of what she wanted. I seem actually to have been somewhat blind to the depth of her feelings for me. I would learn this only when it was too late, from friends, and from a final letter she wrote a few minutes before the end. One old and close friend of Gilly's had invited us down to her place in the West Indies for the Christmas holidays that year. Gilly had dashed off a letter to her on December 22, the friend wrote me, saying "that you and she would not be coming down to visit because of your book. . . . She spoke of not being able to leave you even for a short ten days."

In my thickheadedness I had not realized that Gilly's devotion had reached such a pitch. We talked over our plight during two or three days at the friends' country place just before Christmas. I told Gilly that I would have to spend Christmas at the farm with my family. The children would be coming up for the holiday. I promised Gilly that we would get together during the week and perhaps have New Year's together. She seemed to accept this, or so I thought. She would spend Christmas then with her daughter and son-in-law and their young child at their country retreat not far from our friends' farmhouse. I would drop in on them Christmas day. We exchanged presents and parted. I had no idea how unhappy she was. She had not been exactly joyous as we said good-bye, but neither was she melancholy or, so far as I could see, unduly depressed.

It began to snow early that afternoon; and as the day darkened into Christmas Eve, it had turned into a blizzard, with a raging wind that piled the deepening snow high into drifts. Two or three times that evening we went out to shovel a place before the kitchen door and also to watch the blinding storm. There was something awesome about it and beautiful. We had our Christmas Eve dinner and later sat around the fire and opened presents as we had done nearly every Christmas

Eve since acquiring the farm nineteen years before. It was still home, sentimentally at least, to the children. And this was a special evening in the country they said they would always remember. Having lived so long as a sort of vagabond in my early years as a roving correspondent in Europe and Asia, never really having a home, at least for long, and rarely in it, I had savored these holidays with the family on the farm after I returned for good and settled down. Perhaps I had grown sentimental about them, but I could not help it. They gave me most of what happiness I knew. If only one could keep this — and the other, too. I did think of Gilly that evening. I fretted that I could not steal upstairs and phone her. But there was no telephone at her daughter's place.

Still, I felt quite happy and content that blizzardy evening. After the presents we lingered by the fire, taking turns reading from Dickens's *Christmas Carol*, as we had done each Christmas Eve since the children were tots, and then talking, sentimentally no doubt, about earlier holidays on the farm and earlier blizzards that sometimes had left us snowbound, as this one threatened to do. It was another good Christmas Eve, I thought to myself, as finally, around 2 A.M., we broke up and went to bed.

It was late afternoon on Christmas Day when the telephone rang and Gilly's daughter said that her mother had killed herself during the snowy night. I could not believe it; and when it had sunk in on me, I found my vocal chords were paralyzed. I tried to ask what in God's name had happened, but I could not get the words out. "I'll tell you more later," the daughter said, "when we've all recovered a little."

Whatever happened that Christmas Eve with her daughter and son-in-law in the country, Gilly at some point set off in the wild blizzard through the drifting snow for our friends' farmhouse two miles away. How she was able to stumble in the dark through the deep snow up that steep road for two miles we never learned. If only our friends, who out of kindness and generosity had lent us the use of their house, had been there Christmas Eve, as they usually were. But they had remained in New York. Gilly had a key and took refuge in the house. And if it had been only that: a place of refuge. There was a telephone there; and she could have rung me, and I could have talked to her and, if one could get through the snowdrifts in a car, come to her. But she had not.

Sometime after midnight the storm subsided; the snow stopped falling; the wind died down, and Gilly's son-in-law, his wife told me, set off for the house to see if she was all right. He knocked at the door. He tried another and knocked there. If only she had answered. If only he had broken the door down. Instead, he assumed his mother-in-law had gone to bed and did not want to be disturbed. When he and his wife returned early on Christmas morning, it was too late. When there was no response to their knocking, they found a key at a neighbor's, walked in, and found Gilly dead in bed. She had swallowed a bottle of sleeping pills.

It was no consolation to remember that Gilly once before had tried to kill herself and had nearly succeeded. She had written frankly about it in her last book. It should have been a warning. I should have kept it in mind. But then she had publicly vowed in the last moving pages of the book that it would never happen again, that henceforth she would not forget "that my life belongs not to me but to whatever lives it has touched and touches."

And even though on that first occasion she had swallowed a bottle of pills that surely would have killed her in a short time, she had on taking them telephoned the man she loved, who immediately had telephoned her estranged Polish husband, and they both had raced through the traffic of New York City, got her into an ambulance, and rushed her to a hospital in time.

Why on this Christmas Eve she did not telephone me, I shall never know. She did not say in the hastily scrawled note she left for me. But she explained some things.

> You will have to go through a bad moment, but I have seen how you rebound, and you have the blessing of your work. Don't imagine it is your fault. You are the center — I suppose — of the dark mosaic of my mind, but there are lots of other things beside the *absurdity* of the "situation." I was not made for triangles, I have discovered. I am an all or nothing — todos y nada — person that leads me to this tiresomely inconvenient act. *Like* you said, it seems a bit drastic. But how could you know that I am not as "strong" as you figured I was and expected, and, yes, demanded of me to be?
>
> I think it was [your] not calling me in New York that made me understand, finally, that in your life, in fact, I am expendable. So okay, that's natural enough but being expendable, I am now spent. . . .
>
> This note, by the way, is NOT a "whine."
>
> Anyway our times together have been wonderful. You are a [illegible word] and as overwhelmingly sweet and giving as the first movement of the Brahms 4th. . . .
>
> But I am, quite simply, too tired to go on — and only the conviction that I had another book in me would have justified the effort of every new day — but I have not that conviction. All the same, you have been the sun, the evening sun, and I go down in its blaze.

She had reached the bottom of the page. Scrawled on the side of the paper was one more sentence.

"If only *once* you had 'come flying.' "

If only she had held off for another ten months! But that would have been, I realized too late, beyond her weakening power.

As I sat alone in a pew in the St. Jean Baptiste Church on Lexington Avenue in New York on the chilly but sunny morning of January 3, 1967, during the memorial mass for Gilly, I knew that I would never fully recover from this sudden and final separation from her. And walking down Lexington Avenue toward home with heavy heart, I felt I could not be saved by my marriage because I could not save it. It was past saving. Gilly's sad and precipitous end and our respective reactions to it brought home to me, and I think to Tess, that we could not go on the rest of the way together.

The scenes which had taken place from the beginning but for long had been bearable had in the last few years become devastating to Tess and me. In the past couple of years they had reached a frequency and intensity that made a decent life together impossible and a separation necessary if we were to save ourselves. Over the last two summers on the farm, especially, there were confrontations that would string out all night until both of us were utterly exhausted. As dawn broke, I would gather up the manuscript of the France book, along with folders of the most important notes and documents, put them into a large suitcase, throw it into the trunk of the car to make sure they would not be destroyed, and strike out for some haven, an old inn or a squalid motel or some isolated spot in the woods by a lake in search of some peace and quiet, fighting to get my breath back, to calm down and to stave off a nervous breakdown.

Finally, on the afternoon of November 3, 1967, in desperation, I fled for good. It saved, I believe, not only my own life but that of my long-suffering wife. Still, the parting was a terrible wrench. We had been together, in good times and bad, and all over the world, for thirty-six years. Despite our difficulties and my own failings that contributed so much to them, I had somehow hoped we could go on together to the end, however near or far-off that might be. I was sixty-three; Tess was fifty-seven. It was a vain hope and, as I see now, a foolish one. There are times and circumstances when it is more civilized and, yes, I believe, more decent and moral, to break up a marriage that is destroying both partners, than to continue on in utter misery until one or both are broken. There are few things worse in life than a marriage poisoned beyond hope of any cure. When love and tolerance and respect are gone and replaced by poisonous hate, a marriage is finished, and it is evil, in my opinion, to prolong it.

The trauma of getting a divorce was not spared us. Not the usual sordid haggling over money. Not the wrangling of the lawyers, whose fees year after year soaked up much of our modest lifetime savings. Not the bitter recriminations. Not even the lies, as when Tess told the children during the first months of painful separation that I had not left her a cent to live on, whereas the truth was that she was receiving half my income. (The children had castigated me for my foul behavior and offered to send her what sums they could spare to keep her, they said, from starving.) But who was I to complain of lies, I who had lied so often about other women in my life?

Finally, after nearly three years of separation, there came an end to the bickering — and an end to the marriage.

> Lenox, Saturday, July 25, 1970 . . . After two days of wrangling by our respective lawyers in New Haven (Thursday, all day; yesterday from 1:30 P.M. to 6) Tess and I finally came to a parting of the ways. Formal agreements, which took more than two years to hammer out (and cost enormous attorneys' fees) were signed for the separation, and Tess agreed to fly to Mexico next week to get the divorce. Both of us were exhausted by the two-day ordeal. . . .
>
> Instead of the relief I thought I would feel at being free at last from this marriage . . . I feel depressed and sad. . . .
>
> There is an ache at casting off finally from Tess. Some of my sentiments I put in a letter to her today, which I attach to this. We had a full, stormy, meaningful life together and I regret that she was unable (as I see it) to let it continue on a tolerable level. . . .
>
> At New Haven this week, there was no bitter recrimination from either of us. Only at the last minute did she appear as if she might break down, after all the documents were signed and she turned on my lawyer bitterly for holding up the agreements until she carried out her unwritten promise to get an immediate Mexican divorce. . . . She resented deeply our "distrust" in her word, as she put it. . . .
>
> The parting was sad, to me. She stalked out, barely able to control her feelings. I feared she might not be able to drive home as a heat wave had suddenly struck. But obviously . . . she would not accept an offer (from me) to drive her home. We bid good-bye at the door of the office, and she went off alone, a forlorn, unhappy figure, and I wanted to weep that it had all ended this way.

That was my diary, or a part of it. I also got off to Tess a letter.

Lenox, Saturday, July 25, 1970

Dear Tessie:

It was very sad for me, the parting yesterday in the heat of ugly New Haven. Whatever has happened it was depressing to come to an end after so long a time of a shared life that saw so much over many continents that was meaningful and exciting and joyous.

You have often asked how I could forget it. But of course I never forgot, nor could I. A shared experience of such magnitude over so many years is stamped indelibly on any two people of any sensitivity. . . . I kept thinking of it yesterday afternoon — and of how the parting ever came — as the two lawyers haggled over dollars and cents. . . .

I am sorry about the strain to you at the very end. . . . It was none of my doing. . . .

I do not believe that love between a man and woman, however flawed by the cruelties of life and by their own mistakes and shortcomings, ever dies. Mine for you will not, ever. . . . Despite all our problems and the impossibilities of the later years, we had a rich life together and fuller than most people will ever have or know. This cannot be lost , no matter what happens. It remains part of one, of both persons. It cannot be wiped out by the signing of piles of documents the lawyers have thought up. . . .

I wish you well, much happiness, and your state will always be of concern to me far beyond the obligations assumed in writing and duly signed yesterday. . . . Of immediate import, I hope you recover from the ordeal we've gone through together in the last days, especially the last two in New Haven.

Love,
Bill

On July 31, I noted in my diary receipt of a note from Tess saying she would be flying to Mexico for the divorce that very day. The diary ends: "I feel an awful void, a deep ache in the heart."

I saw Tess again on August 6 at the farm shortly after she returned from Mexico.

Lenox, Wednesday, August 6 . . . We had a very good and long talk at the farm over sherry and then a sumptuous lunch she prepared: a Coquilles St.-Jacques followed by the wonderful meat and macaroni dish she learned to do our year-off in Spain. I felt quite close to her again. . . . I kept thinking what a failure it was for the both of us not to have been able to resolve our differences those last few years.

Packed a dozen cases of papers and books in a U-Haul van I had brought along and departed late in the afternoon, sad at the finality of the breakup but happy that we had had this decent day together.

Lenox, Wednesday, August 26 . . . Again to the farm to help movers load rest of books, papers and tractor and farm machinery, which Tess suggested I might as well take since she cannot use. Stayed on for another pleasant lunch.

Lenox, Friday, August 28 . . . To farm to spend the day with Inga and her two girls, whom I had not seen for nearly three years. . . . Deirdre, now 7, had changed immensely from a babyish girl to a handsome young thing, and very sensitive. Caitlin, more outgoing, who had been a crawling baby last time I saw her, now at 4 was very interesting and attractive. I had a fine time playing with them and afterward lunch with Tess and Inga. Much good talk. . . .

I bid farewell for the last time to the farm, which had brought so much pleasure and relaxation to my wife and children and me for twenty years, a place where I had renewed my roots with the soil and the fields and the woods and written the better part of most of my books. In a diary entry on New Year's Eve, 1970, I would recall the

late summer day at the farm when I fetched my last books and papers and we sat on the lawn looking over the fields I loved so deeply and had worked so rather hard on, having a drink and later the splendid lunch she prepared with the fine, dry, white Burgundy wine.

And I recalled too

another such scene in October in New York, fetching the books and papers there, and having my last look at the lovely place we had on the East River, and more good drinks and a superb dinner and wine and much good talk until for a while I wondered how all this had happened — my leaving, finally, seemed so unreal — and she telling me the next morning when I came with the movers that she could not stand another such meeting. . . . I suppose one never fully gets over such a split-up after being together so long. But why should one?

A year went by:

Lenox, Monday, February 1, 1971 . . . Tess called from New York to ask if "a little thing" she had sent arrived. It hadn't. It came out after some talk that it had to do with our wedding anniversary. . . . We would have had 40 years together yesterday, married, if it had lasted.

Lenox, Wednesday, February 3 . . . The anniversary present arrived this morning. A silver-banded Dunhill pipe, with my initials engraved on the silver band . . . the most beautiful pipe I've ever had. . . . I phoned Tess in New York and thanked her.

Lenox, Tuesday, February 23 . . . 67 today! . . . Yesterday an expensive pipe bowl (Dunhill, N.Y.) from Tess. (She had already sent a Dunhill pipe for our wedding anniversary, Jan. 31.) Very nice, generous of her, but it opens wounds.

They would never completely heal, and I would remember Tess mostly for the good times, for sharing with me the ups and downs of so many wonderful years in Europe, India, and here at home in America, for bringing into the world two beautiful daughters and shepherding them through childhood and adolescence while I was necessarily away so much, for making homes whenever, wherever we settled down for a bit — in Vienna, in the village by the sea in Spain, in Paris and Berlin and Geneva and finally in New York and on the Connecticut farm. She was a beautiful woman, sensitive, intelligent, vivacious, full of — when she let go — Viennese charm and unlike any other woman I have ever known. And I remembered her talents. She was a fine linguist, at home in five languages. After studying at the Arts Students League in New York, she became a promising painter, later abandoning the brush to take up the study of ancient and modern Greek, which led her to the field of Greek archaeology, in which she made a name.

CHAPTER 2

S omehow, in the midst of the bitterness and the sorrow I managed to finish the book on the fall of France. It took me even longer to research and write than *The Rise and Fall of the Third Reich*. It was a sad story to recount, just as it had been to witness.

Suddenly and swiftly, in the lovely first month of summer in 1940, the nation was conquered by the Germans. Accepting their defeat with astonishing alacrity, a surprisingly large number of French had turned to ape their barbaric Teutonic conqueror and turned against most of the things that had made their country great. A liberal democracy was scrapped and a mindless French version of Nazi totalitarianism set up. A great people had lost itself.

After the war, when the French began to find themselves, it was natural for them to want to forget the terrible defeat and what followed. It was a slice of their long history most were not proud of and did not want to be reminded of. Understandably, few French historians could bring themselves to try to write of what happened and why.

"You must give us time," Pierre Renouvin, the doyen of historians at the Sorbonne, had told me. "Time to let things heal." He himself had been placed by the government in charge of organizing and releasing documents pertinent to the defeat; but his efforts had been hamstrung by successive governments, parliaments, and the bureaucracy. As late as 1958, thirteen years after the end of the war, he was complaining that "the French archives . . . are still not accessible, even to privileged scholars." Privately he admitted that not many French scholars were pressing to see them. He encouraged me to go ahead. As an American, I would have fewer prejudices and, therefore, I could be more objective, he thought, than his French *confrères*.

It was not easy to go ahead. Whereas the victorious Allies had captured the archives of the Nazi German government nearly intact, along with the confidential and highly secret papers of the German High Command, the navy, the party, and soon made them available to scholars who wanted to write the history of Nazi Germany, the French government, insofar as its own records were concerned, had clamped on an infamous law — *"la loi de cinquante ans"* — which forbade making available to researchers confidential state papers until they were at least fifty years old. That made difficult any documented history of the decline and fall of the French Third Republic.

But even after fifty years the French government held back. I had a letter from the Ministry of the Armies saying that "unfortunately" the archives of the Historical Section of the Army were not available to scholars — "not even," it said, "to generals of the French army" — for any period later than 1900. That would include confidential military documents of *both* world wars.* The French Foreign Office responded to my queries by sending me a copy of an order releasing for the perusal of scholars certain dossiers up to 1815 (presumably about the Napoleonic wars and the Congress of Vienna), others up to 1848, still others up to 1896. It seemed to shy away from the twentieth century. Even when I appealed to André Chamson, director of the National Archives, in the belief that he, as a noted author and a member of the prestigious Academie Française, would be sympathetic to authors, I got nowhere. After a lengthy personal discussion he wrote me that he was "deeply grieved" about the situation. "But we have to stick firmly to the law of 50 years, especially in the matter of papers covering the last war and the occupation."

This was at first discouraging, especially to one who had worked for years with mountains of the most confidential documents of the Third Reich. But in time I found that I could get most of the French material I was looking for without ever having to break the law. For one thing, the former political leaders and the generals, particularly the latter, were making them available either in their memoirs or in their sworn testimony at the postwar trials of collaborators, especially those of Pétain and Laval, and during exhaustive questioning by the Parliamentary Investigating Committee, which after the war was charged by the National Assembly to look into the events from 1933 to 1945 which had brought the country to its knees. It became a rather common sight to see former cabinet members, politicians, diplomats, generals, and admirals appear on these occasions and, as they testified, pull out of bulging briefcases sheafs of secret documents that they had stashed away and that they were now using to defend themselves and clear their names.

Once a key French general, whose confidence I had gained after some initial difficulties by impressing him with the results of my initial

---

* Fortunately for history the government long ago had published most of the pertinent records for the First World War.

research (i.e., that I had learned quite a bit about my subject), suddenly broke off a conversation we were having at his home, got up without a word, left the room, and returned lugging in three trunks of confidential material he had been guarding that covered an important part of the story I had not been able to document fully.

The publication in France of *The Rise and Fall of the Third Reich* undoubtedly helped me. It brought a certain respect from French academic historians that I had not received from their American counterparts. A surprisingly large number of them, including some of France's most illustrious historians, helped me in numerous ways, not only in my research but also in understanding the complex factors that brought about the debacle. Some of the politicians, too. Edouard Daladier and Paul Reynaud, the last two premiers of the Third Republic and, therefore, the two most important politicians of the last years before France's fall, went out of their way to help me. With them I put to practice an idea I had found valuable in my work as a journalist: that statesmen open up most to a reporter who can provide them information in return for what they are giving. It makes the relationship a two-way street.

Daladier was especially appreciative of certain revelations in my Third Reich book. He wrote in the press that I had revealed a great deal that would have moved him to act differently had he known it when he was in office.

Both former premiers complained to me that because of the "law of 50 years" they were being denied access to their own state papers, though Reynaud must have taken an awful lot of them with him when he left office, for they were largely the basis of his own memoirs. At numerous meetings at his home he showed me a number of them. Over the years of research in Paris, Reynaud turned out to be one of my chief sources of information. I realized that he, like every other politician, hoped that the material he gave me would bolster his own defense of what he had done. So I approached it with a certain skepticism and made due allowances. But it was not only historical material that he gave me: he opened doors to other politicians, military chiefs, historians, editors, diplomats. For some Americans, the French are often difficult to deal with. They gave me more help and cooperation than I had ever received in any other country, including my own.

This was all the more remarkable, because I was prying into an unpleasant subject for the French: their failures, mistakes, shortcomings, that had brought their country down. I had feared they might greet me coolly and suggest that I leave the recounting of France's fall to them; a foreigner had no business poking into it.* But none of the hundreds I talked to over a period of five years took this view.

I tried to spend either a whole morning or a whole afternoon — and sometimes both when I could — at a very special library I had stumbled on. This was the Bibliothèque de Documentation International Contemporaine, or BDIC, as it was known for short. It was a unique library and, as its name suggests, was devoted to documentation of contemporary history, especially that of World War II and the events that led up to it. Though it was then housed in a ramshackle old palace off the Etoile (it has since moved to the complex of the University of Paris at Nanterre just outside the city), which was too small to provide space for all its holdings, it had a warehouse on the outskirts of the capital and a brash motorcyclist raced to and fro all day long through the mad Parisian traffic to fetch you the documentation you needed. In some miraculous way the BDIC was also able to obtain for you material from the Bibliothèque Nationale and the library of the University of Paris in much less time than you could get it by going yourself to these venerable institutions. Anyone who has tried to work at the Bibliothèque Nationale, one of the great libraries of the world but one where haste is unknown (or was in the old days), will appreciate this shortcutting. There was an assistant director at BDIC who was a walking encyclopedia of knowledge about documenting contemporary history. And there were four very learned and attractive lady librarians, one of whom has remained a personal friend and adviser on modern French history to this day, twenty-five years later.

Without the collaboration of the BDIC, I doubt if I ever would have acquired the material I had to have to go ahead and write the France book. Without the permanent desk the library provided me in the cluttered office of the librarians, I doubt if I would have gotten it all down in the time I had.

Even before I began my research in Paris, I thought I might have a problem with the two rival key political figures I have mentioned, Edouard Daladier and Paul Reynaud. It was scarcely a secret among the correspondents and diplomats in Paris that both politicians had mistresses, who played important roles in the careers of their men, especially in the case of Reynaud. Ordinarily when I am writing history, a statesman's mistress may interest me, but she does not

* That was the attitude of many Germans toward my Third Reich book.

concern me unless she has had an influence on events — either through her man or on her own or both.

"History has a right to discuss her," wrote Pertinax (André Géraud), the forthright Parisian editor-columnist, in his book on the fall of France. He was referring to the mistress of Daladier, but he exercised that right to make even fuller comment on the mistress of Reynaud. What made the situation especially delicate for the country was that the two women had become deadly enemies. At one weekend gathering in the country the spring the war came, one official reported that the good ladies "had almost come to blows."

Reynaud did not mention his close friend in his voluminous memoirs nor in the conversations and correspondence I had with him after the war. Obviously he regarded the matter as his private and personal affair, which others had no right to pry into. Daladier, when I saw him, took the same attitude, and I respected it in both cases, and did not bring the matter up with either of them. Still, as I got further in my investigations, I found that the role of these two women — especially that of Reynaud's mistress — was such that it was no longer merely a personal matter. It was a small but important bit of history. Some French writers began to compare the position of the Comtesse de Portes, Reynaud's Egeria, with that of the Marquise de Maintenon in the reign of Louis XIV and even more with that of the Marquise de Pompadour in the time of Louis XV. The latter lady, it was remembered, virtually ruled France for twenty years (1745–1764). Madame de Portes never got that far — her time was too short — but many thought she tried. I decided that her story would have to find due notice in my narrative of the fall of France. And there would have to be at least mention of her great rival, who had the same exalted title, marquise, as that of the mistresses of the two French kings.

The background of the two women was strangely similar. Both came from wealthy bourgeois families, both married into the aristocracy, and with titles and money for a base proceeded to seek political power by liaisons with politicians who seemed most likely to reach the top.

The Marquise de Crussol was born Jeanne Beziers, daughter of a businessman at Nantes, who had made a fortune canning sardines. Seeking a suitable title, she had married the Marquis de Crussol, grandson of the redoubtable Duchesse d'Uzes. Seeking a more interesting life, she had moved on to Paris where she met Daladier some years after the death of his wife. He was then living alone in a modest apartment. They quickly warmed to each other and Madame de Crussol began to further his career in the more fashionable places in Paris.

To Pertinax "she was a spirited woman, rather attractive . . . but grasping and covetous" and dominating. To the writer André Maurois, she was "a graceful and beautiful woman but with a taste for power and an unfortunate passion for economic and political doctrines" — about which apparently she knew very little. Still, both observers agreed, she was, unlike her enemy, content to keep herself in the background and exercise her power and influence discreetly.

Hélène de Portes was the daughter of a wealthy contractor and shipping magnate in Marseilles named Rebuffel. Bright, intelligent, full of energy and ambition, she married Comte Jean de Portes, son of the Marquis de Portes and the Duchesse de Gadagne, who soon became employed in one of her father's establishments in Marseilles. As Pierre Lazareff, the brilliant, youthful editor of *Paris-Soir* remarked, the two titled husbands "left their wives a good deal of freedom." Like the marquise, the comtesse set off to conquer Paris. There she was soon introduced to Reynaud, a middle-of-the-road conservative, who was on the political rise. At first there seems to have been merely a flirtation, and Hélène de Portes became a close friend of Reynaud's wife. But when his political fortunes began to prosper and he became an important cabinet member, Madame de Portes became his mistress. Bitter clashes, often public and embarrassing, began to ensue between the wife and mistress. Reynaud finally moved out of his home and took a bachelor apartment on the Place du Palais-Bourbon, where he lived to the end of his long life. There the comtesse had him to herself. I never could penetrate the mystery of her strong hold on this brilliant and strong-willed man. Those who had to deal with her were far from flattering.

To General Sir Edward L. Spears, who had occasion to see her at a critical moment of France's fall — and more often than he could stand — she was

> of medium height, dark, [and] her curly hair brushed upwards looked untidy. . . . Her mouth was big and the voice that issued from it was unharmonious. . . . She seemed to the ordinary male observer to be devoid of charm.

Lazareff, who also saw her more often than he cared to, thought her "a little dumpy . . . with pretty eyes and pretty legs, always dressed badly and with an untidy hairdo." He saw in her slightly protruding teeth a mark of "one who loved power."

André Maurois, usually very gentle and gallant in his comments on women in the public eye, could scarcely hold back his thoughts of Hélène de Portes.

> She was slightly mad, excitable, meddlesome and, as the course of events was to show, dangerous. . . . Her dominant characteristic seemed to be ambition. It was not enough for her that Reynaud was Minister of Finance; she was determined at all costs to make him Premier. She filled the salons of Paris with accounts of Daladier's lack of energy, and gave everyone to understand that Reynaud should succeed him.

Reynaud did become premier toward the end of March 1940, replacing Daladier, who retained the Ministry of Defense, a post he had held for four years, even while he was prime minister. This change, to be sure, was not due to Madame de Portes's intrigues, though they may have helped, but to the general feeling in the country and in Parliament that Daladier was not prosecuting the war energetically enough. The Phony War had gone on in the West for six months but there were signs that it was coming to an end and that at last the Western Allies, Britain and France, might clash militarily with the Germans — if not immediately in France, where there had been no fighting at all, then in Scandinavia.

There are numerous accounts of how Hélène de Portes, now that her lover was top man, tried to help him run a country torn with political dissension and defeatism and bracing for a German attack. At times she appeared to be trying to run the country on her own.

Maurois recalled calling on the new premier at his home.

> He was depressed and nervous. On his desk were three telephones, one connected with the Ministry, the second with the outside, the third with the room of Madame de Portes. This last instrument rang unceasingly. Reynaud would lift the receiver, listen for a second and then cry out in an exasperated tone: "Yes . . . Yes, of course . . . But that's understood . . . But I implore you to let me do my work . . ." Finally he stopped answering.

On April 27, 1940, shortly after Hitler had conquered Norway and driven the hapless Franco-British contingents out of the country, Reynaud fell ill and his doctor ordered him to bed at his residence on the Place du Palais-Bourbon. There Pierre Lazareff tried to phone him in regard to a matter he considered important. Hélène de Portes answered the phone.

"We are horribly busy, my dear," she said, "but come over anyway."

When I arrived I found Hélène de Portes sitting behind Paul Reynaud's desk. Surrounded by generals, high officials, members of parliament, and functionaries, she was presiding over a council. She did most of the talking, speaking rapidly in a peremptory tone, advising and giving orders. From time to time she opened a door and I could hear her saying:

"How are you feeling, Paul? Keep resting. You need the rest. We are carrying on."

A couple of months later, after the German tanks had swept through France to the Channel in a few days and the French government had paused at the Loire on its flight from Paris to Bordeaux, General Spears, the British liaison officer with the French government, ran into Premier Reynaud's formidable mistress. The French armies were disintegrating and the defeatists in the government and army were demanding that Reynaud ask the Germans for an immediate armistice. At this crucial moment in France's history, Madame de Portes was siding with the defeatists and trying to get her lover to agree. Thus far he had been holding out for further resistance, first in Brittany and then in North Africa, to which he wanted to move the French government. Prime Minister Churchill had flown over to the Loire on June 11 to plead with the French government and army not to give in. The situation was admittedly desperate. Paris was about to fall. The venerable Marshal Pétain, hero of Verdun in the first war, and General Weygand, commander in chief of the retreating French armies, were insisting to Reynaud that he give up and ask the Germans for an armistice. Madame de Portes was backing them.

General Spears ran into her as he drove to the Château de Chissay to see the premier.

In the courtyard I saw to my utter astonishment Madame de Portes in a dressing gown over red pyjamas directing the traffic from the steps of the entrance. She was shouting to the drivers where to park.

The astounded British general parked his own car "so as to avoid the lady," he says, and went inside. Among other things he wanted to see a "Most Secret" telegram from London, which he had been told had been sent him but which he had not received. He questioned Roland de Margerie, Reynaud's *chef de cabinet*, who told him the message had been lost but that they were searching for it. Finally someone brought it in, all crumpled.

"*Chut!*" Margerie exclaimed. "It was in Madame de Portes's bed!"

The redoubtable lady kept popping in, says Spears, "this time in normal female garb, whispering mysteriously to one or another." Later at lunch the British ambassador told Spears "that as soon as any of us left the premier she dashed in asking what had been said and assailing him with reproaches. 'What did he say? What is the sense of going on?' "

"What an unattractive woman," Spears said he thought again. "She was certainly not pretty and quite as certainly untidy."

Even when Churchill flew back to the Loire a second time to try to shore up the faltering French, Madame de Portes kept trying to intervene to make the premier capitulate to the Germans. During an intense meeting of the two prime ministers, the good lady, according to a reporter of the *Petit Parisien*, kept flitting about between the conference hall and the courtyard, sending for Paul Baudoin, undersecretary of the Foreign Office, who sat in on the talks, and insisting that he keep Reynaud informed of *her* views.

"Tell Paul," she said, "that we must give up. We must make an end to it. There must be an armistice."

To Reynaud's credit, he opposed the armistice with the Germans to the last and was replaced by Marshal Pétain as premier, who promptly asked for it. But some thought Reynaud could have been stronger in the last crucial days in Bordeaux and that he might have arranged, as General de Gaulle, his military adviser, was urging, as were several members of his cabinet, for the French government to move to its colonies in North Africa, from where France could have made a prolonged stand. But his dogged mistress had worn him down.

The account of the two lady-friends of the two French leaders took up but three or four pages in a book of a thousand pages. The reasons why France fell so swiftly that June of 1940 were many and complex and went far back in French history. The Third Republic was probably doomed from the beginning because of its deep divisions at the very outset, which were never resolved — the majority of the members of the elected Assembly had preferred another monarchy. The role of the comtesse and the marquise had added a little spice to the last chapter of the story of a Republic that had had its moments of glory and achievement but also of appalling failures and a dismal, shabby ending. And it had touched on a theme that is as old as history itself: the influence of women, of wives and mistresses, on the course of events. The history of Nazi Germany had lacked that. The women in Adolf Hitler's life were of no consequence. *His* mistress was a cipher.

*　　*　　*

During the course of my research in Paris, I had one shocking moment of disillusionment. It came during a talk with Raymond Aron at his home on the Quai de Passy on July 7, 1961. Aron was an important figure in France's postwar intellectual, political, and journalistic life, a man of immense prestige in conservative circles in France and very dear to American academics and political commentators, even those of the liberal persuasion. He had had a distinguished academic career in Paris and when I saw him, he was devoting much of his time and mind to a regular front-page column he wrote for *Le Figaro*, the leading conservative daily newspaper in the capital. His many admirers in France and elsewhere, particularly in America, regarded him as a great philosopher-sage. Though I admired Aron and read him regularly when I was in France, I did not share in this immense admiration. He seemed to me too narrow in his conservatism, in his view of politics, economics, and the general situation in the world. But he was someone, I thought, whom it would benefit me to see. I was looking for all viewpoints.

During our talk he advanced what I noted in my diary as an "interesting (surprising) thesis." But by the time I wrote up the notes of our conversation and mulled over them, I began to be appalled by what he said. It still troubles me when I think of it twenty-seven years later. I had not expected such a view from him.

His idea was that in the long run France gained from its quick and early defeat and surrender to the Germans in June 1940, and he was now glad of it. He argued that if France had been able to stop Hitler's armies and continue the war, as in 1914–1918, she again would have lost the cream of her youth — some one million and a half men — as in the First World War. It was her small losses in men and material and wealth in 1940 that enabled her to come back so quickly and well after 1945.

> Neither Aron nor other French [I wrote in my diary] seem to realize that it was the Allied armies which saved France, that it was those nations that did fight — Britain, Russia, the U.S.A. — that made the recovery of France possible.

It is better to be rescued by others than not to be rescued at all. But it is better for a nation if it can save itself. One can understand, and sympathize with, the French rejoicing that the lives of their youth had been spared in the Second World War after such horrible losses in the First. France and, to a certain extent, Great Britain never recovered from the staggering loss of life and property in the First World War.

But what if Britain, the United States, and the Soviet Union had not liberated France? The country would have remained under the savage heel of the Nazi Germans, who probably would have destroyed it as a nation, as Hitler planned to destroy Poland and Russia. What good would it have done to save the lives of a million and a half young men if, with the rest of the French, they would become permanent slaves of the Nazi Germans?

Philosopher and great sage though Aron was regarded by many in France and abroad to be, he and those French who thought like him had really not faced that question. Nor, I gathered, did they want to. I put it to Aron as politely as I could, but he did not answer.

CHAPTER 3

Lenox, February 3, 1969 . . . At 1:15 P.M. today I finished the French book, writing "The End" on page 1618. Eight years of labor over. I feel exultant but also sad. It has been such a major part of my life all these years, that it will be strange to have to live without it. And my last big book, probably. With it and the German book, I've lived for 15 years. And though my personal life was unhappy — until a year ago when I left home — my working life has been exciting, each day.

Later. Forgot brief epilogue — on what happened to the chief characters. . . . Some of them executed, almost all imprisoned. So by midnight, when I finished, manuscript had come to 1620 pages!

Lenox, August 7 . . . The France book now scheduled to come out November 13. A Book-of-the-Month Club selection for January. *Look* to do an extract next month. I wonder how it, which represents eight years of hard labor, will be received. One never knows.

The reception by the *New York Times* was an example. It was surprising. The distinguished newspaper clobbered the book — not once but twice, in its daily review of books and in its Sunday *Book Review*. For good measure its news department, which had asked me to talk with a *Times* reporter and pose for pictures by a *Times* photographer for a story it said it had to have by publication date, November 13, did not print it until December 29, six weeks later, when the appearance of the book was no longer news. The reporter's piece itself was harmless enough, but the photographer turned out to be a problem. He had greeted me on arriving at my home in Lenox by saying that the last time we met I had shoved him off the stage onto the floor of Carnegie Hall in New York while he was trying to photograph me — an unlikely story, since I could not recall ever having been on the stage of Carnegie Hall and I had never pushed anyone off a stage anywhere, especially a man bigger than I, as this cameraman was. The photograph of his which the *Times* used was far from flattering, to say the least.

One paragraph in the story must have struck some readers as a bit strange. On December 29 that year, when it appeared, the entire East was being buried under one of the worst blizzards in years. Blowing, drifting snow had tied up the region. Yet the paragraph began: "On a recent cold and rainy day Mr. Shirer sat in the library of the white frame house in which he lives. . . ." As I read the piece, the snow was coming down so hard I could not see across the street. It had been a "cold and rainy" autumn day six weeks before when the *Times* men arrived. But winter had set in early that December, as it usually does in our Berkshire Hills, blanketing us with snow.

Was it a conspiracy at the *Times* to try to destroy this book, as my publishers and some friends thought? Or was it just a coincidence? I wondered. Scotty Reston, the *Times* bureau chief and columnist in Washington, and an old friend, wrote me he was sure "there was no conspiracy at the *Times* to be beastly to Shirer." He himself, he said, had been "surprised by the two reviews and personally hurt by them."

I cannot say I was personally hurt myself. But I was certainly resentful that the two reviewers in so good a newspaper would deliberately distort and misrepresent to their readers what I had written, and one of them with surprising vulgarity. Surprising for the *Times*, at any rate.

This last was a staff reviewer for the *Times* daily book column by the name of Lehmann-Haupt. I was surprised he had been given the book to review, because in previous pieces he had shown, I thought, a singular lack of understanding of history.

After noting that I was "a popular historian" and that "Lord knows there's nothing wrong with that" he gave his readers, despite his obvious ignorance of the subject, a little lecture on "written history," which he asserted was "a distortion of reality." But "Mr. Shirer," he complained, "does not buy that. He is bent on reproducing history in its pristine state."

This irked him. For one thing, he wrote, he did not think that the fall of France and the collapse of the Third Republic in 1940 was important enough to warrant so long and detailed a book as I wrote. After all, he said, France had been defeated by Germany before, in 1870. Why all the fuss about its defeat in 1940 by the same Germans?

Well, I thought, with such an ignorance of history — and history recent enough for him perhaps to make an effort to understand — what could you expect but such drivel? Obviously he had not comprehended the lines I had quoted in the book from an eminent French historian, who shortly after writing them had been executed by the Nazi Germans. This was Marc Bloch, who wrote that France's fall that June "was the most terrible collapse in all the long history of our national life." To the French Catholic philosopher Jacques Maritain it was an "unprecedented humiliation of a great nation." For me personally, as I noted in my diary in Paris on June 17, 1940, my feeling was "that what we are witnessing here is the complete breakdown of French society — a collapse of the army, of government, of the morale of the people. It is almost too tremendous to believe."

It could not be compared to the surrender to the Prussians in 1870 as the reviewer thought. As I read on, I could discern that he seemed miffed that I was what he called "a best-selling author" and that my new book, like the previous one, was a Book-of-the-Month Club selection. He saved his punchline for the last. After informing his readers that there were a few parts in the book worth reading, he gave them this parting advice: "Tear out the rest of the pages and use them to line the gerbil's cage, or something." In other words, as toilet paper for your pet rat.

It was the first time I had seen this reviewer resort to vulgarity — and the *Times* print it — though it may have popped up in pieces I had skipped, of which there were many.

The editor of the Sunday *Times Book Review* had given my book for review to an unknown teacher of history at Columbia. The editor, or his predecessor, had given my *Rise and Fall of the Third Reich* nine years before to an eminent Oxford historian in the belief, my publishers suspected, that such a British authority would give a history by an upstart American journalist the drubbing it probably deserved. Instead, H. R. Trevor-Roper, later the Regis Professor of Modern History at Oxford, had praised the book to the skies on the front page, finding it to be a "monumental work . . . a splendid work of scholarship, objective in judgment, inescapable in its conclusions." My publishers believed, I'm sure wrongly, that the *Times Book Review* editor never forgave Trevor-Roper for crossing him up. At any rate, some of the editors at Simon and Schuster thought the *Review* was not going to take any chances this time with a noted historian. So it chose an obscure young instructor at nearby Columbia.

The man was as condescending as most American academics were to my works. But he turned out to be more adept than most in his deliberate distortions and falsifications of what I had written. He began by dismissing my book on the Third Reich, which he said "reached millions who, against the advice of scholars, found in its very bulk a reassurance of the final word."

Against the advice of what scholars? Peter Schwed, an editor at Simon and Schuster, posed the question in a brief note to the *Times Book Review* editor. Schwed pointed out that the *Book Review* itself had front-paged the laudatory appraisal of the book by Trevor-Roper. For good measure, he added a comment by another scholar, Frederick L. Schuman of Williams College, who called the Third Reich book "the definitive work on Nazi Germany: massive, monumental, meticulously documented."

Like the *Times* daily reviewer, the young Columbia teacher seemed resentful that some of my previous books, *Berlin Diary* and *The Rise and Fall of the Third Reich,* had been "best-sellers" and were selections of the Book-of-the-Month Club. "Now 'The Collapse of the Third Republic,' " he added as if it irked him, "is also a Book-of-the-Month selection." Apparently to this young university instructor, as to many of his academic brethren, if a book was selected by the Book-of-the-Month Club and sold well, it had to be bad. He could scarcely get off the subject. He snidely suggested that in my case there was "the commercial calculation by which a best-seller [my book on Nazi Germany] has its pre-sold sequel [my France book]." If he were a wiser young man, he might have known that invariably an author who tries consciously to write a best-seller ends up with a book that no one will buy or read. At any rate there was never any such "commercial calculation" on my part. No one had believed the Third Reich book would sell at all. And as a matter of fact, the France book never sold enough to pay back the advance.

The Columbia instructor was resentful at something else. He did not like a comment I made in my "Acknowledgments" about the difference in the attitude between European and American professors toward nonacademics like myself who tried to write history. I had expressed my appreciation to some dozen distinguished French university historians for the help and guidance they had given me, and I had named them, adding that none of them shared the "disdain their American academic colleagues have for former journalists breaking into their sacred field — that stupidity is unknown in Europe, where *teaching* history is not considered the only qualification for *writing* it." The young instructor thought such a comment "unnecessary."

He complained that one of the grave faults of the book was that I did not have a "major theme." As if the terrible collapse of the Third Republic or the rise and fall of the Third Reich were not great themes, as if, to go to a higher league beyond me, the decline and fall of the Roman Empire by Gibbon and the story of the decline of Athens as the result of the Peloponnesian War by Thucydides were not "major themes."

Not all professors missed the theme of the book. An unsolicited letter from Eric F. Goldman, professor of history at Princeton, noted: "This is certainly history in the grand tradition — a theme of sweeping significance illuminated by tremendous research and a skeptical but always warmly humane intelligence."

There was a beauty at the end of the young Columbia instructor's long piece. Despite all the solid documentation, which had taken years in France to gather and which I had checked with many of France's most illustrious historians, this reviewer told his readers that in the main my book "on closer inspection" turned out to derive "from 1940 potboilers."

I dwell on these two *Times* reviews for two reasons. First: my book on the fall of France was surely marked by flaws as most long, narrative histories are. Any reviewer worth his salt would have had to point them out if he were knowledgeable enough to detect them. A writer does not gripe about such reviews. What is harder for him to take are reviews which deliberately — as in these two cases — decline to give the reader the faintest idea of a book, its scope, its sweep, its story, its scholarship, its documentation, its judgments and conclusions, how-ever controversial — but instead give a false and distorted picture. And he does not much enjoy being the victim of petty prejudices and jealousies even when they come from academics. To write that the France book — any part of it — was based on "1940 potboilers" was not only cheap and petty but also a deliberate deception.

Second: an American writer was concerned about the fairness and adequacy of reviews in the *Times*, especially in the Sunday *Book Review*, because the newspaper, by 1969, had a near-monopoly in the greater New York area insofar as reviewing books was concerned. The only competition in the city came from a morning and an afternoon tabloid that did not bother about such things as books. And the greater New York area was the place where more books were published, sold, and read than in any other section of the country.

The *Times* with its monopoly could kill a play in New York — and often did — with its one review. It could not kill a book, but it could damage one, especially if there was a one-two punch from the daily and then the Sunday editions.

This had not been true until the lamentable demise of the *New York Herald-Tribune* three years before. The *Tribune's* daily book column, pioneered by Lewis Gannett, was excellent as was the *Tribune*'s Sunday *Books*, edited by Irita Van Doren, a worthy rival to the *Times* Sunday review. In both cases the *Tribune* provided a fair balance to the reviews in the *Times*. Now that balance was gone.

The serious reviews of the book from coast to coast displayed a healthy variety of opinion. *Time* was condescending as it had been with my Third Reich book. In both cases *Time* concluded that I was not qualified to write on such important subjects. Its sister, *Life*, came to just the opposite conclusion. Its reviewer hailed the book as the "most illuminating one ever written" on the fall of France. "The essential merit of his book is that it explains the fall of France in 1940 not only as a military defeat but as the collapse of a political system and a society."

Though finding a good deal to criticize in the book — its style was not "particularly distinguished," its treatment of the history of the nineteenth century was "sketchy, without much original interpretation and with some rather facile generalizations" — the reviewer in *The Atlantic* ended up by finding that the France book in the "sense of compassionate involvement, of genuine tragedy" was "a more moving book than its great predecessor, *The Rise and Fall of the Third Reich*."

> Shirer succeeds magnificently in the main task he sets himself. . . . He is fair, scholarly and superbly dramatic. Few readers at the end of these thousand pages will not feel a new understanding of the French people and their past ordeals.

On the other hand, a reviewer in the *Washington Post* thought I skipped too briefly over the relevant facts about the cost to the French of their victory in 1918, whereupon he purported to reveal those facts himself — all of them, I thought, taken from the lengthy section I had devoted to the subject. A reviewer in the *Wall Street Journal* faulted me, as had the man in the Sunday *Times Book Review*, for spending more time scandalizing over the mistresses of Daladier and Reynaud than I did "analyzing the atmosphere and psychology of deceit and defeat that felled in 20 years" the Third Republic. One wonders about their arithmetic. There were some 810 pages devoted to the latter; three or four pages, in all, to the former.

Some journalist-reviewers touched on the question of whether journalists should leave the writing of history exclusively to the academics. They seemed unanimous that they should not. A few even went farther and thought that some journalists had turned out to be historians. Thus a reviewer in the *Kansas City Star* commented:

> "The Collapse of the Third Republic" is a popular history but it is written by a journalist who became a professional historian.

A promotion for me!

Though he insisted on dividing journalists and historians, a professor of history at Towson State College in the *Baltimore Sun* sort of promoted me also.

> William L. Shirer both profits and suffers from the rich experiences of his life as a veteran reporter and a recently ordained historian.
>
> He is not quite able to reconcile the conflicts inherent in these two roles. To his credit, it must be said that he succeeds as well as any man could. . . .

In fact, he went on to say that I "succeeded amazingly well in describing the human beings torn by conflicting motives rather than leaden dummies stereotyped as heroes or villains." Finally,

> Someday, when the definitive history of the War of 1939 is written, Mr. Shirer's work will be an important primary source in itself. Until then, it will provide adequate subject for debate and many hours of profitable and satisfying reading.

From Princeton, Professor Eric F. Goldman tried to cheer me up. He had written first:

> Last night I finished reading your book on the collapse of France and I want to write you. I was fascinated by the book and I was moved by it. . . .

Then followed his specific comment, which I have quoted. When I write to him later asking why most of his colleagues attacked me, he responded:

> So far as the academics are concerned, as you know, a lot of them have always gone after anybody who writes well. Their dismal canon is that if history is to be significant, it must be dull. I'm afraid the trend is increasing. . . .

He thought the trend was also increasing among critics who dismissed any book that was "too successful."

> I believe you are entirely right to dismiss these smears, even if it would be more than human not to be annoyed by them. The great distinction of your historical works speaks for itself, and has not only

been widely recognized but will be — I am sure — recognized more and more as times go by. They stand as monuments of superb history, immune to pettiness.

The British reviewers, as usual, were condescending. They seemed annoyed that an American, and a journalist to boot, should try to write of Europe and of their tight little isle. The British did it better.

Most of them echoed A. J. P. Taylor, the eminent Oxford historian and author, among other works, of the silliest book ever written about the origins of the Second World War (he practically exonerated Hitler of any responsibility for it), in the *London Observer*. He claimed there was nothing new in the book. A well-read Englishman knew it all already. Taylor also found my "command of English not impeccable" and as an example cited a quotation I had used from a Belgian statesman, as if I were responsible for the Belgian's language.

Only one British reviewer liked the book. This was William McElwee in the London *Sunday Telegraph*. He and Taylor did not seem to have read the same book. Noting that in my subtitle I had called the book "an inquiry," McElwee thought *The Collapse of the Third Republic* is more likely to remain for many years as an authoritative answer."

> Considering the rigidity with which the French archivists interpret their fifty-year rule, it is staggeringly well documented; and I suspect that when all is revealed in 1990, few of these conclusions will be seriously challenged.
>
> Shirer the journalist does indeed intrude, but only to add vivid detail to authenticated events. In no sense is this reportage or "contemporary" history. It is a highly professional piece of research; and it holds the reader's interest for every one of its 921 pages.

Taylor had derided an early section of the book giving a brief résumé of the history of the Third Republic as a "scamper over French history." To McElwee that same section was "itself a minor historical masterpiece."

I wondered what the reaction in France would be when the French translation came out in the late fall of 1970. As I've indicated, the subject was very painful for the French. No people, no nation, likes to be reminded of such a crushing defeat, such a breakdown of their whole society in such a shabby end as the one in Vichy. And there was always that touch of chauvinism in the French (as in most peoples, including the American and British). I suspected a lot of reviewers would ask why a foreigner would poke his nose into their sorrows. Or if not that, that they would conclude that no foreigner, and especially one from distant America across the ocean and a journalist to boot, could possibly understand French history. In both cases they would dismiss the book as the *Times* had done so cavalierly in New York.

But this did not happen. The reviews found plenty to criticize. Some of my views and interpretations were attacked, my shortcomings pointed out. But the book as a work of history was taken seriously and seriously reviewed. The French, however much they disagreed with it, concluded that it was an important work, a considerable contribution to their history and more objective, despite my prejudices, than it was yet possible for a French historian to be.

None of the French reviewers, some of whom were university professors, seemed to care a whit whether I was an academic or a journalist-historian. They judged the book on its contents. Some from the universities even conceded that my having been a journalist eyewitness to the last years of the Third Republic added color and authoritativeness to the chronicle.

The most telling attack on the book came from Professor René Rémond, director of studies and research at the Fondation Nationale des Sciences Politiques in Paris. This was a prestigious academic post and the review appeared in what was then (and perhaps still is) France's most prestigious daily newspaper, *Le Monde* of Paris, a sort of French equivalent to the *New York Times* and the *Times* of London, which gave it half a *page*. I was grateful that the leading newspaper in Paris would devote so much space to the book. I was somewhat surprised by the review itself. Professor Rémond had been most helpful to me, not only in my research and in putting me in touch with some of the country's best historians, but also in discussing the history of France's fall. We had hours of talks about it. We argued many points but on the whole, I thought, we had pretty much the same approach to the story — he perhaps a little more conservative than I. I knew he was a leading layman of the Catholic Church. But he seemed to be a moderate, and I knew he was an authority about the right wing in the country — he had written a fine book about it: *La Droite en France*.

In his review, I must say, he seemed like a man who had drastically changed. Though he found some good things to say, he was severely critical of a great deal — he thought I had "half-failed" in what I set out to do. Though I thought some of his criticism was certainly deserved, I found I did not mind those parts which I thought unreasonable and distortions of what I had written. (He was critical even of conceptions I had received from him.) This probably was because, after all, his taking a whole half-page in *Le Monde* to air his reaction to the book — and the newspaper giving him that much space — was proof, I thought, of the importance he and the newspaper gave the book. The piece in *Le Monde* stirred up a great deal of controversy and provoked many, many letters to the newspaper. This was all to the good.

Most of the rest of the reviews in France were more understanding. Lord knows they found plenty to criticize. But on the whole they thought well of the book. A few examples:

Temoinage Chrétien: "Shirer has constructed a monument. He has known how to mix his personal memories with the work of research. Every new work will henceforth have to refer to this." Jean-Pierre Rioux in three pages in the *Magazin Littéraire* questioned some of my interpretations and emphasis in regard to the strengths and weaknesses of the Third Republic, but added "that few authors before him have brought forth so much labor" in "a spectacular and vibrant book." For "Akademois" in the Paris *Journal* the work "is more than a large work, it's a great book." The review of the early history of the Third Republic, which I had written for American readers as background, so that they could understand the last chapters, and which might well have been left out of the French edition, found an enthusiast in this reviewer. He thought it "a vast and interesting prologue." As for the whole work, it was for him "magistral, impartial, with an extraordinary power of evocation" and finally: "The book reestablishes the responsibilities . . . and makes the truth triumph."

So in France, I got brickbats and flowers, favorable and unfavorable comments, criticism that I deserved and some that I didn't. But the important thing for me was that the French took the book, painful as it must have been to read, seriously, and they wrote seriously about it.

Some of the war veterans groups in France did go after me. I had rather expected it, since the book, I thought, exploded a number of myths that were dear to them in explaining the debacle, such as that the French were inferior in tanks to the Germans and vastly inferior in the air. I had shown that the French had more and better tanks and that even in the air, if you took the planes of the R.A.F. stationed in France into account, they had enough aircraft to give the Germans a good deal of trouble. And I mentioned that, strangely enough, the French had more planes at the end of the Battle of France than at its outset. This had puzzled General Gamelin, the commander in chief.

But my analysis of tank and plane strength did not convince the French veterans. They wrote in protest to the press, especially to *Le Monde*. And they published a manifesto attacking the book. I must say they were civilized about it. At the end of the declaration they wrote: "We invite W. Shirer to come and discuss this with us."

Other veterans rose to my defense. Colonel Adolphe Goutard, for instance, a noted military historian, wrote a lengthy reply to veterans. After that the ruckus died down. But I felt good that a mere book could arouse such interest.

Late that fall of 1970, after the book came out in Paris, I had a novel experience. My French publisher sent me off on a six-week tour of the country to promote the book — something it had not done with the Third Reich book, something that French publishers, more staid than those in the United States, rarely did. It turned out for me to be a wonderful and hilarious trip.

At Bordeaux, I was given something I had never received at home. The mayor gave me a gala luncheon to launch the book. No American mayor had ever done that or, to the best of my knowledge, ever heard of a book of mine. But before I got too puffed up, the mayor of Bordeaux took me down a notch or two. In a gracious speech he said that one thing bothered him about me. I had given a local interview praising red Bordeaux but condemning the white vintages as too sweet. There were no *dry* Bordeaux white wines, as in Burgundy. On the contrary, the mayor said, gently rebuking me before the local TV cameras. He had brought along to the lunch three bottles of *dry* Bordeaux *white*, and he invited me to taste them. I did. They were very dry. And wonderful. And I publicly apologized.

All went smoothly in the next stops, Marseilles, Toulouse, and Nice. I would arrive, as at Bordeaux, be interviewed by the press, then go to the regional radio-TV headquarters for interviews there. After lunch there would be autographing parties in two or three local bookstores — a rather new happening, I gathered, in France. I was sure many French came to see what an American writer looked like and how well he spoke their language. Some came to show off their English.

It was not until I got to Grenoble, a gem of an old city nestled in the Savoy Alps, that the fun really began. There I was to be interviewed on TV by the head of the regional station, a former literary journalist in Paris with whom I had a slight acquaintance. He had written to say he wanted to do the show himself. But when I arrived, I found he had been abruptly dismissed, apparently by General de Gaulle, the president of the Republic, and had returned to Paris. At the TV station I was ushered into a studio where I remained alone as the minutes ticked off to air-time. Some thirty seconds before we were to begin, a young man arrived, seated himself at the table, glanced at me, and said: "Excuse me, monsieur, but who are you?"

"I'm the author of this book," I said, pointing to a copy I had lugged into the studio with me. I looked up to the clock. About twelve seconds to go.

"What book is that? I have not heard of it," he said. "Someone sent me in to talk to someone about something," he added, "but that's all I know. What is your name, by the way?" I started to answer: "By the way, I'm —" when I noticed the engineer in the control room waving frantically at us. And the red light went on in the camera facing me. The young man finally realized we were on the air.

"Ladies and gentlemen," he said breezily, "we have with us to-day . . ." He paused. "Uh . . . we have with us today . . . uh . . ." I thrust the book under his nose. "Ah, yes, we have with us today . . ." He stopped to read the lettering on the book cover. "Uh . . . the celebrated American writer . . ." He looked down again at the jacket. "Uh . . . William L. Shirer . . ." He had trouble, as the French do, with the *w*, which is rarely used in French and then only for foreign words and names, and he did not find my last name easy — it came out something like "Sheer–ere."

". . . who is the author of . . ." He had to stop again to look down at the book. ". . . the author of . . . uh . . . *La Chute de la Troisième Republique.*"

There was a dead silence. The young man for the first time appeared flustered. What to say when you had not read the book or even, two minutes ago, ever heard of it and the author? I thought it was time for me to take over. A few seconds of silence on the air can seem an eternity.

"I'd like to talk to you a little about this book," I said.

"Yes. Please do," the man said, immensely relieved. "I'm sure our audience would be interested in what you say." The fool might have mentioned the subject of the book, I thought, and added that it was one of particular interest to the French, since it was about their recent history. But how could he? He hadn't the faintest idea. The title, on the jacket, apparently did not connote anything to him. That must have been something that had happened before he came along.

I launched into a lecture in the best French I could command. It had a strong American accent, I knew. A Frenchwoman who had interviewed me in Paris had said she liked the way I spoke her language. It was *"très drôle."* The broadcast at Grenoble, too.

At Nancy in the north of France where I autographed copies of my work in the biggest bookstore I had ever seen — a seven-story building full of books — there was some kind of snafu between the promotion people and the publisher. So when I arrived at the bookstore after lunch, the mayor of the city, who was also a deputy in the National Assembly, politely but pointedly expressed his regret that I had not appeared at the luncheon he had given for me, to which, he said, he had invited a number of French historians from the northern universities as well as some political luminaries. It was an embarrassing moment. The publicity woman and my publishers had neglected to mention the luncheon to me.

Driving east that afternoon for a TV show at Strasbourg on the Rhine, it began to fog up and we had to crawl along the last couple of hours, which made us late. We were greeted at the door of the studios by a bouncy young man, who said he would be interviewing me. I suggested that since we were late, we go immediately to a studio and begin.

"I have arranged something better," he said with great enthusiasm. "You see, I aspire to get a job in American television. I see tapes of many of your shows. I love American TV. It's so innovative. So imaginative. So let us do this interview the American way. We'll do it strolling through the park. It is just a few meters from here." He pointed toward a space lost in the fog.

"You can photograph in such a dense fog?" I said.

"Oui. We have special cameras. Equipped with infrared rays, or something. They can see through the fog."

"I think it would be better to do it in a studio," I said. No TV camera, I was sure, could penetrate that thick fog. But he would not have it. He wanted very much to do it the "American way." He would make a copy for the résumé he was sending to America for a job.

So we hurried down to an adjacent park. The fog was even thicker than on the road. You couldn't see more than eight or nine feet ahead of you.

"We'll walk along the delightful paths of the park," the young man said. "And talk. Informally, you know, about your book. Like they do in the 'States.' "

We began, a man with a mike at the end of a long pole and a second man lugging what looked like a very heavy TV camera back-pedaling a few feet in front of us as we strolled and talked.

We did not stroll and talk very long. Suddenly out of the fog loomed two figures who looked like the derelicts you see sleeping along the *quais* and under the bridges of the Seine in Paris.

"*Bonjour!*" they said, happily. "What's going on here?"

"Don't disturb us, please," the young interviewer said. "Can't you see? We're filming a talk here with this American writer."

"Ah! You're an American writer?" one of the men broke in. "All Americans are rich, *n'est-ce pas? Donnez-nous cent francs.*"

"I haven't got a hundred francs on me," I told them.

"Please! You are disturbing the interview!" the young man kept saying.

"Please!" both tramps persisted. "Give us one hundred francs! You're an American, he says. All Americans rich, *très riche, n'est-ce pas?* A hundred francs, please!"

Finally between the interviewer, the two technicians, and myself, we scraped up fifty or sixty francs. The vagabonds thanked us and disappeared into the fog.

The cameraman had continued to roll his camera during most of the incident, and the sound man had picked it up.

"Wonderful!" said the pro-American interviewer. "We'll put it all in. Like they would in America. It will *enhance* the interview, *n'est-ce pas?*"

That evening the director of the regional radio-TV network gave a fine dinner for us at a local hotel on the Rhine. Later we were to watch the late evening news broadcast, which the director said would feature our interview. But about 10:00 P.M. the chief engineer called the director, who left the table to take the call in another room. He looked a trifle baffled when he returned.

"We need not hurry," he said. "I am sorry, Mr. Shirer. But your broadcast didn't come off. The audio part was fine. But there was no picture. Just fog. Thick, gray fog."

Shortly before noon on November 9, I arrived at the TV center in Lyon for another interview about the book. The place was in great commotion. Perhaps, I thought, some big story had just broken. Someone ushered me to a studio. I could see men and women rushing in and out of the control room. Finally one of them burst into the studio.

"Your broadcast is canceled," he said. "All regular programs are canceled. General de Gaulle has just died."

I felt the same shock as he did, as everyone at the broadcasting house seemed to feel. As almost everyone in France and soon many in the whole wide world felt. I had spoken up for de Gaulle in my broadcasts after he flew from Bordeaux to London in June 1940, to denounce the surrender of the French to the Germans. Like his friend Paul Reynaud, he had been for continuing resistance from the French colonies in North Africa. He broadcast to his fellow countrymen from London that the war was not over. It would go on, and Hitler in the end would lose.

The pro-Nazi French government under Pétain and Pierre Laval at Vichy declared him a traitor. During the next couple of years of the war, Churchill in London encouraged him in his efforts to build up the "Free French" as a fighting force but found him, with his imperious manners and his stubbornness, difficult to deal with. President Roosevelt didn't even try, and remained hostile to him to the end of the war — a stupid mistake, I always thought.

The Allies brought him back to Paris after the successful landings in France in the summer of 1944 and he became head of the provisional government, was elected president the next year, and resigned in 1946 because his support on the left crumbled. He was called out of retirement twelve years later, in 1958, when it seemed France might fall apart over its failures in North Africa. He quickly restored confidence, drafted a new constitution that he hoped would dampen the bitter party strife that had been the bane of French politics for nearly a century, and he was elected president of the Fifth Republic. In the new Republic the president was given much more power and the elected Assembly less.

Personally de Gaulle was rather authoritarian but he did not aspire, as many charged, to dictatorship. He thought a strong democracy could stand a strong president — that, in fact, it needed one.

A few days later, back in Paris, I watched on television the state funeral for the general at Notre Dame. While I was watching, a messenger arrived at my room from my French publisher, Stock. He handed me a letter that had come in that morning to the director of Stock from General de Gaulle.

"This must be one of the very last letters General de Gaulle wrote," a note from the director said. "And it concerns you."

It was dated November 3, 1970, on his personal stationery with "Le General de Gaulle" printed at the top of the page.

Monsieur:

You gave me a great pleasure in sending me the work of William L. Shirer "La Chute de la Troisième Republique" at the moment it came off the press.

I thank you for having given me to read this very remarkable book and interesting inquiry into the causes of defeat of 1940.

De Gaulle had already read the book in the original English language version — or had had it read to him. One year before, when the book came out in New York, I had sent him a copy and he had written me on November 13, 1969:

Monsieur:

I thank you very sincerely for having had the happy thought of sending me your book "The Collapse of the Third Republic."

I have read it with great interest and I appreciated the objectivity which you have shown.

CHAPTER 4

That six weeks of barnstorming for the book in France as 1970 came to an end was, with one exception, the last assignment I would have in Europe, to which I had first come as a budding journalist nearly half a century before — forty-five years, to be exact. I was twenty-one then; now I was sixty-six. It was time to begin to slow down. If I didn't, the process of aging would soon do it for me.

I had had my say about Europe in the two long books about the rise and fall of the Third Reich and on the collapse of the Third Republic. Previously, as a newspaperman and a broadcaster, I had written and spoken a million words about it in my dispatches and broadcasts. I still felt at home on the old Continent, especially in Paris. This last fling there and in the rest of France had been a lark. But I had no yearning to return for good. Over the quarter of a century since I came home at the end of the war, Europe had faded away as the center of my existence.

I had a feeling as I returned from France that year, in time for a snowy New England Christmas, that I would be spending almost all of the rest of my life — which could not be long — in my village in the Berkshires of western Massachusetts, writing (but no more massively documented thousand-page books!), reading (there would never be time to read all the books I wanted to, even those in my own small library), having a try at learning Russian, listening to classical music at nearby Tanglewood, where the Boston Symphony Orchestra played eight weeks in summer, doing a little skiing and sailing, cultivating my garden (if I could triumph over the woodchucks), chewing the fat with old friends — now dwindling in numbers — and with new, younger friends . . . if they could stand an old fogy, seeing my two daughters and watching their children grow.

By now I preferred life in the country. I loved the green hills and valleys of the Berkshires, the streams and the forests, the lakes and the fields, the mountain air, the moody skies and the changing seasons. I needed more space than I could get in a city — space to have a garden to putter in, a lake on which to sail, woods to tramp through, slopes to ski. After so long in the great, dynamic cities of Europe and in Chicago and New York, I liked the slower pace of the countryside. Not that I wanted to lose contact entirely with the city. One reason I settled in Lenox, Massachusetts, was that New York and Boston were but 150 miles away. Every once in a while I could steal away to them to get a recharge of their electricity and get fired up by their stimulation.

Over the years I drifted slowly and, for the most part, happily, actively and in relative good health, into old age. I did not retire. A writer rarely retires. But I began to ease up a bit, trying to face up to the fact that at seventy and then eighty, one could no longer pursue fully the strenuous life of youth and middle age. It was not easy at first to face. The illusion that old age would never creep up on me stubbornly persisted. I forgot the advice George Bernard Shaw once gave to a friend: "Don't try to live forever. You will never succeed."

It was a rather interesting time in which to come to the end of a long life. Interesting because much that was new and daring and exciting was happening, but depressing too and discouraging, because the appalling follies of men, their selfishness, their greed, their lust for power and their downright sadism was making life so wretched for so many.

The 1960s raced by and because I was absorbed in writing the book on France, they somewhat passed me by. I followed events as reported in the newspapers and over the air and reacted to them. But my diaries for that decade dealt mostly with the problems of the book and with the ups and downs of my personal life.

I cannot say that I had a very clear idea of the 1960s as they came to an end though I felt, like everyone else, I suppose, that they had been tumultuous and violent.

Later, looking back, some observers would take a dim view of the decade. Richard Rovere, the correspondent of *The New Yorker* in Washington, thought the 1960s had "been perfectly awful." They made up for him "a slum of a Decade." Benjamin de Mott, the astute literary critic and teacher from Amherst, believed the 1960s had produced "a cultural revolution" and that life in America could never be the same again. Richard Hofstader, the historian, took an opposite view. "If I get around to writing a general history of the recent past, I'm going to call the chapter on the sixties 'The Age of Rubbish.' "

But this disregarded the fact that the 1960s was a time of revolt: of the youth, particularly the college students, of blacks, of women. The students tore up the campuses at Columbia, Berkeley, Cornell, even Harvard. The blacks called for "Black Power." At Cornell they brandished arms as they took over some of the buildings. "Women's Liberation" was born and grew.

And the civil rights movement, spurred on by the courageous, imaginative leadership of Martin Luther King, began to break down the barriers that had kept the blacks from having their constitutional freedoms. The nation could no longer ignore it, especially after the spectacular march on Washington in the sweltering August days of 1963 when two hundred thousand blacks and several thousand whites gathered in the capital to demand the end of racial inequality. Because the nation watched it on television, the conscience of the country was aroused. And millions of listeners, after following a series of rather florid but unaffective speeches from the platform in front of the Lincoln Memorial, were galvanized, as were those in the vast throng, by the electrifying words of King.

"I have a dream," he sang out in that deep, rich, southern voice of his.

> a dream that one day the nation will rise up, live out the true meaning of its creed: "We hold these truths to be self-evident that all men are created equal."
>
> I have a dream that one day on the red hills of Georgia the sons of former slaves and the sons of former slave owners will be able to sit down together at the table of brotherhood. I have a dream . . .

And he went on, telling of his dreams that "even Mississippi" one day would be transformed "into an oasis of freedom and justice"; that his four little children would "one day live in a nation where they will not be judged by the color of their skin, but by the content of their character."

Few of the millions who heard the eloquent words, I fancy, would ever forget them.

It was silly to brand as "rubbish" these events and many more such as the Selma March, Woodstock, the brutality of Mayor Daley's Chicago police against the young peaceniks at the Democratic Convention in 1968, or other massive demonstrations against the Vietnam War, the angry reaction against the U.S. Army's atrocities at My Lai in Vietnam, and the mindless killings by the Ohio National Guard at Kent State. And I was surprised to see the usually balanced Teddy White, a witness at the scene, castigate the youthful demonstrators at Chicago and an equally balanced commentator, George Kennan, criticize the nation's youths for their uncouth behavior.

I applauded their revolt. The college generation of the 1950s, to which I had often lectured, had been cowered by McCarthyism, it seemed to me. It had chosen to play it safe as our collegians would do in the seventies and eighties: go for a good job in business and refrain from having or expressing any dangerous — or serious — thoughts.

In many instances in the sixties the students, in the heady excitement of revolt, may have gone too far as they did at Columbia when they seized President Kirk's office and destroyed valuable papers or at Cornell where black students took up arms. But on the whole, shaking up the staid and insensitive administrations of our colleges and universities was probably overdue. At any rate, I liked young people who stood for something beyond achieving safe careers and were willing to risk life and limb against the billy clubs and bayoneted rifles of the police and the National Guard to express it. I joined them in their opposition to the Vietnam War.

Some things about them, I confess, I did not understand. Their obsession with rock music — the louder the better. Their gathering at Woodstock, New York, in August 1969, for example, to listen to a whole weekend of it. Originally the promoters had hoped to draw fifty thousand youths to their rock music festival. But four hundred thousand showed up, blocking the roads, seeking food, drink, and shelter in vain, and milling about in some disorder before they settled down. Two cloudbursts turned the area into a quagmire. Reporters for the New York daily newspapers predicted disaster. There was no one to keep order for nearly a half million people, full of youthful energy not to mention, they said, "grass" and liquor. The *Times*'s reporters, it seemed to me, were particularly hostile to the youths. The newspaper's editorials condemned them.

Yet, on the whole, the young people conducted themselves admirably in difficult circumstances. Sandwiched in as they were, with little food or even water and minimal sanitary facilities, they did not panic or riot. The tone was set by one of the first entertainers. Looking over the vast throng, standing shoulder to shoulder, he said over the loudspeaker: "If we're going to make it, you had better remember that the guy next to you is your brother." It set the tone for the gathering that grew into a sort of feeling of generational unity. Later many participants would talk of the "Woodstock Nation."

After so much turmoil an event occurred at the end of the decade that staggered the imagination and united Americans in a great common pride. On July 20, 1969, man landed and walked on the moon.

Two American astronauts, Neil A. Armstrong, a civilian, and Colonel

Edwin E. Aldrin, Jr., of the air force, detached their lunar module "The Eagle" from the Apollo spaceship, which had been circling the moon, after taking off from Earth three days earlier, and steered it down to safe landing on the rock-strewn surface of the moon.

What mankind had speculated on and dreamed of for millennia had taken place. Human beings from Earth had traveled to another planet. It was almost too tremendous to believe. But there was no doubting. Hundreds of millions throughout the world could see it on television. They watched Neil Armstrong slowly descend the ladder of his frail craft, and as his foot touched the barren surface, exclaim: "One small step for man, one giant leap for mankind."

Like almost everyone else on our planet, I dropped whatever I was doing and sat glued before the TV set, watching. The moon landing was a triumph for man's spirit, for his resolve, for his creation of the incredible technology necessary and for bravery — bravery of two American men. The great voyage had been made. But could the astronauts blast off in what looked like a very rickety contraption, return safely to their spaceship, and then fly back to Earth? I put the question in my diary and added: "One prays that they'll get back. But I feel a pit in my stomach about it. The blast-off machinery, though tested at home, has never been tested on the moon." If it didn't work, two splendid human beings would be left to die on this desolate place when their oxygen gave out — in a day or two.

Listening to the countdown to blast-off was one of the most excruciating moments of my life.

My diary, Monday, July 21, 1969:

> The two astronauts successfully blasted off the moon today in their frail craft and rejoined the spaceship, which had been orbiting the moon while they were there. Another incredible feat — beyond the imagination.

> Thursday, July 24, 1969 . . . The astronauts returned safely to earth today. A happy, wonderful conclusion to man's first trip to the moon.

Looking over my diary nineteen years later, in July of 1988, I was a little surprised to see that in it I had also raised some questions about this awesome achievement. The pictures the television gave us of the moon were so bleak.

> Was it worth it — some 35 billion dollars and the risk of lives? To get to so dismal a place? And what, except for scientific data, is the good of the moon to earthbound men? No atmosphere, no air there to support

human life. Probably nothing worth much on the moon's surface. And even if there were, how could it be brought back? . . .

All right, it was a mighty feat, tremendous . . . perhaps man's greatest feat in his entire existence, the discoveries of Columbus, of Magellan, etc. paling beside it. But at least *they* journeyed through the unknown oceans to a new continent where life was easily supportable.

I suppose it's typical of man, especially in America, that he will spend billions to get to the moon but simply will not spend an equal amount to make this place on earth a bit more habitable . . . to easing the misery of the millions of the poor, giving them enough food and decent shelter, and rebuilding the slums of the great cities where most of them live.

I cited other dire needs in our great country. Better education, adequate housing, medical care.

Now nineteen years later, I wonder about my carping. It seems petty in the midst of so much celebration of a tremendous human achievement. It occurs to me now that the same gripes might have been made in Spain and Portugal about the expeditions of Columbus and Magellan. If the outcry against spending so much money for such a dubious purpose had been loud enough, the expeditions might never have taken place; America might have remained undiscovered, and I and a few hundred million others might not be here today.

Still, glancing through the yellowing pages of the *New York Times* for Monday, July 21, 1969, with its huge banner headline in type one inch high, "MAN WALKS ON MOON," I noticed that this great organ of the establishment took a view somewhat similar to mine.

Man has realized the unrealizable because he dared to conceive the inconceivable. . . .

And there lies the irony inherent in the most extraordinary expression of man's prowess. . . .

For all his resplendent glory as he steps forth on another planet, man is still a pathetic creature, able to master outer space and yet unable to control his inner self; able to conquer new worlds yet unable to live in peace on this one; able to create miracles of science and yet unable properly to house and clothe and feed all his fellow men; able eventually to colonize an alien and hostile environment and yet increasingly unable to come to terms with his natural environment that is his home.

The great question, the *Times* concluded, was

whether the magnificent accomplishment celebrated throughout the world today will at last inspire man to achieve the age-old goals of which he is capable: life in harmony with nature, peace with his fellow men and a just society on this no longer lonely planet.

Nineteen years later, as this is written, it can hardly be said that the moon landing inspired any such thing.

On Wednesday, November 8, 1972, I began my diary by noting Richard Nixon's reelection the previous day. He had beaten Senator George McGovern in a landslide. "Incredible!" I exclaimed. "Incredible that the vast majority would choose this devious man." I mentioned the growing corruption in his administration and added:

> Recently his operatives were caught bugging Democratic National Headquarters and pilfering it. As Henry Commager said in a recent piece, no Administration in history has been so crooked, so lying, etc. But the citizens didn't care.

The break-in at the headquarters of the Democratic party in Washington in an apartment complex called "Watergate" had scarcely threatened to become a scandal. During the last week of the presidential election campaign supporters of McGovern had miraculously raised enough money to buy television time for one last speech by the candidate, who was faring terribly in the polls. McGovern spent most of his broadcast denouncing Nixon for the "Watergate Affair," predicting that it would turn out to be one of the worst political scandals in the history of the American presidency. The speech impressed me and many others in Massachusetts, the only state in the Union that would go for McGovern. But it made little impression on the country. Reporters covering the election largely ignored it. The nation's newspaper editorials were silent about it. I remember one TV network reporter asking a farmer's wife in Wisconsin what she thought of Watergate. "Watergate? Never heard of it. What is it? A fountain or something?"

The great country, enthusiastic about four more years of Nixon, would take a good deal of time before it began to take Watergate seriously. Nixon's press secretary called it "the Watergate caper" and "a third-rate burglary" and refused further comment, he said, on so trifling a matter. But gradually the country, thanks to the brilliant reporting of Bob Woodward and Carl Bernstein of the *Washington Post*, became conscious of it, conscious that something was wrong at the Nixon White House, that the reelected president and his men may have been up to serious crimes and were trying to cover them up. Within a year what up to then had seemed the unbelievable, the unspeakable, was beginning to be spoken or at least whispered: the possible impeachment of the president of the United States. Not since the presidency of Andrew Johnson in 1868, when the House of Representatives voted to impeach him, had this happened to a president.*

In 1974 matters reached a climax and a denouement, the most extraordinary the nation had ever experienced. It was the most exciting year I had lived through since coming home twenty-nine years before. To the veteran Washington correspondent, TRB, summing up the year in the *New Republic:*

> In 50 years of Washington reporting this has been the most dramatic year I have ever known. Historians will come to it with a sense of disbelief, and for us who saw it unfold at first hand . . . there was the same incredulity.

Toward the end of the previous year the vice-president of the United States, Spiro Agnew, had resigned to escape prison. In a sordid deal, as I put it in my diary, the Department of Justice allowed Agnew, who, like the president, had been lecturing Americans for six years about morality, to resign in return for promising not to prosecute him except for income tax fraud, for which he received only a fine. Nixon appointed Gerald Ford, the genial, loyal, plodding Republican minority leader in the House, to succeed him. Since then Ford had gone around for months proclaiming President Nixon innocent of any involvement in the Watergate affair or its coverup. He had seen the documents, he said, and they cleared the president. The chief documents consisted of tapes of conversations Nixon had with his men in the White House — he himself set up the unusual process of taping them.

All through the previous summer, 1973, a special Senate committee under Senator Sam Erwin had held televised hearings about Watergate. It had begun to unravel the story, among other things establishing that Nixon had set up special units to break into the offices and homes of former officials suspected of leaking documents damaging to the administration or of Americans who merely dissented from the dictates of Richard Nixon. But the Senate committee had not found "the smoking gun" — the evidence that would convict the president of willful obstruction of justice, an impeachable offense. Neither had the House Judiciary Committee under a folksy New Jersey lawyer, Peter Rodino, which as 1974 progressed began to press for impeachment. The evidence, both

---

* By a narrow margin the Senate failed to convict President Johnson.

committees were sure, would be found in the tapes. But Nixon refused to hand them over, despite court-issued subpoenas. The investigators, though, continued to close in on him, and on April 29, 1974, my diary reminds me, the president went on national television to announce that he was making public twelve hundred pages of transcripts of his taped Watergate conversations — "all that was relevant," he said, except the profanity.

This was a lie, as we would soon learn. But even that night, as I watched and listened to the president speaking from his Oval Office in the White House with stacks of the transcripts piled up behind him, I felt he was perpetrating a fraud. If he had nothing to hide, why didn't he produce the tapes themselves — all of them? Already the Senate committee had discovered that eighteen and a half minutes of one tape of a conversation he had with J. R. Haldeman, his right-hand man at the White House, about the Watergate cover-up had been "erased" — inadvertently, Nixon claimed. And wasn't it suspicious that the president was fighting in the courts to prevent the subpoenaed tapes from being turned over to the special prosecutor and the House Judiciary Committee?

That litigation was soon settled. I noted it in my diary, summing up the unbelievable year.

> . . . On July 19 [1974], John Doar, chief counsel to the House Judiciary Committee, presented it with a devastating Bill of Particulars for impeachment. Still, most Republicans on the committee argued that there still was not evidence. It was shortly to come, even for them. At the end of July the Supreme Court unanimously ordered Nixon to hand over to the special prosecutor all the tapes he had asked for. One was particularly damaging and when the president saw that it could no longer be withheld he released it himself.

This was the tape of a conversation Nixon had with his chief of staff, Haldeman, on June 23, 1972, on how they could hush up the scandal of the Watergate break-in. Nixon had succeeded in getting the Justice Department and the CIA to lay off any further investigations. In the case of the latter it was explained that the CIA had decided that "national security" interests were involved and had to be protected. But the FBI insisted on pursuing its investigation. Nixon had tried to call them off but to no avail. On June 23, 1972, Nixon and Haldeman had had a long conference at the end of which Nixon, plainly exasperated by the FBI's stubbornness in carrying on its queries, told Haldeman to call in the FBI and say to them on behalf of the president: *"Don't go any further into this case. Period."*

This was the evidence [I wrote in my diary] of the president's obstruction of justice the special prosecutor and the House Judiciary Committee had been waiting for. Nixon issued a statement of regret* and pleaded that he did not think it was sufficiently serious to warrant impeachment. But even the Republicans on the Committee, who now felt double-crossed by Nixon, thought otherwise and joined the others in approving impeachment. The die was cast. Senate Republican leaders finally got up nerve enough to tell him that he was certain to be impeached. If so, he would lose his presidential pension and other monetary benefits. If he resigned, he would save them.

Lenox, Friday, August 9, 1974. For the first time in our history a president has resigned. Shortly after 9 P.M. last night Richard M. Nixon went on TV and announced his resignation. Though he and his toady aides had insisted to the last moment that he would not quit ("I am not a quitter!") his going became inevitable last Monday (Aug. 5). Forced by the Supreme Court to turn over the tapes of the June 23, 1972, meeting with Haldeman and realizing that they would soon become known and published, he released them last Monday. They destroyed what was left of this devious, hollow man, whom the American people reelected in 1972 by the biggest majority in history. They showed, what he had tried to deny to the last moment, that he had obstructed justice, an impeachable offense. . . . It exposed the president as a liar. He was finished.

A brazen man, he could not quite face it. He tried to squirm out all day Monday and Tuesday. But on Wednesday a group of conservative Republican senators called on him to tell him that as the result of Monday's disclosures he would certainly be found guilty by an overwhelming majority in an impeachment trial in the Senate (that the House would vote to impeach, even he finally admitted Monday), he saw he could squirm no further and decided to resign. Today at noon, Vice-President Gerald Ford will be sworn in as the 38th president.†

---

* "This was a serious act of omission," he said, "for which I take full responsibility and which I deeply regret."

† Ford pardoned Nixon a month later. As TRB put it: "For crimes identified or yet to be revealed, he gave him a 'full and free and absolute' pardon, sight unseen. He did this out of compassion, he said. He did it without an admission of guilt from Nixon. . . . Nixon gulled Ford and made a fool of him."

Despite his disgrace, unique in the history of American presidents, Nixon would stage a comeback of sorts, his sins, his crimes, his lies apparently forgiven, if not forgotten, by a surprisingly large number of Americans, especially on the right. Were there no longer in our country any standards of morals, of ethics, of decency?

. . . Good riddance! What I felt about him from the first finally got through to the American people.

Lenox, New Years Day, 1976. . . . So ended a tumultuous year. We have now for the first time a president and a vice-president (Ford and Rockefeller) who were appointed by presidents and approved by Congress, but not elected by the people.*

Nineteen seventy-four was remarkable for another happening that much occupied our good people. My diary review of the year began with it.

The Arab oil embargo and the quadrupling of oil prices suddenly threatened the very existence of the Western countries, especially our own, since their economies, social structure and way of life were based on cheap crude oil which enable the motorcar civilization and even the heating of our homes to function. The central assumption of our age in the West (and in Japan) was that we were living through an indefinite period of unlimited growth and infinite resources. . . . We must now adjust to the hard fact of life that resources are limited and that an affluent existence based on what we thought were unlimited resources is over.

---

* On becoming president, Ford had appointed Nelson Rockefeller vice-president.

CHAPTER 5

$\mathbf{B}$ack on February 23, 1971, I began my diary:

> 67 today! . . . Will I write anything important still? Some have, after
> 67. . . .

The France book over, I had decided to have a try at some memoirs.
I had lived through nearly three-quarters of the tumultuous twentieth
century — from the horse-and-buggy age to the nuclear and space era.
Those seventy-odd years had seen more changes on earth than in the
previous two thousand years. I had had the luck to witness some of the
historic occasions and turning points of the century: the revolution in
India and the rise of Gandhi, the breakdown of the old order in Europe,
the advent of Communism and Fascism, the seeming decay of Western
democracy, the eroding of the two great European empires, British and
French, and the weakening of Britain and France, the resurgence of
Germany under a brutal but popular dictator and a mindless but also
popular Nazi ideology, and the coming of the greatest, bloodiest, and
most costly world war ever fought. I thought what I had seen and tried
to learn might be of some interest to American readers.

My publishers were not so sure. Simon and Schuster had made a
small fortune on *The Rise and Fall of the Third Reich,* and it had not
done too badly with the next book, on the fall of France. Perhaps it
thought that no more "big" books — that is, very profitable books —
were in me. Perhaps it was because this fine publishing house, founded
during the Depression by Dick Simon and Max Schuster, had been
taken over by a conglomerate, Gulf & Western, which had no particular
interest in book publishing except that it show a profit — and the
bigger the better.

At any rate, Simon and Schuster showed no great enthusiasm for my
doing some memoirs. My new editor seemed to share that skepticism.
I have a stubborn streak, and despite my publisher's misgivings I went
ahead with the first volume. I hoped to make it not so much a memoir
of myself but of the times I had lived through — a journey through the

twentieth century and from one world to another, or to several others.

Even for writing memoirs, a good deal of research is necessary. If you try to write about your life and the times you've lived through solely from memory, without a note, as a friend of mine, a distinguished poet and critic, tried to do, you are liable to end up with very little — at best, with a novel.

My family and friends kidded me for never throwing anything away. But as I plunged into *Memoirs I*, as I called it, I was glad I never had. My diaries, my correspondence, my clippings, were not only invaluable — without them I never could have written the books.

But for the early years there was very little to go on. So I took off to Chicago, where I had been born in 1904, and spent days going over old files to see what it was like in this raucous, dynamic city at the turn of the century. That was where I first put down my American roots. That was where I began to be formed.

To my surprise, even the *Chicago Tribune*, which once had fired me and later on the front page had told its readers what a lousy foreign correspondent I had been for it, was friendly and helpful. Colonel McCormick, the old tyrant publisher and chief owner who had so poisoned the paper with his outlandish prejudices, was dead. The *Tribune* had improved greatly since his demise. The new managing editor put the paper's archives at my disposal. From these and other sources I began to get the flavor of the Midwest metropolis where I was born and, for that matter, of the whole Midwest where I grew up.

I knew very little about my father, who had died in Chicago in 1913 when he was only forty-two and I, nine. I did not know much either about my mother; she was always very reticent about talking of herself.

But some of their papers came into my hands on my brother's death, and I learned more: that they had grown up in Iowa, she in Cedar Rapids and he on a farm near LaPorte; that they had met while students at Cornell College in Mt. Vernon, Iowa, and married after he moved on to Chicago to pursue a career as a lawyer. Her forebears had fought in the American Revolution; her father had joined the Union Army at seventeen when the Civil War began and had seen action at Gettysburg and other places. My father's ancestors were German, having emigrated from the Rhineland around 1840 to seek freedom on our shores. His father was the first to be born in the family in America and to speak English without a German accent. He was a farmer in Wisconsin, Illinois, and Iowa and a cattle breeder. But in the 1880s he sold a prosperous Iowa farm and moved to Mt. Vernon in order to give his four children a college education.

Such was my American background. But I did not put it down at once. I began the book by describing my escape from Iowa to Paris, the year I graduated from Coe College, a small but excellent Presbyterian institution of learning, in June 1925. That was where my real life and work began. Everything else, grade school, high school, and college, had been a preparation.

I finished the first volume of the memoirs early in 1975, and it was published in the fall of the following year. The overall title of the memoirs was *20th Century Journey — A Memoir of a Life and the Times*. I called the first volume *The Start: 1904–1930*.

The reviews were varied and on the whole good, though a couple of reviewers found the book "strangely disappointing." I was reminded of how differently various persons see the same thing.

Robert Kirsch, an old favorite of mine though I did not know him personally, wrote in the *Los Angeles Times* some things about me that I was not much aware of:

> . . . his life and experience formed Shirer, forced him to see beyond illusion and stereotype. That shaping . . . energizes the deepest levels of this memoir. This is . . . to be found . . . in Shirer's ability to evoke people, times and places with the excitement of a Midwestern small-town boy and the sophistication of a man who has been around. . . .
>
> His life has paralleled history and he illuminates it in this narrative, informal, detailed, honest searching.

I did not know Alden Whitman personally either, but I had liked his book reviews and obituaries when he was on the *New York Times*. Now writing in *Newsday*, he thought that "*Journey* belongs to the great tradition of autobiographical history." Since it was autobiography, Whitman, like some other reviewers, speculated about what kind of a person I was. He liked my "lifelong skepticism" and my "moral passion," which he thought I

> translated into an active sympathy for the men and women who produce society's goods and services yet reap so few of its benefits. What gives it [the depiction of life in America during the first quarter of the century] its special life is Shirer's liberal and humane point of view, his deadly shots at piosity and cant.

This was a time when the word "liberal" was beginning to be looked upon by Richard Nixon, Ronald Reagan, George Bush, and their followers as a dirty word, denoting, as they put it, some poor American slob "out in left field." I was, and am, proud to bear that label whether I deserve it or not. Though the Nixons, the Reagans, and the Bushes did not know it, it is the term most Americans use when they think of Jefferson and Jackson and Lincoln and Wilson and Franklin Roosevelt, not to mention Walt Whitman and Thoreau among others.

Somewhat to my surprise Alden Whitman thought I came across in the book as "a patient and very pleasant school master."

"In a trench coat?" he asked. He could not tell. (Most of us wore trench coats in those days in Europe and Asia. It was the only kind of all-weather coat there was.)

Finally I reminded Whitman of Lincoln Steffens, actually one of my youthful idols, whose autobiography enriched us all.

> Shirer has Steffens' humaneness of spirit. But above all he has his own exciting inquisitiveness. Good reporters . . . never lose their childhood curiosity. When this is fused, as in Shirer's case, with an abiding faith in man's potential capacity to handle the truth about himself, the result is a book that is a must reading.

"Must reading" was the sort of admonition my publishers liked. They thought the reviews coming in were "terrific." Some were, like those of Whitman and Kirsch. Ted Morgan wrote a four-column piece in the *Saturday Review,* which my editor, who sent it on to me, exclaimed was "just terrific." "The 'smalltown boy makes good' story is one of the things," he wrote, "that make William Shirer's *20th Century Journey* so affecting and so eminently worth reading." He liked, especially, the first part, which he called a "meditation on America."

> Shirer had to leave America to understand it. Only after his European experience could he appreciate the virtues of his upbringing and realize that what he had left behind was not as undeserving as he had imagined.

Some reviewers went overboard, I thought, in their enthusiasm for the book. Caspar Nannes in the *Washington Star* concluded a long review:

> "20th Century Journey" is a masterpiece in its genre. It is not only the chronicle of an individual but an illuminating picture of the history of Europe and America from 1904 to 1930. Shirer writes superbly and with an undeviating clarity. Based upon a journalist's experience, the book moves up to the high reaches of great literature. It is one of the few books of our time that should last indefinitely.

Even the *Wall Street Journal* and the *National Observer* were kind and understanding, despite views that must have seemed anathema to such conservative journals.

If the *Washington Star* man thought the book "a masterpiece," a reviewer in the rival *Washington Post* thought it was "largely a disappointment."

For Shirer tries to tell too much and ends up by not telling us enough. . . . His memoirs therefore are somewhat superfluous.

Richard J. Margolis in *Bookletter* also found the first volume of memoirs "oddly disappointing." He did not like my disparagement of Main Street Babbittry America, from which so many of us fled in the 1920s, claiming that we set out "in pursuit of fame and fortune" and that what "many" of us wanted "most of all was to impress the folks back home."

Shirer was among "those crazy boatloads of Americans," as Fitzgerald called them, who for one brief moment thought they had found the right side of paradise.

A staff reporter, Mark Green, in the esteemed *Patriot Ledger* of Quincy, Massachusetts, really went after me. The book was a "phony," he pronounced. It was also "absurdly pretentious." He thought my quoting Euripides, Pindar, Pascal, Mark Twain, and other such at the beginning of my book and citing William Allen White, Isadora Duncan, Emily Dickinson, George Santayana, Stendhal (which he misspelled) in the introduction was an example of my pretentiousness.*

And to this intellectual name-dropping the narrative adds social name-dropping, for this is all his life-experience boils down to, as he boils it down.

This time the *New York Times* did not clobber me, as it had done with my previous book. The memoirs were given for the Sunday *Review* to that veteran critic and chronicler of the "lost generation" in Paris, Malcolm Cowley, who was most generous in his comments. Naturally he liked the Paris chapters the best, but he took notice of the part that history played in the narrative. In fact, he found the book to be "another contemporary history rather than a true memoir." Amidst all the

* Gerald W. Johnson, the eminent journalist-historian and sage of the old *Baltimore Sun*, writing in the *Chicago Sun-Times*, had a different impression of the introduction.

It is an introduction that is a syllabus of his philosophy of history and comprises seven pages of the best philosophical discourse turned out by an American writer in many years.

characters in the book he found one was missing. "The missing person," he concluded, "is William L. Shirer."

The daily review in the *Times* this time was written by someone I could not identify: Maurice Carroll, apparently a reporter on the newspaper. He found the memoirs "a good book by a good reporter." He looked forward to the next volume. But he seemed a little concerned about being too enthusiastic. "Maybe," he wrote, "I liked the book more than I should have."

The review of Stanley Karnow, himself a veteran foreign correspondent, in the *Washington Post* raised for me, at least, an interesting question. He did not like my writing about the early years of the century in America in which I had tried to sketch the background of the years I was growing up. (Some reviewers thought it was the best part of the book.) "All this material," he argued, "is too familiar to bear repeating."

This is a common complaint of many reviewers and I think it is silly. The last word about any period of history has not, and never will be, said. There are always new insights. Perhaps my account lacked them. But to put historical eras "off limits" and proclaim that they are "too familiar to bear repeating" is to be blind to the past. It shows arrogance and ignorance.

The first reviews of a book in this country, my publishers reminded me, come out in *Publishers Weekly* and *Kirkus Reviews*, and many bookstores base their orders on these initial reports. So when they came out, though the review in *Publishers Weekly* was quite favorable, the one in *Kirkus Reviews* was, as my editor wrote me, "snotty." It certainly seemed to me to be an odd reaction to the book. The anonymous reviewer concluded, "sadly," he said, that I was "mean-spirited." He was particularly shocked by "my sheer aggressiveness" when "at nine or so he pummeled his 'bitchy, ugly, old grandma' into submission, an incident he relates without embarrassment."

To the reviewer that seemed to be the most important event of a book that tried to tell of growing up in America at the turn of the century and what the country was like then and reporting contemporary history in Europe during the 1920s. And he slanted his account of that rather unimportant happening. I, of course, never "pummeled" my grandmother "into submission." As I related, one day, after years of taking her thrashings, I hit back and that ended the practice. It was a tiny tale of boyhood. *Kirkus Reviews* blew it up into a major battle that proved my "sheer aggressiveness" and my "mean spirit."

The publishers were afraid this initial bit of foolish and irresponsible reporting might discourage the bookstores from trying to sell the book. But apparently it was not taken seriously. At any rate, the first volume of memoirs got off to a good start, was a featured alternate of the Book-of-the-Month Club, and did fairly well.

If my publisher was lukewarm about the first volume of memoirs, it was positively chilly about the next book, a memoir of Gandhi. I had tried to write it first as the opening section of the second volume of memoirs, since the first volume had ended with my receipt in Vienna of a three-word cable from Colonel McCormick, the lord of the *Chicago Tribune:* "SHIRER FLY INDIA."

Eventually I agreed with Simon and Schuster that the Gandhi part did not fit into the volume, which was going to be mostly about my life and work in Nazi Germany. I thereupon proposed that we take it out and make it a separate book. It seemed to me that Gandhi had been the greatest man of our time, that it had been a lucky break for me to get to know him while covering the revolution against British rule in India in 1930 and 1931 and that this small book about him, a work of love on my part, was worth publishing.

Simon and Schuster did not agree. The publishing house, now quite changed, I thought, under the ownership of Gulf & Western, was not interested, it said, in bringing out a memoir of Gandhi. In fact, it objected to my publishing such a memoir. It wanted me to go back to the second volume of the memoirs, take out the Gandhi section, and go ahead with the time in Nazi Germany and the coming of World War II and its aftermath, completing the whole project. They wanted no Volume III.

"The American reading public," my editor wrote me, "does not take to multi-volume autobiographies. Two is really the limit. To try to spread it past that is an act of self-destruction."

After wrapping up the memoirs in the second volume, I could go on, if I liked, and do a big biography of Gandhi. But I must not make it a memoir. That, said Simon and Schuster, would detract from the two-volume general memoir.

Having agreed to take the Gandhi section out of *Memoirs II*, I tried to persuade Simon and Schuster to change its mind and publish it as a separate book, calling it a memoir, which it was. I was not interested, I said, in doing a straight biography. It was probably beyond my capacity at my age. I was turning seventy-six. But a memoir springing out of my experience in India with Gandhi — a unique experience for an American journalist, I thought — was already written, ready to be published.

Perhaps I wore them down by my perseverance. In the end, and most reluctantly, they promised to publish the book. After a long struggle they even agreed to calling it a "memoir" in the title: *Gandhi — A Memoir.*

It came out January 14, 1980, amidst the usual complaints from the author, all of them, I thought, justified. In June, I had written my editor of "my shock and deep disappointment" ("shock" was a little strong, I admit) that the book would not be published in the fall, as promised, in time for Christmas when more books are sold than at any other season. We had proofs already at the beginning of June. I wrote that bookstore managers had always assured me that January is the worst month of the year, except for August, to sell books. Most people have done their book-buying for Christmas and are in no mood to buy further books until spring. An owner-manager of a big bookstore in Washington had even written me a memo to that effect.

"You had assured me of 'fall publication,' " I wrote my editor. "January is not the fall — in any calendar."

"It certainly is, Bill, in the book-publishing world," he replied in a letter that astonished me. There were only two seasons for book publishers, he explained, spring and fall. The latter season, he wrote, "went from September through February."

So January publication was "a fall publication"!

He went on. "November really is a bum month in which to publish, whereas January, regardless of what you've been told, is one of the very best — country miles better than November." The book, he said, wouldn't have done very well for Christmas even if it had been available in the bookstores.

> To be honest, Bill, in our opinion, GANDHI isn't exactly a natural and obvious choice for a Christmas present despite its appeal to the spirit.

I griped about the steep price of the 240-page book. Simon and Schuster had listed it in its fall catalogue at $9.95. But when it came out, they jumped the price to $12.95, an increase of three dollars a book or twenty-three percent. When I asked the head of the firm why there was such a steep and sudden rise in the price, he replied that if I "looked around, I would see 'a world-wide inflation going on.' " I had looked around and, like everyone else, been aware of inflation. But I had not noticed it rising by twenty-three percent in three months at the end of 1979, and it hadn't.

And, of course, like all authors I complained about the publisher's not pushing the book. As they said in the trade, Simon and Schuster *printed* the book but scarcely *published* it. A full-page ad in the Sunday *New York Times Book Review* got the work off to a good start but then sales fell off shortly to nothing. I did what I could to promote the book: dozens of interviews in the press and on the talk shows. The Book-of-the-Month Club made *Gandhi* an alternate selection. And despite prominently displayed reviews, many of them controversial, several favorable, the book did not make the best-seller lists; and Simon and Schuster soon dropped it. Until . . . a few years later word got around that Richard Attenborough was doing what I thought would have been impossible: a film about Gandhi. Then there were rumors that it was a masterpiece.* Over at Simon and Schuster there was sudden interest. A new paperback edition was hastily brought out to appear about the time the film opened.

Reviews of the Gandhi book were mixed — most favorable, some controversial, a few hostile and highly critical. Two or three, I thought, were simply silly. The piece by Robert Kirsch in the *Los Angeles Times* was typical of the reviewers who found much to admire. He saw the book as "a moving and tough-minded memoir of Gandhi."

The review in the *Chicago Tribune*, which had sent me out to India to cover Gandhi, was, to my surprise, quite favorable and understanding. I had been caustic and unsparing in depicting Colonel Robert R. McCormick, the authoritarian monarch of the *Tribune*, in my first volume of memoirs. The colonel now was gone and the present editors apparently did not mind what I had written about our former czar. Milton Viorst, an old *Washington Post* hand, who wrote the *Tribune* review, concluded that "what Shirer has written is more cameo than psychobiography, but its very modesty is enduring, and from it emerges an authentic figure."

The *Washington Post* again clobbered me, this time with a review by one of its foreign correspondents who, it said, had served in Southeast Asia for the last ten years. He pooh-poohed my admiration of Gandhi and insisted that there was in Gandhi "a great deal of hokus-pokus, of showmanship, of the shrewd politico who knew how to play to the

---

* Which on viewing it later I thought it was.

grandstands at home and abroad." Such demeaning of a man who Lord Louis Mountbatten, the last British viceroy in India, had said would "go down in history on a par with Buddha and Jesus" and who made Einstein exclaim: "Generations to come, it may well be, will scarce believe that such a man as this ever in flesh and blood walked upon this earth." Was the generation of foreign correspondents which had followed mine trying to show how tough and realistic (and mindless) it was? Gandhi — "a hokus-pokus politico"?

In the *New York Times*, I batted .500. In the Sunday *Times Book Review*, I did quite well. James Cameron, a distinguished British foreign correspondent who knew India well, discussed the Gandhi book seriously and thoughtfully.

John Leonard in the daily *Times* poked fun at Gandhi and the author in his familiar Manhattan wise-cracking, smart-alec way. Decidedly I did not have too much luck with the daily reviewers in the *Times*. Leonard's piece, I thought, was typical of some book reviews in this country by staff writers who seek to cover up their ignorance of a subject by wise-cracking their way through their reviews. They do not subscribe to a rule scrupulously followed by Lewis Gannett, in his daily reviews in the *New York Herald-Tribune*, that no matter whether you liked the book or not, no matter how ignorant you were of its subject matter, you were obliged in all honesty to try to give the reader some idea of what the book was all about. Leonard was obsessed with reports of Gandhi's smile, which, he pontificated, "was the center of Gandhi's myth." He found that "Shirer positively babbles about it." He himself prattled on for most of his column on the subject, oblivious to anything more important or interesting about the great Hindu leader.

> We demand to know whether or not behind the smile — Buddha? Gioconda? Cheshire cat? — there was an arrogance of humility, a masochism and perfectionism, an ambition for power through self-denial.

I was not around when the reviews came out. An insert in a review on a page called "Friday's Bookshelf" in the *Milwaukee Journal*, January 11, 1980, explained why.

> Shirer was in satisfactory condition Thursday after undergoing open heart surgery at Mount Sinai Medical Center. Shirer, 75, of Lenox, Mass., underwent eight hours of surgery Wednesday. He received three bypasses.

Again I had been lucky.

I had flown down to Sarasota, Florida, to spend the Christmas–New Year holidays that year with friends. As usual I had eaten too much and had a few extra drinks and was feeling like many do after New Year's Eve — a little under the weather.

I had had a slight scare shortly before Christmas up in Lenox when my doctor had discovered a little angina. But I had taken a stress test and apparently passed it satisfactorily. The results had been sent off to Boston for further analysis, but the heart doctor had given me a copy of his report. I did not understand its technical language, but I put it in my pocket and forgot it.

A day or two before my flight home from Sarasota the head of the family I was staying with, a doctor, suggested I see a heart specialist just as a precaution. He knew a young cardiologist who had come down from New York recently to practice in the town. I waved aside the suggestion, but my friend grew insistent, and finally I gave in. We called on the doctor on a Saturday afternoon, January 5, 1980. His staff was off, but he had agreed to see me anyway. I regarded it as sort of a "courtesy" call. As I sat down in his office with my friends, he asked me if I had a copy of the recent stress test in Lenox. I pulled it out of my pocket, remarking that perhaps he could give me a layman's explanation of it. He glanced over it with sort of a poker face, looked up, and asked me to go down the hall to a room where he said he would like to do another stress test. As the door closed behind me, he turned to my friends, they told me later, and said: "This is the second worst stress test report I have ever seen. I'm afraid this man is about finished."

I flunked his stress test. I gave up, out of breath, after a couple of minutes on the treadmill. The doctor then advised doing an immediate catheterization. In this the physician inserts a small tube up a vein from the thigh to the heart. At its end is a small camera that miraculously photographs the heart and, in fact, flashes pictures on a screen. Though I am usually squeamish about such things, I remember watching it with utter fascination. The conclusion was that there were severe blockages in three main arteries that carry blood to the heart; two of them were almost completely stopped up — ninety-nine percent, the doctor said.

He explained that I couldn't last many more days with such blockages and advised immediate open heart surgery. After telephoning to several heart surgeons around the country, he picked Dr. Dudley Johnson, who was then practicing at the Mount Sinai Medical Center in Milwaukee. Before I knew it he had me on a plane to that destination. Such was my first meeting with Dr. Gene E. Myers of Sarasota. He saved my life as, of course, did Dr. Johnson, who successfully performed the eight-hour operation after running into three or four unforeseen complications.

For several years after it I felt better than I had for a long time. Recently, though, as I began to advance through my eighties — I'm eighty-four at this writing — I found that I had to slow up. Plenty of exercise and a good diet is the secret of survival for most heart patients. But I have had of late to curtail the first a little, giving up skiing and heavy gardening and long walks but keeping up the sailing, puttering in the garden, and doing twenty-five minutes of exercises, including five minutes of shadow-boxing (cut down from nine) and ten minutes on a stationary bike each morning. Up to now the heart surgery in 1980 prolonged my life by eight years — and healthy years to boot.

I must say I've been grateful to have had them. Though I know I gripe more about the sad state of the world than the average citizen and still resent life's inequalities, brutality, the plight of the poor and the homeless, the greed and arrogance of the rich, and much more, I myself have continued to have an enormous appetite for life, a zest for it. Work and play and good health have enabled me to love every minute of the last eight years.

And finally, like everyone else, I survived eight years of Ronald Reagan's reign in the White House. He was one of the great phenomena of modern politics. The worse he did, in my opinion, the more shortcomings he exhibited, the more popular he became among our people. He was tough on unions, and organized labor voted for him. He favored the rich, who got richer while the poor got poorer. He deprived the poor of more and more benefits until millions lived in disgraceful poverty, but the poor voted for him. He piled up more public debt than all the previous presidents put together, but the American people did not hold it against him. He spent billions of their tax dollars on Star Wars, which surely will turn out to have been a hoax; but the people applauded him.

For the entire eight years of his administration, in violation of solemn treaties by which we swore not to interfere directly in the affairs of other countries, he waged a lethal war of his own against Nicaragua with "contra" troops he armed, trained, and financed for the purpose of overthrowing a government that we formally recognized as sovereign and indeed maintained diplomatic relations with. And he had the effrontery to call these U.S.A.-backed mercenaries "freedom fighters," though their military commander and many of his lieutenants had been loyal members of the unsavory Nicaraguan National Guard run by the hated, corrupt, barbarian dictator Somoza. They cared about as much about freedom for Nicaraguans as Somoza, who brutally suppressed it, did.

But Reagan was obsessed with Nicaragua, insisting that the "contra" leaders, whose troops in eight years had never captured a major town or inspired even a local uprising against a shoddy Communist dictatorship, were to be compared to our own Founding Fathers, which was an insult to the latter and to the great Republic they founded — and, of course, a tasteless travesty of history. So thousands were slain by the "contras," including Nicaraguan women and children, so that Ronald Reagan could pursue his little war, doomed though it was to failure. And a surprisingly large number of Americans, and the Republican party itself, along with many Democrats, supported him. Just as at first, at least, they had backed our war "against Communism" in faraway Vietnam. For Vietnam, though, the backing melted away. For Nicaragua it held steady over eight years, though the majority of citizens — if the polls are to be believed — gradually turned against the dismal war.

Communism, which had failed in Russia and in the Iron Curtain countries, had its greatest triumph in the way it befuddled the American people and their government. Any old bloody dictator obtained our support if he prattled his "anti-Communism" loudly enough. I never understood how we became such suckers. We are not normally so naïve and so stupid.

My diary for Sarasota, January 7, 1981, reviewed the previous year: the heart surgery at its beginning, the gradual six months' recovery, the prospects for the future. My life had been saved, but for how long?

> . . . I won't say I'm ready to go. I'm not. I'd like to finish the Memoirs. . . . And maybe have a few more years in such a pleasant place as Lenox, with the music at Tanglewood, the gardening and sailing, and M's love. . . .
>
> . . . Much trouble over the year with my publisher, S&S, which since it was taken over by a conglomerate, has been hard to deal with. . . . S&S let me down on the Gandhi book. And for the first time since I began, with *Berlin Diary*, writing books that were immediately published, they turned down a manuscript of mine, Vol. II of my memoirs.*. . . No discussion, as a writer used to have with a publisher. They just said they wouldn't publish it.

---

* My memory was faulty. Knopf, my first publisher, had rejected the manuscript of my second book after *Berlin Diary*.

There had been a letter from my new editor explaining why, in *my* interest as well as theirs, my manuscript of the second volume would not be published. And there were some telephone calls from Simon and Schuster urging me to accept its decision — again in *my* interest as well as theirs. It was touching how solicitous my publisher, in rejecting me, was of *my* "interests." The same editor had argued for hours on the phone that the repayable advance was a better proposition for the author of the Gandhi book than a nonrepayable one.

In our dispute Simon and Schuster certainly had a point. It had contracted for a second volume of my memoirs that would carry the story through my years in Nazi Germany and the war — from 1934 to 1945. The manuscript I had submitted, which was pretty much the one I had originally written, minus the Gandhi portion, covered only the years 1930–1934. But I felt, I told the publisher, that period was an important one in my life and the times.

To publish my manuscript, Simon and Schuster replied, could "do neither of us anything but harm." The editor did not like the "down-beat" nature of the book, especially the expression of my sense of failure. "To segregate them in a volume is self-destructive from a reputation standpoint, nor is it even commercial — very few copies would be sold, and most certainly no book clubs or reprint action."

It was the old shibboleth that in America you had always to be successful. There was no place for failure. If it happened in your life, in your career, don't mention it.

To Simon and Schuster's objections to publishing the book I made two answers: that it was a logical successor to Volume I and was not a bad book; second, that, as all publishers knew from experience, many a book did not turn out as its creator and its publisher envisioned. Manuscripts have a life of their own. The creative process brings strange results that no man can predict. My first book for Simon and Schuster, *The Rise and Fall of the Third Reich*, I pointed out, had come out quite differently from what any of us foresaw. Simon and Schuster had contracted for a relatively short book to be finished in a couple of years. In the end it had become a very long book and it was years behind schedule when it was finished. Nevertheless, Simon and Schuster had dared to publish it as is.

But this time, no. My editor finally agreed I could offer the new volume to another publisher if I wished, but Simon and Schuster still retained its rights to bringing out the ensuing volume on the years in Nazi Germany and the war years.

This I could not accept. Finally, after several months of bickering,

Simon and Schuster agreed to release me to take the rest of my memoirs elsewhere, subject to my repaying the advance, which I did. But there was one hitch. There remained between us, it said, the matter of Simon and Schuster's "collecting" from me the interest on the advance. In the end it demanded twelve percent over the years the sum had been in my possession.

This astonished me, coming from a company that for twenty years had had the use of a very much larger sum from my royalties that had been withheld by mutual consent. (So as not to pay taxes all at once on royalties from the Third Reich book, the IRS allowed the author, since it was stipulated in his contract, to receive only "X" number of dollars per year and thus spread the tax burden. The money belonged to the writer; he had earned it in royalties. But the publisher had the use of it. It remained in his possession.)

For years Simon and Schuster kept after me to pay interest at the rate of twelve percent on that advance. I refused, and finally the matter just faded away.

The whole episode was a reminder that despite all the talk to the contrary, the true relationship between a publisher and a writer is essentially an adversarial one. It may not be so in every single case, especially in regard to an author whose books continue to be best-sellers, but it is true of most relationships, and a lot of misunderstanding and bad feeling between author and publisher would be alleviated if this were recognized. I suspect most publishers do, though they won't admit it publicly, but many writers don't. Until, as usually happens in the end, they get hurt.

Thanks mainly to the Authors Guild, book contracts today are much fairer to the writer than they were seventy-five years ago when the Guild was founded. (Ex-president Theodore Roosevelt was one of its most militant early members.) Gradually the Guild was able, largely by persuasion, to get the publishers to agree to decent terms. But it was a long, hard struggle. Many publishers resisted change as long as they could.

Even today most contracts strike most writers as still unfair. They do not see why they should give hardcover publishers fifty percent of paperback royalties or the same split on the sale of a book to a book club. The paperback publishers and the book clubs choose a book not because of the way it was published but because of the appeal of the writing. True, if a hardcover publisher has really pushed a book and greatly helped it to become widely known, he deserves something for his effort. Surely twenty-five percent would be more than fair. But he insists, in almost all cases, on fifty percent. I have heard some hardcover publishers argue that if they gave up their fifty-fifty cut, they would go broke. But since most of them are now part of giant corporations, this argument weakens.

A few hardcover publishers will stick to an author through his ups and downs, bringing out the books that sell well and those that don't. But not many these days, and not often. They'll publish you when you make a lot of money for them and drop you when you don't. I was dropped by Knopf one book after *Berlin Diary*, which had done well enough to help rescue it from financial difficulty, and by Simon and Schuster one book after *The Rise and Fall of the Third Reich* had netted it a fortune. Many other authors have similar tales to tell. It was in my case, I concluded, as if the publisher had decided I had one big book in me, so far as sales went, and that was it. No need to bother with the guy again. Recently I had come to think that this practice of picking up the booty and then beating it was due mainly to the old individual publishing houses being taken over by the large corporations, which were interested only in profits and regarded a book as a commodity no different from soap. I liked to think that in the old days a writer had personal friends in the old publishing houses. You were on friendly terms with the publisher and your editor, who stuck by you through thick and thin. I know that was the case with John Gunther at Harper's. Cass Canfield, its head, was one of John's closest friends. I gather that is the relationship William Manchester has with Little, Brown. There are, no doubt, other such instances. But they are happy exceptions.

Ironically, I returned with a new version of my second volume of memoirs to Little, Brown, from which I had been forced to depart when the then chief editor rejected the very idea of publishing a book I proposed to do on the rise and fall of the Third Reich. I must say I received a warm welcome back, and our consultations were among the most pleasant I have ever had with a publisher. The book, to be fair, was better than the one Simon and Schuster had rejected. The core of it now was my long assignment in Nazi Germany, the nightmare years in that oppressive land. It was the personal side of the story I had told in the book of history about the Third Reich. The people at Little, Brown, especially Roger Donald, my editor, liked it. And they pushed it when it came out. The title: *The Nightmare Years — 1930–1940*.

The reviews were the best I had ever had. Not because most of them were very favorable but because so many of them were so discerning, showing a deep understanding of what I had tried to do. Even the five-column review in *The American Scholar*, that citadel of academia, was perceptive and sympathetic, though certainly not uncritical. The reviewer thought, for instance, that "the vocabulary of tragedy" was "beyond my reach." "Yet," he continued, "I can think of no other narrative that gives you the disturbing sensation of having lived in suspense throughout the period, not knowing how it was to the end." *The American Scholar* is essentially literary, and its reviewer was the only one who noticed what I wrote about the reaction of France's greatest living writers to the surrender to the Germans in June 1940.

> Shirer prods us with a sad reminder of what happened in 1940 to men who lived by the word, those keepers of the flame whom we now see celebrated without moderation every year in our literary quarterlies. When the doddering Marshal Pétain accepted a prostrate France, before the French army itself had surrendered, not a single man of letters repudiated him. Quite the contrary.

And he quoted my account of what happened to Paul Claudel, François Mauriac, Paul Valéry, and André Gide — the giants of contemporary French literature. They praised Pétain to the skies and meekly accepted France's surrender to the Germans. André Gide thought it might be a good thing for France.

Naomi Bliven's two-page review in *The New Yorker* was one of the most beautiful and eloquent I had ever had. *Time*, for the first time, liked a book of mine. In a signed review John Skow called it "an admirable memoir" and added: "At 80 . . . he still writes an unusually fine book." The *Philadelphia Inquirer*, which had belabored the first volume of memoirs, went overboard on this second volume calling me "the Thucydides of our time," which, of course, I am not. Even *Kirkus Reviews*, on which bookstores depend for the first word about a book, wrote what my publishers thought was "a rave review." This was quite a contrast to its blast against me for Volume I.

As usual, I got a pretty good review in my hometown newspaper, the *Cedar Rapids Gazette*, for which I had worked briefly while in college. The reviewer thought I got "off to a slow start." He did not find interesting my adventures in Afghanistan, Ur, Babylon, Bagdad, and Constantinople or the account of my return to Vienna, where I was married and fired, or of the year-off in Spain, whose young Republic was being undermined by Fascism and would soon fall to Franco and his Nazi German and Fascist Italian supporters. He thought the book "seemed to catch on" when I got to Berlin.

Once more I was lucky with the *New York Times*, the most influential of all newspapers when it comes to new books. The review in the daily edition was written by Herbert Mitgang, a cultural writer but not a regular staff reviewer. He liked my "strong" views and opinions and thought my books had "elevated" me to "the position of contemporary historian." (As we shall see, one academic strongly disagreed.)

John Chancellor, the NBC commentator, reviewed the book in the Sunday *Times Book Review*. He wrote a genial piece about foreign correspondents, of whom he had been one after the war, expressing admiration for those of us of the previous generation. He did not go overboard about the book, by any means. There was too much history in the work for him. The writing, he felt, was "sometimes repetitive and hurried." But there was "enough adventure in it," he concluded, "to make it well worth reading." I had hoped he would see more in it than "adventure" — the nightmare years in Berlin were beyond adventure — and the last cliché, "well worth reading," struck some as a little condescending but it probably did no harm.

This time not many academics weighed in against me. Some may not have liked the enthusiastic review in *The American Scholar* or the pieces by some of their brethren in several newspapers in which they hailed me as a historian. But, if so, they did not take to print to attack me.

There was one notable exception, and he bitterly resented anyone's calling me "a historian" or my books, especially *The Rise and Fall of the Third Reich*, "histories." This was one William Sheridan Allen, writing in the *Boston Sunday Globe*, a newspaper whose reviewers had in the past dismissed most of what I had written. The newspaper identified him as a professor of history at the State University of New York at Buffalo and the author of two books on Nazism, one of which I knew, *The Nazi Seizure of Power*, based on his studies of a single small town in Germany. I had concluded the sample was too small to explain such a large and fateful event. This led him into the fatal error of absolving the German people of any guilt for Nazism. Professor Allen lost no time in going after me. His piece began:

> To begin with, let me be honest: Professional historians do not esteem William L. Shirer. His historical books are simplistic in interpretation, unbalanced in coverage, superficially researched and full of wrong-headed theories. Worst of all, they sell like crazy. His *Rise and Fall of*

the Third Reich sold over ten million copies. Not a single work by a professional historian comes near that. This is exasperating.

Actually, the professor professed a sneaking liking for *The Nightmare Years*. For one thing, he conceded, it was well-written — "professional historians could learn from him what the public likes to read."*

So read it, he suggested,

> as a gripping account of the personal experiences of a young American midwesterner inside Hitler's inferno, complete with badly flawed data. But I certainly would not accept it as an accurate description of anything except what Shirer observed firsthand, including his own uncorrected misconceptions.

Apparently among my "misconceptions" was my view of the Holocaust. Allen stated I had exaggerated the number of Jews slaughtered in the extermination camps by one million (no one knows, or will ever know, the exact number). He complained that though I "was appalled by the persecution of the Jews," I "never knew that the people of Berlin hid 500 Jews throughout the entire war."

The lives of five hundred Jews in Berlin saved — out of tens of thousands who were slain! Out of some six or seven million, in all, exterminated! Did that excuse the Holocaust?

Allen's review, appalling as it was, and his own works, brought up, I thought, some interesting points. One was the academic's obsession with mere data about Germany collected after the war by university historians who were too young to have observed Nazism at first hand and who resented the writings of those of us who had. It is certainly not necessary in writing history "to have been there," but as we learn from Thucydides, it helps. John Wheeler-Bennett, the eminent British historian and well known for his fine books on Germany, thought there was no substitute for firsthand experience, of which he had had a great deal in Berlin.

Also, I was troubled by the practice of Allen and other young academic historians of drawing historical conclusions from their detailed studies of a tiny part of the picture. It reminded me of a weekend meeting at Harvard, some years before, of historians from Germany, France, Britain, and the United States to discuss the history of Nazi Germany. I was invited to participate and was, I believe, the only

---

* Perhaps Prof. Allen was too immature to know that, like most writers, I certainly never knew what the public liked to read and never gave the matter any thought.

nonacademic present. Many who came discussed their own detailed studies of towns, a single city block, of the party or the press in a province. Almost all of the talk had an air of unreality about it. There was no attempt to assess the whole picture or to delve into fundamental questions such as why it was, and how, that the citizens of an ancient, cultured, cultivated Christian land allowed their great country to be demeaned and destroyed by the Nazi barbarians — and with enthusiasm. I, who had seen it happen, had never been able to fully explain it, but I thought all historians should make the attempt. But these young academics, some of them already of great repute, but all too young to have known Nazi Germany at first hand as adults, kept dodging important questions. They were more interested in their data on how, for example, Germans in one city block in Cologne voted in the years that led up to Hitler's triumph.

The last day of the seminar, one of those attending, an elderly man, came up to me in frustration and exasperation. He had been a refugee from Nazi Germany and for many years a distinguished professor of history at the University of Paris. I knew him by reputation, and the day before he had said he admired my own works on Germany.

"This is all so unreal," he whispered to me. "Let's ask the chair if we can interrupt the program for a few minutes and tell some of these young historians what it was like to live in Nazi Germany and just what happened to bring such a calamity on the German people. We can tell them how the people really behaved, which is quite different from what the dry data tells them."

He got the attention of the chair, apologized for breaking into the agenda, and explained that much of the talk over the weekend had seemed to him to be so lacking in reality — as sometimes happened to scholars who worked only from arid documents — that the conference might be interested in hearing from two historians who had lived through at first hand the Nazi nightmare. He mentioned himself and me.

The presiding academic historian listened patiently, a little bemused, I thought, and said: "Thank you very much," and promptly, without batting an eye, called on the next speaker on the agenda.

CHAPTER 6

More and more, as I grew older, my diaries, when I summed up the year past or on the occasion of another birthday, speculated about how many years I might have left and what I intended to do with them. Thus an entry for January 19, 1982, after reviewing 1981, peered into the new year.

> . . . I'll be 78 this coming Feb. 23. I feel lucky to be alive and in good health and writing well, my days filled to the limit with work, exercise, reading, listening to music, seeing friends. Life in many ways may be a swindle, terribly unfair to many who are poor or unemployed or rejected. But it has been good to me and interesting, and I wouldn't mind having a little more of it, tho I have to face the fact that at 78 my days are decidedly numbered.
>
> I'd like to finish my memoirs — another 3 or 4 years work. And love deeply a woman again and be loved, and read more and really study Russian and sail and garden and see my children and their mother, estranged though Tess and I are, and my grandchildren and friends. Am I too greedy for life? Too selfish?

I recalled reading something from Virginia Woolf — I think in her diaries toward the end of her life — that she realized finally she would never learn Russian as she had once hoped to do. There was an air of sadness in her words, for she had had a passion for Russian literature, in which she had read widely in English translation, and she wanted very much to read it again in the original, realizing how much was lost in translation.

I had had the same ambition, had begun to study it as I approached seventy, and then my teacher had returned to Europe, and I had not found another and had given it up. Then in 1982, when I was seventy-eight, I again found a tutor, a Russian woman teaching the language in a nearby college, and I resumed my studies. This also had rekindled a fire under a related and long-held ambition: to go to Russia. For fifty years I had been trying to get into that country and the Bolsheviks had always turned me down.

In Kabul back in 1930, I thought I had made it when the Soviet ambassador invited me to stop over in Russia on my way back to my post in Vienna. But the Foreign Office in Moscow had rebuked him for issuing any such invitation to a correspondent of the *Chicago Tribune*, which had been lambasting the Bolsheviks since the advent of Lenin and Trotsky, and the trip was off. I thought finally I would get there twenty-one years later, in 1953, when the Soviet embassy in Washington advised me I could pick up my visa in Helsinki. But when I arrived at the embassy in the Finnish capital, they informed me that Josef Stalin had died, that the border was closed, and that no visas could be issued for the moment. Two or three times subsequently my attempts to get a visa failed.

I could not understand why. I had never written much about the Soviet Union because I had never been there. I knew that the Kremlin had not liked what I wrote about the Nazi–Soviet Pact and had only permitted the publication of my two books, which assailed Stalin for having signed it, *Berlin Diary* and *The Rise and Fall of the Third Reich*, after that had been cut out (without my permission or prior knowledge). But I was not a professional Bolshevik-hater. I had hailed the courageous fight of the Russians against the German invaders during the Second World War. I had written of my love for Russian literature and my fascination with the language. Still, over all the years, no visa. No explanation. *Nichevo!*

Then one day in 1982, Marge Champion, the dancer, a dear friend and neighbor in the Berkshires, phoned that a member of a group she was going to the Soviet Union with, the Society of Stage Directors and Choreographers, had fallen ill and that I could take his place. The visa, one of thirty issued to the group, could simply be stapled to my passport.

"Can you act like a dancer?" Marge teased me. "Most of us in the group are dancers."

"Sure," I said. "Look at all the great dancers I've known. Isadora Duncan, Mary Wigman, Tilly Losch, you. It will be easy."

For a decrepit old man not long recovered from heart surgery it was ludicrous, of course, to assume any such pose. Though I was certainly not known in Russia, the KGB surely had a dossier on me if only because of my books. But the worst that could happen to me, if I were found out, I figured, would be to be thrown out.

I told Marge I would go. After waiting for half a century, I was determined to get into Russia under any pretense.

Harrison Salisbury, also an old friend and neighbor in the Berkshires and a former *Times* correspondent in Moscow who had just returned from shepherding a group of American writers through the Soviet Union, was not so sure I should take the chance. The authorities in Moscow, he said, had been in a vile mood about Americans. They were still resentful of President Reagan's crack about "the evil empire" and of all the other attacks by the Reagan administration.

"If they think you have tried to put something over on them," he added, "they might throw you out."

But I was determined.

Actually it took the KGB in Moscow two days to find out who I was. But from the very first moment we landed at Sheremetyevo Airport, I established a certain contact with the famed secret police. When I walked through the metal detector, all the bells of Moscow seemed to ring out. A suspicious official ordered me to empty my pockets and try again. The bells continued to ring. Finally after half a dozen attempts he called a superior, who turned out to be almost a picture-book specimen of what I imagined a KGB operative to be. Very suave. Almost genial. Obviously competent.

"What's the problem?" he asked, in almost perfect American.

By this time I realized that the probable cause of my setting off the alarm was that I still carried a number of metal clasps that had been inserted after heart surgery to hold the chest area together. I had had this problem at airports at home. I explained this to the KGB officer, who seemed skeptical.

"Try again," he ordered.

Same result. Again and again and again. Finally in frustration he shook his head and said, "Very strange. Quite unusual. But okay. I accept your explanation. You can go pick up your luggage." That, too, had just had a narrow escape of its own.

While he was inspecting me, I had looked over his shoulder to see a very interesting sight. A Russian friend at home had asked me to take some things to her mother in Moscow, and one of the items had been an old-fashioned Flit-pump to spray cockroaches, which invade many, if not all, Moscow apartments. As my suitcase passed through the detector, its contents were shown on a TV screen, and the Flit-pump looked exactly like a good-sized bomb. However, the Russian inspector checking the screen was looking the other way, and my KGB friend was looking at me, his back to the screen, and the clear outline of what looked like a deadly bomb faded from the screen and I was again home safe. And my friend's Moscow mother was assured of a tool to wage her war against the cockroaches.

On the late afternoon of our second day in Moscow, our Intourist guide took me aside as we arrived back at the hotel and said she had to speak to me alone. She was so attractive a woman and so intelligent that I had assumed from the first that she was not only an Intourist guide but, as many of them were said to be, a member in good standing of the KGB. In my years in Nazi Germany, I had developed a pretty good sense for detecting agents of the secret police, especially women.

So I had been identified, I thought. And probably the woman was about to tell me to get ready to catch the first plane out of the Soviet Union. Everyone in our group had been so taken with her that we already were first-naming her, as Americans like to do.

"Sonia," I said (I am not giving her real name), "may I suggest that we go to the bar and that you give me the pleasure of buying you a drink." Over drinks in the bar, I thought, we would at least be civilized. She readily assented.

After a little small-talk at the bar, she turned to me and said, "Why did you do this to us? We are not dumb, you know. We know perfectly well who you are."

"Well, Sonia," I said, "it's an honor to be recognized in the Soviet Union." She really had a beautiful, intelligent, sensitive face and was an enormously attractive person. She certainly didn't seem grim, and I began to hope.

"Are you a member of this society of dancers?" she asked.

"No." And I explained why I had come with the group and how for years the Soviet government, for reasons I could not comprehend, had denied me a visa.

"Did you come over to write about us?"

"No. I came over to see what I could of a country and a people that has always fascinated me and whose language I'm trying to learn."

"I suspect you speak more Russian than you have shown me," she said. Why were Russians so suspicious? I wondered. Sonia would entertain that suspicion to the end.

"No, I really can't speak it yet," I said. "I'm learning it mostly to read. So I can read Pushkin and Tolstoy and Dostoyevski and all the rest, including your Soviet writers, in the original."

"Good luck!" she said and broke into a broad smile. I felt better now about the verdict. Sonia certainly didn't look as if she were going to tell me to pack my bags. She sipped her sherry, took a long and somewhat quizzical look at me, broke into another smile, and said: "What can we do for you? Since you're a writer, you probably would like to see some things on your own."

"Sonia," I said, when I had recovered my breath, "I thank you very much. I really appreciate it." I paused for more breath. I was still savoring the pleasant surprise. "There is something I would like very much to see. I've been trying for years to write a play about Tolstoy."

"You have? That interests me very much."

"And since it is laid mostly in his country place, where he spent most of his life, I would very much like to go down to Yasnaya Polyana." It was one hundred and thirty-five miles south of Moscow.

"I'll try to arrange it," she said.

"Sonia, I love you," I said. "You're wonderful!"

Alas, the next day I came down with the flu; my temperature soared to 102°, and the hotel doctor ordered me to bed. On the following day Sonia came by to see how I was.

"It's all arranged," she said. "I've got you a car, a driver, and, since you claim you don't speak Russian, an interpreter. You start at six o'clock tomorrow morning."

I thanked her profusely. But the doctor, when she came in later, would not allow it. Did I realize, she asked, that in Russian cars the heater almost never worked? It was the end of October. Winter was setting in. It had already begun to snow. It was getting colder. It would take eight hours to drive to Yasnaya Polyana and back on the clogged Tula road. I would freeze to death. Or, at the very least, catch pneumonia and die that way. No. *Nyet! Nelzya!*

It was a bitter disappointment. But I recovered quickly enough to meander around Moscow toward the end of the week and then for another whole week in Leningrad. In Moscow there was a subway station in front of the Hotel Kosmos, and I would take a subway train there, ride a few stations, get off, and wander around the district, ask my way back to the station (to try out my extremely limited Russian), embark on another line, get off again, and look over a new area. One day I found myself at a station unable to figure out what line to take to get to Red Square, where I had an appointment with a friend for lunch at the nearby Hotel National. I paused to ask directions from two young men who were passing by. They listened patiently for a moment to my attempts at Russian and then broke out in an almost unaccented American. They turned out to be a couple of young instructors at the University of Moscow. They got off with me at a stop on Gorky Street, and as I was early for my luncheon appointment, we had a long talk as we circled around Red Square. I began to get a feel, however slight, for what the Russian people were thinking.

In Leningrad, I met a professor from the university in a still more curious way. I had gone with my group to some institute to hear some Russians speak about their peace movement. But the speeches were so long and so boring, what with the translations, and so full of propaganda baloney, that I was looking for a way out when a young Russian secretary tapped my shoulder and whispered that a professor from the university was outside in the reception hall and wanted to see me.

"She says she has read all your books," the secretary whispered.

"Most unlikely," I said.

However, I was glad of the opportunity to escape, and I followed the young lady out to the reception hall. There waited a middle-aged woman who said she was a professor of history at the University of Leningrad. She spoke very good English.

"I've read all your books," she said eagerly.

"Well, you honor me, madame. But how is that possible? None of them, so far as I know, except for *Berlin Diary* and *The Rise and Fall of the Third Reich,* have been published in the Soviet Union, and then only in a very limited way."

"We have the American editions of all of them in our library," she said rather triumphantly, "and I've read them all," whereupon she proceeded to run through the titles of each, a few of which I myself had almost forgotten. "They are required reading in my classes," she claimed.

She was genial enough and warm and friendly. But I found myself watching my words as we launched into a long discussion of what I had written about Nazi Germany. I kept wondering how this woman professor knew that I was at this particular meeting or, for that matter, in Leningrad or even in Russia. Who had tipped her off? The KGB in Moscow? Sonia, who was supposed to terminate her guiding of us when we left the capital but who had come on to Leningrad with us? Obviously this woman was in good standing with the powers-that-be.

So though I was wary, I learned a good deal from her, I think, and from a colleague of hers on the faculty of the university to whom she introduced me and who, I gathered, was also in the good graces of the party.

This late autumn of 1982 marked the end of the long Brezhnev era — he would die on November 10 in Moscow, four days after we departed the Soviet Union. Short as my stay in the country had been, it was long enough to see that he had almost ruined it and that the system itself was failing. The Soviet Union was mired in a terrible stagnation and had been for years. Nothing much worked except the space program and the arming of the military. The vast country — by far the largest in the world — could not even properly feed its people nor house them nor provide them with hardly any of the amenities that were commonplace in the West. And the situation was getting worse, the lines before the shops longer. Russia was falling rapidly behind the West in almost every way.

And the people, it was clear, knew all these things. They had lost hope of an improvement in their lives under this system. They had nothing but contempt for the Communist party and its leaders, who were running the country into the ground, the bigwigs leading lives of luxury, complacency, and corruption and, in turn, contemptuous of the common people, who were barely able to survive. The so-called dictatorship of the proletariat was a joke to most Russians. The workers, deprived of independent free-trade unions and the right to strike, not only did not run the country — or have any say in its running — they lacked the freedoms of the workers in the West, with their really independent free-trade unions and the right to strike.

All these failures were a revelation to me. If the American press had reported them, I had missed it, though I read a number of newspapers and magazines. It had all come out in bits and pieces from talks with a few Russians themselves and from the feel you got as you mingled with the throngs on Gorky Street or on the Nevsky Prospect and watched the long lines before the shops and went into them to see the shabby goods, the scrawny scraps of meat and decaying vegetables, and the barren shelves.

The intellectuals I met, except for those who had sold out — and even some of them — were chafing at the lack of freedom of writers and artists and journalists and teachers. The line laid down for them by the party bureaucrats seemed to them inane. And stifling. They were no longer in fear of their lives as they had been under Stalin. But dissidents were still being arrested, given mock trials, and sent off to Siberia. Andrei Sakharov himself was under virtual house arrest and confined to the city of Gorki, where he was subjected to indignities and humiliations by the KGB.

Brezhnev, who had let the country slide down into such a morass, was about finished. His health was failing. I caught him on TV the night before we left Moscow for Leningrad at the end of October. He was presiding over a meeting with his military chiefs, one of the preliminaries to celebrating on November 7 the sixty-fifth anniversary of the Bolshevik Revolution. You could tell he was a dying man. He had to be half-carried to the rostrum by a couple of generals. His speech was badly slurred. He could hardly read the words.

Who would replace him? Nobody you spoke to seemed to care. His successor would be, they knew, another ailing, aging party boss. The Bolshevik Old Guard was clinging to power no matter what happened to the country. This was shown — not once but twice. First there was Yuri Andropov, the former head of the KGB, and then Konstantine Chernenko, a handsome, fumbling, elderly party regular. The first because he was too ill, the second because he was too old and mediocre, did little to stem the decline. Both died shortly after attaining office.

When I returned to Russia four years later, in 1986, there was a new kind of man at the top in the Kremlin, and he was filling the people with a hope that at last something would really be done to drag the country out of its stagnation, reduce tensions with the West, join the U.S.A. in reducing nuclear arms, provide the citizens with adequate food and decent housing, cut down the long lines before the shops, open up the whole moribund society and give the people some of the freedoms they had been deprived of. He even talked about introducing some democracy in the monolithic party and in the country, though it certainly would be limited. No Russian believed the Kremlin was about to relinquish its iron control.

On the second visit I was on my own. A Russian friend would be meeting me in Moscow, helping me with the language, guiding me about and taking me into Russian homes. She was now an American citizen living and working in the States, but she had visited her ailing mother in Moscow nearly every summer for years and was enormously interested in the goings-on in her native land.

Once again the Soviet embassy in Washington had not even acknowledged my request for a visa, but I had obtained one through a travel bureau in New York. Thanks to its Moscow connections it had also persuaded Intourist to renew its offer to take me down to Yasnaya Polyana to visit Tolstoy's estate. Though I was anxious to see how the Soviet Union had changed in the four years since I was last there, especially the last year under an amazing new leader, one of the main purposes of my journey this time was to do background research in Moscow and Yasnaya Polyana for a play and possibly a book on Tolstoy.

The new man in charge in the Soviet Union was Mikhail Gorbachev, and my Russian friend could scarcely believe how much Russia had changed even in the short interval since he took over. A good deal of her excitement rubbed off on me. That summer of 1986, despite one of the worst heat spells in living memory, despite the worst disaster ever to hit an atomic generating plant — the one at Chernobyl two or three weeks before I arrived — was a heady time to be in Moscow. You could feel the winds of change beginning to sweep over the country. My Russian friend was amazed that her friends and acquaintances and relatives were suddenly speaking out in the open about things they had not dared to mention two or three years before. *Glasnost* — openness — so long suppressed in the country, was now publicly proclaimed by Gorbachev as one of the first immediate goals. Books that had long been banned began to appear. Plays that it had been verboten to produce suddenly popped up in some of Moscow's theaters. The dreary, controlled press that for so long had been confined to boasting of the party's progress and its good works was more lively, opening for the first time its columns to contradictory views.

Readers now dared to write in, and the newspapers — even *Pravda* and *Isvestia* — dared to print their criticism of what had long gone wrong in the Soviet Union: the shortage of food and its terrible quality, the lack of decent housing, the lines at the shops with their shoddy goods, the suppression of books and plays, the restraints on free speech and free assembly.

Even the wooden prime-time evening news show on Soviet television, *Vremya*, which had bored Russians to death, began to loosen up and present some actual news.

The Russians we saw were excited about the change and, on the whole, approving. But they were also skeptical. After nearly a year and a half of *perestroika* there had been no noticeable improvement in the food supply or its quality. The lines before the shops still stretched out far down the street. A new apartment was almost impossible to find. Whole families were still crowded in one room. The great apartment complexes on the outskirts of the capital were beginning to decay, though many were only three or four years old. Prices were going up, though salaries and wages remained unchanged.

Above all, I think, Russians feared that Gorbachev might not survive for long. Khrushchev had tried to introduce some drastic reforms, they said, and had been overthrown by the Old Guard in the Kremlin. It was still strong, and the immense party bureaucracy was probably out to get Gorbachev and return to the old corrupt, stagnant ways. The mass of the Russian people, it was said, were inherently conservative, fearing change and hating it if it came too fast and was too drastic. A tumultuous history had taught them to value stability. It had also taught them to be wary of leaders who promised better times.

Many, also, were still afraid. Afraid that if they spoke out too frankly, too publicly, now, it would be held against them if a new repressive regime gained control of the Kremlin. In that case they might again end up in a Gulag for something they said or wrote.

They were also fearful that their security might be threatened. Though their standard of living had been miserable compared to the West, at least their lives had been secure. They were guaranteed a job. There was no unemployment in Russia as there was in the West. Health care was free, and education. Many of the necessities of life were subsidized by the government and cost them little. Bread, the staple of their diet, was cheap because it was heavily subsidized. Rents were much lower than in the West. Transportation was almost free. A ride on the excellent Moscow subway cost four cents. If you went by bus, it was a cent cheaper.

Now Gorbachev was telling the people that in order to pull the economic machine out of the quagmire and improve the standard of living, certain drastic measures that would temporarily make things seem worse had to be taken. Subsidies would have to be reduced and even, in some cases, eliminated. Giant state monopolies would have to be decentralized so as to allow competition between the various parts and also from more private enterprise. Government-run industries that were operated at a loss, as so many were, would have to be reorganized or eliminated unless they could bring a profit to the state. To produce more food, which was the country's most pressing need, competition to the badly run state farms and farm collectives would be introduced by giving the peasants more land to till on their own.

The introduction of some form of competition in many parts of the Soviet economy, which would provide the incentives to produce more and distribute it better, seemed to be one of the most important foundations of Gorbachev's proposed reforms. Drastic improvement in transportation and marketing, he said, was absolutely necessary. Apparently the railroads, good as they were in comparison with the appalling state of them in the U.S.A., could not solve all of the problem. The Soviet Union needed good roads for its increasing truck traffic. One could understand why Russia, going back to the time of the czars and continuing through the Bolshevik era, had deliberately neglected building good roads. It was because they feared invasion. Bad roads, which in Russia are almost impassable in the autumn and spring "muddy" seasons, not to mention when the heavy winter snows come, helped hold back the invader, as happened to Napoleon and the Nazi

Germans when they advanced into Russia, only to be hampered and slowed by the miserable roads as autumn and then winter came.

For lack of adequate transportation and marketing facilities, some twenty percent of the fruit and vegetables in the country, I was told, was spoiled before reaching the consumer. The Crimea and the Caucasus, especially, raised great quantities of fruit and vegetables but there was no way the authorities could find to get them all to the vast markets of the great cities of the north — at least while they were fresh. Refrigerated railway cars and automotive trucks seemed to be unknown in the Soviet Union.

Fundamental reforms in the economy and in agriculture, Gorbachev warned the people, would bring higher prices — and faster at first than wages and salaries could be raised. This did not go down well with the populace. They wondered how they could make both ends meet. It had been hard enough to do it before.

While most Russians we met were excited and happy about the new cultural freedoms, I could understand their wariness. They could scarcely believe their eyes when they read in the press articles that attacked Stalin for his brutality and regime of terror and others that blamed Brezhnev for the glaring failures of the economy. They were astounded when the Kremlin began to rehabilitate most of the old Bolsheviks, Bukharin, for example, whom Stalin had shot after mock trials. All this was heady stuff, as were new plays and books that castigated Stalin and criticized a good deal that had happened since his death. But, as I learned by personal experience, there were limits to *glasnost*.

When my Russian friend telephoned old friends of hers in Moscow asking if she could drop in on them with me, an American, some of them hesitated to say yes. They were frankly afraid that my presence might get them into trouble with the party spy at their apartment house, who would report to higher party officials. One hesitant family assented only after we promised not to speak a word of English when we entered the building. The old woman who had the first room on the left beyond the entrance, we were warned, was the Communist stooge for the apartment house, who checked on everyone entering. She had not yet heard, my hosts joked after we were safely in their fourth-floor apartment, of Gorbachev's *glasnost*.

Neither, it was obvious, had a lot of higher-ups. Jews, who had waited for years to emigrate, were still being denied permission to leave. If they protested too loudly and especially to a foreigner and more especially to an American, they might well find themselves in trouble.

One very hot day we were invited to lunch by an eminent Jewish physician. His wife, who was not Jewish, had been a brilliant young scientist whose career was cut short by the authorities when she married him. I had had no idea that official anti-Semitism applied to such persons. Seven years before they had asked for permission to emigrate to Australia. Because of their eminence in their respective fields, they had been assured there would be no difficulty. As a result, they had shipped their furniture and their library to Australia, expecting that they would arrive by air before their goods did. But year after year their exit visas had been held up.

The afternoon we sat down to lunch with them they were desperate. They felt they had been humiliated long enough. Even the way we arrived had been a small humiliation, the doctor said. In the first place, our rendezvous had been arranged only after he and we had resorted to pay telephones in Moscow's side streets. I never telephoned from my room in the hotel, and he was careful about whom he phoned from his home or office. He insisted on fetching us for lunch. But he warned it would not be advisable to drive up to the hotel, swarming with agents of the KGB — not advisable for him or for us. So he arranged to pick us up on a small side street several blocks from the hotel.

We had much good talk at their table, for they were a very civilized couple. But as the meal wore on, they appeared to me to grow more and more nervous. And bitter. Finally, the doctor told us why.

At 5:00 P.M., he said, he and his wife and their three young children were going to join another family, which was in a similar fix, and go out in the street and stage a miniature demonstration. They had painted placards telling of their plight. They had also called a French TV correspondent, who had said he would arrive with a cameraman to film them.

"I don't have much hope this will move the authorities," the doctor said. "But we're desperate. They won't let my wife work at her profession. And I can't stand it any longer to be persecuted for my race."

He drove us back to a small street some distance from the hotel and we wished him well. We said we would call him later from a pay phone down the street to see how they made out.

When we phoned around 10:00 P.M., the doctor's telephone line had been cut. We thought of taking a taxi to their home but realized it might further endanger them. How my Russian friend soon found out what had happened to them she declined to tell me. She would only say, jokingly, that in Russia there was a vast underground grapevine by which people learned a great deal of what was going on. Anyway, within a couple of days, my friend found out that the militia had broken up the little demonstration of the two families, but not until the French TV had photographed it. The doctor was arrested and sentenced to two weeks in jail "for blocking the traffic." His wife and the children were put under house arrest. This prevented us from visiting her before we left.

We did not write them for fear of making their situation even worse. It would not have been helpful to them if they were found having further contacts with an American. But somehow my Russian friend found out that eventually there was a happy ending to their story after all. Gorbachev's more tolerant policy had an effect. Two years later the family was allowed to emigrate to Australia.

I had come, as I have noted, to Russia this time not only to see how things had begun to change under Gorbachev but also to do some background work for a play about Tolstoy. Above all, I wanted to get the feel for the two homes he had spent his life in, his house in Moscow and, more important, his country place at Yasnaya Polyana, an old family estate on which he passed most of his years, particularly the great creative ones during which he wrote his two masterpieces, *War and Peace* and *Anna Karenina*. The scenes of any play about him, or of any book, for that matter, would be laid mostly there. It was important to visit the Tolstoy home in the capital not only for its intrinsic interest but also because the Tolstoy Museum was located there, and I hoped to find some material that had been unavailable in the Russian bookstores. A new book about Tolstoy in Moscow had just been acclaimed by the Soviet reviewers, but I had tried in vain to find a copy of it in the bookshops. I thought perhaps I would find it at the Tolstoy Museum. Maybe the curator would have a spare copy.

But when we arrived one morning at the Tolstoy house, a guide informed us that the curator would not be in that day. Before we left, several hours later, I had found out that doing research in the Soviet Union was interesting in ways one had not anticipated.

The guide, it seemed to us, began to offer a very perfunctory tour of the old house as if she were most anxious to get rid of us as soon as possible — she had expressed surprise that a foreigner could be interested in Tolstoy. By the time we climbed to the second floor and entered the spacious living room with its grand piano in one corner and a long table in another, my Russian friend, whom we might as well start calling Tania, which is not her name, became so exasperated that she turned on the guide and burst out in a torrent of words spoken so rapidly and so emotionally that I could scarcely catch a word. But I got the gist. Here, she was saying, albeit with some exaggeration, was a distinguished American writer, a student of Tolstoy, who had come a long way to visit this house and museum and who deserved better than this insultingly perfunctory tour the guide was giving us. Mr. Shirer, she said, loved Russia, loved Tolstoy, had come here to learn more about the Master, but he was certainly not learning anything from her.

I must say the woman, in her middle fifties, I guessed, who had mentioned that she was a former actress, seemed shocked by Tania's outburst. She started to apologize.

"I'm very sorry," she said. "I mistook you for the kind of tourists we get here every day, who don't give a damn really about Tolstoy. I heard you speaking a foreign language — German is it? — and I thought you probably cared even less than our Russian tourists."

The good lady, who had been so haughty, became very humble.

"We will start all over," she said, and led us back downstairs. She was now quite a different person. Someone had stuffed a lot of knowledge of Tolstoy in this house into her. It was several hours before we finished. In fact, almost the entire day had passed; it was closing time. And I had learned a great deal.

Most reluctantly in 1881 Tolstoy with his family had moved for the winter from his country place at Yasnaya Polyana, which he loved, to Moscow, which he hated. He had not always felt that way about it. In his mid-twenties he had sowed his wild oats there, gambling, drinking, and patronizing the city's many brothels. But now he was fifty-three, with a wife and several children. With his flowing beard turning white, he had begun to look like an old patriarch. He was also, after writing *War and Peace* and *Anna Karenina,* the most famous writer in Russia and perhaps in the world. And since he turned fifty he had been undergoing a conversion that he hoped would transform his life. It was a grave middle-age crisis. He was seeking to find himself as a Christian. He believed he must give up the good life of the rich and privileged aristocracy and live like a peasant, and if possible like a saint. And that his wife and children should try to follow him.

But Countess Tolstoy was not interested. She had eight children who had been growing up in the isolated countryside without formal education except that provided by none-too-bright tutors. It was time for the family, she urged her husband, to return at least for the winter to Moscow, where she had grown up, and put the children in regular schools. The eldest son, Sergei, was eighteen and ready for the university. After much argument between the spouses, Tolstoy grudgingly agreed. But he professed to hate almost every minute of it. On October 5, 1881, only a month after arriving, he jotted down in his diary: "Moscow. A month gone by, the hardest month of my life."

Old friends were puzzled. Here was a man acclaimed worldwide as a great novelist, an original thinker. He was a wealthy aristocrat with two or three great estates. He was blessed with an attractive and intelligent wife and eight fine children. What more could he want out of life? Such a man had to be happy. But here he was proclaiming his misery, his discontent with himself, his life, his family. And though outsiders might not suspect it, the great man and his formidable wife had fallen into a rut of horrendous quarreling that would plague them all the rest of their days.

After spending the first winter in a large house that Sophia Tolstoy had rented and her husband detested, he had found a place he liked and the next year bought: a wooden house of sixteen rooms with a large garden, located in a factory district that included a distillery, a stocking manufacturer, a brewery, and a spinning mill. Tolstoy was pleased that he could live among the workers, even though in style — he had brought along twelve servants from the country.

It was in this house that Tania and I found ourselves the summer of 1986, a century later, as I continued my search for the true Tolstoy. For the next nineteen years the Tolstoy family would spend a good part of the winters here. In it, after he had settled down, he would turn out some one hundred works, including *Confession, The Kreuzer Sonata, The Death of Ivan Illych,* and his famous *Response to the Synod's Edict of Excommunication* — after the Orthodox Church in 1961 had thrown out this passionate but unorthodox Christian.

The study in which he turned out these great works was of special interest to me. It was not a large room, but it had space enough for a large desk and several chairs covered in black leather — rather ugly, I thought, but comfortable and probably appreciated by Tolstoy's literary friends who sometimes gathered there. The chair in which he sat at the desk seemed very short, and the guide explained that Tolstoy himself had sawed off several inches of the legs so that his chin was only a few inches above the table level when he worked. He was shortsighted but hated to wear glasses. Out of vanity? I wondered. Obviously when he was writing, he was alone and no one could notice how he looked in glasses. When the guests arrived, he could have taken them off.

When we returned to the big living room on the second floor, the guide was more forthcoming. It was a spacious room with the walls painted white and three large windows looking out on the garden. It was sparsely, rather than elegantly, furnished. A long table in one corner was set for a meal for fourteen, its white tablecloth, white china, and a large candelabrum laid out exactly as in Tolstoy's time, though I had noticed a large dining room downstairs. There were no pictures on the walls, only two large mirrors. At the opposite end of the room was a small round table in a corner, the rest of the space being taken by a grand piano. Tolstoy himself and his wife were fair pianists. They often played duets together, and he himself loved to have a go at Chopin and Beethoven. And it was here that Russia's great composers and musicians came to play: Tchaikovsky, Rimski-Korsakov, Rubinstein, Rachmaninoff, and Scriabin. On a memorable evening a young Chaliapin, accompanied at the piano by Rachmaninoff, sang arias from several operas.

There were also literary evenings in this room when writers gathered to discuss each other's works or read from their latest pieces. The guide mentioned Gorky, Korolenko, Leskov, among others. But the names of two other great writers, Tolstoy's rivals, Turgenev and Dostoyevski, were missing. Turgenev, whom a young Tolstoy had once challenged to a duel though they were later reconciled, visited Tolstoy at Yasnaya Polyana, which was near his own estate, but apparently never in Moscow.

Strangely enough, the two literary giants of that time, Tolstoy and Dostoyevski, never met. Each seemed to be wary of the other. Tolstoy could not stand much of what Dostoyevski wrote. Perhaps he did not try very hard. At the end, though, when he learned of Dostoyevski's death in 1881, he was deeply moved.

> I never saw the man [he wrote to his publisher] and never had any direct relations with him, and suddenly when he died, I realized that he was the very closest, dearest and most necessary man for me. . . . I was overcome: but then it became clear how precious he was to me, and I cried and am still crying.

Though Countess Tolstoy was glad to be back in her native Moscow after twenty years of life in the country, pleased that she could put the children in school and exhilarated at renewing her old social life, entertaining, going out to gala balls, attending concerts, she was far from happy with her distinguished husband. She, like him, kept a diary, but there are only three entries for 1882, the year they moved into the new house. In the first, for February 28, she writes: "Our life in Moscow would be quite delightful if only it did not make Lyovochka so unhappy." Then on August 26:

> It was twenty years ago, when I was young and happy, that I started writing the story of my love for Lyovochka in this book. Twenty years later, here I am sitting up all night on my own, reading and mourning its loss. For the first time in our life Lyovochka has run off to sleep alone in the study. We were quarreling about such silly things. . . . Today he shouted at the top of his voice that his dearest wish was to leave his family. I shall carry the memory of that heartfelt, heartrending cry of his to my grave.

In a sense she did. From that time on, though this quarrel, like so many others, would end in their tearful making up, the threat of his leaving, often imagined by her as it was, would haunt her — until it became a terrifying reality twenty-eight years later.

"I'm sorry your curator is not here today," I said to the guide at the end of the day as we went downstairs to the vestibule. "I was looking forward to talking to her. And perhaps to get some material."

"Oh, she's here," said the guide with the straightest of faces. "I will take you to her. I'm sure she would like to meet a writer from America. I do not believe we have had any before."

And off she went to find the curator, whom she had told us earlier was not there and would not be there that day. We had a fine talk with this lady. She had a good deal of material she was more than willing to provide me. Monographs by various Russian authors on Tolstoy. And booklets. I started to ask her if there were any way I could get the new book, *Tolstoy in Moscow*. It had, among other things, I was told, some wonderful pictures of each room in the Tolstoy house. It had dozens of photographs of paintings of the old Moscow of the mid-nineteenth century.

Before I could finish the sentence she got up, disappeared into what appeared to be a storeroom, and returned with a small truck with three big cartons.

"I was given 150 copies of the new *Tolstoy in Moscow* book," she said. "I was told by the party people to have plenty in stock for the delegates to the Twentieth Party Congress that ended here a few days ago. Would you believe it, not a single party delegate visited us? They were not much interested in Tolstoy, it appears. I believe they were more interested in shopping. So I have all these books. How many do you want?"

"I'll take half a dozen," I said. An American who taught Russian and Russian studies at one of our universities had begged me to try to get a copy for her. She had been in Moscow a few weeks before while on a sabbatical but had been unable to find it in any bookstore. I knew other teachers at home who would want a copy.

The good curator went out again and returned with an empty box, which we filled with the six books and other material she gave me. She talked as if I had made her day. She had certainly made mine.

Finally the morning came when I could fulfill an old dream: set out on the road to Yasnaya Polyana. Tania and I met the Intourist guide at 7:00 A.M. in front of the hotel. She and two or three men, whom I took to be KGB, were talking rather loudly with the driver of our car. He must not under any circumstances take this American into Tula, which one passed just before reaching Yasnaya Polyana. I already had been told by someone that Tula, a city of a million people and the center of the arms industry in Russia, was off limits to foreigners. That was why they could not allow me to stay overnight in a hotel there, as I had first requested. It made no difference to me. I was not interested in seeing the Soviet Union's armament manufacturing center. When they had finished with the driver, the guide, a rather prissy lady, I thought, in her early forties, turned to me and said in English: "You understand? We are not to go into Tula. You cannot stay overnight there after visiting Yasnaya Polyana. We must return to Moscow!"

"I understand," I said. *"Ya panimayu."*

"The driver has strict orders."

"It's fine with me," I said.

She and her colleagues looked at me rather suspiciously. This surprised me, for I was sure the whole trip with Tania had been cleared with the proper authorities. They knew who I was. And I didn't think I looked like a spy.

But then I aroused their suspicion anew. It was innocent enough. I turned to the Intourist guide and said that if she didn't want to make the long, tiring drive to Yasnaya Polyana and back, it was all right with me, since my friend spoke Russian and could be my interpreter.

The lady was outraged.

"I am your interpreter for today," she said sharply. "And your guide until we get to Yasnaya Polyana. There we will have a special guide."

Why she thought I needed an interpreter and guide to sit in a bouncing car for eight hours on the bumpy, dusty Tula road choked with fumes from bumper-to-bumper giant trucks that spewed exhaust smoke like little Mt. Vesuviuses (I had first observed the phenomenon when we met the Red Army in Berlin in 1945) was a naïve question I did not pose. We all understood that she was going along to keep track of us and report back to Intourist and probably to the KGB, though it seemed silly that the secret police could be interested in Tania and me. At any rate, we were stuck with her, and, after all, I realized she was just doing her job and trying to earn her living.

She turned to the others and apparently repeated in Russian what I said. They thought it was funny. They sort of chuckled. Tania and I climbed into the back seat, and our guide primly and sternly took her place next to the driver in the front seat and we were off.

Friends who had tried to make the trip without supervision had told me how they were stopped repeatedly at checkpoints every few miles by the militia. A friend from home who had made the journey a few weeks before with her husband had been halted at one checkpoint after another and finally at the last one, a few miles from Tula, told that she could not go on. Only by staging a hysterical scene had the militia finally relented and let her through. But now as we sped south, we whizzed by one checkpoint after another without even slowing down. Occasionally a guard acknowledged us with a sloppy salute.

"There must be some special sign on our car," Tania whispered to me. "Otherwise, why should they let us through? They've never done that with me before."

Later Tania concluded that there must have been a special KGB insignia on the license plate.

As we neared Tula nearly four hours later, the driver, a healthy peasant type but not too bright, slowed down to read the road signs. I saw plainly a large one that pointed to the left and said in large letters TULA. He hesitated a moment and then turned left onto what turned out to be the road into the great armaments center that was supposed to be off limits to the likes of me.

Soon we were hopelessly lost in the big city. The driver would stop to ask a worker the road to Yasnaya Polyana. None knew. Tolstoy's place, after all, was a tiny village. So we drove about for an hour, in the course of which I am sure I saw every damned armament works in Tula. They all seemed to be humming. But for all I knew, that was to be expected. Probably their counterparts at home were also going full blast, though I hadn't the slightest idea where the arms manufacturing center was in America, assuming we had one.

Our effort to get out of Tula seemed unending. We were losing valuable time. But finally we made it and drove on the five or six miles to Yasnaya Polyana. There was a café-restaurant opposite the gate to the estate, and we stopped there for a bite to eat. Our guide, obviously battered by the rugged ride, frustrated by the delay in Tula, and probably wondering darkly how she was going to explain to her superiors that she had taken this American writer into the forbidden city, sat down beside me at the table when Tania went off to the ladies' room. Tired as she was, our guide looked suspicious. I wondered what it was now.

"Your friend," she said. "How come she speaks such good Russian?"

She and Tania had had a few exchanges in Russian during the trip that I had not attempted to follow; and I did not know what, if anything, my friend had told her of herself. Tania, though she had an American passport, was always very careful what she said in her native country. If the guide were more intelligent, I thought, she would have seen that Tania spoke good Russian because it was her native language. But I was not going to get her involved, so I merely replied:

"Why don't you ask her?"

"You do not know?" she asked, surprised.

"*Da. Ya znayu,*" I said, calling on my few words of Russian. "Yes. I know. But it is better if *you* ask her."

It was easy to see why Tolstoy loved Yasnaya Polyana so passionately. Nature had made it a place of beauty and Tolstoy had endowed it with his own great spirit.

"The landscape, the view, the houses, the rooms," Ilya Repin, Russia's foremost nineteenth-century painter, remarked after his first visit, ". . . all is imbued here with a special, touching charm."

It was a gently rolling countryside, not unlike the Iowa where I had grown up, except that the soil here was not so rich. But it was more forested, especially with white-barked birches, which dominated the landscape, a tree Russians love above all others — as Tolstoy had. To him, his two thousand acres was Russia itself. "Without Yasnaya Polyana," he said, "I could hardly imagine Russia."

He was born there, in 1828, spent his childhood and early youth there, returned there after some years in Kazan and in military service in the Caucasus and at Sebastopol in the Crimea, brought his eighteen-year-old bride home there when he was thirty-four, and lived the rest of his life there, except for some winters in Moscow, until that dramatic early dawn of October 28, 1910, when, aged eighty-two, he stole out on tiptoe of the house in the autumn cold and darkness, abandoning his wife of forty-eight years to seek a little peace and quiet before he died. Ten days later, in the stationmaster's lonely little cottage opposite the railroad station in the small town of Ostapovo, he was dead.

Such a surprising tragedy and pathetic end for so great a man had haunted me since I first read about it in my youth. How could it have happened? And more important, why? In the beginning most critics, in Russia and abroad, blamed Tolstoy's formidable wife, Sophia Andreyevna, who they said had made life unbearable for her distinguished husband by her constant nagging and by the ugly quarrels and hysterical scenes she provoked. But later, when more was learned of the turbulent life of the Tolstoys and especially after the diary of Countess Tolstoy was published, it became evident that not all the blame, by any means, could be put on Sophia; that the old man himself carried a heavy responsibility, and that it was a very complicated story, which could not be depicted in blacks and whites. One critic, the French biographer Martine de Courcel, wrote a very civilized book, *Tolstoy — the Ultimate Reconciliation*, to prove that he finally left home in his old age, abandoning wife and family, because he had to get away to resume writing — a thesis that was not convincing to me.

My own conclusion, reached after years of thinking about it and reading all the material I could find — and it was vast — was that the final, tragic break had come as the inevitable climax of nearly half a century of a wonderful but stormy marriage of two very great personalities of tremendous ego, the man a genius, the woman formidable in her intelligence, drive, stubbornness, and love of her family. Both had strong temperaments, and Sophia, as she grew older, was subject to terrible outbursts of hysteria that jarred on the other. On that October evening there had been a final provocation that the fatigued and sorely tried author could no longer take from his wife. It caused something within him to snap. It forced him to a desperate act, to flee the family and home he loved in the dead of the freezing night. He sought not a place to resume writing — at eighty-two his *oeuvre* was pretty well finished — but a refuge from the hell of matrimonial strife, a place where he could have a little peace and quiet at the end of a long and stormy life.

Perhaps on this visit to Yasnaya Polyana, I could come across some new insights.

*   *   *

We entered the grounds between two old pillars that stood at the bottom of the birch-lined avenue that led up to the main house. The entrance itself was on the old Kiev road on which passed by, season after season, year after year, pilgrims setting off for or returning from the holy places that dotted the Russian land. Many would be on their way to Kiev and the famous Pechersky monastery there. Tolstoy, in his peasant blouse and high boots, often went down to the road to talk with them, "the fools of God," as they were called. He was fascinated by their tales. He often felt an urge to join them.

It was a very warm day — the record-breaking heat spell was relentless — and because of the heat and my heart condition, I had to take the ascending path to the main house slowly. It was not a grand palace by any means but a comfortably large country house of some twenty rooms. In 1862, when Tolstoy had brought his bride there from Moscow, it was much less imposing. The once-great mansion in which he was born had been broken up and most of it moved away to pay for gambling debts the young Tolstoy had run up while in the army. Only one small wing had remained for the bride and groom to start their life in — not nearly big enough to house the family when the children began to appear, as they did regularly nearly every year. So as his literary fortunes prospered and growing royalties came in, Tolstoy had added on one wing to each side of the main building.

Inside it seemed somewhat austere. Most rooms had floors of rough, wide planks without rugs or carpets, and were relatively small and not well lit. Not well heated, either, I judged, in Tolstoy's time. Now in 1986 central heating had replaced the old wood stoves. There was very little upholstered furniture in the house, though there was a large leather-covered couch in Tolstoy's study on which he and his brothers and sister and most of his children were born.

The Grande Salle was the most spacious room in the house, and it was there that the lively family life was centered. Meals were taken at a long table at one end. At the other end were two grand pianos at which Tolstoy and his wife often played, as well as visiting guests. I saw a photograph somewhere in the house taken by Countess Tolstoy of Alexander Goldenwieser, the pianist, and S. T. Taneyev, the composer and pianist, playing the pianos. Goldenwieser would become an ardent Tolstoyan and Taneyev the object of a strange, unrequited love of Sophia Tolstoy — much to the annoyance of her husband, who even before this bizarre happening used to say that Taneyev got on his nerves.

At a round table in one corner other visiting luminaries, Turgenev,

Fet, Chekhov, Leskov, Korolenko, Gorky, and others sometimes gathered to discuss the latest news from Moscow and Petersburg and sometimes to read their works.

More often Tolstoy gathered there in the evening to chat with his wife and children and to read to them from his latest writing. On many an evening, if he could find a partner, Tolstoy would steal away to another corner of the room to play chess, which for him as for many Russians became a lifelong passion.

With the acquiescence of our special guide, a pleasant and attractive young woman who appeared to have memorized her remarks, which were informative but not very insightful, we moved quickly to the rooms that interested me most, where Tolstoy had worked at his writing and pondered the fate of Russia, mankind, and the world, where he and his wife had slept, the very rooms in which had taken place the dramatic denouement of the lives of Leo and Sophia Tolstoy on that October night of 1910. They were all on the second floor.

The library was too small to hold Tolstoy's twenty-two thousand books, so they were scattered in bookshelves all over the house. But the thousands of volumes that were there shed light on the great man's intellectual growth. There were books, for instance, in Greek and Hebrew, which Tolstoy had learned after his "conversion" at fifty when he had sought to achieve a better understanding of the New Testament, especially the Gospels, and of the Old Testament than he believed he was getting from the Orthodox Church. There were books in English, French, and German as well as Russian, on history, literature, philosophy, and science. There must have been a thousand books, Russian and foreign, autographed and inscribed to Tolstoy. The guide allowed me to thumb through a few of the books. There were dozens of annotations in the margins in Tolstoy's handwriting. In nearly every book he read, he noted down his reactions.

There were more books to peruse in Tolstoy's study, a room I found fascinating. According to the guide, the books in a two-tiered bookrack on the wall above his desk had been burned by German troops when they occupied the house between October 29, 1941 and early November of the following year, but they had been replaced after the war by identical copies. One of them on the second tier attracted my attention: a book in English by one Joseph D. Doke entitled *M. K. Gandhi — Indian Patriot in South Africa*.

In my time in India, Gandhi had often talked to me of the immense influence of Tolstoy on him.

"Have you read him?" he asked once.

"Yes. Most of the great novels, I think. Besides *War and Peace* and *Anna Karenina*, I've read *Resurrection* and *The Kreuzer Sonata*."

But Gandhi was not interested in Tolstoy's fiction.

"I mean," he said, "have you read *The Kingdom of God Is Within You, The Gospels in Brief, What Can Be Done?*, and his other great works on religion and philosophy?"

In his autobiography Gandhi wrote: "Tolstoy's *The Kingdom of God Is Within You* overwhelmed me. It left an abiding impression on me. Before the independent thinking, profound morality and the truthfulness of this book, all the books [that he had previously been reading] seemed to pale into insignificance."

Later, Gandhi wrote, he made "an intensive study of Tolstoy's other books." They caused him to realize, he said, "the infinite possibilities of universal love."*

No wonder that when Gandhi set up his commune in the Transvaal in South Africa in 1910, the year of the great writer's death, he called it "Tolstoy Farm."

Gandhi and Tolstoy had come into contact with each other by correspondence in 1909 when the young leader of the Indians in South Africa had written to the Russian writer about the condition of the Indians in the Transvaal and asked permission to publish a letter Tolstoy had written to an Indian editor in India. Tolstoy had answered (in English) from Yasnaya Polyana on September 25, 1909, saying that Gandhi's letter had given him "great pleasure" and that he was free to publish his letter.

"God help our dear brothers and workers in the Transvaal," he added. "I greet you fraternally and am glad to have intercourse with you."

A year later, on September 7, 1910, only seven weeks before his hasty departure from Yasnaya Polyana, Tolstoy again wrote Gandhi, this time a letter of some two thousand words and this time in Russian (translated by his chief disciple, Vladimir Chertkov) apparently so he could express his thoughts with greater precision and clarity. It is a long summary of his views of nonviolence and passive resistance and their relation to Christianity, written at a moment, he said, when he felt the "nearness of death." Gandhi published it in his Transvaal journal *Indian Opinion* on November 26, 1910, a few days after Tolstoy's death.

* *Gandhi — The Story of My Experiments with Truth.* Beacon Press. Boston. Paperback ed., pp. 137, 160.

Glancing at the books in English in Tolstoy's study, I recalled a letter he had written, also in English, to Edward Garnet, the British critic, who had asked the Russian writer for a statement to American readers that he could insert in an article he was writing for *Harper's Magazine* on Tolstoy's new book, *Resurrection*. Replying on June 21, 1900, from Yasnaya Polyana (probably doing it in this very study), Tolstoy wrote that at first he hesitated to "send any message to the American people" but that on reflection

> it came to me that if I had to address the American people, I should like to thank them for the great help from their writers who flourished about [the] fifties. I would mention Garrison, Parker, Emerson, Ballou, Thoreau, not as the greatest, but as those who I think specially influenced me. Other names are Channing, Whittier, Lowell, Walt Whitman — a bright constellation, such as is rarely to be found in the literatures of the world.*
>
> And I should like to ask the American people why they do not pay more attention to these voices (hardly to be replaced by those of Gould, Rockefeller and Carnegie) and continue the good work in which they made such hopeful progress.

It was a good question, I thought. Apparently Americans at the beginning of the century valued their poets no more than they did at its end.

We had never had a writer who was so revered by the masses as Tolstoy. There was a reminder of this on his desk, a heavy, greenish, crystal paperweight sent to him by the workers at the Matltsov glassworks at Bryannsk. He took much pride in the inscription.

* Tolstoy forgot to include in his list the American writer who he often said had the most influence on him: Henry George, the single-tax advocate. As I glanced at the wall in Tolstoy's study in the midst of this recollection, I saw a portrait of Henry George on the wall above his desk. Tolstoy's admiration for Henry George and his idea of the single tax never waned. In a letter to an American correspondent in 1894, Tolstoy wrote: "Henry George has sent me all his books. I knew some of them before, but some others as the 'Perplexed Philosopher' and others were new to me. The more I know of him, the more I esteem him, and am astonished at the indifference of the civilized world to his work."

Tolstoy added that should the new czar ask his advice on how to run Russia, he would ask him to introduce "the single-tax system."

On close inspection, there were portraits of other Americans on the walls of his study. One was a photograph of an American I had never heard of, Ernest H. Crosby. I made a note to look up his name and I found it in the American edition of Tolstoy's letters. There the editor, R. F. Christian, revealed that Crosby (1856–1906) had served in the New York State Assembly and later as a judge in the International Court in Egypt, resigning after having been converted to Tolstoy's beliefs. He visited Yasnaya Polyana in 1894. Tolstoy advised him to work with Henry George for the single tax.

Near one window was a portrait of William Lloyd Garrison with the inscription in English: "Liberty for each, for all, and forever!" Wm. Lloyd Garrison. Boston. October 23, 1873.

Most Esteemed Leo Nikolayevich:
You have shared the fate of numerous great men who surpassed their century. Formerly they were burned at the stake or they were left to rot in prisons or in exile. The "great priests," Pharisees, can excommunicate you as they wish. The Russian people will always be proud of you, their great, their dear, their beloved Tolstoy.

Scores of letters, not only from Russians of all sorts but also from foreigners all over the world, arrived at Yasnaya Polyana daily and were answered, many by Tolstoy himself, many at his direction by a full-time secretary and by his wife and children. To help them with the correspondence and also with copying manuscripts, a Remington typewriter, with Russian letters, had been sent the family from America. Though puzzled by the new-fangled contraption, the household soon got the hang of it and found it invaluable. Tolstoy's almost indecipherable manuscripts, which previously had been copied by hand by Sophia were henceforth typed. So were the letters, all on the old Remington set up in the secretary's office. The children called it the "Remington Room." All in all, Tolstoy received some fifty thousand letters in his lifetime. The letters he himself wrote occupy thirty volumes out of the ninety volumes of *The Complete Works of Tolstoy*, published in Moscow over a long period beginning in 1928, the hundredth anniversary of his birth.

I noticed another American gadget as I was leaving Tolstoy's study. In 1908, Thomas Edison had sent the Russian writer a phonograph. The gift caused great excitement in the household. Tolstoy was persuaded to use it in dictating letters and even articles. But he found it difficult to operate and after a few months gave it up. In the process, luckily, his voice was preserved on the recordings. But as I recalled hearing it some years before, it came out high pitched and scratchy, due probably to the state of the art at the beginning of the century.

A door led from the study into Tolstoy's bedroom. Beyond it was the bedroom of his wife. It was in these rooms and in the study that the brief acts took place on that October night of 1910 that led to the great writer's final flight from home.

Tolstoy's bedroom reflected the ascetic tastes of the last years of his life. A narrow brass bed (the guide called it an "iron bed") and next to it a night table, a trunk, and a wash-table. Only two pictures on the walls. No rugs or carpets covered the rough, wide-planked floor. In this room, the guide said, as in some of the others, the Germans had spread straw and set it afire as they left. The fire, she added, destroyed half the floor, a part of one wall, and the ceiling.

Sophia's bedroom, in contrast, which occupied the front corner of the upstairs, was crammed with furniture and with pictures of her husband, children, grandchildren, parents, and friends. There was a high commode and several small tables and a larger writing desk. At this desk Countess Tolstoy had spent a good part of her days, for she kept the daily accounts of the estate, wrote out the daily menus, kept up a large correspondence, made clear copies of her husband's manuscripts for the printer, corrected his proofs, and wrote daily entries in her diary. In one corner of the room was an old sewing machine, old even, she said, when she was given it by her mother, and on which she made all the blouses and underwear of her husband and repaired her own clothing and that of the children.

Obviously Sophia Andreyevna was a busy woman, which her husband, absorbed in his writing and his teaching, often seemed to have forgotten. If only she had contented herself with doing these things she did so well. But she was suspicious of her husband (not without reason) and this had gnawed at her for years until toward the end it had ended in a terrible obsession. She was sure he had made a secret will, at the instigation of her archenemy Vladimir Chertkov, a former guards officer who had turned Tolstoyan and pretty much taken over the man he worshipped, a will, she believed, that turned over the rest of the writer's copyrights and perhaps the estate itself to the Foundation Chertkov had set up to preserve the works of the master — leaving Sophia and the children penniless.

Her pervasive suspicion was what, late on the night of October 28, 1910, had caused her to jump up from her bed, light a candle, peep into her husband's bedroom to see that he was asleep, and proceed into his study to rummage through the drawers of his desk and tables and even under the leather covering of the old couch to find his secret diary for the last few days, which might give a clue to the whereabouts of the will or even its contents, or better still, to discover the will itself.

Her prowling awakened her husband. He told what followed in a diary entry the next day, jotted down in the Optina Monastery, the first stop on his precipitate flight.

October 28 [1910]. Went to bed at 11.30. Slept until after two. Woke up, and again, as on previous nights, I heard the opening of doors and footsteps. On previous nights I hadn't looked at my door, but this time I did look and saw through the crack a bright light in my study and heard rustling. It was Sophia Andreyevna looking for something and probably reading. The day before she was asking and insisting that I shouldn't lock my doors. Both her doors were open so that she could hear my slightest movement. Day and night all my movements and words have to be known to her and under her control. There were footsteps again, again the door opened carefully and she walked through the room.

I don't know why, but this aroused indignation and uncontrollable revulsion in me. I wanted to go back to sleep but couldn't; I tossed about for an hour or so, lit a candle and sat up. Sophia Andreyevna opened the door and came in, asking about 'my health' and expressing surprise at the light which she had seen in my room.

My indignation and revulsion grew. I gasped for breath, counted my pulse: 97. I couldn't go on lying there, and suddenly I took the final decision to leave. I wrote her a letter and began to pack the most necessary things, just so that I could leave. I woke Dusan and then Sasha* and they helped me pack. I trembled at the thought that she would hear and come out — that there would be a scene, hysterics — and I wouldn't be able to leave her without a scene.

Everything was packed somehow or other before 6; I walked to the stables to tell them to harness the horses. . . . The night was pitch black, I lost my way to the outhouse, found myself in a thicket, pricked myself, bumped into some trees, fell over, lost my cap, couldn't find it, made my way out again with an effort, went back home, took another cap and with the aid of a lantern made my way to the stables and ordered the horses to be harnessed. . . . I trembled as I waited to be pursued. But then we were on our way.

At that little railroad station at Shchekino a few kilometers from Yasnaya Polyana, they had to wait an hour for the train and Tolstoy wrote that "every minute I expected her to appear." But finally the train arrived, Tolstoy and Dusan got in (Sasha was left behind to give her mother the news and to report to her father on her mother's reaction) and the fugitive's trembling fear subsided. "Pity for her," he says, "rose up within me, but no doubt about having done what I had to do."

Considering the circumstances in which it was written, the desperation of the old man, the fear and trembling that he might be caught before he could escape, Tolstoy's departing letter to his wife of forty-eight years is remarkably composed. Sophia did not awaken the next morning until 11 A.M. Sasha then handed her the letter.

My departure will distress you. I'm sorry about this, but do understand and believe that I couldn't do otherwise. My position in the house

---

* Dr. Dusan Makovitsky, a Slovak and ardent Tolstoyan, was the family doctor, who lived in the house. Sasha was Alexandra, Tolstoy's youngest daughter, who sided with her father against her mother.

is becoming, or has become, unbearable. Apart from everything else, I can't live any longer in these conditions of luxury in which I have been living, and I'm doing what old men of my age commonly do; leaving this worldly life in order to live the last days of my life in peace and solitude.

Please understand this and don't come after me, even if you find out where I am. Your coming would only make your position and mine worse and wouldn't alter my decision. I thank you for your honorable 48 years of life with me, and I beg you to forgive me for everything for which I am to blame towards you, just as I forgive you with all my soul for everything for which you may have been to blame towards me. I advise you to reconcile yourself to this new situation which my departure puts you in, and to have no unkind feelings toward me. If you want to let me know anything, tell Sasha; she will know where I am and will send on what is necessary; but she can't tell you where I am because I have made her promise not to tell anyone.

He signed it "Leo Tolstoy."

Sophia Tolstoy did not see her husband again until he was breathing his last and was unconscious of her presence. At Astapovo as he lay dying in the modest station-master house their children and her old enemy, Chertkov, would not let her into the house even to say farewell and to ask, as she pleaded she wanted to do, forgiveness from the husband she realized she had driven from home. I have seen a haunting photograph, taken I believe from a movie film shot by a Pathé News photographer, one of a thousand journalists who milled about the little railroad station, that shows Countess Tolstoy, a *platok* over her head and a long dark coat enveloping the rest of her body, standing on tiptoe at a window of the room where she knew her husband's life was ebbing away and stretching to see through it to him. Then she was taken away to a railroad car on a siding in which she was staying. On the last day, after he had lost consciousness, she was finally permitted to enter the room and embrace her husband and, though he could not hear her, ask for his forgiveness.

It was time to leave Yasnaya Polyana. Tania and the Intourist guide had gone over to see Tolstoy's grave, a simple mound without a mark of identification on it deep in the woods. I could not go along because of the heat and my faltering heart and because I needed to be alone for a few moments to collect my thoughts. I sat down on a bench near the porch of the old residence. The sun was going down beyond the birch and lime trees behind the house. The old writer had seen so many sunsets from this very spot and they made him rejoice over life that at other gloomier times seemed to him so cruel and meaningless. I remembered his elation at watching one sunset in particular and what he had written about it in a diary entry for 1904.

> I looked at the sunset. What a joy! And I thought: no, this world is not a mere bubble, an ordeal only before passing into a better and eternal world, but is itself one of the eternal worlds which is beautiful and radiant, and in which we not only can but must make more beautiful and radiant for people who live with us and who will live after us.

As I sat on that hard bench my thoughts also turned to the Germans. They had occupied Yasnaya Polyana, and according to books I had read and now the testimony of the guide this day they had behaved like beasts, pilfering or destroying various objects in the house which the Russians had not been able to carry away and finally barbarously setting fire to the great house as they left. It had been saved, though not without some damage, by the heroic efforts of peasants, police, and volunteer firemen from the neighborhood, none of whom, perhaps like the German soldiers, probably had read Tolstoy but who revered a great writer and a great soul.

Why, I wondered, I who had sat in Berlin in the 1930s and watched the Nazi Germans march off to conquer the world, and who had seen them try to destroy their own fine culture, a part of Western civilization, after all — why did the Germans have this barbaric mania for destroying the great cultural works in the lands they occupied? In Russia, perhaps, especially? I had seen another terrible example of it four years before at the palace of Catherine at Pushkin, formerly Tsarskoye Selo (the czar's village), fifteen miles from Leningrad. It was a splendid work of art, of which the Russians were immensely proud — both before and after the Bolshevik Revolution.

German troops had arrived in September 1941, to begin the siege of Leningrad, which they were unable to take, and had departed in January 1944 when the general German retreat had forced them to abandon the siege. According to the Russians, German army detachments, stationed in the palace during the long siege, used the immense Throne Room, a work of art in itself, as a stable for their horses. Our guides produced photographs of the great hall, the floors strewn with straw, and horses scattered about. The Germans also pilfered numerous works of art that had not been carted away in time by the Russians. All this was bad enough, but much worse was to follow. As they were departing, the Russians swear, the Germans blew up the palace, destroying it.

In 1982, Russian workmen were still rebuilding the palace. But most of it had been restored — just as it was before, in all its splendor, and the Russians were very proud of it. But they wondered why the Germans had behaved so barbarously. One of the guides approached me. He had heard from someone in our party, he said, that I had been an American correspondent in Germany during the Nazi horror.

"You know the Germans, they tell me. Then perhaps you can tell me. Why do they blow up a palace like this? Did we blow up their palaces when our troops got to Berlin? Perhaps you were there at the end, and can tell me."

"Yes," I said. "I was in Berlin at the end, and the Russians did not blow up any palaces. All they blew up was Hitler's bunker. Our bombing pretty well destroyed the kaiser's old palace in the center of Berlin. But the old imperial palaces at Potsdam largely escaped the bombing. In fact, your Marshal Zukov occupied the crown prince's palace at Potsdam. But he did not use any part of it as a stable. I was invited out there once, to a party he gave on the anniversary of your revolution. The place was spick and span. And Marshal Zukov did not blow it up when he left."

"Then why do the Germans do it?" he persisted.

"I cannot explain it," I said. "All one can say is that's the way they are."

We arrived in Moscow that summer of 1986 exactly four weeks after the Russian nuclear plant at Chernobyl overheated and blew up, causing the worst atomic disaster in history. The poisonous fallout from the burnt-out reactor, which had spread more than a thousand miles to the far corners of western and northern Europe and done great damage to fields, lakes, and streams and to crops and grazing animals, had pretty much subsided. But the political fallout from the Soviet government's irresponsibility in first refusing to inform its own people and those countries which lay in the path of the windblown nuclear fumes had not dissipated.

The Kremlin itself was still in disarray about what to do, or at least what to tell. Despite *glasnost* — Gorbachev had been in power fourteen months — the government had not yet come clean about the facts. The blowout at Reactor Number Four at Chernobyl had occurred at 1:24 A.M. on Saturday, April 26. An explosion followed by a raging graphite fire that was so hot it melted the uranium and plutonium in the pressure tubes threatened to release thousands of tons of radioactive clouds into the atmosphere. Yet Moscow said not a word, not even when the Swedish government, which had detected incoming waves of radioactive air, asked it on Sunday, the twenty-seventh, if something was amiss in any of its nuclear plants. The answer, from an official of the Soviet Atomic Energy Commission in Moscow, was that he had no knowledge of any damage to a Russian reactor. It was not until the evening of Monday, April 28, two and a half days after the reactor blew, that Tass, the official Soviet news agency, issued a curt announcement that there had been "an accident" at the atomic energy plant at Chernobyl and that it was being investigated. There was no warning to the public as to what the consequences might be, though secretly the government had begun the evacuation of more than one hundred thousand people from the area around the stricken plant. When later in the week a little more information was given out, it was accompanied by an attack on the West, "for artificially stirring up a public outcry over Chernobyl."

In Moscow, in the absence of a press that was trusted by Russians, the wildest rumors spread and were still afloat when we arrived. One was that thousands of people had been killed and tens of thousands stricken by fallout. Refugees from Kiev, just south of the disaster area, were still packing the trains that arrived at the Kiev station in Moscow. But out of fear of the KGB, apparently, they said little. Russians were still skeptical about *glasnost*. They had learned to keep their mouths shut.

During our stay in Moscow, the silliest stories about Chernobyl continued to appear in the press, designed to assure the public that there was nothing to worry about. One day at the beginning of June, Tania called my attention to a piece in one — I think it was *Isvestia*, the newspaper of the government (*Pravda* was the daily paper of the party) — which was astonishing, but typical. A reporter and his photographer had chartered a boat at Kiev and motored up the Dnieper River to Chernobyl, where the Pripyat River empties into the Dnieper. They reported having a jolly time. Despite all the lies in the foreign press about the waters around Chernobyl being contaminated, they reported they had taken a long swim in the river, spent pleasant hours fishing off their boat, and had eaten the fish for supper. And this in an area where, as we learned later from the official Soviet account, a thousand square miles had to be decontaminated, one hundred and twelve thousand people evacuated and where besides twenty-nine killed, hundreds were severely injured by the fallout and thousands more subject to amounts of radioactivity so strong as to imperil their health for the rest of their lives.

What stands out in my memory of those tense days in Russia just after the inferno at Chernobyl was the realization that man had not yet learned to prevent or to cope with disasters to our nuclear power-generating plants. For the first forty-eight hours after it happened, the Soviet government was paralyzed by the news. It was as if its leaders could not believe it. When we were in Moscow, we heard that perhaps the Kremlin didn't really know what had occurred because the truth was being withheld from them by the party boss of the Ukraine, one Vladimir Shscherbitsky, who was also a member of the Politbureau. But this was not true. One of the leading Soviet nuclear scientists, V. A. Legasov, disclosed that he was told of the accident around 10 A.M. of the morning it happened and by noon he had been appointed a member of a government commission to go immediately to the scene and decide what should be done to stop the fire and halt the emission of radioactivity. He got there early enough that evening, he later testified, to see from eight to ten miles away the sky over Chernobyl lit up in an awesome crimson glow. He also found the Russian engineers at the plant and public officials "at loggerheads." They couldn't agree on how to put out the raging graphite fire.

Eventually the Soviet government did come clean about the Chernobyl blowout. In its report to the International Atomic Energy Agency in Vienna, it disclosed for the first time the immense amount of fallout. "In all about 100 million curies of radioactivity were released into the atmosphere, about 3½ percent of the reactor's total inventory, including all the gaseous fission products, about 20 percent of the iodine and 10 percent of the caesium."

The Kremlin put the blame for the accident on the engineers who were on duty that night it happened, conducting an unauthorized experiment that ironically was meant to test the safety of the reactor. But in so doing, they committed six violations of their own rules. The government also acknowledged defects in the Russian designs for atomic reactors.

But the causes went deeper. The principal one was noted, in of all places, the columns of *Pravda* a couple of years later. In an article that could not have been published even when we were in Moscow in 1986, Legasov enumerated all the mistakes that had culminated in the disaster to Reactor Number Four at Chernobyl. The system of safeguards, he wrote, was defective and "the scientists knew it." But nothing was done to remedy the situation. "There were mistakes at every turn," he continued — human mistakes of the operators, mistakes in the projects and plans. The scientist said his blood "ran cold" when he read the transcript of telephone conversations between the operators the night of the catastrophe.

> One operator rings another and asks: "The manual says what has to be done but there's a lot crossed out. What shall I do?" The man on the other end of the line thinks for a moment and replies: "Do what's crossed out."

But apart from all the blunders in operation and all the faults in design, there was one overriding, fundamental conclusion reached by Legasov that helps explain not only the blowup at Chernobyl but what had happened to the whole of industry, to the very economy of the Soviet Union after seventy years of Communism.

"The accident at Chernobyl," he concluded, *"was the apotheosis and the highest point of all that was wrong in the management of our country's economy, and had been for many decades."*

It was a statement that would have cost him his life under Stalin and a long spell in a Siberian Gulag under Khrushchev and Brezhnev, but now under Gorbachev was being published in the party's newspaper itself. The piece appeared in *Pravda* on May 20, 1988. Three weeks before, Legasov had killed himself.

Like us, after our own disaster at Three Mile Island, the Russians in the end learned a significant lesson from Chernobyl. They agreed that a serious accident to a nuclear plant henceforth would no longer be regarded as a Russian problem but as an international problem, that a damage to a plant on the Dnieper might pollute the atmosphere above Iceland or Lapland or any other far place and cause grievous damage. From now on, the Kremlin would join other governments in a frank and honest and timely warning system.

In a cynical, quarreling world, this was progress.

There was another lesson to be pondered by Chernobyl, it seemed to me. If the relatively simple operation of nuclear power-generating plants and also those that made nuclear ammunition for the big bombs was subject to human error, despite all the marvelous computers and other gadgets that were supposed to regulate and control them, then President Ronald Reagan's proposed Star Wars defense against a Soviet nuclear attack was also subject to the mistakes human beings inevitably make. And that since this was so, we could not depend on it to repel a nuclear assault from abroad.

For years, I had been saying in lectures, in articles, and in letters to our newspapers that, in my opinion, Star Wars was a hoax, a delusion of the president that unfortunately had fooled most Americans. Worse,

I thought the president's massive propaganda for it was deceiving the American people into believing that there could be an absolute defense against nuclear attack.

I believe Star Wars will shortly be exposed as an impossible dream, a massively expensive project that could not work, and that there is no way in the foreseeable future, given our limited knowledge of space technology, to turn back an assault in the skies launched by either side. But even if there eventually were such a possibility and a space defensive system run by computers more advanced than we can imagine today, it would be subject to human error. Computers would break down or run amok. Men would lose control as they did at Chernobyl. The human race would be wiped out.

On the train from Moscow to Leningrad and on to Helsinki, I watched from the window the fields of wheat and the great forests pass by. Tania remarked that there was something about those fields and especially about those forests that was unlike the ones she had seen elsewhere — in Western Europe and in America — and that she still passionately loved them, as all Russians did. The visit to Yasnaya Polyana had impressed me with how deep that love was. I myself had begun to have a special feeling for this land and its people and I regretted that at my age and with my infirmities I probably would never see them again. I wished I had started earlier to visit them and learn the language but I had not been able, in time, to persuade the Soviet government to let me try.

CHAPTER 7

In 1985, before it was too late, I had made one last trip back to Western Europe, to London, Paris, and Berlin, where I had worked and lived for most of the twenty years between the wars. Surprisingly enough, CBS had asked me to go back to Berlin, from which I had broadcast for it during the Hitler years and into the first fifteen months of the war. It would be on May 8, the fortieth anniversary of VE-Day, when Germany surrendered to the Allies. President Ronald Reagan had, unwisely I thought, decided not to celebrate the victory or pay homage to Americans killed in the war, but to mark the day by honoring the German war dead at a military ceremony at Bitburg, Germany. The heads of state of our Western Allies in the war, the queen of England, the president of France, would be honoring their own war dead and celebrating the victory over Nazi barbarism.

A storm had blown up in America when it was discovered that among the twenty-eight hundred German soldiers buried at Bitburg, some forty-nine had served in the Waffen-S.S., a particularly odious Nazi party military outfit that had carried out some of the worst atrocities against the Jews and other victims. Some of the S.S. men buried at Bitburg, according to a report in the *New York Times*, had belonged to the infamous Second S.S. Panzer Division, Das Reich, which had carried out one of the most horrible massacres of World War II, the slaughter of 642 men, women, and children in the French village of Oradour-sûr-Glane.

The president of the United States was going to honor such murderers, along with other German war dead? Not only the Jews, but the American Legion and others protested. But Reagan stuck to his guns. He had promised the chancellor of West Germany, Helmut Kohl, that he would join him in honoring the German war dead at Bitburg on the anniversary of VE-Day. He would keep his promise.

The president made his position worse by foolish remarks which offended the victims of Nazism, particularly the Jews, and which showed up his abysmal ignorance of history. In defending his decision, he had said, among other things, that most of the German soldiers buried at Bitburg were as much victims of the Nazis as those done to death in the German concentration camps.

This seemed to me to be shocking and it moved me to write a letter to the *New York Times,* which was published on April 25, the eve of the president's departure for Germany. To equate the German soldiers buried at Bitburg, I wrote, with the victims done to death in the Nazi concentration camps, "seems to me a horrible violation of the truth." As a neutral war correspondent following the German Army through Poland in the fall of 1939 and through the Netherlands, Belgium, and France in the spring of 1940, I had talked with hundreds of German soldiers and not one had ever considered himself a victim of Nazism. On the contrary, they had fought for the Führer and Fatherland, as they put it, with "immense enthusiasm and dedication and very bravely." Even the German prisoners I helped interrogate on the U.S. First Army front four years later, at a time when the war must have seemed lost to them, expressed their complete loyalty to Hitler and the Nazi Reich.

> The idea that most German soldiers felt themselves "victims of Nazism" is false. It saddens me that the President has embraced it and that he cannot see the difference between those loyal soldiers of the Third Reich and the millions the Germans butchered in the camps. I do not believe he can further reconciliation with the Germans on the basis of a falsehood.*

At first, after his Bitburg trip was announced, the president had refused to add to his itinerary a trip to a Nazi death camp, for fear of offending his German hosts.

"I didn't see any way," he told the foreign broadcasters, "that I as a guest of the state and of the government of Germany could take off on my own and go [to a camp], and that might look as if I was trying to do something different than the purpose that we had in mind."

But giving in to protests at home, he had finally agreed to visit a camp the same day as he laid a wreath at the Bitburg military cemetery. Chancellor Kohl eased the change of mind by inviting him to come with him to Bergen-Belsen.

---

* The president made a curious remark at a press conference on April 29 at the White House with representatives of foreign radio and television, mostly German. Asked if he knew that some of the S.S. men buried at Bitburg may have participated in the massacre at Oradour, Mr. Reagan replied: "Yes. I know all about the bad things that happened in the war. I was in uniform for four years myself." But in Hollywood, rather far from any front. One wondered how he could know of such things as a soldier in Hollywood. Just as the correspondents in Washington, I was told, wondered how Reagan could say that he knew what had happened in the concentration camps because he had been in on the liberation of some of them.

The raging controversy over Bitburg raised questions about the Germans and ourselves that had been bothering me for years. I had not been back to Berlin since the Airlift of 1948 — thirty-seven years before. I had set out for Germany in the summer of 1961, when *The Rise and Fall of the Third Reich* was published in Germany. But a German lawyer friend had called me and stopped me in Paris. A good many libel suits were being brought against me by Nazis. Even a firm that made the ovens for some of the concentration camps was suing. He thought it best not to take any chances with German courts imposing fines or even imprisonment.*

I accepted the invitation of CBS to return to Berlin that spring of 1985 to comment on German reaction to Bitburg and see how the Germans were faring forty years after the end of Hitler. Their attitude toward Reagan's visit to honor their war dead might give a clue. Bitburg had aroused so many old passions on all sides. I wanted to see if the Germans, who had behaved so savagely in the Nazi time when I was there, had much changed. And whether at last they had honestly tried to come to terms with their past. In a sense, in the Soviet Union I had felt the Russians faced a somewhat similar problem: to look back honestly at the crimes of Stalin. Khrushchev had made a beginning by his exposure of Stalin in an address to his Party Congress. But he had not dared to publish the speech in Russia. Under the drift of Brezhnev, the Kremlin had flinched from coming to grips with Stalin's past. It had continued to suppress history that conflicted with the party line.

Before I left for Berlin, I realized that this would almost certainly be my last experience with the Germans. Since the days of the Weimar Republic back in the late 1920s, I had been reporting on them, and yet they had always baffled me. Many German critics and also some at home had insisted that I didn't understand the Germans. They noted that I had occasionally admitted it, but these were times of despair, after the whole German people seemed to me to have embraced the

---

* One early morning in New York the German consul-general in New York had knocked at my door and served me court papers from Hamburg on behalf of one of the worst of the Nazi party criminals, who claimed I had libeled him. Such is German justice even today that he had been able to hold up the publication of the German edition of the book all through the weeks preceding Christmas, when Germans traditionally buy a great many books.

The firm that made the ovens for some of the Nazi concentration camps threatened to sue me in New York and I hoped it would, but it dropped the idea and instead brought suit against my publisher in Munich. Its argument was that it was a respectable, upright firm that had been making ovens for a century and did not know what its product would be used for in the concentration camps. But I had copies of its correspondence with the S.S., showing it knew perfectly well what its ovens were going to be used for. In the face of this, the firm, so far as I remember, dropped the suit.

madness of Nazism and I wrote that I could not understand how a folk who had given us Bach and Kant and Goethe and Schiller and Beethoven and even Wagner, among others, and who had been such ardent Christians, could connive in so much evil.

In Berlin that May, it was easy to ascertain the reaction of the Germans to Reagan's visit. They welcomed it. They loved it. The government, the press, radio and TV, and the people you talked to were almost unanimous. To the Germans — and the government and the press hammered it in — the president's visit meant the U.S.A. and the rest of the free world it led recognized at last that Germany's aggressive wars were a thing of the past, that Nazism had been dead for forty years, and that the world ought, as Reagan urged, forgive and forget. This solved the German guilt problem. They no longer would be reminded of history, that the Germans started World War II by attacking Poland on September 1, 1939, that they had also been the aggressor when German troops moved into Austria in March 1938, into Czechoslovakia in March 1939, into neutral, peaceful Denmark and Norway in April 1940 and into neutral, peaceful Belgium and the Netherlands in May. After the American president's gesture of reconciliation and his insistence that Nazism was the product of one man, Adolf Hitler, and that the conscripts in the German Army (all German soldiers were drafted) were as much victims of the Nazi tyranny as were the millions slain by the Germans in the death camps, after all this, the Germans seemed to think, they would no longer have to be reminded that the German government had cold-bloodedly carried out the massacre of millions of Jews and Slavs.

The German press I read and the Germans I talked to could not understand the fuss in America about there being Waffen-S.S. men buried in the cemetery President Reagan would be visiting. They made no distinction themselves. All had died for the Fatherland. Why single out an S.S. soldier? He too had given his life for the country.

The Germans did resent the uproar in America against Reagan's visit. The press howled about it. But it was dismissed by the Germans, as I believe Reagan had tried to dismiss it, as the work of "the American news media." And by many Germans as the work also "of the American Jews."

I was a little surprised at the anti-Semitism still lingering in Germany. I had supposed that at least was finished. (Complacently I forgot that it was far from extinct in my own country.) But anti-Semitism kept creeping into the articles in the press blaming the Jews in America for the opposition to Bitburg, in the remarks of some of the angered politicians, and in conversations I overheard in the cafés and restaurants.

Down the street from the Kürfurstendam hotel I was staying at, I noted, was a Jewish Community House, which, if my memory was correct, had been built on the very site of the largest synagogue in Berlin, itself set fire and destroyed by a Nazi mob egged on by Goebbels on *Krystallnacht* in November 1938. In strolling past it on one of my first days in Berlin, I had noticed two policemen patrolling back and forth before it, and wondered why. About dusk on May 7, I happened to look out my hotel window and noticed a large crowd gathered in the street before the building. I hurried down to see what was up. Most of the crowd consisted of Jews, but there were also representatives of the Trade Union Federation and a youth group, identifiable by their banners. My diary tells the rest.

> . . . The occasion, I saw, was a protest against President Reagan going to Bitburg. A platoon of police stood on the street curb. A rabbi, apparently from West Germany, was speaking, deploring the president's insistence of going to Bitburg to honor the German war dead in a cemetery where 49 Waffen-S.S. men . . . lay buried next to the German soldiers. He made one remark that surprised me, after all the talk about the Germans having changed since the Nazi time. Calling attention to the band of police protecting the meeting, he said: "It is significant that in this country today Jewish buildings and institutions have to be guarded by the police — because the past threatens to catch up with us."
>
> I must say that skeptical as I am about the Germans, I was shocked. This morning the Berlin newspapers give the meeting but a few lines and say only "a few hundred" were at the gathering. I went down to check this morning if the Jewish Community House was really guarded around the clock, as someone had told me. Two policemen sauntered up and down the sidewalk outside.

By this time, Reagan had departed Germany and indeed on the morning of May 8, the actual anniversary of VE-Day, the *Morganpost*, one of Berlin's leading newspapers, played down the occasion, and put at the top of its front page a large photograph of Nancy Reagan dancing the flamenco with a young Spaniard. The president and his party had hopped off to Spain for a day before circling back to mark VE-Day with an address to the European Parliament at Strasbourg.

There had been no speeches at the brief ceremony at the Bitburg military cemetery. President Reagan and Chancellor Helmut Kohl, who was at his side throughout the day, laid their wreaths at the base of a cemetery tower in silence. Mr. Reagan, the reporters said, appeared not to see two S.S. graves a few feet away from where he and the German leader stood. He could not have seen the wreaths that had lain on the two graves shortly before he arrived. One had a banner: "To the Waffen-S.S. who fell at Leningrad." The other read: "To the fallen comrades of the Waffen-S.S." They had been removed temporarily during the president's appearance and restored as soon as he left.

At the Bergen-Belsen concentration camp, where fifty thousand Jews murdered there lay buried in mass graves, President Reagan spoke movingly. But twice, he alluded to the Nazi evil as being the work of "one man." "The awful evil started by one man," he said, "led to the deaths in the camps." And, "until that man and his evil were destroyed," he added, the killing went on.

After the wreath-laying at the military cemetery, the president spoke at a gathering of some five thousand American soldiers, their families, and a scattering of Germans at a U.S. air base at Bitburg, a mile from the military cemetery. He told of just coming from the ceremony there and of the emotions it raised in him. The war, he said, had been "against one man's totalitarian dictatorship." So we could "mourn the German war dead today as human beings crushed by a vicious ideology." It was an extenuation of his remarks made earlier in Washington that German soldiers drafted into service were just as much victims of Nazism as those done to death in the concentration camps, a contention, as I have written, that was a horrible distortion of the truth.

Reagan's misleading remarks about the innocence of German soldiers seemed to reflect his blind acceptance of a view propagandized by successive Bonn governments that the German armed forces and especially the army had no responsibility at all for what the Third Reich had done to humanity and that therefore its successor, the army of the Federal Republic, the Bundewehr, had no stains from the past.*

The truth was that the German Army bore a grave responsibility for the evils Hitler wrought — for his wars of aggression which it fought so fiercely and well, for his brutal treatment of the occupied lands, for the deaths by deliberate starvation and exposure of more than two million Russian prisoners-of-war, and even, in part at least, for the massacre of the Jews.

* As a symbolic gesture, the president had arranged for two old generals from World War II, one American, the other German, to meet and shake hands at the close of the wreath-laying at the Bitburg military cemetery. The American was General Matthew B. Ridgway, ninety years old and a former commander of the 82nd Airborne Division under General Eisenhower. The German was General Johannes Steinhof, seventy-one, a former ace in Göring's Luftwaffe.

Although the Nuremberg Tribunal, through a technicality, found the German High Command and the General Staff not guilty of Nazi crimes, it castigated the German field marshals and generals who had done Hitler's bidding.

They have been a disgrace to the honorable profession of arms. Without their military guidance, the aggressive ambitions of Hitler and his fellow Nazis would have been academic and sterile. Although they were not a group . . . they were certainly a military caste. . . . Many of them have made a mockery of the soldier's oath of obedience to military orders. . . . The truth is that they actively participated in all these crimes, or sat silent and acquiescent, witnessing the commission of crimes on a scale larger and more shocking than the world ever has had the misfortune of knowing.

To emphasize the participation of the German Army in Hitler's war crimes, the court found the Führer's two top generals, Field Marshal Wilhelm Keitel, chief of the High Command, and General Alfred Jodl, chief of operations, guilty on all four counts of the indictment and sentenced them to be hanged.

At Nuremberg and at the subsequent trials of several German generals before an American court, gruesome evidence turned up against some of the most prominent leaders of the German Army. Field Marshal Walter von Reichenau, commander of Army Group South in Russia, issued an order on October 10, 1941, which rivaled some of those of Hitler. He called the German attack on the Soviet Union "a war against the Jewish-Bolshevist system" and told his troops that they must understand "the necessity of a severe but just revenge on sub-human Jewry."

As early as September 8, 1941, less than three months after the launching of the attack on Russia, General Hermann Reinecke, who was in charge of prisoner-of-war camps in the east, ordered that captured Russians not be treated according to the Geneva Conventions. A directive from the High Command itself backed him up. The result was that of 5,700,000 Russian prisoners-of-war, only 2,000,000 survived the war. According to German official figures, 473,000 were executed. More than 2,000,000 were left to die of hunger and exposure. The order for this odious crime came from Hitler and Göring. But the Russian war prisoners were in the custody of the German Army, which was responsible for treating them humanely, according to rules laid down by the Geneva Conventions.

Of course, American POWs on the western front were also killed, seventy-two in cold blood on December 17, 1944, near Malmedy, Belgium, during the Battle of the Bulge. But the number was extremely small compared to the Russians, and the killings were carried out by the Waffen-S.S., not the regular army. At Malmedy, a combat group of the First S.S. Panzer Division was responsible.*

At Nuremberg, I recalled, there came to light three highly secret directives that besmirched the honor of the German Army though, to their credit, many generals refused to obey them. The first of them was the so-called Commissar Order. Hitler himself, on the eve of the attack on the Soviet Union in 1941, called in the chiefs of the three armed services and the key army field commanders and told them of his order to execute without court-martial and without delay all political commissars attached to captured Red Army units. Field Marshal Erich von Manstein, on the stand at Nuremberg, recalled the dilemma this odious order created. "It was the first time," he testified, "that I found myself involved in a conflict between my soldierly concepts and my duty to obey."

Manstein decided not to obey. He did not say so to Hitler at the conference — that would have meant his head — but he says he informed the commander of the army group under which he served. Others also declined to carry out the decree. Some obeyed. Many turned the job over to S.S. units and thus eased their consciences.

It was the same with Hitler's order, which he issued through the High Command, to exterminate all British and American commandos captured in the west. They were "to be slaughtered to the last man." General Jodl himself became involved in the infamous order. He issued instructions that "this order is intended for commanders only and must not under any circumstances fall into enemy hands." The generals were told by Jodl to destroy all copies of the order as soon as they had taken due note.

On the stand in Nuremberg, Field Marshal Keitel told the court that he was forced by Hitler to order many war crimes but the worst, he said, was the *Nacht und Nebel Erlass* — the "Night and Fog Decree." This one concerned the west and was issued by Hitler on December 7, 1941. It called for the arrest of all persons "endangering German security." If they were not immediately executed, they were to be

* In the spring of 1946, an American military tribunal sitting at Dachau sentenced forty-three officers of the S.S. group to death. But a hue and cry against the sentences arose in the U.S. Senate, led by Senator Joseph McCarthy. So in March 1948, thirty-one of the death sentences were commuted by the court. In 1951, General Lucius D. Clay reduced the death sentences from twelve to six, and in 1951, John J. McCloy, the U.S. high commissioner in Germany, commuted the remaining sentences to life imprisonment. Soon all were released from prison.

taken to Germany and made to vanish into the night and fog of the unknown. No information was to be given their families as to their fate even when it was merely a question of where they were buried. They were to be made to disappear forever.

Five days later, on December 12, Field Marshal Keitel, in the name of the High Command, issued a directive explaining the order.

> In general the punishment for offenses committed against the German State is a death penalty. . . . Effective intimidation can only be achieved either by capital punishment or by measures by which the relatives of the criminal and the population do not know his fate.

In case anyone still misunderstood the order or hesitated to carry it out, Keitel sent out another instruction in the name of the High Command. Where the death penalty was not meted out within eight days of a person's arrest,

> the prisoners are to be transported to Germany secretly. These measures will have a deterrent effect because
> (a) the prisoners will vanish without leaving a trace,
> (b) no information may be given as to their whereabouts or their fate.

How many Western Europeans (mostly the French were involved) disappeared into the "Night and Fog" was never established at Nuremberg. There were no records and no marked graves.

What responsibility the army shared with purely Nazi organizations in the "Final Solution" for the Jews was much debated at Nuremberg. On the whole, the army commands left the dirty work to the S.S., which ran the camps and did the actual exterminating. But as the courts at Nuremberg found, the German Army officers knew what was going on, knew that millions of Jews were being done to death in the camps and looked the other way. At times, they aided the S.S. in rounding up the Jews in the occupied territories and helped organize their transport — often across half of Europe — to the death camps. This was especially true in Russia, Belgium, France, Yugoslavia, and Greece, where the German military had much to answer for in what it did to the Jews.

The German Army had long had a tradition of anti-Semitism. In the Prussian Army which marched off to war in 1914, no Jew could be an officer, though during the war such restrictions were relaxed, especially in the non-Prussian units, and some Jews became officers. Some thirty-five thousand Jewish soldiers received the Iron Cross for bravery. No Jew, though, could be awarded the highest decoration, *Pour le Mérite*. The German Army that served Hitler so well was "not friendly to Jews," General Siegfried Westphal once declared, "but it was not anti-Semitically inclined." However, no Jews were allowed to serve in the armed forces under Hitler. And there is no doubt that in the Second World War a number of German commanders of the highest rank, though certainly not all, indoctrinated their troops with a violent hatred of the Jews, calling them, as Field Marshal von Reichenau did, "subhumans," and that furthermore they sometimes assisted the S.S. in the persecution and massacre of the Jews.

As we have seen, the Jews were not the only victims of Nazi savagery in which the German Army was implicated. One had to remember the Russian war prisoners who were deliberately left to die of starvation and exposure, and the Russian commissars and the Anglo-American commandos executed after their capture. And the unknown number of human beings in the German occupied lands in the west rounded up under the *Nacht und Nebel* decree and made to disappear forever in the "night and fog" of Germany. And the shooting of hostages by German Army commanders — 29,660 in France alone.

It was the dead of this German Army and of this German S.S. that President Reagan honored at Bitburg. No doubt he did it with the best of intentions. But also out of ignorance of the past. I'm sure he sincerely believed, as he recently had said, that the German soldiers who died under Hitler were as much victims of Nazism as were the Jews murdered in the death camps. But it was not true, and the reconciliation he sought, and that we all seek in the end, could not be based on a falsehood.

President Reagan came to Bitburg under another illusion. Chancellor Kohl apparently had convinced him that the Waffen-S.S. men buried at the military cemetery had, like himself, been drafted into its ranks at the age of fifteen or sixteen in the closing months of the war when replacements were badly needed.

This was not true, at least in the case of ten of the forty-nine Waffen-S.S. soldiers who lay at rest at Bitburg. On May 3, two days before the president visited the cemetery, I was able to obtain in Berlin the complete army records of these ten. The papers disclosed that all ten were veteran Nazis. All were over thirty when they were killed, all had been decorated for being part of the German Armed Forces that invaded Austria in 1938, Czechoslovakia the next year, and Poland later that same year. One had served for a time as a guard at the Dachau concentration camp.

President Reagan's view of Germany's Nazi past was based on ignorance. He probably would have been the first to admit that he was no great student of history, and his American advisers who had arranged the trip could easily make the same admission. But Chancellor Kohl, who had given the president most of his ideas, and the German people had no such excuse. They knew the terrible past that had climaxed in the Holocaust. The question was whether they could face it. After forty years since the Allies, not the Germans, made an end of Hitler, could the Germans confront the principal question: How was it possible for this nation to have committed the horrendous crimes it did under Hitler? Until the question was at least posed, it seemed to me, and an answer at least sought, until the past, that is, was squarely faced, it would be very difficult, if not impossible, to build up a new, decent, civilized Germany.

My feeling was that most Germans had not faced that question, had no wish to come to terms with the past or even understand it.

Probably many of them already had taken themselves off the hook. I read as many German newspapers as I could, and listened for hours to German television, and both the press and TV left me with the impression that Mr. Reagan's visit had made the Germans more complacent than ever about their Nazi past. Let's forget it, they seemed to say, and they rejoiced that Mr. Reagan was saying the same thing. They were annoyed that so many Americans wanted to distinguish between the dead of the army and those of the Waffen-S.S. And they resented the U.S. Senate and the U.S. House of Representatives for voting overwhelmingly to ask the president not to go to Bitburg.

There was another view being increasingly expressed in Germany that spring of 1985 that disturbed me. One evening in a talk in a *Bierkeller,* a German acquaintance who, I knew, had not supported the Nazis, though like others he had gone along, brought it up. Yes, he said, the Nazis had committed some horrible crimes, but so had the Allies, especially the Russians. War made barbarians of men — on both sides. Why not let bygones be bygones? So German guilt was relative. Actually in some of the German newspapers, I had, to my surprise, noticed somewhat similar comments.

I concluded in the end that they may have first been inspired by the editor of an influential weekly German journal, *Der Spiegel,* Rudolf Augstein. His lengthy piece early in 1985 was an angry diatribe against the Bitburg ceremonies. "Let them [the Allies] celebrate," he wrote, "because they won the war. We can watch and need not participate."

But what most bothered Augstein was the constant reminder of the outside world that the Germans bore a terrible guilt for the crimes of Adolf Hitler. Why put all the blame on the Germans? he asked. "Whether the anti-Hitler Allies committed fewer crimes than Hitler is not at all certain. The one who initiated such crimes against humanity was, in any case, Stalin in 1928."

As to the extermination of the Jews by the Nazis, this influential German editor did not deny that it took place, though he remarked that mostly "foreign Jews" were slain — "within the Reich there were only 50,000 of them."

The Jews themselves, he went on, were far from blameless. In this regard, he brought up Henry Morgenthau, President Roosevelt's secretary of the treasury, who was a Jew. The "Morgenthau Plan," he told his readers, would have subjugated a defeated Germany and reduced it to a terrible state. (Though he did not say so, this was what Hitler had in store for Poland and Russia.) In fact, he added, Morgenthau would have been "a good follower of Hitler."

But not only Morgenthau. Augstein claimed that in 1941, "when nobody knew anything yet about Hitler's gas chambers," Theodore Nathan Kaufman, president of the American Peace Society, proposed that the German people be sterilized so that they would disappear. Finally, the German editor appeared to equate the brutal German treatment of Russians in the occupied territories with the Russian-Polish expulsion of Germans in the east after the war.

The same effort to balance war crimes was made by a five-part television series that drew a big audience in West Germany that spring. It was entitled "The War of the Bombers," and its theme was that whatever destruction German bombers wrought on the enemy was no worse than what Allied bombers did to German cities, climaxed by the terrible American firebombing of Dresden. Polls showed that the motive of the film was not lost on most Germans, who believed that both sides were equally to blame for the bombing of innocent citizens in the great cities. The polls also showed that most Germans were fed up with all the documentary reports on the crimes of the Nazis and of World War II.

Apparently, as I feared at the time, the lessons of the Nuremberg trials had been lost on the Germans. Whatever the crimes of the Allies in the war, the Germans could not see, or did not wish to remember, that the Third Reich had started the war by attacking Poland, had started the massive bombing of the great cities, and that it was the only nation which had systematically tried to wipe out a whole race of people and, in massacring six million of them before it was defeated, had almost succeeded.

And finally on this subject: I kept hearing in Germany that May a terrible story that I was told had been circulating in the country for years. It was about the fifteen-year-old Anne Frank, whom President Reagan had alluded to in his remarks at the Bergen-Belsen death camp and who had been murdered and presumably buried there. The story told of a German woman who had attended a performance of the play based on *The Diary of Anne Frank*. She was deeply moved by the drama and leaving the theater, she turned to someone and in a shaken voice said, "Yes, but really, at least that girl ought to have been allowed to live."

I left Berlin that bright spring of 1985 in a state of deep depression. I felt worse, I believe, than that snowy December day in 1940, forty-five years before when I departed from Nazi Germany for the last time. By then, Hitler had conquered Poland in the East and Denmark, Norway, the Netherlands, Belgium, and France in the West. Great Britain, the cream of its army lost in France that summer, held out alone against the conquering Germans. I still held out hope she would survive, somehow, but few, especially at home, gave her much chance. A Europe enslaved by the Nazi barbarians seemed too awful to contemplate, but one had to face the possibility, even, as it seemed to many, the probability. The very prospect brought a man to the depths of despair. I was in a black mood. But it was lightened somewhat by my selfishness. I felt such a relief to be getting out alive from the Nazi inferno that I was almost happy. When I returned to Germany four years later, at the end of the war, she lay in ruins. However much you hated Nazism and what these people had done under Nazism, you were saddened by their plight.

But now, forty years later, they had risen from the rubble. They had, with Allied help, rebuilt their country. They were once again prosperous and proud. I did not begrudge them their happy state. Welcome to it. But I was depressed deep down by their failure to face the past. They did not even want to remember it.

Not all, to be sure. There was one in high office who on that very VE-Day looked back unblinkingly and remembered. This was the president of the Federal Republic, Richard von Weizsaecker. I had known his father, the permanent state secretary and the brains of the Nazi German Foreign Office, who after the war claimed to have been an anti-Nazi all along but who had served Hitler well. He did not escape Allied justice in the end, receiving as I recall, a five-year prison sentence of which he served eighteen months. At Nuremberg, his son had defended his father but this may have been more out of filial loyalty than conviction. Still, many Germans — and certainly I — were surprised by his speech on the Bundestag on May 8, for the like of it had not been heard very often, if ever, in postwar West Germany. He insisted that Germans remember the past and face its consequences. As I listened to the broadcast, I regretted that Mr. Reagan could not have been present to hear it, but the president, dodging any anniversary celebration of the Allied triumph over Germany (so as not to offend the Germans?), was addressing the European Parliament in Strasbourg that day, warning it of the Russian danger.

First, the German president faced squarely what the Germans under Hitler had done to the Jews. "The genocide of the Jews," he said, "is unparalleled in history." Why had the German people ignored it?

There were many ways of not burdening one's conscience, of shirking responsibility, looking away, keeping mum. When the unspeakable truth of the Holocaust became known at the end of the war, all too many of us claimed that they had known nothing about it or even suspected anything.

All of us, whether guilty or not, whether old or young, must accept the past. We are all affected by its consequences and liable for it. . . .
It is not a case of coming to terms with the past. That is not possible. It can not be subsequently modified or undone. However, anyone who closes his mind to the past is blind to the present. Whoever refuses to remember the inhumanity is prone to new risks of infection.

He quoted an old Jewish proverb: "Seeking to forget makes exiles of us all the longer. The secret of redemption lies in remembrance."*

I wondered why Chancellor Kohl, who inveigled Reagan into making his unfortunate trip to Bitburg and had filled him with what I

* Three and a half years later, in October 1988, Weisaecker took on German revisionist historians who had been peddling the thesis that German guilt for the Nazi crimes was relative, that other nations had behaved just as badly. The issue had sharply divided the historians in West Germany, who had convoked a Congress at Bamberg to try to resolve it.

The West German president left no doubt on whose side he was. The revisionists, he said, had sought to raise a multitude of comparisons and parallels that would cause "the dark chapter of our history to disappear, to be reduced to a mere episode."

But the German nation [he answered] cannot make others responsible for what it and its neighbors endured under National Socialism. It was led by criminals and allowed itself to be led by them.
Auschwitz remains unique. It was perpetrated by Germans in the name of Germany. The truth is immutable and will not be forgotten.

believed to be historical untruths, had not spoken out as frankly and honestly as his German president. Why couldn't he too face the past?

I was wrong about Kohl, as I discovered after I left Germany. At home I came across a speech he had made on April 21, 1985, a month before Reagan's visit at the Bergen-Belsen concentration camp. It had not been widely reported, at least over here. The chancellor's remarks were as blunt about Germans facing the past as were those of Wiezsaecker. If only he had uttered similar words in the presence of Ronald Reagan!

Reconciliation, he said, was only possible

> if we accept our history as it really was. If we Germans acknowledge our shame and our historical responsibility. . . . For twelve years . . . Germany under the National Socialist regime filled the world with fear and horror. That era of slaughter, indeed of genocide, is the darkest, most painful chapter in German history. One of our country's paramount tasks is to . . . keep alive an awareness of the full extent of this historical burden. We must not, nor shall we ever forget the atrocities committed under the Hitler regime, . . . the systematic inhumanity of the Nazi dictatorship. A nation that abandons its history forsakes itself.

Kohl then came to what he called the decisive question.

> The decisive question is why so many people remained apathetic, did not listen properly, closed their eyes to reality.*

Kohl might have gone further and asked why so many Germans fanatically backed Hitler from the beginning to the bitter end.

It was a question that aroused such a furor in West Germany three and a half years later in November 1988, just as I was writing these lines, that it forced Philipp Jenninger, the president of the Bundestag, to resign.

It was a curious happening involving on the one hand the clumsiness and insensitivity of the well-meaning House Speaker, which many of his colleagues resented, and on the other hand his maladroit but truthful reminder of how the German people had given their ardent support to the barbarian German dictator.

---

* Chancellor Kohl revealed something about the Bergen-Belsen camp that few people were aware of — one wonders whether he told Mr. Reagan of it when they visited the camp together.

> When the camp was set up [he said] Russian prisoners-of-war were first brought here. Their accommodation and treatment amounted to no less than torture. Over 50,000 died alone in this region. This we must also remember today and in the future: of the almost six million Soviet soldiers who were captured by the Germans as prisoners-of-war, far less than half survived.

That his remarks, or the way he had drafted them and delivered them, were given at a special session of the Bundestag which he had called to mark the fiftieth anniversary of *Krystallnacht* was unfortunate. For that was the "night of the broken glass" on November 9–10, 1938, when the German government had carried out a pogrom against the Jews, burning down their synagogues, meeting houses, places of business and homes, killing several hundred, carting thirty thousand off to concentration camps and then fining what was left of the Jewish community a billion marks. On that gruesome night, Nazi Germany had turned down a dark and savage road that would lead to the Holocaust.

It was on the fiftieth anniversary of that night that Philipp Jenninger chose to speak out and remind his fellow Germans that the Nazi regime which had perpetrated such horrors had the enthusiastic support of most Germans. This was true, as all of us who lived in Germany in those days knew, but, as we have seen, the Bonn government, starting with Adenauer, had denied it. Unfortunately Jenninger, a moderate, a friend actually of the Jews and of Israel, which he had often visited, was so clumsy in presenting this truth that many of his listeners thought he was defending the Nazi past and they walked out in indignation.

You could scarcely blame them. For here was the House Speaker saying that the years between 1933 and 1938 remained "fascinating" because "there was hardly a parallel in history to Hitler's triumphs during those first years."

He then proceeded to recount them: the return of the Saar, the introduction of a conscript army in defiance of Versailles, the Anglo-German naval accords, which released Germany from the naval restrictions of the peace treaty, the Olympic summer games in Berlin, the annexation of Austria, the Munich agreement, the dismemberment of Czechoslovakia.

> And not only that: mass unemployment turned into full employment; from mass misery there was something like prosperity for the widest section of the population. Instead of desperation and hopelessness, optimism and self-confidence reigned.

This was all true. This is the way I reported it at the time. Hitler was giving the Germans what they wanted. That is why they backed him. But it sounded to the audience as if the Speaker was heaping praise on the Nazi regime.

> Did not Hitler [the Speaker continued] make into reality what was only promised under Wilhelm II, that is, to bring wonderful times to the

Germans? Was not Hitler someone selected by Providence, a leader who was only given to a people once in a thousand years? . . . Who could doubt that in 1938 a majority of Germans stood behind him and identified themselves with his politics.

I certainly never doubted it. But by this time in his speech, the Speaker apparently was making it sound as if he agreed with the Germans of fifty years before, which he didn't.

"Perhaps," he went on,

one enjoyed fewer freedoms in some areas of life but one's lot was better than before and the Reich was greater again, bigger and more powerful than ever before. Had not the leaders of Britain, France and Italy visited Hitler in Munich and helped him achieve greater successes than were thought possible?

What about the Nazi brutality toward the Jews? Here the Speaker lost his way and, as it turned out, his job.

And as for the Jews, hadn't they in the past, after all, sought a position that was not their place? Mustn't they now accept a bit of curbing? Hadn't they, in fact, earned being put in their place? . . . And when things got much too ugly, as in November 1938, one could always say, in the words of a contemporary: what does that have to do with us?

Indeed that was what the Germans were saying of the Jews in my time in Nazi Germany. But to be reminded of it fifty years later, and in a way that seemed to reflect the views of the distinguished Speaker, was too much. He was forced to resign, pleading that his speech was not understood in the way he meant it to be.

But lost in the furor was the fact that the Bundestag president had told some important truths about the past, and that this did not go down well with many Germans.

While Israel and many Jews worldwide protested Jenninger's remarks, the vice-president of the Central Council of Jews in West Germany, Michael Fuerst, praised them. He applauded the Speaker's bringing "such clarity about what the situation was like in Germany between 1933 and 1938. . . . It expressed the fact that everything Hitler did was supported by the whole German people."*

Indeed, if the Speaker got that across, he deserved, I thought, the thanks not only of the present-day Germans but of the present-day Americans, who for too long had professed to believe that it was not so,

---

* A few days later, Fuerst himself was forced to resign by the Council of Jews for applauding Jenninger's speech.

though it was. Facing the past started here. Believing in an ugly lie was no longer excusable.

And so for the last time that spring of 1985, I took leave of the Germans, among whom I had spent so many years that went back more than half a century. My life and work had been intertwined with theirs during, as Kohl himself put it, the worst, the darkest period in their history. It had been a horror to live through. What perhaps had made it worse for me was that my ancestors, on my father's side, had been Germans, my very name had been Anglicized from the German, and from boyhood I had felt a certain affinity for these kindred people and their philosophers, poets, and composers.

As a human being, I would have preferred to have escaped this long German chapter in my life. But as a journalist and eventual writer, I did not regret it. The long Nazi night had given me much to think and write about, first as a newspaperman and broadcaster and then as a historian of those times. It was an experience such as was given to few foreigners: to have seen Hitler at work, at the dizzy Nuremberg party rallies, at the moments of crisis when he addressed the Reichstag, at Munich the night he humbled Chamberlain and Daladier over Czechoslovakia, in Poland during his first armed conquest, and at Compiègne in June 1940 when he humbled France at the Franco-German armistice proceedings. I had also seen at close quarters the other Nazi monsters at their jobs, Göring, the corpulent swashbuckling number-two man, Goebbels, the nimble, cynical, warped propaganda minister, number three, Himmler, the terrible, sadistic killer, chief of the S.S. and Gestapo, and the arrogant, ignorant Ribbentrop, who did so much harm as foreign minister.

And I had seen them all again, minus Hitler, Goebbels, and Himmler, at Nuremberg at the end of the war, witnessing something I had never expected to see in this unjust world: the bringing to justice of these shabby criminals whom the German people had followed so enthusiastically so long. Ten were hanged, Ribbentrop the first of all. Göring escaped the gallows at the last hour by swallowing a vial of poison. By that time, Hitler, Goebbels, and Himmler had also killed themselves.

After the Nazi years, I no longer felt any affinity for the Germans. A people who could behave so bestially, who could treat others with so much brutality, who could try to massacre a whole people because of their race, who had such a lust for conquest and domination, who so savagely violated the human spirit — were they not barbarians who had to be watched and restrained? How could you trust them not to break out again, as they had under Bismarck, Wilhelm II, and then Hitler? Philosophers and statesmen and historians said you could not condemn an entire people. But this entire people, with a few honorable exceptions, had joined together under the primitive swastika to participate in unspeakable crimes. They were not to be condemned for it? They were not to be held responsible? They were to be trusted? Certainly in that brief period of my return to Berlin in 1985, forty years after the destruction of the Nazis by the Allies, the Germans seemed like a normal people. One sat on the café terraces or in the *Bierkellers* or in their homes talking to them as one human being to another. Had they changed? For good? Does any great people change fundamentally?

I kept mulling the questions but I came up with no answers. One had to leave it at that. Time, as they said, would tell. But I would not be around if and when it did. I felt no bitterness toward these people. I had had some of the best friends of my life among them. It was not as individuals but as a people that I had my doubts and fears about them.

Goethe, a great German and a great poet, had this feeling too. As my plane for Paris took off and we flew over the divided city with the abominable wall separating East and West and as I glanced down for what I was sure was the last time at Berlin, Goethe's words came back to me and seemed near to my own thoughts:

> I have often felt a bitter sorrow at the thought of the German people, which is so estimable in the individual and so wretched in the generality.

CHAPTER 8

I took a final farewell of London and Paris too.

To celebrate VE-Day, CBS had arranged a reunion of its old foreign correspondents, Murrow's boys who had covered the war for it. We were to reminisce about the old days in a broadcast from the Café Royal. Walker Cronkite, who had been with the United Press in London during the war, joined us and Dan Rather, the anchor of the CBS Evening News, who was too young for the war, was flown over from New York to preside over our meeting.

> Some friction [I noted in my diary] between Dan and Walter, who may have wanted to anchor the program himself. Dan started the broadcast with a question to Walter, who sat at his right, and Walter promptly put him down. "Well," he said in his richly avuncular fashion, "I think, Dan, I would put the question a little different," which he proceeded to do.

It was good to see some of my old comrades again, especially Eric Sevareid and Charles Collingwood, whom Murrow had recruited at the beginning of the war. Later, the three of us had dinner together, talking about the old times and catching up on each other's news, for I had not seen either of them for years. Sevareid seemed a little bitter that CBS had forced him to retire at sixty-five (as it had Cronkite; only Bill Paley, the chief, was exempted — by himself — from the rules) and somewhat at loose ends apparently because he had not found enough work elsewhere to make him happy. He seemed to regret too that he had not done more writing. As his autobiography showed, he was a talented writer, but he had chosen to stick with his broadcasting until he was retired. Collingwood still had a job at CBS, but he had been shunted aside for new and younger talent, though this did not seem to have embittered him. He took it philosophically. As he did something much more troubling.

"Bill," he said toward the end of the meal, "I've got cancer."

He was taking chemotherapy, he said, and hoping for the best. He did not dwell on it. He was facing it bravely. A few months later, in New York, he died.

I had only the weekend in London, most of it devoted to the broadcast and to doing some taping for CBS. There was no time to get out into the streets to get the feel of the place or to see the few friends still living, who might bring me up to date on the state of the island. Maggie Thatcher, the Tory prime minister, seemed firmly in charge. She was a great survivor and had been in power, or soon would be, longer than any British prime minister in modern history. Thatcher was a sort of British Ronald Reagan in her ultra-conservatism and she was popular for about the same reasons he was. The Labour party, in which most of my friends had been, seemed in disarray, unable to decide on a program that might attract a majority of the electorate. The Social Democrats, consisting mostly of former moderate Labourites, and their ally, the Liberals, were no longer a challenge to the Tories. Maggie Thatcher ruled supreme. The British had had their ruling queens, they had one now in Elizabeth, but Mrs. Thatcher, I believe, was their first woman prime minister.

Since most of my friends had been a little older than me, most of them were gone. Russell Strauss, now retired, the old left-winger of the Labour party, but growing more conservative as the years passed by, survived as "Lord Strauss."

And Jennie Lee had become Baroness Lee of Asheridge.

Lady Lee? Sitting in the sedate House of Lords? For some of us among her friends who remembered her impassioned speeches in the House of Commons on behalf of the underprivileged, it was hard to imagine.* Jennie survived her husband, Nye Bevin, by twenty-eight years. She died in London at eighty-four on November 16, 1988.

After my deep depression in Berlin, I thought a week in Paris might restore my spirits. I very much wanted to see it once again before it was too late.

Always before when I returned to Paris I had a job to do, for decades reporting and then in the 1960s to research a book on the fall of France, and finally to beat the drums for the French editions of my books by submitting to endless interviews on the air for television and radio, and off the air for the press.

But now in May 1985, after Berlin, I came for the first time in my

---

* Even for the *New York Times.* "How Scotland's fiery Jennie," it commented editorially, "would have scorned the robes of a baroness early in her Labor Party career."

life, not to work but just to see my old haunts and to say farewell to the city and country that had given me so much.

Paris in May was as lovely as ever; it was always at its best in springtime. The chestnut trees were about to blossom along the boulevards, people in every neighborhood were filling the terraces of the cafés to enjoy the season or milling up and down the boulevards. In my favorite park, the Luxembourg Garden, where I had spent so many happy hours, the youngsters were sailing their little boats on the waters beneath the fountain opposite the Medici Palace, and in another area old men were playing *Balle* — just as the children and the elderly had done in this park sixty years before when I first discovered it. And just as before, barges moved slowly up and down the Seine, beneath the graceful bridges, past Notre Dame and the Isle St. Louis.

And yet I did not find in Paris the solace I sought. There were three reasons, I finally realized. I had no assignment, and for this reason, I felt somewhat at loose ends. Second, most of my French friends were gone, including Yvonne, who had been five years older than I, though it had made no difference when we first fell in love fifty-nine years ago. She would have been eighty-six that spring. Eventually, we had gone separate ways but remained friends.

Gone too at a ripe old age was Jennie Bradley, a Frenchwoman long widowed by her American husband. As a youngster, she had sat on the knee of Anatole France and had known most of France's great writers since. For many years, she had been my French literary agent and she had invited to lunch and dinner parties that she had given for me in her attractive apartment in the Isle St. Louis most of the literary and political luminaries in France.

Sylviane, with whom I had spent much of my time when I was researching my book on the fall of France in the 1960s, was working abroad for a year in an exchange program. I did have lunch with my French publisher, but the editors who had worked with me on the French edition of my books had dispersed. And I spent a pleasant weekend with Benjamin Barber, on a sabbatical from Rutgers to work on another book, and Leah, his wife, who was dancing in Paris that spring.

But for the most part, I was alone. Usually I like it that way, to be left to myself, especially in Paris. But thinking of that led me to understand the third reason for my low spirits. I was simply getting too old and too decrepit to partake any longer of the moveable feast here that Hemingway had written about and from which I had taken large portions in the heady 1920s in Paris.

To experience the great city, to appreciate it, to savor it, you had to walk . . . and walk . . . for hours; walk through the parks, up and down the boulevards and the long halls of the great museums, starting with the Louvre. You had to roam through the narrow winding streets of the Left Bank or of hilly Montmartre and along the quays of the Seine. You had to walk some distance to take in the cathedral and churches, Notre Dame, Ste. Chapelle, St. Sulpice, and the Church of St. Germain-des-Pres with its lovely eleventh-century Romanesque tower.

There were a hundred or more walks to take in Paris and another hundred in its environs. But I could no longer take them. Age and a heart condition had finally forced me, reluctantly to realize it.

I tried, though, to go on as before. I was staying at a familiar hotel just off the Boulevard St. Germain. From there I set off to roam through my old haunts, up the boulevard to St. Germain des Pres to have an aperitif on the terrace of the Deux Magots, where one could look across at the lovely old church that had the same name as the square. In my youth, I had sometimes gone in there to meditate. With its thick walls, it was cool on a hot day. During the war, I knew, the Resistance had used the church as a place to meet and as a drop for messages, and it was there that Suzanne, who later became a friend and who was a courier for the Resistance, was nabbed by the German Gestapo after being betrayed by a French collaborator. She had been frightfully tortured by the Germans, had not broken and finally had been shipped half-dead off to Ravensbrück, a Nazi concentration camp for women, where miraculously, despite further abuse by the Germans, she survived.

From the Deux Magots, I crossed the street to Lipp's, which had been an Alsatian brasserie much frequented by American writers and journalists in the old days but now was upgraded into a rather fancy restaurant. Like a lot of other places in Paris, it was no longer the same. Most of the customers seemed to be German and American tourists. The Alsatian beer and the *choucroute-garnie*, however, were still good. After lunch, up the rue de Rennes to the Place St. Sulpice and into the spacious church there. It had one of the finest pipe-organs in the world and when I first came to Paris, and lived around the corner in the Rue de Vaugirard, I used to drop in on a late afternoon before going to work on the *Tribune* to hear the renowned Marcel Dupré play. I had first met him when he came to inaugurate a new organ donated to my Iowa college by a wealthy benefactor. Dupré, of course, was no longer living and someone else was practicing on the organ.

I had gone into the church principally to rest and to catch my breath for a further excursion, but I still felt tired when I emerged. I pressed on, though, up to the Place de L'Odeon, noting that the rambling bookstalls in the archways of the State Theatre, where I had purchased my first French books, were gone. Then up the rue de Vaugirard to the sagging old Hôtel de Lisbonne, where I had lived the first three years in Paris when my salary was fifteen dollars a week. It had a few modern conveniences, not a single bath in the whole place, and only one stand-up toilet on each of its five floors, but it had character, its rooms were rather spacious and cheap and, after all, as a plaque on the façade reminded us, two great French poets, Baudelaire and Verlaine, once had lived there. The wild spirit of the mad, drunken Verlaine hung over our fair abode.

It was only a stone's throw from the hotel to the Luxembourg Garden, but when I got there I found I was too tired to meander through it. I slumped on a bench to get my breath. I had planned to walk down the Boulevard St. Michel, past the Sorbonne, and down to the Seine and then over to Notre Dame — so much of my early life had been spent along that broad avenue — but I realized I could never make it. I was exhausted. I would not be able to do much more walking in this magic city. Despondent, I hailed a taxi and returned to my hotel. A good nap, followed by a good dinner at a nearby restaurant, bucked me up, but nonetheless I felt it was time to bid farewell to this city with which I had had a love affair for more than half a century, and book a plane home.

For much of my adulthood, Europe had been the center of my life and work. Wonderful years! In many ways, the best, certainly the most adventurous, the most filled with excitement, the most meaningful, the deepest, as one lived through the rise of the totalitarian powers, the decline of the West, the advent of the Second World War, the cruelest, most destructive of all, with its slaughter of tens of millions not only at the front but at home (in the bombings), and finally the Holocaust of the European Jews.

For a journalist and an author, there had been much to write about — and to think about.

And now I was saying good-bye to it, to return to the placid life of an old man in a quiet village in the hills of the Berkshires. It had been a rough but wonderful passage through the twentieth century. My own country had grown from a second-rate, rather provincial, power to be, with the Soviet Union, the colossus of the world. I had found plenty to criticize in it, especially after it became powerful, dominating, conservative, and rich. The greed and selfishness of the well-off, the plight of the poor and the homeless, sickened me. And I was appalled at, among other things, our warm support of despotic totalitarian governments abroad if they were run by a right-wing dictator or a shabby military junta, no matter how murderous or corrupt, while determined to overthrow a dictatorship if it was left-wing. Such deviousness demeaned us.

But we could also be a generous nation, as we had shown with the Marshall Plan, which had helped rebuild a bombed-out, war-ravaged Europe after the last war. If we were erratic, we were often well-meaning. And we had sought to preserve freedom not only for ourselves but for others, if not for all. This had given me the freedom as a citizen to live as I liked and to me as both a citizen and a writer, the most precious freedom of all: to express and publish my thoughts and opinions, however unpopular and wrong. In how many countries had writers who tried to exercise that freedom been jailed!

My country had given me no public honors, but I did not seek or want any. It was enough that it had been good to me, as life had been, and fate, and the gods.

So as the tumultuous twentieth century began to wind down to its end, I remained settled in my Berkshire village, happy to live out there my allotted time, which at eighty-five could not be long. Despite the heart condition, which, after all, many old men had, and another handicap or two, I was in relative good health,* able still in the summer to do a little gardening and sailing, and get over to nearby Tanglewood for some classical music and over to Jacob's Pillow, also nearby, for the dance.

A year ago, as this is written, I suffered a tear in the retina of the only eye I have, and this has slowed my writing and curtailed my reading. But with the help of special lenses, I can still see enough to write and read. Even without them, I can glimpse the great outdoors, the hills and valleys and the bright blue sky above, the fields, the streams, lakes and woods, the tree-lined village streets, and from my home a harvest moon rising full blown in the dusk of autumn, a sun setting beneath a pink sky.

* Better apparently than Paul Claudel, the French poet, at eighty.

> 80 years old! [he wrote in his diary.] No eyes left, no ears, no teeth, no legs, no wind! And when all is said and done, how astonishingly well one does without them!

A few friends still survive in the area: Marge Champion, the dancer and still a ball of fire who refuses to retire or even slow down; Jim (James McGregor) Burns, the genial, thoughtful historian at nearby Williams College, among others. Inga, my elder daughter, who came to the village some years before to write, has made life easier and richer, as has Tania, my Russian friend, who recently became my bride. Linda, my younger daughter, who lives but two hours away by car, drives up, despite her busy life, with her two children, to visit and help. Tess, in New York, and I chat on the telephone and see each other at one of the children's homes at holidays, especially Christmas. Four grandchildren, two of them now grown up and scattered, have helped to keep me young.

So much life! Despite death waiting over the hill,* I find myself keeping too busy writing, reading, gardening, sailing, listening to music, attending the theater and the dance and chewing the fat with friends, to think of death. I wonder why so many fear it, even the great Tolstoy, for instance, who dreaded its coming and cursed it for destroying life.

I don't look forward to it. I would like to linger on a little longer, to write another book or two and a play, read more of the books there has never been time to get to and return to many I have loved. (All the plays and sonnets of Shakespeare, which I have in one volume; all the plays of the great Greek dramatists, Aeschylus, Euripides, Sophocles, and Aristophanes, the novels of Dostoyevski, Tolstoy, Dickens, Balzac, and Stendhal, the plays and short stories of Chekhov — the list is long — listen to music, not only symphonic but chamber music, my greatest love, from Bach, Mozart, Beethoven, Schubert, and Brahms.) To do all that — and more, including clarifying my thoughts about the history I've lived through and written about. And continuing my pursuit of Russian, which still eludes me.

There will never be enough time, I know. Death will come. And then what? A life of some kind hereafter? We do not know. There is no evidence, no proof, that there is life after death. Yet all the great

---

* Some thought one day a few years ago that it had already come. It was mentioned in the esteemed *Springfield* (Mass.) *Union* on February 26, 1974.

Lenox. Reports of the death of author William L. Shirer, which appeared in the Gardner syndicated column in *The Union* last Saturday reached Shirer during his 70th birthday celebration.
In the column, he was referred to as "the *late* William L. Shirer, author of *Berlin Diary.* . . ."
Shirer, paraphrasing Mark Twain, said, "The reports of my death are exaggerated and premature."

religions have promised it. Even that of the Greeks, who were so skeptical, who believed above all else in Reason. Obviously, one couldn't take one's body to the hereafter. But the religions said the soul ascended to it. I had tried to imagine the soul but I could not. I have never understood it or found it. There was much, of course, beyond my paltry comprehension, beyond my imagination and vision. But try as I could, I could never bring myself to believe in a heaven and a hell. I could not prove that they did not exist nor could I prove the opposite. At the moment, I am content to wait and see.

Religion, no doubt, would have given me the faith to believe in a hereafter, but I lost it along the way. I was baptized in the Presbyterian Church and went to Sunday school and church regularly as a child. In college, the first doubts began to rise. And they grew rapidly as I went abroad as a correspondent and came into contact with other cultures, other religions. I found it increasingly difficult to believe in the very foundations of the Christianity I had been born into, the "miracles" of the virgin birth of Jesus, his resurrection, and ascension. I was filled with doubts about Jesus being the Son of God.

I suppose it was my sojourn in India and my experience with Mahatma Gandhi that caused me to begin to lose faith in my own religion. The other great religions I encountered there, Islam, Hinduism, and Buddhism, did not recognize that Jesus was the Son of God. They had their own conception of God, which was different from ours.

I often discussed this with the Mahatma, a devout Hindu, but tolerant of other faiths, from which he drew much of his thinking, especially the Christianity of the New Testament, a work he knew well and loved. He certainly made no attempt to pry me loose from Christianity. Just the opposite. But he did try to interest me in what he called "comparative religion," in which he himself believed, and which was based on taking the best from all the religions, not just one's own. Gandhi could not believe, as some of his Christian friends tried to convince him, that he could attain salvation and go to heaven only by becoming a Christian.

> It was more than I could believe [he wrote] that Jesus was the only incarnate son of God, and that only he who believed in him would have everlasting life. If God could have sons, all of us were his sons. If Jesus was like God, or God himself, then all men were like God and could be God himself.
>
> My reason was not ready to believe literally that Jesus by his death and by his blood redeemed the sins of the world. . . . I could accept

Jesus as a martyr, an embodiment of sacrifice and a divine teacher but not as the most perfect man ever born. His death on the Cross was a great example to the world, but that there was anything like a mysterious or miraculous virtue in it, my heart could not accept. The pious lives of Christians did not give me anything that the lives of men of other faiths had failed to give me. . . . Philosophically there was nothing extraordinary in Christian principles.

Thomas Jefferson, in a remarkable essay, had expressed a similar view of Christ, and this also had influenced me. (Had Jefferson lived in our time and run for president and expounded publicly that view, he never could have been elected.)

One thing that bothered me in all religions I studied was the idea of a "just and powerful God," or for the Hindus, gods. If God is just, I asked myself, then why does he permit so much human suffering: all the wars, for example, in which millions have died? Why allow the terrible massacres, of which our time has seen probably the worst? Why go along with the humiliation of the human spirit?

How, I've asked myself, could one believe in God after the Holocaust in our own day? How could a Christian worship a God who permitted Christians to perpetrate such an unspeakable crime? How could a Jew believe in his God who permitted the killing by the Nazi beasts of a good part of his race?

Albert Einstein, a Jew, who was deeply affected by the Nazi attempt to exterminate the Jews in their death camps (had he remained in Germany, he probably would have been a victim), was inclined to let God off the hook.

> The idea of a Being [he wrote] who interferes in the world is absolutely impossible. . . . A God who rewards and punishes is unthinkable because man acts in accordance with an inner and outer necessity, and would, in the eyes of God, be as little responsible as an inanimate object for the movements it makes.

But most religions, including the Christian, did believe that God, or the gods, rewarded and punished. And most good Christians credited God for all the good in this world. I have kept wondering why they did not hold God responsible, then, for all the bad.

Arnold Toynbee, the British historian and Christian philosopher, pondered this question. "Christianity," he concluded, "does not — and cannot — explain how a God who is infinitely powerful and infinitely loving came to create a universe which turned out to be not very good." Toynbee himself, born a Christian and, judging by his writing, a very devout one, eventually became, in his words, "an ex-Christian," no longer able, he said, to believe in the virgin birth, the resurrection and ascension, or that Jesus was the Son of God.

After my experience with India, I could never believe that Christianity was the only religion, as millions of my fundamentalist compatriots did. The idea that hundreds of millions of Moslems, Hindus, and Buddhists were destined to go to hell because they were not Christians was not only absurd but repulsive. If there was an afterlife — and they believed there was — then they were due as good a reception above as Christians.

In the end, after meditating over it all my adult life, I was prepared to believe that religion, from the dawn of civilization, answered the most deeply felt need of mankind. Every society, so far as we know, had a religion, with its god or gods and goddesses. I could understand that religion offered a solace to human beings as they made their rocky, sorrowful way through life. Religion promised them a better life hereafter. With all the misery in the world, this was what millions craved. The universality of the human need for religion made me regret that I could not share it. I knew I was in a minority.

I did not care to go on as did Ernest Renan, the nineteenth-century French religious historian and author of a French classic, *The Life of Jesus.*

"My life," he said toward its end, "is still governed by a faith I no longer have."

I could not accept such a life for myself. The pretense and the hypocrisy would have been too much.

But if at eighty-five I faced soon departing this life without the consolation of religion and a belief in a life hereafter, I felt enriched by the poetry and the philosophy which I had found in the religions I knew.

There was one other question I sought an answer to in vain. How did the universe originate? The scientists told us that it began with gases that over hundreds of millions of years cooled and solidified into the stars and planets we know. Some say it started with a big bang. But from where and from what did the gases come? How can something be created from nothing? It became, at least for me, more a question of philosophy than of physics. Before the beginning of the formation of the universe, there must have been nothing — a great void. Then how did the gases spring up? They could not have come from nothing. I read the physicists who were trying to explain the origins of the universe. They dodged, it seemed to me, the fundamental question. Perhaps there was no answer, at least that we could understand. This was something beyond our comprehension.

One thing we did know: how puny was our tiny Earth in the great cosmos, a mere speck, actually. And for thousands of years, the inhabitants of Earth had believed that our planet was the center of the universe! Was the universe limited in its extent? Or did it stretch into the infinite? We do not know. And if there are no limits, how can we even imagine the infinite, the boundless?

Like everyone else, I suppose, I did not give much thought to all these things when I was busy trying to make it in a materialistic world. Only as I grew older, and found time for meditation and contemplation, did these matters occupy my thoughts.

Whatever happens now, and whenever, I am glad to have lived through the turbulent, tumultuous twentieth century, with all its tremendous changes, despite all its upheavals and violence. And as an American, whose country came of age in his lifetime and, despite all its shortcomings, achieved greatness.

It was a complex fate, maybe, as Henry James said, to be an American and one, I realize, not especially admired by some in other countries and other cultures, who perceived us as "the ugly Americans." Still, as I wrote in the last line of the general introduction, I am glad it was mine.

INDEX